Policin
Communities

Understanding Crime and Solving Problems

An Anthology

Ronald W. Glensor
Deputy Chief, Reno Police Department

Mark E. Correia
University of Nevada, Reno

Kenneth J. Peak
University of Nevada, Reno

Roxbury Publishing Company
Los Angeles, California

Library of Congress Cataloging-in-Publication Data

Policing Communitites: Understanding Crime and Solving Problems
  Ronald W. Glensor, Mark E. Correia, and Kenneth J. Peak
p. cm.
Includes bibliographical references
ISBN 1-891487-07-8
1. Community policing. 2. Crime prevention. 3. Crime prevention-citizen participation. I. Glensor, Ronald W., 1953– II. Correia, Mark, 1967–. III. Peak, Kenneth J., 1947–.
  Policing Communities.
HV7936.C83P655 2000
363–150dc21

98-19442
CIP

Policing Communities: Understanding Crime and Solving Problems

Publisher: Claude Teweles
Managing Editor: Dawn VanDercreek
Production Editor: Renée M. Burkhammer
Assistant Editor: Josh Levine
Typography: Synergistic Data Systems
Cover Design: Marnie Kenney
Cover Photo: Corbis

Printed on acid-free paper in the United States of America. This paper meets the standards for recycling of the Environmental Protection Agency.

ISBN 1-891487-07-8

Roxbury Publishing Company
P.O. Box 491044
Los Angeles, California 90049-9044
Tel: (310) 473-3312 • Fax: (310) 473-4490
Email: roxbury@crl.com
Website: www.roxbury.net

Dedications

To my wife, Kristy, and my children, Breanne and Ronnie, for their continued support, and for keeping me focused on the more important things in life.
R.W.G.

To my family and friends for the tremendous amount of support and encouragement they have provided. They are, and continue to be, the source of meaning in my work.
M.E.C.

To my parents, Bill and Jo.
K.J.P.

Contents

Part I: The Emergence of a New Policing

   Herman Goldstein

   Concerned about policing's overemphasis on process
   versus substance, the author recommends that police
   improve their approach to crime and disorder through
   a more systematic process for examining those problems.

   George L. Kelling

   This article discusses whether reasonable levels of civic
   order can be maintained amid the complex interplay
   between the community and police that is essential for
   neighborhood civility.

   John E. Eck and Dennis P. Rosenbaum

   A conceptual framework for community policing centers on three essential components: effectiveness, efficiency, and equity.

   Dennis P. Rosenbaum

   This exploration of the more recent evolution of policing focuses on the important role that community partnerships play in improving its effectiveness.

Part II: Mobilizing Communities Toward the Control and Prevention of Crime

   John Gardner

   This article presents a theoretical analysis of the essential ingredients in building more cohesive and responsive communities.

   Mark E. Correia

   According to this argument, building strong social cohesion is paramount to solving complex community problems.

   *Edmund F. McGarrell, Andrew L. Giacomazzi, and
     Quint C. Thurman*

   The authors discuss the debilitating effects of fear on neighborhoods and the potential of new policing techniques for understanding and responding to its causes.

   Susan Sadd and Randolph M. Grinc

   An evaluation of eight U.S. cities that implemented innovative neighborhood-oriented policing (INOP) programs presents the challenges and problems that were encountered.

   Ronald W. Glensor and Kenneth J. Peak

   This article discusses the systems being developed to maintain neighborhood order.

Part III: Street-Level Criminology: What Police Need to Know About Crime

Part IV: Implementing Change in Police Organizations

Part V: Epilogue: Future Trends and Challenges

Acknowledgments

The editors wish to thank the following reviewers for their insights and comments, which contributed tremendously to this manuscript: Mark Alley (Michigan State University), Michael Blankenship (Eastern Tennessee State University), Steven Brandl (University of Wisconsin, Milwaukee), David Carter (Michigan State University), Dean Champion (Minot State University), William Doerner (Florida State University), Bryan Forst (American University), Ron Hunter (Jacksonville State University), Lynette Lee-Sammons (California State University, Sacramento), Roy Roberg (San Jose State University), Clinton Terry (Florida International University), Quint Thurman (University of Wichita), Lawrence Travis (University of Cincinnati), and Gennaro Vito (University of Louisville). ✦

About the Editors

Ronald W. Glensor, Ph.D., is a deputy chief of the Reno, Nevada, Police department (RPD). He has more than 23 years of police experience and has commanded the department's patrol, administration, and detective divisions. In addition to being active in the development of, and training for, the RPD's community-oriented policing and problem solving (COPPS) initiative since 1987, he has provided COPPS training for more than 250 police agencies throughout the United States and in Canada, Australia, and the United Kingdom. He was the 1997 recipient of the prestigious Gary P. Hayes Award conferred by the Police Executive Research Forum, recognizing his contributions and leadership in the policing field. He has spoken at numerous national conferences on the implementation of COPPS and the utilization of citizen surveys. He also served a six-month fellowship as problem-oriented policing coordinator with the Police Executive Research Forum in Washington, D.C., and received an Atlantic Fellowship in public policy, studying repeat victimization at the Home Office in London. Dr. Glensor has published *Police Supervision, Community Policing and Problem Solving: Strategies and Practices* (2nd ed.) as well as numerous articles in journals and trade magazines. He is an adjunct professor at the University of Nevada, Reno (in the criminal justice department's bachelor of arts program in COPPS) and instructs at area police academies and criminal justice programs. His education includes a doctorate in political science and a master's degree of public administration from the University of Nevada, Reno.

Mark E. Correia, Ph.D., received his doctoral degree from Washington State University in 1998. His dissertation, *Social Capital, Civic Engagement, and Social Equity* explored the underlying factors affecting the communal acceptance of community policing on both the philosophical and programmatic levels. Dr. Correia's general interests relate to public administration, methods of survey research, and applied statistical applications. Recent publications include *Filling the Gap: Critical Readings in Criminal Justice* and *Citizen Involvement in Community Policing: How Community Factors Affect Success*.

Kenneth J. Peak, Ph.D., is professor and former chairman of the criminal justice department at the University of Nevada, Reno (UNR), where he was named "Teacher of the Year" (1984–1985) by the UNR Honor Society and served as acting director of public safety in 1989. Recent publications include *Policing America: Methods, Issues, and Challenges* (3rd ed.); *Police Supervision, Community Policing, and Problem Solving: Strategies and Practices* (2nd ed.); and *Justice Administration: Police, Courts, and Corrections Management* (2nd ed., 1998). He has published nearly 50 journal articles and book chapters on a wide range of justice-related subjects. Peak is a past chairman of the Police Section, Academy of Criminal Justice Sciences, and past president of the Western and Pacific Association of Criminal Justice Educators. He entered municipal policing in Kansas in 1970 and subsequently held positions as criminal justice planner for southeast Kansas; director of the Technical Assistance Institute, Washburn University of Topeka; director of university police, Pittsburg State University; and assistant professor at Wichita State University. He received two gubernatorial appointments to statewide criminal justice committees while in Kansas and holds a doctorate from the University of Kansas. ✦

About the Contributors

Michael E. Buerger is an associate professor in the College of Criminal Justice at Northeastern University in Boston, Massachusetts. He was the field director for RECAP and the Hot Spots of Crime Experiment in Minneapolis, Minnesota, and recently concluded a National Institute of Justice Locally Initiated Research Project as research director for the Jersey City (NJ) Police Department. A former police officer, his current interests include police organizational change; police response to domestic violence; improving preservice education of prospective police officers and better integration of education and training; and the evolution of police-community dynamics. He has published articles on street-level drug markets, police problem-solving efforts, and the limits of community policing, and is writing a book about the community policing movement.

David L. Carter, Ph.D., earned his doctoral degree at Sam Houston State University in 1980, and came to the School of Criminal Justice in 1985. His research interests include police administration and behavior. Specific current interests include police education, international crime and justice, violent crime, community policing, law enforcement intelligence operations, and computer crime.

Ronald V. Clarke is University Professor at the Rutgers School of Criminal Justice. He was the Dean of the school for more than ten years, and before that was head of the Home Research and Planning Unit (the British government's criminological department). While at the Home Office, Dr. Clarke played a significant part in the development of situational crime prevention and in the launching of the British Crime Survey. He is the editor of *Crime Prevention Studies* and the author of more than 150 books and articles. His most recent book is *Situational Crime Prevention: Successful Case Studies,* of which the second edition was published in 1997.

Ellen G. Cohn received her Ph.D., in criminology from Cambridge University in 1991 and currently is an associate professor of criminal justice in the School of Policy and Management at Florida International University. She has published extensively in criminology and psychology journals both in the United States and the United Kingdom, and is the lead author of *Examining Criminology and Criminal Justice* (1998). Her research and writing to date focus primarily on the relationships between weather and criminal behavior, the use of citation analysis, and the development of community policing programs.

John Eck is associate professor of criminal justice at the University of Cincinnati. He has conducted research on criminal investigations, problem-oriented policing, community policing, and drug control strategies. His interests include how police organizations address community problems, crime and place, how crime places develop, and methods for controlling crime in and around places.

John Gardner is currently the Miriam and Peter Haas Centennial Professor of Public Service at Stanford University, and has long been an active participant in America's educational, philanthropic, and political life. He has been the president of the Carnegie Corporation of New York, and the Carnegie Foundation for the Advancement of Teaching. Mr. Gardner has served as the Secretary of Health, Education, and Welfare; Chairperson of the National Urban Coalition; and was a founding chairperson of "Common Cause." In 1964 he received the Presidential Medal of Freedom, the nation's highest civil honor.

Andrew L. Giacomazzi, Ph.D., is assistant professor of criminal justice at Boise State University. He is co-author of a forthcoming book entitled *Community Policing* *in a Community Era: An Introduction*. His recent articles have appeared in journals such as the *American Journal of Police, Crime and Delinquency, Police Studies, Justice Quarterly*, and *Policing: An International Journal of Police Strategies and Management*. Currently, Giacomazzi is involved in a number of research projects, including an impact assessment of a grass roots problem-oriented approach to reduce crime and disorder in public housing, assessing organizational change in policing, strategic planning, and collaborative problem-solving to reduce family violence against women, an NIJ funded research project. In addition, Giacomazzi is principal investigator of an evaluation to determine the impacts of the Western Regional Institute for Community-Oriented Public Safety's technical assistance program within its five-state region.

Herman Goldstein is Evjue-Bascum Professor of Law at the Law School, University of Wisconsin, Madison. He has written extensively on the police, including the following: *The Urban Police Function* (1973), *Policing a Free Society* (1977), and *Problem-Oriented Policing* (1990).

Sheldon F. Greenberg, Ph.D., is chair of the Department of Interdisciplinary Programs and director of the Police Executive Leadership Program at Johns Hopkins University. He has co-authored several books, including *Stress and the Helping Professions*, *Stress and the Teaching Profession*, and *On the Dotted Line*.

Randolph M. Grinc earned his Ph.D. in sociology from New York University. He has worked as a research associate at the Vera Institute of Justice, where he helped the New York Police Department develop a performance system for community policing. He has also worked with the Bureau of Justice Assistance on their Innovative Neighborhood Oriented Policing (INOP) projects.

Adele V. Harrell is director of the Program on Law and Behavior at the Urban Institute in Washington, D.C. She is currently evaluating the Brooklyn Treatment Court and Breaking the Cycle, a program linking court and treatment services for drug-involved defendants. Prior research includes an evaluation of the system-wide drug testing in case management at pretrial, probation, and parole, and studies of the relationship between arrestee urinalysis results and community indicators of drug problems among adults and juveniles.

George Kelling received his B.A degree in philosophy from St. Olaf College, a master's degree in Social Work from the University of Wisconsin-Milwaukee, and a Ph.D. in social welfare from the University of Wisconsin-Madison. He is currently a Fellow in the program of Criminal Justice Policy and Management in the Kennedy School of Government at Harvard University. His areas of special interest are the police; the relationships among fear, crime, and disorder; community crime control; and the evolution of policing strategies and tactics.

Nicholas P. Lovrich is the Cladius O. and Mary W. Johnson Distinguished Professor of Political Science at Washington State University. He has served as Director of Governmental Studies and Services since 1977, and currently serves as the leader of applied research for the Western Regional Institute for Community Oriented Public Safety. His research on law enforcement has appeared in *Journal of Criminal Justice, Policing, Women and Criminal Justice, American Journal of Police, Justice Quarterly, Journal of Urban Affairs, Social Science Journal*, and *Social Science Quarterly*.

Arthur Lurigio, a social psychologist, is Professor and Chair of the Criminal Justice Department at Loyola University Chicago, and a member of the graduate faculty at Loyola University. Dr. Lurigio has done research in local and state community corrections and court systems for nearly twenty years, and served as Director of Research and Evaluation for the Cook County Adult Probation Department from 1982 through 1997. He has published extensively in such areas as substance abuse, community corrections, mental disorders and crime, crime prevention and crime victimization.

Susan E. Martin currently is a health scientist administrator in the Prevention Research Branch of the National Institute on Alcohol Abuse and Alcoholism (NIAAA) of the National Institute of Health (NIH), where she manages that Institute's research portfolio on alcohol-related violence, drunk driving, alcohol-related problems in the worksite, and public policies designed to reduce alcohol misuse. Previously, she was a project director at the Police Foundation in Washington, D.C., and a study director with the Committee on Research on Law Enforcement and the Administration of Justice at the National Research Council. She is the editor of several NIAAA monographs, including *Alcohol and Interpersonal Violence*, and author of articles on various aspects of alcohol-related injury, hate crime, and police work. She has a Ph.D. in Sociology from American University. Her recent research and writing have focused on women in criminal justice as well as on alcohol-related violence and unintentional injuries.

Edmund F. McGarrell holds a Ph.D. in criminal justice. He has specialized in the study of juvenile justice, especially juvenile corrections. His dissertation study about two decades of reform in New York state's juvenile justice system led to the publication of *Juvenile Correctional Reform: Two Decades of Policy and Procedural Change* (SUNY Press, 1988). He has published articles on case studies of criminal law reform, public and elite attitudes toward criminal justice, cross-state analyses of correctional processes and structures, and racial disproportionality in the juvenile justice system. Professor McGarrell is the co-author of *Community Corrections: A Community Field Approach* (Anderson Press, 1990) and has been a fellow at the National Center for Juvenile Justice. His recent research involves studying community-based responses to crime. He is currently completing a National Institute of Justice sponsored study of a crime-, fear-, and disorder-reduction program in public housing and is beginning related projects involving the Indianapolis Police Department and the Marion County juvenile court and prosecutor's office.

Anthony Petrosino received his Ph.D. in criminal justice from Rutgers University and is currently a Spencer Fellow at Harvard University. He is formerly a Graduate Research Fellow at the National Institute of Justice and a visiting assistant professor at Northeastern University's College of Criminal Justice. Petrosino plans a meta-analytic research project to study the efficacy of school-based interventions designed to reduce problem behavior.

Michael D. Reisig is an assistant professor of criminal justice at Michigan State University. His interests include organization theory, survey research, and applied statistical models. His research has been published in *Crime & Delinquency*, *Policing*, and the *Journal of Criminal Justice*.

Dennis P. Rosenbaum is a member of the Psychology Department at Loyola University, Chicago. He has conducted many research and evaluation studies focusing on police, community, school, and media initiatives to prevent violence, disorder, and drug abuse. His interests include community crime prevention, community policing, interagency partnerships, and drug abuse prevention. He has served as an advisor to local, state, and national organizations interested in community-based initiatives to prevent crime. He is currently directing longitudinal studies of community policing and school-based drug education, as well as participating in national evaluations funded by the National Institute of Justice.

Susan Sadd received her Ph.D. in Social Psychology from New York University and is currently the director of Research and Planning for the Bronx District. She has worked at the Vera's NIJ-funded evaluation of Innovative Neighborhood Oriented Policing programs. Her primary area of research has been evaluations of police departments and developing performance measures for community policing.

Allen Sapp, Ph.D. is a Professor of Criminal Justice at Central Missouri State University. His research interests encompass most areas of law enforcement and the study of the "future" of policing. He has published numerous articles on law enforcement.

Susan Sapp, Ph.D., is Director of Research and Planning for the Bronx District. While at the Vera Institute she gained considerable experience evaluating police programs. Sapp is co-author of *Community Policing: The CPOP in New York*.

Lawrence W. Sherman is the Greenfield Professor of Human Relations and Director of the Fels Center of Government at the University of Pennsylvania. For three decades, he has collaborated with police agencies in a wide range of policy research projects, on such topics as policing domestic violence, gun crime, drug raids, restorative justice, drunk driving, crime mapping, and problem-oriented policing. His research on police use of deadly force was cited by the U.S. Supreme Court in the case of *Tennessee v. Garner*, and he is currently working in a research partnership with the Philadelphia Police Department.

Wesley G. Skogan, Ph.D., has focused his research on citizens as producers and consumers of law. Most of his research involves sample surveys. He has conducted evaluations of police innovations and community organizations, and studies on the impact of crime and citizen participation in crime related programs. His most recent book is *Community Policing, Chicago Style*, and his book *Victims of Crime: Problems, Policies and Programs* has just been reprinted in a second edition.

William Spelman, an urban policy specialist, holds a Ph.D. in public policy from Harvard University's John F. Kennedy School of Government. He has a background in operations research and evaluation, and in local government, law, administration, and finance. His numerous publications focus on criminal justice policies, mainly in the areas of community crime prevention, repeat offenders, and neighborhood problem solving.

William Tafoya, Ph.D., received his degree from the University of Maryland and currently is Professor of Criminal Justice at Governors State University. Previously, he was Director of Research for the Office of International Criminal Justice at the University of Illinois, Chicago. Internationally recognized, he is an authority on the law enforcement use of high technology and the future of policing. Prior to teaching, he served in the FBI, most recently, as a senior faculty member of the Computer Crimes Unit and the Behavioral Sciences Units.

Ralph B. Taylor received his Ph.D. in social psychology at Johns Hopkins University in 1977 and is currently professor of criminal justice at Temple University where he has been since 1984. He is the editor of *Urban Neighborhoods* (Praeger, 1986) and the author of *Human Territorial Functioning* (Cambridge, 1988), *Research Methods in Criminal Justice* (McGraw Hill, 1994), and the forthcoming *Crime, Grime, Fear and Decline: The Incivilities Thesis in the Context of Community Structure* (Westview). He recently completed research examining connections between crime, deterioration, structural changes, and residents' reactions to crime over several years.

Quint C. Thurman is Professor of Criminal Justice and director of the Midwest Criminal Justice Institute in the School of Community Affairs at Wichita State University. Dr. Thurman received his Ph.D. in Sociology at the University of Massachusetts (Amherst) in 1987 and has since published articles that have appeared in the *American Behavioral Scientist, Crime and Delinquency, Social Science Quarterly, Public Finance, Justice Quarterly*, and the *Journal of Quantitative Criminology*. In 1997 he edited *Community Policing in a Rural Setting* with co-author Edmund McGarrell. His latest book, *Community Policing in a Community Era*, is forthcoming from Roxbury Press and co-authored with Jihong Zhao and Andrew Giacomazzi.

Deborah L. Weisel joined PERF in 1987. She has conducted numerous studies on policing, including case studies of decision making in municipal law enforcement agencies, a national study of the various forms of community policing, an assessment of alternative drug enforcement tactics use by police agencies, and extensive work on safety and security in public housing environments. She recently conducted a national study for NIJ to determine the ways in which youth gangs evolve into more highly organized groups over time. She also conducted a national survey of law enforcement agencies to learn more about the varieties of gangs in their cities, with more intensive studies of four gangs—two in San Diego and two in Chicago. Ms. Weisel is participating in implementation of a problem-solving model to address gang problems as part of the Comprehensive Communities program funded by the Bureau of Justice Assistance. She has a Bachelor's degree from the University of North Carolina at Chapel Hill, a Master's degree in Public Affairs from North Carolina State University and is a doctoral candidate in Public Policy Analysis at the University of Illinois at Chicago.

Jihong Zhao is an assistant professor in the Department of Criminal Justice at the University of Nebraska-Omaha. His interests include organization theory, police organizational change, and an organizational culture approach to the study of criminal justice organizations. He is author of *Why Police Organizations Change: A Study of Community-Oriented Policing* published by the Police Executive Research Forum. ✦

Introduction

Community-oriented policing and problem solving (COPPS) has evolved to the point of being generally accepted by both police practitioners and criminal justice academics in the United States and abroad. This innovative approach to addressing crime and disorder and promoting police-citizen collaboration engenders more thoughtful strategies for controlling and preventing crime control and prevention strategies. Essential to COPPS is the view that police should examine the underlying causes of disorder and crime in order to develop long-term solutions.

Despite its acceptance, the implementation of this "new policing" has achieved varying degrees of success, and long-term citizen engagement has varied from place to place. Much of this variation has been the result of diminishing community support after the initial surge of enthusiasm. The editor's of this book believe that what is needed is greater insight and clarity into the context in which a crime is committed, prevention occurs, and citizens become engaged. As a result, more effective measures of crime control and prevention may be realized through the collaborative efforts of the police, other government agencies, service organizations, local businesses, and citizens.

This collection of articles addresses these issues. It does so by using a three-pronged approach. First, it brings to the fore the importance of social capital and cohesion in building more civil and safe neighborhoods. Second, it uses a problem analysis triangle as a framework, viewing crime through the lenses of the location, the offender, and the victim. Third, it draws upon research focusing on change in police organization. Overall, this book integrates the current research on the important elements of police and community, advancing an understanding of their nexus.

Policing Communities is divided into five parts. Part I, "The Emergence of a New Policing," provides a historical perspective on the evolution of policing. The readings emphasize the importance of partnerships, problem solving, and organizational change. Additionally, they provide the reader with those elements necessary for a fundamental understanding of the new direction of policing.

Part II, "Mobilizing Communities Toward the Control and Prevention of Crime," emphasizes the important role citizens play in social control and prevention of crime. Such important topics as social capital and community building, neighborhood disorder and fear, and the importance of maintaining order following interventions are explored. The experiences and challenges of eight U.S. cities are also presented.

Part III, "Street-Level Criminology: What the Police Need to Know About Crime," brings the context of crime and its causes into focus. It argues that police officers should become street-level criminologists to be effective in addressing the complexities of disorder, fear of crime, and occurrences of crime. Specifically, officers will benefit from developing a more complete understanding of the victims, the offender's behavior, and the context in which crime is committed, in order to develop effective solutions. It is only through comprehensive understanding and thoughtful analysis that appropriate long-term solutions are possible. In addition, these readings introduce situational crime prevention and crime prevention through environmental design as new tools for addressing community crime problems.

Part IV, "Implementing Change in Police Organizations," describes how the implementation of new ideas and methods requires major change in an organization's philosophical structure, processes, and personnel behaviors. New evaluation measures should also be considered. Change within policing organizations is difficult and often resisted. Winning the hearts and minds of police officers is not a simple task but one that requires strong leadership and strategic planning.

The conclusion, "Epilogue: Future Trends and Challenges," examines the future of po-

licing. The editor's feel it is imperative that police and citizens not only address current problems but also look beyond the horizon to prepare effectively for the future. In this light, the views and future projections of leading academics and practitioners in policing are presented.

In summary, this book describes and analyzes the important changes that are occurring in policing. The editor's emphasize the role that the community plays in developing effective strategies to control and prevent crime, the new methods by which the police are examining the context of crime, and the methods by which they are implementing these changes. ✦

Part I

The Emergence of a New Policing

This book—as exemplified by the four readings selected for Part I—proposes that the field of policing is evolving. This development has been prompted by a recognition that police methods of the past are no longer effective, given the following: the overall complexity of crime and its changing patterns in the United States, a general reorientation of police from means to ends, the willingness of the community to become engaged in seeking order, a shift in police focus from mere numbers of crimes to the context of crimes, and the new challenges facing the police today.

In the first article, H. Goldstein argues that police officers need to move beyond just handling incidents, recognizing that incidents are often merely overt symptoms of underlying problems. Officers will wisely take a more in-depth interest in incidents by understanding some of the conditions that cause them. This problem-oriented approach represents a radical change in the direction of policing. Goldstein proposes a new framework that moves the police from process driven quantitative measures, such as response time, numbers of arrests, and calls for service, toward more direct and thoughtful approaches to addressing substantive problems. He also suggests that this new style of policing will have implications for staffing, organization, and management.

The second reading, by G. Kelling, explores the source of police authority within the context of neighborhoods and communities. Kelling identifies how, in the late 1960s, problems began to overwhelm what has been termed the professional model of policing; crime increased, citizen fear of crime rose, many minority citizens did not perceive the police as being equitable or adequate, and several myths on which policing was founded could no longer be sustained.

One of several things that police are challenged to do is to assess their role toward the community. Do a majority of citizens today feel they are valued customers when visiting a police station, or some other agency of criminal justice, or indeed any agency of government? History has demonstrated that people want to have input and some measure of control over their environments.

As J. Eck and D. Rosenbaum state in the third article, "Community policing is the only form of policing available for anyone who seeks to improve police operations, management, or relations with the public." The authors present three important components: effectiveness (reducing neighborhood crime and fear of crime, and enhancing the quality of life); efficiency (getting the most impact from available resources); and equity (providing equal access to police service by all citizens, equal treatment of all individuals according to the Constitution, and equal distribution of police services and resources among communities).

Finally, the reading by D. Rosenbaum adeptly explains the changing role of the police and the current transition to community policing. He discusses attempts by police to rethink and restructure their role in society as well as their relationship with the community.

In sum, Part I "sets the table," explaining the who, what, why, and how of a "new policing." As Oliver Wendell Holmes observed, "To understand what *is*, we need to know what has *been*, and what it tends to become." These four readings collectively explain the roots of, and the rationale for, this emerging paradigm. ✦

1

Improving Policing

A Problem-Oriented Approach

Herman Goldstein

H. *Goldstein was the architect of the move-ment that is now known as problem-oriented policing. In the following reading, which has become a classic, he explains what prompted his thinking about the need for a paradigm shift in policing. At the nexus of this belief was the view that the police had become susceptible to what he terms the "means over ends" syn-drome, placing more emphasis on department organization and operating methods in their improvement efforts than on the substantive outcome of their work. In short, the police had become more concerned about such matters as how rapidly they arrived at a call for service than the long-term, end product of their efforts after arrival. Thus, Goldstein recommends that the police improve their approach to crime and disorder through a more systematic pro-cess for examining and addressing problems that the public expects them to handle. This reading helps in large measure to set the stage for those articles that follow.*

Introduction

The police have been particularly suscepti-ble to the "means over ends" syndrome, plac-ing more emphasis in their improvement ef-forts on organization and operating methods than on the substantive outcome of their work. This condition has been fed by the pro-fessional movement within the police field, with its concentration on the staffing, man-agement, and organization of police agen-cies. More and more persons are questioning the widely held assumption that improve-ments in the internal management of police departments will enable the police to deal more effectively with the problems they are called upon to handle. If the police are to re-alize a greater return on the investment made in improving their operations, and if they are to mature as a profession, they must concern themselves more directly with the end prod-uct of their efforts.

Meeting this need requires that the police develop a more systematic process for exam-ining and addressing the problems that the public expects them to handle. It requires identifying these problems in more precise terms, researching each problem, document-ing the nature of the current police response, assessing its adequacy and the adequacy of existing authority and resources, engaging in a broad exploration of alternatives to present responses, weighing the merits of these alter-natives, and choosing from among them.

Improvements in staffing, organization, and management remain important, but they should be achieved—and may, in fact, be more achievable—within the context of a more direct concern with the outcome of po-licing.

> Complaints from passengers wishing to use the Bagnall to Greenfields bus service that "the drivers were speeding past queues of up to 30 people with a smile and a wave of a hand" have been met by a statement pointing out that "it is impossi-ble for the drivers to keep their timetable if they have to stop for passengers."[1]

All bureaucracies risk becoming so preoc-cupied with running their organizations and getting so involved in their methods of oper-ating that they lose sight of the primary pur-poses for which they were created. The police seem unusually susceptible to this phenome-non.

One of the most popular new develop-ments in policing is the use of officers as de-coys to apprehend offenders in high-crime areas. A speaker at a recent conference for police administrators, when asked to sum-marize new developments in the field, re-ported on a sixteen-week experiment in his agency with the use of decoys, aimed at re-ducing street robberies.

One major value of the project, the speaker claimed, was its contribution to the police department's public image. Apparently, the public was intrigued by the clever, seductive character of the project, especially by the widely publicized demonstrations of the makeup artists' ability to disguise burly officers. The speaker also claimed that the project greatly increased the morale of the personnel working in the unit. The officers found the assignment exciting and challenging, a welcome change from the tedious routine that characterizes so much of regular police work, and they developed a high *esprit de corps*.

The effect on robberies, however, was much less clear. The methodology used and the problems in measuring crime apparently prevented the project staff from reaching any firm conclusions. But it was reported that, of the 216 persons arrested by the unit for robbery during the experiment, more than half would not have committed a robbery, in the judgment of the unit members, if they had not been tempted by the situation presented by the police decoys. Thus, while the total impact of the project remains unclear, it can be said with certainty that the experiment actually increased the number of robberies by over 100 in the sixteen weeks of the experiment.

The account of this particular decoy project (others have claimed greater success) is an especially poignant reminder of just how serious an imbalance there is within the police field between the interest in organizational and procedural matters and the concern for the substance of policing. The assumption, of course, is that the two are related, that improvements in internal management will eventually increase the capacity of the police to meet the objectives for which police agencies are created. But the relationship is not that clear and direct and is increasingly being questioned.

Perhaps the best example of such questioning relates to response time. Tremendous resources were invested during the past decade in personnel, vehicles, communications equipment, and new procedures in order to increase the speed with which the police respond to calls for assistance. Much less attention was given in this same period to what the officer does in handling the variety of problems he confronts on arriving, albeit fast, where he is summoned. Now, ironically, even the value of a quick response is being questioned.[2]

This article summarizes the nature of the "means over ends" syndrome in policing and explores ways of focusing greater attention on the results of policing—on the effect that police efforts have on the problems that the police are expected to handle.

The 'Means over Ends' Syndrome

Until the late 1960s, efforts to improve policing in this country concentrated almost exclusively on internal management: streamlining the organization, upgrading personnel, modernizing equipment, and establishing more businesslike operating procedures. All of the major commentators on the police since the beginning of the century—Leonard F. Fuld (1909), Raymond B. Fosdick (1915), August Vollmer (1936), Bruce Smith (1940), and O. W. Wilson (1950)—stressed the need to improve the organization and management of police agencies. Indeed, the emphasis on internal management was so strong that professional policing was defined primarily as the application of modern management concepts to the running of a police department.

The sharp increase in the demands made on the police in the late 1960s (increased crime, civil rights demonstrations, and political protest) led to several national assessments of the state of policing.[3] The published findings contained some criticism of the professional model of police organization, primarily because of its impersonal character and failure to respond to legitimate pressures from within the community.[4] Many recommendations were made for introducing a greater concern for the human factors in policing, but the vast majority of the recommendations that emerged from the reassessments demonstrated a continuing belief that the way to improve the police was to improve the organization. Higher recruitment standards, college education for police personnel, reassignment and reallocation of personnel, additional training, and greater mobility were proposed. Thus the management-dominated concept of police reform spread and gained greater stature.

The emphasis on secondary goals—on improving the organization—continues to this day, reflected in the prevailing interests of police administrators, in the factors considered in the selection of police chiefs and the promotion of subordinates, in the subject matter of police periodicals and texts, in the content of recently developed educational programs for the police, and even in the focus of major research projects.

At one time this emphasis was appropriate. When Vollmer, Smith, and Wilson formulated their prescriptions for improved policing, the state of the vast majority of police agencies was chaotic: Personnel were disorganized, poorly equipped, poorly trained, inefficient, lacking accountability, and often corrupt. The first priority was putting the police house in order. Otherwise, the endless crises that are produced by an organization out of control would be totally consuming. Without a minimum level of order and accountability, an agency cannot be redirected—however committed its administrators may be to addressing more substantive matters.

What is troubling is that administrators of those agencies that have succeeded in developing a high level of operating efficiency have not gone on to concern themselves with the end results of their efforts—with the actual impact that their streamlined organizations have on the problems the police are called upon to handle.

The police seem to have reached a plateau at which the highest objective to which they aspire is administrative competence. And, with some scattered exceptions, they seem reluctant to move beyond this plateau—toward creating a more systematic concern for the end product of their efforts. But strong pressures generated by several new developments may now force them to do so.

1. The Financial Crisis

The growing cost of police services and the financial plight of most city governments, especially those under threat of Proposition 13

movements, are making municipal officials increasingly reluctant to appropriate still more money for police service without greater assurance that their investment will have an impact on the problems that the police are expected to handle. Those cities that are already reducing their budgets are being forced to make some of the hard choices that must be made in weighing the impact of such cuts on the nature of the service rendered to the public.

2. Research Findings

Recently completed research questions the value of two major aspects of police operations—preventive patrol and investigations conducted by detectives.[5] Some police administrators have challenged the finding;[6] others are awaiting the results of replication.[7] But those who concur with the results have begun to search for alternatives, aware of the need to measure the effectiveness of a new response before making a substantial investment in it.

3. Growth of a Consumer Orientation

Policing has not yet felt the full impact of consumer advocacy. As citizens press for improvement in police service, improvement will increasingly be measured in terms of results. Those concerned about battered wives, for example, could not care less whether the police who respond to such calls operate with one or two officers in a car, whether the officers are short or tall, or whether they have a college education. Their attention is on what the police do for the battered wife.

4. Questioning the Effectiveness of the Best-Managed Agencies

A number of police departments have carried out most, if not all, of the numerous recommendations for strengthening a police organization and enjoy a national reputation for their efficiency, their high standards of personnel selection and training, and their application of modern technology to their operations. Nevertheless, their communities apparently continue to have the same problems as do others with less advanced police agencies.[8]

5. Increased Resistance to Organizational Change

Intended improvements that are primarily in the form of organizational change, such as team policing, almost invariably run into resistance from rank-and-file personnel. Stronger and more militant unions have engaged some police administrators in bitter and prolonged fights over such changes.[9] Because the costs in terms of disruption and discontent are so great, police administrators initiating change will be under increasing pressure to demonstrate in advance that the results of their efforts will make the struggle worthwhile.

Against this background, the exceptions to the dominant concern with the police organization and its personnel take on greater significance. Although scattered and quite modest, a number of projects and training programs carried out in recent years have focused on a single problem that the public expects the police to handle, such as child abuse, sexual assault, arson, or the drunk driver.[10] These projects and programs, by their very nature, subordinate the customary priorities of police reform, such as staffing, management, and equipment, to a concern about a specific problem and the police response to it.

Some of the earliest support for this type of effort was reflected in the crime-specific projects funded by the Law Enforcement Assistance Administration.[11] Communities—not just the police—were encouraged to direct their attention to a specific type of crime and to make those changes in existing operations that were deemed necessary to reduce its incidence. The widespread move to fashion a more effective police response to domestic disturbances is probably the best example of a major reform that has, as its principal objective, improvement in the quality of service delivered, and that calls for changes in organization, staffing, and training only as these are necessary to achieve the primary goal.

Are these scattered efforts a harbinger of things to come? Are they a natural development in the steadily evolving search for ways to improve police operations? Or are they, like the programs dealing with sexual assault and child abuse, simply the result of the sudden availability of funds because of intensified citizen concern about a specific problem? Whatever their origin, those projects that do subordinate administrative considerations to the task of improving police effectiveness in dealing with a specific problem have a refreshing quality to them.

What Is the End Product of Policing?

To urge a more direct focus on the primary objectives of a police agency requires spelling out these objectives more clearly. But this is no easy task, given the conglomeration of unrelated, ill-defined, and often inseparable jobs that the police are expected to handle.

The task is complicated further because so many people believe that the job of the police is, first and foremost, to enforce the law: to regulate conduct by applying the criminal law of the jurisdiction. One commentator on the police recently claimed: "We do not say to the police: 'Here is the problem. Deal with it.' We say: 'Here is a detailed code. Enforce it.'"[12] In reality, the police job is perhaps most accurately described as dealing with problems.[13] Moreover, enforcing the criminal code is itself only a means to an end—one of several that the police employ in getting their job done.[14] The emphasis on law enforcement, therefore, is nothing more than a continuing preoccupation with means.

Considerable effort has been invested in recent years in attempting to define the police function: inventorying the wide range of police responsibilities, categorizing various aspects of policing, and identifying some of the characteristics common to all police tasks.[15] This work will be of great value in refocusing attention on the end product of policing, but the fact that it is still going on is not cause to delay giving greater attention to substantive matters. It is sufficient, for our purposes here, simply to acknowledge that the police job requires that they deal with a wide range of behavioral and social problems that arise in a community—that the end product of policing consists of dealing with these *problems*.

By problems, I mean the incredibly broad range of troublesome situations that prompt citizens to turn to the police, such as street robberies, residential burglaries, battered wives, vandalism, speeding cars, runaway children, accidents, acts of terrorism, even fear. These and other similar problems are the essence of police work. They are the reason for having a police agency.

Problems of this nature are to be distinguished from those that frequently occupy police administrators, such as lack of manpower, inadequate supervision, inadequate training, or strained relations with police unions. They differ from those most often identified by operating personnel, such as lack of adequate equipment, frustrations in the prosecution of criminal cases, or inequities in working conditions. And they differ, too, from the problems that have occupied those advocating police reform, such as the multiplicity of police agencies, the lack of lateral entry, and the absence of effective controls over police conduct.

Many of the problems coming to the attention of the police become their responsibility because no other means has been found to solve them. They are the residual problems of society. It follows that expecting the police to solve or eliminate them is expecting too much. It is more realistic to aim at reducing their volume, preventing repetition, alleviating suffering, and minimizing the other adverse effects they produce.

Developing the Overall Process

To address the substantive problems of the police requires developing a commitment to a more systematic process for inquiring into these problems. Initially, this calls for identifying in precise terms the problems that citizens look to the police to handle. Once identified, each problem must be explored in great detail. What do we know about the problem? Has it been researched? If so, with what results? What more should we know? Is it a proper concern of government? What authority and resources are available for dealing with it? What is the current police response? In the broadest-ranging search for solutions, what would constitute the most intelligent response? What factors should be considered in choosing from among alternatives? If a new response is adopted, how does

one go about evaluating its effectiveness? And finally, what changes, if any, does implementation of a more effective response require in the police organization?

This type of inquiry is not foreign to the police. Many departments conduct rigorous studies of administrative and operational problems. A police agency may undertake a detailed study of the relative merits of adopting one of several different types of uniforms. And it may regularly develop military-like plans for handling special events that require the assignment of large numbers of personnel.[16] However, systematic analysis and planning have rarely been applied to the specific behavioral and social problems that constitute the agency's routine business. The situation is somewhat like that of a private industry that studies the speed of its assembly line, the productivity of its employees, and the nature of its public relations program, but does not examine the quality of its product.

Perhaps the closest police agencies have come to developing a system for addressing substantive problems has been their work in crime analysis. Police routinely analyze information on reported crimes to identify patterns of criminal conduct, with the goal of enabling operating personnel to apprehend specific offenders or develop strategies to prevent similar offenses from occurring. Some police departments have, through the use of computers, developed sophisticated programs to analyze reported crimes.[17] Unfortunately, these analyses are almost always put to very limited use—to apprehend a professional car thief or to deter a well-known cat burglar—rather than serving as a basis for rethinking the overall police response to the problem of car theft or cat burglaries. Nevertheless, the practice of planning operational responses based on an analysis of hard data, now a familiar concept to the police, is a helpful point of reference in advocating development of more broadly based research and planning.

The most significant effort to use a problem orientation for improving police responses was embodied in the crime-specific concept initiated in California in 1971[18] and later promoted with LEAA funds throughout the country. The concept was made an integral part of the anticrime program launched in eight cities in January 1972, aimed at bringing about reductions in five crime categories: murder, rape, assault, robbery, and burglary.[19] This would have provided an excellent opportunity to develop and test the concept, were it not for the commitment that this politically motivated program carried to achieving fast and dramatic results: a 5 percent reduction in each category in two years and a 20 percent reduction in five years. These rather naive, unrealistic goals and the emphasis on quantifying the results placed a heavy shadow over the program from the outset. With the eventual abandonment of the projects, the crime-specific concept seems to have lost ground as well. However, the national evaluation of the program makes it clear that progress was made, despite the various pressures, in planning a community's approach to the five general crime categories. The "crime-oriented planning, implementation and evaluation" process employed in all eight cities had many of the elements one would want to include in a problem-oriented approach to improving police service.[20]

Defining Problems With Greater Specificity

The importance of defining problems more precisely becomes apparent when one reflects on the long-standing practice of using overly broad categories to describe police business. Attacking police problems under a categorical heading—"crime" or "disorder," "delinquency," or even "violence"—is bound to be futile. While police business is often further subdivided by means of the labels tied to the criminal code, such as robbery, burglary, and theft, these are not adequate, for several reasons.

First, they frequently mask diverse forms of behavior. Thus, for example, incidents classified under "arson" might include fires set by teenagers as a form of vandalism, fires set by persons suffering severe psychological problems, fires set for the purpose of destroying evidence of a crime, fires set by persons (or their hired agents) to collect insurance, and fires set by organized criminal interests to intimidate. Each type of incident poses a radically different problem for the police.

Second, if police depend heavily on categories of criminal offenses to define problems of concern to them, others may be misled to believe that, if a given form of behavior is not criminal, it is of no concern to the police. This is perhaps best reflected in the proposals for decriminalizing prostitution, gambling, narcotic use, vagrancy, and public intoxication. The argument, made over and over again, is that removing the criminal label will reduce the magnitude and complexity of the police function, freeing personnel to work on more serious matters and ridding the police of some of the negative side effects, such as corruption, that these problems produce. But decriminalization does not relieve the police of responsibility. The public expects drunks to be picked up if only because they find their presence on the street annoying or because they feel that the government has an obligation to care for persons who cannot care for themselves. The public expects prostitutes who solicit openly on the streets to be stopped, because such conduct is offensive to innocent passersby, blocks pedestrian or motor traffic, and contributes to the deterioration of a neighborhood. The problem is a problem for the police whether or not it is defined as a criminal offense.

Finally, use of offense categories as descriptive of police problems implies that the police role is restricted to arresting and prosecuting offenders. In fact, the police job is much broader, extending, in the case of burglary, to encouraging citizens to lock their premises more securely, to eliminating some of the conditions that might attract potential burglars, to counseling burglary victims on ways they can avoid similar attacks in the future, and to recovering and returning burglarized property.

Until recently, the police role in regard to the crime of rape was perceived primarily as responding quickly when a report of a rape was received, determining whether a rape had really occurred (given current legal definitions), and then attempting to identify and apprehend the perpetrator. Today, the police role has been radically redefined to include teaching women how to avoid attack, organizing transit programs to provide safe movement in areas where there is a high risk of attack, dealing with the full range of sexual assault not previously covered by the narrowly drawn rape statutes, and—perhaps most important— providing needed care and support to the rape victim to minimize the physical and mental damage resulting from such an attack. Police are now concerned with sexual assault not simply because they have a direct role in the arrest and prosecution of violators, but also because sexual assault is a community problem which the police and others can affect in a variety of ways.

It seems desirable, at least initially in the development of a problem-solving approach to improved policing, to press for as detailed a breakdown of problems as possible. In addition to distinguishing different forms of behavior and the apparent motivation, as in the case of incidents commonly grouped under the heading of "arson," it is helpful to be much more precise regarding locale and time of day, the type of people involved, and the type of people victimized. Different combinations of these variables may present different problems, posing different policy questions and calling for radically different solutions.[21]

For example, most police agencies already separate the problem of purse snatching in which force is used from the various other forms of conduct commonly grouped under robbery. But an agency is likely to find it much more helpful to go further—to pinpoint, for example, the problem of teenagers snatching the purses of elderly women waiting for buses in the downtown section of the city during the hours of early darkness. Likewise, a police agency might find it helpful to isolate the robberies of grocery stores that are open all night and are typically staffed by a lone attendant; or the theft of vehicles by a highly organized group engaged in the business of transporting them for sale in another jurisdiction; or the problem posed by teenagers who gather around hamburger stands each evening to the annoyance of neighbors, customers, and management. Eventually, similar problems calling for similar responses may be grouped together, but one cannot be certain that they are similar until they have been analyzed.

In the analysis of a given problem, one may find, for example, that the concern of the citizenry is primarily fear of attack, but the fear is not warranted, given the pattern of actual offenses. Where this situation becomes apparent, the police have two quite different problems: to deal more effectively with the actual incidents where they occur, and to respond to the groundless fears. Each calls for a different response.

The importance of subdividing problems was dramatically illustrated by the recent experience of the New York City Police department in its effort to deal more constructively with domestic disturbances. An experimental program in which police were trained to use mediation techniques was undertaken with obvious public support. But, in applying the mediation techniques, the department apparently failed to distinguish sufficiently those cases in which wives were repeatedly subject to physical abuse. The aggravated nature of the latter cases resulted in a suit against the department in which the plaintiffs argued that the police are mandated to enforce the law when any violation comes to their attention. In the settlement, the department agreed that its personnel would not attempt to reconcile the parties or to mediate when a felony was committed.[22] However, the net effect of the suit is likely to be more far reaching. The vulnerability of the department to criticism for not having dealt more aggressively with the aggravated cases has dampened support—in New York and elsewhere—for the use of alternatives to arrest in less serious cases, even though alternatives still appear to represent the more intelligent response.

One of the major values in subdividing police business is that it gives visibility to some problems which have traditionally been given short shrift, but which warrant more careful attention. The seemingly minor problem of noise, for example, is typically buried in the mass of police business lumped together under such headings as "complaints," "miscellaneous," "noncriminal incidents," or "disturbances." Both police officers and unaffected citizens would most likely be inclined to rank it at the bottom in any list of problems. Yet the number of complaints about noise is high in many communities—in fact, noise is probably among the most common problems brought by the public to the police.[23] While some of those complaining may be petty or unreasonable, many are seriously aggrieved and justified in their appeal for relief: Sleep is lost, schedules are disrupted, mental and emotional problems are aggravated. departments may become uninhabitable. The elderly woman living alone, whose life has been made miserable by inconsiderate neighbors, is not easily convinced that the daily intrusion into her life of their noise is any less serious than other forms of intrusion. For this person, and for many like her, improved policing would mean a more effective response to the problem of the noise created by her neighbors.

Researching the Problem

Without a tradition for viewing in sufficiently discrete terms the various problems making up the police job, gathering even the most basic information about a specific problem—such as complaints about noise—can be extremely difficult.

First, the magnitude of the problem and the various forms in which it surfaces must be established. One is inclined to turn initially to police reports for such information. But overgeneralization in categorizing incidents, the impossibility of separating some problems, variations in the reporting practices of the community, and inadequacies in report writing seriously limit their value for purposes of obtaining a full picture of the problem. However, if used cautiously, some of the information in police files may be helpful. Police agencies routinely collect and store large amounts of data, even though they may not use them to evaluate the effectiveness of their responses. Moreover, if needed information is not available, often it can be collected expeditiously in a well-managed department, owing to the high degree of centralized control of field operations.

How does one discover the nature of the current police response? Administrators and their immediate subordinates are not a good source. Quite naturally, they have a desire to provide an answer that reflects well on the agency, is consistent with legal requirements, and meets the formal expectations of both the public and other agencies that might have a responsibility relating to the problem. But even if these concerns did not color their answers, top administrators are often so far removed from street operations, in both distance and time, that they would have great difficulty describing current responses accurately.

Inquiry, then, must focus on the operating level. But mere questioning of line officers is not likely to be any more productive. We know from the various efforts to document police activity in the field that there is often tremendous variation in the way in which different officers respond to the same type of incident.[24] Yet the high value placed on uniformity and on adhering to formal requirements and the pressures from peers inhibit officers from candidly discussing the manner in which they respond to the multitude of problems they handle—especially if the inquiry comes from outside the agency. But one cannot afford to give up at this point, for the individualized practices of police officers and the vast amount of knowledge they acquire about the situations they handle, taken together, are an extremely rich resource that is too often overlooked by those concerned about improving the quality of police services. Serious research into the problems police handle requires observing police officers over a period of time. This means accompanying them as they perform their regular assignments and cultivating the kind of relationship that enables them to talk candidly about the way in which they handle specific aspects of their job. The differences in the way in which police respond, even in dealing with relatively simple matters, may be significant. When a runaway child is reported, one officer may limit himself to obtaining the basic facts. Another officer, sensing as much of a responsibility for dealing with the parents' fears as for finding the child and looking out for the child's interests, may endeavor to relieve the parents' anxiety by providing information about the runaway problem and about what they might expect. From the standpoint of the consumers—in this case, the parents—the response of the second officer is vastly superior to that of the first.

In handling more complicated matters, the need to improvise has prompted some officers to develop what appear to be unusually effective ways of dealing with specific problems. Many officers develop a unique understanding of problems that frequently come to their attention, learning to make important distinctions among different forms of the same problem and becoming familiar with the many complicating factors that are often present. And they develop a feel for what, under the circumstances, constitute the most effective responses. After careful evaluation, these types of responses might profitably be adopted as standard for an entire police agency. If the knowledge of officers at the operating level were more readily available, it might be useful to those responsible for drafting crime-related legislation. Many of the difficulties in implementing recent changes in statutes relating to sexual assault, public drunkenness, drunk driving, and child abuse could have been avoided had police expertise been tapped.

By way of example, if a police agency were to decide to explore the problem of noise, the following questions might be asked. What is the magnitude of the problem as reflected by the number of complaints received? What is the source of the complaints: industry, traffic, groups of people gathered outdoors, or neighbors? How do noise complaints from residents break down between private dwellings and department houses? How often are the police summoned to the same location? How often are other forms of misconduct, such as fights, attributable to conflicts over noise? What is the responsibility of a landlord or an department house manager regarding noise complaints? What do the police now do in responding to such complaints? How much of the police procedure has been thought through and formalized? What is the authority of the police in such situations? Is it directly applicable or must they lean on somewhat nebulous authority, such as threatening to arrest for disorderly conduct or for failure to obey a lawful order, if the parties fail to quiet down? What works in police practice and what does not work?

Are specific officers recognized as more capable of handling such complaints? If so, what makes them more effective? Do factors outside the control of a police agency influence the frequency with which complaints are received? Are noise complaints from department dwellers related to the manner in which the buildings are constructed? And what influence, if any, does the relative effectiveness of the police in handling noise complaints have on the complaining citizen's willingness to cooperate with the police in dealing with other problems including criminal conduct traditionally defined as much more serious?

Considerable knowledge about some of the problems with which the police struggle has been generated outside police agencies by criminologists, sociologists, psychologists, and psychiatrists. But as has been pointed out frequently, relatively few of these findings have influenced the formal policies and operating decisions of practitioners.[25] Admittedly, the quality of many such studies is poor. Often the practitioner finds it difficult to draw out from the research its significance for his operations. But most important, the police have not needed to employ these studies because they have not been expected to address specific problems in a systematic manner. If the police were pressured to examine in great detail the problems they are expected to handle, a review of the literature would become routine. If convinced that research findings had practical value, police administrators would develop into more sophisticated users of such research; their responsible criticism could, in turn, contribute to upgrading the quality and usefulness of future research efforts.

Exploring Alternatives

After the information assembled about a specific problem is analyzed, a fresh, uninhibited search should be made for alternative responses that might be an improvement over what is currently being done. The nature of such a search will differ from past efforts in that, presumably, the problem itself will be better defined and understood, the commitment to past approaches (such as focusing primarily on the identification and prosecution of offenders) will be shelved temporarily, and the search will be much broader, extending well beyond the present or future potential of just the police.

But caution is in order. Those intent on improving the operations of the criminal justice system (by divesting it of some of its current burdens) and those who are principally occupied with improving the operating efficiency of police agencies frequently recommend that the problem simply be shifted to some other agency of government or to the private sector. Such recommendations often glibly imply that a health department or a social work agency, for example, is better equipped to handle the problem. Experience over the past decade, however, shows that this is rarely the case.[26] Merely shifting responsibility for the problem, without some assurance that more adequate provisions have been made for dealing with it, achieves nothing.

Police in many jurisdictions, in a commendable effort to employ alternatives to the criminal justice system, have arranged to make referrals to various social, health, and legal agencies. By tying into the services provided by the whole range of other helping agencies in the community, the police in these cities have taken a giant step toward improving the quality of their response. But there is a great danger that referral will come to be an end in itself, that the police and others advocating the use of such a system will not concern themselves adequately with the consequences of referral. If referral does not lead to reducing the citizens' problem, nothing will have been gained by this change. It may even cause harm: Expectations that are raised and not fulfilled may lead to further frustration; the original problem may, as a consequence, be compounded; and the resulting bitterness about government services may feed the tensions that develop in urban areas.

The search for alternatives obviously need not start from scratch. There is much to build on. Crime prevention efforts of some police agencies and experiments with developing alternatives to the criminal justice system and with diverting cases from the system should

be reassessed for their impact on specific problems; those that appear to have the greatest potential should be developed and promoted.[27] Several alternatives should be explored for each problem.

1. Physical and Technical Changes

Can the problem be reduced or eliminated through physical or technical changes? Some refer to this as part of a program of "reducing opportunities" or "target hardening." Extensive effort has already gone into reducing, through urban design, factors that contribute to behavior requiring police attention.[28] Improved locks on homes and cars, the requirement of exact fares on buses,[29] and the provision for mailing social security checks directly to the recipients' banks exemplify recent efforts to control crime through this alternative.

What additional physical or technical changes might be made that would have an effect on the problem? Should such changes be mandatory, or can they be voluntary? What incentives might be offered to encourage their implementation?

2. Changes in the Provision of Government Services

Can the problem be alleviated by changes in other government services? Some of the most petty but annoying problems the police must handle originate in the policies, operating practices, and inadequacies of other public agencies: the scattering of garbage because of delays in collection, poor housing conditions because of lax code enforcement, the interference with traffic by children playing because they have not been provided with adequate playground facilities, the uncapping of hydrants on hot summer nights because available pools are closed. Most police agencies long ago developed procedures for relaying reports on such conditions to the appropriate government service. But relatively few police agencies see their role as pressing for changes in policies and operations that would eliminate the recurrence of the same problems. Yet the police are the only people who see and who must become responsible for the collective negative consequences of current policies.

3. Conveying Reliable Information?

What many people want, when they turn to the police with their problems, is simply reliable information.[30] The tenant who is locked out by his landlord for failure to pay the rent wants to know his rights to his property. The car owner whose license plates are lost or stolen wants to know what reporting obligations he has, how he goes about replacing the plates, and whether he can drive his car in the meantime. The person who suspects his neighbors of abusing their child wants to know whether he is warranted in reporting the matter to the police. And the person who receives a series of obscene telephone calls wants to know what can be done about them. Even if citizens do not ask specific questions, the best response the police can make to many requests for help is to provide accurate, concise information.

4. Developing New Skills Among Police Officers

The greatest potential for improvement in the handling of some problems is in providing police officers with new forms of specialized training. This is illustrated by several recent developments. For example, the major component in the family-crisis intervention projects launched all over the country is instruction of police officers in the peculiar skills required to de-escalate highly emotional family quarrels. First aid training for police is being expanded, consistent with the current trend toward greater use of paramedics. One unpleasant task faced by the police, seldom noted by outsiders, is notifying families of the death of a family member. Often, this problem is handled poorly. In 1976, a film was made specifically to demonstrate how police should carry out this responsibility.[31] Against this background of recent developments, one should ask whether specialized training can bring about needed improvement in the handling of each specific problem.

5. New Forms of Authority

Do the police need a specific, limited form of authority which they do not now have? If the most intelligent response to a problem, such as a person causing a disturbance in a bar, is to order the person to leave, should the police be authorized to issue such an order, or should they be compelled to arrest the individual in order to stop the disturbance? The same question can be asked about the estranged husband who has returned to his wife's department or about the group of teenagers annoying passersby at a street corner. Police are called upon to resolve these common problems, but their authority is questionable unless the behavior constitutes a criminal offense. And even then, it may not be desirable to prosecute the offender. Another type of problem is presented by the intoxicated person who is not sufficiently incapacitated to warrant being taken into protective custody, but who apparently intends to drive his car. Should a police officer have the authority to prevent the person from driving by temporarily confiscating the car keys or, as a last resort, by taking him into protective custody? Or must the officer wait for the individual to get behind the wheel and actually attempt to drive and then make an arrest? Limited specific authority may enable the police to deal more directly and intelligently with a number of comparable situations.

6. Developing New Community Resources

Analysis of a problem may lead to the conclusion that assistance is needed from another government agency. But often the problem is not clearly within the province of an existing agency, or the agency may be unaware of the problem or, if aware, without the resources to do anything about it. In such cases, since the problem is likely to be of little concern to the community as a whole, it will probably remain the responsibility of the police, unless they themselves take the initiative, as a sort of community ombudsman, in getting others to address it.

A substantial percentage of all police business involves dealing with persons suffering from mental illness. In the most acute cases, where the individual may cause immediate harm to himself or others, the police are usually authorized to initiate an emergency commitment. Many other cases that do not warrant hospitalization nevertheless require some form of attention: The number of these situations has increased dramatically as the mental health system has begun treating more and more of its patients in the community. If the conduct of these persons, who are being taught to cope with the world around them, creates problems for others or exceeds community tolerance, should they be referred back to a mental health agency? Or, because they are being encouraged to adjust to the reality of the community, should they be arrested if their behavior constitutes a criminal offense? How are the police to distinguish between those who have never received any assistance, and who should therefore be referred to a mental health agency, and those who are in community treatment? Should a community agency establish services for these persons comparable to the crisis-intervention services now offered by specially organized units operating in some communities?

Such crisis-intervention units are among a number of new resources that have been established in the past few years for dealing with several long-neglected problems: detoxification centers for those incapacitated by alcohol, shelters and counseling for runaways, shelters for battered wives, and support services for the victims of sexual assault. Programs are now being designed to provide a better response to citizen disputes and grievances, another long-neglected problem. Variously labeled, these programs set up quasi-judicial forums that are intended to be inexpensive, easily accessible, and geared to the specific needs of their neighborhoods. LEAA has recently funded three such experimental programs, which they call Neighborhood Justice Centers.[32] These centers will receive many of their cases from the police.

Thus, the pattern of creating new services that bear a relationship with police operations is now well established, and one would expect that problem-oriented policing will lead to more services in greater variety.

7. Increased Regulation

Can the problem be handled through a tightening of regulatory codes? Where easy access to private premises is a factor, should city building codes be amended to require improved lock systems? To reduce the noise problem, should more soundproofing be re-

quired in construction? The incidence of shoplifting is determined, in part, by the number of salespeople employed, the manner in which merchandise is displayed, and the use made of various antishoplifting devices. Should the police be expected to combat shoplifting without regard to the merchandising practices by a given merchant, or should merchants be required by a "merchandising code" to meet some minimum standards before they can turn to the police for assistance?

8. Increased Use of City Ordinances

Does the problem call for some community sanction less drastic than a criminal sanction? Many small communities process through their local courts, as ordinance violations, as many cases of minor misconduct as possible. Of course, this requires that the community have written ordinances, usually patterned after the state statutes, that define such misconduct. Several factors make this form of processing desirable for certain offenses: It is less formal than criminal action; physical detention is not necessary; cases may be disposed of without a court appearance; the judge may select from a wide range of alternative penalties; and the offender is spared the burden of a criminal record. Some jurisdictions now use a system of civil forfeitures in proceeding against persons found to be in possession of marijuana, though the legal status of the procedure is unclear in those states whose statutes define possession as criminal and call for a more severe fine or for imprisonment.

9. Use of Zoning

Much policing involves resolving disputes between those who have competing interests in the use made of a given sidewalk, street, park, or neighborhood. Bigger and more basic conflicts in land-use were resolved long ago by zoning, a concept that is now firmly established. Recently, zoning has been used by a number of cities to limit the pornography stores and adult movie houses in a given area. And at least one city has experimented with the opposite approach, creating an adult entertainment zone with the hope of curtailing the spread of such establishments and simplifying the management of attendant problems. Much more experimentation is needed before any judgment can be made as to the value of zoning in such situations.

Implementing the Process

A fully developed process for systematically addressing the problems that make up police business would call for more than the three steps just explored—defining the problem, researching it, and exploring alternatives. I have focused on these three because describing them may be the most effective way of communicating the nature of a problem-oriented approach to improving police service. A number of intervening steps are required to fill out the processes: methods for evaluating the effectiveness of current responses, procedures for choosing from among available alternatives, means of involving the community in the decision making, procedures for obtaining the approval of the municipal officials to whom the police are formally accountable, methods for obtaining any additional funding that may be necessary, adjustments in the organization and staffing of the agency that may be required to implement an agreed-upon change, and methods for evaluating the effectiveness of the change.

How does a police agency make the shift to problem-oriented policing? Ideally, the initiative will come from police administrators. What is needed is not a single decision implementing a specific program or a single memorandum announcing a unique way of running the organization. The concept represents a new way of looking at the process of improving police functioning. It is a way of thinking about the police and their function that, carried out over an extended period, would be reflected in all that the administrator does: in the relationship with personnel, in the priorities he sets in his own work schedule, in what he focuses on in addressing community groups, in the choice of training curriculums, and in the questions raised with local and state legislators. Once introduced, this orientation would affect subordinates, gradually filter through the rest of the organization, and reach other administrators and agencies as well.

An administrator's success will depend heavily, in particular, on the use made of planning staff, for systematic analysis of substantive problems requires developing a capacity within the organization to collect and analyze data and to conduct evaluations of the effectiveness of police operations. Police planners (now employed in significant numbers) will have to move beyond their traditional concern with operating procedures into what might best be characterized as "product research." The police administrator who focuses on the substance of policing should be able to count on support from others in key positions in the police field. Colleges with programs especially designed for police personnel may exert considerable leadership through their choice of offerings and through the subject matter of individual courses. In an occupation in which so much deference is paid to the value of a college education, if college instructors reinforce the impression that purely administrative matters are the most important issues in policing, police personnel understandably will not develop their interests beyond this concern.

Likewise, the LEAA, its state and local offspring, and other grant-making organizations have a unique opportunity to draw the attention of operating personnel to the importance of addressing substantive problems. The manner in which these organizations invest their funds sends a strong message to the police about what is thought to be worthwhile.

Effect on the Organization

In the context of this reordering of police priorities, efforts to improve the staffing, management, and procedures of police agencies must continue. Those who have been strongly committed to improving policing through better administration and organization may be disturbed by any move to subordinate their interests to a broader concern with the end product of policing. However, a problem-oriented approach to police improvement may actually contribute in several important ways to achieving their objectives.

The approach calls for the police to take greater initiative in attempting to deal with problems rather than resign themselves to living with them. It calls for tapping police expertise. It calls for the police to be more aggressive partners with other public agencies. These changes, which would place the police in a much more positive light in the community, would also contribute significantly to improving the working environment within a police agency—an environment that suffers much from the tendency of the police to assume responsibility for problems which are insolvable or ignored by others. And an improved working environment increases, in turn, the potential for recruiting and keeping qualified personnel and for bringing about needed organizational change.

Focusing on problems, because it is a practical and concrete approach, is attractive to both citizens and the police. By contrast, some of the most frequent proposals for improving police operations, because they do not produce immediate and specifically identifiable results, have no such attraction. A problem-oriented approach, with its greater appeal, has the potential for becoming a vehicle through which long-sought organizational change might be more effectively and more rapidly achieved.

Administrative rule making, for example, has gained considerable support from policy makers and some police administrators as a way of structuring police discretion, with the expectation that applying the concept would improve the quality of the decisions made by the police in the field. Yet many police administrators regard administrative rule making as an idea without practical significance. By contrast, police administrators are usually enthusiastic if invited to explore the problem of car theft or vandalism. And within such exploration, there is the opportunity to demonstrate the value of structuring police discretion in responding to reports of vandalism and car theft. Approached from this practical point of view, the concept of administrative rule making is more likely to be implemented.

Long-advocated changes in the structure and operations of police agencies have been achieved because of a concentrated concern with a given problem: The focus on the domestic disturbance, originally in New York and now elsewhere, introduced the generalist-specialist concept that has enabled many police agencies to make more effective use of their personnel; the problem in controlling narcotics and the high mobility of drug sellers motivated police agencies in many metropolitan areas to pool their resources in special investigative units, thereby achieving in a limited way one of the objectives of those who have urged consolidation of police agencies; and the recent interest in the crime of rape has resulted in widespread backing for the establishment of victim-support programs. Probably the support for any of these changes could not have been generated without the problem-oriented context in which they have been advocated.

An important factor contributing to these successes is that a problem-oriented approach to improvement is less likely to be seen as a direct challenge to the police establishment and the prevailing police value system. As a consequence, rank-and-file personnel do not resist and subvert the resulting changes. Traditional programs to improve the police—labeled as efforts to "change," "upgrade," or "reform" the police or to "achieve minimum standards"—require that police officers openly acknowledge their own deficiencies. Rank-and-file officers are much more likely to support an innovation that is cast in the form of a new response to an old problem—a problem with which they have struggled for many years and which they would like to see handled more effectively. It may be that addressing the quality of the police product will turn out to be the most effective way of achieving the objectives that have for so long been the goal of police reform.

Notes

1. Newspaper report from the Midlands of England, cited in Patrick Ryan, "Get Rid of the People, and the System Runs Fine," *Smithsonian*, September 1977, p. 140.
2. The recent study of Kansas City found that the effect of response time in the capacity of the police to deal with crime was negligible, primarily because delays by citizens in reporting

crimes make the minutes saved by the police insignificant. See Kansas City, Missouri, Police department, *Response Time Analysis*, Executive Summary (Kansas City, 1977).

3. See President's Commission on Law Enforcement and Administration of Justice, *The Challenge of Crime in a Free Society* (Washington, D.C.: Govt. Printing Office, 1967); National Advisory Commission on Civil Disorders, *Report on the National Advisory Commission on Civil Disorders* (Washington, D.C.: Govt. Printing Office 1968); National Commission on the Causes and Prevention of Violence, *To Establish Justice, to Insure Domestic Tranquility*, Final Report (Washington, D.C.; Govt. Printing Office 1969); President's Commission on Campus Unrest, *Report of the President's Commission on Campus Unrest* (Washington, D.C.; Govt. Printing Office, 1970); and National Advisory Commission on Criminal Justice Standards and Goals, *Police* (Washington, D.C.; Govt. Printing Office, 1973).

4. See, for example, National Advisory Commission on Civil Disorders, *Report*, p. 158.

5. George L. Kelling et al., *The Kansas City Preventive Patrol Experiment: A Summary Report* (Washington, D.C.: Police Foundation, 1974); and Peter W. Greenwood et al., *The Criminal Investigation Process*, 3 vols. (Santa Monica, Calif.: Rand Corp., 1976).

6. For questioning by a police administrator of the findings of the Kansas City Preventive Patrol Project, see Edward M. Davis and Lyle Knowles, "A Critique of the Report: An Evaluation of review of the Rand Corporation's Analysis of the Criminal Investigation Process," *Police Chief*, July 1976, p. 20. Each of the two pages is followed by a response from the authors of the original studies. In addition, for the position of the International Association of Chiefs of Police on the results of the Kansas City project, see "IACP Position Paper on the Kansas City Preventive Patrol Experiment," *Police Chief*, September 1975. p. 16

7. The National Institute of Law Enforcement and Criminal Justice is sponsoring a replication of the Kansas City Preventive Patrol Experiment and is supporting further explorations of the criminal investigation process. See National Institute of Law Enforcement and Criminal Justice, *Program Plan, Fiscal Year 1978* (Washington, D.C.: Govt. Printing Office, 1977), p.12

8. Admittedly, precise appraisals and comparisons are difficult. For a recent example of an examination by the press of one department that has enjoyed a reputation for good management, see "The LAPD: How Good Is It?" *Los Angeles Times*, Dec. 18, 1977.

9. Examples of cities in which police unions recently have fought vigorously to oppose innovations introduced by police administrators are Boston, Massachusetts, and Troy, New York.

10. These programs are reflected in the training opportunities routinely listed is such publications as *Police Chief, Criminal Law Reporter, Law Enforcement News, and Crime Control Digest*, and by the abstracting service of the National Criminal Justice Reference Center.

11. See, for example, National Institute of Law Enforcement and Criminal Justice, Law Enforcement Assistance Administration, "Planning Guidelines and Program to Reduce Crime," mimeographed (Washington, D.C., 1972), pp. vi–xiii. For a discussion of the concept, see Paul K. Wormeli and Steve E. Kolodney, "The Crime-Specific Model: A New Criminal Justice Perspective," *Journal of Research in Crime and Delinquency*, January 1972, pp. 54-65.

12. Ronald J. Allen, "The Police and Substantive Rulemaking: Reconciling Principle and Expediency," *University of Pennsylvania Law Review*, November 1976, p. 97.

13. Egon Bittner comes close to this point of view when he describes police functioning as applying immediate solutions to an endless array of problems. See Egon Bittner, "Florence Nightingale in Pursuit of Willie Sutton," in *The Potential for Reform of Criminal Justice*, Herbert Jacob, ed. (Beverly Hills, CA.: Sage, 1974), p. 30. James Q. Wilson does also when he describes policing as handling situations. See James Q. Wilson, *Varieties of Police Behavior: The Management of Law and Order in Eight Communities* (Cambridge, Mass.: Harvard University Press, 1968), p. 31.

14. I develop this point in an earlier work. See Herman Goldstein, *Policing a Free Society* (Cambridge, Mass.: Ballinger, 1977), pp. 30, 34-35.

15. In the 1977 book I presented a brief summary of these studies. Ibid., pp. 26-28.

16. For an up-to-date description of the concept of planning and research as it has evolved in police agencies, see O.W. Wilson and Roy C. McLaren, *Police Administration*, 4th ed. (New York: McGraw-Hill, 1977), pp. 157-81.

17. For example, see National Institute of Law Enforcement and Criminal Justice, *Police Crime Analysis Unit Handbook* (Washington, D.C.: Govt. Printing Office, 1973), pp. 90–92, 113–21.

18. For a brief description, see Joanne W. Rockwell, "Crime Specific. . . An Answer?" *Police Chief*, September 1972, p. 38.

19. The program is described in Eleanor Chelimsky, *High Impact Anti-Crime Program*, Final Report, vol. 2 (Washington, D.C.: Govt. Printing Office, 1976), pp. 19–38.

20. Ibid., pp. 145–50, 418–21.

21. For an excellent example of what is needed, see the typography of vandalism developed by the British sociologist Stanley Cohen, quoted in Albert M. Williams, Jr., "Vandalism," *Management Information Service Report* (Washington, D.C.: International City Management Association May, 1976), pp. 1–2. Another excellent example of an effort to break down a problem of concern to the police—in this case, heroin—is found in Mark Harrison Moore, *Buy and Bust: The Effective Regulation of an Illicit Market in Heroin* (Lexington, Mass.: Lexington Books, 1977), p. 83.

22. See *Bruno v. Codd*, 90 Misc. 2d 1047, 396 N.Y.S. 2d 974 (1977), finding a cause of action against the New York City Police department for failing to protect battered wives. On June 26, 1978, the city agreed to a settlement with the plaintiffs in which it committed the police to arrest in all cases in which "there is reasonable cause to believe that a husband has committed a felony against his wife and/or has violated an Order of Protection or Temporary Order of Protection." See Consent Decree, *Bruno against McGuire*, New York Appelate Court, First department, July 1978 [#3020] dismissed an appeal in the case as moot in so far as it involved the police department. From a reading of the court's reversal as to the other parts of the case, however, it appears that it would also have reversed the decision of the lower court in sustaining the action against the police department if there had not been a consent decree.)

23. It was reported that, on a recent three-day holiday weekend in Madison, Wisconsin, police handled slightly more than 1,000 calls, of which 118 were for loud parties and other types of noise disturbances. See "Over 1,000 Calls Made to Police on Weekend," *Wisconsin State Journal* (Madison, Wisc.: June 1, 1978).

24. See, for example, the detailed accounts of police functioning in Minneapolis, in Joseph M. Livermore, "Policing," *Minnesota Law Review*, March 1971, pp. 649–729. Among the works describing the police officers' varying styles in responding to similar situations are Wilson, *Varieties of Police Behavior*; Albert J. Reiss, Jr., *The Police and the Public* (New Haven, Conn.: Yale University Press, 1971); Jerome H. Skolnick, *Justice without Trial: Law Enforcement in Democratic Society* (New York: John Wiley, 1966); and Egon Bittner, *The Functions of the Police in Modern Society: A Review of Background Factors, Current Practices, and Possible Role Models* (Washington, D.C.: Govt. Printing Office, 1970).

25. See, for example, the comments of Marvin Wolfgang in a Congressionally sponsored discussion of federal support for criminal justice research, reported in the U.S. House Committee on the Judiciary, Subcommittee on Crime, *New Directions for Federal Involvement in Crime Control* (Washington, D.C.: Govt. Printing Office, 1977). Wolfgang claims that research in criminology and criminal justice has had little impact on the administration of justice or on major decision makers.

26. For further discussion of this point, see American Bar Association, *The Urban Police Function*, Approved Draft (Chicago: American Bar Association, 1973), pp. 41–42.

27. Many of these programs are summarized in David E. Aaronson et al., *The New Justice: Alternatives to Conventional Criminal Adjudication* (Washington, D.C.: Govt. Printing Office, 1977); and David E. Aaronson et al., *Alternatives to Conventional Criminal Adjudication: Guidebook for Planners and Practitioners*, Caroline S. Cooper, ed. (Washington, D.C.: Govt. Printing Office, 1977).

28. The leading work on the subject is Oscar Newman, *Defensible Space: Crime Prevention through Urban Design* (New York: Macmillan, 1972). See also Westinghouse National Issues Center, *Crime Prevention through Environment Design—A Special Report* (Washington, D.C.: National League of Cities, 1977).

29. For a summary of a survey designed to assess the effect of this change, see Russell Grindle and Thomas Aceituno, "Innovations in Robbery Control," in *The Prevention and Control of Robbery*, vol. 1, Floyd Feeney and Adrianne Weir, eds. (Davis, Calif.: University of California, 1973), pp. 315–20.

30. In one of the most recent of a growing number of studies of how police spend their time, it was reported that, of the 18,012 calls made to the police serving a community of 24,000 peo-

ple in a four-month period, 59.98 percent were requests for information. Police responded to 65 percent of the calls they received by providing information by telephone. See J. Robert Lilly, "What Are the Police Now Doing?" *Journal of Police Science and Administration,* January 1978, p. 56.

31. Death Notification (New York: Harper & Row, 1976).

32. The concept is described in Daniel McGillis and Joan Mullen, *Neighborhood Justice Centers: An Analysis of Potential Models* (Wash-ington, D.C.: Govt. Printing Office, 1977). See also R. F. Conner and R. Suretta. *The Citizen Dispute Settlement Program: Resolving Disputes outside the Courts—Orlando, Florida* (Washington, D.C.: American Bar Association, 1977).

Reprinted from: Herman Goldstein, "Improving Policing: A Problem-Oriented Approach." In *Crime and Delinquency,* 25 (25), pp. 236–258. Copyright © 1979 by Sage Publications, Inc. Reprinted by permission. ✦

2

Acquiring a Taste for Order

The Community and Police

George L. Kelling

What is disorder, and what can and should the police do about it? These are key questions, especially where community policing and problem solving are concerned. Also of importance is whether or not reasonable levels of order can be maintained in our communities, and whether or not order can ever be defined in terms that will satisfy citizens seeking predictability in their daily lives. The flip side is that the police function of maintaining order lies at the heart of the tension between individual freedoms and neighborhood security. Who should determine the level and nature of social control in our communities—the police, the citizen, or both? Although such control seems to be a police function, many citizens today are reluctant to delegate this job to strangers. G. Kelling brings this quandary into focus, discussing the delicate and controversial interplay between community and police. As you read, consider what both the community and the police can do to preserve order in our neighborhoods—and, just as important, how this goal might be divided between the two entities.

In recent writings (Kelling, 1981; Wilson and Kelling, 1983; Moore and Kelling, 1983; Kelling, 1986) I have discussed and advocated aggressive order maintenance activities by the police. Implicit in such advocacy are assumptions about the source of authority for police activity. The purpose of this article is to explore in more detail a particular source of police authority: neighborhoods and communities. The article begins with a brief description of an event I witnessed in Chicago.

> It was a late warm afternoon on north Michigan Avenue: Chicago's Gold Coast. Two young rollerskaters were taking advantage of Michigan Avenue's long slope toward the Watertower, John Hancock Building, and ultimately Lake Shore Drive. As they gyrated, dipped, and wove among pedestrians they appeared able to turn and stop on a dime. Whether intended or not, they were the center of attention and a source of some fear: some citizens moved against buildings; others stepped off of the sidewalk into the street; still others "froze" in place; and a few tried to ignore the whole thing.

Reflecting on this observation, I assume the skaters were reasonably intelligent high-spirited young people who, in their own minds, were doing nothing more than "showboating." Taken by itself the event was not particularly noteworthy. It had some dangerous potential, especially for the elderly who could not move quickly and for whom an accident could be serious, but given the catalogue of evils that afflict cities, it was a minor event. Had a police officer seen the skaters, he or she might have asked them to stop skating in such a crowded area. Most citizens would have appreciated such an intervention. In other places or times, they may well have intervened on their own. Undoubtedly, some citizens would cluck their indignation at the youths (or, at least, feel like doing so) and hope that an officer would "run them in;" others would feel empathy with the youths, but would understand the need for intervention and hope the officer would exercise good humor and patience; a few, and I suspect a *very* few, would object to police action. In any case, odds are that the skaters would have acquiesced to the officer's request.

But alas, there's a rub. Despite the relative unimportance of such events, they have within them the seeds of mischief. What if the youths had not been of good spirit? What if they would not stop or slow down and had refused the officer's request or skated away in an insulting fashion? After all, what legal right does a police officer have to order roller skaters to slow down and what recourse does the officer have if the request is ignored or defied?

If the only issue at stake were two youths roller skating on a busy street, then most of us might be quite content for the officer to do nothing if he or she were ignored or defied. Other values are at stake, however. Earlier I mentioned the danger of injury to elderly persons. Other people, less at jeopardy but equally committed to being able to walk on sidewalks, might wish to do so without having to dodge fast-moving roller skaters. What if other youths decided that Michigan Avenue was a great place for roller skating and inundated the area? Do we want civil requests from police officers to be ignored with impunity? What about bystanders who would witness disrespect for a police officer and decide that they too, perhaps in more serious circumstances, could choose whether or not to abide by an officer's request? What of the response of the police officer to being ignored? Do we want police officers to develop a "What the hell" attitude toward disorderly or dangerous behavior, even if it is not technically illegal?

Maintaining Order in Cities

At stake in the roller skating incident is whether reasonable levels of order can be maintained on city streets—that is, whether citizens and government can define, through tradition and law, what order is and devise methods to maintain it—without substantially threatening essential rights of citizens. This is an important, but controversial issue. It is important because civility, order, and predictability in daily contacts with strangers are important values in all aspects of urban life: commerce, industry, transportation, communication, education, and public safety. It is controversial because order maintenance lies at the heart of the tension between individual freedom and communal security.

The Importance of Maintaining Order

Citizens in public areas, especially [on] city streets, are obligated by a common sense of propriety. Civility allows citizens both to move safely through city streets and to enjoy street life—the simple freedom from the inti-macy of homes and intensity of domestic relationships. Without civility—the sense of reciprocity with strangers—every stranger would be a source of fear and no basis would exist for resolving conflicts. Street life since the early 1960s has been characterized by an erosion of reciprocity. Streets have become stages for the drama of what Wilson (1983) has called "the psychology of radical individualism and the philosophy of individual rights" and, more cryptically, what Tom Wolfe has labeled the "Me Decade." This era has emphasized individual liberty over communal security, privilege over responsibility, self-expression over restraint, and egalitarianism over meritocracy.[1]

Public policy has fostered this individualistic ethos. Drunkenness, vagrancy, loitering, and minor drug use have been decriminalized. Emotionally disturbed persons have been turned out onto city streets and juvenile courts have backed away from controlling obstreperous youth. The ideology of radical individualism and preoccupation with mounting crime has kept us from fully comprehending the consequences of these public policies. While government policy and police concentrated on serious crime during the 1960s and 1970s, prostitutes, gangs, hustlers, drunks, and others lacking commitment to civic virtue increasingly behaved in outrageous ways. Despite professional and academic absorption with crime, citizens were bothered by the consequences of radical individualism and public policy: increasingly outrageous street disorder. Police officials recall that citizens' groups meeting with police during this period were concerned primarily about "quality of life" problems in their neighborhoods—drunks, gangs, unruly youth, and other sources of disorder. Yet public policy concentrated on crime: It was not unusual for police and other government officials to attempt to "educate" citizens about the *real* problem—crime—and convince them of the need to concentrate police resources on it.

In the early 1980s research caught up with public sentiment when it recognized that public fear stemmed more from disorder than from serious crime (Kelling, 1981; Skogan and Maxfield 1981; Trojanowicz, 1981). Research showed that maintaining order—keeping subways free of graffiti or keeping dirty and messy people off the street—was not merely a cosmetic treatment. Drunks, gangs, prostitutes, obstreperous youth, as well as panhandling and other behaviors considered disorderly, were linked in citizens' minds to personal danger and serious crime. Moreover, as James Q. Wilson and I have argued, citizens may be right: Just as unrepaired broken windows in buildings may signal that nobody cares and lead to additional vandalism and damage, so untended disorderly behavior may also communicate that nobody cares (or that nobody can or will do anything about disorder) and thus lead to increasingly aggressive criminal and dangerous predatory behavior (Wilson and Kelling, 1982).

Whether or not Wilson and I are correct in this latter point, the consequences of fear for both citizens and cities have been dramatic: Citizens have abandoned neighborhoods, cities, shopping areas, public transportation systems, churches, and other public and private facilities. Even areas once rejuvenated—Chicago's Old Town, for example—are again troubled due primarily to street disorder. And, citizens have become increasingly skeptical of government's ability to ameliorate these problems.

One final point about the importance of order maintenance: it is deceptive to think that the majority of urban residents who are intolerant of street barbarism and support protecting neighborhood and traditional values are white, conservative, and middle class. Those demanding increased order are people of all races wanting to walk streets or ride buses without feeling under constant siege by others asserting their "rights" to say anything or behave any way they wish. These people have a deep concern for propriety and civility. Even in the most crime ridden and disorderly neighborhoods, a majority of citizens are deeply troubled about the quality of neighborhood life. Many of these people are minorities. Despite the contrary belief of some citizens and police that minority residents do not respect police, the great majority do. For many of them, police presence is the difference between being a prisoner in their own homes and being free to move about and con-

duct their daily business. Some minorities are indeed frustrated with police, as police have sensed, but their frustration is different from that portrayed by journalistic and professional elites who have focused on police brutality and abuse of authority. Most urban minorities are frustrated because police have been strangers in their communities, whisking in and out and responding to calls for service in a brusque fashion. They believe that police have not been a tangible presence, engaged with citizens to develop neighborhood peace and security. A sadness of contemporary policing is its alienation from good people in minority neighborhoods.

The Controversial Aspects of Maintaining Order

Despite the importance of maintaining order, it is also controversial—for at least two reasons. First, there is no clear and consistent definition of disorder. Unlike criminal laws that define *acts*, public disorder is a *condition*. Criminal acts are relatively easy to define (threatening someone with a weapon and taking his or her money, for example) and there is almost universal agreement among citizens of all social classes that such activities are indeed reprehensible, threaten communal life, and deserve drastic public response. Disorder as a condition may depend on the number of persons or events involved. One prostitute or one person drinking on the street may not create disorder in any community; two prostitutes or drunks may. Every community has perceptual thresholds that when approached threaten basic order. The perception of disorder may be caused by the timing of behavior. Revelry and noisemaking that are appropriate on New Year's Eve, Halloween, and the Fourth of July (indeed, often sanctioned and promoted by communities and cities), usually are not appropriate at other times. More commonly, behavior considered tolerable [on] Friday and Saturday nights may not be condoned on other nights. Location is also important: partying and noisemaking are commonplace and accepted in some neighborhoods, but rare and unacceptable in others.

Disorder then, is a condition resulting from behavior that, depending on location, time, and local traditions, is offensive in its violation of local expectations for normalcy and peace in a community. Whether malevolent or innocent in intent, disorderly behavior powerfully shapes the quality of urban life and citizens' views both of their own safety and the ability of government to ensure it.

The relativity and ambiguity that characterize definitions of disorder lead to the second controversial aspect of order maintenance: that is, the basis upon which responses to it are justified. The justification for intervening in serious criminal events is clear: there is evidence of the commission of a crime, or else it has been committed in view of a police officer. With elaborate procedural safeguards for the alleged perpetrator, the police officer can make an arrest, detain the suspect, and initiate prosecution. Maintenance of order is different: many behaviors that may create disorder are not illegal. Those that *are* illegal present, at least in theory, little difficulty for the police officer who can order the behavior stopped and make an arrest if the person will not desist. However, many disruptive behaviors have never been illegal (roller skating for example), and over the past 20 years the list of disorderly behaviors categorized as illegal has shrunk considerably (vagrancy, drunkenness, and so on).

When activities of individuals threaten order but are not illegal, perplexing problems arise for citizens and police officers. On the one hand, we all respect constitutional principles that prevent police interference with citizens' essential rights. Yet whether disorder originates from lack of civic virtue or sheer meanness, it demands action of limited scope and duration by citizens or police. The fact that public drunkenness has been decriminalized does not change the situation for police—it is a social problem about which something must be done. Likewise, deinstitutionalization of the emotionally disturbed may have been conceptually wise, but lack of community resources has resulted in the addition of one more source of urban disorder and fear: the mentally ill—another police problem. Gangs are an additional example. There is nothing illegal about the existence of a gang or its meeting on a street corner. Nevertheless, depending on where members

congregate and what they do, their very presence may terrorize many citizens. And citizens may well demand, in fact *do* demand, that police respond to gangs and gang activities, as well as drunkenness and the mentally ill. To the extent that police do respond—except when gangs, drunks, or mentally ill are involved in illegal behaviors, and for the most part they are not—police are involved in order maintenance activities that have as their goal the establishment and maintenance of some vision of civic morality.

Authorizing Order Maintenance Activities

Many citizens as well as police are squeamish about acknowledging police involvement in establishing and maintaining civic morality. Yet, every shred of empirical evidence is that police are deeply involved in order maintenance (Wycoff, 1982). It is not a question of whether police have been involved in such activities or whether they will continue to be, it is instead a question of whether they are going to acknowledge and manage their activities fully and properly to maintain order. George Will's comment, "Government would do better what it does if it would admit what it is doing" (1983), is especially apt for police. The deep-seated American inclination to be suspicious of government and especially distrustful of police ought not to divert citizens and police from the real world. Since police, as part of government, are inextricably involved in the business of defining and maintaining civic morality, it is important that police and policymakers be clear about the sources of their authority to do so. Certainly law is important. Professional wisdom is as well. What has been lost, however, is the realization and acknowledgment that community traditions are also a basic source of public authority.

The Origins of Civic Responsibility

Political theory from Aristotle to contemporary times has affirmed the centrality of the community in the development of individual character and morality. This concept has been especially important in the shaping of American political thought. Tocqueville

(1945, p. 71) describes the link between community life and good citizenship in his description of political life in New England townships.

> The native of New England is attached to his township because it is independent and free: his cooperation in its affairs ensures his attachment to its interests; the well-being it affords him secures his affection; and its welfare is the aim of his ambition and of his future expectations. He takes a part in every occurrence in the place; he practices the art of government in the small sphere within his reach; he accustoms himself to those forms without which liberty can only advance by revolutions; he imbibes their spirit; he acquires a taste for order, comprehends the balance of powers, and collects clear practical notions on the nature of his duties and the extent of his rights.

Assertion of the primacy of the community as a force shaping citizen duties and rights shifts attention from the current emphasis on the constitution and law as basic or sole repositories of society's values and virtues. That we should have come to emphasize legal sources of social control in our attempts to find a base for moral action in America is not hard to understand. During periods of rapid social change, both the constitution and laws represent a broad political and moral consensus about the role of government in economic and social life and acceptable limits on official and citizen behavior. Yet the foundations of moral and civic life are more complicated: legal codes represent a small portion of the norms, mores, taboos, and traditions that define goodness, propriety, and ultimately, legal codes. Any human society, and certainly a society as pluralistic as the United States, is characterized by both a relatively monolithic formal legal system and informal social control systems that complement and compete with the formal system.

Moreover, powerful institutions encourage and enforce adherence to both formal legal and informal social control codes: The constitution and laws are shored up by the police and courts; other basic values and norms are buttressed by the family, church, neighborhood, and community. The power of these later institutions of social control to encourage and enforce morality is found in their capacity to provide care, nurture, education, and opportunity, as well as structure and discipline. Despite the potential of neighborhoods and communities to mold and shape behavior, it can be argued that public policy has weakened many informal institutions of social control. Of particular interest here are those deliberate political, governmental, and professional policies that have weakened the political and moral authority of neighborhoods and communities.

Opposition to and elimination of powerful neighborhood governance can be traced to turn-of-the-century reformers. For the most part white Anglo-Saxon Protestants confronted by ethnic minorities and wishing to maintain their political control and traditional values, reformers came to see political methods of maintaining values, resolving disputes, and allocating services to communities as ineffective and inherently distasteful. That they should have wished to change those methods is not surprising: Consensus was not hard to achieve in the relative homogeneous New England villages described by De Tocqueville. Later, when ethnic minorities claimed their rights to their own values and used the decentralized political system to their advantage, it was another matter. Reformers moved to protect their urban vision and interests by "freeing" cities from politics. Politics became synonymous with corruption, and neighborhood and community power became equated with "ward bosses." City management came to be seen as primarily a technical matter.

According to this view, fire and police protection, garbage collection, and other urban services could best be planned and administered by professional managers serving the city at large rather than local neighborhoods. Touting efficiency and clean government, and motivated by moral zeal, reformers advocated removing control of service functions from neighborhoods and assigning them to the city at large, and when all else failed—as in the case of the police in many cities—transferring city functions to the state. During the 1950s, urban renewal and highway construction further eroded neighborhoods. Many administrators of such programs openly claimed that social good came from the obliteration of ethnic neighborhoods. When I was a student in Milwaukee during the early 1960s, for example, a former director of urban renewal justified the eradication of an Italian neighborhood for an expressway on the basis that it was "time" for second- and third-generation Italians to be integrated into the community at large. The wide dispersal of these citizens throughout Milwaukee and its suburbs suggested to administrators that Italians had been ready and wanted to disperse, rather than that these citizens had no choice but to disperse.

Preemption of political authority from neighborhoods has radically separated urban service systems from neighborhoods. While this separation was characteristic of all services, it became the keystone of the police version of professionalism. Independence from neighborhood, community, and, ultimately, city government became so central to police orthodoxy that most police administrators viewed any political attempts to influence them as tantamount to corruption. To ensure maximum separation of police officers from neighborhoods, many cities enforced legislation that police officers could not live in the neighborhoods they patrolled. "Good" services were seen as those delivered by remote professionals acting independently with little or no investment in, or accountability to, neighborhoods. This model has dominated urban administration and ideals to the present time.

In actuality, neighborhoods and communities were not easily subdued and in many cities, including Boston, New York, Philadelphia, Chicago, San Francisco, and others, they have maintained considerable political authority. For example, in New York City neighborhood representatives have regularly monitored allocation of police personnel and precluded administrative attempts to alter them appreciably. It is for this reason that it is not unlikely that when New York City allocates the 1,500 officers it is now hiring, the current district proportions will be perpetuated. Likewise, citizens in Boston have prevented neighborhood fire and police stations from closing despite the "efficiencies" to be gained from centralization. The strength of Chicago's traditional ethnic neighborhoods is well known. But generally, neighborhood political activity has been considered a throwback to earlier, less progressive forms of government-inefficient, perhaps having a particular charm, but certainly not in accord with reformers' perceptions of proper urban administration.

It is arguable whether centralizing control of urban service has resulted in the efficiencies both hoped for and promised by reformers. Perhaps in the case of fire protection and garbage collection, it has—although even that is debatable. In the case of neighborhood protection and safety, it has not. Despite increases in the number of police, narrowed responsibilities, improved management, reduced corruption, and most recently, improved treatment of minorities, police have not notably improved their record with respect to crime rates, citizen fear, disorder, or service delivery. Although police have developed an impressive capacity to respond rapidly to calls for service, the primary result of this ability has been an increase in the demand for rapid response to calls for service without any measurable impact. It has, however, widened the chasm between the police and citizens: If police are to respond rapidly to calls for service, they must remain on standby in their cars—not out of their cars with citizens.

The removal of control of police services from neighborhoods is felt most acutely when the informal controls exercised by families and neighborhoods break down and are in need of buttressing. If the breakdown in a neighborhood consists primarily of serious crime, police are increasingly positioned to know it and target an impressive array of resources at the problem. Although serious crime is a common problem in many neighborhoods, most often residents are troubled by less dramatic but, from a citizen's point of view, a more vexatious problem: chronic and demoralizing disorder. Yet rarely have police routinely collected data about chronic disorder and citizens' response to it or used such data to formulate personnel allocations or police tactics. As a result, neighborhoods have often been left to their own devices to deal with disorder. Some communities have had the resources to do so; but in other communities citizens could not make a significant impact on disorder without substantial police assistance. Indeed, disorder has become so severe in certain communities it would have been foolhardy for citizens to try. Under such circumstances, residents want and need assistance from police—not necessarily to arrest those creating disorder, but to bring them in line with community ideas of appropriate behavior. Centralizing police authority and narrowing police functioning have preempted the authority of neighborhoods and left them bereft of back-up force when things start to get out of control.

Today, circumstances are changing. Neighborhood political awareness is growing stronger and spreading—not just in the cities mentioned above that have maintained a strong sense of neighborhoods, but also in cities like Houston, Columbia (S.C.), Detroit, Milwaukee, Seattle, Minneapolis, Washington D. C., and others not generally known for having politically viable neighborhoods. Neighborhoods are organizing both to provide their own neighborhood security and to structure new relations with local politicians, police, fire departments, prosecutor's offices, courts, and other agencies responsible for citizen safety. As these groups coalesce, they become means by which citizens collectively press their interests and demands on the police.

And, just as nineteenth-century Progressives were fueled by moral zeal and civic virtue, so too are the new generation of reformers. To be sure, their vision of cities is different than the Progressive view, but it is no less fervent. At its core is a sense that citizens are no longer prepared to tolerate their own lack of control over urban services, especially given the level of urban incivility and barbarity and the apparent helplessness of centralized government to cope with it.

Increasingly, neighborhood political groups are rejecting protective services that are remote and not accountable to them. Citizens do not want to delegate social control to strangers in their communities. This is not limited to the police: It explains the recent conflicts between the Guardian Angels and citizens in the Manhattan area of Boston. Stranger guardians may be fine in neutral and impersonal territories like subways, but citizens want to know and have significant influence over anyone exercising authority in their territory. The persistence of small-town police departments, despite their "inefficiencies" evidences the same political fact: Residents of small towns are simply not prepared to give power over police to outsiders. Neighborhoods are slowly, but inexorably, learning this basic political reality. Police are starting to adjust to it.

Does this mean that local residents should completely control neighborhood standards, police should be accountable solely to communities, and police behavior should be circumscribed by neighborhood interests? Clearly, the answer is no. Such an orientation has gotten police into much difficulty in the past. Communities exist within cities, states, and the country, and alongside other communities. Each polity imposes obligations and opportunities on citizens as well as the police. Values compete with and contradict each other. For example, constitutional rights of strangers to express themselves freely can conflict with community rights of citizens to determine the character of their neighborhoods. No easy or fully satisfactory resolutions to such contradictions are available. They are inherent in a liberal democracy with competing interests and values. As much as police may want to avoid such ambiguities, the very nature of our society and its problems ensures that they cannot. Paraphrasing George Will (1983: 93), do we want citizens to enjoy freedom of expression? Yes, up to a point. Do we want police to encourage self-expression? Up to a point. Do we want police to control citizen behavior that offends and frightens other persons? Up to a point. Identifying excesses and encouraging citizen restraint is the honor, privilege, and duty of police. The fact that it is hard to define standards, reconcile competing values, and prescribe police activities to enforce them does not mean that individual citizens, groups, collectives, and police and other representatives of government should be free from the responsibility of trying to do so. If the police do become involved in such processes earnestly, their contributions may be small and indirect; but they stand a chance of strengthening those institutions that have the primary task of social control—family and community.

Note

1. Such trends have contributed much to our society. They have reduced the consequences of racism, sexism, and other forms of inequality based on personal characteristics. They have also fostered creative thinking and expression. The same trends, however, have given rise to selfishness, incivility, and unlimited behavior. Unfortunately, city streets have borne the brunt of radical individualism. And, they have been seriously, if not irreparably, harmed.

References

Kelling, George L. 1986. "Order Maintenance, the Quality of Urban Life, and the Police: A Line of Argument." In *Police Leadership in America: Crisis and Opportunity,* edited by William A. Geller. New York: Praeger.

Moore, Mark H. and George L. Kelling. 1983. "To Serve and Protect: Learning from Police History." *The Public Interest,* 70 (Winter): 49–65.

The Newark Foot Patrol Experiment. 1981. Washington, D.C.: Police Foundation. (See especially, "Conclusions," pp. 111–129.)

Skogan, Wesley G. and Michael G. Maxfield. 1981. *Coping with Crime: Individual and Neighborhood Reactions.* Beverly Hills, CA: Sage.

Tocqueville, Alexis de. 1945. *Democracy in America. vol. I* New York: Vintage.

Trojanowicz, Robert C. Unpublished. "An Evaluation Report: The Flint Neighborhood Foot Patrol."

Will, George F. 1983. *Statecraft as Soulcraft: What Government Does.* New York: Simon & Schuster.

Wilson, James Q. 1983. "Crime and American Culture." *The Public Interest,* 70 (Winter): 22–48.

Wilson, James Q. and George L. Kelling. 1983. "Broken Windows." *The Atlantic Monthly.* (March): 29–38.

Wycoff, Mary Ann. 1982. "The Role of Municipal Police: Research as a Prelude to Changing it." Washington, DC: Police Foundation.

3

The New Police Order

Effectiveness, Equity, and Efficiency in Community Policing

John E. Eck
Dennis P. Rosenbaum

If anyone needed a strong argument for community-oriented policing and problem solving, the following reading by J. Eck and D. Rosenbaum provides it. As these authors state, "Community policing is the only form of policing available for anyone who seeks to improve police operations, management, or relations with the public." The dominance of the community-policing strategy today is said to represent the new "orthodoxy" for the police. Generally, the authors provide a conceptual framework for understanding what community policing is and is not. At the heart of the matter are discussions of three important components of community policing and the need for evaluations of its effectiveness. As you read, consider how policing in a community might vary if the police and the citizens were not at all concerned with effectiveness, efficiency, and equity.

Community policing has become the new orthodoxy for cops. Simultaneously ambitious and ambiguous, community policing promises to change radically the relationship between the police and the public, address underlying community problems, and improve the living conditions in neighborhoods. One reason for its popularity is that community policing is a plastic concept, meaning different things to different people.

There are many perspectives on community policing, and each of them is built on assumptions that are only partially supported by empirical evidence.

This chapter will establish a conceptual framework for understanding what community policing is and is not in contemporary discourse. By articulating some of the central (although sometimes conflicting) expectations that we hold for community policing, we are able to distinguish this reform movement from previous initiatives and make its unique features more amenable to critical policy analysis and scientific evaluation.

In both theory and practice, the dominance of the community policing movement is evident. First, there is a large and growing literature on this topic. The growth of this literature began in the mid-1980s, but exploded with the publication of Greene and Mastrofski's (1988) anthology, *Community Policing: Rhetoric or Reality*. There are at least six other books on this subject (Goldstein, 1990; McElroy, Cosgrove, & Sadd, 1993; Skolnick & Bayley, 1986; Sparrow, Moore, & Kennedy, 1990; Trojanowicz & Bucqueroux, 1989; and Toch & Grant, 1991). Police executives also have written extensively on this subject (Brown, 1985, 1989; Couper & Lobitz, 1991; Stamper, 1992; Wadman & Olson, 1990; Williams & Sloan, 1990).

At the conferences of major police executive organizations—Police Executive Research Forum (PERF), International Association of Chiefs of Police (IACP), and National Sheriff's Association (NSA)—sessions on community policing are prominent and well attended. In fall 1992, four national conferences were held on community policing. In 1993 at least three such conferences were held. The Federal Government has recognized the emergence of community policing by funding various projects through various branches of the Department of Justice.[1] Presidents Bush and Clinton have made community policing a key element in their administrations' efforts to fight crime and rebuild cities.

Proponents of community policing can no longer claim to be fighting the battle alone against a sea of opposition. Although internal resistance to such innovation continues to be formidable in many departments, the fact remains that community policing is the only form of policing available for anyone who seeks to improve police operations, management, or relations with the public. The reason for this is simple. Community policing is part of a larger set of practices that community policing advocates—decentralizing decision making, problem-solving teams, attention to customer needs, and others—are used widely in industry. Racial fairness, another theme in community policing, is a resurgent theme throughout society. Community policing is only one manifestation of a larger social concern with quality of life issues. And renewed faith in community empowerment and self-help pervades discussions of how to address virtually any social problem. In short, there are many forces in society that support the full-scale adaptation of community policing and discourage the decline of this reform movement. With all this interest and activity, one might assume that community policing is a well-defined idea. As early as 1985, however, concern being expressed that community policing was not a unitary concept (Murphy & Muir, 1985). Bayley (1988) expanded on this concern:

> Despite the benefits claimed for community policing, programmatic implementation of police has been very uneven. Although widely, almost universally, said to be important, it means different things to different people—public relations campaigns, shopfronts and mini-stations, rescaled patrol beats, liaison with ethnic groups, permission for rank-and-file to speak to the press, Neighborhood Watch, foot patrols, patrol-detective teams, and door-to-door visits by police officers. Community policing on the ground often seems less a program than a set of aspirations wrapped in a slogan. (p. 225)

The diversity of police programs that fit under the community policing umbrella can be seen in the programs operating under a single Bureau of Justice Assistance initiative, the Innovative Neighborhood Oriented Policing (INOP) program. The eight sites initiated a variety of projects within this program, including ombudsmen, coordinating councils, mobile and stationary mini-stations, enforcement crackdowns, advertising campaigns, problem-solving efforts, and foot patrols. This range of approaches to community policing is indicative of the flexibility of the concept as well as the difficulty of defining what it is. The diversity and the lack of definition of community policing has generated critical discussion. Manning (1988), Mastrofski (1988), and Klockars (1988) attack the vagueness of community policing and question whether it can result in the performance of the police. Weatheritt (1988) describes how this vagueness was used by police in Great Britain to enhance their public image without having to change their organizations or the behavior of their constables.

Organizing the diverse views on community policing into a coherent whole is a daunting and possibly futile task. So much has been said by so many police officials, policy analysts, researchers, and theoreticians that one sometimes wonders if they are talking about the same thing. So many claims have been made about community policing—with and without evidence— that one wonders if it is possible for community policing to deliver on all or even most of them.

Framework for Understanding Community Policing Expectations

The public asks a number of things of the police. First, it asks that the police be effective at carrying out their function. This question requires us to determine what the police function is. Some of the discussions of community policing, and all of the discussions of problem-oriented policing, are primarily with the effectiveness of police services. The next question we ask is that these services be equitably distributed. That is, that the police act in a fair and responsive manner while carrying out their functions. Equity issues are at the core of many forms of community policing, especially those advocated in response to serious crises resulting from police abuses of force. Finally, we ask that effectiveness be achieved at minimal cost or that the resources provided the police be used in the most productive manner possible. Efficiency concerns are about the means of policing: hiring, training, performance measurement, organizational structure, technology, integrity, morale, policies, and procedures. Efficiency dominates most discussions of community policing, just as it has dominated discussions of the styles of policing that preceded it.

Community policing developed in response to increased realization that established forms of policing were far less effective, equitable, and efficient than had been imagined. But discussions of community policing seldom distinguish effectiveness, equity, and efficiency, in part because these are often inseparable. Attempts to redress one deficiency, say equity, are often seen as addressing the other two. For example, it has been asserted, with little hard evidence, that involving members of the community in police decision making (equity) simultaneously makes people feel that the police are responsive (equity), helps reduce neighborhood crime (effectiveness), and can reduce the police workload (efficiency). Similarly, it has been claimed that decentralizing decision making (efficiency) makes officers better able to address community problems (effectiveness), makes officers more accountable to citizens (equity), and makes better use of police resources (efficiency). By not distinguishing among these three requirements, and by not clearly separating the means of policing from the ends it serves, community policing advocates have made it more difficult to achieve meaningful improvements in policing and have made it easier for some police administrators to enact cosmetic changes disguised as fundamental reforms. Confusing these conceptually distinct requirements also has led to exaggerated claims that have the potential of undermining legitimate claims. Finally, confusing effectiveness, equity, and efficiency makes it more difficult to evaluate the successes of community policing.

In this chapter we will examine community policing in terms of effectiveness, equity, and efficiency. In doing so, we will compare how earlier forms of policing have applied these three concepts to how they have been applied in community policing. This will reveal those features that distinguish community policing from the forms of policing that

it grew out of. We will also use these concepts to critically examine a number of claims for community policing. Finally, we will describe how these three concepts can be used to measure the performance of community policing so that the claims can be empirically verified.

Effectiveness and Police Function

The function of policing always has been a subject of discussion and policing has undergone several changes in function (Fogelson, 1977; Monkkonen, 1992). Community policing is, in part, the latest attempt to answer the question, Why do we have a police force and what services should it deliver? There are a number of histories of policing and this chapter is not the place to recount past debates over the appropriate role of policing in society. To understand how community policing departs from police practice of a decade ago, however, we need to examine the principal functions the police performed.

First, police are a part of society's attempts to control crime. The fact that much of what police do appears to have little to do with crime (Reiss, 1971) does not diminish the fact that police agencies are the principal arm of local government that have crime control as one of its mandates. The traditional approach to carrying out this function is through the criminal justice system. There are three traditional methods the police could use to control crime in this manner, and each requires the apprehension of criminal offenders. First, through the application of deterrence, potential offenders might be frightened into keeping to the straight and narrow, and active offenders might be scared into abating their criminal careers. Second, locking the most active offenders away for prolonged periods could prevent them from preying on members of the public. Or, third, once caught, offenders could be rehabilitated to lead more socially acceptable lives.

A series of National Academy of Sciences studies has cast doubt on the efficacy of each of these traditional means of crime prevention and control (Blumstein, Cohen, & Nagin, 1978; Blumstein, Cohen, Roth, & Visher, 1986; Sechrest, White, & Brown, 1979). Police-specific studies questioned whether the standard police strategies of random patrolling, rapid response, and follow-up investigative work resulted in more arrests and less crime (Greenwood, Chaiken, & Petersilia, 1977; Kelling, Pate, Dieckman, & Brown, 1974; Spelman & Brown, 1984). Despite evidence that police are unlikely to have a great impact on crime on a large scale, crime control has remained an important function of policing.

A second function of policing is the rendering of immediate aid to people in crisis. The emergency response function is related to crime control, but can be considered independent of its impact on crime. Even if arriving rapidly at the scene of a crime or other emergency does not prevent future reoccurrences of that type of event, police can provide aid and assistance to people in trouble. A 911 system may not frighten offenders, but it probably gives comfort to members of the public who feel that if something goes terribly wrong they can get assistance quickly.

Also related to the crime control function, but conceptually distinct, is the police role in serving justice. Again, even if arresting a suspect does not reduce future criminal acts, it is important that people who misbehave are given some measure of punishment. The saturation of the criminal justice system with offenders has undermined this important function of the police, but the function still exists and is unlikely to be removed from the police.

The fourth and last traditional function of policing is the delivery of a variety of nonemergency services. These include such tasks as giving directions to lost tourists, controlling traffic, helping motorists whose cars have broken down, and so forth. These services are often placed in secondary importance to crime related functions, but they occupy a great deal of police time. Nevertheless, the police have slowly divested themselves of many of these services as other specialized agencies of government have taken them over (Monkkonen, 1992).

These functions—crime control, emergency aid, nonemergency services, and justice—have not been discarded by community policing advocates. Instead, community policing rearranges priorities among functions and adds new ones.

Nonemergency services take on greater importance. Crime control, emergency aid, and justice become less prominent relative to nonemergency services for four reasons: They make up such a small portion of police work that police organizations should not be organized around these functions; research has shown that the police are not particularly effective in carrying out these functions; when asked, the public is more frequently concerned about noncriminal, nonemergency quality-of-life problems; and researchers have suggested that the presence of social and physical disorder, if left unchecked, can lead to more serious neighborhood problems, including criminality (Skogan, 1990).

For some police executives community policing has to do with their beliefs (and social science theories) about the role of community in preventing crime. Community theories suggest that social order is maintained primarily by informal social processes within the neighborhood and not by police activity, thus underscoring the importance of citizen participation and the utilization of available community resources for preventing crime (Bursik & Grasmick, 1993; Byrne & Sampson, 1986; Rosenbaum, 1988). Because police have been given the public resources and mandate to fight crime, however, they have been encouraged to take a leadership role in stimulating community action and developing partnerships with community organizations and agencies (Lavrakas, 1985; Rosenbaum, Hernandez, & Daughtry, 1991). A fundamental objective of this community engagement perspective is to help create self-regulating, self-sufficient communities where levels of crime and disorder are contained by the efforts of local residents and local institutions.

Unfortunately, there is limited evidence that informal social control processes and collective crime prevention behaviors can be "implanted" in neighborhoods characterized by social disorganization and the absence of these behaviors, although comprehensive efforts certainly hold some promise (see Rosenbaum, 1986, 1988; Skogan, 1990). Furthermore, there is concern on the part of both the police and community leaders about whether police should be in the business of organizing communities, given the complex politics represented by diverse ethnic and racial needs.

A community's ability to regulate and defend itself is in part related to individuals' perceptions about crime. So community policing added fear of crime to the portfolio of police concerns. The rationale behind this was twofold: Research had shown that fear of crime was influenced by many factors other than objective risks of crime (Rosenbaum et al., 1991; Skogan & Maxfield, 1981), and it was suggested that fear of crime undermined neighborhood cohesiveness and led to the deterioration of communities (Skogan, 1990; Wilson & Kelling, 1982). Making fear of crime a center piece of community policing presents two difficulties. First, police do not claim expertise on factors that contribute to fear or effective methods of reducing fear. Second, because fear of crime is often associated with the presence of racially or ethnically dissimilar groups within the community (Anderson, 1990; Heitgerd & Bursik, 1987; Merry, 1981; Suttles, 1968; Taub, Taylor, & Dunham, 1984), police can find it difficult simultaneously to reduce fear, respond to divergent community desires and provide equitable services (Gottlieb, 1993). Nevertheless, there is some evidence that increased contact with the public can have a fear-reducing effect (Pate, Wycoff, Skogan, & Sherman, 1986; Skogan, 1990).

When the Baltimore County Police Department added fear of crime to the problems it would address, it took a problem-oriented approach (Cordner, 1986; Goldstein, 1979). A problem-oriented approach does not start with a tactical solution to a problem and seek to apply it to all occurrences of the problem. Instead, it begins with the peculiar circumstances that give rise to the problem and then looks for a situational solution (Clarke, 1992; Goldstein, 1979, 1990). That this solution may be unique—and never used again—is of little concern. The situational strategy of problem-oriented policing is a radical departure from the generic posture of traditional policing and some forms of community policing (Eck, 1993). Community policing experts should not be concerned by the repeated application of police tactics or methods to *identify or analyze* local problems (e.g., interviews, meetings, or door-to-door visits with citizens), but rather by their repeated application as *solutions* to local problems.

When one examines the fear-fighting experiments that are associated with community policing, some of these efforts represent a departure from traditional means-oriented policing, while others do not (see Pate et al., 1986; Police Foundation, 1981; Skogan, 1990). The decision to operationalize community policing as foot patrol, for example, would not be a departure from means-oriented policing unless officers were specifically instructed to gather information about possible fear-inducing problems or the police department was responding to a known fear problem. Whenever problem-oriented goals and objectives are built into this process, a police organization cannot be accused of engaging in foot patrol "for the sake of foot patrol"—a motivation that is all too common these days.

Problem-oriented policing reorganizes the police role. Emergency aid and justice are still important functions, but crime and nonemergency services are now seen as two broad classes of problems, as are fear of crime and quality of life concerns. The problem is a primary unit of police work (for the justice function the offender or victim is the unit of work and for emergency aid the event or incident is the unit of work). Goldstein (1990) defined a problem as

> a cluster of similar, related, or recurring incidents rather than a single incident; a substantive community concern; a unit of police business. (p. 66)

This definition emphasizes the importance of the public in defining a problem. Ideally, problem solving needs a high level of community engagement to identify problems, to develop an understanding of the particular circumstances that that give rise to them, to craft enduring preventive remedies, and to evaluate the effectiveness of the remedies. Without community engagement many problems will be difficult to detect,it will be hard for the police to learn about the circumstances that give rise to them, solutions will be harder to craft, and police will have limited means for determining their effectiveness (Eck & Spelman, 1987). In reality, the extent to which police agencies have solicited community input and participation in the problem-solving process varies significantly from one jurisdiction to the next, and community leaders sometimes complain about having limited input (see Sunset Park Restoration Committee, 1993). The nature, extent, and productivity of community participation in community policing is an important question for research and policy analysis.

Goldstein's definition of problems also emphasized that they are made up of events and events are potential symptoms of problems. An incident that occurs once and has little chance of occurring again is not a problem. The implication is that the purpose behind addressing problems is not to redress past wrongs but to prevent future harmful events.

Problem handling represents a departure from the past in another way. The theoretical basis for traditional police crime control has been deterrence, incapacitation, or rehabilitation. All three rely on the application of the criminal law, and as noted above, the efficacy of such a strategy of crime control is dubious. A problem-oriented approach adds a variety of ways to control crime that do not rely on the application of the criminal law. Some might be classified as situational crime prevention (Clarke, 1992). Other tactics could be classified as social prevention, addressing the root causes of crime, and relying on education and redirection of potential offenders before they get into trouble (see Rosenbaum & Lurigio, in press). And other tactics rely on the use of the civil law to change behaviors.

Community policing changes the way effectiveness is measured. Numbers of arrests and prosecutions may be crude measures of how well the police contribute to achieving justice, and response time may still be a useful gauge for measuring police handling of emergency incidents, but other measures take on greater importance. In particular, two effectiveness questions are critical: Do the police detect problems that are important to most members of the community? And do the problems the police handle decline in magnitude or seriousness as a result? If the police do not detect important problems, then they cannot address them. But even if they address them, they may not reduce the harmful effects of the problems.

Equity and the Engagement of the Public

Another long-standing concern to policing is the relationship between the police and the public. This concern was central to the debates leading to the formation of the first uniformed civil police force in London (Critchley, 1979), it shaped the form policing took when the London model was adapted to the United States (Miller, 1977), and it is a central theme in recent reform commission reports calling for community policing (Independent Commission on the Los Angeles Police Department, 1991; Philadelphia Police Study Task Force, 1987).

There are two common methods of judging the equity, or fairness, of modern policing. The first is based on legal principles. Here, police are judged to be fair if they follow the rules, that is, due process based on constitutional principles as interpreted by court decisions, legislatures, and legal authorities (the local prosecutor, city attorney, or department legal advisor). If a citizen or group of citizens complains about the fairness of police actions, then the police defend themselves by claiming that officers are simply enforcing the laws and following the procedures laid down by others. Wilson (1968) describes the extreme reliance on this way of justifying police action as the "legalistic" form of policing. Skolnick (1966) points out that the ideals of due process often run counter to other demands on policing, principally efficiency. The second method of judging equity involves the distribution of resources or outcomes. A complaint that a community does not receive the same level of police service might be met by a police claim that response times, the number of officers per capita, the number of officers per crime, or the number of crimes per resident is the same across all communities.

These approaches to equity may be acceptable if the population is homogeneous or no group feels excluded from local politics. If, however, a sizable group feels that the local political system and its government bureaucracies are unresponsive, then appeals to procedure or statistics will not address claims of inequitable treatment. Community policing is sometimes a response to the inadequacy of these methods for judging equity. Though steeped in euphemistic rhetoric, the "community" in community policing often, but not always, refers to groups who have not traditionally been in the mainstream of society.

Following recent crises in public confidence in large city policing, public commissions have called for the implementation of community policing (Independent Commission on the Los Angeles Police Department, 1991; Philadelphia Police Study Task Force, 1987). Though reports of commissions established to investigate policing address effectiveness, the precipitating events that created a sense of crisis have little to do with effectiveness. Instead they almost always involve the use of force against a nonwhite citizen and a long history of complaints by minority groups about unresponsive and inequitable treatment by the police. For some cities, though not all, community policing is an attempt to forge links between police and previously excluded communities. In this context community policing can be viewed as an outgrowth of the civil rights movement and the ascendancy to power of non-European groups in large cities. And in this sense community policing is a professional approach to Wilson's (1968) watchman style of policing, in that fairness in both styles is particularistic and personal, rather than rule bound and bureaucratic.

Equity is no longer simply defined as adherence to due process or numerical parity. Instead, community policing seeks to build trust and change the perceptions of communities toward the police, and of police officers toward communities. The principal means for achieving a sense that the police are fair and responsive is through personal contacts. The methods for community engagement vary from the deployment of foot officers to community organizing. Apart from any substantive impact on problems, one of the central objectives of these efforts is to place police employees in close prolonged contact with the same group of residents. This contact is intended to close the physical and psychological distance between the police and the community. Unless there is an explicit emphasis on addressing other problems, however, community does not necessarily require that problems be addressed or solved. Thus working directly to achieve equity will not necessarily produce more effective police, but working to solve community problems may build partnerships and improve equity as a by-product (cf. Goldstein, 1990).

Regardless of whether high-crime neighborhoods can be "turned around" through community empowerment initiatives, on a more limited scale the community perspective calls for greater citizen involvement in police decision making and problem-solving efforts. Equity concerns typically imply a passive role for citizens ("Did we get our fair share of police service?"), but in a growing number of urban communities with active neighborhood groups, equity is more about participatory management and power sharing ("Did the police ask us which problems are the most important for our community?" or "Did the police demonstrate a desire to work with us as equal partners in developing anticrime and antidrug initiatives?"). In sum, although equity efforts in the context of community policing are typically limited to increasing the number of police-citizen contacts, the community outreach perspective can be, and has been, taken to another level. New police-community relationships (established by additional contact) can be used to enhance citizen involvement in decision making, problem solving, community self-defense, and various community empowerment actions. The popular methods for communication with the public (e.g., door-to-door interviews, foot patrols, community meetings, mini-stations) can provide vehicles for attacking specific local problems if police management will use them as such.

The appropriate measure of equity changes with a move to community policing. Traditional measures such as compliance with due process, use of force, and the distribution of services remain important gauges of equity. However, the most relevant measures are the perceptions of the various publics served by police. How people feel about the police is as critical, if not more critical, than other measures of equity. Both the quantity and quality of police-citizen contacts are considered important measures of police performance under many community policing programs. It is for this reason that police agencies in Reno (NV) and Madison (WI) routinely use surveys to assess public opinion about their services. Periodic samples of public opinion can show changes in community concerns about the police and show how perceptions vary by neighborhood, age, race, gender and other characteristics. Large stable differences among groups may be indicators of perceptions of inequity.

Efficiency in Resource Deployment and Control

Finally, there is the concern with police organization and management. Whether based on the management principles of the British military (Critchley, 1979), Taylorist theories (Wilson, 1950), or current management styles (Moore & Stephens, 1991), how the police mobilized their resources to fulfill their mission has been a recurring theme within the writings on policing. Given demands to deliver services effectively and equitably, which management procedures help achieve these goals with the minimal cost? In particular, two concerns are paramount: How should resources be deployed in a police organization? And how should the behaviors of officers be controlled so these resources are put to use in the most effective and equitable manner?

Until recently, the resources of concern to the police could be itemized within the police operating and capital budgets. These resources included equipment, facilities, and most importantly, its personnel. If the people, equipment, or facilities were not included in the police organization, then police managers did not view them as assets. The police saw themselves as self-contained and did not ask assistance in carrying out their functions. The primary task for police managers was to allocate their resources among various divisions and deploy their personnel geographically and functionally. The decision to decentralize or centralize commands was based on whether it would reduce costs for the same results or achieve more results for the same costs.

The Achilles' heel of this approach is readily appreciated when one looks at the actual number of officers deployed on the street at any given time. Out of every 100 sworn personnel, seldom are more than 60 in the uniform patrol division (Police Executive Research Forum, 1981). Once these personnel are divided among three shifts and allowing for time off, weekends, and holidays, few are on duty at any given time. This number is further reduced because some of these officers are managers who are not engaged in street work, and many of the street officers may be in court or other off-street activities. Of the remaining officers, many others will be handling calls (Levine & McEwen, 1985). This leaves very few officers patrolling the street as a deterrent to crime. The simple arithmetic of policing suggests that in any neighborhood it is not the police who are keeping the peace, it is the public. So for the purposes of controlling crime, the assets of the police extend far beyond the police organization. The same is true of the other functions of the police; in order to pursue justice and provide emergency and nonemergency services, the police rely on citizens to report events and pass on vital information.

At the same time as the police discounted their assets they ignored their limits for taking on more work. To an individual considering whether to request police help, policing is free. Though the public does pay for policing through their taxes, people can consume unlimited amounts of police services without their individual tax bill being affected. As with all free services, customers will use much more of it than they would if there was a cost for its use. By making it easier to get this service, the telephone, radio, and squad car increased the demand for it. Without a phone, a citizen with a problem would have to seek out an officer. The inconvenience of going to a police station kept the demand for policing down prior to the widespread access to telephones and the adoption of two-way radios and cars. Call handling would be effective and efficient if answering calls prevented future calls from the same location, but recent studies of repeat calls indicate that responding to events does little to control them (Pierce, Spaar, & Briggs, 1986; Sherman, Gartin, & Buerger, 1989). So from the standpoint of simple economics, there is no staffing level for policing that would ever keep the call workload in check, as long as calling is free and easy.

Community policing departs from previous styles of policing by the way resources are counted and the methods by which control over officer behavior is exerted. Many of the assets needed to address problems are outside the boundaries of police organizations. These assets are the powers and resources of other government agencies, businesses, and the community itself. Bolstering the capacities of others can help the police become more effective without requiring proportional increases in police controlled resources. When officers of the Baltimore County police discovered that the county needed a detoxification center to handle chronic alcoholics to address a panhandler problem around a shopping center, the department requested that the county establish such a facility. When San Diego police officers found that violent crimes at a trolley stop were facilitated by the station's physical design, they asked the trolley authority to make the required changes. When a Newport News police detective wanted to reduce domestic homicides he established a multiagency task force involving local hospitals, the prosecutor, the newspaper, women's groups, military bases, and various other stakeholders in the problem. The common theme to these examples is that the police expand their capacity to address community concerns by using the resources of other groups. This stands in stark contrast to the standard practices of trying to carry out the police function with existing police resources or by requesting greater resources.

Community policing advocates have advanced the idea that organized citizens can control crime and improve neighborhood conditions, and therefore police should mobilize neighborhood groups. As noted earlier,

the empirical support for this idea is limited (Rosenbaum, 1988; Skogan, 1990). The weak empirical support may be because insufficient research has been conducted on the precise mechanisms by which organized communities could control crime and improve the quality of community life. There are five means by which citizens can help accomplish these ends. First, they can watch and report suspicious behavior and other information to police officials. Police have promoted passive involvement through the formation of Neighborhood Watch groups. Second, citizens can patrol areas, confront suspicious people, and ask that they leave the area or change their behaviors. Active involvement is less common than passive involvement, and police agencies often try to thwart active involvement because of safety concerns. Nevertheless, some police have encouraged such actions. Third, citizens can change their own behavior to reduce their chances of becoming victims of crime or inadvertently contributing to a deterioration of the quality of life in a neighborhood. Police crime prevention programs frequently promote personal safety precautions. Fourth, citizens can put pressure on others to act: They can demand more police resources, they can pressure businesses to change their practices, they can lobby local government agencies to obtain services and get favorable rulings from regulators, and they can threaten property owners and organizations with civil suits to change behaviors and physical conditions. Unlike the first and third methods, here citizens do not directly confront the problem with their own resources, but use their legal and political powers to gain external resources. Exerting pressure is a tactic that has been highly effective for many community organizations, as documented in case studies (Rosenbaum, 1993). Fifth, citizens can authorize the police to act on their behalf. Knowing this, community police officers will meet with community members and gain their acquiescence, thereby allowing the police to act. By building a rapport with neighborhood residents, officers can carry out enforcement actions that would be otherwise unacceptable (Eck,

1993; Weisburd, McElroy, & Hardyman, 1988).

Though these methods of contributing to neighborhood safety are important, many of these actions are indirect, operating through the police or other organizations. This is because to take direct action on problems one must have resources and special powers, which community organizations often lack. For example, the residents of an apartment complex may want a drug dealer to leave the complex, but only the landlord can evict him. A community may want a local liquor store to stop selling fortified wine to chronic alcoholics, but only the owner of the store can curtail this behavior. Citizens can pressure the landlord or liquor store owner (threatening a rent boycott, picketing, adverse publicity, or a suit), or they can get the police or a regulatory agency to apply pressure on their behalf. Sometimes, these pressures can be very effective if the community has the necessary organizing skills or clout. Other times, community frustrations are not translated into action.

Therefore, when the police go to a community to help address a problem, there are limits on what the community can deliver and what the police can realistically expect. If police feel that community consent is not problematic, they think that they understand the problem, and they believe that they can get the help of other city agencies, the police often will handle the problem without community help (e.g., threaten the landlord with a nuisance abatement proceeding that could result in the confiscation of the apartment building unless the drug dealer is evicted, or threaten the liquor store owner with the revocation of his license to sell alcohol unless he controls whom he sells to). It can be more efficient not to involve the community. Police are especially likely to act this way in disorganized neighborhoods with little political clout and where knowledge of how to access government agencies is limited. Interestingly enough, research suggests that *if* the police were to invite community input in these neighborhoods, many, if not most, residents would support aggressive (and sometimes unconstitutional) enforcement actions by the police (Rosenbaum, 1993).[2]

Organizing resources to cope with demands for service presents one set of problems for efficiently running a police agency. Another set of problems involves control over police employees. To be effective and deliver services equitably, police officers must use their powers for the ends of the organization. Miller (1977) shows that the police in the United States have always been endowed with more discretion than their British counterparts, in large part for efficiency reasons; to save costs police agencies in the United States hired fewer officers and gave them wider latitude to make decisions while police forces in Great Britain hired more constables and gave them less discretion. Police organizations attempt to limit the discretionary authority of police officers through rules and procedures and a system of command and control. This approach is topdown and rule driven. The limits of this approach to controlling officer behavior have been widely documented (Brown, 1981; Davis, 1975; Krantz, Gilman, Benda, Hallstrom, & Nadworny, 1979; LaFave, 1965; Punch, 1983). Officers operate out of sight of their supervisors and make decisions that seldom can be directly monitored (Goldstein, 1960). Rules and procedures are more likely to proscribe behaviors than to help officers determine the appropriate behavior (Goldstein, 1977). Further, the police organization often makes demands on officers that cannot be fulfilled without violating some rule or procedure (Skolnick, 1966).

At the same time that community policing advocates promote the idea that networking with other organizations and communities is important, they also promote the idea that police organizations need to make better use of the experience and knowledge of street officers. This has taken a variety of forms from decentralization of decision making from headquarters to substations and the establishment of fixed beat assignments (Brown, 1989; Koller, 1990; Sparrow, 1988) to experiments in replacing rule-based/top-down decision making with bottom-up/value-driven decision making (Couper & Lobitz, 1991; Sparrow, 1988; Wasserman & Moore, 1988). The rationale for these changes is that to be responsive to community members and to address problems, decision makers need more information than is usually available to high-level commanders, and the police need to be more flexible than is possible by following the chain of command. These changes will bring officers closer to the communities they serve and provide them with the authority to act on their behalf.

In the process of attempting these organizational changes, police administrators and researchers recognize that community residents are not the only clients (or targets) of community policing and that internal changes may benefit police personnel as well. Authors have suggested that decentralization and participatory management, for example, will improve the morale of officers (Trojanowicz & Banas, 1985; Wycoff, 1988), despite internal resistance to change. These ideas are well grounded in organizational theory (e.g., Hackman & Oldham, 1976), but there is a paucity of well-designed studies capable of testing these and other hypotheses. For the most part, community policing efforts are relatively new and the officers involved are either specially selected for special assignments or the officers decided to get on board early. In either case, it is difficult to determine if changes in the administration of the department had an effect on the behavior and attitudes of the officers or whether the officers were predisposed to this type of work and already had a different view of their work as police officers before their involvement in community policing.

As community policing becomes more pervasive within police agencies, and officers do not have the option of keeping away from it, these management concepts will be put to a more rigorous test. It seems unlikely that police agencies will be able to abandon totally their many rules and procedures in deference to a mission-driven organization, or that police agencies will become fully democratic institutions instead of command bureaucracies. Instead, these newer management ideas may be layered on top of more traditional management techniques.

A major barrier to newer management ideas is the political environment that police departments must work within. Local officials with authority over the police will have to give police agencies broad authority to work with communities, address problems, and adopt a mission-driven perspective. But the police, with their monopoly on the use of force, 24-hour responsibilities, and broad mandate, will always be the center of conflicting demands. The uncertain nature of the police chief's job will maintain a demand for rules that curtail officers' authority and centralize decision making.

Because efficiency is a gauge of how well resources are used to obtain a given level of effectiveness, two yardsticks for efficiency are appropriate for community policing. First, given two equally effective community policing agencies, the agency that makes the greatest use of resources beyond its direct control should be viewed as the most efficient. These resources include those of other government and private organizations and citizens' groups. By this measure of efficiency, police agencies that are well integrated into local government service delivery systems, have extensive networks with private institutions, and have well-developed partnerships with community groups should be able to leverage their resources more than police agencies that operate autonomously.

One would expect, if proponents of community policing are correct, that police agencies that have extensive collaborative arrangements will need fewer resources to achieve a given level of effectiveness than police agencies that do not.

Second, given comparable levels of effectiveness, police agencies with the fewest internal layers of bureaucratic control are more efficient than police agencies with a greater number of ranks. The parts of a police agency that directly serve the public are those parts that have direct contact with people outside the organization. The greater the ratio of service deliverers to administrators, the more services that can be provided or leveraged for a given level of resources. Agencies that find ways to guide officers to activities that are effective and equitable, with few levels of supervision, will be more efficient than agencies that are equally effective and equitable, but have more layers of supervision.

Future of Community Policing

We began this discussion by noting that a reason community policing is so difficult to define is that different proponents emphasize different aspects while using the same terminology. We have shown that organizing a discussion of community policing around effectiveness, equity, and efficiency helps clarify the concept by highlighting the aspects of community policing that are different from previous practices and suggesting methods for gauging performance.

This discussion raises the question of priority among the three concerns. Does it matter if community policing is framed in terms of efficiency, equity, or effectiveness? Which concern—effectiveness, equity, or efficiency— should be the starting point for implementing community policing? Or will beginning with any one of these concerns naturally and inevitably lead to addressing the other two? Will a police agency that starts by changing the decision-making processes of the organization also end up improving trust between the police and the public and effectively addressing problems? Will a department that starts by building trust between members of the public and the police inevitably come to addressing problems, developing partnerships with other organizations, and decentralizing decision-making authority? Will a police agency that begins by promoting effective problem solving have to engage members of communities, decentralize authority, and develop collaborative arrangements with other organizations? The answers to these questions are unclear, but we suggest three related hypotheses.

Historically, police have emphasized efficiency and equity concerns relative to effectiveness. This emphasis on means over ends was the basis for Goldstein's (1979) critique of policing and led to his development of problem-oriented policing. If a police agency begins by focusing on substantive community problems, the need to improve relationships with the public, decentralize decision-making, and create networks with other groups may become rather obvious. Most problems cannot be successfully addressed without the involvement of others and collaboration requires a level of trust. Effective problem solving also seems to require a high level of delegation of authority to line personnel. Further, the process of working on problems is likely to build trust between the police and community. Therefore, a police agency that begins by focusing on effectiveness and continually looks for ways of making the agency more effective, is likely to address equity and efficiency concerns as well. There is nothing that is inevitable about this, but if communities, other agencies, and officers' experiences are crucial to effective problem solving, then beginning with effectiveness will lead to the more equitable and efficient policing.

An agency that begins by focusing on equity may not make fundamental changes to improve the effectiveness of the police. One could reduce conflicts between the police and the public by hiring more minority officers, conducting cultural sensitivity training for officers, reducing police use of force, developing open citizen-complaint handling processes, creating stable beat assignments, and enacting a host of other policies and procedures. As important as these changes may be, none of them require the police to change their basic functions. It is not difficult to imagine a police force that focuses exclusively on handling emergency and nonemergency calls and making sure offenders are brought to justice and is seen as responsive and trustworthy by the communities it serves. In such instances, other institutions may handle community problems, with or without police assistance. A responsive police agency can easily increase the level of patrolling when community groups ask. A responsive police agency can enlist the help of local organizations to make sure officers handle incidents better. If the police are particularly good at building trust, it is quite likely that they will be able to use their support in the community to increase staffing and resources, resulting in a decrease in efficiency. In short, a focus on equity concerns without a major effort to improve effectiveness and efficiency may only change how the police are perceived by members of the public.

This improvement should not be taken lightly in inner-city neighborhoods where massive distrust between the police and the community may prohibit the development of a problem-solving partnership. But even here, our point is that unless a plan is eventually developed to attack specific crime and disorder problems, the improved attitudes about the police are unlikely to portend any major improvements in the quality of neighborhood life.

Finally, addressing efficiency issues alone is unlikely to lead to changes in police effectiveness or improvements in equity. For example, a police agency that changes the way nonemergency calls are handled—from a rapid response by an officer to taking a report over the telephone or a follow-up by a civilian employee—may reduce officers' workloads and reduce costs. But unless the time officers no longer have to spend on these calls is used to address problems, there will be no improvement in effectiveness. Neither are such policies likely to project a feeling of responsiveness to community needs. Officers may be delegated a great deal of decision-making authority but unless they are directed to address problems, and unless they are shown the appropriate ways to interact with the public, effectiveness and equity will not be addressed.

Though effectiveness is unlikely to be improved without improving equity and efficiency also, it is possible to make improvements in equity or efficiency and leave the other two areas untouched. If this is true, then three forms of community policing may develop in U.S. cities. Equitable community policing agencies would seek to improve the way police are perceived by minority communities and groups that have been traditionally left out of the mainstream. Such agencies may not necessarily be more effective or efficient than police agencies are today. Efficient community police agencies would have a few highly trained officers carry out the police function without layers of management. These agencies also could have highly developed networks with other organizations. The officers would use these networks to divert cases and shift workload. Because this may be accomplished without preventing the incidents that create the workload, efficiency would improve but effectiveness would remain unchanged. In these agencies police community relations might not be appreciably different than we see them today, Effective community policing, or problem-oriented policing agencies could be more preventive and thereby improve their effectiveness. But because prevention would require them to be responsive to communities, to collaborate with other agencies, and to decentralize decision making, these agencies might have to make strides in all three areas.

Developing performance measures for community policing and stronger evaluations will allow the testing of these hypotheses. By longitudinally measuring effectiveness, equity, and efficiency in police agencies we could determine how police agencies change and if changes in one domain influence changes in the other two. These measures would allow us to determine if community policing substantially improves police effectiveness, the equitable distribution of police services, or the efficient use of police resources.

Notes

1. In 1992 the Bureau of Justice Assistance funded a consortium of the IACP, PERF, Police Foundation, and NSA to develop a model community policing strategy and deliver technical assistance to four demonstration sites to be selected in 1993.

2. We should note that although police often act without community involvement or total consent, the reverse is also true when residents have lost confidence in the ability of the police to solve their local problems. Citizen patrols and direct actions against drug dealers have become common occurrences in neighborhoods where drug markets have emerged and citizens have come to realize that no one outside the neighborhood is going to rescue them (see Davis, Lurigio, & Rosenbaum, 1993).

References

Anderson, E. (1990). *Streetwise*. Chicago: University of Chicago Press.

Bayley, D. H. (1988). Community policing: A report from the devil's advocate. In J. R. Greene & S. D. Mastrofski (Eds.), *Community policing: Rhetoric or reality?* (pp. 225–238). New York: Praeger.

Blumstein, A., Cohen, J., & Nagin, D. (Eds.). (1978). *Deterrence and incapacitation: Estimating the effects of criminal sanctions on crime rates*. Washington, DC: National Academy of Sciences.

Blumstein, A., Cohen, J., Roth, J., & Visher, C. (1986). *Criminal careers and "career criminals"* (Vol. 1). Washington, DC: National Academy of Sciences.

Brown, L. P. (1985). Community-policing power sharing. In W. A. Geller (Ed.), *Police leadership in America: Crisis and opportunity* (pp. 70–83). New York: Praeger.

Brown, L. P. (1989). *Community policing: A Practical guide for police officials* (Perspectives in Policing No. 12). Washington, DC: National Institute of Justice.

Brown, M. K. (1981). *Working the street: Police discretion and the dilemmas of reform*. New York: Russell Sage Foundation.

Bursik, R. J., & Grasmick, H. G. (1993). *Neighborhoods and crime: The dimensions of effective community control*. New York: Lexington.

Byrne, J. M. & Sampson, R. J. (Eds.). (1986). *The social ecology of crime*. New York: Springer.

Clarke, R. V. (Ed.). (1992). *Situational crime prevention: Successful case studies*. New York: Harrow & Heston.

Cordner, G. W. (1986). Fear of crime and the police: An evaluation of a fear-reduction strategy. *Journal of Police Science and Administration, 14*, 223–233.

Couper, D. C., & Lobitz, S. H. (1991). *Quality policing: The Madison experience*. Washington, DC: Police Executive Research Forum.

Critchley, T. A. (1979). *A history of police in England and Wales*. Montclair, NJ: Patterson Smith.

Davis, K. C. (1975). *Police discretion*. St. Paul, MN: West.

Davis, R. C., Lurigio, A. J., & Rosenbaum, D. P. (Eds.). (1993). *Drugs and the community*. Springfield, IL: Charles C. Thomas.

Eck, J. E. (1993). Alternative futures for policing. In D. Weisburd & C. Uchida (Eds.), *Police innovation and control of the police* (pp. 59–79). New York: Springer.

Eck, J. E., & Spelman, W. (1987). *Problem solving: Problem-oriented policing in Newport News*. Washington, DC: Police Executive Research Forum.

Fogelson, R. M. (1977). *Big city police*. Cambridge, MA: Harvard University Press.

Goldstein, H. (1977). *Policing a free society*. Cambridge, MA: Ballinger.

Goldstein, H. (1979). Improving policing: A problem-oriented approach. *Crime and Delinquency, 25*, 236–258.

Goldstein, H. (1990). *Problem-oriented policing*. New York: McGraw-Hill.

Goldstein, J. (1960). Police discretion not to invoke the criminal process: Low-visibility decisions in the administration of justice. *Yale Law Journal, 69*, 543–594.

Gottlieb, M. (1993, July 21). Crown Heights study finds Dinkins and police at fault in letting unrest escalate. *The New York Times*, p. 1.

Greene, J. R., & Mastrofski, S. D. (Eds.). (1988). *Community policing: Rhetoric or reality?* New York: Praeger.

Greenwood, P. W., Chaiken, J. M., & Petersilia, J. (1977). *The criminal investigation process*. Lexington, MA: D. C. Heath.

Hackman, J. R., & Oldham, G. R. (1976). Motivation through the design of work: Test of a theory. *Organizational Behavior and Human Performance, 16*, 250–279.

Heitgerd, J. L., & Bursik, R. L., Jr. (1987). Extracommunity dynamics and the ecology of delinquency. *American Journal of Sociology, 92*, 775–787.

Independent Commission on the Los Angeles Police Department. (1991). *Report of the Independent Commission on the Los Angeles Police Department*. Los Angeles, CA: Author.

Kelling, G. L., Pate, T., Dieckman, D., & Brown, C. E. (1974). *The Kansas City preventive patrol experiment: A technical report*. Washington, DC: Police Foundation.

Klockars, C. B. (1988). The rhetoric of community policing. In J. R. Greene & S. D. Mastrofski (Eds.), *Community policing: Rhetoric or reality?* (pp. 239–258). New York: Praeger.

Koller, K. (1990). *Working the beat: The Edmonton neighborhood foot patrol*. Edmonton, Alberta: Edmonton Police Service.

Krantz, S., Gilman, B., Benda, C., Hallstrom, C., and Nadworny, E. (1979). *Police policymaking*. Lexington, MA: D. C. Heath.

LaFave, W. R. (1965). *Arrest: The decision to take a suspect into custody*. Boston: Little, Brown.

Lavrakas, P. J. (1985). Citizen self-help and neighborhood crime prevention policy. In L. A. Curtis (Ed.), *American violence and public policy* (pp. 87–116). New Haven, CT: Yale University Press.

Levine, M. J. & McEwen, J. T. (1985). *Patrol deployment*. Washington, DC: National Institute of Justice.

Manning, P. K. (1988). Community policing as a drama of control. In J. R. Greene & S. D. Mastrofski (Eds.), *Community policing: Rhetoric or reality?* (pp. 27–46). New York: Praeger.

Mastrofski, S. D. (1988). Community policing as reform: A cautionary tale. In J. R. Greene & S. D. Mastrofski (Eds.), *Community policing: Rhetoric or reality?* (pp. 47–68). New York: Praeger.

McElroy, J. E., Cosgrove, C. A., & Sadd, S. (1993). *Community policing: The CPOP in New York.* Newbury Park, CA.: Sage.

Merry, S. F. (1981). Defensible space undefended: Social factors in crime prevention through environmental design. *Urban Affairs Quarterly, 16*, 397–422.

Miller, W. R. (1977). *Cops and Bobbies: Police authority in New York and London, 1830–1870.* Chicago: University of Chicago Press.

Monkkonen, E. (1992). History of urban police. In M. Tonry & N. Morris (Eds.), *Crime and justice: Vol. 15. Modern policing* (pp. 547–580). Chicago: University of Chicago Press.

Moore, M. H., & Stephens, D. W. (1991). *Beyond command and control: The strategic management of police departments.* Washington, DC: Police Executive Research Forum.

Murphy, C., & Muir, G. (1985). *Community-based policing: A review of the critical issues.* Ottawa: Solicitor General of Canada.

Pate, A. M., Wycoff, M. A., Skogan, W. G., & Sherman, L. W. (1986). *Reducing fear of crime in Houston and Newark: A summary report.* Washington, DC: Police Foundation.

Philadelphia Police Study Task Force. (1987). *Philadelphia and its police: Toward a new partnership.* Philadelphia: Philadelphia Police Department.

Pierce, G. L., Spaar, S., & Briggs L. R. (1986). *The character of police work: Strategic and tactical implications.* Boston: Center for Applied Social Research, Northeastern University.

Police Executive Research Forum. (1981). *Survey of police operational and administrative practices.* Washington, DC: Author.

Punch, M. (Ed.). (1983). *Control in the police organization.* Cambridge: MIT Press.

Reiss, A. J., Jr. (1971). *The police and the public.* New Haven, CT: Yale University Press.

Rosenbaum, D. P. (1986). *Community crime prevention: Does it work?* Beverly Hills, CA: Sage.

Rosenbaum, D. P. (1988). Community crime prevention: A review and synthesis of the literature. *Justice Quarterly 5*, 323–395.

Rosenbaum, D. P. (1993). Civil liberties and aggressive enforcement: Balancing the rights of individuals and society in the drug war. In R. C. Davis, A. J. Lurigio, & D. P. Rosenbaum

(Eds.), *Drugs and the community* (pp. 55–82). Springfield, IL: Charles C. Thomas.

Rosenbaum, D. P., & Lurigio, A. J. (in press). *Fighting back: Two sides of citizen reactions to crime.* Pacific Grove, CA: Wadsworth.

Rosenbaum, D. P., Hernandez, E., & Daughtry, S., Jr. (1991). Crime prevention, fear reduction, and the community. In W. A. Geller (Ed.), *Local government police management* (Golden Anniversary ed.) (pp. 96–130). Washington, DC: International City Management Association.

Sechrest, L. B., White, S. O., & Brown, E. D. (Eds.). (1979). *The rehabilitation of criminal offenders: Problems and prospects.* Washington, DC: National Academy of Sciences.

Sherman, L. W., Gartin, P. R., & Buerger, M. E. (1989). Hot spots of predatory crime: Routine activities and the criminology of place. *Criminology, 27*, 27–55.

Skogan, W. G. (1990). *Disorder and decline: Crime and the spiral of decay in American neighborhoods.* New York: Free Press.

Skogan, W. G., & Maxfield, M. (1981). *Coping with crime: Individual and neighborhood reactions.* Beverly Hills, CA: Sage.

Skolnick, J. (1966). *Justice without trial: Law enforcement in a democratic society.* New York: John Wiley.

Skolnick, J. H., & Bayley, D. H. (1986). *The new blue line: Police innovations in six American cities.* New York: Free Press.

Sparrow, M. K. (1988). *Implementing community policing* (Perspectives on Policing No. 9). Washington, DC: National Institute of Justice.

Sparrow, M. K., Moore, M. H., & Kennedy, D. M. (1990). *Beyond 911: A new era for policing.* New York: Basic Books.

Spelman, W., & Brown, D. K. (1984). *Calling the police: Citizen reporting of serious crime.* Washington, DC: Government Printing Office.

Stamper, N. (1992). *Removing managerial barriers to effective police leadership.* Washington, DC: Police Executive Research Forum.

Sunset Park Restoration Committee, Inc. (1993). *The model precinct: A community review of the 72nd Police Precinct.* Brooklyn, NY: Author.

Suttles, G. D. (1968). *Social order of the slum: Ethnicity and territory in the inner city.* Chicago: University of Chicago Press.

Taub, R. D., Taylor, G. S., Dunham, J. (1984). *Patterns of neighborhood change: Race and crime in urban America.* Chicago: University of Chicago Press.

Toch, H., & Grant, J. D. (1991). *Police as problem-solvers.* New York: Plenum.

Trojanowicz, R. C., & Banas, D. (1985). *Job satisfaction: A comparison of foot patrol versus mo-*

tor patrol officers (Community Policing Series No. 2). East Lansing: Michigan State University, National Neighborhood Foot Patrol Center.

Trojanowicz, R. C., & Bucqueroux, B. (1989). *Community policing: A contemporary perspective*. Cincinnati: Anderson.

Wadman, R. C., & Olson, R. K. (1990). *Community wellness: A new theory of policing*. Washington, DC: Police Executive Research Forum.

Wasserman, R., & Moore, M. H. (1988). Values in policing (Perspectives in Policing No. 8). Washington, DC: National Institute of Justice.

Weatheritt, M. (1988). Community policing: Rhetoric or reality. In J. R. Greene & S. D. Mastrofski (Eds.), *Community policing: Rhetoric or reality?* (pp. 153–176). New York: Praeger.

Weisburd, D., McElroy, J. E., & Hardyman, P. (1988). Challenges to supervision in community policing: Observations on a pilot project. *American Journal of Police, 7*, 29–59.

Williams, J., & Sloan, R. (1990). *Turning concept into practice: The Aurora, Colorado story* (Community Policing Series No. 19). East Lansing: Michigan State University, National Center for Community Policing.

Wilson, J. Q. (1968). Varieties of police behavior. New York: Athenaeum.

Wilson, J. Q., & Kelling, G. L. (1982, March). Broken windows: The police and neighborhood safety. *The Atlantic Monthly*, pp. 29–38.

Wilson, 0. W. (1950). *Police administration*. New York: McGraw-Hill.

Wycoff, M. A. (1988). The benefits of community policing: Evidence and conjecture. In J. R. Greene & S. D. Mastrofski (Eds.), *Community policing: Rhetoric or reality?* (pp. 103–121). New York: Praeger.

4

The Changing Role of the Police

Assessing the Current Transition to Community Policing

Dennis P. Rosenbaum

Beginning with a metaphor that community policing is "like a summer breeze that opens the door to new possibilities," D. Rosenbaum proceeds to assess community policing as a reform movement, replacing the traditional, law enforcement-oriented approach. Included are community policing's main features, the changing role of police, and how police "effectiveness" is to be viewed within this model. Community engagements and partnerships— two essential features that lie at the heart of the community-policing approach because of the fundamental notion that police cannot fight crime alone—are also examined. Rosenbaum attaches tremendous importance to the need for forming police-community partnerships in order for community policing to be effective. This reading is key to the understanding of this strategy's components. Preventing problems is seen as holding the most promise for arresting a wide range of social problems, through early and intensive interventions by citizens and their police. After reading this selection, contemplate how community policing represents a true reform movement and whether or not it would have any hope of success without community input.

This is an exciting and challenging time in the world of policing. The winds of change are moving through the hallways of many police organizations in Northern America. For some, these winds are like a summer breeze that opens the door to new possibilities. For others, they signal the onset of a cold, uncertain winter. Regardless of how one experiences it, something is happening, and this "something" is an attempt to rethink and restructure the role of police in society.

This reform movement is both promising and threatening; it promises to improve public safety, yet it offers no simple formula or road map to get there; it promises to reform police agencies and stimulate community involvement in public safety, yet police officers and community residents are often left to imagine how this will happen. In any event, there is no debate about the magnitude of this push to create a new model of policing. The concept of community policing has spread rapidly in many countries and is touted highly by police executives in Canada and the United States (Leighton, 1991; Normandeau & Leighton, 1990; Wycoff, 1995). In the United States, community policing is the centerpiece of the 1994 national crime bill, which provides funding for 100,000 new community policing officers over 6 years (see 42 USC 3796dd, Sec. 1701; Office of Community Oriented Policing Services, 1994). In Canada, community policing has been promoted aggressively by the federal government through official publications and conferences (e.g., Normandeau & Leighton, 1990; Solicitor General of Canada, 1990).

Although this reform movement may seem mature and well advanced to those who have been advocating such change over the past few years, in the larger picture it is (at best) only the beginning of what is likely to be a long and arduous journey down a new road. The future is very uncertain, the tasks ahead are complex, and the obstacles are numerous. Community policing is still in what might be called the conceptualization phase of development. At this stage, we are still grappling with some very basic questions, such as: What is the appropriate role for the police in society, and do we really want to move in a new direction without reservation? What are the central elements of community policing, and how is it different from what police have traditionally done under the "reform era" (Kelling & Moore, 1988)? What is the theory that provides the foundation and justification for changing the role of police in society? If community policing sounds good in theory, what about when the "rubber meets the road"?—what implementation problems can be expected? What evidence exists to suggest that community policing will be more effective than the current model of policing? At this point, there are more questions than answers, but we should expect this state of affairs during conceptualization phase. Police administrators, government officials, academics, and community leaders are struggling with the concept of community policing and are experimenting with a wide range of operational translations.

The task here is to explore the changing role of police in North America. Because community policing is the only real alternative to the traditional model (at this point in time), comparisons between these two approaches can be found throughout this analysis. First, this chapter offers a brief historical account of the forces driving this latest reform movement. Second, and more important, some key components of community policing theory are developed and analyzed. Third, the question of whether community policing is a cost effective investment in times of budget austerity is explored. Finally, some concerns about the future of this reform movement are examined.

The Context of Reform

A full historical account of this reform movement is beyond the scope of this chapter and would include a reexamination of a century and a half of organized policing (see Fogelson, 1977; Kelling & Moore, 1988; Sparrow, Moore, & Kennedy, 1990; Walker, 1983). Suffice it to say that over the past 20 years, the traditional model (present in the United States since the 1930s) has been under serious attack. Several factors have contributed to this latest round of criticism and to a rethinking of the police role in the United States and Canada. The growing violence and civil unrest in the United States during the 1960s led the President's Commission on Law Enforcement and Administration of Justice (1967) to recommend "team policing" in 1967 as a means of closing tasks the physical

and psychological distance between the beat officer and the community. This precursor to community policing was attempted in U.S. police departments in the 1970s, but serious implementation problems were encountered when management resisted plans for decentralization (see Anderson, 1978; Bloch & Specht, 1972; Schwartz & Clarren, 1977; Sherman, Milton, & Kelly, 1973). This opposition delayed any future community oriented reforms for a full decade, but research in the 1970s and 1980s continued to highlight the limitations of the traditional model. Although cities have their own reasons for pursuing community policing, a growing dissatisfaction with "business as usual" can be attributed, at least in part, to two decades of research that suggest that the traditional model is ineffective, inefficient, and inequitable (see Eck & Rosenbaum, 1994).

Meanwhile, community crime prevention initiatives were receiving substantial publicity during the 1980s in both Canada and the United States (Lavrakas, 1985; Linden, Barker, & Frisbie, 1984; Rosenbaum, 1986, 1988), and the concept of community involvement became especially attractive as the level of government funding began to decline.[1] Furthermore, as violence, drugs, gang activity, and police brutality received growing media attention in the late 1980s and early 1990s, police chiefs and politicians in the United States were under growing pressure to develop more effective response strategies. By this point, several demonstration programs had been developed and tested through the National Institute of Justice, and were ready to be marketed—Foot patrol in Newark, New Jersey (Pate, 1986), and Flint, Michigan (Trojanowicz, 1986); problem solving in Newport News, Virginia (Eck & Spelman, 1987a); and a variety of community-oriented initiatives in Newark and Houston (Pate, Wycoff, Skogan, & Sherman, 1986) including storefront mini-stations, newsletters, door-to-door contacts, and the creation of voluntary community organizations. Meanwhile, throughout the 1980s, hundreds of police departments were experimenting independently with various community-oriented initiatives, the most popular being foot patrol.

Community policing in Canada did not emerge from the same conditions of urban crisis, but nevertheless followed a similar pattern of development. Some Canadian scholars have suggested that, in the absence of other political pressures, the pursuit of community policing in Canada has followed recent trends in the United States, where a larger body of experimental programs and scientific evaluations is available (Murphy, 1988). Others have suggested that Canadian police "simply returned to their 19th century origins" (referring to Robert Peel's Metropolitan London Police Bobbies) after "a few decades of flirting with the professional policing model" (Leighton, 1994, p. 211). In any event, what is clear to the observer is that Canadian scholars have worked very closely with the federal government and local police officials throughout Canada to help establish a clear agenda for police reform and to evaluate promising initiatives.

Changing the Role of Police: Community Versus Enforcement-Oriented Policing

What is "community policing" and what, if anything, is so special about it? *Community policing* is a very popular term but one that has a multitude of definitions. The popularity and ambiguity of this concept are both a blessing and a curse. On the positive side, the term is something that everyone can identify with (after all, who is opposed to the concept of "community" or to "mother" and "apple pie," for that matter?), thus providing the popular support that is needed to engender police reform in the long run. On the negative side, the concept has been badly abused by police chiefs and politicians who use this nebulous term to justify any and every program of their liking. Granted, programs must be tailored to local circumstances, but the label of community policing can produce a "halo effect" around pet programs and prevent outside observers from being able to distinguish true police innovation from traditional policing. The question is whether "community policing" in practice is truly innovative, or, as Bayley (1988) put it, simply "another attempt to put old wine into new bottles?" In addition, Goldstein (1993) warns us that the popularity of the community po-

licing concept increases public expectations and "create[s] the impression that, somehow, on implementation, community policing will provide a panacea for not only crime, disorder, and racial tensions, but many of the other acute problems that plague our urban areas"(p. 1).

Hence, one of the challenges that we face today is to figure out what community policing is and is not, and how to distinguish it from the current model. Providing such a clarification will help to set the stage for a critical discussion of the merits and limitations of this reform movement. Unfortunately, criminal justice scholars and police administrators have yet to articulate the full theory behind community policing with all of its assumptions and implications.[2] This theoretical imprecision has contributed to the criticism of community policing by many police researchers (see, for example, Klockars, 1988; Manning, 1988; Mastrofski, 1988).

While definition problems abound, it would be a mistake to leave the impression that this reform movement is all rhetoric and no substance, or that there exists no consensus as to what constitutes the core elements of this new model of policing. Although community policing has been operationalized through a variety of programs and practices, the concept appears to be supported by a common set of guiding principles and assumptions (see Eck & Spelman, 1987a; Goldstein, 1990; Greene & Mastrofski, 1988; Leighton, 1991; McElroy, Cosgrove, & Sadd, 1993; Murphy & Muir, 1984; Rosenbaum,1994; Skogan & Hartnett, 1997; Skolnick & Bayley, 1986; Sparrow et al., 1990; Toch & Grant, 1991; Trojanowicz & Bucqueroux, 1990). Some of the commonly cited elements of this model include: (a) a broader definition of police work; (b) a reordering of police priorities, giving greater attention to "soft" crime and disorder; (c) a focus on problem solving and prevention rather than incident-driven policing; (d) a recognition that the "community," however defined, plays a critical role in solving neighborhood problems; and (e) a recognition that police organizations must be restructured and reorganized to be responsive to the demands of this new approach and to encourage a new set of police behaviors.

More and more, these shared concepts and assumptions are being translated into common practices, such as decentralized organizational structures, permanent beat assignments, new mechanisms for community participation and problem solving, new training programs, and revised performance evaluation systems. (Nevertheless, the tendency to call nearly everything "community policing" is also a widespread practice.)

To explore some of these changes in policing, community policing can be compared to the current model on the key dimensions of police effectiveness, equity, and efficiency (Eck & Rosenbaum, 1994). The public expects the police to be *effective* in the services they provide; to offer services in a manner that is *equitable and fair* to the community; and to make every effort to see that these equitable and effective services are provided at *minimal cost* to society (i.e., efficiency). The community policing model turns the spotlight on police effectiveness in a way that previous approaches do not. Consequently, this chapter will give disproportionate attention to the issue of effectiveness. Furthermore, given the current fiscal concerns in Canada and the United States, this chapter also gives considerable attention to the question of police efficiency.

Police Effectiveness

When someone asks whether the police are "effective," the first thought that comes to mind is—"effective at doing what?" The proper role of police in society has been a debated subject for many years, but there can be little doubt that the job of controlling crime is considered the highest priority of the police under the traditional model (other key functions include providing emergency services, administering justice by means of arrest, and offering a wide range of nonemergency services). The traditional methods used to fight crime include deterrence (through preventive patrol and arrest), incapacitation, and rehabilitation. Several major studies have questioned the effectiveness of these general strategies for controlling or preventing crime (Blumstein, Cohen, & Nagin, 1978; Blumstein, Cohen, Roth, & Visher, 1986; Sechrest, White, & Brown,

1979). Furthermore, research on the police in particular has failed to support the hypothesis that random patrols, rapid response, follow-up investigations—practices at the core of enforcement-oriented policing—would produce more arrests and less crime (Greenwood, Petersilia, & Chaiken, 1977; Kelling, Pate, Dieckman, & Brown, 1974b; Spelman & Brown, 1984). Nevertheless, police have fully adopted (and, over the years, have promoted) the image of "crime fighter," while taxpayers continue to demand that crime control (via law enforcement) is the primary function of the police.

Under the community policing model, traditional police functions have not been discontinued; rather, the priorities have been rearranged to give greater attention to some functions and less to others. Moreover, additional police functions have been added under the new model. Most important, the manner in which these functions are executed is entirely different under community policing—a topic that deserves additional treatment later on.

Under community policing theory, crime control, emergency aid, and justice—as traditionally conceived—receive less attention, while nonemergency services receive greater attention. This reprioritizing has been justified on several grounds. First, the crime control, emergency, and justice functions constitute a small proportion of the total demand for police service, and thus, it is argued, should not be the hub of the police organizational structure and response system. Second, prior research (cited earlier) suggests that the police have not been very effective at these functions. Third, noncriminal, nonemergency problems represent the most frequent concern of neighborhood residents (Skogan, 1990a; Skogan & Hartnett, 1997).

The fourth, and most compelling, rationale for reordering the priority assigned to different police functions has to do with the nature of urban life and forces that contribute to neighborhood decline. The community policing model does not call for different policing *goals* (e.g., reducing crime is still a major police goal), but rather, it suggests that alternative *means* of achieving these goals should be given more attention (e.g., indirect strategies involving other police functions). The problem of neighborhood disorder will be used to illustrate how the community policing model is fundamentally different from previous models of policing. It is hoped that this example will also help to further elaborate and clarify the theory so that policymakers and critics can more easily distinguish this approach from its predecessors. For practitioners who are unsure whether community policing is anything more than cosmetic change ("old wine in new bottles"), the theory and research behind this approach are especially important.

Police researchers, policy analysts, and administrators have, in my opinion, underestimated the importance of social and physical disorders in their efforts to develop effective strategies for controlling crime and improving urban neighborhoods. When community residents are asked about the biggest problems in their neighborhood, they consistently mention various types of physical and social disorders that are low on the list of police priorities. In Skogan's analysis of 40 neighborhoods, for example, the biggest physical disorder problem was vandalism (including graffiti), followed by litter and trash, garbage handling, and unkempt vacant lots. In some neighborhoods, abandoned buildings were the biggest concern to local residents. In the realm of social problems, public drinking was the biggest concern, followed by loitering youth, and drug use. (More recent data from Chicago neighborhoods suggest that street-level drug transactions are also a major concern of neighborhood residents; Skogan & Hartnett, 1997.)

The ranking of problems can vary significantly by neighborhood, but the pattern is consistent—disorders are the most frequently mentioned set of "big problems" facing urban residents.

As Skogan (1990a) notes, historically, dealing with disorder was a central function of the police as they walked the beat and listened to the concerns of local residents and business owners. Yet with the rise of serious crime, the centralization of the police bureaucracy, and the push for greater efficiency in handling a growing number of calls, disorder and other neighborhood problems were given less and less attention by the police.

The question here is this: Why should disorder and related community concerns be given a higher priority under this new model of policing? This question is especially important today, as a conservative backlash against "soft" policing gains momentum in the United States. In the context of a growing debate about "soft" versus "hard" policing, the answer to this question is fairly simple: There is a growing evidence to suggest that soft and hard problems are highly related; that the failure to attend to soft problems will only exacerbate serious crime; and that an indirect attack on crime through order maintenance may be a more effective, efficient, and just means of policing in urban areas.

Both advocates and critics of community policing should have a solid understanding of the theory behind this form of policing before they become too opinionated in either direction. A good place to start is by examining the forces that contribute to neighborhood crime. The concept of neighborhood disorder is at the heart of current thinking about the relationship between crime, community, and policing, and suggests how a community's capacity for self-regulation can be undermined (see Bursik & Grasmick, 1993; Lewis & Salem, 1986; Skogan, 1990a; Wilson & Kelling, 1982). The failure of a community and its police to respond decisively to the early signs of disorder is analogous to the failure of a patient and his or her doctor to detect and treat cancer in the early stages—the problem will spread uncontrollably. Disorder, although not easily defined, is something that "locals" will "know when they see or hear it" (i.e., various behaviors and physical conditions that violate the social norms of the local community). Research suggests that disorder is extremely important because it sends a clear signal to residents and others who use the local environment that the social order has broken down. Shattered windows, abandoned buildings, graffiti, litter on the streets, loud music, unsupervised kids hanging out—the message is clear to everyone—people are either unable or unwilling to intervene in defense of their neighborhood and their neighbors. The message to potential offenders is clear—because the social order has broken down in this area, no one is going to intervene if you decide to tag a grocery store, break a window in an apartment, mug an elderly women, or even shoot someone. The message to potential victims is clear—this is an unsafe area and one where you are likely to be victimized by crime. Indeed, research indicates that the higher the level of disorder in a neighborhood, the higher the level of fear of victimization (Hope & Hough,1988; Skogan, 1990a). A large-scale field study using qualitative data also supports the hypothesis that disorder stimulates fear of crime (Lewis & Salem, 1986).[3]

Fear of crime generates its own set of problems. Fear causes residents and nonresidents alike to use the local environment less frequently and to withdraw behind locked doors (Lavrakas et al., 1980; Skogan & Maxfield, 1981). This avoidance of public areas reduces a neighborhood's capacity to regulate social behavior, thus providing additional opportunities for potential offenders to engage in antisocial and criminal conduct without sanction. This absence of "guardianship" is a critical element in opportunity theories of crime (e.g., Cohen & Felson, 1979). In sum, there is reason to believe that disorder undermines a community's ability to exercise control over the behavior of those who use the area, and it increases the opportunities for criminal behavior.

The curious nature of disorder is that it feeds on itself, working to multiply and escalate urban problems. As Wilson and Kelling (1982) note, one broken window, if not repaired, will result in many broken windows. Furthermore, this process of decline can stimulate more serious criminal activity for the reasons stated earlier. Community research documents this relationship—the higher the level of neighborhood disorder, the higher the level of serious criminal activity (Skogan, 1990a). Clearly, crime and disorder are strongly correlated and both represent serious threats to the quality of urban life—contrary to conventional wisdom, disorder is not a "soft" problem that is unrelated to the "hard" problems that consume the thoughts of traditional enforcement officers. Hence, an indirect attack on crime (via disorder)

may be an effective strategy of policing while not losing sight of the importance of crime.

Similar to disorder, the concept of "fear of crime" is another lightning rod for critics who argue that community policing is soft on crime. They claim that switching the focus of policing from fighting crime to maintaining order and reducing fear of crime is simply a "smoke and mirrors" tactic to make citizens feel good about themselves, the police department, and their neighborhood. These critics argue that such a "warm fuzzy" approach to policing will divert police attention away from the real job of arresting criminals. Again, this argument fails to appreciate the critical role of fear of crime in undermining urban neighborhoods and housing markets. As implied earlier, fear is one of the driving forces behind patterns of residential mobility and neighborhood decline (Skogan, 1986). Research by Taub, Taylor, and Dunham (1984) in eight Chicago neighborhoods shows that residents' perceptions of safety can influence their assessment of the housing market and their investment plans. For people considering a residential move, the issues are similar.

Every day, families in urban areas make decisions about whether a particular neighborhood is a good place to raise children, and safety concerns are at the top of their list.[4] When current or potential residents get nervous about the quality of life in a neighborhood, sociodemographic transition can be set in motion, and the neighborhood can be thrust into a cycle of decline (see Skogan, 1990a). The presence of graffiti, broken windows, and vacant lots not only arouses fear, but sends a clear message to move out or stay out of the area if possible.

In sum, disorder is the primary concern of neighborhood residents, and these problems can have a significant impact on residents' perceptions of, and reactions to, crime. These reactions, including the fear response, play a critical role in determining the residential stability of the neighborhood. In essence, disorder, if left unchecked, will undermine the social control processes by which communities maintain social order, stimulate fear of crime, exacerbate more serious crime, and destabilize the housing market. Collectively, these forces can lead to neighborhood decline and give rise to additional serious crime as part of a vicious cycle.

If disorder is a powerful contributor to urban crime, and if police have a renewed interest in pursuing effective anticrime strategies, then such incivilities should be given a higher priority on the problem-solving agenda. If police officers work with local residents to reduce the social and physical signs of disorder in their neighborhood, perhaps an area can be stabilized before it reaches the "tipping point."[5] In theory, a reduction in the signs of disorder will lead to a reduction in residents' fear. As a result, local residents should be more inclined to use the streets, interact with one another, develop social networks and exercise greater informal control over what happens in their neighborhood. In the end, hopefully their desire to move away will subside and their pride in, and perceived ownership of, the area will increase.

How police go about reducing disorder and fear is another matter. The enforcement tactics used in the 1970s and 1980s were generally ineffective and judged to be unconstitutional. Rounding up groups of kids hanging out on street corners did not solve the problem. More creative and less aggressive policies will be needed. One of the greatest problems with traditional policing has been the overreliance on law enforcement as the primary tool of controlling crime and disorder. Whatever the problem, the first inclination of the police is to make an arrest, and this tendency is due to community pressure as much as pressure within the police organization. As a result, we now have a criminal justice system in the United States that is completely overwhelmed by the volume of cases, and that only serves as a revolving door for many criminal suspects. Consequently, the system has lost its ability to punish and deter potential offenders by using the threat of arrest.[6]

The community policing model gives police officers considerable latitude to help solve neighborhood problems. As Herman Goldstein (1993) notes, the community policing officer is expected to "exhaust a wide range of alternatives before resorting to arrest for minor offenses; to exercise broad discretion; and to depend more on resourceful-

ness, persuasion, and cajoling than on coercion, image, and bluff" (p. 8). Given the highly dysfunctional nature of the present criminal justice system, I would argue that the community policing officer should attempt to resolve problems outside of this bureaucracy, pursuing a new goal of decreasing (rather than increasing) the number of cases that have contact with the judicial system. When contact is unavoidable, the new goal should be to reduce the depth of penetration into the system by offering effective alternatives for young offenders.

This brings us to another distinguishing feature of the community policing model, namely, the focus on problem solving. If neighborhood problems are the source of community discontent and contribute to a cycle of urban decline, then effective policing will involve identifying the source and nature of these problems and working to develop effective solutions. In contrast, the traditional model—also known as "incident-driven policing" (Eck & Spelman, 1987a)—requires no thinking about persistent problems. Instead, the officer's responsibility ends when he or she responds to a citizen's complaint about a single incident.[7] Hence, the police are encouraged to drive around randomly in their beat until they are dispatched to an incident, but they are not required to look for, or address, patterns of incidents or "hot spots" that would suggest a persistent neighborhood problem.

A closer look at the problem-solving process highlights the most fundamental difference between the community policing and the traditional models. Problem solving is not done in isolation—it requires a high degree of community participation. This fact takes us to the heart of community policing theory.

Community Engagement and Partnerships

The role of the community is essential to community policing as conceived in theory, and constitutes the most distinguishing feature of this new approach. At the heart of this new model of policing is the empirically supported idea that the police cannot successfully fight crime alone, and must rely on resources in the community to address neighborhood problems effectively. Perhaps the biggest mistake in the history of modern policing was to give the police *full* responsibility and accountability for public safety. With the emergence of community policing, emphasis is now given to the "co-production" of public safety (Lavrakas, 1985; Murphy & Muir, 1984; Rosenbaum, 1988; Wilson & Kelling, 1982). In this framework, safety is viewed as a commodity that is produced by the joint efforts of the police and the community, working together in ways that were not envisioned or encouraged in the past.[8]

The rationale for this new orientation should be made clear to those who criticize the role of "community" in community policing. If we are interested in reducing crime, disorder, fear of crime, and other factors that lower the quality of urban life, we must be attentive to research findings (and personal experience) that remind us that crime-related outcomes are controlled by the social and economic forces in the community (see Bursik & Grasmick, 1993, for a review).

Jane Jacobs (1961) described this reality very clearly in her classic work, *The Death and Life of Great American Cities:*

> The first thing to understand is that the public peace—the sidewalk and the street peace—of cities is not kept primarily by the police, necessary as police are. It is kept primarily by an intricate, almost unconscious network of voluntary controls and standards among the people themselves, and enforced by the people themselves. (pp. 31–32)

This perspective is radically different from the one that is implied by the conventional crime-fighting model. In contrast to the widely accepted view that citizens are supplemental to the police ("eyes and ears" at best),the assumption here is that the police are supplemental to the community in fighting neighborhood problems. This is not to suggest that the police are irrelevant or unimportant. To the contrary, because our tax dollars for fighting crime at the street level have been invested almost exclusively in the police, it is incumbent upon the police to take a lead role and serve as a catalyst for commu-

nity change. The challenge for police today and into the 21st is to find creative ways to help communities help themselves.[9]

To prevent crime, we must first understand the forces behind crime at the neighborhood level. A growing body of research provides support for social disorganization theory, which is derived from the classic work of Clifford Shaw and Henry McKay (1942). According to this revived model, criminal activity is encouraged when a neighborhood is socially disorganized, meaning that it is unable to exercise effective informal social control over its residents and achieve common goals, such as reducing the threat of crime (see Bursik & Grasmick, 1993; Byrne & Sampson, 1986). Socially disorganized neighborhoods are unable to create and sustain local institutions. Because of population turnover and heterogeneity, residents are unlikely to develop primary relationships with each other and unlikely to work jointly to solve neighborhood problems.

Disadvantaged neighborhoods need outside intervention (on a large scale) if they are to have any hope for a better environment, but the options for citizen participation and empowerment within the neighborhood are numerous. Local residents can take many different actions to help prevent crime and disorder (DuBow, McCabe, & Kaplan, 1979; Lab, 1988; Lavrakas, 1985; Lewis & Salem, 1986; Rosenbaum, 1988). They can get involved in protecting themselves, their families, their property, and their neighborhood through individual or collective actions. Expanding the role of ordinary citizens in anticrime efforts has been recommended by several national commissions in the United States. Today, the community policing officer must take these ideas to the next level—to engage the community in experimental ways to solve neighborhood problems. Two key roles for the community are immediately apparent—community building and problem solving.

Community Building. If communities suffer from social disorganization, then efforts can be made to strengthen social networks and bolster residents' attachment to the area. Getting residents to work together to achieve common, neighborhood goals is one way to stimulate social interaction and build social relationships. The involvement of local community residents in neighborhood anticrime or youth-oriented projects may strengthen informal social controls at the neighborhood level, and *may* contribute to the overall goal of creating *self-regulating* communities. By organizing local residents and encouraging, more frequent social interaction, the hope is to create a social environment where people become more territorial about the neighborhood—that is, they increase their surveillance of suspicious behavior, provide greater supervision of local youths, and demonstrate a stronger willingness to intervene as needed to stop or deter antisocial behavior. The possibilities for involvement are limitless, although the outcomes remain uncertain. Continued experimentation is needed.

At this point, the talk about getting citizens involved in community policing has far exceeded the reality. For a variety of reasons, community participation in community policing has been limited in many cities (see Sadd & Grinc, 1994). In highly disorganized, highly disadvantaged neighborhoods, it may be too much to expect individual citizens or voluntary grassroots organizations to play a major role in stopping crime, drug activity, and disorder, except in narrowly defined geographic spaces. Therefore, I will appeal to a much broader definition of "community" and suggest that the primary task at hand is to mobilize local institutions and agencies that are invested in the neighborhood, such as churches, schools, and social service agencies (more about this topic below). In theory, the coordinated and persistent application of additional resources should help to empower local residents over time if the resources are used to reinforce independent, self-regulating behaviors.

There are unlimited roles for the police in the community-building process, but few of these roles resemble what was expected under the traditional model. Here we are talking about efforts to facilitate the creation of self-regulating and self-defended neighborhoods. The new community policing officer may pursue many different paths to achieve these goals, but the fundamental objectives are: (a)

to seek community input and participation in defining local problems, (b) to work with the community to develop proposed solutions to these problems, and (c) to identify and mobilize the necessary resources—both inside and outside the community—to respond effectively to these problems. In this new role as facilitator, coordinator, and referral agent, the fundamental goal of the new community police officer is to strengthen the ability of local organizations, institutions, and individuals to build a physical and social environment that has fewer opportunities for antisocial and criminal behavior. This brings us to the second community function, and one where the progressive police agencies are making inroads, namely, problem solving through partnerships.

Problem Solving and Partnership Formation. As suggested above, one of the unique characteristics of the community policing model is its focus on problem solving, and this orientation has clear implications for community participation. As John Eck and I have observed, "Ideally, problem solving needs a high level of community engagement to identify problems, to develop an understanding of the particular circumstances that give rise to them, to craft enduring preventive remedies, and to evaluate the effectiveness of the remedies" (Eck & Rosenbaum, 1994, p. 9). Community policing officers know firsthand that community residents play a major role in solving neighborhood problems. We have witnessed how the new police role can involve seeking community input about local problems through door-to-door surveys, community meetings, the analysis of calls for service, and other data derived from citizen feedback.

The means by which identified problems are solved are often unique to the community policing model. Oftentimes, these remedies do *not* involve the application of criminal law. Solutions may be as simple as calling the sanitation department to report a persistent garbage problem or as complex as developing a long-term education and job training program to prevent youth violence in the neighborhood. In academia, we talk about a wide range of "situational crime prevention" measures that can be implemented to reduce opportunities for crime (Clarke, 1992), and "social crime prevention" measures that can be developed to attack the root causes of crime (Rosenbaum, 1988). In any event, the options are numerous and the appropriate choice will depend on how the problem is defined and what resources are available.

In addition to less reliance on criminal sanctions to solve problems, another critical and distinguishing feature of community policing is the development of partnerships with other institutions and agencies to mobilize additional resources. Today, the formation of "partnerships" and "coalitions" is a preferred strategy among social engineers seeking to "make a difference" in urban communities. From a police perspective, the creation and utilization of interagency partnerships represents a significant departure from the traditional police role. Not only does this co-production activity recognize the limitations of the police as a self-reliant organization, but it underscores the importance of community resources as key elements in a comprehensive crime control plan.

The theory underlying partnerships is worth noting. The basic idea is that the problems being addressed are too complex and intractable for a single organization to solve. The process of accurately defining the problem and responding effectively requires the coordination and application of resources from multiple sources. Hence, partnerships are typically created for the purpose of developing and implementing comprehensive, co-ordinated strategies (see Cook & Roehl, 1993; Florin, Chavis, Wandersman, & Rich, 1992; Klitzner, 1993; Prestby & Wandersman, 1985).

In recent years, we have witnessed the formation of partnerships to combat violence and drug abuse, and this activity is part of a broader movement to develop community-wide strategies in response to a wide range of social problems. For example, promising evaluation results have been obtained from studying partnerships in the areas of health promotion (Shea & Basch, 1990) and drug abuse prevention (Johnson et al., 1990; Pentz et al., 1989), where parents, schools, the mass media, and other agents of change have teamed up to prevent the onset of these prob-

lems. With a grant from the National Institute of Justice, my colleagues and I recently evaluated the Community Responses to Drug Abuse Program in nine cities and found that police and community organizations can work effectively with other agencies at the level of both enforcement and youth-oriented prevention (Rosenbaum, Bennett, Lindsay, & Wilkinson, 1994). Two other projects—the Robert Wood Johnson Foundation's 15-site Fighting Back project (Klitzner, 1993), and the 250-site Community Partnership Program (Cook & Roehl, 1993) funded by the Center for Substance Abuse Prevention, represent major efforts to build coalitions to fight neighborhood drug abuse. More recently, the Justice Department has funded the Comprehensive Communities Program in 12 cities to support the development of multiagency partnerships to attack gangs and violence, with focus on community policing.[10]

Coalitions or partnerships might include representatives from government agencies such as criminal justice, health, welfare, and social services; elected officials; private businesses; voluntary organizations; community/grassroots organizations; churches; and other groups that have a vested interest in the neighborhood. In theory, the more resources that can be applied, the better the chances of impacting the problem. Although larger coalitions seek to be all-inclusive, in reality, the number of agencies involved is often limited, and the program is often located in, and controlled by, one agency.

Partnerships can vary in size and type (e.g., grassroots vs. professional members), number of committees, ethnic diversity, number of staff, membership criteria, decision-making processes, and the group's approach/orientation to the target problem (Cook & Roehl, 1993). The dynamics among the members of the partnership can be especially important for determining the partnership's success. The levels of cooperation, conflict, and participation that exist among coalition members can be important for determining whether the problem is properly addressed or solved. Success is often linked to the presence of a key coordinating individual who has a vision, who believes in the importance of the initiative, is highly motivated to see it succeed, and has access to the resources and political influence needed to make it happen. A coalition must be able to achieve internal goals, such as planning, securing resources, recruiting all key organizations, maintaining stability, and keeping members satisfied about the group's progress. In the final analysis, holding partnership meetings is a desirable objective but the "bottom line" is whether the group can develop and implement a plan of action that will effectively address the target problem. This remains an empirical question in many cases.

In any event, the door is now open for police to play an important role by creating and/or facilitating partnerships to address neighborhood problems related to crime and disorder. As organizers, facilitators, coordinators, or service providers, under the full community policing model, police organizations are expected to "step up to bat" in a multiagency context. From command personnel to the officers on the street, partnerships can provide work for everyone. Who gets involved will depend on the size of the initiative and how easily the problem can be solved. When the problem is relatively small, a smaller partnership with fewer members will be sufficient. Under these conditions, line officers should be able to represent the police organization with limited involvement from top management. However, when the problem is characterized as large, visible, and perceptibly political, then the police organization (and the community) is best served by requiring the participation of management personnel.

Every neighborhood and every problem is unique, which means that the community policing officer will need considerable freedom to develop relationships with other agencies and make decisions about appropriate courses of action. This concept of empowering individual officers is both exciting and troublesome, depending on your perspective, but it is a central component of the new model. The exciting aspect is that individual police officers are expected to use their talents to think creatively about ways to solve neighborhood problems, unlike the current state of affairs in many agencies where offi-

cers are reluctant to do anything unusual for fear of punishment. Coincidentally, in addition to helping solve problems, this new approach to police work should yield happier employees. There is good evidence to indicate that police officers are more satisfied with their jobs under these arrangements (see Lurigio & Rosenbaum, 1994, for a review).

However, the idea of empowering police is troublesome to those who fear a return to the days of corruption and abuse of police powers. Obviously, in agencies where such problems are rampant, giving the beat officer more freedom could be very problematical. I am hoping that this concern will prove to be unwarranted. Most police organizations do not suffer from widespread corruption, and preventive measures can be instituted to prevent the spread of unethical conduct. The bigger concern should be whether beat officers have the training and skill level to function in this new capacity, and whether supervisors are prepared to supervise under these new arrangements.

Efficiency of Community Policing

During these times of fiscal austerity, the most important question facing many police administrators and city politicians is whether they can afford community policing and whether it is worth the investment. There are two related questions that should be addressed. First: What is the cost of community policing, and is it more or less expensive than traditional, reactive policing? Second: What are the benefits or gains associated with this new model of policing? Each of these questions is briefly addressed.

Regarding the cost question, I am unwilling to argue (as I know others have done in the past) that community policing is cheaper than traditional policing or that it will be cheaper in the near future when it becomes fully operational. In my judgment, cities can expect to spend *considerably more* on community policing in the next few years if police administrators continue to follow the current implementation plan. For the many organizations that simply want cosmetic changes, rather than substantive changes, cost should not be a major concern. But for those that are determined to introduce fundamental changes in the police organization and function, the present course of action is certain to bring added costs. To drive home this point, the question should be reversed. Specifically, how could it *not* cost more to (a) intensively retrain and restructure the entire police organization from top to bottom; (b) add *new* police roles and responsibilities; *and* (c) keep all of the existing police functions?

Who promised the taxpayer that real, substantive reform would be cheap? Cosmetic reform is cheap. Real reform is expensive, as it should be! For example, I'm not talking about a one-hour or one-day classroom training seminar, which I often see. Community policing is an entirely new way of thinking and behaving that will require months and even years of retooling in the classroom and in the field.

The biggest cost problem, however, is point (c) above, namely, the desire to add new police functions *without eliminating* or cutting back on current police responsibilities. If the community expects the police to attend community meetings, organize and maintain partnerships with other agencies, and so on, then beat officers cannot be expected to give the same response to all 911 calls. This is perhaps the most common and most serious implementation problem facing police organizations in large urban areas, namely, the failure to re-market police services to the public. Repeatedly, police organizations attempt to introduce new community policing activities on the present budget while continuing business as usual or making minor adjustments in the dispatching process. Unless existing activities are dropped or reduced in priority, cities should expect that additional police officers will be needed in the short run to achieve successful implementation. Fortunately, in the United States, police departments are able to add more police officers under the federally funded "COPS" (Community Oriented Policing Services) program. Unfortunately, local municipalities must be prepared to absorb the long-term cost of these additional resources once the COPS money has been phased out.

The debate about how many police officers are needed to fight crime is an old one, and the emergence of community policing has only reignited this discussion. Historically, the budget requests of police chiefs in the United States have been met by city government—every year, as the crime rate rose in the 1960s and 1970s, so did the municipal police budget (Jacob & Lineberry, 1982). Those budget days are now history, but police departments face the issue of whether they need more police to implement community policing. During the transition period, when police organizations are in the process of converting from the traditional to the community policing model (and the length of this transition will depend on local circumstances), the argument can be made for increasing the size of the police force. This request for additional personnel assumes that police officers will take on new functions and responsibilities, yet will continue to operate within a traditional bureaucracy with few, if any, changes in the public's demand for service. There are several reasons, however, why community policing may *not* be more expensive than traditional policing when fully operational: (a) unnecessary layers of bureaucracy can be eliminated or scaled down as the organization becomes more decentralized; (b) decentralization will mean that officers on the street can handle many of the complaints that are currently fed through the 911 system; (c) the de-marketing of 911 and marketing of new procedures should reduce the demand for a dispatched car; and (d) by adopting a problem-oriented approach to policing, the volume of calls for service should decline as beat officers work with residents to resolve the underlying problems.

These are reasons why community policing may *someday* reach the point of not being more expensive than traditional enforcement policing. I believe, however, that this entire discussion of cost is misguided and reflects our inability as a society to engage in long-term planning or implement effective reform. The issue is not cost, but cost-effectiveness. The important question is this: Do we have any reason(s) to believe that community policing will yield more beneficial effects for society than reactive, enforcement-oriented policing? If so, we can then ask ourselves: Is it worth the investment—do the benefits outweigh the costs?

If community policing is more expensive, so be it. The real question is how much "bang for our buck" can we expect under this new model? If community policing is more expensive in absolute monetary terms, but yields a significantly greater impact on neighborhood problems in the long run, by all means, we should continue on the current path of reform.

The problem we face is the uncertainty about both costs and benefits. The potential costs are more tangible than the gains, but I have tried to suggest here that the gains could be substantial if community policing is exploited to the fullest extent. Let me continue this discussion of whether community policing is affordable by *briefly* summarizing what we know about the positive, short-term effects of these interventions, and then move into the realm of informed speculation regarding long-term benefits.

Short and Long-Term Effects. Controlled evaluations of community policing are few and far between (see Rosenbaum, 1994, for a collection of recent evaluations). In Canada, there have been only two widely publicized, quantitative evaluations—in Victoria (Walker & Walker, 1989) and in Edmonton (Hornick, Burrows, Phillips, & Leighton, 1991). The results of these evaluations can be viewed as encouraging, but not definitive. In Victoria, where mini-stations were introduced, official crime rates declined in five categories, but fear of crime did not change in the target areas (unfortunately, control citizens, and greater groups were not used). In Edmonton, where foot patrols were introduced and measured in the context of a more controlled quasi-experimental design, two thirds of the target beats reported significant reductions in repeat calls, and citizens gave higher evaluations to foot patrol officers than to officers patrolling in cars. In the United States, Skogan's (1994b) reanalysis of 14 target neighborhoods in six cities (involving quasi-experimental pretest-posttest control group designs) provides the most systematic, rigorous look at the effects of community policing programs on residential neighborhoods. Across these 14 areas, Skogan found that 9 had experienced statistically significant improvements in residents' attitudes about the police, 7 experienced reductions in fear of crime, 6 showed declines in perceived neighborhood disorder, and 3 had experienced reductions in victimization rates. Recently, I conducted comprehensive evaluation of community policing in Joliet, Illinois, and the results were mixed (Rosenbaum et al., 1994). After nearly 2 years, residents in the main target area reported significantly greater satisfaction with police contacts, but fear of crime and perceptions of neighborhood problems were unchanged. Residents reported a marginally significant drop in victimization experiences. The most positive findings came from our evaluation of intensive problem-solving activities along the main commercial strip in Joliet (Wilkinson, Rosenbaum, Bruni, & Yeh, 1994). Police records over a 4-year period showed *dramatic* declines in Part I crimes and disorders. The total number of reported incidents declined 68 percent—substantially greater than the citywide trends. Consistent declines were observed for violent crime, property crime, disorder, and other code violations.

Unfortunately, as critical methodologists have noted (Greene & Taylor, 1988; Lurigio & Rosenbaum, 1986), evaluations of community-based interventions often suffer from weak research designs and measures, thus making it difficult to draw any firm conclusions. Fortunately, the state of the art has improved in recent years. A series of stronger longitudinal evaluations funded by the National Institute of Justice is currently in progress and should yield more definitive findings.

In the literature on community and team policing, the benefits to police personnel are easier to document. Lurigio and Rosenbaum (1994) reviewed 12 studies that measured the effects of community-oriented programs and organizational changes on police officers. The results are generally encouraging, indicating positive effects in the areas of job satisfaction, perceived broadening of police functions, improved relations with co-workers and citizens, and greater expectations for citizen participation in crime prevention.

Again, my own research shows fewer benefits for police officers, but more implementation time may be needed (Rosenbaum, Yeh, & Wilkinson, 1994).

In sum, early experiments with community policing show some promise for producing positive changes in police personnel, community residents, and (to a lesser extent) community crime rates. Despite these encouraging signs, some of the most basic questions remain unanswered: Are these effects long-lasting or short-lived? Do observed reductions in crime and disorder occur at the expense of other neighborhoods or other forms of crime where displacement is likely? Can community policing initiatives alter the nature or scope of social relations within high-crime neighborhoods? Can such programs strengthen local institutions or build lasting partnerships? Will the most innovative programs or reforms be institutionalized and sustained or will they be dropped with the next change of administration? Notwithstanding these uncertainties, community policing advocates can point to a fairly encouraging start, especially given the limited intensity of these early field tests.

A closer look at costs and benefits takes us beyond an assessment of immediate program effects into the realm of possible long-term gains from this reform movement. Unfortunately, there exist insufficient data on long-term outcomes, which forces us to think about these impacts from a rational and theoretical perspective. To this point, this chapter has tried to underscore some of the advantages of this new model from a *theoretical* (and to a lesser extent, *empirical*) standpoint. Let us revisit that discussion from an *economic* point of view, drawing attention to the potential cost savings that are inherent in this new approach as we look into the future.

The central purpose of cost-benefit and cost-effectiveness analyses is to determine whether the preferred program is one that "produces the most impact on the most targets for a given level of expenditure" (Rossi & Freeman, 1985, p. 325). Cost-effectiveness analyses compare monetary costs to some standard program outcome (e.g., percentage reduction in crime or fear of crime). Cost-benefit analyses compare monetary costs to

monetary gains. In the final analysis, police officials and policymakers may be interested in a cost-benefit analysis, but the data are simply not available. Nevertheless, let us think in terms of monetary costs and gains for the moment.

At the core of this new model of policing is the idea that police organizations need to think differently about the resources (monetary costs?) that are needed, and are available, to combat crime. Eck and Rosenbaum (1994) characterized the problem this way:

> Many of the assets needed to address problems are outside the boundaries of police organizations. These assets are the powers and resources of other government agencies, businesses, and the leveraging resources in the community itself. (p. 14)

The basic idea of police-community partnerships is to enhance our capacity to solve neighborhood problems. In theory, this is an excellent means of multiplying the resources available to the police without necessarily increasing the police budget. The multiplier effect of "community involvement" allows the police to maximize program effectiveness without a proportional increase in costs. When we begin to talk about "police efficiency" in the 21st century, we need to think in terms of identifying police organizations that have done a good job of mobilizing community resources to fight crime and disorder.

Turning from costs to benefits, I want to emphasize that utilizing *nonpolice* resources is more than a multiplication of assets, more than the provision of intensive, "high dosage" treatments, although this is certainly a welcome improvement. The community policing model, if fully implemented, should be not only quantitatively superior to the traditional model—but if the model is correct, it should be *qualitatively* different as well. In particular, the activation of local institutions and agencies, as well as other governmental agencies, reflects a commitment to pursue *preventive* strategies, as opposed to merely reactive approaches to neighborhood problems.

One of the most basic lessons that our society has yet to learn is that preventive programs yield larger benefit-cost ratios than reactive programs (in terms of national crime policy, the United States continues to move in the opposite direction, preferring after-the-fact over all other strategies). The second lesson we have learned about prevention is equally clear: The earlier we can intervene in the process of human development, the larger the program's effects on crime and disorder, and the larger the monetary savings (see Schorr, 1988, for examples).

In economic terms, direct program benefits can be defined as "estimations of savings on direct costs" (Bootman, Rowland, & Wertheimer, 1979), and this includes the cost of prevention, enforcement, treatment, incarceration (including capital investments), and other tangible services. In 1992, for example U.S. taxpayers spent approximately 93.7 billion dollars to operate a totally reactive justice system (Maguire & Pastore, 1994). These massive costs do not include the costs of personal crime for Americans. Data from 1990 indicate that personal crime costs Americans an estimated 450 billion dollars annually, including medical costs, lost earnings, pain and suffering, reduced quality of life, and public program costs related to victim assistance (Miller, Cohen, & Wierseman, 1996). The point is clear: To the extent that leveraging resources in the community will prevent even a small percentage of criminal and delinquent acts, taxpayers and potential victims can avoid paying the future costs associated with these transgressions. Given the possible economic savings, how can a society that has become increasingly self-interested with regard to taxation say "No" so quickly to prevention?

Admittedly, at this moment in time, there is a paucity of data to demonstrate the long-term crime prevention benefits of community-oriented policing initiatives (see Rosenbaum, 1988, 1994). There are many reasons for this shortage of compelling, conclusive data, including the fact that previous programs have been poorly funded, poorly implemented, and/or poorly evaluated, which makes it difficult to learn very much. The main reason, however, is that politicians are unwilling to wait 5 to 10 years for the results. Given this political reality, we are forced to move ahead using the best available data, our best theorizing about the possible program costs and benefits, and our own anecdotes.

Conclusion

By highlighting some distinguishing features of the community policing model, I have attempted to illustrate how this approach represents more than just a set of fancy slogans. I have tried to suggest that key components of the underlying theory are consistent with research on neighborhood disorder, fear of crime, community crime prevention, coalition building, and organizational reform. To be clear, this is not the same as rhetorically advocating community policing or stating that community policing has been shown to be a cost-effective response to crime and disorder. Although the available evidence is supportive of the model, many questions remain unanswered.

I hope that this delineation of key components of the theory and research behind community policing will help to debunk the common misconception that community policing will be "soft on crime." By promising to attack the social problems that contribute to crime, one could argue that community policing is "harder" on crime than traditional enforcement strategies. By the definition proposed here, to be tough on crime is to employ strategies that are *believed to be effective* in fighting crime (based on available theory and research), not strategies that are *known to be ineffective*. Given what we currently know about the causes of neighborhood crime, I have suggested that fighting fear of crime and local signs of disorder are promising, potentially effective means of attacking crime, and that creating police-community partnerships that lead to prevention strategies is another sensible strategy for being "hard" on crime.

My optimism about the future of community policing, however, should be tempered by widespread problems with program implementation. Whether these difficulties can be overcome remains to be seen and, in the final analysis, will determine the future of this reform movement. The internal and external obstacles to successful planning and implementation have been well documented through several process evaluations (see Rosenbaum, 1994). Problems within the organization that threaten to derail the reform process are numerous, and include inadequate training and supervision, top-down rule-driven bureaucracies that work to undermine officers' discretion, outdated performance evaluation systems that reward "bean counting" on enforcement activities, limited resources to carry out additional police functions, and, above all, employee resistance to change in general. In a nutshell, most police organizations are simply *not ready* for serious police reform, and even the most progressive administrators would prefer to develop special units or small programs within the department than to upset the status quo by introducing large-scale reform initiatives. "Organizational readiness," as I have defined it, implies that the agency "has in place the structure, policies, procedures, knowledge, and officer skills needed to deliver a new set of police services and a new approach to crime prevention and control" (Rosenbaum et al., 1994, p. 350). In the short history of community policing, one of the main lessons yet to be learned is that serious organizational changes are a fundamental prerequisite to *sustained* community policing. Anyone can start the process of change without much money or without much internal support from police personnel, but past experience reminds us that such reform efforts will not survive unless formal mechanisms are established to create a new work environment and, eventually, a new police culture. Most essentially, the behavior of police officers (like that of all human beings) is shaped and controlled by rewards and punishments in their immediate environment. Thus, in the absence of a totally new system of performance evaluation—one that identifies and encourages community-oriented, problem-solving behaviors and discourages traditional responses—street-level police behavior will remain unchanged. Police chiefs and academics can talk about community policing until they are "blue in the face," but the day-to-day behavioral repertoire of the beat officer will remain unchanged.

Outside the organization, the problems with community participation are more serious than many experts suspect (Grinc, 1994). Public education through a professional marketing (and de-marketing) strategy will help to build a more functional relationship between the police and the community, but the problem of mobilizing local residents runs deeper. In the inner city, the new community policing officer must understand that a lack of citizen participation is due to feelings of hopelessness and despair, fear of gang/offender retaliation, and deep-seated distrust of and anger toward police officers, among other factors.

For these reasons, the future of community policing in disadvantaged neighborhoods should not be built entirely upon lofty assumptions about citizen mobilization and empowerment. Alternatively, in this context, the primary thrust of the community-oriented approach is best conceptualized in terms of *resource mobilization* and skills training rather than citizen mobilization. When neighborhoods reach a certain level of decline, community mobilization must go beyond traditional community organizing tactics to focus on the provision of needed services and opportunities for self-improvement. As I have noted in previous writings (Rosenbaum, 1987, 1988), past research has been unable to demonstrate that social order and residential cohesiveness can be "implanted" in neighborhoods characterized by high levels of social disorder and crime. This does not mean that this goal is impossible to achieve; only that it has yet to be documented. Along these lines, we must remember that economic instability is likely to have an adverse effect on residential transition, and, therefore, on efforts to build cohesive, self-regulating neighborhoods. In essence, police and other community-minded persons will be hard-pressed to find shortcuts to rebuilding inner-city communities where legitimate jobs and businesses are virtually nonexistent.

In this chapter, I have suggested that *prevention* is a unique and important characteristic of the community policing model. In the literature beyond policing, comprehensive community-based programs have shown considerable promise for arresting a wide range of social problems, especially when interventions are early and intensive. In the area of crime, the victims and perpetrators of violence are becoming younger each year, and this fact provides additional justification for police officers playing an active role in multiagency partnerships. Other agencies would benefit greatly from the police officer's firsthand knowledge of juvenile delinquency, juvenile justice, and various street-level youth problems.

In closing, the fundamental challenge behind current attempts to enhance police effectiveness is best articulated through an old (modified) parable: Once there was a young couple standing on the bank of a swift river, enjoying a sunny day, when they noticed a young boy swimming for his life and calling for help. They responded quickly and managed to rescue him, but before they could catch their breath, they noticed another young person calling for help from the middle of the river. They proceeded to rescue him as well, but the problem continued, as more kids were discovered in this treacherous river, struggling for survival. The couple quickly realized that they, alone, could not save all of these children, so they sought help from the citizens of the nearby town. Before long, dozens of helpers were pulling drowning children from the river. This crisis continued until everyone was approaching the point of exhaustion. Finally, one woman became angry. "That does it!" she said in a loud voice, and then took off running up the river bank. Her friends called out—"Where are you going? She turned and said—"I'm going up stream to find out who is throwing these kids in the water and put a stop to it!"

Whether or not she can "put a stop to it," and how much it will cost, is another story. But to stop her from venturing up stream to investigate the problem would be foolish.

Notes

1. Interestingly enough, "community empowerment" began as a liberal concept to encourage citizens to demand their share of government resources, but in the 1980s and 1990s, conservatives found the empowerment concept very appealing as a cost-cutting strategy. With the latter interpretation, volunteerism was proposed as an alternative to many government-funded programs.

2. This is not the place to develop a complete theory of community policing, but I will attend to a few key areas that have been neglected or misunderstood in past discussions.

3. Taylor, Shumaker, and Gottfredson (1985) did not find a link between physical decay and fear after controlling for area, race, income, and home ownership. However, the bulk of extant data suggest a causal linkage, including studies with similar controls. Nevertheless, the disorder model has engendered serious criticism (e.g., Greene & Taylor, 1988), suggesting that additional work is needed on this topic.

4. *Money* magazine's annual survey of the best places to live in the United States illustrates, however unscientifically, the importance of crime in the housing market. Their 1994 readers' poll found that the desire for a low crime rate ranked first among 43 factors that people consider when choosing a place to live (September 1994 issue). Hence, crime rate was weighted heavily when ranking cities.

5. If we begin to think of crime as an epidemic (cf. Gladwell, 1996), and of neighborhoods in terms of reaching some critical threshold of crime-related problems, then perhaps we will better understand the process of rapid neighborhood decline or improvement. The tipping point, however, is likely to be different from one neighborhood to another.

6. To make matters worse, the emphasis on arrest has led to drug enforcement practices that are disproportionately focused on minority communities, thus producing differential increases in the Hispanic and African American prison populations.

7. To distinguish incidents from problems, Goldstein (1990) defines a problem as "a cluster of similar, related, or recurring incidents rather than a single incident; a substantive community concern; a unit of police business." (p. 66)

8. I should note that community policing was born in several major U.S. cities because the minority communities expressed dissatisfaction with unresponsive and apparent inequitable treatment by the police. In these cases, the emergence of community policing can be viewed as an attempt by the police to build trust and establish better relations with inner-city neighborhoods.

9. Even the traditional, enforcement-oriented police agency is forced to recognize that there is little it can accomplish without the full cooperation of local residents who serve as witnesses and informants regarding crime incidents.

10. This demonstration program is being funded by the Bureau of Justice Assistance, with the evaluation supported by the National Institute of Justice. The research team includes George Kelling, Ann Marie Rocheleau, Jeff Roth, Wes Skogan, and Dennis Rosenbaum.

Reprinted from: Dennis P. Rosenbaum, "The Changing Role of the Police: Assessing the Current Transition to Community Policing." In *How to Recognize Good Policing: Problems and Issues*, pp. 3–29. Copyright © 1998 by Sage Publications, Inc. Reprinted by permission. ✦

Part II

Mobilizing Communities Toward the Control and Prevention of Crime

While changes in policing over the past few decades have generated substantial research, few studies have focused outside the policing agency. Specifically, little attention has been given to understanding the complex relationship between police departments and the communities they serve. The lack of a comprehensive understanding of the political, cultural, and social realities of community mobilization and collaboration, however, will inhibit the success of efforts to combat crime.

Effective crime control and prevention are grounded in the collaborative efforts of police, community-based organizations, and citizens. But society still needs a better understanding of the underlying social processes responsible for developing the necessary attributes for effective collaboration. That is, strong efforts to control and prevent crime depend on the ability of citizens to come together to solve their problems. The articles here show that developing a more comprehensive view of the processes behind these collaborative efforts may bring clarity to the problem of sustaining long-term citizen involvement.

Several studies have suggested two interesting trends: first, citizen involvement tends to be high at the outset of a program but eventually tapers off; second, most citizens simply do not become involved. The lack of initial or continued citizen involvement is detrimental to long-term efforts to prevent crime. This fact raises important questions: What motivates citizens to engage in crime prevention? Why are some citizens more likely to participate? What are the responsibilities of citizens in crime prevention? To what degree must they be held accountable? Can police departments provide the impetus for citizen participation? The articles in this section explore these important issues.

Part II begins with J. Gardner's discussion of the elements necessary to build an effective community based on shared values, trust, and collaboration. He stresses the importance of community structure when solving problems. Drawing on Gardner's research, M. Correia then examines the critical role of strong social cohesion in maintaining neighborhood order. Next, E.F. McGarrell, A.L. Giacomazzi, and Q.C. Thurman explain social cohesion, disorder, and the fear of crime. Integrating these elements into one overall perspective, the authors suggest, is a more effective way of understanding fear of crime. More specifically, citizen cohesion, trust, and informal social control mechanisms are together capable of reducing levels of fear of crime.

Through a case study analysis, S. Sadd and R.M. Grinc illustrate the effectiveness of community mobilization in eight cities. The concluding reading, by R.W. Glensor and K.J. Peak, highlights the problems associated with citizens maintaining their neighborhoods after collaborative problem-solving efforts have been implemented.

The readings in Part II maintain that both citizen participation and community engagement are necessary for effective crime control and prevention. They also indicate that effective programs rely on a comprehensive understanding of the context in which crime occurs; the cohesiveness of citizens, and their willingness, accountability, and responsibility to engage in collective problem solving. ✦

5

Building a Responsive Community

John Gardner

Mobilizing and maintaining citizen involvement in efforts to control and prevent crime have been problematic. Through the years, criminal justice practitioners, policy makers, and educators have attempted to design and implement more effective programs—many of which have not lived up to their promises. These "failures" may not be indicative of the programs themselves but rather of the structure of the community. In a theoretical analysis, J. Gardner discusses those "ingredients" that he believes are essential for more cohesive and responsive communities. Realizing that most communities do not have all of these characteristics, he also presents steps that communities can take. Overall, he recognizes the diversity in American communities and offers prescriptions to weave them into a more cohesive fabric for heightened problem solving. As you read, assess which steps your community might take to achieve this end.

The Traditional Community

Setting about the contemporary task of building community, one discovers at once that the old, beloved traditional model will not serve our present purposes well. Nostalgia for "the good old days" will not help us through the turbulent times ahead.

The traditional community was homogeneous. Today most of us live with heterogeneity, and it will inevitably affect the design of our communities. Some of the homogeneity of traditional communities was based on exclusionary practices we cannot accept today.

The traditional community experienced relatively little change from one year to the next. The vital contemporary community will not only survive change but, when necessary, seek it.

The traditional community commonly demanded a high degree of conformity. Because of the nature of our world, the best of our contemporary communities today are pluralistic and adaptive, fostering individual freedom and responsibility within a framework of group obligation.

The traditional community was often unwelcoming to strangers, and all too ready to reduce its communication with the external world. Hard realities require that present-day communities be in continuous and effective touch with the outside world, and our values require that they be inclusive.

The traditional community could boast generations of history and continuity. Only a few communities today can hope to enjoy any such heritage. The rest, if they are vital, continuously rebuild their shared culture and consciously foster the norms and values that will ensure their continued integrity.

In short, much as we may value the memory of the traditional community, we shall find ourselves building anew, seeking to reincarnate some of the cherished values in forms appropriate to contemporary social organization. The traditional community, whatever its shortcomings, did create, through the family, through the extended family, and through all the interlocking networks of community life a structure of social interdependency in which individuals gave and received support—all giving, all receiving. With that no longer available, we must seek to reconstruct comparable structures of dependable interdependency wherever we can—in the work place, the church, the school, the youth-serving organizations, and so on.

The Ingredients of Community

I have spoken of the building and rebuilding [of the] community, but so far haven't said what we might expect as a result of our rebuilding. Let me be specific. I think of community as a set of attributes that may appear in diverse settings—a school, a congregation, a town, a suburb, a work place, a neighborhood. I'm going to list ten attributes of a community that would be viable in the contemporary world. There is no value neutrality in my description of the ingredients, but I believe the values explicit in these pages are widely shared. My interest is not to depict Utopia. My interest is to get us away from vague generalizations about "community" and to identify some ingredients we can work on constructively.

One of my purposes is to provide a list of characteristics against which observers can measure any setting in which they find themselves. Many readers, as they review the list, will be asking themselves what steps might be taken in their own setting. So at the same time that I describe the ingredients, I shall be suggesting—under the heading Steps Toward Solutions—some of the ways in which those ingredients might be made to emerge—methods of building community. I do so with some hesitation because my thoughts at this writing are preliminary and incomplete. Yet they may lead to more developed ideas as the subject is pursued further.

Some methods buy community at too high a price, and I shall not advocate them. It is always possible, for example, to build community by creating (or exaggerating) an outside threat. Many cults force new members to divest themselves of old ties and to cast off old identities. Many totalitarian societies create community by cutting off other options for their members.

1. Wholeness Incorporating Diversity

We live in a world of multiple, interacting systems. On the international scene, nations function interdependently or collide. In the city, government officials, business, labor, ethnic groups, and community organizations find—or fail to find—ways of living together. Russia seeks a way of dealing with the Ukraine, Canada a way of dealing with Quebec. Los Angeles copes with its multiple cultures. One encounters religious congregations that are split along class, racial, or doctrinal lines.

In our system, "the common good" is first of all preservation of a system in which all kinds of people can —within the law—pursue their various visions of the common good *and* at the same time accomplish the kinds of mutual accommodation that make a social system livable and workable. The play of conflicting interests in a framework of shared purposes is the drama of a free society. It is a robust exercise and a noisy one, not for the fainthearted or the tidy-minded. Diversity is not simply "good" in that it implies breadth of tolerance and sympathy. A community of diverse elements has greater capacity to adapt and renew itself in a swiftly changing world.

But to speak of community implies *some* degree of wholeness. What we seek, at every level, is pluralism that achieves some kind of coherence, *wholeness incorporating diversity*. I do not think it is venturing beyond the truth to say that wholeness incorporating diversity is the transcendent goal of our time, the task for our generation—close to home and worldwide.

"Wholeness" does not characterize our cities today. They are seriously fragmented. They are torn by everything from momentary political battles to deep and complex ethnic rifts. Separate worlds live side by side but fail to communicate or understand one another. The list of substantive issues facing the city are not the city's main problem. Its main problem is that it can't pull itself together to act on any of the issues. It cannot think as a community or act as a community.

As we look at the world's grimmest trouble spots, wholeness incorporating diversity seems a hopeless quest. But there are a good many cities and even nations where markedly heterogeneous populations live and work together quite peaceably.

Steps Towards Solutions. To prevent the wholeness from smothering diversity, there must be a philosophy of pluralism, an open climate for dissent, and an opportunity for subcommunities to retain their identity and share in the setting of larger group goals.

To prevent the diversity from destroying the wholeness, there must be institutional arrangements for diminishing polarization, for teaching diverse groups to know one another, for coalition-building, dispute resolution, negotiation and mediation. Of course the existence of a healthy community is in itself an instrument of conflict resolution.

A clear part of the problem, particularly in our cities, is the fragmentation of leadership. Most leaders are one-segment leaders, fattening themselves on the loyalty of their own little segment and exhibiting little regard for the city as a whole. Indeed, sometimes they thrive on divisiveness. But in any city there are leaders capable of a broader perspective, capable of joining with leaders of other segments (in and out of government) to define and solve the larger problems of the community. Such networks of responsibility can serve as a kind of constituency for the whole.

In our pluralistic system, each group is given the right to pursue its purposes within the law. Each group may demand recognition, may push for its rights, may engage in the healthy conflict implicit in pluralism—but then, in a healthy community each group will reach back to the whole community of which it is a segment and ask, "How can we help? How can we sing our part in the chorus?"

The nonprofit or voluntary sector can be a significant ally in accomplishing wholeness that incorporates diversity. It is a natural arena for diversity, but it is also capable of the "knitting together" that brings us back to some semblance of wholeness.

2. A Reasonable Base of Shared Values

To require that a community agree on everything would be unrealistic and would violate our concern for diversity. But it has to agree on something. *There has to be some core of shared values. Of all the ingredients of community this is possibly the most important.* The values may be reflected in written laws and rules, in a shared framework of meaning, in unwritten customs, in a shared vision of what constitutes the common good and the future.

To say that the community is characterized by those shared ideas and attributes puts the matter too passively. It will be more truly a community if members see it as an active defender of the shared ground. There should be a sense of social purpose. In our own society, we expect that the community will not only respect but actively pursue such ideals as justice, equality, freedom, the dignity of the individual, the release of human talent and energy, and so on. Thus, programs in education, civil rights, and the like build community. Rampant crime, fraud, and corruption tear it down.

The community teaches. If it is healthy it will impart a coherent value system. If it is chaotic or degenerate, lessons will be taught anyway—but not lessons that heal and strengthen. We treasure images of value education in which an older mentor quietly instructs a child in the rules of behavior, but that is a small part of a larger and more turbulent scene. The child absorbs values, good and bad, on the playground, through the media, on the street—everywhere. It is the community and culture that hold the individual in a framework of values.

None of this should be taken to mean that healthy communities should suppress internal criticism or deny their flaws or agree on everything. Irving Janis has shown how easily shared beliefs can become shared delusions.

Steps Towards Solutions. If the community is very lucky—and few will be in the years ahead—its shared values will be embedded in tradition and history and memory. But most future communities will have to build and continuously repair the framework of shared values. Their norms will have to be explicitly taught. Values that are never expressed are apt to be taken for granted and not adequately conveyed to young people and newcomers. Individuals have a role in the continuous rebuilding of the value framework, and the best thing that they can do is not to preach values but to exemplify them. Teach the truth by living it. All of us celebrate our values in our behavior. It is the universal ministry. The way we act and conduct our lives is saying something to others—perhaps something reprehensible, perhaps something encouraging.

Today we live with many faiths, so we must foster a framework of shared secular values—liberty, justice, and so on—while leaving people free to honor diverse deeper faiths that undergird those values.

3. Caring, Trust, and Teamwork

In some of the primitive tribes studied by anthropologists, the group was almost wholly self-sufficient. The community was responsible for all of the functions essential to human life: the provision of food and shelter, the resolving of internal conflicts, common defense in a hostile environment (human and other), the passing on of survival skills as well as provision of a context of meaning, allegiance, identity, and emotional fulfillment.

Today the community has been stripped of many of these functions by federal and state government, by distant suppliers, by media external to the community, and so on. It is all the more important then that we give attention to the functions that remain. Prominent among those remaining functions is providing the climate of caring, trust, and teamwork that ensures the accomplishment of group purpose.

The members of a good community deal with one another humanely, respect individual differences, and value the integrity of each person. A good community fosters an atmosphere of cooperation and connectedness. There is recognition and thanks for hard work, and the members are aware that they need one another. There is a sense of belonging and identity, a spirit of mutual responsibility. There is the altruism that is so consistently urged by major world religions. There is trust and tolerance and loyalty. Everyone is included. There is room for mavericks, nonconformists, and dissenters; there are no outcasts. Obviously, this describes an ideal community, perhaps beyond our reach. The best communities we know have a long way to go.

But even the approximation of such an environment is powerfully rewarding to individuals and can counteract the tendency of members to drift away that afflicts most American communities today.

Research shows that much of the basis for positive and generous adult relationships can be traced back to a warm and nurturing environment in childhood. But there are measures that can be taken at the adult level.

Steps Towards Solutions. In seeking the goal of caring, trust, and teamwork, the first necessary step is to give all subgroups and individuals reason to believe that they are fully accepted. It is essential that ethnic minorities, women, newcomers, the disabled, and so on—all feel that they count. We know how to fight that battle and should not let up.

Another step, equally critical, is to institutionalize arrangements for resolving disputes. Conflicting purposes and values are inevitable in our pluralistic society and part of the normal functioning of a healthy community. Indeed, groups that have been denied just treatment by the community find it necessary to precipitate conflict. But without processes for conflict resolution we can never achieve the "wholeness incorporating diversity" that we seek. Some systems for resolving disputes have been institutionalized over centuries. Our courts, our representative political institutions, and the economic marketplace resolve many conflicts. Some cities have community boards to deal with neighborhood disputes, commissions to work on racial harmony, or other instruments to diminish polarization.

Beyond that, there is an impressive array of measures that may be taken to resolve disputes. Every competent legislator knows the modes of building consensus and forming coalitions. Wise political leaders have learned the methods of collaboration and compromise.

The arts of reconciling conflicting purposes should be taught in every school and college in the world. Young potential leaders should be exposed to real-life situations—a political campaign, internship in a legislature or action in a community organization—where they learn the arts at first hand. The goal is not to abolish conflict, which is inevitable and even healthy, but to achieve constructive outcomes.

The third step is based on shared tasks. When individuals invest (time, energy, whatever) in their community, their bond with the community is strengthened. If they give something to (or give up something for) the community, they feel closer to it. Community problem-solving activities build community.

A healthy community will provide ample opportunities for the individual to participate in community efforts. Beginning early, boys and girls should take some responsibility for the well-being of any group they are in. This is a seemingly small step but without doubt the first step in responsible community participation, and for that matter the first step in leadership development. Through volunteer community service experiences outside of school, they will learn how the adult [world] works and will have the experience of serving their society. Every organization serving the community should find ways to involve young people.

There should be an Experience Corps through which older citizens can engage in volunteer work. A Volunteer Technical Assistance Center should help every nonprofit institution in the community learn the rather complex art of using volunteers effectively.

4. Participation

A two-way flow of influence and communication is dictated by our value system. Our society requires a dispersed network of leaders spread through every segment of the organization and down through every level. Beyond this wide network of identified leaders, there will be, in a vital community, a large number of individuals voluntarily sharing those leadership tasks that lend themselves to sharing, for example, achieving a workable level of unity, motivating, explaining.

If the system under discussion is a community functioning politically, one would want to add that beyond this voluntary sharing of leadership tasks a very large number of people will be expected to participate in such matters as voting and attending town meetings.

There are those who are opposed to the very concept of "a leader"—and there is much in human experience that makes their attitude easy to understand. But leadership in the mode I've described is not the sort of coercive or exploitative process that we've seen so much of in human history.

For a city, perhaps the most important requirement for effective leadership is the continuous collaboration between city government and all the segments of private-sector leadership, profit and nonprofit. Private-sector groups are beginning to recognize that such participation is a positive duty.

The citizen voting or speaking out in public meetings is participating, but so are the parents who rear their children with a sense of community responsibility, and so is the teenager who volunteers to tutor disadvantaged children. The healthy community has many ways of saying to the individual, "You belong, you have a role to play, and the drama has meaning." It is this more than anything else that accounts for the sense of identity so characteristic of community members.

Steps Towards Solutions. Among the conditions that enhance the possibility of participation are the following:

A. A community culture that enables all members and all subgroups to feel accepted and confident that their needs will be considered.

B. Civic education as to how local government works and why it sometimes doesn't work.

C. Voter registration and "get out the vote" drives.

D. Strong and active neighborhood groups and civic associations.

E. Free and responsible media of communication.

F. An open and responsive political process—restoration of trust in government by making it worthy of trust!

G. A sound educational system that includes preparation for effective leadership and participation.

H. Avoidance of the delusion that experts and professionals will solve all problems—what some have called managerial liberalism—making citizen action necessary.

I. Forums in which community members can "work through" (to use Daniel Yankelovich's phrase) the key issues facing them. Yankelovich points out that the superficial poll responses that are labeled public opinion are not at all the same as public judgment, which can only result from public dialogue.

J. A strong tradition of voluntary public service.

Let me elaborate on "G" above: education for effective leadership and participation. The overwhelming emphasis in contemporary education on individual performance must be supplemented with education in the accomplishment of group purpose. Some of the new cooperative education programs achieve that result. At some point in high school and college, one or another form of community service or political internship is helpful.

Many other institutions in the community can help with the task of civic education. Any citizen group, any advisory commission, every civic task force is a potential training ground for leaders and community builders. In addition, the community should have one or another form of "community leadership program" of the sort sponsored by the National Association for Community Leadership or the American Leadership Forum. All segments of community leadership must be represented in such groups.

It would be wrong to conclude a discussion of participation without mentioning some of the complexities of the subject. First, participation is never total, and those who do participate are always a self-selected group. Some have a higher than average self-interest in participating, some have more energy that participation requires, some are more zealous (or dogmatic) on the issues, some thrive on emotional intensity and combative talk, some have more of the physical or psychological stamina required for interminable meetings. Whatever the basis of selection, the result is not a representative sample of the community.

Among those who do participate, there will be a small group of activists who come to dominate and a large number who play less effective (or downright passive) roles. One cannot change that reality. One can design the system so that the small guiding group is required to act openly and is held firmly accountable by the others.

5. Affirmation

A healthy community reaffirms itself continuously. It builds its own morale. It may face up to its flaws and tolerate criticism, but basically it has confidence in itself. No group, no matter how well established, can take such affirmation entirely for granted. There are always young people to instruct and newcomers to welcome. Even a group with no history or tradition to build on can reaffirm its identity, its purposes, and its shared values. Individuals are generally members of more than one community and there are competing demands on them. The communities that survive the competition are likely to be those that press their claims.

In an earlier era, communities celebrated their beginnings, their roots. But in few American communities today can a majority, or even a sizable fraction of members, claim any link with the community's history. The story of most communities today is acceptance of wave upon wave of newcomers who over generations found a way of living with the culture, influencing it as they accommodated to it. The drama and pride of our communities have been the coming together of many cultures, with the consequent enrichment of all.

Steps Towards Solutions. Of course, a healthy community provides innumerable and ever-present affirmations of shared purpose just by being intact and vital. Everything from its nursery tales and its legendary figures to its structures of law and custom are forever conveying messages of instruction and reinforcement. Its history speaks, its symbols speak. It affirms the framework of meaning so important to community membership.

Normally, communities have ceremonies and celebrations to reaffirm the symbols of group identity, to recognize and reward exemplary members, to provide bonding experiences. In addition, there should be more formal measures to further civic education, not just in the schools and colleges but in the churches, youth organizations, and civic groups. It is everybody's business.

In thinking about the task of affirmation, we face the question of how far one carries a good thing before it becomes a bad thing. It is appropriate in a martial community such as the U.S. Marine Corps to pursue the matter somewhat obsessively. But for the normal community, excessive affirmation may create more pressure for conformity than is compatible with creativity.

6. Institutional Arrangements for Community Maintenance

Every community has institutional arrangements for group maintenance. In a city the most conspicuous arrangements are those we call government. In a nonprofit organization it is the board of trustees, the director and staff, and perhaps some volunteer committees. The forms are infinitely varied, and unwritten codes of conduct play their role.

There are marked variations from one community to the next in the extent to which the institutional arrangements are characterized by structure and control. We can't accept the extremes. Excessive community control does not accord with our ideal of individual freedom and responsibility. At the other extreme is a degree of anarchy that does not permit (or invite) the emergence of shared values, that tolerates a degree of disorder wholly incompatible with a sense of community.

Between the extremes we can tolerate considerable variation in the degree of structure and control.

In a democratic society, a high proportion of the population has some role in the maintenance system. In a town, for example, there are leaders in town government and in the private sector. There are lower level leaders in every segment of the community. And there are a considerable number of individuals throughout the system who "share leadership tasks" on their own initiative, working to maintain group motivation, to heal rifts, to do volunteer work, and the like. And then there are the many members who participate by voting, by setting an example of appropriate individual behavior, by nurturing younger members.

Steps Towards Solutions. Some of the writers who are most concerned about restoring a sense of community today are not inclined to pay much attention to government, but its role is critically important. If it doesn't work, it must be made to work. We cannot take it for granted. It has to be made an instrument of community and of participation, worthy of respect and trust. Politicians are much maligned, but the best of them, skilled in mediating among disparate groups, can make a significant contribution to community.

There must be continuous collaboration between local government and the private sector. There must be an infrastructure of neighborhood associations, churches, citizen groups, youth-serving organizations, and professional groups. Today some of these groups are genuinely interested in the community as a community, but most are highly specialized, each existing in its own little niche, rarely if ever thinking about the fate of the community as a whole. They must learn where their civic duty lies. They are an important part of the fabric of the community.

One of the most important functions in community maintenance is training and development of those who will ensure the continuity of maintenance. For this, the mingling of the generations is crucial. Young people should, from an early age, learn how their community functions and how it can be kept functioning.

Conclusion

Social theorists have pointed out that among the first acts of totalitarian dictators coming to power is to undermine the private associative links of the citizen, so there is nothing left but the state and a mass of separate individuals, easily dominated. Such theorists argue (correctly) that the close-in loyalties—to family, school, church, lodge, union, neighborhood, and community—are essential to the health of a free society. Not only do such loyalties make the rise of an absolutist state far more unlikely, but also they are teaching arenas for the arts of community that we need so desperately at national and world levels.

At first glance, it would seem that no other nation has, or could have, a richer diversity of associations than we do. We have taken pluralism to its limits. So what's the problem? Why aren't we in great shape?

The answer is that the conditions of contemporary life have leached out the ingredients of community from a great many of these potentially nurturing associations. How many congregations have we seen in which the element of community is so thinned out as to be nonfunctional? How many schools have we seen that might be splendid communities but in fact don't even approach that condition? How many neighborhoods might be coherent human settlements but are not?

I had occasion recently to spend considerable time with the local branch of a famous social service organization, committed in its public pronouncements to serve its clients humanely. I have reason to believe that the agency uses its funds carefully and provides its services dutifully. But the rich opportunities it has to provide an experience of community to clients who desperately need that experience are squandered. It is a station for the delivery of social services, but one might find more sense of community among the patrons of the nearest motel.

Another problem is that even for those of our associations that are in fact communities, there is often a reluctance to play their role in relation to the larger wholes of which they are a part. I know of one small business enterprise whose officers and employees constitute a satisfying little community, but they have little or no interest in the disintegrating city in which they are located.

Returning to a point made earlier, I think of community as a set of attributes that may or may not be present in a particular group or social system. I have tried to describe those attributes so that people can assess any particular institution or social system of which

they are a part—school, congregation, village, work place, neighborhood, whatever—and judge whether it is in fact a community.

We must seek to regenerate the sense of community from the ground up. How can people work to make their metropolis a community when most of them have seldom experienced a sense of community in any familiar setting? Men and women who have come to understand, in their own intimate settings, the principles of "wholeness incorporating diversity," the arts of diminishing polarization, the meaning of teamwork and participation, will be strong allies in the effort to build elements of community into the metropolis, the nation, and the world.

It would be a grave mistake to imagine that, in a great burst of energy, we can rebuild our communities and then turn to other tasks. That assumes a degree of stability we once knew but may never see again in our lifetime. We can never stop rebuilding.

The communities we build today may eventually be eroded or torn apart by the crosscurrents of contemporary life. Then we rebuild. We can't know all the forms that community will take, but we know the values and the kinds of supporting structures we want to preserve. We are a community-building species. We might become remarkably ingenious at creating new forms of community for a swiftly changing world.

6

Social Capital and Sense of Community Building

Building Social Cohesion

Mark E. Correia

M. *Correia explores the underlying social processes that affect citizens' ability to collaborate effectively with governmental agencies. He draws upon the works of community psychologists, political scientists, and sociologists in examining the role of social capital and sense of community in building social cohesion. More specifically, he suggests that strong social cohesion is paramount to solving complex community problems. That is, for citizens to work effectively with government agencies (the police), they must be able to get along with one another. Essentially, Correia brings to the fore the importance of community structure in facilitating problem solving. As you read, think about the degree of social cohesion in your own community and consider whether or not its citizens and government agencies would collaboratively address neighborhood crime and disorder.*

Introduction

As discussed throughout this book, an important component of effective policing is the willingness of citizens to engage in problem-solving activities. In fact, a common assumption among proponents of community policing is that this type of broad based citizen participation is both necessary and possible

to elicit in order to overcome the problems of disorder and crime. Indeed, a consistent finding among researchers is that a low level of participation of individuals is detrimental to the programmatic efforts of police departments (Sadd and Grinc, 1994).

This type of citizen behavior is termed *collective action,* and has been defined as "activities which produce collective or public goods, that is, goods with the non-excludability property that their provision to some members of a group means that they cannot be withheld from others in the group" (Oliver, 1984: 602). Within the context of collective action, a collective good is a benefit which, if provided to one member of a group, cannot be withheld from other members (Hardin, 1982). The most common examples of collective goods include commodities such as national defense and use of public lands (e.g., water or grazing rights). Properly conceptualized, neighborhood safety and social order can also be defined as a collective good. Hence, problems of physical and social disorder, as well as crime, are collective action problems — problems that affect all individuals in the area and require a collective response in order to be alleviated.

What are the underlying motivations driving individuals to join together to solve collective action problems? Why are some communities better able to deal with problems of crime and social disorder? This article addresses these questions through an examination of those social processes which affect individual participation in communal problems.

The Effect of 'Size' on Community Participation

Contrary to proponents of community policing, most collective action theorists contend that broad based participation in the achievement of collective goods is normally unnecessary. Instead, if a "critical mass" of individuals is available for mobilization, it is possible to facilitate effective collective action in many circumstances (Inchausti, 1991; Kavial, 1977; Scarce, 1990). In terms of neighborhood safety, it may be the case that only a handful of very active individuals is necessary to ensure this safety, not all of the individuals living in the area.

This perspective was developed by Schelling (1978), who suggests that individual behavior is contingent upon the behavior of others with whom one comes in contact (p. 26). In terms of collective action, he states that "what people do affects what other people do. How well people accomplish what they want to accomplish depends on what others are doing" (p. 26). This perspective suggests that collective action activities may be more determined by psychological and behavioral aspects (i.e., socially- based norms and value aspects) than by rational decision making or group size (see also Kaye, 1990; Prestby, Wandersman, Florin, Rich, and Chavis, 1990; Prestby and Wandersman, 1985). This broader conception of rationality, one that is more applicable to collective action, "recognizes the process by which understandings are reached, communal bonds formed, and collective identities are constructed" (Miller, 1992: 24).

The major contribution put forth by Schelling is that of critical mass, described as "some activity that is self-sustaining once the measure of that activity passes a certain minimum level" (p. 95).[1] This concept indicates that successful collective activity is not dependent on the participation of all individuals involved, but rather requires only enough participation by highly engaged citizens to keep the organization "alive." Similarly, Oliver and Marwell (1988) suggest that,

> The problem of collective action is not whether it is possible to mobilize every single person who would be benefited by a collective good. It is not whether it is possible to mobilize everyone willing to be mobilized. It is not even whether all the members of some organization or social network can be mobilized. Rather, the issue is whether there is some social mechanism that connects enough people who have the appropriate interests and resources so that they can act. (p. 6)

Conceptualization of the collective action problem allows for the incorporation of values, shared ideas, and common interests of individuals within the communities to rise to the center of attention, all being factors which may influence citizens' decisions to become engaged in problem solving activities (see also Oliver, 1984; Oliver, Marwell, and Teixeira, 1985; Marwell, Oliver, and Prahl, 1988; Oliver, 1993).

Further complicating the matter of collective action are the different types of communal structures which may exist: strong or weak communal bonds, larger and heterogeneous community composition, pockets of "community" within a larger community, and lack of any type of communal bonds are all possible contexts for collective action efforts (Taylor and Singleton, 1993: 202). Each of these variations in community structure may affect the manner in which individuals seek to solve their problems collectively. Again, these observations serve to highlight the contention that individual rationality may play only a limited role in many collective activities (see Gardner in this volume).[2]

Collective Action and Innovative Policing

Collective action involves a working partnership between members of the community, the police, other governmental agencies and institutions; together they can solve chronic problems of crime and disorder within the community. As stated by Friedman and Clark (1997),

> [t]he importance of organizing and organization cannot be overemphasized. The community needs to be organized because it is the most effective way to work with a highly organized partner like the police and against often well-organized and frightening adversaries. (p. 12)

While some appreciation as to the importance of collective action exists among police practitioners, COPPS is plagued by the inability to sustain citizen participation in many settings where they are being attempted (see Glensor and Peak in this volume). COPPS strategies often target the community as a whole, attempting to include all individuals in solving a community problem. However, available public resources and policy efforts may be better spent on identifying and supporting that critical mass of individuals which is most likely to engage in civic activities promoting public safety.

Neighboring Behavior, Social Cohesion, and Collective Action

At the most basic level, social interaction among citizens typically occurs between persons who care in close proximity to one another; in most cases this means interactions with neighbors. Hence, "neighbors are an informal resource who may act individually to provide socio-emotional support to each other as well as collectively to ameliorate problems in their residential environment" (Unger and Wandersman, 1982: 493).

Neighboring activities are strongly associated with an individual's psychological attachment, rootedness, and integration into his/her community, and perceived sense of safety (Unger and Wandersman, 1982; Wandersman, Florin, Friedman, and Meier, 1987; Skogan, 1990), and can provide emotional, instrumental, and informational support to individuals (Unger and Wandersman, 1985). In terms of emotional support, neighboring behaviors provide individuals with the opportunity to socially interact, and in so doing generally reduce feelings of disconnectedness and social isolation (Rubin, 1976; Unger and Wandersman, 1983). The level of support provided by these interactions depends on the number of positive interactions that individuals have with one another; of course, negative interactions are also possible.

Instrumental support refers to the commitments and rules of reciprocity within the neighboring environment (Unger and Wandersman, 1985). For example, individuals may exchange resources or watch a neighbor's house and/or property while they are away. The most significant determining factor is length of residence within the particular area (Sampson, 1990; Skogan, 1990; Unger and Wandersman, 1983, 1985); positive interactions over time tend to build a strong basis for instrumental support. High levels of this type of support have also been shown to decrease levels of crime and disorder as well as fear of crime within a community (Skogan, 1990; Taylor, 1995; Taylor, Gottfredson, and Brower, 1984).

Informational support involves individuals sharing information and is critical in keeping residents current on the happenings in the neighborhood as well as the transference of mutual expectations, norms, and values. Again, in order for such support to be provided, residents must have adequate levels of interaction with each other and live in the area for long periods of time for interpersonal familiarity to obtain.

Overall, then, neighboring activity plays an important role in collective action activities. As neighbors become more familiar with each other and have more positive interactions with one another, they are more likely to come together to solve complex social problems. Importantly, neighborhoods have been described as "where the bonds of community are built" and as the "wellsprings of social capital" (Portney and Berry, 1997).

Social Capital and Social Cohesion

The importance of social relationships in understanding collective action has recently been furthered by the development of the concept of social capital. Social capital can be defined as "a variety of different entities having two characteristics in common: . . . some aspect of a social structure, and facilitat[ing] certain actions of individuals who are within the structure" (Coleman, 1990: 302). Putnam (1993, 1995a, 1995b) has refined this definition as those "features of social organization such as networks, norms and trust that facilitate cooperation or coordination for mutual benefits" (Putnam, 1995b: 665). In terms of measuring social capital, Putnam (1995a, 1995b) focuses his attention on levels of civic participation in formal organizations. In American society, he has found significant declines in religious participation, union membership, parent-teacher associations, fraternal organizations (e.g., Elks, Masons), Red Cross, and bowling leagues over the course of the past decades. Consequently, Putnam argues that many social problems within American communities may be a result of this declining reserve of social capital (Ladd, 1996).[3]

This definition of social capital more clearly reflects the embeddedness of individuals into their communal and governmental affairs, which in turn promotes the development of trust among citizens and between citizens and their governmental institutions. More specifically, social capital can be defined as the reserves of trust and *engagement* found in a community.

Building partnerships between citizens and police (e.g., COPPS) is part of a larger community building movement which requires high levels of trust and engagement (see Osborne and Gaebler, 1992). For example, making city services more accessible, increasing citizen volunteers in government agencies, and developing neighborhood-based governing organizations, have helped increase problem solving efforts. In a study assessing the relationship between interpersonal trust and civic engagement, Brehm and Rahn (1997) found that civic participation increases levels of interpersonal trust. Specifically, without high levels of trust, civic engagement would not occur, and that without high levels of civic engagement interpersonal trust could not be generated. Sustaining this reciprocal relationship requires both trust and civic engagement.

In terms of COPPS, community partnerships (i.e., citizens, police, and other organizations) have been shown to be effective in reducing crime and disorder. Efforts in Norfolk, Virginia, for example, show that bringing neighborhood groups, social services and police agencies together can have positive results; in this case, a substantial decrease in overall crime (DOJ, 1994).

These broad-based partnership efforts and, more specifically COPPS, highlight the importance of trust and citizen engagement in solving complex social problems (see Peak and Glensor, 1999: 55–65). More specifically, they indicate that,

> Social capital is important because it constitutes a force that helps to bind society together by transforming individuals from self-seeking and egocentric calculators with little social conscious or sense of mutual obligations, into members of a community with shared interests. (Newton, 1997: 576)

Social Capital and Social Responsibility

According to Putnam (1995b), there are two distinct levels of social capital: local social capital and public social capital. The first, or most basic form of social capital, is found among members of the family and between citizens within a community. At this level, trust and reciprocity among individuals is key. Another important aspect is informal responsibility, which is inherent to trust and reciprocity. This level of responsibility pertains to obligations felt to those informal groups that immediately surround the individual— for example, family and friends— and relies on the ability of the neighborhood and/or friendship networks to enforce informal rules of social conduct through social disapproval (Bursik and Grasmick, 1993).

Community psychologists suggest that an individual's need for emotional safety and feeling of belonging to a group places them in a situation where social disapproval is quite effective (McMillan and Chavis, 1986; see also Braithwaite, 1989). Similarly, strong family cohesiveness has been found to be related to higher levels of educational attainment (Hagan, MacMillan, and Wheaton, 1996) and lower levels of behavioral problems in children (Parcel and Menaghan, 1993).

The second level of social capital (public social capital) consists of those social networks tying the individual to broader community institutions (e.g., churches, schools, civic and voluntary organizations). These informal associations with other citizens help build familiarity and trust among individuals and keep individuals engaged in communal affairs; a necessary component to facilitating collective activities and resisting the spiral effect of social disorder (Wilson and Kelling, 1982; Skogan, 1990). Putnam (1993) suggests that these associational networks are important because "members of associations are much more likely than nonmembers to participate in politics, to spend time with neighbors, to express trust, and so on" (p. 36).

Research across several disciplines has focused on the effect these informal social bonds have on lower levels of fear of crime

(Taylor, Gottfredson, and Brower, 1984), lower rates of victimization and delinquency (Simcha-Fagan and Schwartz, 1986; Shaw and McKay, 1969), lower levels of general disorder (Skogan, 1990), higher levels of sense of community (Chavis and Wandersman, 1990; McMillan and Chavis, 1986), larger stocks of social capital (Putnam, 1995a), stronger neighborhood social control mechanisms (Bursik and Grasmick, 1993; Greenberg and Rohe, 1986), and lower levels of community disorganization (Sampson and Groves, 1989).

Social capital is an important element in social cohesion and collective action. There is, however, the possibility that a "dark side" to social capital exists (Levi, 1996; Edwards and Foley, 1997). As discussed elsewhere (Correia, Reisig, and Pratt, forthcoming), strong ties among individuals can lead to the exclusion of others from participating in their community (see also Granovetter, 1973), or may foster and perpetuate destructive norms and values (e.g., Montana's citizen militia groups). Along similar lines, MacMillan and Chavis (1986) highlight the polarizing characteristics of social cohesion, providing examples of vigilantism, gated communities, and hate groups. Consequently, the results of strong social capital and social cohesion may be either positive or negative for the community, depending upon the context.

This possibility places increased levels of importance on the structure of the community. Those communities better able to balance individual and community rights are more likely to have inclusive social capital than communities unable to provide such a balance (Etzioni, 1993, 1995a, 1995b; Walzer, 1991, 1993; see also Gardner, this volume).

Perceived Sense of Safety, Incivilities and Disorder

An individual's perceived sense of safety affects his/her attachment to the community (Slovak, 1986; Perkins, Florin, Rich, Wandersman, and Chavis, 1990; Taylor, Gottfredson, and Brower, 1985; Riger, LeBailly, and Gordon, 1981) and is related to the incidence of incivilities and disorder within their neighborhood and/or community. That is, incivilities and disorder refer to the erosion of informal social control mechanisms (e.g., graffiti, public drunkenness, and harassment) (Skogan, 1990; Wilson and Kelling, 1982). An increase in these incivilities will increase the fear of crime, and in so doing reduce an individual's perceived sense of safety (Covington and Taylor, 1991; Skogan and Maxfield, 1981; see also Taub, Taylor, and Dunham, 1981).

Though rather inconclusive as to the direct or indirect effects involved, available research on incivilities and disorder suggests that individuals can respond in a variety of ways, including avoidance, protective actions or by engaging in collective activities (Miethe, 1995). Most research focuses on avoidance behavior, where individuals may physically and/or psychologically withdraw from public spaces and isolate themselves from their neighbors. Under these circumstances levels of interpersonal trust and reciprocity are minimal, stocks of social capital are depleted, social cohesion is weakened, and collective action is non-existent (Miethe, 1995; Skogan, 1987, 1990; Taylor and Hall, 1986). Protective actions, which range from fortifying one's residence to carrying a protective device, may also have the same effects as avoidance behavior (Skogan and Maxfield, 1981).

Both of these possible responses have several psychological consequences, which then affect the ability of citizens to engage in problem solving activities. These types of withdrawal reactions will lead to decreased levels of neighboring activity, a decreased willingness to get involved and decreased satisfaction with one's community (Taylor, 1995).

Lastly, it is possible that increased levels of incivilities and disorder may actually bring individuals together (Taylor, 1995; Perkins et al., 1990). For example, instead of psychologically or physically removing themselves from the community, citizens may actually establish crime prevention groups, implement special events (e.g., take back the neighborhood), or create victimization groups and lobby for victim-based legislation. It does appear that individuals have found numerous methods to cope with crime in their communities, with some reactions being more socially productive than others.

Discussion

As the above theoretical perspectives indicate, there appears to be a strong relationship between social cohesion and collective action. More specifically, strong social cohesion (i.e., high levels of informal social control and large stocks of social capital) may be indicative of more effective types of collective action. Given this, a more comprehensive understanding of factors affecting innovative policing techniques should entail these community-based characteristics.

Unfortunately, most research has been directed at the policing organization rather than the policed *community*, consequently overlooking the clear importance of social cohesion. This can negatively affect policing organizations which are implementing COPPS. For example, if communities lack strong social cohesion, citizens are not likely to engage in collective activities, therefore, policing agencies will have difficulty in implementing programs which require long term citizen participation. On the other hand, those communities with strong social cohesion and active citizens may be better able to form effective problem solving partnerships with policing agencies.

Effective policing of American communities appears to require more than changing the policing organization itself. The underlying social processes of a community appear to play an important role in reducing crime and disorder in our communities.

References

Braithwaite, J. (1989). Crime, shame and reintegration. New York, NY: Cambridge University Press.

Brehm, J. and W. Rahn (1997). Individual-level evidence for the causes and consequences of social capital. *American Journal of Political Science* 41: 999–1023.

Brown, L. and D. Ashman (1996). Participation, social capital, and intersectoral problem solving: African and Asian cases. *World Development* 24: 1467–1479.

Bursik, R. and H. Grasmick (1993). *Neighborhoods and crime: The dimensions of effective community control.* New York, NY: Lexington Books.

Chavis, D. and A. Wandersman (1990). Sense of community in the urban environment: a catalyst for participation and community development. *American Journal of Community Psychology* 18: 55–81.

Coleman, J. (1990). *Foundations of social theory.* Cambridge, MA: Belknap.

Correia, M., M. Reisig, T. Pratt (1999). The conceptual ambiguity of "community" policing: Filtering the muddy waters. Forthcoming.

Covington, J. and R. Taylor (1991). Fear of crime in urban residential neighborhoods: implications for between-and- within neighborhood sources for current models. *Sociological Quarterly* 32: 231–247.

Department of Justice (1994). Working as partners with community groups. Bureau of Justice Assistance Bulletin, National Crime Prevention Council. Washington, D.C.: U.S. Department of Justice.

Edwards, B. and M. Foley (1997). Social capital and the political economy of our discontent. *American Behavioral Scientist* 40: 669–679.

Etzioni, A. (1993). *The spirit of community: The reinvention of American Society.* New York, NY: Simon and Schuster.

Etzioni, A. (1995a). Old chestnuts and new spurs. In A. Etzioni (Ed.) *New Communitarian Thinking: Persons, Virtues, Institutions and Communities* (p. 16–36) Charlottesville, VA: University Press of Virginia.

Etzioni, A. (1995b). The attack on community: the grooved debate. *Society* 32: 12–17.

Friedman, W. and M. Clark (1997). Measuring what matters, part two: Developing measures of what the police do. [National Institute of Justice] *Research in Action.*

Granovetter, M. (1973). The strength of weak ties. *American Journal of Sociology* 78: 1360–1380.

Greenberg, S. and W. Rohe (1986). Informal social control and crime prevention in modern urban neighborhoods. In R. Taylor (Ed.) *Urban Neighborhoods: Research and Policy* (pp. 79–112). Westport, CT: Praeger.

Hagan, J., H. Merkens, and K. Boehnke (1995). Delinquency and disdain: Social capital and the control of right-wing extremism among East and West Berlin youth. *American Journal of Sociology* 100: 1028–1052.

Hagan, J., R. MacMillan, and B. Wheaton (1996). New kid in town: Social capital and the life course effects of family migration on children. *American Sociological Review* 61: 368–385.

Hardin, R. (1982). *Collective action.* Baltimore, MD: John Hopkins University Press.

Heying, C. (1997). Civic elites and corporate delocalization: An alternative explanation for declining civic engagement. *American Behavioral Scientist* 40: 657–669.

Inchausti, R. (1991). *The ignorant perfection of ordinary people*. Albany, NY: State University of New York Press.

Kaye, G. (1990). A community organizer's perspective on citizen participation research and the researcher practitioner partnership. *American Journal of Community Psychology* 18: 151–157.

Ladd, E. (Ed)(1996). *A vast empirical record reflects the idea of civic decline. The public perspective: A roper center review of public opinion and policy*. Willimantic, CT: Hall and Bill Printing.

Levi, M. (1996). Social and unsocial capital: A review essay of Robert Putnam's "Making Democracy Work." *Politics and Society* 24: 45–55.

Marwell, G., P. Oliver, and R. Prahl (1988). Social networks and collective action: A theory of the critical mass, III. *American Journal of Sociology* 94: 502–534.

McMillan, D. and D. Chavis (1986). Sense of community: A definition and theory. *Journal of Community Psychology* 14: 6–23.

Miller, B. (1992). Collective action and rational choice: Place, community, and the limits to individual self-interest. *Economic Geography* 68: 22–42.

Oliver, P. (1984). If you don't do it, nobody else will: Collective and token contributors to local collective action. *American Sociological Review* 49: 601–610.

Oliver, P. (1993). Formal models of collective action. *Annual Review of Sociology* 19: 271–300.

Oliver, P. and G. Marwell (1988). The paradox of group size in collective action: A theory of critical mass. II. *American Sociological Review* 53: 108–134.

Oliver, P., G. Marwell, and R. Teixeira (1985). A theory of critical mass I. Interdependence, group heterogeneity, and the production of collective action. *American Journal of Sociology* 91: 522–556.

Olson, M. (1969). *The logic of collective action*. Cambridge, MA: Harvard University Press.

Osborne, D. and T. Gaebler (1993). *Reinventing government: How the entrepreneurial spirit is transforming the public sector*. New York, NY: Plume.

Parcel, T. and E. Menaghan (1993). Family social capital and children's behavior problems. *Social Psychology Quarterly* 56: 120–135.

Peak, K. and R. Glensor (1999). *Community policing & problem solving: Strategies and practices. 2nd ed.* Upper Saddle River, NJ: Prentice Hall.

Perkins, D., P. Florin, R. Rich, A. Wandersman, and D. Chavis (1990). Participation and the social and physical environment of residential blocks: Crime and community context. *American Journal of Community Psychology* 1: 534–557.

Portney, K. and J. Berry (1997). Mobilizing minority communities: Social capital and participation in urban neighborhoods. *American Behavioral Scientist* 40: 631–643.

Putnam, R. (1993). The prosperous community: Social capital and public life. *The American Prospect Spring:* 35–42.

Putnam, R. (1995a). Bowling alone: America's declining social capital. *Journal of Democracy* 6: 65–78.

Putnam, R. (1995b). Tuning in, tuning out: The strange disappearance of social capital in America. *PS: Political Science and Politics* Dec: 664–683.

Prestby, T. and A. Wandersman (1985). An empirical exploration of a framework of organizational viability: Maintaining block organization. *The Journal of Applied Behavioral Science* 21: 287–305.

Prestby, T., A. Wandersman, P. Florin, R. R. Rich, D. Chavis (1990). Benefits, costs, incentive management and participation in voluntary organizations: A means to understanding and promoting empowerment. *American Journal of Community Psychology* 18:117–149.

Riger, S., R. LeBailly and M. Gordon (1981). Community ties and urbanites' fear of crime: An ecological investigation. *American Journal of Community Psychology* 9: 653–665.

Rubin, L. (1976). *Worlds of pain*. New York, NY: Basic Books.

Sadd, S. and R. Grinc (1994). Innovative neighborhood orienting policing: An evaluation of community policing programs in eight cities. In D. Rosenbaum (Ed.) *The Challenge of Community Policing* (pp. 27–52), Thousand Oaks, CA: Sage Publications.

Sampson, R. (1990). The community. In J. Wilson and J. Petersilia (Eds) *Crime* (p. 193–216). San Francisco, CA: ICS Press.

Sampson, R. and B. Groves (1989). Community structure and crime: Testing social–disorganization theory. *American Journal of Sociology* 94: 774–802.

Scarce, R. (1990). Eco-Warriors: *Understanding the radical environment movement*. Chicago, IL: The Noble Press.

Schelling, T. (1988). *Micromotives and macrobehavior*. New York, NY: W.W. Norton Co.

Shaw, C. and H. McKay (1969). *Juvenile delinquency and urban areas*. Chicago, IL: University of Chicago Press.

Simcha-Fagan, O. and J. Schwartz (1986). Neighborhood and delinquency: An assessment of contextual effects. *Criminology* 24: 667–703.

Skogan, W. (1987). The importance of victimization on fear. *Crime and Delinquency* 33: 135-154.

Skogan, W. (1990). *Disorder and decline*. Berkeley, CA: University of California Press.

Skogan, W. and M. Maxfield (1981). *Coping with crime: Individual and neighborhood reactions*. Newbury Park, CA: Sage Publications.

Slovak, J. (1986). Attachments in the nested community: Evidence from a case study. *Urban Affairs Quarterly* 21: 575–592.

Taub, R., G. Taylor, and J. Dunham (1981). Neighborhoods and safety. In D. Lewis (Ed.) *Reactions to Crime* (p. 103–119). Beverly Hills, CA: Sage.

Taylor, R. (1995). The impact of crime on communities. *The Annals of the American Academy of Political and Social Science* 539: 28–45.

Taylor, R. and M. Hall (1986). Testing alternative models of fear of crime. *Journal of Criminal Law and Criminology* 77: 151–179.

Taylor, R. and S. Singleton (1993). The communal resource: Transaction costs and the solution of collective action problems. *Politics and Society* 21: 195–214.

Taylor, R., S. Gottfredson, and S. Brower (1984). Block crime and fear: Defensible space, local social ties, and territorial functioning. *Journal of Crime and Delinquency* 21: 303–331.

Unger, D. and A. Wandersman (1982). Neighboring in an urban environment. *American Journal of Community Psychology* 10: 493–509.

Unger, D. and A. Wandersman (1983). Neighboring and its role in block organizations: An exploratory report. *American Journal of Community Psychology* 11: 291–300.

Unger, D. and A. Wandersman (1985). The importance of neighbors: The social, cognitive and affective components of neighboring. *American Journal of Community Psychology* 13: 139–169.

Walzer, M.(1991). The idea of civil society: A path to social reconstruction. *Dissent* 38: 293–304.

Walzer, M.(1993). Exclusion, injustice, and the democratic state. *Dissent* 40: 55–64.

Wandersman, A., P. Florin, R. Friedman, and R. Meier (1987). Who participates, who does not, and why? An analysis of voluntary neighborhood organizations in the United States and Israel. *Sociological Forum* 2: 534–555.

Wilson, J. and G. Kelling (1982). The police and neighborhood safety: Broken windows. *Atlantic Monthly* 128: 29–38.

7

Neighborhood Disorder, Integration, and the Fear of Crime

Edmund F. McGarrell
Andrew L. Giacomazzi
Quint C. Thurman

A major part of new policing techniques is aimed at reducing citizens' fear of crime. In order to do so, we must first answer the question, "What is fear of crime based on?" E.F. McGarrell, A. Giacomazzi, and Q. Thurman assess the dominant explanations, provide an analysis of fear of crime, and develop a more comprehensive explanation. As you read, think about what might be your underlying fears. Are they based on physical disorder in your neighborhood (e.g., graffiti, abandoned vehicles, and so on)? Have you or someone you know been a victim of crime? Do you hold high levels of concern for your neighborhood? In addition, how would you reduce your fear of crime? What could the police or other public agencies do to help? Finally, try to weigh the amount of emotional devastation felt by people who suffer from living in fear of crime.

In the past two decades, scholars have conducted considerable research on fear of crime. Much of this research has focused on the facilitators of fear. These factors include victimization and vicarious victimization, disorder, vulnerability to crime, and the demographic traits thought to relate to vulnerability. Less attention has been given to potential inhibitors of fear such as social in-tegration, local social control, and responsiveness of governmental institutions.[1]

Related to this theoretical development is the recent emergence of the community policing movement. This movement operates on the assumption that increasing police and governmental responsiveness to community members, as well as increasing social partnerships at the neighborhood level, can reduce fear of crime and improve the quality of community life (see Wilson and Kelling 1982). Despite some empirical support for these assumptions, such as the finding that foot patrol reduces fear (Kelling 1986; Pate 1986; Skogan 1990), other studies have been less encouraging (Greene and Taylor 1988).

In the following analysis we attempt to address these issues by examining both the facilitators and the inhibitors of individual fear of crime. By including a number of indicators drawn from the victimization, disorder, and community concern perspectives, we test a more complete model of fear of crime. We also examine whether the model holds in neighborhoods reporting low, medium, and high levels of disorder.

Models of Fear of Crime

The Victimization Model

Several distinct but related theoretical models of fear of crime have emerged. Early studies of fear were based on a victimization model, which posited higher levels of fear in people who had been victims of crime. Although some researchers found a relationship between victimization and fear (Skogan and Maxfield 1981), others found that victimization was either unrelated or only marginally related to fear (Gates and Rohe 1987; Liska, Sanchirico, and Reed 1988). Further, this model was called into question by the common finding that those most likely to be victims (young males) had relatively low levels of fear, whereas those least likely to be victims (elderly females) had high levels of fear (Garofalo and Laub 1978). In light of these findings, a revised version of the model, the indirect victimization model, has emerged.

The indirect victimization framework is based on the finding that groups vulnerable to crime have high levels of fear. Thus the finding that fear is greatest among women and the elderly (e.g., Hindelang, Gottfredson, and Garofalo 1978; Kennedy and Silverman 1985; Taylor, Gottfredson, and Brower 1984; Taylor and Hale 1986; Will and McGrath 1995) is attributed to these groups' perception of greater physical vulnerability to crime. Similarly, the finding of a negative relationship between income and fear (Taylor et al. 1984; Taylor and Hale 1986; Will and McGrath 1995) and a relationship between race and fear (Covington and Taylor 1991) is interpreted as the consequence of heightened social vulnerability (Taylor and Hale 1986). The indirect victimization model also predicts higher rates of fear for those embedded in social networks (where they are likely to learn of another's victimization) and for those concerned about the crime problem (Lewis and Salem 1986; Skogan and Maxfield 1981).

The Disorder Model

The disorder model is based on the finding of a relationship between fear and perceived social and physical disorder (Gates and Rohe 1987; LaGrange, Ferraro, and Supancic 1992; Lewis and Salem 1986; Skogan 1990; Skogan and Maxfield 1981). Disorder indicates weakened local social control and the attenuation of traditional norms. Physical decay signals a lack of concern about the neighborhood; both "social and physical incivilities are signs of lack of adherence to norms of public behavior" (Taylor and Hale 1986: 154). Skogan (1990) observed that disorderly persons are perceived as unpredictable and potentially violent. Similarly, Lewis and Salem (1986) found that disorderly activities such as gang graffiti, loitering teens, and public drinking were associated with the perception of a high risk of victimization. In a national sample of residents in Great Britain, Hope and Hough (1988) found that the association between disorder and fear was strong even when other aspects of community life were controlled.[2]

The Community Concern Model

A third model of fear of crime has been labeled the "community concern perspective" (Taylor and Hale 1986). Closely related to the disorder model, this perspective holds that fear rises as concerns about the neighborhood increase. Taylor and Hale (1986) found more fear among citizens who reported that they were concerned about neighborhood deterioration and those who found the neighborhood less satisfying. Lewis and Salem (1986: xiv) attribute this community concern to the "erosion of commonly accepted standards and values." They maintain that fear "is a consequence of the erosion of social control as it is perceived by urban residents" (1986:xiii). This view is consistent with Garofalo and Laub's (1978) argument that fear may reflect "urban unease." The other side of the breakdown of social control—that is, urban unease—is the finding that fear is low in well-integrated neighborhoods (Lewis and Salem 1986; but see Hartnagel 1979). Similarly, Taylor et al. (1984) found that social ties were related negatively to fear. According to Hunter and Baumer (1982), citizens who could distinguish strangers from neighbors and who claimed to feel part of the neighborhood reported less fear. Homeownership, indicative of "rootedness" (Lewis and Salem 1986), also is negatively related to fear (Kennedy and Silverman 1985; Taylor and Hale 1986).

Of the three models, the community concern framework appears to be the least developed. As Bursik and Grasmick (1993) observe, there has been considerable variation in the conceptualization and measurement of social integration. Indeed, some studies focus on integration, others on community responsiveness, and still others on involvement and social networks. Consequently one purpose of the present analysis is to examine the role of these various community dimensions in explaining fear of crime.

The factors that have been related to fear of crime in these three theoretical models can be regarded as facilitators and inhibitors of fear. For example, those personal traits thought to relate to vulnerability (e.g., age, gender, class, race) can be considered facilitators. Higher levels of actual or perceived social and physical disorder also facilitate fear. In contrast, dimensions of social integration, community responsiveness, social control, and social support can be regarded as inhibitors of fear of crime. In this paper we seek to examine how well the combination of facilitators and inhibitors can account for variation in fear. We also seek to extend past research by clarifying the role of these various aspects of the perceived neighborhood. Finally, we examine the external validity of the model in low-, medium-, and high-disorder neighborhoods.

Method

The data presented below were gathered from respondents to a self-administered questionnaire sent to citizens of Spokane Washington, in the fall of 1994 by the Division of Governmental Studies and Services at Washington State University. We conducted the survey through the mail, following Dillman's total design method (Dillman 1978). An initial survey was sent to 2,785 randomly selected potential respondents, with up to three additional follow-up requests to nonrespondents. When 266 unusable addresses are eliminated, the 1,134 completed surveys represent a 45 percent response rate.[34] This rather low rate appears to be largely due to timing: The survey was conducted at the same time as a hotly contested election involving presiding House Speaker Thomas Foley. It is estimated that Spokane was the fourth most frequently surveyed city in the country during 1994 (Thurman and McGarrell 1995).

Despite the low response rate, comparisons of the characteristics of the sample with data from the 1990 census indicate that the sample closely matches the city's population. The only exceptions are that the sample is slightly older, is better educated, and contains more males than the population as a whole (Thurman and McGarrell 1995). Given that the purpose of this analysis is to test theoretical propositions about the fear of crime, as opposed to strict inference to the city population, the sample seems adequate. In view of the response rate, however, the findings may have been affected by nonresponse bias.

Measures[5]

Demographic Characteristics. In keeping with previous research, we predict that women and older citizens will have higher levels of fear because of their greater vulnerability to crime. We also predict that social class and race will be related to fear because of the heightened social vulnerability of the lower class and of racial and ethnic minorities. We examined two measures of class: education and household income. In the analyses that follow, we use income rather than education because it has a stronger and more consistent relationship to fear in the multivariate analyses. The measure of race/ethnicity contrasts whites with nonwhites. Spokane is a relatively homogeneous city; only 6.7 percent of the residents are non-Caucasian. The nonwhite category is divided relatively evenly among African Americans, Asian Americans, Native Americans, and Hispanics and Latinos.

Victimization. As noted earlier, research has not found the consistent relationship between victimization and fear that is predicted by the victimization model. Yet because some studies (e.g., Skogan and Maxfield 1981) have found such a relationship, we include it here. The measure is based on whether the respondent indicated that he/she had been a victim of one of the following types of crime within the past six months: assault, robbery, burglary, larceny-theft, racial/sexual harassment, automobile theft, vandalism. Just over one-fifth of the respondents indicated that they had been victimized during that period.

Concern About Victimization. Lewis and Salem (1986) found that concern about victimization had a positive relationship to fear. In measuring citizens' concern about victimization, they asked the extent to which burglary, robbery, assault, and rape were serious problems in the respondents' neighborhood. The measure we employ here is very similar but is based only on burglary, robbery, and assault. The scale for concern about victimization has an alpha of .77 and is predicted to relate positively to fear.

Perceived Characteristics of the Neighborhood

Disorder. The indicator of perceived disorder is a scale based on nine items, which combines physical and social disorder. Respondents were asked to rate the seriousness of the following problems in their neighborhood: people drinking in public, groups of teens hanging out and harassing, youth gangs, people using illegal drugs, vandalism, physical decay, garbage on streets and sidewalks, noise, and drunk drivers. The disorder scale has an alpha of .86. In accordance with the disorder model, we predict that the scale relates positively to fear of crime.

Residential Character of the Neighborhood. Greenberg and Rohe (1984) found that the more commercial property in an area, the higher the level of fear. Consequently, individuals living in predominantly residential neighborhoods are predicted to be less fearful. Here the measure was based on a single item that asked respondents whether there were stores, bars, or business offices in their neighborhoods. Responses were based on an ordinal scale: many, a few, none.

Single-Family Homes Predominant. Past research suggests that the proportion of single-family housing will relate to neighboring and protective activities (Gates and Rohe 1987). These types of activities, in turn, are likely to lead to lower levels of fear. We employed a dichotomous measure which contrasted respondents who claimed that their neighborhood consisted mostly of single-family homes with those who replied that it was composed mostly of apartments, or a mix of homes and apartments.

Social Control in the Neighborhood. We examined several indicators of social control in the neighborhood. Adult responsibility is based on an item that asked whether adults in the neighborhood take responsibility for the behavior of youths other than their own children. The suspicious person indicator relates to an item asking whether someone would be likely to call the police if a suspicious person were hanging around in the block. As in Lewis and Salem (1986), respondents indicating that "adults take responsibility" and that "someone is likely to call the police" are predicted to be less fearful of crime because of the more effective exercise of social control in the neighborhood.

A third indicator of social control, neighbors respond, contrasts reliance on the police with informal responses by neighbors. We asked respondents whether, in a situation where a neighbor was having trouble with rowdy teens, the neighbors would be more likely to get together to address the problem or to call the police. We predict that reliance on informal community control is related negatively to fear.[6]

The final indicator of social control in the neighborhood is a block watch scale based on whether the neighborhood has a Block Watch program and on whether the respondent has attended Block Watch meetings. The scale has a modest alpha of .53; we predict that it relates to lower levels of fear (Fisher 1993).[7]

Responsiveness. One of the assumptions of the community policing movement is that increasing neighborhood and government responsiveness to crime will reduce the fear of crime. We examine this assumption with a scale of city government, police, and neighborhood responsiveness. The scale is based on five variables: whether inadequate police and city services are problems in the neighborhood (two items), whether police-community relations are a problem in the neighborhood, how likely is it that local groups will get government to respond to problems, and whether there is a lack of community interest in crime prevention. The scale has an alpha of .71.

Neighborhood Integration. Several studies suggest that neighborhood integration may reduce fear (Lewis and Salem 1986; Taylor et al. 1984). Following Lewis and Salem (1986), we predict that informal integration and residential rootedness are related to lower fear of crime. Informal integration is based on a two-item scale: whether the neighborhood is the type of place where people mostly help one another or go their own way, and whether the neighborhood is a real home or just a place to live. The scale alpha is .70. Residential rootedness is based on homeownership (Kennedy and Silverman 1985; Lewis and Salem 1986).

Fear of crime. Our measure of the fear of crime follows a long line of research that uses these items from the National Crime Victimization Survey (NCVS): "How safe do you feel being outside and alone in your neighborhood at night (during the day)?" (Covington and Taylor 1991; Lewis and Salem 1986; Skogan and Maxfield 1981). Our fear scale combines responses to the "day" and the "night" items. The alpha for the scale is .71.[8]

Analysis

Initially we examined zero-order correlations of fear with the variables listed above. All of the variables except race and the block watch scale had significant bivariate correlations with the fear scale. Given prior findings of the relationship between race and fear (Covington and Taylor 1991) and between participation in block watch and fear (Fisher 1993), we decided not to eliminate these variables before conducting the multivariate analysis. Consequently, as a first step in the analysis, we entered all of the independent variables into a multiple regression equation (OLS). The results of this equation suggested that four of the variables—victim, block watch, single-family homes, and suspicious person—were not significant predictors of fear.

As a second step, we entered the same independent variables into multiple regression equations, using stepwise and backward methods of entering the variables. The two methods resulted in virtually identical models and suggested that the four variables noted above could be trimmed from the model. Once the model was identified, we undertook a number of regression diagnostic steps. Inspection of residuals showed that assumptions of normality and of equal variances were met. Like Skogan (1990), we found a high correlation ($r = .67$) between two of the independent variables, disorder and concern about victimization, which thus created a potential problem of multicollinearity. Consequently we eliminated concern about victimization from the multivariate analysis.[9] Subsequent analysis showed that inclusion of concern about victimization had virtually no effect on the overall model and did not alter substantive conclusions. When included, concern about victimization enters the multivariate equation; this suggests that it has an effect even after the effects of perceived disorder are controlled. Given concerns about multicollinearity, however, we present the model excluding concern about victimization.[10]

Table 7.1
Multiple Regression Analysis of Fear, Full Sample

Variables	B	Beta	SE	t-value	Significance
DEMOGRAPHICS					
Age	.009	.087	.003	2.69	.007
Race	-.302	-.046	.204	-1.48	.139
Gender	1.01	.281	.112	9.02	.000
Income	-.082	-.096	.029	-2.83	.005
FACILITATORS					
Disorder	.126	.299	.016	8.05	.000
INHIBITORS					
Residential	-.179	-.070	.082	-2.18	.030
Homeowner	-.384	-.086	.151	-2.54	.011
Responsiveness	-.064	-.085	.028	-2.31	.021
Integration	-.227	-.108	.075	-3.03	.002
INFORMAL SOCIAL CONTROL					
Adults Responsible	-2.06	-.099	.070	-2.96	.003
Neighbors Respond	-.315	-.091	.108	-2.91	.004

Notes: Multiple R = .661; Adjusted R2 = .427; F = 43.77; Significance = .000

Results

Table 7.1 presents the results of the OLS multiple regression analysis. The model is statistically significant and explains 43 percent of the variance in fear. With the exception of race, all the individual variables are statistically significant and in the expected direction.

As found in prior research, gender and age were related significantly to fear: Women and older respondents tended to be more fearful of crime. The beta coefficient showed that gender was one of the two most powerful variables in the model.[11] Income also was related to fear: Lower-income respondents reported higher levels of fear.

Again, in keeping with prior research, perception of neighborhood disorder was related significantly to fear. Indeed, disorder had the greatest influence on fear when the other variables in the equation were held constant. As predicted, perceptions of disorder acted as a facilitator of fear.

Several perceived dimensions of the neighborhood appeared to inhibit fear. Respondents living in predominantly residential neighborhoods expressed less fear than did respondents in mixed or commercial areas. Individuals rooted in the neighborhood through homeownership also were less fearful. Informal integration, based on descriptions of the neighborhood as a place where people mostly help one another and on the perception of the neighborhood as a real home, also was related to lower levels of fear. Citizens who perceived more responsiveness to neighborhood problems on the part of city government, the police, and the neighborhood itself reported less fear. Finally, both indicators of informal social control were related negatively to fear: Respondents who indicated that neighborhood adults take responsibility for youths other than their own children were less fearful, as were respondents who stated that they would likely get together with neighbors to deal with rowdy teens as opposed to calling the police.

As noted earlier, several variables failed to enter the multivariate equations and thus were dropped from the model. Victim, the block watch scale, the predominance of sin-gle-family homes versus apartments, and the likelihood that someone would call the police if a suspicious person were observed did not relate significantly to fear at the multivariate level.

Examining the Models for Subsamples

Given the importance of disorder in explaining fear of crime in this analysis and in prior research, we thought it would be valuable to ask whether the same basic model of fear would apply to individuals living in various types of neighborhoods. Do the same variables explain fear of crimes for individuals living in a low-disorder neighborhood as for individuals living in a high-disorder neighborhood?

We examined this issue by dividing the sample into three groups of neighborhoods based on the aggregated disorder scores. That is, we calculated mean disorder scores for the 20 Spokane neighborhoods.[12] The aggregated neighborhood disorder scores ranged from 10.77 to 16.96, with a mean of 13.69. Examination of the distribution of neighborhood means suggested that the neighborhoods could be classified into three groups. All of the low-disorder neighborhoods had mean scores below 12.0 (range 10.77 to 11.85; n = 5 neighborhoods containing 146 respondents). The medium-disorder neighborhoods had mean scores ranging from 12.73 to 14.69 (n = 9 neighborhoods containing 422 respondents). The high-disorder neighborhoods had mean scores ranging from 14.98 to 16.96 (n = 6 neighborhoods containing 205 respondents). The mean disorder scores for respondents in the low-, medium-, and high-disorder neighborhoods were 11.62, 13.62, and 15.82 respectively.

As would be expected in view of the relationship between disorder and fear, the mean fear scores varied for the three groups of neighborhoods as well (low-disorder neighborhoods = 3.51; medium-disorder neighborhoods = 4.46; high-disorder neighborhoods = 5.16). The groupings apparently have face validity: The neighborhoods categorized as high-disorder neighborhoods are those identified by the police and in local lore as the centers of crime and disorder. In contrast, the low-disorder neighborhoods are predominantly residential and wealthier areas. Consequently, we are confident that modeling fear for respondents living in these different neighborhoods captures a meaningful dimension of neighborhood context.

Several cautions are necessary, however. It would be ideal to formally model both contextual and individual-level effects (e.g., Covington and Taylor 1991). Unfortunately, however, because of the limited number of neighborhoods in our study, we cannot do so. In addition, once we begin to aggregate the data, as we did by creating neighborhood disorder scores, we run the risk of violating the OLS multiple regression assumption of independence (Taylor and Hale 1986). We address this concern by using regression diagnostic techniques to examine whether regression assumptions were violated by grouping the sample into relatively homogeneous subgroups.[13]

Subsample Findings

Table 7.2 presents the results of the models in the three types of neighborhood. Overall, on the basis of the amount of explained variance, the set of variables appears to be a reasonable model of fear in all three contexts. The medium-disorder subsample contains more unexplained variance than the others;

yet even there, one-third of the variation is explained. Some of the individual variables, however, appear to have different effects in different contexts.

One interesting pattern emerges in relation to demographic characteristics. As the analysis moves from the low-disorder to the high-disorder subsample, the demographic traits appear to exert less influence on fear of crime. Although this was not true of the gender effect, which was significant for all three subsamples, age, race, and income were not significantly related to fear in the high-disorder neighborhoods. They were so related in the low-disorder neighborhoods (though race was related only marginally). In contrast, concern about victimization,[14] which was not significantly related to fear in the low-disorder neighborhoods was a significant predictor of fear in the medium- and high-disorder subsamples.

Among the neighborhood characteristics, living in a primarily residential neighborhood was not significant in any of the three subsamples. This may be the case because, once the sample was broken down into subsamples, the within-subsample variation in residential makeup no longer was present to explain much of the variance in fear. Being a homeowner was related negatively to fear in

Table 7.2

Multiple Regression Analysis of Fear for Samples from Neighborhoods with Varying Levels of Reported Disorder

Variables	Low-Disorder Neighborhoods				Medium-Disorder Neighborhoods				High-Disorder Neighborhoods			
	B	Beta	SE	t-value	B	Beta	SE	t-value	B	Beta	SE	t-value
DEMOGRAPHICS												
Age	.016	.161	.008	2.07*	.010	.106	.005	1.94	-.001	-.010	.007	-1.06
Race	-.790	-.130	.466	-1.69	-.084	-.013	.318	-0.26	-.220	-.034	.409	-0.54
Gender	.910	.274	.255	3.56***	1.06	.321	.163	6.52***	.884	.227	.247	3.58***
Income	-.188	-.186	.083	-2.26*	-.032	-.039	.044	-0.71	-.075	-.083	.062	-1.21
FACILITATORS												
Concern About Victimization	.135	.114	.104	1.30	.304	.277	.062	4.94***	.271	.213	.090	3.02**
INHIBITORS												
Residential	-.044	-.019	.182	-0.24	-.012	-.004	.130	-0.89	-.224	-.060	.245	-0.91
Homeowner	-1.18	-.194	.498	-2.41*	-.075	-.019	.211	-0.36	-.784	-.175	.303	-2.59*
Responsiveness	-.095	-.116	.071	-1.33	-.067	-.097	.041	-1.65	-.192	-.226	.061	-3.13**
Integration	-.370	-.160	.178	-2.08*	-.264	-.135	.114	-2.32*	-.204	-.093	.161	-1.27
INFORMAL SOCIAL CONTROL												
Adults Responsible	-.345	-.183	.156	-2.21*	-.191	-.102	.103	-1.86	-.287	-.109	.191	-1.50
Neighbors Respond	-.172	-.055	.248	-0.69	-.275	-.085	.161	-1.71	-.409	-.105	.246	-1.66

Notes: Low-disorder Neighborhoods: Multiple R = .710; R^2 = .446 (adjusted); F = 8.60; Significance = .000. Medium-disorder Neighborhoods: Multiple R = .570; R^2 = (adjusted); F = 12.63;

the low- and high-disorder subsamples but not in the medium-disorder group.

Community responsiveness and informal integration appeared to operate differently in the three subsamples. Community responsiveness had a significant negative relation to fear in the high-disorder neighborhoods but not in either of the other sets of neighborhoods. In contrast, informal integration was related negatively to fear in the low- and medium-disorder neighborhoods but not in the high-disorder neighborhoods. Similarly, the likelihood of adults taking responsibility for youths other than their own children was related negatively to fear in the low- and medium-disorder subsamples but did not relate to fear in the high-disorder neighborhoods. Finally, the "neighbors respond" item, regarding whether neighbors would be more likely to respond directly to teen rowdiness or to rely on the police, was not significantly related to fear in the low-disorder subsample and was related only marginally in the other two subsamples.

Discussion

One notable finding from these analyses is the increase in explanatory power created by including the "perceptions of the neighborhood" variables along with demographic characteristics and perceived disorder. Indeed, when the four demographic variables and the disorder variable are included in a multiple regression equation, the adjusted R' equals .314. As noted above, the addition of the six neighborhood and community dimensions results in an adjusted R1 of .427. This finding suggests the need to include the community concerns/informal social control model along with the victimization and disorder models of fear of crime.

In a related vein, the analysis also suggests that several dimensions of neighborhoods are important. Researchers who have examined the community concerns/informal social control model have analyzed homogeneity (Covington and Taylor 1991), informal social control (Lewis and Salem 1986), and integration (Hunter and Baumer 1982; Lewis and Salem 1986). The present analysis suggests that all three dimensions are important,

along with a fourth dimension, community responsiveness. We have described these dimensions as inhibitors of fear of crime; empirically they appear to act as such. They also appear to be consistent with Cullen's (1994) concept of social support. That is, respondents who report that they and their neighbors are likely to engage in informal control, who perceive their neighborhood as a real home where people mostly help one another, and who perceive the overall neighborhood, the city, and the police as more responsive tend to be less fearful.

Among the demographic characteristics, gender emerged as the most powerful and most consistent predictor of fear (see note 11). Females expressed more fear after a number of other characteristics were controlled, and across all three types of neighborhood.

Along with gender, another powerful predictor of fear is perceived disorder. Further, it appears that the role of disorder has both a neighborhood-level and an individual-level component. In a separate analysis we attempted to disentangle the neighborhood-level dimension from the individual-level component by including a neighborhood score, a mean-centered individual-level score of disorder, and gender.[15] These three variables produced an adjusted R^2 of .305 (F = 107.60; ≤.0000). All three variables were significantly related to fear (gender beta = .318; aggregate disorder beta = .305; mean-centered disorder beta = .306). This finding suggests that disorder affects fear both as a contextual dimension and as an individual trait.

The subsample analysis produced two interesting findings. First, it appears that demographic characteristics may determine fear more strongly in a low-disorder than in a high-disorder context. This point is consistent with Maxfield's (1984) finding that age, considered a measure of physical vulnerability, did not predict fear in high-crime neighborhoods. This finding is further evidenced in supplemental analyses in which we entered the four demographic traits alone into multiple regression equations for the three subsamples. For the low-disorder subsample, the four demographic variables accounted for over one-quarter of the variance in fear (adjusted R^2 = .264). In contrast, the same four variables accounted for less than 14 percent of the variance in the medium- and high-disorder neighborhoods. Perhaps in those neighborhoods, the reality of crime, disorder, and incivility makes fear of crime more salient in everyday experience and hence less dependent on personal traits. In the low-disorder neighborhoods, however, where crime and disorder may be less immediate, fear may be governed by demographic traits related to vulnerability. In other words, vulnerability may be more equally distributed, and thus less explanatory, where disorder is high.

A second suggestive finding from the subsample analysis relates to the impact of informal integration and social control in different neighborhoods. In the low- and medium-disorder neighborhoods, perceptions of informal integration and informal social control (adults responsible) related to fear.[16] These two measures did not relate to fear in the high-disorder subsample. A broader measure of community responsiveness did so, however. This finding may indicate that informal measures alone may be sufficient to influence fear in low- and medium-disorder contexts, whereas more extensive community responses (e.g., city hall, police, neighborhood associations) may be needed to influence fear in a high-disorder setting.

Several variables were not related to fear. As in other studies, direct victimization experience had little influence on fear of crime. In addition, the block watch scale did not enter the multivariate equation. Yet in light of Fisher's (1993) research, which was better able to measure actual experience in Block Watch, this variable may merit further investigation, at least as a potential indicator of the effects of participation in Block Watch programs.

Conclusion

Like Bennett and Flavins (1994) recent cross-cultural research on fear, this study suggests the need to combine the victimization, disorder, and community concern frameworks into an overall model of fear of crime. In this analysis we extend the re-

search, however, by clarifying the role of the various dimensions of the community concern/social control perspective. Whereas the breakdown of community indeed may lead to a sense of "urban unease" and to greater fear, the perception of informal social control, social support, and integration relates to lower levels of fear. The more one perceives neighbors as responding to rowdy youths, the more one feels rooted in the community, the more one feels that the neighborhood is a real home where people mostly help one another, and the more responsive one perceives local institutions to be, the less fear. Thus it is not only the case that disorder and the breakdown of community facilitate fear; in addition, integration, social control, social support, and responsiveness appear to inhibit fear.

Although this study extends a line of research examining the role of various community dimensions in fear of crime (e.g., Lewis and Salem 1986; Skogan 1990; Taylor and Hale 1986), continued specification of these community dimensions is warranted. For example, our measure of responsiveness is similar to other researchers' conception of formal social control. Are these concepts distinct? How are they related? What are their separate and joint effects on fear? Similarly, our measures are based on individual perceptions. It would be both theoretically and practically important to assess the connection between these perceptions and more objective measures. For example, what is the relationship between perceived responsiveness and actual delivery of government services?

Our findings also have practical implications for the community policing movement. One of the ironies of past research is that the neighborhoods which have been organized most readily to address crime and disorder are the more homogeneous, middle-class neighborhoods with fewer crime problems. Poorer, crime-ridden, inner-city neighborhoods have been less amenable to such efforts (Skogan 1990).[17] The present analysis suggests that despite this difficulty, meaningful intervention may have an effect in the high-disorder neighborhoods, at least in regard to fear. The subsample analysis suggested that responsiveness by city hall, the police, and neighborhood associations had the greatest influence on fear in these neighborhoods.

Although a cross-sectional study (like the present research) cannot identify an effect of attempts at intervention, the correlations suggest the validity of the assumption that increasing the responsiveness of these institutions will reduce fear and improve the quality of life. Further, when coupled with evaluations of programs designed to develop police-citizen-city government partnerships in high-disorder neighborhoods (e.g., Giacomazzi 1995), the results suggest that these efforts to increase responsiveness indeed may reduce the fear of crime.

Notes

1. An exception would be Taylor and colleagues' studies of territorial functioning and defensible space (e.g., Taylor, Gottfredson, and Brower 1984; Taylor, Shumaker, and Gottfredson 1985).

2. In contrast, Taylor et al. (1985) found the relationship between disorder and fear to be conditional. This relationship held in moderate-income neighborhoods but not in full sample of neighborhoods, once controls for social class were introduced.

3. Of the 1,134 respondents, we eliminated 114 from the analyses presented here because they answered "uncertain" on four or more of the nine items constituting the "perception of disorder" scale. For respondents answering "uncertain" on three or fewer items, we used mean substitution in creating the scale. This step resulted in a usable N of 1,020. Appendix A presents the actual number of respondents for each specific variable. The discrepancy between the usable sample ($N \leq 1,020$) and the number of responses for each variable is due to nonresponses to specific items. In the multiple regression analyses presented in tables 1 and 2, we employed listwise deletion of cases, using only those cases which show valid values for all the variables in the analysis.

4. This is a conservative estimate of the response rate. Subsequent analysis revealed that approximately 9 percent of the original addresses represented households outside the city. Spokane, like many western U.S. cities, has undergone annexation processes that produce a checkerboard of city and county residences. Consequently, urban neighbors may be classified as city residents on one side of the street and county on the other. When we plotted each respondent's address, we found that 9 percent were actually outside the city (often across the street or across an intersection from a valid city address). We removed these respondents' surveys from the total number of usable surveys. It is clear that among the nonrespondents, approximately 9 percent would be noncity residents. We do not have the precise figure, however, and therefore do not exclude these as "bad addresses." If the precise figure were known, the overall response rate apparently would exceed 50 percent.

5. Details of the variables and descriptive statistics are presented in Appendix A.

6. The item (neighbors respond) on how rowdy teens would likely be handled (call police or get together with neighbors) included a third response option, "not get involved." Fewer than 7 percent of the respondents indicated that they would not get involved. Consequently we excluded them from the analysis, which contrasted informal neighborhood social control with reliance on the police. Individuals responding "not get involved" had fear scores similar (mean ≤ 4.63) to those of respondents indicating that they would call the police (mean ≤ 4.77). In contrast, respondents indicating that they would get together with their neighbors to handle the problem had lower fear scores (mean ≤ 3.87). Inclusion of the respondents indicating that they would not get involved had no appreciable influence on the multivariate models.

7. We also examined each of the individual components of the Block Watch scale. Neither variable related to fear in the multivariate analysis.

8. Ferraro and LaGrange (1987) observe that the NCVS items include both a risk of victimization dimension and an emotion-based fear dimension (also see LaGrange et al. 1992; Warr 1984). We agree, but we believe that this measure has several advantages. First, because it has been used in a number of studies, it offers comparability and opportunities for replication. Second, analyses employing the NCVS item have policy implications: Unwillingness to venture forth in one's neighborhood has clear implications for quality of life. We agree, however, that this global fear measure does not allow us to clearly distinguish assessments of risk from emotional fear.

9. Our decision to include perceptions of disorder rather than concern about victimization was based primarily on theoretical grounds. The disorder model suggests that perceived disorder leads both to heightened concern about crime and to fear (Lewis and Salem 1986; Skogan 1990).

10. The alternative analyses discussed throughout are available from the authors.

11. Given the powerful effect of gender, the *JQ* editors raised the concern that gender differences might be governing the overall model. To investigate this possibility we took two steps. First we conducted the analyses for males only and for females only. Although the R^2 values were reduced, as one would expect from the removal of gender, the model held for both subsamples($R^2 \le .32$ for males, .39 for females). Then we examined the partial *r*s for each and fear, controlling for gender. All variables but race were significantly related to fear. (see Appendix B for results).

12. Identifying neighborhoods is a key question in ecological research. In Spokane, 20 distinct neighborhoods traditionally have been recognized through the existence of formal neighborhood associations. Most respondents can identify these neighborhoods by name. We coded respondents according to these traditional neighborhood boundaries. The neighborhoods comprise several census tracts but do not correspond neatly to the boundaries of the tracts.

13. We examined plots of studentized deleted residuals, box plots of residuals, Q-Q plots, scatterplots of residuals versus predicted values, and Durbin-Watson and Cook's distance statistics. The only apparent problem was curvilinearity between income and fear (for the low-disorder subsample) between homeownership and fear. A multiple regression model with appropriate log transformation yielded findings virtually indistinguishable from those presented here.

14. Because the sample was divided on the basis of neighborhood disorder scores, we removed disorder as an independent variable. Concern about victimization was included in the multiple regression equation. One of the *JQ* reviewers raised the legitimate point that reintroducing concern about victimization in the subsample analyses made these models noncomparable to the overall model. Consequently we conducted the subsample analyses with concern about victimization excluded. These models were virtually identi-cal to those presented in table 2. The explained variance was reduced slightly (R^2 = .441, .242, and .454 respectively in the low-, medium-, and high-disorder neighborhood samples). Among the individual predictor variables, the only change was that responsiveness was related significantly in all three subsamples. When we included concern about victimization, however, it was significant only in the high-disorder neighborhoods.

15. The mean-centered score is the difference between the neighborhood aggregate disorder score and the individual's disorder score. Thus an individual reporting more disorder than his or her neighbors would have a higher score on the mean-centered scale. In effect this decomposes the variation in disorder scores into a between-neighborhoods and a within-neighborhoods component. For details see Covington and Taylor (1991).

16. In terms of informal social control, the item "Adults responsible," concerning whether or not adults take responsibility, was related significantly. A second item (neighbors respond), asking whether neighbors would be likely to get together to deal with rowdy teens, was not related to fear in any of the three subsamples.

17. Similarly, Weisburd and McElroy (1988) suggest that the promise of community policing often is more rhetorical than attainable in highly disorganized social settings. Other research undertaken in Spokane, however (see Giacomazzi, McGarrell, and Thurman 1995; Thurman 1995), confirms that at least in this city, crime-ridden areas can be affected positively by community policing innovations in concert with a mobilized citizenry.

References

Bennett, R.R. and J.M. Flavin. 1994. "Determinants of Fear of Crime: The Effect of Cultural Setting." *Justice Quarterly* 11:357–81.

Bursik, R.J. and H.G. Grasmick. 1993. *Neighborhoods and Crime: The Dimensions of Effective Community Control.* New York: Lexington Books.

Covington, J. and R.B. Taylor. 1991. "Fear of Crime in Urban Residential Neighborhoods: Implications of Between- and Within-Neighborhood Sources for Current Models." *Sociological Quarterly* 32:231–49.

Cullen. F.T. 1994. "Social Support as an Organizing Concept for Criminology: Presidential Address to the Academy of Criminal Justice Sciences." *Justice Quarterly* 11:527–59.

Dillman, D. 1978. *Mail and Telephone Surveys: The Total Design Method.* New York: Wiley.

Ferraro, K.F. and R.L. LaGrange. 1987. "The Measurement of Fear of Crime." *Sociological Inquiry* 57:70–101.

Fisher, B. 1993. "What Works: Block Watch Meetings or Crime Prevention Seminars?" *Journal of Crime and Justice* 16:1–27.

Garofalo, J. and J. Laub. 1978. "The Fear of Crime: Broadening Our Perspectives." *Victimology* 3:242–53.

Gates, L.B. and W.M. Rohe. 1987. "Fear and Reactions to Crime: A Revised Model." *Urban Affairs Quarterly* 22:425–53.

Giacomazzi, A.L. 1995. "Community Crime Prevention, Community Policing, and Public Housing: An Evaluation of a Multi-Level, Collaborative Drug-Crime Elimination Program in Spokane, Washington." Doctoral dissertation, Washington State University.

Giacomazzi, A.L., E.F. McGarrell, and Q.C. Thurman. 1995. "Community Crime Prevention and Public Housing—A Preliminary Assessment of a Multi-Level, Collaborative Drug-Crime Elimination Strategy." Presented at the annual meetings of the American Society of Criminology, Boston.

Greenberg, G.S. and W.M. Rohe. 1984. "Neighborhood Design and Crime." *Journal of the American Planning Association* 50:48–61.

Greene, J.R. and R.B. Taylor. 1988. "Community-Based Policing and Foot Patrol: Issues of Theory and Evaluation." Pp. 195–223 in *Community Policing: Rhetoric or Reality?*, edited by J.R. Greene and S.D. Mastrofski. New York: Praeger.

Hartnagel, T. 1979. "The Perception and Fear of Crime: Implications for Neighborhood Cohesion, Social Activity and Community Affect." *Social Forces* 58:176–93.

Hindelang, M.J., M.R. Gottfredson, and J. Garofalo. 1978. *Victims of Personal Crime.* Cambridge, MA: Ballinger.

Hope, T. and M. Hough. 1988. "Community Approaches to Reducing Crime." Pp. 1–29 in *Communities and Crime Reduction*, edited by T. Hope and M. Shaw. London: Her Majesty's Stationery Office.

Hunter, A.J. and T.L. Baumer. 1982. "Street Traffic, Social Integration and Fear of Crime." *Sociological Inquiry* 52:122–31.

Kelling, G. 1986. *Foot Patrol.* Washington, DC: National Institute of Justice.

Kennedy, L.W. and R.A. Silverman. 1985. "Perceptions of Social Diversity and Fear of Crime." *Environment and Behavior* 17:275–95.

LaGrange, R.L., F.F. Ferraro, and M. Supancic. 1992. "Perceived Risk and Fear of Crime: Role of Social and Physical Incivilities." *Journal of Research in Crime and Delinquency* 29:311–34.

Lewis, D.A. and G. Salem. 1986. *Fear of Crime: Incivility and the Production of a Social Problem.* New Brunswick, NJ: Transaction Books.

Liska, A.E., A. Sanchirico, and M.D. Reed. 1988. "Fear of Crime and Constrained Behavior: Specifying and Estimating a Reciprocal Effects Model." *Social Forces* 66:827–37.

Maxfield, M.G. 1984. "The Limits of Vulnerability in Explaining Fear of Crime." *Journal of Research in Crime and Delinquency* 21:233–50.

Pate, A.M. 1986. *Reducing Fear of Crime in Houston and Newark: A Summary Report.* Washington, DC: The Police Foundation and National Institute of Justice.

Skogan, W.G. 1990. *Disorder and Decline: Crime and the Spiral of Decay in American Neighborhoods.* New York: Free Press.

Skogan, W.G. and M.G. Maxfield. 1981. *Coping with Crime.* Beverly Hills: Sage.

Taylor, R.B., S.D. Gottfredson, and S. Brower. 1984. "Block Crime and Fear: Defensible Space, Local Social Ties, and Territorial Functioning." *Journal of Research in Crime and Delinquency* 21:303–31.

Taylor, R.B. and M. Hale. 1986. "Testing Alternative Models of Fear of Crime." *Journal of Criminal Law and Criminology* 77:151–89.

Taylor, R.B., S.A. Shumaker, and S.D. Gottfredson. 1985. "Neighborhood-Level Link between Physical Features and Local Sentiments: Deterioration, Fear of Crime, and Confidence." *Journal of Architectural Planning Research* 2:261–75.

Thurman, Q.C. 1995. "Community Policing: The Police as a Community Resource." Pp. 175–187 in *Reinventing Human Services: Community and Family-Centered Practice*, edited by P. Adams and K Nelson. New York: Aldine de Gruyter.

Thurman, Q.C. and E.F. McGarrell. 1995. *Findings from the 1994 Spokane Police Department Citizen Survey: Final Report.* Spokane: Washington State Institute for Community Oriented Policing.

Warr, M. 1984. "Fear of Victimization: Why Are Women and the Elderly More Afraid?" *Social Science Quarterly* 65:681–702.

Weisburd, D. and J.E. McElroy. 1988. "Enacting the CPO Role: Findings from the New York City Pilot Program in Community Policing."

Pp. 89–101 in *Community Policing: Rhetoric or Reality?*, edited by J.R. Greene and S.E. Mastrofski. New York: Praeger.

Will, J.A. and J.H. McGrath. 1995. "Crime, Neighborhood Perceptions, and the Underclass: The Relationship between Fear of Crime and Class Position." *Journal of Criminal Justice* 23:163–176.

Wilson, J.Q. and G.L. Kelling. 1982. "Broken Windows." *Atlantic Monthly,* March, pp. 29–38.

Reprinted from: Edmund F. McGarrell, Andrew L. Giacomazzi, and Quint C. Thurman, "Neighborhood Disorder, Integration, and the Fear of Crime." In *Justice Quarterly, 14 (3), pp. 479-500.* Copyright © 1997 by Academy of Criminal Justice Sciences. Reprinted by permission. ✦

Appendix 7A
Correlation Matrix and Partial Rs

	Fear	Age	Race	Gender	Income	Disorder	Residential	Homeowner	Responsiveness	Integration	Adults Respons	Neighbors	Concern V
FEAR	1.0												
AGE	.07*	1.0											
RACE	-.04	.05	1.0										
GENDER	.35***	.03	.02	1.0									
INCOME	-.31***	-.18***	-.07*	-.24***	1.0								
DISORDER	.42***	-.16***	-.00	.03	-.13***	1.0							
RESIDENTIAL	-.22***	.11***	-.07*	-.05	.18***	-.21***	1.0						
HOMEOWNER	-.21***	.13***	.05	-.08*	.33***	-.16***	.18***	1.0					
RESPONSIVENESS	-.34***	.18***	.05	-.06	.11***	-.53***	.17***	.16***	1.0				
INTEGRATION	-.32***	.14***	.02	-.06	.16***	-.27***	.18***	.30***	.29***	1.0			
ADULTS RESPONSIBLE	-.31***	.04	.02	-.13***	.14***	-.22***	.14***	.11***	.25***	.37***	1.0		
NEIGHBORS	-.26***	-.07	.07*	-.10**	.10**	-.14***	.10**	.05	.14***	.15***	.18***	1.0	
CONCERN V	.39***	-.10**	.01	.07*	-.11***	.67***	-.19***	-.14***	-.47***	-.21***	-.16***	-.09**	1.0

Partial *rs* with FEAR controlling for GENDER

	Age	Race	Gender	Income	Disorder	Residential	Homeowner	Responsiveness	Integration	Adults Respons	Neighbors	Concern V
FEAR	.07*	-.06	.NA	-.25***	.44***	-.24***	-.21***	-.34***	-.34	-.28***	-.24***	.42***

*$p \leq .05$; **$p \leq .01$; *** $p \leq .001$

Appendix 7B

Description of Variables

VARIABLES(coding values)	Percentage	N
AGE Mean = 53.8 Range = 19-94		981
RACE		
White(2)	92.6	981
Nonwhite(1)	7.4	
INCOME		
<$4,000	1.1	944
$4,000-$6,999	3.2	
$7,000-$9,999	4.3	
$10,000-$14,999	9.3	
$15,000-$19,999	10.1	
$20,000-$24,999	12.2	
$25,000-$29,999	10.3	
$30,000-$49,999	26.7	
$50,000+	22.9	
VICTIM		
No(0)	78.5	1,020
Yes(1)	21.5	

Yes response indicates that respondent reported being the victim of at least one of the following offense types within the previous six months: assault; robbery; burglary; larceny-theft; racial/sexual harassment; automobile theft; vandalism.

DISORDER
Additive scale based on rating of the following as a serious problem (3), a problem (2), or no problem within neighborhood: drinking in public; teen vagrancy; youth gangs; illegal drug use; vandalism, physical decay; garbage/litter; noise, drunk drivers.

      Mean = 13.66   Range = 9-27   899
      Alpha = .8665

SINGLE-FAMILY HOMES PREDOMINANT
Single-family homes (1)	66.0	1,005
Apartments or mix (2)	34.0	

RESIDENTIAL NEIGHBORHOOD
Q: "Are there stores, bars, or business offices in your neighborhood (within a 15-minute walk of your home)?"

Many (1)	24.1	1,009
A few (2)	54.0	
None (3)	21.9	

ADULTS RESPONSIBLE
Q: "Do adults in this neighborhood take responsibility for the behavior of youths other than their own children?"

Often (4)	9.2	926
Sometimes (3)	40.6	
Rarely (2)	37.7	
Never (1)	12.5	

SUSPICIOUS PERSON
Q: "If there is a suspicious person hanging around my block someone is bound to call the police."

Strongly agree (1)	8.7	999
Agree (2)	40.0	
Neither agree or disagree (3)	30.3	
Disagree (4)	16.3	
Strongly Disagree (5)	4.6	

Description of Variables

	Percentage	N

NEIGHBORS RESPOND
Q: "If a neighbor of yours was having trouble with rowdy teenagers parking in front of their residence, which of the following would you be most likely to do?"

Do nothing	6.9	987
Get with neighbors (1)	47.2	
Call police (2)	45.9	

BLOCK WATCH
Additive scale based on whether the neighborhood has a block watch program and whether the respondent has attended a block watch meeting (yes = 4; no = 2).

      Mean = 5.06   Range = 4-8   985
      Alpha = .53

CONCERN ABOUT VICTIMIZATION
Additive scale based on rating of the following as a serious problem (3), a problem (2), or no problem (1) within neighborhood: burglary; robbery; assault.

      Mean = 4.69   Range = 3-9   919
      Alpha = .77

FEAR SCALE
Additive scale based on two items: Q: "How safe would you feel walking alone during the day in your neighborhood?" Q: "How safe would you feel being outside and alone in your neighborhood at night?"

      Mean = 4.33   Range = 2-10   998
      Alpha = .71

RESPONSIVENESS (reverse coded so high scores indicate high responsiveness)
Additive scale based on rating of the following as a serious problem (3), a problem (2), or no problem (1) within neighborhood: inadequate police services; inadequate city services; lack of community interest in crime prevention; police-community relations; how likely is it for local groups to get government to respond to local problems (four-point Likert scale ranging from very likely to very unlikely).

      Mean = 8.76   Range = 5-16   858
      Alpha = .71

INTEGRATION
Additive scale based two items: Q: "Would you describe your neighborhood as a place where people mostly help one another (1) or where people mostly go their own way (0)?" Q: "Do you feel your neighborhood is more of a 'real home' (1) or more like 'just a place to live' (0)?"

      Mean = 1.32   Range = 0-2   994
      Alpha = .70

HOMEOWNERSHIP (reverse coded so high score indicates homeownership)
Own (1)	79.5	994
Rent (2)	20.5	

8

Implementation Challenges in Community Policing

Innovative Neighborhood-Oriented Policing in Eight Cities

Susan Sadd
Randolph M. Grinc

Through a multi-site evaluation, these authors assess eight Innovative Neighborhood Oriented Policing (INOP) programs which focused on neighborhood drug problems, and the use of community oriented policing techniques to alleviate these problems. This evaluation focuses its efforts on several areas, in particular measuring the effects on crime, implementation issues and the timing of the evaluation. After presenting a brief description of each city under analysis, the authors present several broad findings: that in order for this new policing to be effective, other governmental agencies must become involved; and that agencies must work to increase citizen involvement. Lastly, the authors examine the effectiveness of INOP in reducing drug related problems. Through an evaluation, these authors are able to highlight many problems encountered by similar programs and offer suggestions to alleviate them. As you read this article, consider how an INOP approach to drug problems might succeed in your community. Would citizens assist the police to the extent

necessary to effect the desired results? Why or why not?

Community policing could arguably be called the new orthodoxy of law enforcement in the United States. It has become an increasingly popular alternative to what many police administrators perceive as the failure of traditional policing to deal effectively with street crime, especially crimes of violence and drug trafficking. Although the concept is defined in varying ways and its ability to meet its goals remains largely untested, community policing has gained widespread acceptance. According to one source, about 40 percent of the nation's larger police departments have adopted it.[1]

Community-Centered Drug Demand Reduction

If community policing has been a central aspect of emerging police agendas in many jurisdictions throughout the country, so has drug demand reduction. Innovative Neighborhood-Oriented Policing (INOP) is unique in drawing on the principles of community policing and applying them to drug demand reduction. One of these principles—a major component of community policing—is that partnerships between the police and the community can be effective in reducing crime and fear. In focusing on a particular issue, INOP also draws on the principles of problem-solving policing.

Demand reduction can involve intensive local street-level enforcement, which makes it more difficult for buyers and sellers to link up with each other and may dissuade new users from becoming addicted. Beyond intensive enforcement, which is the more common focus of police initiatives directed at illegal drug use, demand reduction can also include prevention and treatment. What is unique about INOP is its attempt to supplement traditional enforcement with long-term community-based prevention, education, and treatment referral. Combining all these components, INOP projects approximate a comprehensive approach to demand reduction. Ideally, all components are represented in a given project. In the INOP projects analyzed in this Research in Brief, each contained some but not all the components.

The INOP Program

INOP was designed in 1990 by the Bureau of Justice Assistance (BJA), U.S. Department of Justice, as a demonstration program to further the National Drug Control Strategy by focusing on and broadening the scope of community-based approaches to drug demand reduction. INOP projects are based on the notion that crime and drug problems must be addressed by the entire community, not just by the police department. Because of the nature and extent of the drug problem, traditional police tactics are limited in their ability to control it. Proactive and interactive approaches by communities and the police have thus become essential to accomplish both law enforcement and community objectives. INOP's goal is to develop strategies for demand reduction that are centered in the community and anchored in the police-community partnership. Police departments are to act as catalysts for developing and sustaining a coordinated network of neighborhood services.[2]

Eight jurisdictions were selected by BJA as the sites of initial INOP demonstration projects. (See table 8.1.) Each site was awarded between $100,000 and $200,000 for the first year of its program.[3] The sites differed greatly in population size and consequently in the size of the police agency that served them. They also differed in their relationships to other neighborhood-oriented policing initia-

tives within the jurisdiction. In several, for example, the INOP project was the police department's first effort at implementing a neighborhood-oriented style of policing. In others, it was a relatively small component of a larger, citywide neighborhood-oriented policing initiative that was either new or well established.

In general, the projects shared a police enforcement component (except in New York), a focus on target neighborhoods, community involvement, and interagency planning and partnerships. Drug demand reduction was the goal shared by all, but the approaches differed substantially. Some sites featured components that met particular community needs, such as an extensive public advertising campaign or reliance on volunteers.

Evaluation Issues and Methods

The INOP projects were evaluated by the Vera Institute of Justice under National Institute of Justice (NIJ) sponsorship, about one year after each had been launched. The process evaluation presented indepth descriptions of the sites and cross-site comparisons of program structure and operations and expectations of the various groups—police personnel, municipal and community leaders, and others—who had roles in the projects.

Measuring Effects on Crime. The impact evaluation, which is discussed in this document, examined the effects of the INOP projects on drug demand, public safety, and the quality of life of the communities and identified the characteristics of the projects that

Table 8.1
Size of INOP Jurisdictions and Police Departments

Jurisdiction	Population	Police Department Size (Sworn Staff)
Hayward, California	120,000	156
Houston, Texas	1,700,000	3,950
Louisville, Kentucky	300,000	671
New York, New York	8,000,000	25,869
Norfolk, Virginia	261,000	684
Portland, Oregon	418,000	850
Prince George's County, Maryland	700,000	1,230
Tempe, Arizona	145,000	234

Note: The figures reflect the information available at the time of the study.

contributed to (or tended to detract from) program effectiveness.

The effects were measured in terms of the perceptions of the people involved in the projects—police officers and administrators, other police agency personnel, residents, and business people. Effects were measured both within each site and across the sites. Specifically, the individuals interviewed (a total of 552 in the eight sites) were asked for their views of the effects on drug use and drug trafficking, drug-related crime and other crime, fear, quality of life in the area, police-community relations, and level of community organization and involvement.

Implementation Issues. Another part of the evaluation analyzed project implementation based on comparisons among all sites. The research conducted for this analysis employed a variety of methods: interviews, focus groups, field observations by the researchers, and review of evaluations conducted locally when these were available. The implementation issues included police acceptance of/resistance to INOP, extent of community organization and involvement, and extent of involvement of public agencies other than the police.

One of the most significant findings—but one that may come as no surprise—was that early stages of implementing community policing are not easy. This was the experience in all eight jurisdictions. For one thing, it was difficult to convince police officers to accept the new roles and behaviors required for community policing. Citizen involvement— the linchpin of community policing—was particularly challenging. Despite acknowledgment by some residents (largely community leaders) of community policing as valuable, activism was generally confined to a small group of dedicated individuals. The comprehensive approach that is another hallmark of community policing was not carried out to the extent it might have been because the involvement of agencies other than the police was, at best, limited at most sites.

Evaluation Timing. The timing of the evaluation goes a long way to explain the findings regarding implementation difficul-

---

Recent Developments in Tempe, Arizona

Tempe began its INOP project in November 1990 as a pilot program in a single police administration, designated as Beat 16. Since then the police department has used its experiences in Beat 16 to expand community policing.

Expansion of community policing. The department expanded community policing citywide in mid-1993 and continues to be committed to the approach. One reflection of this commitment is the streamlining of command: The number of ranks has been reduced from eight to five, and the rank of detective has been eliminated.

Continued community organizing. The citizens' Coordinating Committee turned over its responsibilities to the parent organization, the Escalante Neighborhood Association (ENA). Since then the Beat 16 officers and ENA have held discussions concerning police activity and problem solving. The department also has a citizen volunteer program that has grown from three members in 1988 to more than 200. Its motto, created by a volunteer, is "We are not an arm of the police; we are the heart of the community."

The department also continues to operate a Citizens Police Academy, begun during the Beat 16 project, that offers citizens an opportunity to learn about the department and its responsibilities. Many citizens who attend the 6 week evening course become volunteers with the department.

The department recently initiated a citywide multi-unit housing program that had been in the planning stages for more than a year. It aims to alleviate drugs and crime in apartments and other multi-unit dwellings, and it includes landlord and tenant education supported by community policing activities.

ties. The evaluation began in mid-1991, with data collection ending about a year later. (The timing of the evaluation was determined by receipt of funding from NIJ.) Most of the projects were launched in mid-1990—only a year before the start of the evaluation. These dates are important to keep in mind because they indicate that the INOP projects were at varying stages of implementation, most of them up and running only a short time before they were subjected to evaluation. In other words, they did not have much time to become fully operational.

The project in Hayward, California, is one example. It began fairly late—in 1991—and its central component, a mobile van, was not put into operation until the researchers' final site visit. The projects continued to progress after the evaluations were completed. In Tempe, Arizona, follow up through mid-1993 revealed the extent of progress achieved. (See "Recent Developments in Tempe, Arizona.")

Because the INOP projects had little time to establish a "track record," it is not possible to come to any definitive conclusions regarding long-term outcomes. Many of the difficulties the projects encountered need to be considered in light of this timeframe. For this reason, the evaluation is best interpreted as an assessment of the INOP projects at a very early stage of their development and over a brief period of time. Nevertheless, the findings also make clear that much remains to be learned about the optimal approach to structuring the various components of this type of program.

Applying the Lessons. In addition, it is important to note the small scale of many of these INOP projects, which often constituted only a single component of a police department's operations. For this reason it would be difficult to apply the lessons of their experiences to those of police departments generally. Moreover, because the evaluation was not national in scope, the same reasoning would apply.

The challenges in implementing INOP led to the conclusion that the evaluation findings would be particularly useful for jurisdictions that have community policing initiatives in the planning stages. The experiences of the eight INOP demonstration sites could help

these jurisdictions avoid some of the difficulties they might otherwise encounter and influence them not to abandon their plans but to improve the likelihood of their success. In this way, implementation of community policing at the neighborhood level could be accomplished more smoothly and productively.

Eight Distinctive Jurisdictions and Programs

Hayward, California— Community-Oriented Policing and Problem Solving (COPPS)

Hayward is a relatively low-income community in which a majority of the population is white, but there is also a great deal of ethnic diversity. The entire city was targeted for INOP, although one area with a pervasive drug problem received more attention than others.

Community policing was a fairly recent development, introduced in 1991. The department reorganized to accommodate the new approach by decentralizing patrol, and all officers became community policing officers. The cornerstone of INOP was a large van, the Neighborhood Access Vehicle, intended for use as a mobile office and community meeting place. It was to serve as a source of referral information and to make the police more accessible and more visible in neighborhoods where it was deployed. INOP was also to include drug enforcement in the schools that would involve cooperation between the police and school principals. Enforcement through a Tactical Narcotics Team took place on a parallel track.

COPPS training was held for all police personnel. The volunteers of Neighborhood Alert, a block watch group active in the city for 20 years, were also trained in a range of topics, and training for rental unit managers in recognizing drug abuse was planned. Plans were also made to increase the number of Neighborhood Alert groups.

INOP helped solidify the interagency cooperation that had existed for several years in the "Beat Health Team," which addressed issues of public health and disorder. INOP developed an information and referral resource guide to facilitate citizen access to other agencies' services and a guide to alcoholism, drug abuse, and family support services.

Houston, Texas—Operation Siege

There were two INOP target areas in Houston. In one, which experienced the city's most serious crime, the major problems were prostitution, crack cocaine, and abandoned buildings used by crack dealers. The other contained many "cantinas" (bars) that residents associated with criminal activity.

Houston's experience with neighborhood-oriented, problem-solving policing dated to 1982, and 5 years later plans were made (but then abandoned) to adopt community policing department-wide INOP emphasized enforcement through a strategy of high-visibility patrol aimed at open-air drug activity, monitoring of the cantinas, and covert operations and intelligence gathering targeted to drug sellers and suspects.

The emphasis on enforcement did not preclude community involvement. Operation Siege opened with a series of meetings with community groups to identify problems and plan strategy. The police enhanced their relationship with Neighborhood Watch, which monitored the cantinas; in this target area citizens formed a patrol and were given CB radios to contact the police. In the other target area the police helped revitalize a community organization, which in turn helped supply information and aided the police in other ways. The police also helped elderly homeowners in "target hardening," providing locks and doors free of charge to a number of them. No formal partnerships were established with other city agencies, but some informal links were made with individuals within these agencies.

Louisville, Kentucky— Community-Oriented Policing (COP)

INOP was adopted in one (and subsequently a second) of the six police districts in Louisville. The initial district was selected because it had the highest level of violent crime in the city and had been the center of heroin trafficking. It was also plagued by high unemployment, and a substantial number of liquor stores and bars had been identified as drug-trafficking locations. INOP had two phases, planning and problem identification, followed by strategy development and implementation. Phase two focused on problem solving, primarily in a park identified as a site of drug activity.

Since the police were involved district wide, there was no recruitment, and all officers were expected ultimately to participate. The enforcement strategy used almost exclusively was a task force of officers who employed a variety of techniques (surveillance, for example) for a few weeks to a few months, depending on the problem. Prevention/education was also part of the strategy, with some community members trained in drug abuse prevention, and an education campaign to create awareness of drug issues was planned.

A project committee and a strategy committee, consisting of police officers and community members, were formed and later consolidated into one. Among other activities, the committee conducted an "advertising" campaign and held community forums to define priority issues. Community involvement was built on the foundation of a number of active, organized block associations that predated INOP. Several block association leaders became active members of the project committee.

In enforcement, the police department received cooperation and assistance from the city-county narcotics unit whose director pledged support. INOP created 12 partnerships with city agencies, including those responsible for job training, housing, health, and parks and recreation. The mayor formally endorsed "COP" (as INOP was called) and mandated cooperation by all supporting agencies. COP also became a member of the city-county drug rehabilitation, education, and enforcement program, which linked the project to a consortium of treatment and prevention initiatives.

New York City—Community Patrol Officer Program (CPOP)

By 1988, community policing in New York had been instituted citywide, although the approach has since evolved. The INOP project targeted three precincts: in East Harlem, the Bronx, and Brooklyn. Each had a substantial drug problem, a large proportion of low-income residents, and a large proportion of minority residents.

The INOP precincts each had a van (a converted motor home) parked outside an elementary or junior high school in areas of active drug markets. Services (such as youth counseling) were provided in them and the adjacent schools. Information on drug prevention was also available. The vans were not used for citizen reporting of crime or providing other information about crime. Rather, citizens who had this type of information were instructed to go to the precinct or to call in reports. The presence of the vans was expected to encourage school attendance. Because the vans were to be seen as a community—not a police—resource, they were not to be staffed by police. However, lack of volunteers led to assignment of a police coordinator.

The Tactical Narcotics Teams, a street-level, buy-and-bust enforcement program, conducted drug sweeps at the time the vans were set up. Otherwise, the enforcement component was not large. Community Patrol Officers, who were assigned walking beats, provided drug prevention activities and referrals to treatment, and they patrolled the area around the vans to take information about drug use in the area and to ensure the safety of people using them.

Community volunteers were recruited through the Parent-Teacher Associations and received training, and the Manhattan District Attorney's office also trained volunteers. Outreach also included introduction of the Neighborhood Resource Centers (the vans) to residents, with requests for volunteers to staff them.

Several public and private agencies were involved: the Board of Education; Victim Services Agency; the Department of Health; the Department of Youth Services; the non-profit Citizens Committee for New York City; MOSAIC, a Bronx community center; and the District Attorney's Office. The Department of Health, for example, provided an injury-prevention component, and Youth Services provided a counselor.

Norfolk, Virginia—Police-Assisted Community Enforcement (PACE)

Although concentrated in and around public housing, the INOP project in Norfolk was part of a citywide program called PACE, which involved all city agencies. By the end of the evaluation research, PACE had been established in 10 areas, with plans for 2 more. Crime and calls for service were to be reduced in a 3 stage process of sweeps, stepped-up patrols, and community partnerships. PACE included all officers, although some were involved more than others. All officers, including the chief, received introductory training, followed by ongoing inservice training.

Stage 1 was an assault on street drug activity through intelligence gathering, undercover operations, and saturation patrols. The major component of drug prevention was an athletic league for young people. Other features included working with the D.A.R.E. (Drug Abuse Resistance Education) program in the schools, demolition of abandoned buildings, attention to physical disorder, evictions of drug dealers, and screening of rental applicants.

Police outreach began in Stage 2, with introduction of the program to the community. Police met with community leaders to organize Neighborhood Watch and Operation Identification. PACE representatives attended community meetings and other functions. "Community Service Days," featuring representatives of city agencies, were organized. Stage 3, whose goal was full community partnership and a reduced burden on the police, was not fully implemented.

Interagency coordination was extensive and mandated, and all city agencies had a role. The Support Services Committee, which coordinated the services of police and other city agencies, addressed specific issues like family services and signs of physical disorder.

Portland, Oregon—Iris Court Community Policing Demonstration Project

Portland INOP was a demonstration project, one of three established in each of the city's three police precincts as part of community policing, which began in 1989.

The focus was a public-housing complex where most of the units were occupied by low-income residents. Evidence suggested that many of them were drug-dependent. This site and three adjacent housing projects were selected primarily because of high levels of open-air drug dealing, calls for service to the police, and gang violence. The project served the 159 residents of the housing complexes.

The projects had several related components: enforcement/high-visibility patrol, a "Neighborhood Response Team" of two uniformed patrol officers, a civilian project coordinator, a community health nurse, a community policing contact office, partnerships between residents and social service providers, use of Crime Prevention Through Environmental Design (CPTED) principles, and resident organizing and empowerment. The emphasis on human services partnerships with other agencies made this project unique among the INOP sites.

The primary method of drug demand reduction was coordination and provision of social services. The contact office provided referral to services rather than functioning as a police ministation. The project coordinator, a civilian employee of the police department, worked full time in the contact office linking residents with service providers, making referrals, and coordinating outreach. Training landlords in how to keep drug activity out of their properties was another INOP component (though not in Iris Court).

Service provision aimed at improving the quality of life of the Iris Court residents to make drug use less attractive to at-risk youths. The enforcement/high-visibility patrol component was begun, however, just before INOP was launched and was intended to convince residents the neighborhood was safe to some degree. The rationale was that before Iris Court residents would take advantage of the social services based in their neighborhood, they needed to feel safe. The means to that end were eviction of suspected drug traffickers and people engaged in other illegal activities, enforcement of the trespass ordinance, and street-level drug enforcement.

Community outreach responsibility lay primarily with the Neighborhood Response Team; its two members attended resident association meetings, and they worked with the residents' council and in the contact office. Through the city housing authority and the project coordinator's outreach efforts, the residents' council and a tenants' association were organized.

Prince George's County, Maryland—Community-Oriented Policing Squad (COPS)

The INOP project was located in a single patrol sector of one police district of this bedroom suburb of Washington, D.C. The area is a "line" district, so-called because it shares some of the problems of crime and poverty that characterize the adjacent areas of its urban neighbor. Problem-solving policing was not unknown, but the project was part of an expansion of the police force. The aim of the expansion was to devote staff for the first time to continuous neighborhood-oriented problem solving in a department long known for its sometimes strained relations with the community. COPS officers were selected after a call for volunteers.

Satellite offices established in problem-ridden apartment complexes offered information about community services. The COPS officers' presence several hours a week was designed to reduce fear and increase police visibility. The officers patrolled (sometimes on foot), conducted community outreach, provided service referrals, and identified and addressed neighborhood problems. Information about prevention was available at the offices, and COPS officers were involved in drug prevention and treatment activities.

Enforcement included police use of information from community sources to identify narcotics locations. The COPS officers also conducted traffic checks at entrances of apartment complexes known for drug activity and explored avenues of civil enforcement.

Community members were represented on the planning committee, the project's advisory group, which consisted also of representatives of several county agencies. COPS officers established small planning committees on their beats and worked with church groups, Neighborhood Watch and Business Watch, tenant organizations, and municipal officials.

Tempe, Arizona—Beat 16

Beat 16, an economically disadvantaged but stable area of Tempe, had a long-standing heroin trafficking problem and a large number of calls for service. INOP, Tempe's introduction to community policing, was centered in a police ministation created as a modular unit in a park. It was established as a pilot project in a single beat, with assignment to a single squad of officers on a long-term basis.

The approach differed more philosophically than operationally from traditional policing. The responsibilities of Beat 16 were like those of routine operations except that its officers were not responsible for calls outside their beat and could set priorities and delay response to calls. The project focused primarily on education and prevention, and the ministation was the site of a drug information hotline. Ties were established with several prevention programs for youths. There was also an enforcement component that began with a drug sweep of the area.

The officers recruited for the project received intensive training and were encouraged to become familiar with problems of the beat and to interact with residents. Several members of the citizens' Coordinating Committee were also trained at the department's Citizen Police Academy.

Each officer on the Beat 16 squad attended meetings of a specific homeowners' association or other neighborhood group. The Coordinating Committee—consisting of representatives of community groups, business leaders, service providers, and city officials—was a central feature. It created links with other agencies, and it was to have had an active role in defining problems and identifying resources but was disbanded because of lack of interest on the part of community residents and difficulties in defining its role and that of its members. The activities of the committee were then taken over by another group.

Evaluation Findings

Police Understanding and Support

Gaining police acceptance was one of the major implementation challenges of INOP. Like many other jurisdictions that have adopted community policing, the INOP sites experienced resistance from many patrol officers. Some resistance may have derived from labor-management problems and from problems at the institutional level. In this respect, the sites resembled other organizations in which management has had difficulty communicating its goals to employees. In other words, the resistance of patrol officers may not always have been to community policing itself; rather, it may have resulted from the low credibility accorded to any management-instituted change or reform. Because most of the projects had been in operation less than a year before the evaluation began, they had little time to overcome this obstacle.[4]

Lack of Knowledge. The majority of the INOP projects consisted of pilot or experimental community policing units in target areas rather than jurisdictionwide undertakings, and the officers not involved in them had little knowledge of them. This lack of knowledge, which may be traced to inadequate communication of project goals at the outset, was a major factor in the limited support for community policing among police officers.

Most INOP projects expended considerable effort in explaining project goals and operations as part of their training of INOP officers. However, the bulk of the training focused on these officers alone, and even the officers who were trained often displayed only a rudimentary understanding of community policing. (See "Preparatory Steps: Training and Technical Assistance.")

In general, when officers (both those involved in the INOP projects and those not involved) were asked about the INOP project goals or for their definition of community policing, they would note its emphasis on community outreach and the new relationship envisioned between police and community residents. Only occasionally did officers mention problem-solving activities or interagency cooperation as elements of community policing or the INOP projects. Most police officers defined "real" police work as work involving crime-related tasks.

The lack of understanding is not unique to the INOP sites. Because community policing is still relatively new, inadequate definition and understanding of its goals and means have complicated implementation. The officers themselves did not have a single definition, although all their definitions shared some common elements (such as involvement of the community) that can be conveyed in training.

The ambitious nature of the community policing mission calling for a new role for the patrol officer—also creates implementation difficulties. Community policing is a fight for the "hearts and minds" of patrol officers and the public. It may be that the INOP sites underestimated the difficulties of this challenge. Officers who eventually embraced the idea of community policing enough to volunteer for the INOP projects recognized the scope of this challenge when they noted that because of their nontraditional nature, the projects needed not just to be described by management but to be actively "sold" to patrol officers. Such an undertaking, involving a shift in the culture of policing, would no doubt take more time to produce results than was available to these projects—more time than the period of the evaluation. In New York and Houston, even after 10 years experience with community policing, many officers contended that there was little support

among the rank and file. This suggests that acceptance by officers may take a very long time.

Opposition to Special-Unit Status. Because for most of the police departments INOP was the first experience with community policing, the projects were usually established as distinct units within patrol, rather than departmentwide. The introduction of special units set apart from the rest of the department seemed to exacerbate the conflict between community policing's reform agenda and the more traditional outlook and hierarchical structure of the departments.

The perception of elitism is ironic because community policing is meant to close the gap between patrol and special units and to empower and value the rank-and-file patrol officer as the most important agent for police work. But INOP projects were themselves special units and as such created distrust between police management and rank-and-file patrol officers and between officers assigned to traditional policing and those assigned to community policing.

A certain amount of this intradepartment resentment can be attributed to the general antagonism that may exist to one degree or another between patrol and any special unit. Therefore, this problem in the INOP projects may have had little to do with community policing itself. Such rivalries are common in most police departments large enough to have special units, and evidence suggests that police departments in the INOP sites were no exception.

To build knowledge and to develop skills in organizing, strategy development, leadership, and other areas, a systematic program of training and technical assistance was carried out as an integral part of INOP. The Police Executive Research Forum and the National Crime Prevention Council were awarded a grant, separate from that of the evaluation, to design and deliver training and technical assistance.

Needs assessment. The assistance, which was tailored to the specific needs of each of the eight sites, was preceded by assessments conducted to identify these needs. Input for the assessments came from individuals at each site—representatives of the community, the police, and other agencies and organizations. A range of needs was identified, but two appeared to dominate the agenda: strengthening collaboration among agencies and citizen mobilization/leadership development for both active and prospective community leaders. In Hayward, California, for example, the police expressed the desire that the current collaboration of the department with the building inspector's agency, a community preservation group, and the city attorney be expanded to other groups, including schools and churches.

Leadership development might require training in such skills as chairing a meeting and in the roles and responsibilities of tenants' organizations. Citizens were also interested in receiving training that was more directly related to crime reduction and control. They wanted to find out, for example, the effects of various illicit substances and how to locate prevention programs, geared to young people and to substance abuse, that could be replicated in their jurisdiction.

The police departments also identified training needs in the areas of crime control, management, and information systems support. For example, they wanted training in innovative narcotics abatement strategies and in CPTED (Crime Prevention Through Environmental Design), as well as in strategic planning, problem identification and analysis, and the development of computer-based information systems.

Training/technical assistance received. Assistance focused on the areas identified in the needs assessment: building and sustaining interagency collaboration and community partnerships, mobilizing citizens/developing citizen powerment to address crime and crime—related problems and, for both the police and citizens, enhancing problem-solving capabilities. In Tempe, for example, citizens were taught how to implement drug abuse prevention strategies and how to build and maintain positive police-community relationships and relationships with public and private agencies. Hayward received training in team building and conflict resolution, problem solving, and resource allocation. In Louisville, training in cooperation between the police and other agencies focused on where to go for what type of assistance *outside* the police department and where to go for what type of assistance *inside* the police department.

Typically, participants included representatives of local governments and government agencies, business, representatives of religious organizations, and community residents, as well as sworn and civilian police personnel. In Hayward, for example, the mayor, the deputy police chief, leaders of the religious community, business people, and community residents were among those taking part. In Louisville, staff from the city's public housing authority, other community agencies, and the schools were trained, as were patrol officers, first-line supervisors, and two district commanders.

'Cluster conferences.' These meetings of INOP project participants were held to promote information sharing among the sites. A series of these conferences was held throughout the course of the projects and functioned as "peer technical assistance." In addition to representatives of each site, participants included the evaluation researchers, representatives of the Bureau of Justice Assistance and the National Institute of Justice, and the technical assistance providers.

Spaced 6 to 9 months apart and beginning early in the life of the INOP projects (December 1990), the conferences were an opportunity to present project updates that covered successes achieved thus far, challenges faced, and steps to be taken next. Workshops were held on such topics as landlord training, an overview of drug supply and demand, effective drug demand reduction, and sustaining interagency collaboration.

It was evident from the interviews that senior patrol officers seemed to make up the backbone of resistance to the INOP projects and the reforms they represented. This was largely because of long-standing working styles cultivated from performing years of traditional patrol work but also because they felt disenfranchised by a management system that takes the best and brightest out of patrol and that has left them behind.

The intrusion of the INOP projects and their community policing agenda into the long-standing promotional structure of departments that rely on the distinctions between patrol and specialized units caused many senior patrol officers in some INOP sites to become embittered and resistant to reforms. By contrast, it also inspired some officers to become involved in community policing. This was particularly the case in departments that expressed intentions to expand their community policing initiatives. An officer in Prince George's County (Maryland), for example, indicated that the department's plans for expanding INOP and adopting community policing as an important element of patrol deployment had led some officers to believe that the INOP projects were the new career path to promotion. An administrator in Louisville saw community policing as the perfect solution to the problems he associated with a department structured around special units because of the value that the approach places on the individual patrol officer and the power and responsibility it assigns to each one.

Officers involved in the INOP projects often expressed their belief that acceptance would take a long time. Community policing would gain widespread acceptance in their department, they felt, only after a generation of younger officers, trained in community policing from the beginning of their careers, had filled the ranks.

Productivity Issues. Some objections stemmed from officers' belief that community policing is a less productive form of policing than traditional patrol. (They perceived that fewer arrests are made, for example). Because police departments face resource constraints, these supposedly less productive units come in for particular criticism.

Many non-INOP patrol officers felt that the community policing projects were safe havens for officers who did not want to work hard. This perception was particularly common in sites where community policing officers were not required to answer 911 calls. Patrol officers generally believed that community police officers should respond to calls in their beats, if only as backup for regular patrol.

Concern for Resources. Related fiscal and human resources issues played an important part in the way police officers viewed INOP. Most police officers (and many community residents) felt their police departments were understaffed and overworked. At all eight sites, officers raised concerns about the effect of community policing on scarce departmental resources. In addition to believing that

community policing was less productive than traditional policing, they also saw it as more time consuming and requiring more police resources. Community outreach and problem solving were the two specific activities that officers identified as being the most labor intensive, as well as the most difficult to integrate with their more additional duties.

In general, officers recognized that community policing activities necessarily would consume extra time, and there was a general consensus that they also required a different *kind* of time from that spent on traditional police functions. Just as an officer in Tempe said she needed large blocks of uncommitted time to develop a relationship with school children in her beat, so, too, officers in Norfolk felt that working with community residents demanded a new work flexibility.

Officers also indicated that the press of 911 calls made it difficult to meet the need for community outreach, problem solving, and networking with other agencies required of community policing. That perception may be based on the notion that the key to easing crime conditions is additional resources. Some officers did believe that community policing would in the long run reduce 911 calls and ease staffing constraints.

Officers were also concerned about the size of the area for which they were responsible. In contrast to conventional police work, which rotates officers in and out of districts according to a prearranged schedule, community policing builds the officer's relationship with and accountability to the community in which he or she works through relatively permanent assignment to a specific geographic area. These "beats" are typically smaller than those of radio motor patrols. Most [departments] on the INOP projects, however, did not subdivide their pre-existing system of geographical deployment to accommodate the community policing agenda, and the officers viewed their beats as too large.

Expectations too High. Police managers in many of the INOP sites who were trying to sell resistant officers on the merits of the program may have described the potential benefits too broadly and optimistically. As a result, officers opposed to community policing had the opportunity to criticize the project if it failed to deliver. But in all the sites, INOP officers saw these criticisms as premature and recognized that community policing needed time if it was to demonstrate the effects and efficiencies it was trying to produce. They felt that critics of the projects were pointing prematurely to failures that had not had sufficient time to mature into successes.

Reliance on Individual Officers. INOP creates a new role for the police officer, one that requires a new outlook and a new set of skills. The scale of the change in the police officer's basic job description and therefore in his/her occupational identity also generated resistance to INOP among regular patrol officers.

Whether they were assigned to INOP projects or not, officers believed that certain individual "styles" of policing were more suitable than others to community policing. The importance of the characteristics of individual police officers in the success of the INOP projects was a theme in all sites, and it manifested itself in several ways. For example, in some sites, a few dedicated and knowledgeable police officers essentially carried the entire INOP effort. At the supervisory level, the newness and complexity of community policing increased the latitude for individual interpretation of its goals.

If responsibility for success resides in a small core group of officers, supervisors, and project administrators, this highlights the necessity of developing recruitment standards that will enable police departments to select officers who are most likely to embrace a community policing approach.

Labor-Management Tension. Most of the officers interviewed felt that community policing was happening *to* them rather than *with* them and that there was no attempt to involve the rank and file in decision making. This perception was due in part to their skepticism about new programs in general and their strained relations with management. While officers throughout the sites expressed distaste for specific aspects of community policing, they were almost unanimous in criticizing what they saw as heavy-handed implementation by management. Community policing emphasizes community empowerment and involving citizens in decision making. Rank-and-file patrol officers, however, generally argued that administrators had excluded them from decision making.

Some police officers perceived that changes in their job descriptions are driven by political rather than law enforcement considerations. Some took comfort from the fact that a long list of new projects and restructurings had come and gone without significantly changing the way policing is performed. This rapid succession of "repackagings" in policing since the current round of reforms began in the 1970's convinced many officers that all new projects are driven by political pressures on police and city managers and are thus inherently of dubious value.

A 'New Old' Idea. In virtually every site, most of the officers who took part in focus groups described the kind of policing implemented by the INOP projects as nothing new but rather as just "good, old-fashioned policing." This was the view of officers who were trying to make a case in favor of community policing, but it was expressed more often by officers who were skeptical about reform. By arguing that INOP essentially requires officers to engage in the same kind of sound policing that many of them have been practicing for years, resistant officers made a case for continuing the status quo. This view, which focused largely on the community outreach component of community policing, was rooted mainly in the general lack of knowledge of community policing. But it may also have been an expression of a generic resistance to change of any sort rather than to INOP. Again, it reflects the distrust of management, which officers raised without prompting, and that underlies some of their resistance.

Perceived Loss of Enforcement Power. The parallel with an idyllic period in the past when the "beat cop" and citizens enjoyed a more trusting relationship was contradicted by the officers' perception that community policing placed too many restraints on police power. The officers were concerned their enforcement powers would be limited. In most sites, the lack of an aggressive enforcement component was consistently reported by officers not assigned to INOP as the biggest stumbling block to acceptance of it.

Some skeptical officers did express a willingness to change their minds if community policing could achieve traditional law enforcement goals. The key to community policing's credibility, they claimed, was its ability to reduce 911 calls, reduce criminal activity, and produce arrests. At least in part, community policing's perceived directives to "smile and wave" (rather than enforce) were disdained because they came from management.

Involvement of Other Agencies

If community policing is to be successful, it must include problem solving, and this in turn requires the active involvement of other city agencies. Although most of the INOP sites made some attempts to involve city agencies, this is the area in which opportunities for better implementation were greatest. Interagency involvement was limited and informal. Many of the INOP projects were perceived to depend not on cooperative efforts among agencies but on the efforts of one or two individuals—a police administrator or a beat officer.

Norfolk was the sole exception; in fact, the active, mandated involvement of *all* city agencies was the component that made Norfolk's program notable. The mayor made it clear to every department head that all city departments were part of the Police-Assisted Community Enforcement program. The program was promoted and training was provided to administrative staff from every city agency. Organizational structure was provided by the PACE Support Services Committee on which all city agencies were represented. The committee focused on team-centered assessment of family service needs and quality-of-life issues in the neighborhoods.

Traditional enforcement strategies—e.g., making arrests, filing reports, and issuing summonses—do not involve public agencies other than the police. But many problems cannot be solved through traditional means alone and require input from other agencies and from community residents. This is especially true of quality-of-life problems (such as abandoned cars, noise, graffiti, and other signs of neighborhood disorder or decay).

Reliance on Personal Networking. Most police officers are not experienced in dealing with other public or private agencies, nor are there effective mechanisms to make such interactions work smoothly and predictably. If an officer at an INOP site believed that another public agency could be helpful in dealing with a particular problem, he or she most often relied on personal contact with someone at the agency. This was done because there was no structured relationship between the department and the agency and no formalized procedures to follow. If the contact person should leave the agency, the officer would have no quick, effective means of dealing with similar, subsequent problems. This business-as-usual approach was taken in most of the INOP sites during the period of the study.

In some sites there was little support for the program from even the city (or county) government. For such cities, community policing is *de facto* an isolated police department phenomenon.

Community Involvement

Definitions of community policing may vary, but all share the idea that the police and the community must work together to identify problems affecting the community and to develop solutions. This is a radical departure from the era of "professionalism" in policing in which police claimed a monopoly of the responsibility for crime control and actively discouraged citizen involvement in police business.

Despite the central role of the police-citizen partnership, many of the police departments paid little attention to the education and inclusion of the community. All the INOP sites experienced difficulty in establishing a solid community infrastructure upon which to build their programs. Although they did not have much time in which to organize the communities, their experience nonetheless suggests that the question of how to unleash the potential for effective organization may prove to be the greatest challenge for community policing.

Familiarity With INOP and Community Policing. Understanding precedes involvement. Respondents' knowledge of a project— its existence, goals, and tactics—varied greatly at all the sites, and the interview data indicate that the level of understanding about INOP or community policing in general was closely linked to a person's status in the community and to the frequency of his or her interaction with the police.[5] Thus, in Hayward and Houston, block watch leaders knew a great deal more about the INOP project than did either their members or average citizens, and the same was true of residents' council members in Portland.

This phenomenon is hardly limited to INOP, however. Almost by definition, local leaders will make it their business to become familiar with issues affecting their community. This was the case in the INOP sites, where community leaders who interacted frequently with the police knew more about INOP than did residents who belonged to no community group. In all the INOP sites, however, even the most knowledgeable community leaders had only limited familiarity with project goals, tactics, and the role of the community.

Some residents, particularly older people, were unaware of the program. Community leaders and other residents tended to lay blame for lack of knowledge on the police, who they claimed did not adequately inform or educate the general population. Even assuming the best education campaign, however, it would have been difficult for the INOP projects to become a familiar community fixture in the short timespan they were in operation.

Type of Knowledge. Residents of public housing or other disadvantaged neighborhoods that were INOP sites often defined community policing or a specific INOP project solely in terms of the picnics, block parties, and events for children that were so often used as methods of community outreach. They were familiar with little of the substance of community policing or the INOP projects. While social events like block parties do little to inform or educate community residents about community policing and their role in it, it is possible that they may create solidarity in the community and thus could be considered the beginnings of attempts to organize. In addition, these events

allow residents to meet police officers in a nonthreatening situation.

Perception of Community Organization. Many residents at all eight sites believed the projects had positive effects on the level of community organization and involvement. In many instances, however, their responses indicated they equated community organization with large turnouts for social events, such as barbecues and picnics. Again, although larger turnouts for community meetings or significant increases in the number of people volunteering to help with problem solving would be better indicators of community involvement, the rudiments of community organization might be detected in people's equating it with these social events.

Issues in Stimulating Community Involvement

Both practitioners and theorists of community policing often assume that because the approach offers such evident benefits to the community, once educated about these benefits, residents will actively aid in the effort. The evidence from these eight sites strongly suggests, however, that community residents generally may not want to become involved, and from their perspective, the reasons are sound.

Fear of Retaliation. The reason most frequently cited in all eight communities for lack of involvement was residents' fear of retaliation from drug dealers. In several communities, residents also specifically expressed fear of reprisals when they were identified as "snitches" as a result of their calls to the police. Responding police officers would come to their homes and thus they would be observed by the drug dealers.

In all theories of community policing, the perception of fear is a central concern. Implicitly or explicitly, most adherents of community policing incorporate the theory of "broken windows"[6] into their programs. This theory holds that the police need to emphasize their order-maintenance function; for example, attending to disorderly behaviors such as loitering or public drunkenness. Such behavior, if neglected by the police, leads to increased incivilities, lower levels of informal social control, and greater fear among community residents. The resulting condition, left unattended, increases the level of community decay, both social and physical, and makes the area ripe for intrusion by outside criminal elements. This in turn generates even more fear.

The role of the community policing officer is to make residents feel safer because he or she will concentrate on the incivilities and order-maintenance problems that inspire fear in residents. It may be, however, that fear is too deeply ingrained among residents of some low-income urban areas. If so, community policing may be unable to reduce fear to the degree necessary to allow residents to feel safe enough to police themselves and take back the streets.

Community policing may find itself confronted by a major contradiction as a result. If community policing is to attain its goal of reducing fear, the streets must first be made safe from the perspective of community residents. According to the residents of these eight communities, for this to happen, the level of crime, not merely the perception of it, must fall. However, most theories of community policing seem to assert that without the active participation of the community, the police cannot reduce the incidence of crime and disorder and thus reduce fear.

The Transitory Nature of Projects to Assist Disadvantaged Neighborhoods. The designers of many of the INOP projects realized this and began or preceded their projects with intensive, traditional law enforcement efforts.[7] Such actions may produce unintended effects, however. Residents almost unanimously applaud police attempts to increase enforcement in their neighborhoods, and during such crackdowns they report feeling safer. But many of these intensive enforcement initiatives are (intentionally) short lived and therefore do not produce the desired effect of reducing fear in the long run. When this happens, residents begin to define community policing as "just another program" in which services are here today but gone tomorrow. Residents attributed lack of community involvement to the fleeting nature of the NOP projects. The perceived view of projects as transitory was most apparent

where a strong enforcement effort—one of short duration—preceded an INOP project.

Historically Poor Police-Community Relations. One of the untested assumptions of community policing is that residents really want closer contact with the police and want to work with them to reduce crime. The assumption is itself based on the notion that people who do not routinely violate the law and who will eventually come to work cooperatively with the police are the logical audience for the community policing approach. Again, data collected in the interviews for this study cast doubt on these assumptions.

A large number of the community residents indicated that a major reason for lack of involvement or even outright hostility was the historically negative relationship between the police and residents of economically disadvantaged communities. Such relationships, most common in areas of the city usually chosen as the target sites for community policing demonstration projects, will not be easily changed. Police officers in many of the sites interpreted the refusal of residents to become involved as apathy or lack of interest in bettering their own lives. The lack of involvement may, however, be due less to apathy than to this long-standing antagonism.

Lack of Outreach by the Police. Nearly all the INOP sites were hampered in their attempts to generate community organization and involvement by lack of resources and experience. The exceptions were Hayward and Houston, which had strong block watch groups in the target areas. While the police departments recognized the need to train officers in the strategy and tactics of community policing, they did not provide the same level of training to members of the community.

One evident need is for training in the fundamental principles of community policing and the role of the community. Confusion about the role of the community in "community policing" was common. As noted earlier, although community leaders had some notion of community policing, ordinary residents had very limited knowledge. Most of the INOP projects did, however, attempt to involve residents in some manner. In Tempe and New York, police recruited citizens as volunteers; in Portland, they helped residents form councils; and in Norfolk, they involved citizens in interagency problem solving.

The Nature of the Target Neighborhoods. The economically disadvantaged urban areas that generally serve as testing grounds for community policing tend to be highly disorganized, characterized by poverty, unemployment, inadequate educational services, and high crime rates. In areas encumbered by such an array of problems, it is often difficult to find well-organized community groups that are attempting to address quality-of-life issues.

Most residents in the eight INOP sites reported that the level of community organization was only average or low and that this had been the case for some time. Most attributed this lack of community activism to fear. In several sites (particularly Tempe, Houston, and Hayward), the police were particularly feared by the illegal immigrants who lived there in large numbers.

The initial responsibility for generating community organization in troubled areas must fall to the police because it is they who are asking the public to assist them. This police effort is best undertaken in association with other city agencies. Thus, in Portland, where the Iris Court project serves people living in public housing, the police asked the city's Housing Authority to assist the residents in forming a residents' council; and in Hayward, the police built on the solid foundation provided by the citywide "Neighborhood Alert" groups.

Intragroup Conflict. A common barrier to organizing, according to both residents and police officers, was conflict among community leaders and residents. In some sites this took the form of disagreement about what issues were to be addressed, how tasks were to be delegated, and similar strategic and tactical questions. In several sites, personality conflicts with community leaders were cited as a major reason residents refused to become involved with a block watch, residents' council, or other civic association linked to INOP.

The intragroup conflicts suggest that references to an ideal "community" often fail to consider that, in reality, the community is often an aggregate of competing groups. Simply because people live in the same geographic area and share the same racial and class backgrounds does not guarantee that they share all the same values or define problems the same way.

The Portland site took a step toward solving this problem by offering training for the Iris Court residents. The aim of the training, offered to residents' council members, was broader participation in the project, and it also focused on resolving intragroup conflict.

Finding Out What the Community Wants. One of the principles guiding community policing is recognition that the police must be guided by the values of the community. Identifying those values may not be easy, especially when neighborhoods are heterogeneous.

Residents of the INOP sites were asked how they would improve the project and how they would improve community policing or policing in general. A number of patterned responses emerged across the sites, among them the desire for continuity in assignment of beat officers. Residents wanted a beat officer assigned for an extended period of time. In Portland, for example, a Neighborhood Response Team, consisting of two officers, spent a great deal of time at the start of the INOP project in the public housing complex to which they were assigned and established rapport with a large number of residents. Residents reported that after a time, however, the presence of these officers declined dramatically.

It is clear from the INOP sites that residents took the problem of "revolving beat officers" very seriously. The beat officer is the most visible manifestation of the community policing approach, and, in fact, it was common for residents to *define* community policing in terms of the beat officer.

Another community expectation, as expressed by residents, was for police to be crime fighters above all else, and they defined the success of community policing in terms of reducing crime and fear. However, a great many residents also noted other, equally important criteria, one of which was better relations among residents and the police, which often seemed to hinge on the idea of having long-term beat officers.

The Perceived Impact of INOP on Crime and Quality of Life

Drug Trafficking. All the projects had one goal in common: reducing drug demand. The purpose of INOP was to develop innovative approaches to that end. The general perception of residents and others who were interviewed was that drug trafficking had been displaced, either from one area to another, from street level to indoors, or to a different time of day.

Some differences in this overall impression were found in specific sites. In Hayward, Houston, and New York City, for example, some people interviewed believed the INOP project had no effect on drug trafficking. In Portland and Tempe, by contrast (see "Attitudes Towards INOP"), the project was seen as extremely effective. In the other sites, the predominant view was that drug dealing had been displaced to an area receiving less attention from the project, to a few blocks away but within the same area, to locations indoors rather than on the street, or to another time during the day.

Drug-Related Crime. The people interviewed found it more difficult to assess the effects of the INOP projects on drug-related crime. Often they noted they were not really able to distinguish crimes that were drug related from those that were not, but despite this difficulty they were able to make an assessment. Responses ranged from "no effect" to "very strong" impact, with a full range of responses in between. New York City was the only site reporting "no effect" on drug-related crime, while Portland, Tempe, and Norfolk said the INOP project had a "very strong" impact. In fact, almost all respondents in Portland believed the INOP project had a very large impact on crime in Iris Court, with dramatic changes in gang activity, violent

---

Attitudes Toward INOP

Citizens. As part of the Beat 16 project in Tempe, citizens were asked how they felt about the project and its effects. This was done through surveys—conducted just after the project began and again a little over a year later—after INOP was in full operation. The initial survey was conducted to provide baseline data, the second to register any change over time.

The results were encouraging. For example, when residents were initially asked about the number of times they saw police officers patrolling their neighborhood, 38 percent answered more than 10 times per month, but in the survey conducted after the INOP project was in operation, the percentage rose to 65. In the baseline survey, 24 percent of the respondents said they personally had seen drug activity in the neighborhood, but this number dropped by almost half (to 13 percent) in the second survey. Only 9 percent initially said they were active in the neighborhood association, and this number doubled when the second survey was taken.

Officers. The nine beat officers involved in the INOP project were also asked, about 2 years after Beat 16's inception, how they felt about the project. All nine said it was working well. They especially liked the idea of staying in one beat and having time to get to know the area and the residents. One officer noted, "I now take ownership of problems instead of slapping a band aid on them."

All nine officers thought the attitudes of residents toward the police had become more favorable, and they felt more empowered and free to pursue more independent avenues of policing and dealing with citizens. Several said they felt more effective now than before when they were limited to random patrol. The officers also believed they enjoyed a greater sense of responsibility for their work. Among the weaknesses they identified were reluctance of officers from other beats to help out, the feeling that not all officers were "pulling their own weight," the need for more training, and the feeling that at times things were moving too fast.

crime, robberies, and burglaries. In Prince George's County, people believed that crime rates had declined, and the County Executive proclaimed the program a "true success." In Hayward, Houston, and Louisville, respondents were divided in their assessments.

Fear and Drug-Related Crime. Theories holding that social disorder and crime generate fear suggest that it will decline where drug trafficking and crime are perceived to have declined. Accordingly, respondents in Hayward, Houston, and New York City believed the INOP projects had little or no effect on drugs and crime (or only a temporary effect), and the levels of citizens' fear in those cities changed little. By contrast, in Portland, where the project was viewed as effective in reducing drug trafficking, respondents were overwhelmingly positive about the project's effect on fear, as were respondents from Tempe and Prince George's County. Responses from Norfolk and Louisville were mixed.

Police-Community Relations. There appeared to be little relationship between perceptions of effects on drugs, crime, and fear and perceptions of how the projects affected police-community relations; it did not necessarily follow that respondents who saw INOP as having little effect on crime also saw it as having little effect on the relationship of the community to the police. Most respondents reported better relationships between the police and community residents. Even in sites where INOP's effect on drugs, crime, and fear was perceived as minimal (Hayward, Houston, and New York City), respondents generally believed the relationship between the police and the community had improved.

Community Organization and Involvement. Respondents found it more difficult to assess INOP's effect on community organization and involvement, but in most sites they indicated that levels of community organization and involvement had increased since the start of the INOP project. It was not clear, however, whether the increases were attributable to INOP or to other factors. Even in Hayward, where citizens' groups were the most organized among the eight sites, it appeared that the increased organization was more likely the result of a grassroots effort by the community that predated the INOP pro-

gram. Nevertheless, the police and residents all indicated that more Neighborhood Alert groups had been formed and attendance in existing groups had improved since community policing began.

The response of a police administrator from Louisville may help explain the general view of respondents that community organization had increased. The administrator indicated that the many interventions taking place, some not related to INOP, made residents feel "there is some interest in them." Residents of many of the INOP neighborhoods to whom the police were paying attention for the first time may have felt that any intervention was better than no attention at all.

Easing the Transition to Community Policing

Community policing holds great promise for citizen participation, increased responsiveness on the part of the police to the concerns of residents, and greater police accountability. But if community policing is to be granted legitimacy by the public, its proponents need to demonstrate that it works. The INOP projects provided an opportunity to meet the need for information about the effectiveness of the approach and about the implementation challenges community policing faces.

In achieving the crime-reduction goals of community policing, the INOP projects had mixed success, but this conclusion needs to be seen in light of the limited amount of time the projects had been in operation before their results were assessed. Community policing represents major shifts, both for the police and community residents, and—particularly because of its emphasis on prevention—is likely to take a long time before it approaches institutionalization.

Aside from the effects of the projects in reducing crime and fear, the assessment brought to light a number of areas in which implementation could be improved. The experiences of the eight INOP sites clearly revealed that in the transition to community policing, jurisdictions need to pay particular attention to three issues: overcoming patrol officer resistance, generating interagency support, and building community involvement. The assessment findings suggest that helping to ensure a better *product*—crime reduction—may require greater attention to *process*.

Overcoming Patrol Officer Resistance. Resistance by police officers to community policing is due in part to inadequate understanding of the principles on which the approach is based, which in turn stems from insufficient training. Police officials who envision the transition of their own departments to community policing can learn from the experience of the INOP sites about the need for a commitment to training all officers.

Jurisdictions contemplating adopting community policing may also want to rethink the special-unit status accorded many of the INOP project officers because of its potential for generating intradepartmental rivalry and consequent resentment and resistance. Moreover, the view of community policing as a drain on resources, one in which not all officers are seen as pulling their own weight or performing traditional duties (such as responding to 911 calls), was also revealed in the INOP sites as a problem that needs to be overcome. For community policing to be successful in attracting the most talented personnel, police departments might want to make it a career path—an exception to the current rule that advancement does not run through patrol.

New recruitment strategies may also be needed. In some INOP sites, it appeared that the continued existence of the program rested on a single officer or administrator. The nature of community policing also makes it susceptible to variations in supervisory style, and because of the emphasis on interaction with the community, a single officer or supervisor can strongly influence the public's perceptions of the program. Officers who are favorably disposed toward community policing may positively influence community residents, while officers who have not bought into the concept may cause residents to develop a negative impression. New recruitment strategies could help police departments select candidates committed to the ideals of working with and for the community.

Becoming a City Agencywide Phenomenon. At the INOP sites, the police tended to rely on personal contacts with other agencies to secure their involvement, and community policing was almost always an isolated police department phenomenon. This approach highlights the need for an organized, systematic involvement of agencies citywide. This need is particularly acute because community policing involves crime prevention and quality-of-life issues, not all of which fall within the purview of the police.

The experience of the INOP sites suggests that at the very least, employees of other agencies should understand how they can contribute to problem solving; in short, they need to be instructed in their role in community policing, which is no less important than that of beat officers or concerned community residents.

Involving the Community. That the INOP sites in general had limited success in stimulating community organization is not surprising, given the brief time in which to involve the community and the limited experience of the police in this area. The evaluation findings indicate that neighborhood organizing is a skill the police will want to develop if they hope to involve the community. Other city agencies can play a role in this process. If police departments involve them from the beginning of the implementation process, they could be useful in stimulating community involvement by educating the public.

By the same token, the experience of the INOP projects can be useful for police administrators in recognizing community education and training as equal in importance with police training and education (though far more difficult to accomplish). Existing community organizations and leaders are the logical first audience, but it should be kept in mind that neighborhoods that commonly serve as community policing pilot sites generally have few viable community groups. The police, in concert with other public and private agencies, should create organization where it does not exist, although it may be argued that a high level of community organization is *not* necessary for community policing to function effectively.

To address residents' concerns about the transitory nature of policing projects, departments considering adopting community policing will want to gauge as accurately as possible, before it is instituted, the resources required to practice it. Almost all the INOP sites promised communities regular beat officers who would be permanent fixtures of the neighborhood, but these officers were in fact rotated, preventing residents from getting to know them. If the police do not accurately estimate resources, the result may be broken promises to the community and a loss of police credibility.

Conclusion

At least initially, community policing will require more resources. That means jurisdictions will find themselves faced with committing to larger budgets in an increasingly harsh fiscal climate. This need highlights the importance of involving other agencies. Not only are they essential to the problem-solving approach to policing, but resource constraints on police departments make them even more valuable because their involvement provides the opportunity to leverage additional expertise and resources.

Given the monumental nature of the tasks, the transition to community policing will take a considerable amount of time—much more time than these eight sites had to "prove themselves." It remains to be seen whether an already impatient public will accept this fact. In large cities with extremely diverse populations and large police bureaucracies, the process is likely to take far longer.

The transition may be faster and ultimately more productive if the jurisdiction itself makes a commitment to a transition that assigns equal value to training the police, the public, and the staffs of all public agencies. The training provided to the INOP sites introduced the key players to the concepts and principles of community policing and to related procedures and practices. It was intended only to set community policing in motion. However, the need for training persists throughout the life of a project, particularly because the new philosophy entails so many and such profound changes. The resistance of many officers at these sites to community policing is a strong argument for offering training on an ongoing basis. Ultimately, training may prove to be a key to long-term success.

Notes

1. Wycoff, Mary Ann, "Community Policing Strategies," draft final report, U.S. Department of Justice, National Institute of Justice, November 1994 (grant 91–IJ–CX–KO008):45. The data for this Police Foundation study are from a survey conducted in 1993. The figure is for municipal police departments with staffs of 100 or more. Figures for county police and sheriffs' departments with staffs of this size are 23 percent and 20 percent, respectively. The community policing provisions of the Violent Crime Control and Law Enforcement Act of 1994 will undoubtedly cause these figures to rise. A two-page summary of the report is available from the National Criminal Justice Reference Service. Call 800-851-3420. Ask for FS 000126.

2. This description of the INOP program was drawn from the Bureau of Justice Assistance's initial solicitation for proposals to establish INOP programs.

3. The total amount awarded to the eight INOP sites was $2.4 million. All but one received funding for 2 years.

4. The police reaction to INOP documented in this section was obtained from individual interviews and focus group sessions (comprising up to eight people) conducted at all the sites, which included the officers involved in INOP and those not involved. Supervisors (sergeants and lieutenants) were interviewed both individually and in groups.

5. The information regarding familiarity with INOP and community policing was obtained from focus groups and interviews with individuals—police officers and police management, representatives of other local government agencies, and community leaders and other residents.

6. Wilson, James Q., and George L. Kelling, "Broken Windows," *Atlantic Monthly*, March 1982:29–38.

7. These law enforcement efforts were not specifically mandated by the Bureau of Justice Assistance, but they were part of the overall demand reduction strategy.

Reprinted from: Susan Sadd and Randolph M. Grinc, "Implementation Challenges in Community Policing: Innovative Neighborhood-Oriented Policing in Eight Cities." In *National Institute of Justice. Research in Brief*, February 1996. ✦

9

Lasting Impact

Maintaining Neighborhood Order

Ronald W. Glensor
Kenneth J. Peak

Community oriented policing and problem solving requires an intensive, systematic approach to neighborhood disorder that may require considerable time, effort, and resources in order to make a difference. However, what happens after the "file" is closed, and the officers are removed from the targeted area? Will neighborhoods tend to return to their previous levels of problems? The authors of this piece correctly suggest that maintaining community safety and enhanced quality of life is of paramount importance; that is, upon successful implementation of community-based policing efforts, attention needs to be paid to maintaining the benefits produced. Through a case study analysis, Glensor and Peak present the SARA model as an effective problem solving tool. The importance of this article lies in the description of the application of the SARA model to an area located in Reno, Nevada, and the findings of this analysis. In particular, the authors note the many problems associated with maintaining the successes, and then present several suggestions for maintaining successful problem solving efforts over the long term.

Introduction

During the past two decades, law enforcement agencies around the country have adopted the combined operational strategies of community oriented policing and problem solving (COPPS) to address a wide range of crime problems and the quality-of-life issues that often surround them. Using the COPPS model, police officers and citizens in communities of every size and demographic makeup have joined together to address these problems in new and creative ways.

However, despite the ever-increasing prevalence of community oriented policing and a growing litany of successful problem solving interventions, few police administrators or scholars have focused on the strategic issues involved in *maintaining* the enhanced quality of life and sense of community safety that successful community-based policing efforts often create. As communities across the country are discovering, maintenance becomes a key issue after the initial problem solving has produced results. To ensure that problem-solving initiatives have a lasting impact on communities, law enforcement agencies should develop practical strategies to ensure that community policing yields long-term solutions rather than short-term fixes.

Long-term Solutions

Much of what has been written about maintenance issues is featured in the important contemporary discussions of crime and its impact on communities. In their landmark "Broken Windows" article, James Q. Wilson and George Kelling describe in very compelling language the potential long-term implications of leaving neighborhood problems unattended.[1] The pioneering work of Herman Goldstein on problem-oriented policing suggests that in-depth analyses of related incidents and the development of tailor-made responses are keys to solving underlying problems within a community.[2] Goldstein's research contributed to the development of the SARA (scanning, analysis, response, and assessment) problem solving process, which would be applied successfully by the Newport News, Virginia, Police Department in the mid-1980s to address long-standing crime problems in specific areas of the city.

Each of these works, and the documented successes of problem solving in Newport News, helped lay the philosophical and operational groundwork for community-oriented policing as it is currently practiced in departments around the country. However, because of their groundbreaking nature, they could only hint at the strategic issues involved in maintaining a problem-solving posture after the initial COPPS interventions had taken place.

Like a patient requiring long-term care, neighborhoods plagued with problems require periodic attention to ensure a healthy environment is preserved. In recent years, a growing number of communities that developed and implemented successful community-oriented intervention strategies have wrestled with the problems of maintaining reduced crime levels after the initial intervention has taken place.

Law enforcement agencies have learned that some crime problems—such as gang violence and drug dealing—tend to resurface. Likewise, certain community environments—public housing developments, high-density apartment complexes, and urban centers—are more prone to rapid degeneration once high-impact intervention policies terminate.

To ensure that community-oriented and problem-solving initiatives have a lasting impact, law enforcement administrators should include maintenance in the strategic planning process. To do so effectively, they first must possess a clear understanding of problem solving as a method to address community problems.

Strategic Response to Persistent Problems

Problem solving is the linchpin of COPPS. It helps agencies adopt long-term solutions to address crime, fear, and disorder. The SARA process provides the police with a useful tool for identifying, analyzing, responding to, and evaluating crime problems and neighborhood concerns. Application of the SARA process leads officers away from short-term, reactive, and incident-driven responses and moves them toward long-term outcomes based on in-depth analysis and collaboration with citizens, municipal agencies, and others.

When formalized, the SARA process serves many useful purposes. These include:

- Providing documentation of initial intervention efforts and their outcomes.

- Producing a record of interested parties, or stakeholders, both internal (specifically, officers and support staff involved in the initial intervention projects) and external (including business and property owners, residents, and other city and government agencies).

- Creating a database of problems, defined by type, area of town, time of day, and other factors. This information provides the who, what, when, where, and how of addressing ongoing problems.

- Developing a training mechanism and resource and a record of information resources for other officers to review and gain ideas about how to address similar conditions.

The information acquired from the SARA process assists officers with ongoing problem assessment and maintenance, as well as helping to mobilize original stakeholders to reestablish neighborhood control. The benefits of formalizing the problem-solving process have led many agencies to develop computer–based programs to support SARA.

Like many agencies, the Reno, Nevada, Police Department has relied on the SARA process to implement problem solving initiatives during the past decade. One of these initiatives, undertaken in a low-income residential area known as Virginia Lake, illustrates how quickly crime problems can return to troubling levels after an initial intervention. The case study that follows demonstrates the importance of maintenance in any problem-solving approach. It also shows how documenting initial efforts can speed the process of repair by providing vital information about strategies and stakeholders.

Case Study: The Virginia Lake Area

In many ways, the Virginia Lake area qualified as a classic candidate for a problem-oriented policing approach. At the time of the initial intervention by the Reno Police Department (RPD), the 1.5 square mile area in the south patrol division was home to approximately 6,600 residents. In 1992, the annual per capita income for area residents was $12,600. Virginia Lake includes five contiguous, high-density apartment complexes, each controlled by absentee owners. The area also consists of several strip-mall shopping centers, numerous retail establishments, and a large public park.

The Initial Intervention

Beginning in the late 1980s, calls for service from the Virginia Lake area increased steadily until February 1992, when two RPD beat officers, working the swing shift (4:00 p.m. to 2 a.m.) in the area, decided to conduct an inquiry to determine the extent of the problem. From February to August 1992, the officers developed and initiated problem-solving efforts in the area. During this six-month period, the officers used periods between service calls, as well as limited additional time provided by their supervisors, to analyze the problems and develop responses. In doing so, the officers used the SARA process to guide and document their efforts. In the period following the initial intervention, this documentation would prove invaluable to subsequent maintenance efforts in the targeted area.

Scanning

Scanning department records revealed that approximately 10,000 calls for service emanated from Virginia Lake annually. The majority of these calls involved domestic violence, burglaries, disturbances, and gang related activities. The area had recently experienced two gang-related homicides, the kidnap-murder of two children, and increased drug activity.

During interviews with the officers, citizens expressed considerable fear of crime but also related an underlying atmosphere of tension, brought about by the influx of gang-related graffiti, assaults, fighting, and shots fired. Residents also expressed concern with the outward signs of neighborhood disorder, including abandoned buildings and vehicles, traffic problems, and uncollected refuse.

Analysis

With the assistance of the department's crime analyst, the officers developed a survey and administered it to 120 business owners, residents, and apartment managers in the Virginia Lake area. The respondents were asked to define the area's problems, discuss their fears, and suggest actions the police, other city agencies, and residents could take to address the area's problems.

The survey produced numerous interesting findings and uncovered several problems that had not been revealed by other forms of crime analysis. For example, residents expressed tremendous fear of gang behavior and its resultant problems, such as random gunfire, graffiti, and the presence of suspicious persons. Residents participating in the survey recommended organizing a formal Neighborhood Watch program.

Business owners in the area, also expressing concern with burglaries and juvenile offenses, inquired about crime prevention programs and supported efforts to organize a business watch. In addition, the survey revealed that apartment managers neither knew nor communicated with one another. As a result, a number of evicted renters simply moved from one complex to another in the same area.

Often, the concerns expressed by tenants in one apartment complex differed considerably from those expressed by tenants in the complex across the street. The varied nature of these concerns convinced the officers that tailored responses to specific problems would succeed better than a generic cookie-cutter approach to problem solving.

In addition to the citizen survey, the department also conducted an environmental survey of the area. Department personnel photographed street intersections and relayed the photographs to the city's streets department. Likewise, officers videotaped abandoned buildings for the fire department. In addition, officers performed speed and traffic surveys, as well as a lighting survey. They also observed that the area's landscaping consisted primarily of rocks, which provided ready ammunition for youths who participated in one of the area's favorite pastimes—throwing stones at vehicle and apartment windows.

Residents expressed considerable enthusiasm about assisting the police department to address the many problems that confronted the area. During an initial neighborhood meeting, residents, police officers, and other stakeholders discussed the problems and possible solutions. During the intervention period, stakeholders continued to share their concerns and ideas and to chart the intervention's progress during monthly follow-up meetings.

Response

When the officers determined the magnitude of the problems facing the area, they began to formulate plans for tailor-made solutions to them. Experience had shown the officers that arresting offenders could be considered *part* of the solution; but arrests alone rarely result in long-term improvements to complex neighborhood problems. The officers knew they would have to explore other options.

Armed with vast amounts of information and data, the officers initiated a collaborative, citywide response to the area's problems. The response comprised a balance of crime control and prevention efforts. The city attorney drafted a graffiti ordinance. A gang enforcement team worked with the beat officers to target gang-related incidents in the area. Pressure on drug dealers and arrests increased in the apartment complexes. The city imposed a curfew at the public park, which had become a focal point for gang activity and drug dealing. At the same time, the police department initiated bike and foot patrols to complement vehicle patrols throughout the area. The enhanced patrols produced immediate results when officers apprehended several juveniles responsible for a string of vehicle burglaries.

With guidance from the police department, landlords and tenants from the five apartment complexes established a resident council; residents and business owners launched Neighborhood and Business Watch programs. Apartment managers received landlord-tenant training and began to exert friendly pressure on one another to proactively address problems on their properties. the manager of one complex initiated a latchkey program to keep young students busy after school.

The beat officers also coordinated efforts to address environmental issues as another means of crime prevention. The local power company evaluated and corrected area lighting problems. The resident council, working with local salvage yards, initiated a program to remove abandoned vehicles. Residents and apartment managers launched a cleanup campaign. The city's parks department and residents jointly cleaned, painted, and repaired the park facilities. Apartment managers arranged to have pyrocantha shrubs planted around fences to make them more formidable crime barriers. The city razed abandoned buildings, and a community service organization purchased recreational equipment and transformed a vacant lot into a neighborhood park.

Assessment

Effective assessment of a problem-solving initiative actually begins in the analysis stage, when the police department collects baseline data on the extent of problems in a targeted area. As the Virginia Lake intervention drew to a close, the beat officers evaluated the overall effectiveness of their efforts and determined whether any remaining issues required additional analysis or responses. They based their outcome evaluations on both quantitative and qualitative data, including calls for service, reported crimes, and results from citizen surveys.

The officers compared calls for service data from February to August 1992 to figures for the same period in 1991. The comparison revealed significant decreases in robberies, assault and battery offenses, assaults with a deadly weapon (ADW), prowlers, commercial and residential burglaries, and auto thefts during the months of the intervention. As often occurs when communities mobilize against crime and citizen trust in the police to respond grows, reports of disturbances, destruction of property, domestic violence, fights, juvenile problems, shots fired, and suspicious persons increased moderately during the intervention.

In a follow-up survey, area residents expressed less fear of crime, cited an improved physical environment in the neighborhood, and pointed with satisfaction to ongoing self-help efforts, as the resident council continued meeting on a regular basis. The reductions in serious criminal activity and calls for service, coupled with improvements to physical environmental conditions throughout the area and the development of citizen-based organizations, led to gradual reduction of the beat officers' efforts, as the police department returned control of the neighborhood to its residents.

Fleeting Success

In the year following the police department's concentrated presence in Virginia Lake, conditions in the area began to worsen. While robbery, ADW, and vehicle theft rates continued to fall, the number of family disturbances, assault and battery offenses, reported prowlers, and residential and vehicle burglaries increased significantly.

In 1994, two years after the police department's intervention efforts, conditions deteriorated further. Crimes against persons increased sharply. ADWs spiked (up 500 percent from 1991 levels), as did robberies and reports of suspicious persons in the area. Commercial burglaries increased 44 percent over 1991 figures. Residents expressed a heightened sense of fear, particularly because of recurring gang-related activities in the neighborhood.

Because of the serious downturn in conditions in the area, the resident council recontacted the two officers who had initiated the 1992 intervention efforts. However, because the officers had since been reassigned to specialized assignments elsewhere, there was little they could do to assist the council. While the new beat officers assigned to the neighborhood and their supervisors were concerned about the declining state of the neighborhood and sought to improve conditions, they were unfamiliar with the area's history. The attrition of area residents and apartment and business managers also had a negative impact on ongoing maintenance and problem-solving efforts in the area.

Eventually, by using information contained in the original project file, the beat officers were able to reclaim the neighborhood and reestablish a network of partnerships with the resident council, apartment managers, business people, and other city departments and government agencies. After renewed police concentration in the area, a new assessment of the crime problem revealed that crime and calls for service data for many of the targeted offenses had returned to the reduced levels achieved during the original intervention effort.

Still, some problems persisted. Commercial, residential, and vehicle burglaries continued to rise significantly, as did reports of prowlers. During the renewed intervention efforts, over 80 shots were fired in the area—a 453 percent increase over 1991 figures. Reports of family disturbances greatly exceeded their 1991 levels as well.

Some criminologists might view these increases as "random noise"—changes in criminal activity that occur routinely in economically deprived areas. However, another characterization might be that the increased crime levels for certain offenses reflect, at least to some degree, the reduction of police-citizen maintenance efforts in the area. This indicates that certain neighborhood conditions can lead to increased crime and disorder and thus demand greater maintenance for stakeholders. The police department must continue to explore ways to address these ongoing problems.

Maintaining the Initial Success

The Virginia Lake case study demonstrates a central truth about problem-oriented policing: law enforcement cannot engage in intensive crime control and prevention efforts and then become essentially inactive in a particular "hot spot." Problems once brought under control quickly can return. Therefore, law enforcement agencies must identify those areas and crime conditions where problems are prone to recur and implement the necessary mechanisms to sustain problem-solving efforts. To ensure a lasting impact, agencies should plan for a long-term approach when implementing community-oriented problem-solving responses.

Documenting Efforts

Law enforcement agencies should document their problem solving efforts using the SARA process. If possible, officers should computerize documentation, such as using automated databases for tracking and retrieving information by type, area, officer assigned, shift, and other factors. Keeping this important information readily accessible will help ensure that maintenance efforts will continue even if the personnel involved in the original intervention effort are assigned elsewhere. Agency administrators should develop methods to periodically update the original project file. Information should include the names of new stakeholders, such as incoming apartment managers, as well as updated crime figures, and service call data for the targeted area. . .

Train All Personnel

Agencies should train all personnel—sworn and support—in COPPS methodologies and develop administrative systems to ensure that officers and supervisors understand the history and status of problems in the areas to which they are assigned. To accomplish this agencywide, commanders might consider posting, in a conspicuous place such as the patrol briefing room, a list of projects by area and officers involved.

Keep Other Agencies Involved

Administrators should also keep municipal agencies that took part in any initial intervention initiatives informed and involved in ongoing efforts to maintain an enhanced quality of life in the targeted area. The police departments in Newport News, Virginia, and San Diego, California, formed analysis advisory committees that serve as vehicles for monthly meetings between police and other government agencies to discuss and monitor ongoing problem-solving efforts.

Keep Stakeholders Informed

Likewise, administrators should ensure that beat officers keep concerned-citizens groups, landlord-tenant associations, business and neighborhood watches, and neighborhood advisory groups, informed about ongoing efforts in target areas. The continued involvement of such groups represents an essential element in any ongoing crime control effort.

Conclusion

Crime is a dynamic force. That is, it tends to respond and adapt to changing environments. Therefore, an effective response to crime also must be dynamic. When law enforcement agencies mobilize for a short-term blitz of activity directed at specific crime problems in particular neighborhoods, they often realize impressive results. But, without ongoing maintenance, conditions in troubled areas can quickly deteriorate to a level as bad, or worse, than those that originally precipitated the intervention.

Therefore, agencies should approach problem solving as a long-term commitment. After the initial intervention has reversed a downward spiral, law enforcement agencies should work to maintain reduced crime and fear levels by continuing to assess and respond to emerging problems. To do so, beat officers and administrators should maintain regular liaison with community leaders, business groups, and other municipal agencies. Law enforcement administrators should view the success of any initial problem-solving intervention effort not as the end of the agency's efforts in the targeted area, but as the beginning of a renewed and ongoing relationship.

References

H. Goldstein, *Problem-oriented Policing* (New York: McGraw-Hill, 1990).

J. Q. Wilson and G. Kelling, "The Police and Neighborhood Safety: Broken Windows," *The Atlantic Monthly*, March 1982, 29–38.

Reprinted from: Ronald W. Glensor and Kenneth J. Peak, "Lasting Impact: Maintaining Neighborhood Order." In FBI Law Enforcement Bulletin, 3, pp. 1–7. 1998 ✦

Part III

Street-Level Criminology: What the Police Need to Know About Crime

As indicated in Part I, one of the most promising developments in policing over the past two decades has been a problem-oriented approach. Attempting to develop more civil neighborhoods, police officers nationwide and abroad have experimented with a problem-solving process commonly known as S.A.R.A., (scanning, analysis, response, and assessment). This protocol involves, to the extent necessary and possible, other government agencies, local businesses, and the public.

Problem solving, as a daily practice of police, asks them to face the context of crime and its causes. This is not a simple task and requires new knowledge, skills, and abilities. It also means that officers need new tools and supporting technologies such as crime analysis and crime mapping.

The linchpin of effective crime control and prevention is knowledge—conducting a thorough *analysis* of problems (the second phase of the S.A.R.A. process). This approach is far different from the mere guesswork that often accompanied conventional police responses. Proper analysis demands a thorough examination of the prevalence and persistence of recurring crime, fear, and disorder. It also requires understanding the conditions that give rise to crime and the developing of long-term tailored responses. Thus, problem solving challenges officers to approach neighborhood concerns more like street-level criminologists and less like street-level bureaucrats.

Three elements must be present for a crime to occur: a victim, a motivated offender, and a location—or, to borrow terms from the reading by W. Spelman and J.E. Eck, "sitting ducks," "ravenous wolves," and "dens of iniquity," respectively. If just *one* of these three elements does not exist in a given situation, a crime cannot occur. These three elements, when conceptualized in the form of a "Problem Analysis Triangle" helps officers visualize their relationships and provides a more complete picture of the crime problem.

In the case of locations—termed "hot spots" in the second reading by M.E. Buerger, E.G. Cohn, and A.J. Petrosino—research has shown that relatively few places account for a high percentage of crime in any given jurisdiction. It is therefore important that officers focus their problem-solving efforts on those troublesome areas.

A few career criminals (commonly known as repeat offenders) also account for a high percentage of crime. The third reading of this section, by S.E. Martin and L.W. Sherman, describes the District of Columbia Metropolitan Police Department's proactive efforts to address their most active and dangerous chronic offenders. It presents the successes in identifying and incarcerating career criminals as well as the difficulties experienced in doing so.

We are also learning a great deal about victimization in general and repeat victimization in particular. Research suggests that past crimes are the best predictors of future criminal events. As with locations and offenders, a few victims appear prone to repeat victimization and also account for a high percentage of crime.

The fourth reading of this section, by R. Glensor, K. Peak, and M. Correia, presents information on repeat victimization and how the problem-solving process can assist officers with identifying it.

Crime prevention is another area of policing that is experiencing rapid change. Historically, police rarely thought about crime prevention outside of specialized programs that dealt with improved locks and bolts or neighborhood watch efforts. Problem solving compels the police to shift their focus to the context in which crime occurs—the physical, organizational, and social environments, which become vital to understanding and responding to crime conditions. The last two readings, by R. Taylor, A. Harrell and R. Clarke, illustrate the benefits of crime prevention through environmental design (CPTED) and the diffusing of situations for crime within the context of problem solving.

There is much for police to learn about crime and its conditions. The process of problem solving will guide officers through a proper analysis of the three elements of crime and their relationship to one another. By addressing multiple offenders, repeat victims, and recurring locations, officers can have a significant impact on crime, fear, and disorder in our communities. ◆

10

Sitting Ducks, Ravenous Wolves, and Helping Hands

New Approaches to Urban Policing

William Spelman
John E. Eck

Social problems of all kinds plague neighborhoods across the nation. Until recently, there was little that our traditionally reactive, incident-driven criminal justice system could do to diminish crime and our fear of it. In more than two decades of research, however, problem-oriented policing has been shown to be more effective than merely throwing more resources at the problem. W. Spelman and J. Eck discuss the three elements that are necessary in order for a crime to be committed and how the police must be able to assess neighborhood crime patterns in order to bring problems— and strategies for their solutions—into focus. With problem-oriented policing also comes the need to recognize that neighborhood problems are linked to other urban concerns; therefore, problem resolution requires a high degree of cooperation with outside agencies, the business sector, and the public. Also required is a change in the structure of the police department and in the role of the police. As you read, consider how, if vulnerable victims ("sitting ducks") are to deal effectively with offenders ("ravenous wolves"), the efforts of many people and agencies ("helping hands") might be linked in this new approach to urban policing.

Drug Dealers have taken over a park. Neighborhood residents, afraid to use the park, feel helpless. Foot patrols and drug raids fail to roust the dealers.

A city is hit with a rash of convenience store robberies. Stakeouts, fast response to robbery calls, and enhanced investigations lead to some arrests—but do not solve the robbery problem.

Disorderly kids invade a peaceful residential neighborhood. Although they have committed no serious crimes, they are noisy and unpredictable; some acts of vandalism have been reported. The kids are black and the residents white—and the police fear a racial incident.

Problems like these plague cities everywhere. Social incivilities, drug dealing and abuse, and violent crime hurt more than the immediate victims: they create fears among the rest of us. We wonder who will be next, but feel incapable of taking action.

Until recently, there was little the criminal justice system could do to help. Police continued to respond to calls for service, and attempted (usually without success) to arrest and punish the most serious criminals. Sometimes they tried to organize a neighborhood watch. But research conducted in the 1970s and early 1980s showed repeatedly that these strategies were severely limited in their effectiveness.

Since the mid-1980s, some innovative police departments have begun to test a new approach to these problems. This "problem-oriented" approach differs from the traditional methods in several ways:

- Police actively seek ways to prevent crime and better the quality of neighborhood life rather than simply react to calls for service and reported crimes.

- Police recognize that crime and disorder problems arise from a variety of conditions and that thorough analysis is needed before they can tailor effective responses to these conditions.

- Police understand that many crime and disorder problems stem from factors beyond the control of any single public or private agency. If these problems are to be solved, they must be attacked on many different fronts, with the police, other agencies, and the public "coproducing" neighborhood security.

Recent research shows that when police adopt a proactive stance, analyze local conditions, and recognize the value of coproduction in framing and implementing a response, they can reduce crime and fear of crime. This new approach has profound implications for the management and operations of police agencies, and for the relationship between the police and the communities they serve.

The Problem: The Incident-Driven Approach

Problem-oriented policing is the culmination of more than two decades of research into the nature of crime and the effectiveness of police response. Many strands of research led to the new approach, but three basic findings were particularly important:

- Additional police resources, if applied in response to individual incidents of crime and disorder, will be ineffective at controlling crime.

- Few incidents are isolated; most are symptoms of some recurring, underlying problem. Problem analysis can help police develop effective, proactive tactics.

- Crime problems are integrally linked to other urban problems, and so the most effective responses require coordinating the activities of private citizens, the business sector, and government agencies outside the criminal justice system.

In short, "incident-driven policing," the prevailing method of delivering police services, consistently treats symptoms, not diseases. By working with others to identify, analyze, and treat the diseases, police can hope to make headway against crime and disorder.

Adding Police Resources Will Be Ineffective

Most police work is reactive—a response to crimes and disorders reported by the public. And current reactive tactics may be effective at controlling crime, to a point. For example, by maintaining some threat of apprehension and punishment, current police actions may deter many would-be offenders.[1]

Nevertheless, twenty years of research into police operations suggest that the marginal value of additional police resources, if applied in the traditional, reactive ways, will be very small.[2] For example, preventive patrol tactics probably will not deter offenders unless the patrol force can be increased dramatically—perhaps by a factor of thirty or more.[3] Only 10 percent of crimes are reported to the police within five minutes of their being committed; thus even the fastest police response to the scene will not result in apprehension of a suspect for the vast majority of crimes.[4] And case solution rates are low because detectives rarely have many leads to work with; even if the number of detectives could be doubled or tripled, it would have virtually no effect on the number of cases solved.[5]

Research has also revealed that alternative deployment methods—split force, investigative case screening, differential response to calls—can succeed in shifting scarce resources to those incidents where they are most needed.[6] In the cases studied, these schemes, often directed by crime analysis, made police operations more efficient and freed up resources for other activities. But they did not make operations more effective.

Crime Analysis Can Lead to More Effective Tactics

Three elements must generally be present before a crime will be committed: someone must be motivated to commit the crime; a suitable target must be present; and the target must be (relatively) unguarded, providing the offender with an opportunity to commit the crime.[7] These elements are more likely to be present at some times and places than at others, forming crime patterns and recurring crime problems. The removal of just one of the elements can alter a crime pattern. Thus, by identifying the elements that are easiest to remove and working to remove them, police can make crime prevention tactics more efficient and effective.

The most obvious crime patterns are spatial. Since the 1930s, researchers have shown that crime types and offender methods of operation—not to mention gross crime rates—differed substantially among neighborhoods.[8] One reason for these differences is that some kinds of neighborhoods have fewer unguarded targets than others. For example, neighborhoods with diverse land uses, single-family houses and garden apartment buildings, and intense street lighting provide criminals with fewer opportunities and incur lower crime rates.[9] Social characteristics such as residential stability, homogeneity of lifestyle, and family orientation empower residents of a neighborhood to "handle" bad actors without calling the police.[10]

Another reason crime rates differ between neighborhoods is that some areas have more potential offenders and victims than others. Adolescents, the poor, and members of minority groups commit property crimes at higher rates. Also, poor youths have few sources of transportation, so it is not surprising that burglary and robbery rates are highest in neighborhoods with many poor Black and Hispanic youths. Some neighborhoods attract more than their share of offenders because open-air drug markets or bars that cater to the especially rowdy or criminal are located there. Potential victims who have the money to do so can make themselves unattractive to offenders by keeping valuables in safe deposit boxes or safes, garaging their cars, and buying houses with sturdy locks and alarms.

Thus neighborhood crime patterns differ in predictable ways, for comprehensible reasons. The implications for crime prevention policies are obvious: if our aim is to reduce the crime rate in a given neighborhood, it is clearly important to know what crimes are committed there, and what might be done either to reduce the number of available offenders or victims or to increase the number of willing and able guardians. Since neighborhoods differ, the best crime prevention strategies will differ from one neighborhood to the next. Officers assigned to an area must study the social and physical conditions there before developing and implementing strategies.

These strategies are given a focus by one regularity that seems to hold for crime problems in all neighborhoods: crime is concentrated. Suppose we took all the criminals active in a community and lined them up in order of the frequency with which they committed crimes. Those who committed crimes most often would go to the head of the line; those who committed crimes only occasionally would go to the end. If all offenders were alike, then it would not matter much where we lined the offenders up; the offenders at the front of the line would commit about as many crimes as those at the end. For example, the "worst" 10 percent of criminals would account for about 10 percent of all crimes. But if there were significant differences among offenders, those at the head of the line would account for far more than their share of all crimes committed; the worst 10 percent would account for much more than 10 percent of all crimes. Analysis of arrest records and offender interviews shows that offenders differ substantially, and that the worst 10 percent of criminals commit about 55 percent of the crimes (see figure 10.1).[11]

The same principle applies to victims and places. A few particularly vulnerable people run risks of victimization that are much higher than average—the most vulnerable 10 percent of victims are involved in about 40 percent of all crimes.[12] And over 60 percent of crimes are committed at a few particularly dangerous locations.[13] Research suggests that there are usually good reasons why these offenders, victims, and locations account for so many crimes. If something can be done about these "ravenous wolves," "sitting ducks," and "dens of iniquity," the crime problem can, in theory, be reduced dramatically.

This is all the more true because current police policies systematically overlook the most crime-prone people and places. For example, until recently, police gave little attention to cases of family violence—even though

Figure 10-1
Ducks, Wolves, and Dens: Crime Is Concentrated

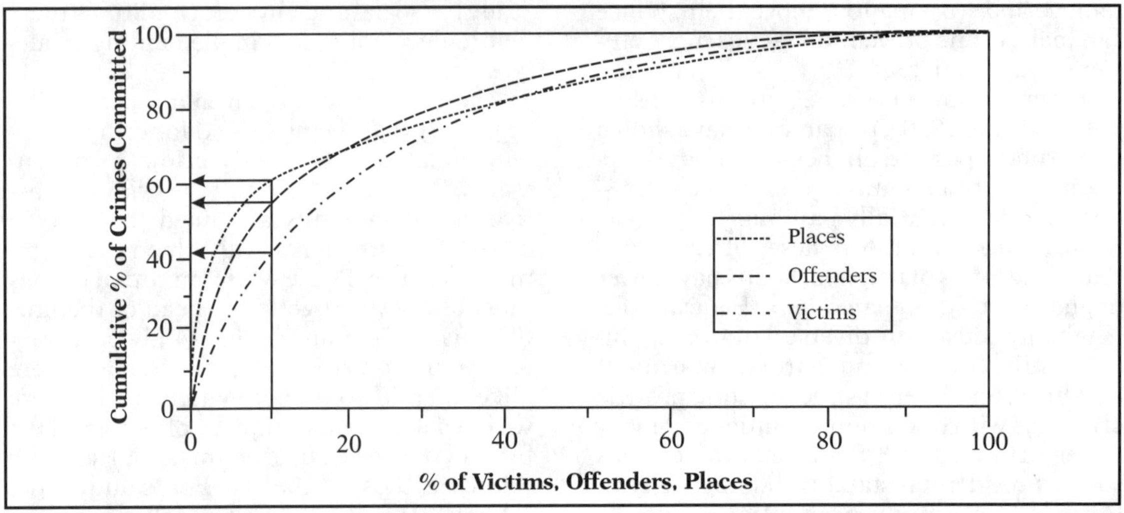

abused family members suffer particularly high risks of being abused again.[14] If repeat calls to a single location are made at different times of the day, they will be distributed over several shifts; thus even the beat officers may not recognize the continuing nature of the problem. The most frequent offenders are also the most successful at evading arrest.[15]

These concentrations of crimes among victims, locations, and offenders are important handles for proactive crime-prevention activity. They are the "problems" that are the focus of problem-oriented policing. Government and private agencies have mounted a wide variety of programs aimed at preventing these most predictable of crimes. For example, police, prosecutors, judges, and patrols boards have adopted programs and policies aimed at deterrence and incapacitation of frequent, serious offenders.[16] Especially vulnerable people—abused spouses and children, the elderly, the mentally disabled—have been the subject of many recent crime prevention efforts. Through directed patrols[17] and environmental and situational crime prevention,[18] police and other agencies have begun to deal with crime-prone locations as well.

But because the nature of these concentrations is different for every problem, standardized responses will not generally succeed. Previous experience can be a guide, but

police must study and create a somewhat different response for each problem they take on.

Neighborhood Problems Are Linked to Other Urban Problems

Knowing whether a given crime or disorder problem results from frequent offenders, high-risk victims, vulnerable locations, or some combination of the three may be helpful, but it is often insufficient to allow the police to identify a workable solution. To solve many problems, the police need the help of outside agencies, the business sector, or the public.

Often this cooperation is necessary because the police lack the authority to remove the offending conditions. If a rowdy bar produces many assaults, it can be closed down—by the state alcoholic beverage control board. If a blind corner produces many automobile accidents, a stop light can be installed—by the city traffic department. If a woman is continually beaten by her husband, she can move out—by her own volition, perhaps with the assistance of a battered women's shelter; the police cannot force her to do so, however.

Perhaps a more important reason for cooperative solutions is that recurring problems have many parts, and no single agency is responsible for all of them. A run-down apartment complex may look like a serious burglary problem to the police. But the fire department sees burnt-out, vacant apartments and a high risk of fire. The housing department sees code violations and the health department sees an abundance of trash and rats. The bank sees a bad risk and refuses to loan the apartment owner the money needed to renovate the vacant apartments taken over by the drug addicts who commit the burglaries. The residents, beset on all sides, see no hope—they cannot afford cleaner and safer housing.

Clearly, no single agency will be able to solve this problem, because the various parts feed off one another. On the other hand, if all the parts could be addressed at the same time, it is possible that the conditions could be removed and the problem solved. This would require the cooperation of the police, fire, housing, and health departments, the bank, and the apartment owner. It might also require the help of the residents, to ensure that the appropriate agencies are notified should the problems start to return.

There is evidence that citizens in particular "coproduce" crime control with public agencies. In addition to cooperating with the police and pressuring public and private agencies to deliver the goods and services the neighborhood needs, citizens sometimes intervene directly in disorderly or criminal incidents. Although some experts maintain that these informal interventions are the most important determinants of a neighborhood's crime rate, they are difficult to maintain in high-crime areas. The physical design of urban neighborhoods—public housing, in particular—discourages surveillance and intervention by neighbors.[19] Often the residents of these poor neighborhoods are fearful of cooperating with the police; they have little in common with one another, they do not expect to stay long; and they do not even recognize one another. These characteristics make it hard for neighbors to control the minor disorders that may contribute to crime. When families are headed by single parents who must work, parents may not even be able to control their own children.[20] On the other hand, the physical and social environment of high-crime neighborhoods can be improved by governments and businesses, in turn in-

creasing the prospects for intervention and cooperation.

All this suggests that crime prevention strategies are incomplete and possibly ineffective unless they recognize the close links between crime, the physical environment, neighborhood culture, and other factors. In general, these links require that the public and outside agencies work with the police to eliminate or ameliorate the conditions that cause the problem.

A Solution: Problem-Oriented Policing

Police could be more effective if they reduced their reliance on traditional methods and instead relied on tailor-made responses that coordinate the activities of people and agencies both inside and outside the criminal justice system. How would such a police department work? How would it be structured? How well would it control crime and disorder? The problem-oriented approach is new, but the experiences of innovative departments suggest some intriguing answers.

Designing Problem-Oriented Policing

The heart of problem-oriented policing is systematic thinking. Although problem solving has been conducted in very different ways in different departments, the most methodical approach has been adopted in Newport News, Virginia.

The Newport News Police Department based its problem-solving system on three principles. First, officers of all ranks, from all units, should be able to use the procedures as part of their daily routine. Second, the system must encourage officers to collect information from a broad range of sources and not limit themselves to conventional police data. Finally, the system should encourage "coproduction" solutions not limited to the criminal justice process.

After several months of work, a department task force developed a problem-solving process that fit these criteria. It consists of four parts:

- Scanning. As part of their daily routine, officers are expected to look for possible problems.

- Analysis. Officers then collect information about the problem. They rely on a Problem Analysis Guide, developed by the task force, which directs officers to examine offenders, victims, the social and physical environment, and previous responses to the problem. The goal is to understand the scope, nature, and causes of the problem.

- Response. The knowledge gained in the analysis stage is then used to develop and implement solutions. Officers seek the assistance of other police units, public and private organizations, and anyone else who can help.

- Assessment. Finally, officers evaluate the effectiveness of their response. They may use the results to revise the response, collect more data, or even redefine the problem.

Newport News's systematic process has since been adopted by other agencies interested in problem solving, including San Diego, Tulsa, Madison, and New York City. Similar approaches have been adopted, although less explicitly, by other police agencies that have experimented with problem-oriented policing.

Problem Solving in Practice

Since the early 1980s, police agencies have applied the problem-solving approach to a wide variety of problems. To illustrate the breadth of problems and solutions that are possible, three case studies are described here. The first two are serious and complex problems—one affecting a residential neighborhood, the other an entire city—that succumbed to careful analysis and comprehensive responses. The third case is an apparently difficult neighborhood problem that was solved in only a few hours through careful observation and a little thought.

New York Retirees Sting Drug Dealers. When out-of-towners think of New York City, they think first of the Empire State Building, Wall Street, and Broadway—the glitz and glitter of Manhattan. But New Yorkers tend to think first of districts like Sunset Park in Brooklyn, a neighborhood of row houses and small businesses peopled by a mix of work-

ing- and middle-class Irish, Italians, Puerto Ricans, and Blacks. Contrary to the national stereotype, Sunset Park is clean. Many streets are lined with trees. The district is dotted with vest-pocket parks containing such amenities as handball and basketball courts for the vigorous, sandboxes and swings for the young, and sunny benches for the relaxed.

Despite these amenities, for years the neighborhood park at the corner of 49th Street and 5th Avenue had lured only drug users looking for a quick score. Respectable residents avoided the park, fearing confrontations with the drug traffickers. The New York Police Department tried to respond to the problem, directing its officers to patrol the park and issue loitering citations to apparent dealers. This dispersed the dealers and users—until the patrol car had turned the corner and disappeared from view. Then business returned to normal. Not surprisingly, the problem persisted.

In May 1986, Officer Vinny Esposito was assigned to the 49th Street beat. As one of the first members of New York's innovative Community Patrol Officer Program (CPOP), Esposito was expected to do more than just handle individual incidents on his beat. His job was to identify and solve recurring problems. The drug-ridden 49th Street park clearly fit the bill, and Esposito went to work.

At first, Esposito used the old tactics. He spent as much time in the park as he could, dispersing dealers and making arrests whenever possible. Unfortunately, his beat was large and the time he could spend in the park was limited. Worse yet, every arrest took him away from the park for an hour or more—and whenever he left, the junkies returned. Weeks passed with no apparent effect on the drug trade. Esposito considered the problem further, and decided to take a different tack.

He began by recognizing that loitering citations and even drug arrests were at worst minor inconveniences to the dealers and users, since few arrests led to jail or prison terms. On the other hand, Esposito reasoned, the threat of losing hundreds or thousands of dollars worth of drugs could be a serious deterrent. Dealers, recognizing their vulnerability in the event of a police field stop, typically hid their stashes in the park. Esposito could seize the dope if he knew where it was hidden, but that required the assistance of local residents.

Esposito held meetings of the tenants in the apartment buildings that overlooked the park. Many tenants were elderly and spent most of their days at home. Esposito asked them to watch the dealers from their windows and report the locations of any drug stashes they saw to the local precinct station. Reassured that their tips would remain completely anonymous, the frustrated tenants readily agreed to help.

Calls began coming in. For each one, a CPOP officer at the precinct station took down the information and radioed the location of the stash to Officer Esposito, who then confiscated the drugs and took them to the station. Within twenty minutes of each tip, Esposito was back on the beat and the dealers were a little bit poorer.

This new strategy had several effects. Some dealers found themselves having to explain to unsympathetic suppliers where their goods had gone. Others began keeping their stashes on their person, making them more vulnerable to arrest. Others simply quit the park. Within one month, all the dealers had gotten the message, and the park was free of drugs.

Today, the park is a different place. Children play on the swings, youths play basketball. Many of the older residents who once sat at home, phoning in anonymous tips, now spend their days sunning themselves on the benches of "their" park. They show no signs of giving it back to the dealers.

The actions taken by Officer Esposito and local residents may not work as well anywhere else. But the thinking that led to their actions can. Like the Sunset Park case, many persistent problems affect residents of small neighborhoods the most. As Officer Esposito's actions illustrate, these problems can often be solved with the resident's help. But other such problems are not restricted to small localities—they affect residents throughout the city. For problems like these, citywide changes in policies and practices are necessary. Sometimes there is a citywide "community of interest" that can be relied

upon to assist the police in much the same way that the elderly residents of Sunset Park helped clear the drug dealers out of their vest-pocket park. Merchant associations, chain retail stores, and citywide community groups may all be of assistance. Even when these communities are uncooperative, however, the police may still be able to solve the problem.

Gainesville Puts the Brakes on QuikStop Crime. When the university town of Gainesville, Florida, was hit with a rash of convenience store robberies in spring 1985, the police recognized that they were dealing with more than just a series of unrelated incidents. The department's crime analysts expected to find that one or two repeat offenders were responsible for the robberies, but suspect descriptions provided by the victims proved otherwise—many different offenders were responsible. Word had apparently spread that convenience stores were an easy target. Police Chief Wayland Clifton, Jr., wondered why, and detailed several members of his department to find out.[21]

Gainesville police officers compared the stores that were robbed to others that were not. Their conclusions were revealing. Many of the stores that had been robbed had posted large advertisements in their front windows, blocking the view from the street. Often, the checkout stand could not be seen by a passing car or pedestrian. Many stores failed to light their parking lots, further limiting visibility. Others kept large sums of money in the cash register, and some provided only one inexperienced employee during the late night hours. The stores that had not been robbed tended to provide better visibility, limit the amount of cash in the register, and train their employees in crime prevention techniques. Thus the criminals seemed to be focusing on the most lucrative and vulnerable targets.

To confirm their findings, the Gainesville Police arranged for a psychologist at a local university to interview sixtyfive offenders who were serving sentences for convenience store robberies. This independent analysis provided even clearer results: would-be robbers avoided stores staffed by two clerks. Many of the robbers were simply taking advantage of available opportunities; if they had had trouble finding stores with only one clerk on duty, many of the robberies might never have been committed at all.

The police department presented these findings to an association of local merchants that had been established to develop a response to the problem. The police asked for a commitment to change the conditions that made robberies easy to commit. They were disappointed: the merchants felt that the solution lay in more frequent police patrols, and they refused to agree to voluntary crime prevention standards. In effect, the merchants argued that the costs of convenience store crime prevention should be borne by the public as a whole rather than by the stores themselves.

Chief Clifton knew that he could not stop the robberies with police presence unless he assigned his officers to stand guard at every convenience store in the city. Instead, he directed his officers to search for another way of mandating crime prevention measures. Their research revealed that the cities of Akron, Ohio, and Coral Gables, Florida, had passed ordinances requiring merchants to take certain crime prevention measures, and that these ordinances had reduced the incidence of robbery. Clifton and his officers began drafting such an ordinance for Gainesville.

By the summer of 1986, the department was ready to present its findings to the City Commission. The proposed ordinance would require convenience stores to remove window advertising, place cash registers in full view of the street, install security cameras and outside lighting, and limit the amount of cash available in the register. Most important, it would require two or more employees, trained in crime prevention techniques, to work late at night. In July, the City Commission overruled the objections of the convenience store owners and passed the ordinance.

The stores fought the ordinance in court, arguing that the crime prevention measures would be costly and ineffective. But the judge found the police department's research to be persuasive. The store owners' injunction was denied, and the ordinance took effect on schedule.

The first year after the adoption of the new ordinance brought encouraging results: con-venience store robberies were down by 65 percent overall, and by 75 percent at night. Best of all, the robbery rate was reduced far below its pre-1985 levels. Convenience stores continue to do a land–office business in Gainesville, and many store owners now admit—a bit grudgingly—that the police department's citywide approach has solved a difficult problem.

Persistent problems are natural targets of problem solving. It is easy to see how time-consuming research and complex crime prevention measures can be worth the effort if they will help to remove a longstanding problem. But many crime and disorder problems are temporary and nagging, rather than persistent and severe; they do not merit lengthy analysis and complicated responses. Still, thinking systematically about even a minor problem can often reveal quick solutions that are easy to implement.

Newport News Skates out of Trouble. The quiet nights of a middle-class Newport News neighborhood were spoiled when groups of rowdy teenagers began to frequent the area on Fridays and Saturdays. There had been no violence, and the kids' primary offenses were loud music, horseplay, and occasional vandalism. But residents felt the teenagers were unpredictable, particularly since they came from the city's mostly Black southeast side, several miles away. The neighborhood became a regular stop for officers working the evening shift.

Sergeant Jim Hogan recognized that responding to these calls took time but accomplished little except to irritate everyone involved. One Friday night he asked the beat officer, Paul Summerfield, to look into the problem and develop a better solution.

Summerfield suspected that the source of the problem might be a roller skating rink. The rink had been trying to increase business by offering reduced rates and transportation on Friday and Saturday nights. As he drove north toward the rink later that night, Summerfield saw several large groups of youths walking south. Other kids were still hanging around the rink, which had closed shortly before. Summerfield talked to several of them and found that they were waiting for a bus. The others, he was told, had become impatient and begun the three-mile walk home. Then Summerfield talked to the rink owner. The owner told him he had leased the bus to pick up and drop off kids who lived far from the rink. But he said there were always more kids needing rides at the end of the night than the bus had picked up earlier.

When Officer Summerfield returned to the skating rink early the next evening, he saw about fifty youngsters get out of the bus rented by the skating rink. But he saw others get out of the public transit buses that stopped running at midnight, and he saw parents in pajamas drop their kids off, then turn around and go home. Clearly the rink's bus would be unable to take home all the kids who would be stranded at closing time.

Summerfield consulted Sergeant Hogan. They agreed that the skating rink owner should be asked to bus the kids home. Summerfield returned to the rink Monday and spoke with the owner. When informed of the size of the problem he had unwittingly created, the owner agreed to lease more buses. By the next weekend, the buses were in use and Summerfield and Hogan saw no kids walking home.

Elapsed time from problem identification to problem solution: one week. Resources used: about four hours of an officer's time. Results: fewer calls, happier kids, satisfied homeowners.

Institutionalizing Problem-Oriented Policing

Problem-oriented policing is a state of mind, not a program, technique, or procedure. Problem-solving procedures and analysis guides can be helpful, but only if they encourage clear-headed analysis of problems and an uninhibited search for solutions. Moreover, there are any number of ways of implementing the approach. The New York Police Department established a special unit to focus on neighborhood problems full time; in Newport News, all officers are obliged to spend some of their time identifying and working out problems. There is a place for problem solving in any agency's standard operating procedures. In the long run, however, it is likely that the problem-oriented approach will have its most dramatic impact on the management structure of American policing and on the relationship between the police, other city agencies, and the public.

Changes in Management Structure. As the case studies considered above suggest, crime and disorder problems are fundamentally local and specialized in nature. As a result, they are best analyzed and responded to on a case-by-case basis by the line officers and detectives assigned to the problem neighborhood or crime type. Implementing this approach will require changes in the centralized, control-oriented organizational structure and management style of most police agencies. Command staff and mid-level managers can structure problem-solving efforts by creating standard operating procedures, such as the problem-solving process created in Newport News. They can also encourage effective and innovative efforts by rewarding the officers who undertake them. But they cannot make the many individual decisions that are required to identify, analyze, and solve problems.

Inevitably, the changes in structure and style will affect line supervisors—sergeants—the most. Problem solving puts a dual burden on supervisors. On the one hand, they must make many of the tough, operational decisions: setting priorities among different problems, facilitating communication and cooperation with other divisions of the police department and outside agencies, and making sure their officers solve the problems they are assigned. On the other hand, sergeants must also provide leadership, encouraging creative analysis and response. As the sergeant's role shifts from taskmaster to team leader, police agencies must take greater care in selecting, training, and rewarding their line supervisors.

As the structure and style of police agencies change, managers must also shift their focus from internal management problems to the external problems of the public. When a few routine procedures such as preventive patrol, rapid response, and follow-up investigations formed the bulk of an agency's activity, the manager's job was mostly to remove barriers to efficient execution of these routines. Good managers streamlined administrative procedures and reduced paperwork;

they implemented new resource deployment schemes; they structured officer discretion.[22] They did not need to emphasize crime and disorder reduction, since crimes and disorders would presumably take care of themselves if the routines were implemented properly.

On the other hand, problem-solving activities are inherently nonroutine; it is far more important to choose the correct response from among many possibilities—to "do the right thing"—than it is to "do things right." Thus managers must shift their attention from internal efficiency measures to external effectiveness measures. And they must shift from global, city- and precinct-wide measures to carefully defined, problem-specific measures. Instead of citywide clearance and arrest rates, police must emphasize neighborhood crime rates; instead of counting the number of tickets written by all officers, they must count the number of auto accidents on particular stretches of road. Implicitly, police must recognize that problem-specific crime rates, accident rates, and the like are partly within their control. Whereas no agency can be held accountable for citywide crime and accident rates, police managers and officers must accept partial responsibility for conditions in their areas.

Changes in Police Role. Of course, crime, disorder, and other evils are only partly the responsibility of the police. As the three case studies illustrate, police cannot solve these problems by themselves; they need help from other public service agencies, the business community, and the public. The need to obtain cooperation and assistance from these "coproducers" of public safety requires that the role of the police agency must change.

One fundamental change will be in the autonomy of the police relative to other public service agencies. Urban bureaucracies are currently structured along functional lines— public works maintains roads and sewers, codes compliance ensures that building codes are met, and so on. But if urban problems are interrelated and concentrated, as the research and case studies presented above suggest, then these functional distinctions begin to blur. The activities of the public works, codes, and other departments affect

(and perhaps worsen) the problems of all the other departments, so at a minimum they must communicate to one another what they are doing about a problem and why. A more ambitious and effective strategy would be for them to develop and implement a common response. In the short run, each agency gives up some of its "turf"; in the long run, each agency saves itself a lot of work.

Problem-oriented police agencies have found that line personnel in other agencies can be "hidden allies," bending procedures to get the job done. For example, one police agency attempted to solve a recurring traffic accident problem at a blind corner by convincing the traffic engineer to install a stop sign. The engineer refused to comply until he had conducted his own study; unfortunately, many similar problems were already awaiting study, so the engineer would not be able to consider the corner for several months. Then a police officer discovered that the public works personnel who actually installed the signs could replace a missing or deteriorated sign within a few days, and that the roadworkers would be happy to install the "missing" stop sign. The work order was placed, and the sign was installed within a week. Now police officers in this jurisdiction regularly bypass the traffic engineer and deal directly with public works officials.

Hidden allies may help get the job done, but in the long run turf difficulties are best surmounted when top managers—city managers and department heads— recognize the value of a cooperative, problem-solving approach and urge their managers and line personnel to comply. This puts the onus on problem-oriented police administrators to educate and lobby their colleagues, running interference for their officers. As will be discussed later, such an education effort may ultimately result in substantial changes in the city bureaucracy.

Problem-oriented policing also requires that police take on a different role with regard to the public it serves. At present, police ask little more of citizens than that they report crimes, be good witnesses, and stand aside to let the professionals do their job. As with public service agencies, however, problem solving requires that the police and the public communicate and cooperate more frequently, on a wider variety of issues. In particular, problem-oriented police agencies recognize that citizens often know their problems more intimately than the police do, and that sometimes citizens know better what must be done.

This raises many difficult questions. Just as different public service agencies see different aspects of a problem, so do different groups of citizens. If there is no consensus among the community of interest as to the nature of the problem, but public cooperation is necessary to solve it, the police must play a role in forging this consensus. Few police agencies are well equipped for such essentially political activities.

The dilemma is even more serious when the conflict is of values, not just perceptions. Quiet residents of an urban neighborhood may see nothing wrong with police harassment of their rowdier neighbors; the rowdies may legitimately claim that they have the right to be raucous so long as they end their loud parties before midnight and do not threaten other residents. In dealing with such a problem, police must balance the rights and needs of the two groups. This is hardly new— police have always had to balance the goals of serving the majority while guarding the liberties of the minority. Because the problem-oriented approach encourages police to seek such difficult situations, however, they may find themselves making such tough choices more often. On the other hand, problem solving also emphasizes the power of information and cooperative action over the power of formal, unilateral authority. If police can develop a broader repertoire of solutions to conflicts like these, they may find that these tough choices are easier to make.

It remains to be seen how the limits on police authority will be set, but it is certain that problem solving will require a new consensus on the role, authority, and limitations of the police in each jurisdiction that adopts it.[23]

The Future: Beyond Problem-Oriented Policing

Problem-oriented policing is new. Traditional procedures die hard, problem solving methods are still under development, and no one knows for sure how successful the approach will be. As a result, no police agency has adopted the approach fully, and it will be a long time before many agencies do. On the other hand, problem-oriented policing is a realistic response to the limitations of traditional, incident-driven policing. It relies on our growing knowledge of the nature of crime and disorder, and it has been successful in a wide variety of police agencies, for a wide variety of urban crime and disorder problems. The problem-oriented approach seems to be where police work is going.

It also seems to be where other urban service agencies are going. Problem-oriented approaches have been implemented on an experimental basis in electric utilities [24] urban transit authorities,[25] and recreation and parks departments.[26] Over the next few years, it makes sense to expect dramatic growth in the use of problem-solving techniques not only in municipal policing but in other areas as well. It is likely, then, that problem-oriented police officers will find problem-oriented fire fighters, housing inspectors, and others to work with.

This seems to be the case in Madison, Wisconsin, where city agencies have been working on problem solving since 1984. The city has implemented a program of quality and productivity improvement, a form of problem solving originally developed in the private sector to improve the quality of manufactured goods. Project teams have been established within most city agencies, consisting of line personnel, supervisors, and managers, often working with a statistical consultant. They identify a recurring problem within their agency, usually an administrative bottleneck, and use methods successful in private industry to analyze and solve it.[27] Although most Madison city agencies have concentrated on administrative problems, some—including the Madison Police Department—are beginning to extend the methods to public problems. When Madison police officers take on a public problem, chances are they will find sympathetic and experienced problem solvers to work with in other agencies.

The growing use of problem-oriented approaches should help to reduce turf problems. As standard operating procedures become more flexible and decision making becomes decentralized, line officials may find that they owe as much allegiance to their colleagues from other agencies as they do to their own bureaucracies. One natural method of institutionalizing these developments would be to adopt a matrix organizational structure. Neighborhood teams, consisting of members of the police, fire, public works, and other departments, would work together on a formal basis to deliver urban services. Although full implementation of a matrix is a long way off, the foundation for such a structure has already been laid in New York City. All urban service agencies are decentralized into eighty-eight districts with identical boundaries; citizens participate in agency decision making through community boards, a permanent part of the city government structure.[28]

A central element of problem-oriented policing is that administrative arrangements are less important than the activities that line officers undertake. But just as the centralized, control-oriented police structure helped police administrators to institutionalize incident-driven policing, so might a decentralized, team-based matrix help city managers to institutionalize problem-oriented urban service provision.

Such an interagency team approach would also provide long-term benefits for the relationship between city government and the public. More problem solvers would be available, with different backgrounds, viewpoints, and opportunities for contact with the public; this would improve the chances of early identification and complete analysis of problems. Because they would report to different bureaucracies, members of problem-solving teams would act as a check on one another, reducing many of the potential dangers of community problem solving. Finally, the teams would provide a unified contact point for frustrated citizens who would otherwise be unable to negotiate their way through the city bureaucracy. If problem-solving teams can be linked to community organizations, the opportunities for cooperative efforts would increase dramatically.

Such benefits, like the interagency team or matrix structure, are speculative. Problem-oriented policing is not. It provides a tested, practical approach for police agencies frustrated with putting Band-Aids on symptoms. By responding to recurring problems, and by working with other agencies, businesses, and the public whenever possible, innovative police agencies have begun to develop an effective strategy for reducing crime and other troubling conditions in our cities.

Notes

1. Philip J. Cook, "Research in Criminal Deterrence: Laying the Groundwork for the Second Decade," in *Crime and Justice: An Annual Review of Research*, vol. 4, ed. Michael Tonry and Norval Morris (Chicago: University of Chicago Press, 1980).

2. John E. Eck and William Spelman, *Problem Solving: Problem-Oriented Policing in Newport News* (Washington, D.C.: Police Executive Research Forum, 1987).

3. J. Schnelle, R. Kirchner, J. Casey, P. Uselton, and M. McNees, "Patrol Evaluation Research: A Multiple-Baseline Analysis of Saturation Police Patrolling During Day and Night Hours," *Journal of Applied Behavior Analysis* 10 (1976): 33–40; George L. Kelling, Tony Pate, Duane Dieckman and Charles E. Brown, *The Kansas City Preventive Patrol Experiment: A Technical Report* (Washington, D.C.: Police Foundation, 1974).

4. William Spelman and Dale K. Brown, *Calling the Police: Citizen Reporting of Serious Crime* (Washington, D.C.: U.S. Government Printing Office, 1984).

5. John E. Eck, *Solving Crimes: The Investigation of Burglary and Robbery* (Washington D.C.: Police Executive Research Forum, 1982); William Spelman, Michael Oshima, and George L. Kelling, *Crime Suppression and Traditional Police Tactics*, final report to the Florence V. Burden Foundation (Cambridge, Mass.: Program in Criminal Justice Policy and Management Harvard University, 1985).

6. James M. Tien, James A. Simon, and Richard C. Larson, *An Alternative Approach in Police Patrol: The Wilmington Split-Force Experiment* (Washington, D.C.: U.S. Government Printing Office, 1978); John E. Eck, Managing Case Assignments: *The Burglary Investigation*

Decision Model Replication (Washington, D.C.: Police Executive Research Forum, 1979); L. Thomas McEwen, Edward F. Connors, and Marcia I. Cohen, Evaluation of the Differential Police Response Field Test (Alexandria, Va.: Research Management Associates, 1984).

7. Lawrence E. Cohen and Marcus Felson, "Social Change and Crime Rate Trends: A Routine Activity Approach," *American Sociological Review* 44 (August 1979): 588–608.

8. For example, Clifford R. Shaw and Henry E. McKay, *Juvenile Delinquency and Urban Areas* (Chicago: University of Chicago Press, 1942); and Thomas A. Reppetto, *Residential Crime* (Cambridge, Mass.: Ballinger, 1974).

9. Jane Jacobs, *The Death and Life of Great American Cities* (New York: Vintage, 1961); Floyd J. Fowler, Jr., Mary Ellen McCalla, and Thomas W. Mangione, *Reducing Residential Crime and Fear: The Hartford Neighborhood Crime Prevention Program* (Washington, D.C.: U.S. Government Printing Office, 1979).

10. Stephanie W. Greenberg, William M. Rohe, and Jay R. Williams, *Safe and Secure Neighborhoods: Physical Characteristics and Informal Territorial Control in High and Low Crime Neighborhoods* (Washington, D.C.: U.S. Government Printing Office, 1984).

11. Alfred Blumstein, Jacqueline Cohen, Jeffrey A. Roth, and Christy A. Visher, *Criminal Careers and "Career Criminals,"* vol. 1 (Washington, D.C.: National Academy Press, 1986).

12. James F. Nelson, "Multiple Victimization in American Cities: A Statistical Analysis of Rare Events," *American Journal of Sociology* 85 (1980):870–91.

13. Glenn L. Pierce, Susan Spaar, and LeBaron R. Briggs, *The Character of Police Work: Strategic and Tactical Implications* (Boston: Center for Applied Social Research, Northeastern University, 1986); Lawrence W. Sherman, "Repeat Calls to Police in Minneapolis," in *Crime Control Reports Number 4* (Washington, D.C.: Crime Control Institute, 1987).

14. Albert J. Reiss, Jr., "Victim Proneness in Repeat Victimization by Type of Crime," in *Indicators of Crime and Criminal Justice: Quantitative Studies,* ed. Stephen E. Fienberg and Albert J. Reiss, Jr. (Washington, D.C.: U.S. Government Printing Office, 1980), pp. 41–53.

15. William Spelman, "The Incapacitation Benefits of Selective Criminal Justice Policies," Ph.D. diss., Harvard University, 1988.

16. Mark H. Moore, Susan R. Estrich, Daniel McGillis, and William Spelman, *Dangerous Offenders:*

The Elusive Target of Justice (Cambridge, Mass.: Harvard University Press, 1985).

17. Tien, Simon, and Larson, *Alternative Approach.*

18. C. Ray Jeffery, *Crime Prevention through Environmental Design* (Beverly Hills, Cal.: Sage, 1971); Ronald V. Clarke and Derek B. Cornish, "Modeling Offenders' Decisions: A Framework for Research and Policy," in *Crime and Justice: An Annual Review of Research,* vol. 6, ed. Michael Tonry and Norval Morris (Chicago: University of Chicago Press, 1985, pp. 147–85).

19. Oscar Newman, *Defensible Space: Crime Prevention through Urban Design* (New York: Macmillan, 1972).

20. Greenberg, Rohe, and Williams, *Safe and Secure Neighborhoods.*

21. Wayland Clifton, Jr., "Convenience Store Robberies in Gainesville, Florida: An Intervention Strategy by the Gainesville Police Department," report by the Gainesville Police Department, Gainesville, Florida, 1987.

22. Herman Goldstein, "Improving Policing: A Problem-Oriented Approach," *Crime and Delinquency* 25 (April 1979): 236–58.

23. Herman Goldstein, "Toward Community-Oriented Policing: Potential Basic Requirements and Threshold Questions," *Crime and Delinquency* 33 (January 1986): 1–30.

24. John Francis Hird, "An Electric Utility," in *Out of the Crisis,* ed. W. Edwards Deming (Cambridge, Mass.: Center for Advanced Engineering Study, Massachusetts Institute of Technology, 1986).

25. Harvey J. Brightman, *Group Problem Solving: An Improved Managerial Approach* (Atlanta: Business Publishing Division, College of Business Administration, Georgia State University, 1988).

26. Joseph J. Bannon, *Problem Solving in Recreation and Parks* (Englewood Cliffs, N.J.: Prentice-Hall, 1972).

27. William Hunter, Jan O'Neill, and Carol Wallen, *Doing More with Less in the Public Sector: A Progress Report from Madison, Wisconsin,* report no. 13 (Madison: Center for Quality and Productivity Improvement, College of Engineering, University of Wisconsin, 1986).

28. John Mudd, *Neighborhood Services* (New Haven, Conn.: Yale University Press, 1984).

11

Defining the Hot Spots of Crime

Operationalizing Theoretical Concepts for Field Research

Michael E. Buerger
Ellen G. Cohn
Anthony J. Petrosino

If crime is to be effectively addressed, certainly the concept of place must be understood by the police and the public. The "hot spots of crime" must be determined in order that the police may deter offending and disorderly behavior. The police must also try to appropriate what is known about the hot spots of crime from their theoretical, computerized depictions and translate that knowledge onto the streets, where fluid conditions make field operations and observations difficult. M.E. Buerger, E.G. Cohn, and A.J. Petrosino analyze how an experiment in Minneapolis focused police presence on hot spots of crime by identifying the smaller places where crime was concentrated, testing the deterrent power of police presence. Several issues, including mapping, public space versus private property, intersections, and the general concept of police presence, had to be addressed and understood in order for the experiment to unfold properly. As you read, consider whether the authors also demonstrate that researchers and officers can combine their skills and abilities in order to effect day-to-day responses to crime and disorder.

The Hot Spots of Crime Experiment (Hereafter referred to as Hot Spots) suggests that there are at least three different points of decision at which abstract concepts of space ("location," "place," or slightly larger aggre-

gates like hot spots) must be negotiated in operational terms: (1) in the nature of the *human techniques and practices* that assign activities to particular addresses in official records; (2) in the attribution of *public space* (which has no "address") *to private property* (which has, or is, an address); and (3) in the conflict over *the nature of boundaries*, which are distinct and discrete in computerized representations but invisible and fluid under conditions of field operations and observations. Of the three, the first is relatively minor and manageable once the patterns are recognized; it is the latter two that pose the greatest difficulty for research. This paper identifies the issues, as well as the debates and their resolutions, that bore on the manner in which the hot spots were ultimately defined and selected.

Introduction

A researcher-practitioner split is widely lamented in conversation but barely acknowledged in the criminological literature. The theoretical questions that motivate researches are of little practical value to those engaged in the day-to-day response to criminal and disorderly behavior, particularly street cops. Aggregate data are required to answer the sociological questions that dominate the criminological portions of criminal justice research, but the data (and even the questions addressed to them) are so attenuated from the legal, social and personal realities of street encounters that they have little bearing on policy—and almost none on practice. Even viewed in their most positive light, these data produce few insights or innovations useful for the patrol officers who must intervene in and resolve individual events.

That "cops are concrete thinkers; they want to be told what to *do*" is a constant management problem recognized by police supervisors from the rank of chief down to that of sergeant. The processes of transforming written policy into onstreet practice are difficult in any police agency, and they are enormously compounded when trying to operationalize the requirements of a social science field experiment in which the agency is participating.

The Hot Spots of Crime Experiment provides one case study in which both dilemmas are present. It was devised to answer a broad sociological question: Does the presence of formal guardianship (represented by the police) deter offending and disorderly behavior? The research was dominated by the demands of experimental design, which required concessions that may have diluted program effects.[1] Hot Spots, which would limit the patrol officers' traditional control over their daily work activities, presented a special set of challenges in transforming theoretical concepts into operational terms.

The Hot Spots Experiment

On December 1, 1988, patrol officers of the Minneapolis (MN) Police Department began a yearlong experiment testing the effect of police presence on crime. Unlike the Kansas City Preventive Patrol Experiment's attempt to create "omnipresence" (Kelling et al., 1974), the Minneapolis experiment focused the police presence in small, tightly defined geographical areas, or "hot spots" of crime. Hot Spots was an experiment that tested the deterrent power of police presence. Its underlying premise was that the Kansas City experiment squandered the availability of police presence by distributing it sporadically throughout large areas where no crime occurred (and thus where none could be deterred). Hot Spots would correct that flaw by identifying the smaller places where crime was concentrated, and focusing police presence there. The experimental design also made corrections for several other shortcomings of the Kansas City study, such as a lack of statistical power and the inability to document true differences in police presence among the beats (Sherman and Weisburd, 1995).[2]

The Hot Spots experiment hypothesized that an increase in the degree of formal public guardianship that was consistent over time—represented by the visible presence of a police officer or officers, without regard to their specific activities—would be sufficient to change the ecological profile of a given place in a positive fashion, reducing the incidence of crime and disorder. This paper examines the Hot-Spot experiment's conceptualization and operationalization of the unit of analysis, the "place."

Mapping the Hot Spots

Drawing upon a distinction between predatory street crime and mere public disorder—"hard" and "soft" crime, respectively—first articulated by Reiss (1985), Sherman and Weisburd describe the process of creating a "hot spot" thus:

> We defined hot spots operationally as small clusters of addresses with frequent 'hard' crime call activity, which also had substantial 'soft' crime calls for service. . . . We then limited the boundaries of each spot conceptually as being easily visible from an epicenter. . . .
>
> . . . A computer mapping program, MAP-INFO, was then employed to locate most of the addresses, so that visual inspection of the computer printouts for each map grid could identify what appeared to be visually connected clusters of these addresses. . . .

All 420 clusters with 20 or more total hard crime calls were inspected by field staff. The inspections had three principle goals. One goal was to reconfigure the boundaries suggested by the computer map, in order to be more consistent with the visual contact definition. The second was to determine whether the type of premises at each address was eligible. In order to limit the sample to places where crime occurred in public and could reasonably be deterred by police presence, we decided to exclude all residential and most commercial buildings over 4 stories (including two hotels), almost all parking garages, department stores and indoor malls, public schools, office buildings, and residential social service institutions (such as homeless shelters). Parks were also excluded because they have their own police. Finally, a few "magnet phone" locations, at which events occurring elsewhere are routinely reported, were excluded.[3]

The third goal was to determine the visual proximity between the clusters, and the possible contamination of each site by patrol car presence in the next closest site. . .The general principles of their re-configurations were these:

1. No hot spot is more than one standard linear street block.

2. No hot spot extends for more than half a block from either side of an intersection.

3. No hot spot is within one standard linear block of another hot spot.

The field inspections were also essential for correcting the errors of the computer mapping program in locating the street addresses in relation to each other. (Sherman and Weisburd, 1988)

These principles were supplemented by a short series of operational refinements directed toward field workers:

When you check the hot spots, please look for:

1)   visual contact (i.e., addresses that should be added or subtracted); and,

2)   likelihood that most activity will not be deterred by police patrol (i.e., most crime occurs indoors—and does not depend on access).

Hot Spot Rules:

1)   All addresses should be visible from one central point.

2)   If you have an intersection you may go 1/2 an average block

3)   You may include two intersections in a hot spot only if you do not go down other streets from the intersection (Sherman Weisburd, 1988).

These rules were the bare bones of the field inspections, which raised a number of questions unanticipated when the original definitions for hot spots were devised.

The Process

A research database was constructed from an archive database of Minneapolis 911 calls maintained by the Crime Control Institute, and each eligible record was coded as hard or soft crime. From the smaller, crime-only database, the MapInfo software package produced clusters of hard crime calls. From 420 potential sites, 110 hot spots were selected and randomly divided into two treatments groups: 55 police presence sites and 55 control sites.

Each of the final 110 sites had to be mapped for the benefit of the police officers covering the patrol hot spots, and for the observers who would be recording the police presence in all of the sites. Where the MapInfo maps plotted only addresses contributing hard crimes, the operational maps were more detailed, containing building "footprints," text descriptions of each property, and identification of the major call-generating addresses (to focus the observers' attention on critical areas). These "footprint maps" would define for both groups of participants the boundaries of each hot spot, with corresponding implications for dosage measurement. Creating the maps in essence saying "this address is part of the hot spot, this one is not"—brought into sharp focus several issues that had been raised but not resolved during the selection phase.

Issues of Definition

Transforming hot spots from statistical constructs to two- and three-dimensional spatial entities introduces several new considerations. Calls archived in the 911 database are attributed primarily to single addresses clearly defined by property lines: the database had no capacity to define public space other than intersections.[4] Permanent and temporary obstructions interfere with visual and sometimes aural perception of activity. The nature of what constitutes "one block" varies, occasionally creating issues of artificial censoring of logical areas. Human variation in perceptions, definitions and behaviors (particularly the ways in which they mobilize the police) have wide-ranging influence in defining logical hot spots (those reflecting human activity patterns rather than statistically compiled reporting patterns).

1. The Issue of Public Space

Most hot spots contain a fairly well-defined "public space," consisting of front yards, sidewalks and the street. However, the majority of residential blocks in Minneapolis are split down the middle by an alleyway, which provides access to rear entrances and parking areas, including garages. Sherman and Weisburd's definition "failed to solve the problem of crimes occurring at rear entrances to addresses listed in the data," but that problem also afflicts the "night-time sight and sound" definition (1988:14).

For all but the most arcane constructions, though, no more than two sides of a building can be seen from any given position on the street or alleyway. In multiple-building configurations, each building obscures part of an observer's view of the next building in most perspectives. There are other semipermanent visual obstructions: trees, shrubs, fences and parked vehicles of varying sizes create an everchanging visual screen that obscures parts of the hot spot. Defining perimeter boundaries had to be done within those limitations, concentrating on the public areas of the streets and fronts of the buildings as the most frequent and logical areas of interaction, and thus of observation. The standard hot spot configuration was that of the linear block, with the "plus-sign" shape of a four-way intersection constituting a strong secondary category.

Except for a handful of idiosyncratic areas (around lakes, the Mississippi River or freeway interchanges), Minneapolis is laid out in a grid pattern. In most residential neighborhoods, the blocks are rectangular: the east-west block sides ("top" and "bottom") are half the length of the north-south block sides. In this context, a hot spot could extend outward along the eastwest axis to include all of the block top (or bottom) to the next intersection in both directions, and contain the same physical dimensions as the "half a block" length pertinent to the longer north-south sides. In some cases, strict adherence to the rule conflicted with a logical sense of the spot under consideration. In most instances, such conflicts were resolved by constructing the boundaries to conform with the social sense of the place under consideration, regardless of what might be permitted under the rules (in some cases, constriction was necessary to preserve the remainder of the hot spot from visual contamination by another nearby site).

The first operational question is what buildings (addresses) constitute a hot spot. The two primary alternatives are to include: (1) just the buildings contributing calls to the analysis database, or (2) both contributing addresses and any noncontributing ones between them. A collateral question is whether to incorporate the noncontributing addresses on the opposite side of the street, in those sites where the contributing addresses are all on one side.[5]

If the hot spot is to be limited to one side of the street, there is a secondary issue of how to treat "street curtilage"—the large open area in front of the property lines where the police will actually be parked.[6] Though a fight in the middle of the street in front of a contributing addresses might not be considered "in" a one-sided hot spot, there are strong logical arguments for including it in the experiment.[7]

Beyond those considerations lies a more important one: where the crimes are being committed. If call activity reflects events occurring in the public space, the "night-time sight and sound" rationale suggests that the deleterious effects of the activity is felt throughout the area, and reporting patterns are largely a matter of happenstance. This argues for a more inclusive hot spot definition. But if the reported criminal activity is primarily occurring inside private space, behind closed doors, there would be no need to include anything more than the handful of addresses that define the statistical hot spots.

That question was keenest in the candidate sites that were primarily residential. Assault calls were coded as hard crime, and "hard crime" was essentially stranger-to-stranger predatory crime, according to Sherman and Weisburd's (1988) definition. However, independent observations indicated that anywhere from one-quarter to two-thirds of the assault calls in a given day were for domestic disputes between familiars and intimates, primarily inside their abode. Domestics were coded as soft crime, so the issue had implications for the process of hot-spot definition through artificial inflation of the hard crime numbers in certain residential areas.[8]

In Minneapolis, a preliminary examination of the call data to resolve the inside/outside issue was ruled out as too time consuming and expensive. Discussions of the problem brought out the point that the "common sense" view of policing—that police can deter activity only in the public spaces, and cannot affect what goes on inside—has no particular empirical basis, and should be open to testing. Accordingly, all Hot Spots decisions contained an assumption that the perpetrators of the crime would either be active within the public spaces or pass through them before committing crimes inside buildings. Even if the crime was domestic in nature (as in spousal assault), or occurred within the confines of buildings that housed both predator and victim (as certain burglaries were), the offender had to leave the building at intervals and would be sensitive to the activity of the neighborhood to some degree.

This "boundaries" question also carried a practical concern, one which helped to resolve the Minneapolis dilemma: police patrol had to be conducted somewhere within the public area. Officers had to walk within view of the buildings, and almost certainly would park their squad cars in locations where they would likely be seen from all sides. While statistical compilations could be limited to individual addresses, the dosage effect would be generalized to all buildings within the sight-and-sound definition. Those addresses would also reap the benefits of any deterrent effects of increased police presence, on the assumption that they were also at risk of victimization by dint of their proximity to the generating addresses.

Moreover, to conclude otherwise led in the direction of hairsplitting that could have been fatal to the operational side of the experiment. To be "in" their hot spot, officers had to be parked on the side of the street where the contributing-address buildings were, but they would be "out" of the hot spot if they parked across the street, equally in view but 20 feet farther away. That violated common sense—particularly as the police would define that commodity—and had the potential to alienate the majority of the patrol force from the experiment. It also artificially censored the deterrent effect the police presence might have on new arrivals in the non-contributing addresses. As a result, hot spots were deemed to include both sides of the street(s), and all buildings leading to, or across from, the last contributing address in each direction.[9]

The Sherman and Weisburd (1995) definition that "the boundaries [will be] easily visible from an epicenter" gives the impression that the hot spot surrounds the observer, and a fast twirl will reveal all of it (or at least the front of all of it). However, the statistical hot spots tended in many instances to be lopsided, with all the defining addresses on one side of a block (partially a product of the MapInfo technology, but equally a function of land use and call distribution). In a few instances, the hot spot "turned the corner," with contributing addresses on only one side of the second blockface. In such cases, the only point from which an observer could see the front doors of all the buildings was from a vantage point on the far corner of an intersection. If the intersection was not itself a contributing address, a case could have been made that one could only see all the addresses of that hot spot from outside the hot spot.

Had the field staff used [the] common understanding of "epicenter" (borrowed from seismology), many around-the-corner addresses would have been dropped, limiting the configurations to intersections and linear block faces only. An alternative method of correction, deleting around-the-corner portions of the original maps, posed several difficulties and was not seriously entertained. It would have been too time consuming; it potentially might erode the "hard-crime" selection threshold and require costly after-the-fact adjustments; and in some sites where corner buildings were missing, even around-the-corner addresses were visible from an epicenter. Of necessity, the "epicenter" was redefined in terms of the rule that "all addresses should be visible from one central point."

Frequently, that "one central point" was the middle of an intersection. That fact, in turn, raised an issue of whether the primary focus was that the police could see all parts of the hot spot (in which case almost all addresses that were "around the corner" would have to be eliminated) or could be seen from points in the hot spot (which raised a similar issue, with slightly different emphasis on line-of-sight from inside buildings). The question was rendered moot by the subsequent adoption of a flexible definition in which both the police and the observers were presumed to be mobile within the hot spot, insuring both surveillance and visibility to others throughout the site.

2. Intersections

Intersections created a novel problem for the mapping process. Unlike building addresses, with definite space and fixed curtilage, the operational definition of intersections, as reflected in the activity attributed to them, was fairly elastic. Although many calls for police service are attributed to intersections, relatively little criminal activity takes place in the intersecting roadways, and for good reason: the routine passage of motor vehicles makes the roadways fairly dangerous for victims and perpetrators alike. Instead, assaults, purse snatchings, and other crimes take place on the sidewalks, in front of and alongside buildings.

The public space associated with "building" and "intersection" thus overlaps, and the boundaries of the intersection tend to creep beyond the curbs of the streets. Bus stops (notorious locations for strong-armed robberies because the victims are stationary, and frequently preoccupied or distracted) are usually set back from the corner, at least by the width of a crosswalk and stop line, and frequently more so. Persons who are accosted or assaulted on the sidewalks tend to give an intersection as their location when they call from nearby pay phones, and intersections function as a place to meet the police.

The human variations of the CAD system input also demonstrated the imprecise definition of "intersection." Observational research on calls in progress[10] and anecdotal evidence from officers indicated a strong possibility that activity that occurred in public spaces might be attributed to a nearby building.[11] If the incident was witnessed by a third person in a building and reported from a phone there, the call could well be attributed to that address rather than to the intersection.[12] Whenever an intersection was included in, or acted as the epicenter of, a four-directional hot spot, this public space fell within the hot-spot boundaries and the question was moot. But when hot spots "turned the corner" of two intersecting blocks, several operational questions resulted: whether or not the intersection was in such a hot spot; whether it included all four corner buildings, which each have a view of the open space that comprises both the technical and the elastic, common-sense intersection; or whether it included just the "pivot building" on the corner where the hot spot "turned."

The same rationale that extended the hot spot to the addresses on the opposite side of the street resolved these questions. The police presence would have an influence through all the public space, to and perhaps into the nearby buildings. Some of this ripple effect was sacrificed beyond the perimeter boundaries, but it did not make sense to drop it altogether in those locations where it would be the strongest. The argument for the "at risk" locations also applied to the buildings on the far side of a hot spot's arc as it "turned the corner."

Here, too, was a practical consideration very similar to the "hairsplitting" discussion of the public space issue. The best observation spots for linear-block and right-angle hot spots were frequently at the intersections, giving the police the most complete view of the public spaces of both blocks. The nature of perspective and necessity (particularly in hot spots where one-way streets restricted the available parking options) often placed those observation spots on the outside of the arc, on the far corner that ordinarily would have been disqualified as "outside the hot spot." The police would be *at* the intersection but not in it, parked a short distance back alongside one of the corner buildings. It made little sense to antagonize the police by handing them counterintuitive instructions, or to limit their effectiveness by restricting their vision. Accordingly, all four corners of an intersection were included in the map definition of the intersection.

A different question was posed when the hot spot's configuration was a full linear block with an intersection at each end. The instructions—"You may include two intersections in a hot spot only if you do not go down other streets from the intersection"— did not provide guidance as to whether including the corner buildings as a *de facto* part of "the intersection" would violate the rule. The dilemma was one of potentially forfeiting some of the calls reporting activity in the intersection, or creating a structural violation of the rules. But all of the rationale applied to other intersection questions applied to this as well. By including the corner buildings, the full potential for capturing intersection activity was retained, and a common definition of "intersection" employed throughout the universe of hot spots.

3. Variants: Where 'One Linear Block' Did Not Apply

Some of the hot spots incorporated large, sprawling parking lots whose area approached or exceeded the "one linear block" yardstick. These potential hot spots added another element that had not been anticipated in the original formulation of the rules: the expanse of open areas. What distinguished them from the public space contained by the two sides of a standard block-face was their greater width. Though the territory covered by these locations was immense compared to the more compact hot spots, the fields of vision within them were wide and clear. These sites, too, had partial obstructions to vision, but a great deal of public space could be scanned from any single point on the perimeter or within the hot spot.

Five hot spots fit this category. Some exceeded the one linear block rule, if the interior of some larger buildings was considered as part of the hot spot. In one patrol hot spot, the front door of a large grocery store with a street address on 26th Avenue actually sat on the east side of what would be 27th Avenue. The building extended eastward to 28th Avenue, encompassing the whole of an entire city block. The store's parking lot encompassed another full block between 27th and 26th Avenues to the west,[13] and the hot spot's out-door "visible space" was primarily that of the parking lot. Though its two-block property was clearly larger than the block-length definition (which did not apply to it because of the idiosyncratic configuration), it and three similar control sites fell easily within the "nighttime sight and sound" definition propounded by Sherman and Weisburd (1988) by virtue of the large open spaces.

One hot spot extended across two short blocks because its primary central space was open. In this case, the definition sprang largely from well-documented knowledge of the social definition of the space. The area had been the scene of gang activity (contesting a small retaining wall between a fast-food restaurant on one block and a strip mall's parking lot on the adjacent one). It was also a hangout for local drunks who panhandled money from customers, then bought and shared alcohol from a liquor store in the shopping mall. Because the street and crime traffic between the two was so closely related, this was deemed to be a single "spot."

Operational Considerations

When the Hot Spots Experiment was devised, Sherman and Weisburd (1995) envisioned a constant parade of squad cars entering areas, staying for a few minutes, then leaving for a few minutes and returning. This pattern, which simulates the intermittent police crackdown model (Sherman, 1990), was urged in order to increase the uncertainty about apprehension for potential offenders, and to stretch the police presence throughout the day. However, low initial totals of police presence were recorded by the observers and noted on police logs. To ensure a proper level of police presence, through their lieutenants and sergeants the precinct commanders began assigning responsibility for specific hot spots meant that a hot spot received one or two "lump-sum" doses of police presence. If possible, a squad would "sit" on the hot spot for the full hour and a half that it was responsible for, then leave.[14]

Operational concessions had to be made to the Minneapolis Emergency Communications Center (MECC), an independent city agency not staffed by or under the control of the police department. Since MECC personnel were rated on the quickness with which they dispatched calls, they looked upon every car on the air as "theirs," and complained when squads were to take themselves off the 911 dispatch queue in order to "get their time in" on a hot spot. The city budget officer intervened to try to force an additional concession, hinting broadly that the experiment might have to be terminated. His objection was answered, but it placed further strain on the police department's ability to establish a steady presence in the hot spots.

One concession was made to the officers themselves, as the request came from some who were doing their best to maintain the sort of police presence that the principal investigators had first envisioned for hot spots. Several officers were in the habit of taking control of their hot spots during their time there, aggressively patrolling on foot, and going up and down the alleyways. Going the length of the block to circle around took them out of the hot spot, and they wanted to know if they would "get credit for" hot spot patrol for the few minutes they were outside the boundaries completing an alley-back-to-the-street circuit. The answer was a rule of thumb that allowed them to walk no more than half a block outside the hot spot on foot patrol, if the squad car was parked inside the hot spot as a visible reminder of their proximity.

The 'If I Were a Mugger' Rule

The observers brought up a question not anticipated in formulating the original set of rules: how to code a patrol car parked just outside the boundary of the hot spot, clearly in sight but not technically "in" the hot spot. This situation could occur when officers answered a call at an address just outside the hot spot, or when a shortage of parking spaces required an assigned car to park just outside the boundaries but in such a way that allowed an officer to observe most of the activity in the public space of the hot spot.

For the observers, this question was a functional equivalent of the "public space" issue that had been raised as part of the definition process. If "presence" was established by visual recognition, and/or an ability to

hear disorderly proceedings nearby, then for all practical purposes a car (or an officer) just outside the boundary exerted a "presence" every bit as real as that of an officer ten feet away but inside the boundary.

The answer was the "if I were a mugger" rule. Observers were told to ask themselves, "If I were a mugger, would I be deterred from mugging someone here and now because of the presence of the police at that particular location?" If the answer to the question was yes, the observers were to record the officers "present" in the hot spot even if they were physically outside the boundaries.

The research staff recognized the potential objection that the lawabiding observers' backgrounds might make them more "deterrable" than a street tough, but the underlying issue was that of presence rather than actual deterrence. Because defiance was a potential element in the street tough's decision to commit a crime despite visible signs of police presence (Sherman, 1993), the critical in/out decision was to be made on a more general basis. As a practical matter, the observers could not second-guess a street tough's decision-making process; they could only code on the basis of their own perceptions. (A similar issue had been raised concerning the observers' sensitivity to "disorderly behavior," and it had been resolved the same way.) Anecdotal reports from the observers indicated that such "on the boundary" decisions were relatively few.

Implications for Research

The Hot-Spots Experiment suggests that there are at least three different points of decision where abstract concepts of space must be negotiated in operational terms: (1) in the nature of the *human techniques* and practices that assign activities to particular addresses in official records; (2) in the attribution of public space (which has no "address") to *private property* (which has, or is, an address); and (3) in the conflict over the nature of boundaries, distinct and discrete in computerized representations but invisible and fluid under field conditions.

Human Practices, Official Records

Maintaining records is subject to human decision making and human error. For instance, a calltaker's practice of entering the address of the caller displayed on the E911 screen could distort the attribution of the problem from the *problem's* location to the *caller's* location.

"Magnet phones" were usually pay phones at convenience stores, gas stations and other locations.[15] Many residents of the low-income neighborhoods (where the large majority of hot spots candidate sites were located) could not afford private phone hookups, and depended upon pay phones. Persons needing the police would go to these public locations, often up to six blocks away, to call 911. Because they waited to meet the police at the phone, the place to which the police were sent to meet the complainant was registered as the address where the phone was located in the "address" line of the dispatch record. Frequently, that address remained as the address of record for the event.

A similar condition of elasticity concerns the intersection as a place, discussed above. As a major landmark more readily identified than a single building on a block, intersections may be used as the "location" of public-space events that are actually farther down a block, and equally applicable to a specific address. But because activities in public space can be mobile, and may not be at the original site upon the arrival of the squad, the intersection acts as a functional "high ground" for the arriving squads. It offers the best possible location for scanning the maximum amount of public space quickly, and a short move forward or back permits observation of the public space of the alleyways.

Public Space and Private Property

In the abstract, the lines between public space and private property are rigid and distinct. In real life, they are not. Behaviors occurring in public space—to which all persons have theoretically equal access—extend into private spaces through the faculties of vision and hearing. Such extensions form the very essence of concepts of "natural surveillance" and "informal control" (see, e.g., Newman,

1972, 1976), though the directionality goes from private to public in those schemes.

Obstreperous behavior on a public corner may not be a problem for the participants in public space, who engage in it by common consent, by virtue of free assembly. The noise that such conduct produces may be a problem for someone located within private space, who objects to one or more of its features: volume, content (obscenity, etc.), participants' ethnic identity or age, or some combination thereof (unsupervised juveniles being raucous on a school night, for example). Similarly, the noise and/or visual clutter produced by individuals who perform repairs on automobiles parked on a public street (even if it is the mechanic's personal vehicle, and not an unlicensed business operation) become "problems" for other residents who view that behavior as a sign of decline (Skogan, 1990).

In cases of such contested legitimacy, police calls-for-service systems frequently attribute the call to the *address* where the activity is a problem (the caller's address), not the *place* where the activity occurs. That creates potential problems for location-specific projects (like the hypothetical "contributing-addresses-only" configuration that hot spots might have been). However, the difficulties are less severe in inclusive schemes such as the actual hot spots configurations, inclusive of all addresses within the perimeter. There may be spillover activities at the boundaries, but the major contributing activity takes place within the hot spot.

'Presence': The Nature of Boundaries

The preceding discussion focuses primarily on the locations at which criminal or disorderly activity occurs, and in which it can be observed by a police officer. The original theoretical definitions of hot spots—all addresses within nighttime sight and sound of each other—center on the patrolling officer and what he or she could observe while on hot-spots patrol. Yet the concept of "police presence" depends more upon the ability of the residents of, and visitors to, the area to perceive the officer.

The hot-spots discussions among field staff, and between field staff and the principal investigators, never addressed directly the abstract concept of "presence." In retrospect, a tacit assumption can be discerned, that a police officer (or a visible symbol, such as a marked patrol car) exerted a uniform level of "presence" or deterrent effect throughout the entire hot spot, regardless of where in the hot spot the officer was. That assumption extended to whether or not the officer moved around within the hot spot on foot patrol, or remained stationary in a parked vehicle.

In the concern over contamination by proximity, however, there is a similarly tacit recognition that the police officer can be observed from farther distances, with varying degrees of influence over the behavior of potential offenders. The "if I were a mugger" rule acknowledges that distinction in practical if subjective terms. Because quantification is almost impossible, it must be assumed that the additional quantum of police presence included under the mugger rule was balanced by an equivalent amount of disturbance from events taking place outside the hot-spot boundary but visible or audible within the hot spot.

In a like vein, the resolution of the debate over "interior" crime and "public-space" crime contains the tacit acknowledgment that deterrence, at least general deterrence, rests upon reciprocal awareness. Police observation of wrongdoers does not constitute a specific deterrent unless and until the wrongdoer is aware of that surveillance. A potentially weaker specific deterrence results from the offender's awareness of the police when the officers are not aware (or not yet aware) of the offender. Over time, a series of specific deterrence encounters may aggregate into a more general deterrent based upon increased awareness of police presence; indeed, the results of the Hot Spots Experiment suggest strongly that such a generalization occurs (Sherman and Weisburd, 1995).

It is tempting to visualize the situation in terms of a fixed square and a moving circle. A hot spot is the fixed square, with firm, clearly delineated, semipermeable boundaries. The moving circle is the "zone of influence" surrounding the figure of the police officer, emanating from his or her person in concentric rings of diminishing force (the closest analogy is that of the "aura"). As he or she moves up and down within the hot spot, the locus of the most powerful influence (the area closest to him or her) shifts back and forth. The immediate influence may fluctuate slightly, depending upon his or her position and whether or not he or she enters one of the buildings in the hot spot, but the residual influence accumulates over time at a constant rate throughout the hot spot. Experimental boundaries are fixed by the predetermined dimensions of the *physical* place, not by the aspects of the more fluid *social* place.

Near the edges of the hot spot, while the officer is inside the patrolled area, part of his or her influence extends beyond the fixed boundaries. In experimental terms, the hot-spot boundary censors that influence, and examines only that part which affects the space inside the perimeter. While the officer's presence nearby may indeed produce a crime-quelling deterrence in the adjacent public and private space, that influence is of no consequence to the experiment because the physical space anchors the issues of measurement.

From outside, however, the hot-spot boundary is semipermeable: an officer's authority extends across the hot-spot boundary through the auspices of the "if I were a mugger" rule, adding a small quantum of "presence" from patrol that occurs outside the formal experimental space. It is primarily the immediate presence, the strongest influence, that is admitted to the quantum of "patrol dosage" in this case: the farther the officer is from the hot-spot boundary, the more attenuated is his or her influence over the behavior in the further reaches of the hot spot.

Social space dominates the observations of activity within and around crime and the physical space, and the hot-spots boundaries are similarly permeable from outside in terms of the sights and sounds that constitute soft crime. However, the disorder and crime incidents were a secondary measure: the primary task of the observers was to verify the differential presence in the patrol and control hot spots. The main effects of the experiment hinged on the effects of patrol presence within the hot spots on reported crime and calls for service.

The Hot Spots fieldwork transformed a series of loosely linked points (the individual addresses that generated three or more "hard crime" calls) into a coherent, three dimensional space. In doing so, it arbitrarily established the "place" for research purposes in terms of an understanding more attuned to the social notion of "place" than any of the possible statistical ones. Research and policy demands thus had a reciprocal, though mismatched, influence upon one [another].

It would have been possible, for instance, to construct different analyses based on combinations of and compromises on the criteria actually used. Operational maps that included all buildings could have been given to patrol officers and observers (thus avoiding the potential "in/out" difficulties described above), but with a statistical analysis conducted only using the contributing addresses. A hot spot might have been defined as the contributing buildings, or all buildings on one side of the street, plus the public space in front of it (up to the front door of the buildings opposite), but at a cost of censoring calls about public space activity reported from the excluded buildings opposite. As the combination of addresses into hot spots acted as a leaven to some of the wide fluctuation of call totals at individual addresses, the inclusion of all contiguous addresses and their opposites across public space stabilized vagaries in reporting activity.

The Minneapolis Hot Spots of Crime Experiment was based upon a year-long manipulation of police practices. The legacy of similar research efforts in the past suggested that sabotage of the experiment by the officers was a potential hazard (Kelling et al., 1974; Sherman and Berk, 1984), and efforts were made to keep officer objections to a minimum in hopes of avoiding such resistance. Perspectives not found in social science design influenced many of the definitional decisions of the experiment. Future research may assess the differences obtained by using contributing-points constructs rather than contiguous-space ones, and distinguishing more fully the tradeoffs between the conceptual realities of the map and those of the territory itself.

Notes

1. Nevertheless, the outcome of the experiment still showed a consistent, statistically significant reduction of crime and disorder in the patrolled hot spots (Sherman and Weisburd, 1995).

2. Patrol officers were to provide a total of three hours of presence in each patrol hot spot daily—an hour and a half in the late morning and afternoon, and another hour and a half in the evening, up until 3 a.m. The observers followed a randomized observation schedule, observing police and street activity in 100 of the 110 hot spots for 70-minute intervals, primarily during the evening hours. They used one checklist to record the type and duration of police presence, and another to record various elements of crime and disorder.

3. Magnet phones are problematic because they represent human reporting patterns more than crime occurrence patterns: a magnet phone artificially concentrates reports of events that take place over a broad geographical area. Time constraints made it impossible to check on the offense report histories of all suspected magnet phones, but an analysis of calls to half a dozen of those spots thought to be magnets found that over 90% of the hard crime activity had occurred in the hot spot itself. In some cases, even though shoplifting calls (THEFT and THEFTH nature codes) for large supermarkets or retail stores dominated the call totals, hot spot status was justified by a sufficient number of other hard crime events (such as robberies occurring in the store parking lots).

   Only one true "magnet phone" was eliminated: a 7–Eleven convenience store on the south side. It was known to be a magnet phone from information developed during the RECAP experiment. Even when the 7–Eleven's address was dropped from the analysis, however, the activity attributed to other addresses, particularly the intersection, still qualified as a hot spot. The people who congregated in the area caused enough problems while there to put the immediate area high on the list of potential hot spots, even without the call-lines contributed by the 7–Eleven store or its outside public phones (though logically, those phones probably reported some of the activity at the intersection). The intersection became part of the experiment as a patrol hot spot.

4. Public parks have addresses in the database, but they are defined by a man and single street address assigned to whatever structure—clubhouse or utility shed—sits on the park, regardless of how large the physical area of the park may be. An area may be half a city block or as large (at the extreme end) as a major lake such as Lake Calhoun or Lake Harriet, which cover many acres.

5. This issue was resolved operationally in December, by Weisburd. After riding with some of the field observers, he suggested that observers position themselves in such a way as to focus their attention on the major contributing addresses. Since the intersections were usually large contributors, and fields of vision included the fronts of almost all addresses, all were included by fiat.

6. In legal terms, curtilage refers to the grounds and outbuildings associated with a particular property, within the limits of deeded property. The term "street curtilage" is an invention of necessity for this discussion, by the first author. It extends the notion of curtilage outward, past the deeded boundaries into the contiguous areas of public space where there are informal expectations of association. The most commonly recognized of those expectations is that of the ability of the property owners to use the street immediately in front of their home for parking, for either themselves or their guests.

7. The Minneapolis CAD system required that a street address be entered in order for the CAD to accept the call. Operational practice was address-based and technology-driven. As a rule, all street activity that was not in or around an intersection was attributed to one of the building addresses in the block, usually to the address from which the call reporting the problem originated. Information that the problem might be in the street or down the block was often conveyed in an "added remarks" field, but no practical means existed to systematically identify such calls.

8. Subsequent negative reactions of patrol supervisors, upon seeing the original lists of hot spots, were based on the intuitive understanding that the call activity in the residential areas was primarily domestic in nature.

9. Even within this definition, however, there were variations and "no man's lands" of excluded-category buildings, though any such properties were clearly marked on the foot-print maps given to police officers and observers.

10. Gathered by the principal author while working on a related project.

11. For examples, see the cases histories of the RECAP addresses at 1025 Portland Av. S and 700 Hennepin Av. S in the RECAP casebook (Buerger, 1992).

12. In doing so, the call-taker provides the responding squads with the origin of the complaint, in case the officers wish to speak with the reporting person. The "outside" location of the call, which frequently includes direction of travel, descriptions, etc., is then given in the "added remarks." Since many of these necessary details would not fit in the address block, and would have to be added in remarks anyway, the call-taker utilizes a certain economy of information-packaging in this way. That, in turn, is necessary in the hectic climate of information-gathering, recording and disseminating when the dispatch center is active.

13. This was one of the spots investigated as a potential magnet phone, developing more detailed information about the nature of the crime calls here. Some of the calls attributed to the address occurred in the block-wide parking lot, but others actually took place inside (purses snatched from grocery carts, money snatched from open cash drawers, etc.).

14. Police officer activity while on a hot spot ranged from an aggressive foot patrol (of a type and quality worthy of the best community policing officers) to an hour and a half spent sitting in the police car, oblivious to activity around them. Anecdotal information supplied by some supervisors late in the experiment suggested that at some busy times, the police "presence" was in fact a "phantom car"—a parked squad with no officer nearby. Overall, however, the police presence was real, if grudging, as the Minneapolis Police responded to a distasteful task with professional commitment. The December foot-dragging was resolved, and there were no attempts to sabotage the project as there had been in Kansas City.

15. Certain apartments—particularly those of resident caretakers—could be magnet phones in apartment buildings, as persons without private phones would go to a friend's apartment or to "the super" to call the police when they were experiencing trouble. However, because those calls reflect activity within

the hot spot, masking only a specific location within a building, they were of no concern to the determination of hot spot sites.

References

Buerger, M. (1992). *The Crime Prevention Casebook: Securing High Crime Locations.* Washington, DC: Crime Control Institute.

Kelling, G., T. Pate, D. Dieckman and C. E. Brown (1974). *The Kansas City Preventive Patrol Experiment: A Summary Report.* Washington, DC: Police Foundation.

Newman, O. (1972). *Defensible Space: Crime Prevention Through Urban Design.* New York, NY: Macmillan.

——(1976). *Design Guidelines for Creating Defensible Space.* Washington, DC: U.S. National Institute of Law Enforcement and Criminal Justice.

Reiss, A.J., Jr. (1985). *Policing A City's Central District: The Oakland Story.* U.S. National Institute of Justice Research Report. Washington, DC.

Sherman, L.W. (1990). "Police Crackdowns: Initial and Residual Deterrence." In: M. Tonry and N. Morris (eds.), *Crime and Justice: A Review of Research,* Vol. 12. Chicago: University of Chicago Press.

——(1993). "Defiance, Deterrence, Irrelevance: A Theory of the Criminal Sanction." *Journal of Research in Crime and Delinquency* 30:445–473.

——and R.A. Berk (1984)."The Specific Deterrent Effects of Arrest for Domestic Assault." *American Sociological Review* 49:261–272.

——and D. Weisburd (1988). "Policing the Hot Spots of Crime: A Redesign of the Kansas City Preventive Patrol Experiment." Research proposal submitted to the U.S. National Institute of Justice, Program on Research in Public Safety and Security.

——and D. Weisburd (1995). "General Deterrent Effects of Police Patrol in Crime 'Hot Spots': A Randomized Study." *Justice Quarterly* 12(4): (forthcoming).

Skogan, W. (1990). *Disorder and Crime: Crime and the Spiral of Decay in American Neighborhoods.* New York, NY: Free Press.

Michael E. Buerger, Ellen G. Cohn, and Anthony J. Petrosino, "Defining the 'Hot Spots of Crime': Operationalizing Theoretical Concepts for Field Research." In *Crime and Place,* pp. 237–257. Copyright © 1995 by Criminal Justice Press. Reprinted by permission. ✦

12

ROP: Catching Career Criminals

Susan E. Martin
Lawrence W. Sherman

Recent offenders-behavior research has shown criminologists what is important for today's problem-oriented policing effort: a small proportion of criminals commit a disproportionate number of crimes. That fact has generated growing interest in the need to apprehend career criminals. In this reading, S. Martin and L. Sherman assess a proactive policing strategy in the Washington, D.C. police department's repeat offender project (ROP) and study its ability to identify and arrest career criminals. The authors sought to determine whether, through ROP, repeat offenders were more likely to be arrested and whether the officers involved in the experiment were able to arrest and convict career offenders. The researchers also observed ROP officers at work and examined their target selection, investigation techniques, and apprehension strategies. The findings provide other police departments with insight concerning the successes and potential problems inherent in the ROP model as part of a problem-oriented policing strategy. While reading, consider whether a ROP strategy is needed and would function well in your community.

Two facts stand out in modern crime control police debates. First, a small proportion of criminals commit a disproportionate number of crimes. Second, most prisons are overcrowded. Together, these facts have generated growing interest in selectively focusing criminal justice system resources on the most active and dangerous chronic offenders.

While police have rarely adopted a proactive targeting approach to apprehending repeat offenders, the Washington, D.C. Metropolitan Police Department adopted precisely this approach in May 1982 when it established an 88-officer (later reduced to 60) Repeat Offender Project (ROP).

The Repeat Offender Project offered a unique opportunity to assess the problems and effectiveness of a proactive police unit formed to carry out a selective apprehension strategy. Between January 1983 and December 1984, the Police Foundation, in cooperation with the D.C. Metropolitan Police Department, conducted a multifaceted evaluation to assess ROP's effectiveness and costs. A controlled experiment sought to determine whether "repeat offenders" identified by ROP were more likely to be arrested by ROP than they were in the absence of ROP activities. A comparative component examined prior arrest histories and current case dispositions of a sample of persons arrested by 40 ROP and 169 non-ROP officers, as well as arrest productivity rates for both groups of officers.

The Police Foundation study addressed the following questions:

1. How does ROP operate and what strategies do officers use in selecting and apprehending their targets?

2. Do ROP's tactics increase the likelihood of arrest for targeted repeat offenders?

3. Are offenders arrested by ROP officers more active and serious than offenders arrested under routine police operations?

4. Are ROP arrestees more likely to be prosecuted, convicted, and incarcerated? and,

5. How does ROP affect the arrest productivity of its officers?

While it is premature to conclude that all police departments would benefit from a proactive repeat offender unit, large departments should consider creating such units, given the magnitude of the repeat offender problem and the findings of this study.

ROP's Design and Initial Implementation

When Maurice Turner, chief of the Washington, D.C. Metropolitan Police Department, requested innovative proposals from senior officers on ways to reduce crime in the nation's capital, Captain (now Inspector) Edward Spurlock responded with a plan to establish a proactive, "perpetrator-oriented" unit. The unit would identify and apprehend two types of active recidivists: those already wanted on one or more warrants who could be arrested on sight, and those believed to be criminally active but not currently wanted. The former were called "warrant targets"; the latter "ROP-initiated" targets.

ROP's Initial Organization

ROP's criterion for selecting both types of targets was "the belief that the person is committing five or more Part 1 offenses per week." The unit's time and effort would be divided equally between the two types of targets. Active apprehension efforts were limited to a 72 hour-or-less time period. This enabled ROP to focus its resources on the most active criminals, since only very active offenders were likely to be observed committing a crime within a three-day period.

ROP's command staff selected a team of 88 officers who varied in age, race, sex, appearance, and previous police experience. The officers were organized into seven-member squads, each including a female and a detective. The squad was led by a sergeant, and became the basic work group to which targets were assigned and credit for arrests given. While officers were allowed ample discretion over their routine activities, the sergeant was responsible for selecting squad targets and worked on the street with officers. A Target Committee of three experienced investigators was responsible for developing new targets and reviewing candidates generated by the squads.

The unit's resources included 20 old cars, other surveillance and investigative equipment, and a computer terminal linked to the department's on-line information system. To aid in target selection, ROP routinely received copies of the department's daily major violators list, criminal histories of recent arrestees, daily crime reports from each district, and specially prepared weekly printouts listing all persons wanted on three or more felony warrants.

To reduce rivalry with other police units that could inhibit the flow of information needed to function effectively, ROP adopted an internal arrest log. This log listed all arrests for which ROP officers were responsible, even if the arrest was formally booked to another officer. This enabled ROP officers to assign formal arrest credit to other officers, while obtaining recognition from their supervisors for the work they had performed.

Prior to commencing operations, ROP's proposed procedures were reviewed by the department's general counsel, the U.S. Attorney, and the local American Civil Liberties Union (ACLU). The ACLU was concerned that ROP would be a "dragnet" operation that harassed and entrapped people. These concerns were satisfied when the ROP commander explained that ROP would use no formula or profile for target selection and that places where citizens have a right to privacy would be put under surveillance only with the permission of the court (Epstein, 1983).

Operational Changes

Difficulties during the first several months led to several modifications of ROP's targeting practices, squad operations, and apprehension tactics. The ROP design anticipated that surveillance would be the principal tactic for apprehending ROP-initiated targets. When constant surveillance failed to produce arrests, and therefore, frustrated ROP officers, the squads increased their proportion of warrant targets to about 75 percent of those selected. The command staff also gradually broadened the officer's repertoire of investigative and undercover infiltration strategies and skills. After several months, surveillance became one of a number of tactics. In addition, the rule that work on a target be terminated after 72 hours was relaxed when it proved difficult to implement.

Target development practices also changed. Initially, the Target Committee selected and developed all targets, mostly on the basis of official record information. However, this information typically was incomplete and an unreliable indicator of criminal activity, and, therefore, was far less desirable than "street" information. With strong encouragement from the ROP command staff, ROP officers built informal information networks and fostered cooperative relations with other units and agencies.

After several months, the unit acquired a reputation for responding to suggestions for targeting and "hot tips" from other police units and informants. Information sources in other departmental units and neighboring police agencies and street informants increased the proportion of targets generated by ROP squads. These squads also initiated a number of joint target investigations with other agencies.

These changes had both positive and negative effects. They allowed ROP to expand its resources and become a center of information about criminal activities in the metropolitan area. But they also resulted in targeting persons who did not meet ROP's selection criteria, diverting limited resources away from a focus on persons committing many Part 1 offenses.

After six months, to streamline operations, ROP was reduced from 88 to 60 officers, the 12 squads were reorganized and reduced to eight, and administrative procedures were tightened. In January 1983, a new theft statute (The District of Columbia's Theft and White Collar Crime Act of 1982) went into effect. At that time, ROP's target selection criteria were expanded to include "persons believed to be trafficking in stolen property."

ROP in Action

Target Selection

Although officers were expected to select criminally active targets, ROP did not establish formal indicators of activity or any system for prioritizing among potential candidates. Selection was based on informal understandings about what makes a "good" target.

Common considerations affecting selection became the target's catchability, deservedness, longer-term yield, and the squad's working style. "Catchability" depended primarily on the quality, recency, type, and amount of information about a warrant target's whereabouts and a ROP initiated target's activities. ROP officers pre-

ferred to use information provided by other officers or an informant. Police recognized that most offender arrest records fail to reflect the full extent of criminal activities. They believe that only criminals in the environment really know what is going on, and that this information helps reduce the amount of preliminary investigation required.

"Deservedness" was related to an officer's belief that the target deserved to be arrested and punished. The primary factors contributing to deservedness were the seriousness and length of the target's criminal history and alleged current criminal activity. Another factor was the target's apparent contempt for the law and police. The former was exemplified by failing to appear in court; the latter encompassed those who were armed or belligerent when arrested on a previous occasion. Concern with "deservedness" helps explain why ROP officers tended to select older persons and suspected fences as targets. Older persons showed a clearer commitment to crime and had an observable modus operandi (in addition to being more likely to be incarcerated if convicted). Fences, although generally not violent, support and facilitate street crime by providing a market for stolen property.

"Yield" was measured by a target's contribution to ROP's information network and public visibility, and the likelihood that the target would result in additional targets and arrests, or in the immediate incarceration of the arrestee. For example, those persons already on pretrial release for another offense and/or on parole were desirable targets because they were more likely to be kept in jail.

ROP squads tended to use three styles for meeting informal pressures to make arrests, and these styles became factors that affected target selection. "Hunter" squads focused almost exclusively on warrant targets, particularly those wanted for violent crimes. "Trapper" squads, which accounted for most ROP initiated arrests, preferred to initiate their own longer-term investigations. These investigations focused on one key target and were designed to close a large number of cases, recover large amounts of stolen property and, subsequently, arrest as many of the target's criminal associates as possible. While an investigation was proceeding, "trappers" also "filled in" with warrant targets, particularly those requested by officers from other units with whom they were working. "Fisherman" squads did not specialize. They made some ROP-initiated arrests on quick buy/bust operations, followed up on "hot tips," arrested some warrant targets, and made many "serendipitous" arrests by street cruising.

Apprehension Strategies

The primary task in apprehending warrant targets was *locating* the target. This was simple if the squad had a current address. But when the officers did not have a good address, the process became more complex. Finding the target usually involved reviewing police and other records or contacting persons likely to know the target's whereabouts. While some contacts were straightforward, others involved deception. For example, a target's relatives might have been told that the target had just won a contest or was being considered for a job and must be contacted. Records to be checked included those at the post office (e.g., mail-forwarding requests), the Department of Motor Vehicles, and the phone company (after getting a court order to gain access to the latter). If these efforts failed, officers sometimes placed the target's girlfriend or close associates under surveillance.

Most warrant targets were wanted in Washington, D.C. as fugitives from justice in neighboring jurisdictions or on felony bench warrants for probation or parole violation or for failure to appear in court. Such targets were frequently selected because they met all informal targeting considerations. They were more catchable than other targets for two reasons. First, D.C. residents being sought by officers from neighboring jurisdictions could be easily located through information provided by these officers. Second, non-ROP D.C. officers were less likely to seek out fugitives and persons wanted on bench warrants than those wanted for Part 1 crimes, despite the seriousness of the underlying charges against the former. In addition, these arrests strengthened cooperative ties between ROP and other units.

To arrest persons not wanted on a warrant, ROP officers had to develop evidence about a specific crime in which targets had participated. This involved a variety of vice and investigative activities such as buy/busts, cultivating informants, investigating "tips," placing targets under surveillance, and tracing stolen property found in the target's possession to its rightful owner. A few prolonged investigations involved undercover penetration of fencing operations. While quite diverse, ROP-initiated target investigations generally focused on property crimes that were more highly organized and, therefore, more easily penetrated through informants and undercover tactics.

Analysis of the ROP-apprehension activities and their outcomes indicated that there was no consistent formula for or primary tactic associated with arrests. Most ROP arrests were made quickly (80 percent within one week of targeting) and did not involve extensive investigative efforts.

Research Design

Experiment

Three research components were used to assess ROP's effectiveness. First, an experiment was conducted to determine whether those selected by ROP as "repeat offenders" were more likely to be arrested because of ROP efforts than they would otherwise. The experiment's design required ROP officers to identify their constantly changing pool of targets, pair any two of the same target type (warrant targets or ROP-initiated targets) and, by coin toss, assign one target to the experimental group and the other to the control group. Experimental targets were investigated by ROP squad officers over a seven-day period. Control targets were off-limits to ROP officers but could be arrested by any other police officer during the seven-day period. The experiment lasted 26 weeks, during which time 212 pairs of randomly assigned targets were investigated.

As is common in field experiments, evidence suggests that some ROP officers manipulated the coin toss (which research staff did not always control) to ensure immediate assignment of desired targets. Others avoided the coin toss by getting the Target Committee to treat the target as an authorized exception even though it did not always fit the rules for exception. In addition, there were difficulties in locating non-ROP arrests, suggesting that some arrests were missed by the researchers. Nevertheless, statistical adjustments designed to eliminate the potential impact of manipulation of random assignment and missed non-ROP arrests did not alter the significance of the experimental outcome.

Comparative Study

The second research component compared ROP officers with a sample of other officers on three factors: 1) criminal histories of those arrested; 2) court dispositions of those arrests; and 3) overall arrest productivity of the officers. ROP officers in this study included 40 officers previously assigned to patrol, tactical/crime prevention, vice, and detective units. The comparison group included a random sample of 95 officers drawn from patrol, vice, and detective assignments; all 60 officers in tactical/crime prevention units; and 14 officers with warrant squad duties. Data were collected on each of the three factors for both groups over two time periods: April 1 to September 30, 1981 (prior to the 1982 establishment of ROP), and April 1 to September 30, 1983.

Information regarding all arrests made by ROP and comparison officers during both time periods was collected from station house arrest logs and a special ROP arrest log. Samples of about 300 ROP-1981, Comparison-1981, and Comparison-1983 arrests were then randomly selected for comparison with all 263 ROP-1983 adult arrests. Arrest histories were obtained from the Metropolitan Police Department. Information on case dispositions was obtained from the Criminal Division of the Superior Court.

Observation and ROP File Data

A third research component involved extensive observation of ROP officers at work, and provided information about ROP target selection, investigative techniques, and apprehension strategies. Various data items also were collected from case jackets of all

persons targeted by ROP during the study period. This included 289 persons involved in the experiment, 100 targets that were authorized exceptions, and 85 persons whom ROP officers serendipitously arrested while working on other assigned targets.

Findings

Experiment

The experimental results clearly showed that ROP *increased the likelihood of arrest of targeted repeat offenders*. ROP arrested 106 (50 percent) of the 212 experimentals. In contrast, only 17 experimentals (8 percent) and 8 controls (4 percent) were arrested by officers in other units. This difference was statistically significant.

Differences in ROP and control arrest rates were found for both warrant and ROP initiated targets. Fifty-five percent of the warrant targets eligible for ROP arrests were arrested by ROP, while only 9 percent of warrant targets eligible for non-ROP arrests were arrested by non-ROP officers. For ROP-initiated targets, the comparable figures were 47 percent and 6 percent. *The magnitude of this finding suggests that despite several problems in implementing and sustaining the experimental design, ROP made a difference by increasing the likelihood of arrest for both warrant and ROP initiated targets.*

Prior Arrest Histories of Arrestees

The study next examined the criminal histories of the samples of 1981 and 1983 ROP and comparison officers' arrestees, after making adjustments for officer's district and assignment and arrestee's age. In 1981, differences between the number of prior arrests for each group's arrestees were minor. *However, in 1983, ROP arrestees had twice as many prior arrests per arrestee as comparison officer arrestees*. ROP 1983 arrestees had an adjusted mean of 8.4 total prior arrests, while comparison officers' arrestees had only 4.2, a statistically significant difference. Assignment to ROP thus led to the expected change in criminal history characteristics of those arrested by ROP officers. The prior arrest records of ROP officer arrestees between 1981 and 1983 became significantly longer and more serious, while the criminal records for [comparison officers'] arrestees became somewhat less serious.

Arrest Seriousness and Case Dispositions

In examining ROP arrests and their outcomes, the study first looked at the seriousness of the arrest charge. There was little difference between ROP and comparison arrest charges in 1981. In 1983, while charges by officer group did not differ in most categories, two categories did differ. Twenty-six percent of ROP arrestees were charged as fugitives, escapees, or probation or parole violators in contrast to only 8 percent of comparison arrestees. Fifteen percent of ROP arrestees and 30 percent of comparison arrestees faced such minor "other" charges as sexual solicitation, gambling, disorderly conduct, unlawful entry, violating vending regulations, and traffic offenses. *Overall, ROP arrests tended to be for more serious offenses.*

The dispositions of the samples of arrests made by ROP and comparison officers were then examined to determine if ROP arrestees were more likely to be prosecuted, convicted, and incarcerated. In 1983, there were substantial differences between case outcomes of ROP and comparison officers' arrests, after adjusting for offense type, offender's age, and arrest history. These differences were not found in 1981 cases.

Although the proportion of cases accepted for prosecution did not change between 1981 and 1983, *there was a substantial increase in the proportion of the ROP officers' new cases accepted for prosecution as felonies.* At the same time, the proportion of the sample of comparison officers' cases prosecuted as felonies fell for officers in all assignments except casual clothes tactical units. As a result, 49 percent of ROP's new cases were accepted for prosecution as felonies while comparison cases charged as felonies in 1983 ranged from 24 to 33 percent.

Total convictions increased from 49 percent of case outcomes in 1981 to 63 percent in 1983 for both ROP and comparison officer groups. The proportion of misdemeanor convictions increased for both groups as well. *However, the proportion of felony convictions resulting from ROP officer cases increased from 19 to 24 percent of all prosecuted cases, whereas the proportion of felony convictions in comparison officers' case outcomes decreased for officers in patrol, vice, and detective assignments and increased for those assigned to tactical units and the warrant squad.*

Finally, incarceration rates for 1983 ROP arrestees remained at about the 1981 level. The rates for comparison officers in all other assignments fell, except for the warrant squad. Although warrant rates rose substantially in 1983, the number of cases involved was quite small.

After statistically controlling the data for offense type, age, and criminal history, the study found that ROP arrestees sentenced to serve time in 1983 appear to have received longer sentences than comparison officer convictees. This apparent effect on sentence length is probably a result of the more serious conviction offenses of ROP arrestees within each of the broad categories of offenses used in this study.

Effects on Officer Arrest Productivity

The third component in the comparative study explored an issue of particular importance to many police administrators: the effect of ROP assignment on officers' productivity as measured by total and specific types of arrests. Changes in the individual arrest rates of each ROP and comparison officer were examined by using two different measures for ROP arrests, and by statistically controlling for differences in district, assignment, time in ROP, and 1981 arrest productivity.

Both measures revealed that *assignment to ROP decreased the total number of arrests made by an officer.* Using the more conservative measure, the study found that in the six-month period in 1983, ROP officers made an adjusted mean of 5.7 arrests per officer and comparison officers an adjusted mean of 12.4 arrests, a statistically significant difference. While ROP officers also made significantly fewer Part 1 arrests than comparison officers in 1983, there was no difference in the number of "serious" arrests (i.e., arrests for Part 1 crimes plus those for distribution and possession with the intent to distribute drugs, weapons charges, and arrests on a felony bench warrant), based on the conservative measure of arrests.

Conclusions

By most measures used in this study, the ROP unit appears to have achieved its goals of selecting, arresting, and contributing to the incarceration of repeat offenders. It increased both the likelihood of arrests of targets, the seriousness of the criminal histories of its arrestees, the probability of prosecution for a felony, the chance of a felony conviction, and the length of the term of those sentenced to incarceration. However, several factors suggest a cautious interpretation of these findings, and the need for other departments to recognize the potential dangers in adopting the ROP model of perpetrator-oriented proactive policing.

Costs

Creating and operating ROP involves costs that cannot be overlooked. First, it took approximately $60,000 in direct expenses to equip the unit. Second, ROP decreased its officers' arrest productivity and, in all likelihood, other aspects of police service as well. Most forgone arrests, however, tended to involve minor offenses such as disorderly conduct and traffic charges. The rate at which ROP officers made "serious" arrests was unaffected, however, and may have increased if the less conservative measure is a more accurate indicator. Thus, the trade-off appears to be reduced-order maintenance activities in exchange for a focus on crime-fighting activities.

The Criminal Activities of Targets

Although ROP arrestees had longer criminal records than comparison arrestees, it cannot be assumed that ROP arrestees are the most active 20 percent of all offenders or are committing five or more Part 1 offenses per week. Other studies have found that prisoners with longer criminal records are more likely than those with short records to be among the highly active group. But prediction instruments, particularly those using official record information, are often unreliable when selecting high-rate criminals (Chaiken and Chaiken, 1982; Greenwood with Abrahamse,

1982; Cohen, 1983; Chaiken and Chaiken, 1985).

Chaiken and Chaiken (1985), for example, used prisoners' self-report of their criminal activities to distinguish three groups of prisoners: "high-rate winners," "high-rate losers," and "low-rate losers." Most of the self-admitted high-rate criminals were "losers" who were often caught and had long criminal records. A small group of "high-rate winners" had avoided apprehension for many years, however, and had official records that made them appear to be low-rate criminals. At the same time, a group of inept "low-rate losers" were not very active but were apprehended nearly every time they committed a crime. The Chaikens suggest that while it is not possible to distinguish accurately among these three groups solely on the basis of criminal record, police and prosecutors have access to additional knowledge that may help them make more accurate distinctions.

This is likely to have been the case with many ROP targets. Criminal history data were generally supplemented by street information upon which ROP officers heavily relied, as well as by data regarding drug use, information from criminal associates, and confessions by targets to many crimes cleared by police but not charged by prosecutors. These sources of information enhanced their ability to select the most criminally active targets. Nevertheless, it was impossible to determine what proportion of ROP targets actually met that unit's targeting criterion of five or more Part 1 crime per week. More important, the ultimate goal of the ROP unit is to reduce crime, and the data from this study do not permit us to determine whether changes in the D.C. crime rate during the study period were related to the program or to other factors.

Legal, Ethical, and Police Issues

ROP activities also pose dangers to civil liberties, especially because of the use of undercover tactics. A proactive plainclothes unit using a variety of unorthodox tactics gives officers an enormous amount of discretion. Without careful supervision, there will be opportunity to harass, entrap, and otherwise violate a citizen's rights.

These problems appear to have been minimized through the ROP supervisors' and officers' careful attention to legality. ROP officers recorded undercover transactions whenever possible and frequently consulted with the U.S. Attorney's office when preparing warrants and carrying out covert operations. Both Inspector Spurlock of the ROP unit and Leslie Harris of the ACLU reported that between May 1982 and September 1985, ROP avoided lawsuits and major complaints of harassment and violation of due process. Nevertheless, the same degree of care may not prevail in other jurisdictions. Nor is it certain that the procedures used by the D.C. ROP unit will stand the test of time.

Proactive units must also make difficult policy choices, either deliberately or by default. These include finding comfortable balances between the emphases to be placed on quantity and quality of targets and arrests, between warrant and unit-initiated targets, and among various types of targets and offenses.

Informal pressure to "put the meat on the table" (i.e., make more arrests) has implications for the type of targets and arrests produced. Emphasis on the number of arrests made results in greater temptations to pick "easy" targets that fail to meet ROP's targetary criteria. An exclusive focus on selecting and arresting only the most active targets, however, is likely to increase the quality of each arrest but decreases their number. Because such a strategy also increases the amount of personnel and other resources devoted to each target, a "failure" (i.e., selection of a low-rate offender or failure to make an arrest) has higher costs and makes accuracy an even more critical part of the target selection process.

Similarly, there is no formula for finding a balance between warrant and unit-initiated targets. The amount of emphasis put on the former must rest, in part, on the effectiveness of existing warrant service procedures and an examination of the types of offenses and offenders left at large in the community due to a failure to serve outstanding warrants. Additionally, warrant targets already "wanted" by the system are likely to pose fewer legal challenges than those initiated by the unit.

Warrant targets also are more likely to be a source of violent-offense arrests and to require less officer time and fewer resources per arrest. An emphasis on warrant targets wanted for violent crimes is also likely to yield a greater proportion of targets detained prior to trial, prosecuted for felonies, and incarcerated if convicted given the greater seriousness of the charges underlying these arrests.

Warrant targets also entail several disadvantages relative to unit-initiated targets. They "belong" to the officer who obtained the warrant and, therefore, yield the unit less information about other crimes and criminal associates upon which to base subsequent targeting activities. The quality of a warrant case depends on evidence developed by another officer. Conversely, proactive investigations enable the police to develop eye-witness evidence and penetrate organized criminal activity networks. Only through systematic proactive efforts are the police likely to develop cases against major fences, professional thieves, and other "high-rate winners."

Difficult police choices also must be made when a proactive unit decides on which types of criminal activities to focus. For example, ROP initiated an investigation of area-wide shoplifting activities that resulted in closure of more than 40 cases in five jurisdictions, recovery of more than $100,000 in stolen property, and more than a dozen arrests. The targets clearly fit the selection criteria; there was ample evidence that they were committing more than five Part 1 offenses per week. Yet, most of the drug-addicted professional shoplifters arrested were neither armed nor violent. The question is thus [one of] balancing potential crime control and other community benefits achieved when apprehending organized, active property offenders against the benefits of apprehending fewer persons believed to be committing violent crimes.

Applicability of the Findings to Other Settings

There are also problems in generalizing from the findings of a single case study. What worked for ROP may be related to the unique characteristics of Washington, D.C., its police department, and ROP's personnel and leadership. In the absence of other comparative units or groups, it is difficult to determine which aspects of ROP's organization and tactics are idiosyncratic, which may be effectively replicated in a different setting, and which might better be altered.

References

Chaiken, J. and M. Chaiken (1982). *Varieties of Criminal Behavior*. Santa Monica: The Rand Corporation.

Chaiken, M. and J. Chaiken (1985). *Who Gets Caught Doing Crime?* Unpublished report. Los Angeles: Hamilton, Rabinovitz, Szanton and Alschuler.

Cohen, J. (1983). "Incapacitation as a Strategy for Crime Control." Pp. 1–85 in M. Tonry and N. Morris, eds. *Crime and Justice: An Annual Review of Research*, Volume 5. Chicago: University of Chicago Press.

Epstein, A. (1983). "Spurlock's Raiders." *Regardies*, 3:41–42. Greenwood, P. with A. Abrahamse (1982). *Selective Incapacitation*. Santa Monica: The Rand Corporation.

13

Focusing on Prey Rather Than Predators

A Problem-Oriented Response to Repeat Victimization

Ronald W. Glensor
Kenneth J. Peak
Mark E. Correia

While police practitioners and academics have been developing and expanding the problem oriented policing strategy in the United States, an important body of research has been undertaken in Great Britain concerning high-rate victimizations. In short, crime is not evenly distributed; some people and places are repeatedly victimized by offenders. Therefore, the concept of repeat victimization—knowing where crime has previously occurred—is a powerful indicator of where future crimes will occur. In reading this article, consider the rationales underlying the study of repeat victimization, the methods and problems that are involved in police attempts to identify patterns of victimization, how the concept of repeat victimization can be incorporated in the problem oriented policing strategy in the United States, and whether our police would be assisted by implementing repeat victimization policy as daily practice.

While police practitioners and academics have been developing and expanding the problem-oriented policing strategy in the United States, an important body of research has been undertaken in Great Britain concerning high-rate victimizations. In short, crime is not evenly distributed; some people

and places are repeatedly victimized by offenders. Therefore, as R. Glesnor, K. Peak, and M. Correia point out, the concept of repeat victimization—knowing where crime has previously occurred—is a powerful indicator of where future crimes will occur. In reading, consider the rationales underlying the study of repeat victimization, the methods and problems that are involved in police attempts to identify patterns of victimization, how the concept of repeat victimization can be incorporated in the problem-oriented policing strategy in the United States, and whether U.S. police would be assisted by implementing repeat-victimization policy as daily practice.

> Crime is contagious.—Louis D. Brandeis

> The innocence that feels no risk is taught no caution, is more vulnerable than guilt, and oftener assaulted.—Nathaniel P. Willis

At the zoo, there always seem to be more spectators around the lions' and tigers' cages than around those of the wildebeest and the antelope; more attention is focused on the predators than their prey. Predator behaviors are more dramatic: they stalk, pursue, attack, and devour, while prey species are comparatively dull—grazing, being constantly nervous, fleeing often, and dying (Titus, 1995).

That predators are more interesting to people than prey might explain why criminology has traditionally been more intrigued with offenders than with victims. There may also be a belief that since offenders commit the crimes, in order to control crime we must concentrate on understanding criminal motivation and behavior (Titus, 1995). These have led police to traditionally base crime control and prevention on the behavior of the offender or the locations where crimes are repeated. More recently, policing agencies in the United States have engaged in problem solving techniques in their daily practices. The wide breadth of problem solving policing incorporates repeat victimization as one of these essential elements (i.e., victim, offender, and location), in the analysis of crime. Yet, the police know the least about the prevalence and persistence of victimization.

Several studies (see Anderson, Chenery, and Pease, 1995; Lloyd, Farrell, and Pease, 1994; Pease, 1996; Farrell and Pease, 1993) in Great Britain have shown that encompassing repeat victimization into police practices increases our understanding of patterns of criminality and enhances prevention activities both of which have led to great reductions in criminal behavior. In the United States, however, where problem oriented policing has spread rapidly across the country, patterns of repeat victimization have not been as thoroughly developed nor understood and have not been assimilated into problem solving. Therefore, broadening the focus of crime prevention to include victims as well as offenders and locations would enable police officers in the United States to become more effective.

Drawing primarily upon the work and British research, this article examines the utility of repeat victimization for identifying complex crime patterns and predicting criminal activity in the United States. It begins with an overview of the research findings related to repeat victimization, followed by a discussion concerning the implementation of repeat victimization and some of the problems which might be encountered. Next, we address the issue of repeat victimization in the United States and how it may be identified, analyzed, and responded to using a problem solving process (S.A.R.A. discussed below). Building on this information, the final section discusses the future of repeat victimization in America, and how the police can begin to incorporate this pattern of crime into their daily practices.

Repeat Victimization

Definition, Rationale, and Extent

Repeat victimization, a relatively new approach to crime analysis and prevention, occurs when the same person or place suffers from more than one incident over a specified period of time (Bridgeman and Hobbs, 1997). Just as a small percentage of offenders and locations account for a disproportionate amount of crime, so do a small percentage of victims account for a disproportionate number of victimizations. And just as repeat offenders typically commit many different types of crime, high-rate victims fall prey to a variety of victimizations (Farrell, 1995). An underlying premise of repeat victimization is that crime is not evenly distributed; that is, certain people and places are repeatedly victimized (Pease and Laycock, 1996). Consequently, repeat victimization is arguably the best single predictor routinely available to the police in the absence of specific intelligence information. In fact, Great Britain has recently adopted repeat victimization as part of the national crime prevention agenda. An awareness of its significance for the deployment of crime prevention efforts came after police examined data in the 1986 Kirkholt burglary prevention project in England (Forrester, 1988). Because too few funds were available to protect all the homes at risk, police had to identify those most at risk. The work was carried out in a public housing project north of Manchester that suffered high levels of residential burglary. What quickly became evident was that most home burglaries involved dwellings that had already been burgled at least once in the past year, and that the best predictor of a future burglary was a *past* burglary. After police took crime prevention measures, repeat burglaries were reduced to almost zero (Pease, 1996).

Looking broadly at repeat victimization, British research found that 5 percent of respondents who experienced 5 or more victimizations suffered 43 percent of all crimes reported; and that half of those victimized in 1992 were repeat victims and suffered 81 percent of reported crimes (Pease, 1996). Additional findings reported by the National Board for Crime Prevention (Anderson, Chenery, and Pease, 1994) determined the following:

- Only 10 percent of domestic violence represented an isolated event.

- Once burglarized, a residence is reburglarized at four times the rate of unburglarized homes.

- Over 39 percent of small businesses were found to have been reburglarized at least once a year.

Though important, the above statistics do not indicate the responses taken by the police to alleviate the problem. Following is an example of how the police can take affirmative measures to address repeat victimization.

Data collected in London (Pease and Laycock, 1996) indicated that 74 of 172 (43 percent) of domestic violence incidents occurring over a 25-month period involved only about 7 percent of 1,450 households (Lloyd et al., 1994). Police took the following measures to help prevent recurrence, apprehend batterers, and enhance victims' sense of security:

- *Development and distribution of neck-pendant alarms to repeat victims.* When a person presses the button on the pendant, it dials a central station that triggers a priority response from police, opens a voice channel so the police can hear what is happening, and provide assurance that help is on the way.

- *Improvement in transfer of injunction information from courts to police.* Police knowledge of injunctions against batterers permits officers to arrive on the scene with a better understanding of their legal authority with the incident at hand.

- *Provision of support and information for victims.* Police employed a domestic violence specialist who developed safety plans for victims and helped them to improve their communication with other agencies.

These measures were warmly welcomed by police and victims alike, and several arrests were made as a result. Although the efficacy of such initiatives is difficult to demonstrate statistically, both researchers and police had no doubt about the project's worth.

Concerning offenders' *rationale* for choosing the persons or places, we may consider burglary as an example. Why do burglars return to burgle the same household again? One could argue that, for several reasons, they might be stupid *not* to return: temporary repairs to a burgled home will make a subsequent burglary easier; the burglar is familiar with the physical layout and surroundings of the property; the burglar knows what items of value were left behind at the prior burglary; and the burglar also knows that items that were taken at the subsequent burglary are likely to have been replaced through an insurance policy.

These reasons for burglaries appear to have empirical support. Anderson and his colleagues (1995) found that revictimization within 11 months for non-residential burglary was 28 percent, and for residential burglary, 16 percent. In fact, other British burglary researchers have determined that in some 80 percent of cases where more than one burglary is cleared with an arrest, the

Table 13.1
General Findings of Research on Repeat Victimization

- An individual's past crime victimization is a good predictor of his or her subsequent victimization.

- The greater the number of prior victimizations, the higher the likelihood the victim will experience future crime (Pease and Laycock, 1996).

- Especially within crime-prone areas, a substantial percentage of victimizations consist of repeat victims (Pease and Laycock, 1996).

- The same perpetrators seem to be responsible for the bulk of repeated offenses against a victim (Pease and Laycock, 1996).

- Many factors, from police shift patterns to computer systems, conspire to mask the true contribution of repeat victimization to the general crime problem (Pease and Laycock, 1996).

- If victimization recurs, it tends to do so soon after the prior occurrence, especially for residential burglary, domestic violence, auto crimes, and retail crimes (Farrell and Pease, 1993). In residential burglary, 40 percent of repeat burglaries occur within one month of the previous burglary (Anderson, et al., 1995).

perpetrator is the same person. This is inconsistent with the long-standing, widely held view among the police that many repeat offenses are the result of criminal associates being told of residual crime opportunities.

In general, the culmination of research conducted in Great Britain on repeat victimization indicates the importance of this pattern and its utility for preventing repeat occurrences. Likewise, these findings have greatly increased our understanding of crime (see table 13.1). Consideration needs to be given to how police utilize repeat victimization data to address recurring crime problems. That is the focus of the next section.

Application of Repeat Victimization: Methods and Problems

There are three primary sources which policing agencies employ for obtaining repeat victimization information: police records, which allow officers to use data from their crime recording system or incident logs; other agencies' records (for example to examine school crime, school records may provide a more complete picture); and interviews or surveys of crime victims providing information concerning the how (method of operation), when, and what happened (Bridgeman and Hobbs, 1997:6). This data should be collected over a 12-month period, to establish any patterns within an adequate framework of time.

After collecting the relevant data, the police can utilize several different analytical techniques to determine patterns of criminality. The first technique, location driven analysis, focuses on the geographical location of the incident or offense. The second technique, object driven analysis, is similar to location, but is used when the location is not fixed. An example is an investigation of crimes against motor vehicles which concentrates on the individual vehicle, rather than the location. Victim driven analysis concentrates on the victim since some forms of repeat victimization, such as racially motivated crimes, focus on the victim. The last technique is hot spot driven analysis. This refers to a site that accounts for a disproportionate number of crimes or incidents, and may include a single location (such as a house or a

park), or a wider area, such as particular street or neighborhood. The ultimate hot spot, the "hot dot," is the individual victim who repeatedly suffers crime (Bridgeman and Hobbs, 1997:7–8).

Utilizing the above data collection methods and analytical techniques, may not provide a clear picture of the extent of repeat victimization, however. Due to several reasons, the prevalence of repeat victimization may be underestimated. For example, the underreporting of crime in general is a problem that has long plagued efforts to measure its extent. People do not report all of the incidents they suffer; this exacerbates any attempt to learn the "crime picture" in general, and compounds attempts to understand repeat victimization. Secondly, many police crime recording systems do not readily identify repeat victims. Also, the police shift systems and beat areas mean that different officers are likely to deal with the same victim, thus reducing the likelihood of links being made between incidents (Bridgeman and Hobbs, 1997:2).

Repeat Victimization and Problem-Oriented Policing in the United States

As the above research findings suggest, utilizing repeat victimization to develop effective crime prevention strategies in Great Britain has shown to be quite effective. Unfortunately, police agencies in the United States have not typically focused on the victim as an important element in crime control. Although the S.A.R.A. problem solving process can be used to identify patterns of repeat victimization within its analysis, police in the United States have primarily used offender behavior and location as the basis for crime prevention. Specifically, the problem-solving process recognizes that three elements must be present before a crime can occur: an offender (someone who is motivated to commit harmful behavior), a victim (a desirable and vulnerable target must be present), and a location (the victim and offender must both be in the same place at the same time)(see figure 13.1). If these elements show up over and over again in patterns and recurring problems, removing one or more of these elements can stop the pattern and prevent future harms (Eck, 1992). Effective removal, however, necessitates gaining as much possible information about these three elements.

Figure 13.1
The Crime Triangle

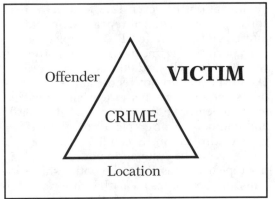

When analysis includes all three elements, a much clearer picture of crime emerges. A study on repeat victimization in 11 industrialized nations found that one in three residential burglaries in the United States is a repeat burglary—a proportion that surpassed all other nations in the study (Farrell and Sousa, 1997). Drawing upon the International Crime Victims Survey (Mayhew and Van Dijik, 1997), this study also found that 48 percent of sexual incidents (i.e., grabbing, touching, and assault), 43-percent of assaults and threats, and 23-percent of vehicle vandalism were repeat victimizations.

Repeat victimization is not limited to the more violent crimes, however. A domestic study of white collar crime (Alexander, personal communication to Farrell and Sousa, 1997) indicated that the same people are victims of fraud and embezzlement time and time again, and that bank robberies also have high rates of repeat victimization (Pease, personal communication to Farrell and Sousa, 1997).

These studies, though somewhat limited, show the value of including repeat victimization in the problem-solving process. An important question, then, is whether problem-oriented policing can utilize patterns of repeat victimization to reduce repeat occurrences. This is the focus of the next section.

Using Problem Solving to Identify Patterns of Victimization

Problem oriented policing was originally framed by Herman Goldstein, who argued for a radical change in policing efforts out of frustration with the dominant model for improving police operations: "More attention (was) being focused on how quickly officers responded to a call than on what they did when they got to their destination" (Goldstein, 1987:2; see also, Goldstein, 1990). Using this as a foundation, Eck (1992) and Spelman and Eck (1987) developed a problem solving process (S.A.R.A.) to determine if problem solving could be applied to the daily practices of the police (see figure 13.2).

Figure 13.2
Using the S.A.R.A. Problem Solving Process to Identify Patterns of Victimization Within the Crime Triangle

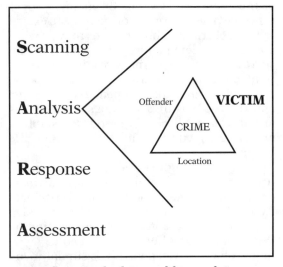

Briefly stated, this problem solving process involves four stages: scanning, analysis, response, and assessment (Spelman and Eck, 1987:43–52). *Scanning* refers to problem identification, where officers identify recurring problems on their beats. The second stage, *analysis*, is the heart of the problem solving process and involves the police learning as much as possible about the problem in order to identify its causes. Third is the *response* stage, with officers looking for long-term, creative, tailor-made solutions to the problem. Finally, in the *assessment* stage, officers evaluate the effectiveness of their responses, for example, checking to see if the number of calls for service regarding the problem decreased.

The S.A.R.A. process has been used very successfully for problem solving efforts in hundreds of communities large, medium, and small in size—across the nation. As examples, this process was used to reduce car burglaries in Seattle, address juvenile drug trafficking in Tulsa, diminish mobile park problems in Reno, against drugs and guns in San Diego, address crimes involving the homeless population in Savannah, and against mall gang problems in Lakewood, Colorado (Peak and Glensor, 1999).

The root of the problem solving process lies in the structured analysis of problems, which leads officers to look for clusters of similar, related, or recurring incidents rather than a single incident. This type of analysis would help police identify repeat offenders, locations (hot spots), and victims. The deflection and prevention of repeat victimization lie in these responses. Spelman (1995:380) articulated the benefits of preventing repeat victimization at the patrol level:

> The primary implication of repeat offenders, vulnerable victims, and dangerous places has always been that long-term activities made sense. In the absence of special attention, these high risk people and places would remain at high risk. Thus they had a claim on a disproportionate share of police resources. Programs to target certain offenders, provide assistance to certain victims, and solve recurring problems at certain locations seem appropriate.

Discussion

Repeat victimization is not new; police officers have always been aware that the same people and places are victimized again and again. However, what *is* new are attempts abroad to incorporate repeat victimization knowledge into formal crime prevention efforts. Research has enabled the police to bring repeat victimization into clearer focus and indicated what must be done—and the kinds of information systems that are required—to identify locations and persons who need the kind of crime prevention attention that is offered through this concept.

British police forces seek to implement repeat victimization policy as daily practice. Police in the United States would also do well to recognize the value of including repeat victimization in their overall crime management policy. To do so requires several philosophical and pragmatic changes to occur (Pease, 1998). Philosophically, police departments must recognize the importance and value of repeat victimization in developing a more comprehensive picture of crime. This recognition puts crime prevention, through detection and deflection, as the sole purpose of policing (Pease, 1996). By viewing crimes as occurring in a sequence, rather than a single incident, detection will enhance future prevention efforts, and prevention will reduce the likelihood of future detection.

The identification of patterns of repeat victimization is dependent upon the available information. Pragmatically, information gathering and computer systems need to reflect repeat victimization. Therefore, greater efforts must be made to gather more information concerning the victim, including those victims who do not report their crimes to the police. This will require implementing community-based surveys to identify patterns of repeat victimization. Integrating this information with information concerning the offender and location into a single database is paramount, and will allow the police to simultaneously consider all three elements of crime offender, place and victim. This, perhaps, poses one of the greatest challenges to American police departments. Currently, very few departments have the resources and/or skills necessary to develop, implement, and maintain adequate computer databases. Those resources that do exist tend to focus on either the offender or the location.

Given that these changes will not come easily, American police departments should continue to draw upon Great Britain as a resource. Their dedication to repeat victimization can contribute greatly to American efforts. At the same time, American police departments can offer their experiences in identifying the offender and location to British police departments, who have long ignored these elements. Together, this international alliance brings all elements of the crime triangle into focus, which can greatly enhance crime prevention efforts in both countries.

References

Anderson, D., Chenery, S., and Pease, K. (1994). *Tackling repeat repeat burglary and car crime.* Crime Detection and Prevention Papers 58. London: Home Office.

Anderson, D., Chenery, S., and Pease, K. (1995). *Preventing repeat victimization: A report on progress in Huddersfield.* London: Home Office Police Research Group Briefing Note 4/95.

Bridgeman, C. and Hobbs, L. (1997). *Preventing repeat victimization: The police officers' guide.* London: Home Office Police Research Group.

Eck, J. (1992). A dissertation prospectus for the study of characteristics of drug dealing places. November.

Farrell, G. (1995). Preventing repeat victimization. In M. Tonry and D.P. Farrington (eds.), *Building a safer society,* (pp. 469–534). Chicago: University of Chicago Press, (1995).

Farrell, G. and Pease, K. (1993). *Once bitten, twice bitten: Repeat victimization and its implications for crime prevention* London: Home Office, Police Research Group, 1993, p. 3.

Farrell, G. and Sousa, W. (1997). Repeat victimization in the United States and ten other industrialized countries. Paper presented at the National Conference on Preventing Crime, Washington, D.C., October 13.

Forrester, D. P. (1988). *The Kirkholt Burglary Prevention Project.* London: Home Office Police Research Group.

Goldstein, H. (1987). Problem-Oriented Policing. Paper presented at the Conference on Policing: State of the Art III, National Institute of Justice, Phoenix, Ariz., June 12.

——. (1990). Problem-Oriented Policing. New York: McGraw-Hill.

Lloyd, S., Farrell, G., and Pease, K. (1994). *Preventing repeated domestic violence: A demonstration project on Merseyside.* London: Home Office Police Research Group, Crime Prevention Unit Paper 49.

Mayhew, P. and J.V. Dijik (1997). *Criminal Victimization in Eleven Industrialized Countries: Key Findings for the 1997 International Crime Victims Survey.* Research and Documentation Center, Dutch Ministry of Justice.

Peak, K. and R. Glensor (1999). *Community Policing and Problem Solving: Strategies and Practices.* New York: Prentice-Hall.

Pease, K. (1996). Repeat Victimization and policing. Unpublished manuscript, University of Huddersfield, West Yorkshire, England, June 30, p. 4.

—— (1998). Repeat victimization: taking stock. Crime Detection and Prevention Series, Paper 90. London: Home Office Police Research Group.

Pease, K. and Laycock, G. (1996). Revictimization: Reducing the heat on hot victims. Washington, D.C.: U.S. Department of Justice, National Institute of Justice, Research Action, November.

Spelman, W. (1995). "Once Bitten, Then What? Cross-Sectional and Time Course Explanations for Repeat Victimization." *British Journal of Criminology,* 35(3):366–380.

Spelman W. and Eck, J. E. (1987). *Problem-Oriented Policing.* Washington, D.C.: U.S. Department of Justice, National Institute of Justice.

Titus, R. M. (1995). Activity theory and the victim. Paper presented to the 4th International Seminar on Environmental Criminology and Crime Analysis, Cambridge, England, July 8, p. 1.

14

Physical Environment and Crime

Ralph B. Taylor
Adele V. Harrell

Crime prevention includes the compelling need for a thorough understanding of the relationship between crime and the surrounding environment. Police and community must understand the settings in which crime occurs. More specifically, R. Taylor and A. Harrell examine how the physical features of the environment affect both an area's potential offenders and its residents, and the reduction of citizens' vulnerability in these settings. Indeed, several studies have shown that many features of the physical environment can assist in predicting crime rates and outcomes, such as the neighborhood's fear or confidence. This reading discusses several important linkages between neighborhood and street block physical features and crime, fear of crime, and other related variables. In sum, it discusses the important relationship between physical environment and crime—which cannot be ignored if a community-policing strategy has hope of success. As you read, appraise some areas in your community to determine how their physical layout may contribute to, or reduce crime.

Can physical features of the environment prevent crime or reduce problems thought to be crime related, such as fear of crime or residents' concerns about neighborhood viability? Crime prevention through environmental design (CPTED) focuses on the settings in which crimes occur and on techniques for reducing vulnerability in these settings. This report discusses assumptions surrounding work in this area and the major studies that link neighborhood and street block physical features with crime, fear of crime, and other related outcomes. Four major sets of physical features are emphasized in the research literature: housing design or block layout, land use and circulation patterns, resident-generated territorial features, and physical deterioration. Each of these approaches is discussed individually, and their policy implications are highlighted. The report ends with a series of questions that have not yet been answered by research.

Assuming a Rational Perspective

How might physical features influence behavior? Researchers have made several assumptions about how physical features affect both potential offenders and residents or users in a setting.

Offenders often operate in a rational fashion; they prefer to commit crimes that require the least effort, provide the highest benefits, and pose the lowest risks. Researchers have applied this rational offender perspective to a range of crimes (Clarke, 1983, 1992; Clarke and Cornish, 1985). This view suggests that crimes are most likely to occur when potential offenders come into contact with a suitable crime target where the chances of detection by others are thought to be low or the criminal, if detected, will be able to exit without being identified or apprehended. In short, the crime site lacks a natural guardian.

Physical environment features can influence the chances of a crime occurring. They affect potential offenders' perceptions about a possible crime site, their evaluations of the circumstances surrounding a potential crime site, and the availability and visibility of one or more natural guardians at or near a site. Offenders may decide whether or not to commit a crime in a location after they determine the following:

- How easy will it be to enter the area?

- How visible, attractive, or vulnerable do targets appear?

- What are the chances of being seen?

- If seen, will the people in the area do something about it?
- Is there a quick, direct route for leaving the location after the crime is committed?

These questions assume a rational offender perspective. The relevance of this perspective to an understanding of crime depends on a range of factors, including the type of crime and the familiarity between offender and victim or target.

The offender-based perspective relates to residents or users in a setting when it suggests potential offenders consider a setting's natural guardians. Much of the work in this area, which relies on empirically grounded models of human territorial functioning (Taylor, 1988), assumes residents or users may respond to potential offenders. The probability and type of response depends on a range of circumstances—social, cultural, and physical. Physical features may influence reactions to potential offenders by altering the chances of detecting them and by shaping the public vs. private nature of the space in question.

Overview of Four Approaches

Assuming that potential offenders and residents or users of a setting are affected by this rational perspective suggests four approaches to making a location more resistant to crime or crime-related problems.

- **Housing design or block layout.** Making it more difficult to commit crimes by (1) reducing the availability of crime targets; (2) removing barriers that prevent easy detection of potential offenders or of an offense in progress; and (3) increasing physical obstacles to committing a crime.
- **Land use and circulation patterns.** Creating safer use of neighborhood space by reducing routine exposure of potential offenders to crime targets. This can be accomplished through careful attention to walkways, paths, streets, traffic patterns, and location and hours of operation of public spaces and facilities.

These strategies may produce broader changes that increase the viability of more micro-level territorial behaviors and signage. For example, street closings or revised traffic patterns that decrease vehicular volume may, under some conditions, encourage residents to better maintain the sidewalk and street in front of their houses.

- **Territorial features.** Encouraging the use of territorial markers or fostering conditions that will lead to more extensive marking to indicate the block or site is occupied by vigilant residents. Sponsoring cleanup and beautification contests and creating controllable, semiprivate outdoor locations may encourage such activities. This strategy focuses on small-scale, private, and semipublic sites, usually within predominantly residential locales (Taylor 1988, chapter 4). It is most relevant at the street block level and below. It enhances the chances that residents themselves will generate semifixed features that demonstrate their involvement in and watchfulness over a particular delimited location. This approach has not proven directly relevant to crime, but it is closely linked to residents' fear of crime.

- **Physical deterioration**. Controlling physical deterioration to reduce offenders' perceptions that areas are vulnerable to crime and that residents are so fearful they would do nothing to stop a crime. Physical improvements may reduce the signals of vulnerability and increase commitment to joint protective activities. Physical deterioration, in all probability, not only influences cognition and behavior of potential offenders but also shapes how residents behave and what they think about other residents.

This focus on physical incivilities or signs of disorder (Skogan, 1990) is distinct from the preceding focus on territorial features.[1] First, there is a difference in scale. Reduction of incivilities addresses larger physical problems than does a territorial focus. An incivilities reduction program might emphasize any of the following:

- Securely closing or "capping" private vacant dwellings to prevent further deterioration and to preserve house values and a neat block appearance.

- Removing trash and abandoned cars from a large vacant lot.

- Razing deteriorated vacant houses.

- Repaving worn sidewalks in a commercial area with bricks.

These efforts often require significant involvement from city agencies or community-development or private corporations. Citizens and neighborhood associations clearly can and do play roles in initiating and assisting such efforts. Whereas a territorial focus concentrates on small-scale, resident-controlled spaces and resident-based dynamics, the incivilities approach is more inclusive. Although it is concerned with the impact on residents, the physical features considered can be located in residential or nonresidential spaces.

Second, the level of physical deterioration is usually too extensive for management by resident-based groups. Residents are not responsible for preventing large numbers of vacant houses or stores in a locale or for removing graffiti from the walls of a large school. One researcher has noted specifically that residents presume that deterioration emerges as a failure, in part, of public agencies (Hunter, 1978).

Third, there is a difference in emphasis. The territorial approach concentrates on cues from resident involvement, maintenance, and protection; the incivilities situation represents large-scale lapses in the local order.

Incivilities reduction, however, may complement improvement strategies based on resident-generated territorial marking and signage. Reductions in larger physical problems may encourage such markers and signage.

Each of the four approaches can reinforce the others separately or collectively. For example, incivilities reduction may complement the strategic focus on building design

and block layout. If two vacant units being used as crack houses on a block are razed, the number of potential offenders may be reduced. The interlocking aspect of the four approaches suggests that where possible, practitioners consider how each may be of help when they look at a particular setting. Stated differently, varying intervention points and levels of intervention may make or encourage physical improvements that may enhance safety and feelings of safety (see "Success Stories").

An in-depth discussion of each approach will show how each of these strategies offers a unique perspective that frequently complements the others.

Success Stories

Research and evaluations have provided examples of situations where physical design or redesign appears to have contributed substantially to lowering crimes or to crime-related public order problems.

- **Designing safer public housing.** Buildings with fewer apartments per entryway, fewer stories, and better views of the outside have residents with lower levels of fear and rates of victimization. (Newman and Franck, 1980, 1982)

- **Erecting barriers and changing street patterns.** In a North Miami neighborhood, building barriers and altering street patterns seem to have helped residents reduce the volume of drug dealers and buyers driving through the area. The result: Crimes such as auto theft and assault declined more rapidly in their neighborhood than in the city as a whole. (Atlas, 1991; Ycaza, 1992)

- **Controlling access to buildings, schools, parks, public housing, or other trouble spots through the use of regulated entry.** Measures used by the Bronx's Community and Clergy Coalition, for example, include requiring an identification card, setting limited hours of usage, diverting traffic through specific checkpoints, and using metal detectors in schools or other public buildings. (Weisel, Gouvis, and Harrell, 1994)

- **Creating safer public places.** Seattle's Adopt-a-Park program removes overgrown trees and bushes and increases lighting in neighborhood parks to deter drug dealing, vandalism, and the presence of homeless persons (Weisel, Gouvis, and Harrell, 1994). Success was reported for a similar project in a major downtown public park in Stockholm. (Knutsson, 1994)

Housing Design Features and Block Layout

Can housing design and block layout make residents less vulnerable and feel safer? The originally formulated idea is that physical features that offer better surveillance, delineation between public and private space, segmentation of outdoor space into locations controlled by smaller groups, and proximity of sites to well–used locations enable stronger resident-based informal control of outdoor, near-home spaces. Such control should lead to less delinquency, less fear, and less victimization (Newman, 1972; Jacobs, 1961).

Studies of varying quality began testing these ideas in the early 1970's and continued at a rapid pace for the next dozen years. In 1980, a theory was formulated that made a distinction between "first generation" and "second generation" defensible space (Taylor, Gottfredson, and Brower, 1980). In the latter version, researchers considered more carefully how the impact of physical features on fear and victimization may depend upon other social and cultural features in the setting, and they made more realistic assumptions about territorial behavior and cognition (see exhibit 14.1).

Defensible space theory has received strong supporting evidence from studies of public housing in Britain and the United States and from studies of residential street blocks in the United States (e.g., Newman and Franck, 1980, 1982; Perkins, Meeks, and Taylor, 1992; Taylor, Gottfredson, and Brower, 1984; see Taylor, 1988, for a review).

Exhibit 14.1
Second Generation Defensible Space Theory

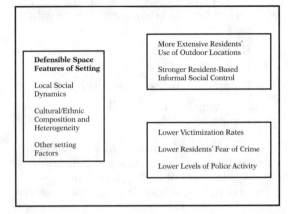

What many consider to be one of the strongest studies focused on 63 public housing sites around the country (Newman and Franck, 1982). The study found that sites with more defensible space features had residents who better controlled outdoor spaces and were less fearful and less victimized.

Practical Implications. This work led to implementation of specific design elements in numerous locations. For example, parking garages with outer walls of glass for the stairwells were constructed. In public housing, this perspective led to the construction of low-rise sites with clear segmentation of private space, clear boundaries between public and private space, and good lines of sight.

Limitations. One of the major limitations to expanding the number of defensible space designs has been the lack of research about how potential offenders view or use the physical features in question. Researchers have recently recast the discussion of defensible space features into a threefold grouping of physical features: prospect, refuge, and escape (e.g., Fisher and Nasar, 1992):

- Settings with high refuge offer concealment for the potential offender.
- Settings with high prospect allow the legitimate user to survey a wide area.
- Settings with high escape potential offer easy escape for the legitimate user.

This view of defensible space focuses explicitly on potential victim-potential offender dynamics in specific locations (see exhibit 14.2). Research confirms that fear is higher in locations that offer good refuge for the potential offender but low prospect and escape for the user.

(see exhibit 14.2)

Exhibit 14.2
Indicators of Refuge, Prospect, and Escape

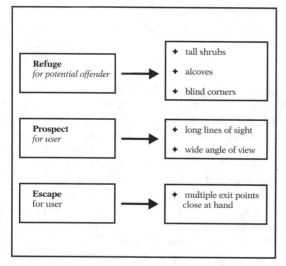

An additional limitation is that the effectiveness of defensible space features depends in part upon the immediate social and cultural context. Defensible space can be left "undefended" (Merry, 1981a). More knowledge is needed about the characteristics of context that allow defensible space features to more effectively support resident-based control. In all fairness, however, this limitation applies to all perspectives that link physical environment features with crime and related outcomes, and it is not unique to this theoretical perspective.

Land Use and Circulation Patterns

The internal layouts, boundary characteristics, and traffic patterns of neighborhoods may encourage or discourage different types of crime. By implication, changes in land uses, boundaries, and traffic patterns may result in higher or lower crime rates because they affect both potential offenders and users. They may alter exposure to potential offenders because they more or less integrate the locale into the offenders' orbits of activity (Rengert and Wasilchick, 1985).

Neighborhood Level. At the neighborhood level, planners classify the relevant features into movement generators, such as high-volume streets, and attractors and nonresidential land uses, such as shopping, that will draw outsiders. Movement generators result in more people moving through a residential locale; attractors and nonresidential land uses generate more people traveling to a residential locale.

Cross-sectional and longitudinal works both suggest strong connections between these physical features and crime levels. Cross-sectional studies in Atlanta (Greenberg and Rohe, 1986; Greenberg, Williams, and Rohe, 1982) and Richmond, Virginia (White, 1990), found that the internal layouts of low-crime neighborhoods were less permeable—more one-way, narrower, and lower volume streets—than those found in higher crime neighborhoods.

A recent study examined effects of physical environment on crime changes. The percentage of lots zoned for commercial use was a significant predictor of increased risk of high robbery rates in Washington, D.C. (Harrell and Gouvis, 1994). But the presence of public housing units, found in many census tracts in Washington, was not significantly related to changes in neighborhood risk of burglary, robbery, or assault in those areas. Longitudinal research in Hartford (Fowler and Mangione, 1986; Fowler, McCalla, and Mangione, 1979) and an unpublished evaluation in Miami (Ycaza, 1992) suggest that physical changes to internal circulation patterns and boundaries were followed by lower crime rates. Planners have routinely worked with neighborhoods across the country to analyze their crime problems and to reduce them by making physical alterations (Gardiner, 1994).

In the studies involving redesign, however, local social or organizational dynamics have often accompanied planned changes. Although it seems likely that design changes themselves have been partially responsible for the impact observed, researchers have not yet precisely estimated their independent contribution to lowering crime, fear, or perceived risk. How much of the benefit has been due to the redesign, and how much has been due to the social and organizational changes surrounding the planned change?

Practical Implications. There are several practical implications of this research at the neighborhood level:

- Social and organizational conditions are important when changes in layout, traffic, or land use are being considered. Community involvement of residents, neighborhood organizations, and local businesspersons is essential for developing a plan free of adverse effects on major interest groups.

- Local involvement may be an important precondition not only for rational, maximally beneficial change but also for achieving a redesign that will actually reduce crime. One study suggests that changes in layout, under conditions of community mobilization, appear to have been partially responsible for decreases in some crimes (Fowler and Mangione, 1986). But the crime-preventive benefits of changes in layout appear to weaken as community mobilization wanes.

- An early step in planning redesign to prevent crime is understanding offender location. For some offenses, such as auto theft, offenders may come from other neighborhoods. For other offenses, such as drug dealing, offenders may live in the area. If they come primarily from outside the neighborhood, can residents readily distinguish between these potential predators and individuals who are in the neighborhood for legitimate purposes? If they can make the distinction, physical impediments to entry and circulation may result in less crimes committed by certain types of offenders.[2]

- Neighborhood layout and boundaries— ease of circulation, a higher proportion of nonresidential land use—appear linked to higher street crimes and more burglary.

These implications need to be tempered by the recognition that crime prevention is just one objective of land use planning. As one of the anonymous reviewers of this report stated:

> Other objectives, such as economic development or equal housing opportunities, might at times conflict with a crime-prevention or fear-reduction objective. The planning process surrounding design or redesign will need to balance these potentially competing goals.

Street Block Level. At the street block level, nonresidential land use and high traffic volume may interfere with residents' ability to manage activities on the block and to recognize people who belong to the neighborhood. Pioneering research found that residents living on higher vehicle traffic streets used their front yards less and withdrew from neighbors (Appleyard, 1981). Higher levels of foot traffic, often associated with nearby commercial or institutional land use, also caused the same social cocooning (Baum, Davis, and Aiello, 1978). Nonresidential land uses and associated higher foot and vehicle traffic levels make it more difficult for residents to get to know one another and to distinguish between legitimate users of the setting and potential offenders. Such dynamics can be understood in the context of resident-based territorial functioning (Taylor, 1988, chapter 8). In short: Nonresidential land uses create holes in the fabric of resident-based informal control, and higher traffic or pedestrian volumes shrink the geographic extent of resident-based informal control.

Consequently, residents living on blocks with higher levels of nonresidential land use are more concerned for their personal safety and less likely to intervene if they see something suspicious; they experience higher victimization rates and call the police more often. These links have been supported by evidence from numerous studies conducted in different cities around the country (Kurtz, Koons, and Taylor, 1995; McPherson, Silloway, and Frey, 1983; Perkins, Florin, Rich, Wandersman, and Chavis, 1990; Roncek and Bell, 1981; Roncek and Faggiani, 1985; Taylor, Kurtz, and Koons, 1994). Not surprisingly, nonresidential land uses, such as bars, are particularly troublesome on residential blocks (Frisbie et al., 1978).

At the same time, increasing the number of people on or around the block in some settings may enhance informal surveillance and reduce some types of offenses. It also may contribute to other neighborhood goals, such as economic development. Good design and management may, to some extent, reduce some crime risks around facilities and public attractions.

Practical Implications. What are the practical implications of these street block dynamics?

- They do not mean that stores and small businesses should be removed from residential settings. As noted earlier, land use planning for crime-prevention purposes may conflict with other legitimate goals, such as economic development. Residents depend on these services. Further, in settings where proprietors have long tenancy or are culturally similar to residents, they make important contributions to the safety and orderliness of street life. (Jablonsky, 1993:80; Jacobs, 1968)

- Nevertheless, in locations where sizable "gaps" exist between residents and entrepreneurs, steps may be needed to draw the personnel staffing nonresidential land uses into contributing to overall street order.

In older urban locations in many cities, residents and entrepreneurs are often of different ethnic backgrounds (e.g., African-American residents vs. Korean entrepreneurs) and therefore have different cultures. It is sometimes difficult for each group to interpret the behavior of the other (Merry, 1981b), which in turn may impede entrepreneurs' contributions to informal control over events on the street. An important role for police community-relations councils and local business organizations may be to develop strategies so these entrepreneurs can contribute meaningfully to resident-based control over street life.[3]

Understanding the effects of nonresidential land use on informal control on the street block is limited by a lack of recent work ex-

amining relationships between entrepreneurs and residents in inner-city neighborhoods. There are several excellent recent ethnographies of inner-city life by, among others, Elijah Anderson, Elliot Liebow, Terry Williams, and Phillipe Bourgois. None, however, provide significant detail about resident-shopkeeper relationships and how they may condition the connection between land use and crime.

Resident-Generated Territorial Signage

Resident-generated signs of caring and proprietorship signal to other residents and to outsiders that people living there care, are vigilant about what happens on the street, and are willing to intervene if needed. Studies to date suggest that the territorial perspective may be more relevant to the goals of fear reduction and bolstering neighborhood confidence than to crime prevention per se.

The theory focuses on street block dynamics and explains how territorial functioning contributes to the smooth running of ongoing residential behavior settings (Brower, 1980; Taylor, 1988, chapter 6). Residents and outsiders alike interpret territorial markers as clues to how residents will act in different situations. Evidence supporting this perspective includes several cross-sectional studies linking territorial markers, local social involvement, and control over nearby public spaces (Brower, 1988; Greenbaum and Greenbaum, 1981). Residents perceive that stronger markers indicate a safer environment: the more threatening the environment, the more markers required to make residents feel safe (Brower, Dockett, and Taylor, 1983).

Practical Implications. In keeping with defensible space ideas, planners and designers want to create delimited, semipublic spaces that can easily be overseen by residents. The current boom in urban gardening on vacant lots in inner-city neighborhoods testifies to what people can do with a space they are allowed to manage. The garden gives them a reason to keep an eye out on the street and involves them more in the neighborhood.

In addition, officials may want to publicly support local initiatives that encourage resident-based territorial strategies. Many local community groups already promote extensive efforts to encourage residents to get involved with cleanup and beautification. Local officials do not want to "take over" these activities. Nevertheless, community groups and residents may be appreciative if officials recognize and support the contributions they are making to create safer blocks and overall neighborhood viability.

The territorial approach as it relates to disorder is limited in three ways relevant to crime-related problems. First, it is not yet understood what happens over time. For example, it is not known how fear of crime can hamper territorial functioning or frustrate intervention in a cycle of increasing concern and weakening jurisdiction. Second, it is difficult to separate the relative contributions to fear reduction of the social and cognitive components of territorial functioning from the physical components emerging from territorial marking. In part, this difficulty emerges from the close, system-like connections between social, cognitive, and behavioral components. Finally, it is not clear how potential offenders respond to territorial signage. Some research suggests that offenders, such as burglars, attend to it (Brown, 1985; Brown and Altman, 1983); other studies theorize that offenders pay attention to different features of house and block context (Bennett and Wright, 1984).

Controlling Physical Deterioration and Disorder

In the 1970's, one researcher proposed that what really made people afraid in cities and concerned about their welfare was not only the crimes they saw and heard about but also the physical and social signs they saw around them that indicated a breakdown in society (J.Q. Wilson, 1975). Another researcher called these indicators "signs of incivility." He argued that such signs made people feel vulnerable because they suggested to resident[s] that the public officials and agencies charged with maintaining order were incapable or unconcerned about following through (Hunter, 1978).

Two researchers then framed the concept of incivilities longitudinally and considered how offenders might respond to signs of incivility (Wilson and Kelling, 1982). They discussed these dynamics in the context of community policing. Their broken windows thesis, depicted in exhibit 14.3, suggests the following chain of events:

- Physical deterioration, wear and tear, and large-scale accumulations of graffiti and trash routinely occur in many older, urban neighborhoods. If, however, people or agencies do not do anything for a significant period about such deterioration or accumulations, residents and shop personnel working in the neighborhood feel increasingly vulnerable.

- Feeling more concerned for their personal safety, residents and store personnel participate less in the maintenance of order in public places. They are less likely to stop teens or adults who are "messing around," "being rowdy," or "hassling people."

- Sensing fewer "eyes on the street" (Jacobs, 1961, 1968), delinquent preteens and teens in the neighborhood become emboldened and harass or vandalize more frequently. Increasingly convinced they can get away with it, delinquents commit more minor crimes, and youths become increasingly disorderly.

- Residents, sensing that some local youths are becoming increasingly troublesome, withdraw further from the public spaces in the neighborhood and become more concerned about protecting their own person and property.

- At this point, potential offenders from outside the neighborhood sense the locale is vulnerable. They are drawn into the neighborhood because crimes committed there will be less likely to be detected and responded to. The neighborhood crime rate increases dramatically.

Another researcher suggested that incivilities may spur subsequent neighborhood decline because the consequences noted above lead ultimately to resident out-migration

Exhibit 14.3
Broken Windows Thesis

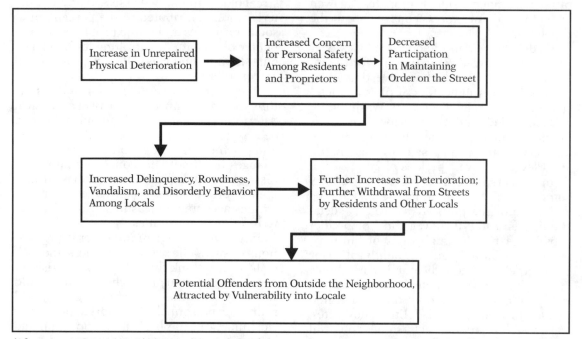

(Skogan, 1986, 1990:2). He proposed the following scenario: Vandalism, abandoned buildings, and other evidence of disrepair may be contagious, stimulating additional disregard for property by attracting potential offenders. The neighborhood declines, sometimes more quickly than would otherwise be the case. The decline may be manifested as increasing vacancy rates, higher conversion rates from owner-occupied to rental properties, more dramatic changes in ethnic or racial composition of residents or store owners, or changes in the socioeconomic status of residents.

These ideas have garnered significant attention from urban theorists and policy planners despite some limitations (Greene and Taylor, 1988). What sound empirical evidence is there that links physical deterioration or signs of incivility with crime, fear of crime, or increases in either?

Cross-sectional studies on signs of disorder, crime, and fear have generated different results, depending upon the unit of analysis and the type of measures used (Miethe, 1995). Studies using residents' perceptions of incivilities have found more consistent ef-

fects than studies based on onsite ratings of physical features, and studies using street blocks generally have provided more consistent results than studies using neighborhoods.[4] In neighborhoods where physical deterioration is more widespread, residents have been more fearful when the future of that neighborhood has appeared uncertain (Taylor, Shumaker, and Gottfredson, 1985). The effect of neighborhood deterioration on residents' fear levels is weakened somewhat when deterioration has reached a high level (Taylor and Shumaker, 1990).

Extensive research has linked perceptions of physical deterioration and social incivilities with fear of crime and other outcomes relevant to neighborhood viability (Lewis and Maxfield, 1980; Skogan, 1990). For example, one study found effects of an incivilities index on perceived crime problems, fear at night, and robbery victimization while controlling for neighborhood poverty, stability, and minority status (Skogan, 1990:193–194).

Both onsite assessments of incivilities and resident perceptions of the incivilities have contributed independently to residents' concerns for personal safety (Covington and Taylor, 1991). This suggests that extant deterioration may make residents more fearful even when they do not express concern about the problems.

Studies of neighborhoods or blocks over time have provided some support for the incivilities thesis. Researchers investigated effects of indirect indicators of physical deterioration and social disorder in Washington, D.C., and Cleveland, Ohio. Prior crime rates predicted subsequent neighborhood risk of burglary, robbery, and assault in Washington and Cleveland across periods of 2 to 5 years. Home ownership, which presumably reflects commitment to maintaining the appearance and value of the property as well as social stability and low turnover, did not predict subsequent risk for high rates of burglary, robbery, or assault independently of prior crime levels. Other indicators of neighborhood decay, however, added significantly to risk prediction based only on prior crime rates. Since arson and delinquency often leave visible scars that act as cues to social and physical incivilities in decaying neighborhoods, arson and delinquency rates predicted changes in neighborhood burglary risk. Family poverty, previously associated with neighborhood disorder (Skogan, 1990), predicted risk of high assault rates in Washington neighborhoods and high robbery rates in Cleveland neighborhoods independently of earlier crime levels (Harrell and Gouvis, 1994).

Physical changes appear to precede crime changes. Using groupings of Los Angeles census tracts and studying them for several decades, researchers found that patterns of owner-to-rental conversion, land use changes, and abandonment predicted the emergence of hardened high-crime areas. The connection remained after controlling for changes in the types of people living there (Schuerman and Kobrin, 1986).

In short, depending upon neighborhood context and other factors, physical deterioration and indirect indicators partially reflecting deterioration appear to be linked to resident fear levels and changing crime rates.

Across street blocks, one study suggested stronger, less conditional connections between incivilities and perceptions of crime-related problems. A study of 50 Baltimore street blocks found that assessed physical deterioration contributed to the perception of social problems and crime problems on particular blocks after controlling for block layout, stability, and class (Perkins, Meeks and Taylor, 1992).

Neighborhood- and block-level results thus indicate connections between physical deterioration, features presumably related to deterioration, or perceptions of deterioration and crime-related problems, crime, or changes in crime. This conclusion, however, rests on a small number of studies. It also ignores divergent perspectives on what constitutes acceptable measures of physical deterioration or incivilities.

Implications. There are several implications of such a link. Local planners and officials, if they think that a locale is "at risk" of experiencing sharply higher crime, could work to coordinate housing, zoning, and sanitation personnel in an effort to prevent or slow increases in physical deterioration and housing abandonment (Taylor and Covington, 1990). Such efforts might block the emergence of higher crime rates, higher fear levels, or declining commitment to the community.

For example, in a partially gentrified neighborhood in Baltimore,Maryland, local leaders urged city personnel to move quickly and "cap" several private, abandoned properties in danger of serious deterioration. According to one leader, the city failed to respond despite several months of repeated requests from the association. The walls of one of the targeted properties finally collapsed into an alley. Alleviation of large-scale deterioration may lead to stronger neighborhood commitment.

Limitations. At the same time, what is known has serious limitations.

- It is not known if changes in physical deterioration and incivilities occur independently of, or simply reflect, neighborhood structural change. Due to ecological processes and social, political, and economic factors, neighborhoods naturally change in three ways: socioeconomic status increases or decreases;

stability, reflected in the balance of owners vs. renters, shifts; and the racial and age composition changes (Hunter, 1974; Taylor and Covington, 1988). Do changes in physical incivilities merely *reflect* these structural changes, or do the physical changes emerge independently of these structural changes? The answer to this question has important policy as well as theoretical implications. For example, suppose physical incivility changes simply reflect socioeconomic status changes.[5] For the long-term purpose of preventing crimes that are already increasing in a neighborhood, it may be more important to provide jobs to residents than to renovate housing.

- At any one point in time, physical incivilities are closely connected to other neighborhood features. For example, blocks with more incivilities also contain a higher proportion of nonresidential land uses (Taylor, Koons, Kurtz, and Greene, in press). It is not yet known if land use mix is more influential in increasing crime than are levels of physical deterioration.

- Little is known about how potential offenders "read" physical incivilities, a key aspect of the broken windows thesis (Wilson and Kelling, 1982). Presumably, offenders from outside read the level of deterioration and base their invasion of a locale partly on those features. Burglars carefully read the environment around contemplated targets (Rengert and Wasilchick, 1985). But it is not known specifically how much attention burglars or other offenders pay to physical deterioration.

Decreasing deterioration also can be problematic. Studies in Britain and the United States suggest that improved physical environments, such as those found in gentrifying neighborhoods, also may be troublesome and associated with higher crime (Bottoms and Wiles, 1986; Covington and Taylor, 1989). Potential offenders inside or outside the location may infer from physical upkeep that more potentially lucrative targets are available for such crimes as larceny and robbery. A key issue influencing such an outcome may be whether a large pool of motivated, potential offenders is extremely close by.

Pending Issues

A fair amount is known about designing and redesigning locations so that a setting's physical features—given certain social and cultural conditions—help discourage crime or make residents or users feel less vulnerable (Crowe, 1991). There are numerous cross-sectional links at the community and street block level and some links over time between physical environment features and these outcomes. Nevertheless, numerous practical and theoretical questions remain about what works in specific situations and why.

- **The sequence of relationships between physical change, crime events, fear of crime, and perceptions of place vulnerability is not well understood.** Does physical decay precede and predict worsening crime rates, is the reverse more generally true, or does it depend? If one factor depends on the others, on what other characteristics of the setting do these processes rely? Where in these processes do residents' feelings of vulnerability and behavioral withdrawal from street life come into play?

- **How do social, cultural, and organizational features contribute to the success of crime reduction through physical environment modifications?** Research to date clearly counters the notion that physical environment features have stand-alone effects on crime and related problems. Their effectiveness depends on other features of the setting in question, especially local social, cultural, and organizational dynamics. Relations between neighbors, ethnic composition, and initiatives emerging from local organizations and churches determine whether physical design or redesign helps reduce crime or related problems, such as fear of crime. With some exceptions, the specific behavioral and social psychological processes that explain how physical effects on crime and related problems depend on nonphysical conditions is not yet understood.

- **What is the effect of the larger social, political, and economic environment on the risk of crime, and how do these broader issues relate to the physical environment features discussed here?** Some types of offenders follow a multistage planning process that begins with the selection of an area or neighborhood where they feel they can operate conformably, with low costs in terms of time and effort, and where they stand a good chance of obtaining a reward for their efforts (Rengert, 149). Subsequently, they select blocks, buildings, or persons within that area (Taylor and Gottfredson, 1986). Features of the larger environment, such as concentrations of potential offenders or concentrated poverty (Bursik and Grasmick, 1993a; Wacquant and Wilson, 1989; Wilson, W.J., 1991), or lack of political power with limited access to resources (Bursik and Grasmick, 1993b), influence an area's locational crime risk. Do physical features have less crime-preventive benefits in areas with high-locational crime risk due to their position in the broader urban ecology? Understanding connections between urban location and crime-prevention benefits of physical design or redesign has important practical implications. Such an understanding can help agencies focus scarce resources on sites likely to produce maximum crime-preventive benefits. If planners have a choice between two equally needy and qualified locales, they would probably want to assist efforts at the site where success is more likely.

- **Housing disrepair and vacancy, certain land use patterns, vandalism, physical layout, and patterns of traffic and pedestrian circulation may increase the risk of crime.** What is the relative importance of these factors? Does their relative importance for crime-prevention purposes depend on the type of crime in question? Does it depend on other features of the context? What is their relative impact on residents' perceptions of safety in the area? How important are the different features, relative to one another, in making the area appealing to potential offenders?

Conclusion

Research has shown that a wide range of features of the physical environment at the street block and neighborhood levels have proven relevant to predicting crime rates and crime-related outcomes, such as fear of crime and neighborhood confidence. In some of these studies, however, it is difficult to separate the relative crime-preventive or fear-reducing effects of redesign from the beneficial effects of ongoing local social dynamics or the organizational development surrounding the redesign effort. In sum, the relevance of the physical environment appears contingent on a range of nonphysical factors and the type of crime or crime-related outcome in question.

Research to date has followed four different theoretical perspectives. To the practitioner, these different views on the issue suggest different points and types of intervention. A more powerful understanding of the relationship between crime and design may emerge from an integration of these different perspectives.

Notes

1. Social as well as physical signs of disorder exist. The authors focus here solely on physical ones.

2. There are two important caveats to this strategy. First, the limitations on entry and circulation must not severely limit other purposes served by the streets and institutions in the neighborhood. In addition, the distinctions drawn between insiders and potential offenders from outside must be empirically founded and not driven by class-based or ethnically based prejudices.

3. The authors are indebted to Angela Taylor for this suggestion.

4. This conclusion is closely parallel to but somewhat more than Miethe's (1995:21): "[T]he empirical evidence on the direct and indirect impact of measures of neighborhood incivilities on individuals' fear of crime is inconclusive."

5. Skogan (1990:173) reports a correlation of .84 between his disorder index and neighborhood unemployment rates.

References

Appleyard, Don. (1981). *Livable Streets*. Berkeley: University of California Press.

Atlas, R. (1991). "The Other Side of CPTED." *Security Management*. March.

Baum, A., A.G. Davis, and J.R. Aiello. (1978). "Crowding and Neighborhood Mediation of Urban Density." *Journal of Population* 1:266-279.

Bennett, T., and J. Wright. (1984). *Burglars on Burglary*. London: Gower.

Bottoms, A.E., and P. Wiles. (1986). "Housing Tenure and Residential Community Crime Careers in Britain." In A.J. Reiss, Jr., and M. Tonry (eds.), *Crime and Justice: A Review Of Research, Communities and Crime*. Chicago: University of Chicago Press, pp. 101–162.

Brower, S. (1980). "Territory in Urban Settings." In Altman et al. (eds.), *Human Behavior in the Environment: Advances in Theory and Research*. New York: Plenum, Volume 4.

Brower, S. (1988). *Design in Familiar Places: What Makes Home Environments Look Good*. New York: Praeger.

Brower, S., K. Dockett, and Ralph B. Taylor. (1983). "Resident's Perceptions Site-level Features." *Environment and Behavior* 15:419-437.

Brown, B.B. (1985). "Residential Territories: Cues to Burglary Vulnerability." *Journal of Architectural Planning and Research* 2:231-243.

Brown, B.B., and I. Altman. (1983). "Territoriality, Defensible Space, and Residential Burglary: An Environmental Analysis." *Journal of Environmental Psychology* 3:203-220.

Bursik, R.J., Jr., and H.G. Grasmick. (1993a). "Economic Deprivation and Neighborhood Crime Rates, 1960-1980." *Law and Society Review* 27.

Bursik, R.J., Jr., and H.G. Grasmick. (1993b). *Neighborhoods and Crime*. New York: Lexington Books.

Clarke, R.V. (1983). "Situational Crime Prevention: Its Theoretical Basis and Practical Scope." In M. Tonry and N. Morris (eds.), *Crime and Justice: An Annual Review of Research*. Chicago: The University of Chicago Press, Volume 4, pp. 225-256.

Clarke, R.V. (ed.). (1992). *Situational Crime Prevention*. Albany: Harrow and Heston.

Clarke, R.V., and D.B. Cornish. (1985). "Modeling Offenders' Decisions: A Framework for Research and Policy." In M. Tonry and N. Morris (eds.), *Crime and Justice: An Annual Review of Research*. Chicago: University of Chicago Press, Volume 6.

Covington, J., and Ralph B. Taylor. (1989). "Gentrification and Crime: Robbery and Larceny Changes in Appreciating Baltimore Neighborhoods in the 1970's." *Urban Affairs Quarterly* 25:142-172.

Covington, J., and Ralph B. Taylor. (1991). "Fear of Crime in Urban Residential Neighborhoods: Implications of Between and Within-Neighborhood Sources for Current Models." *The Sociological Quarterly* 32:231-249.

Crowe, T.D. (1991). *Crime Prevention Through Environmental Design: Applications of Architectural Design and Space Management Concepts*. London: Butterworth-Heinemann.

Fisher, Bonnie, and Jack L. Nasar. (1992). "Fear of Crime in Relation to Three Exterior Site Features: Prospect, Refuge, and Escape." *Environment and Behavior* 24:35-65.

Fowler, F., and T. Mangione. (1986). "A Three-Pronged Effort to Reduce Crime and Fear of Crime: The Hartford Experiment." In D. Rosenbaum (ed.), *Community Crime Prevention*. Newbury Park, CA: Sage, pp. 87-108.

Fowler, F., M.E. McCalla, and T. Mangione. (1979). *Reducing Residential Crime and Fear: The Hartford Neighborhood Crime Prevention Program*. Washington, D.C.: U.S. Government Printing Office.

Frisbie, D., et al. (1978). *Crime in Minneapolis*. MN: Minnesota Crime Prevention Center.

Gardiner, R.A. (1994). Personal communication.

Greenbaum, P.E., and S.D. Greenbaum. (1981). "Territorial Personalization: Group Identity and Social Interaction in a Slavic-American Neighborhood." *Environment and Behavior* 13:574-589.

Greenberg, S., and W. Rohe. (1986). "Informal Social Control." In Ralph B. Taylor (ed.), *Urban Neighborhoods: Research and Policy*. New York: Praeger.

Greenberg, S.W., J.R. Williams, and W.R. Rohe. (1982). "Safety in Urban Neighborhoods: A Comparison of Physical Characteristics and Informal Territorial Control in High and Low Crime Neighborhoods." *Population and Environment* 5:141-165.

Greene, J.R., and Ralph B. Taylor. (1988). "Community-Based Policing and Foot Patrol: Issues of Theory and Evaluation." In J.R. Greene and S.D. Mastrofski (eds.), *Community Policing: Rhetoric or Reality?* New York: Praeger, pp. 195-224.

Harrell, Adele, and C. Gouvis. (1994). "Community Decay and Crime." Washington, D.C.: The Urban Institute. Final report. Grant NU-IJ-CX-KO16.

Hunter, A. (1974). *Symbolic Communities.* Chicago: University of Chicago Press.

Hunter, A. (1978). "Symbols of Incivility." Paper presented at the Annual Meeting of the American Society of Criminology. Dallas, Texas.

Jablonsky, T.J. (1993). *Pride in the Jungle: Community and Everyday Life in Back of the Yards Chicago.* Baltimore: Johns Hopkins University Press.

Jacobs, J. (1961). *The Death and Life of the American City.* New York: Vintage.

Jacobs, J. (1968). "Community on the City Streets." In E.D. Baltzell (ed.), *The Search for Community in Modern America.* New York: Harper and Row, pp. 74-93.

Knutsson, J. (1994). "The Vassapark Project." Paper presented at the Environmental Criminology and Crime Analysis Conference, Rutgers University, Newark, NJ, June.

Kurtz, E., B. Koons, and Ralph B. Taylor. (1995). "Nonresidential Land Use, Informal Resident-based Control, Physical Deterioration, and Calls for Police Service." Paper presented at the Annual Meeting of the Academy for Criminal Justice Sciences, Boston, MA, March.

Lewis, D.A., and M.G. Maxfield. (1980). "Fear in the Neighborhoods: An Investigation of the Impact of Crime." *Journal of Research in Crime and Delinquency* 17:160-189.

McDougall, H.A. (1993). *Black Baltimore: A New Theory of Community.* Philadelphia: Temple University Press.

McPherson, M., G. Silloway, and D.L. Frey. (1983). *Crime, Fear, and Control in Neighborhood Commercial Centers.* Minneapolis: Minnesota Crime Prevention Center.

Merry, S.E. (1981a). "Defensible Space Undefended: Social Factors in Crime Control Through Environmental Design." *Urban Affairs Quarterly* 16:397-422.

Merry, S.E. (1981b). *Urban Danger: Life in a Neighborhood of Strangers.* Philadelphia: Temple University Press.

Miethe, T. (1995). "Fear and Withdrawal from Urban Life." *Annals of the American Academy of Political and Social Science* 539:14-27.

Newman, Oscar. (1972). *Defensible Space.* New York: Macmillan.

Newman, Oscar, and Karen Franck. (1980). *Factors Influencing Crime and Instability in Urban Housing Developments.* Washington, D.C.: U.S. Government Printing Office.

Newman, Oscar, and Karen Franck. (1982). "The Effects of Building Size on Personal Crime and Fear of Crime." *Population and Environment* 5:203-220.

Perkins, D.D., P. Florin, R.C. Rich, A. Wandersman, and D.M. Chavis. (1990). "Participation and the Social and Physical Environment of Residential Blocks: Crime and Community Context." *American Journal of Community Psychology* 18:83-115.

Perkins, D.D., J.W. Meeks, and Ralph B. Taylor. (1992). "The Physical Environment of Street Blocks and Resident Perceptions of Crime and Disorder: Implications for Theory and Measurement." *Journal of Environmental Psychology* 12:21-34.

Rengert, G.F. (1989). "Spatial Justice and Criminal Victimization." *Justice Quarterly* 6:543-564.

Rengert, G., and J. Wasilchick. (1985). *Suburban Burglary.* Springfield, IL: Charles C. Thomas.

Roncek, D.W., and R. Bell. (1981). "Bars, Blocks, and Crime." *Journal of Environmental Systems* 11:35-47.

Roncek, D.W., and D. Faggiani. (1985). "High Schools and Crime: A Replication." *The Sociological Quarterly* 26:491-505

Schuerman, L., and S. Kobrin. (1986). "Community Careers in Crime." In A.J. Reiss and M. Tonry (eds.), *Crime and Justice: A Review of Research, Communities and Crime.* Chicago: University of Chicago Press, pp. 67-100.

Skogan, Wes. (1986). "Fear of Crime and Neighborhood Change." In A.J. Reiss, Jr., and M. Tonry (eds.), *Crime and Justice: A Review of Research, Communities and Crime.* Chicago: University of Chicago Press, 230, Volume 8, p. 203.

Skogan, Wes. (1990). *Disorder and Decline: Crime and the Spiral of Decay in American Cities.* New York: Free Press.

Taylor, Ralph B. (1988). *Human Territorial Functioning.* Cambridge: Cambridge University Press.

Taylor, Ralph B., and J. Covington. (1988). "Neighborhood Changes in Ecology and Violence." *Criminology* 26:553-589.

Taylor, Ralph B., and J. Covington. (1990). "Ecological Change, Changes in Violence, and Risk Prediction." *Journal of Interpersonal Violence* 5:164-175.

Taylor, Ralph B., and S.D. Gottfredson. (1986). "Environmental Design, Crime, and Prevention: An Examination of Community Dynamics." In A.J. Reiss and M. Tonry (eds.), *Crime and Justice: A Review of Research, Communities and Crime*. Chicago: University of Chicago Press, pp. 387-416.

Taylor, Ralph B., S.D. Gottfredson, and S.N. Brower. (1980). "The Defensibility of Defensible Space." In T. Hirschi and M. Gottfredson (eds.), *Understanding Crime*. Beverly Hills: Sage.

Taylor, Ralph B., S.D. Gottfredson, and S. Brower. (1984). "Block Crime and Fear: Local Social Ties and Territorial Functioning." *Journal of Research in Crime and Delinquency* 21:303-331.

Taylor, Ralph B., B. Koons, E. Kurtz, and J. Greene. (In press). "Physical Deterioration and Nonresidential Land Use: Confirmatory Factor Analyses in Two Cities." *Urban Affairs Review* (formerly *Urban Affairs Quarterly*).

Taylor, Ralph B., E. Kurtz, and B. Koons. (1994). "Block-Level Connections Between Land Use Arrangements, Physical Deterioration, and Crime." Paper presented at the Third International Meeting on Situational Crime Prevention, Rutgers University, Newark, NJ, June.

Taylor, Ralph B., and S.A. Shumaker. (1990). "Local Crime as a Natural Hazard: Implications for Understanding the Relationship Between Disorder and Fear of Crime." *American Journal of Community Psychology* 18:619-642.

Taylor, Ralph B., S.A. Shumaker, and S.D. Gottfredson. (1985). "Neighborhood-Level Links Between Physical Features and Local Sentiments: Deterioration, Fear of Crime, and Confidence." *Journal of Architectural Planning and Research* 2:261-275.

Wacquant, L.J.D., and W.J. Wilson. (1989). "The Cost of Racial and Class Exclusion in the Inner City." *Annals of the American Academy of Political and Social Science* 105:8-25.

Weisel, D.L., C. Gouvis, and A.V. Harrell. (1994). "Addressing Community Decay and Crime: Alternative Approaches and Explanations." Washington, D.C.: The Urban Institute. Final report submitted to the National Institute of Justice.

White, G.F. (1990). "Neighborhood Permeability and Burglary Rates." *Justice Quarterly* 7:57-68.

Wilson, James Q. (1975). *Thinking About Crime.* New York: Basic.

Wilson, James Q., and George Kelling. (1982). "Broken Windows." *Atlantic Monthly* 211:29-38.

Wilson, W.J. (1991). "Studying Inner City Dislocations: The Challenge of Public Agenda Research." *American Sociological Review* 56:1-14.

Ycaza, C. (1992). "Crime Rate Drops in Shores." *The Miami Herald*, May 17.

Reprinted from: Ralph. B. Taylor and Adele V. Harrell, "Physical Environment and Crime." In *A Final Summary Report Presented to the National Justice Insitute of Justice*, May 1996. ✦

15

Situational Crime Prevention

Successful Studies

Ronald V. Clarke

One of the tenets of crime prevention is that opportunities for crime must be reduced. Since 1980, there has been a growing movement to develop an approach to crime prevention that makes crime more difficult or too risky. This movement has resulted in situational crime prevention. R. Clarke provides an excellent overview of two related, important concepts: "defensible space" and "crime prevention through environmental design," or CPTED, and how these ideas relate to problem-oriented policing. He provides a further look at the surrounding environment's relationship to crime by including an introduction to the "routine activities" theory. Techniques and case studies of the situational prevention of crime are examined as well as its scope and effectiveness. Issues of philosophy, politics,and policy are included as they concern the situation-prevention approach. Consider how this section takes community policing and problem solving to a higher level, and note the several significant and sophisticated viewpoints and methods offered for reducing opportunities for crime.

Situational crime prevention departs radically from most criminology in its orientation (Clarke, 1980; Clarke and Mayhew, 1980). Proceeding from an analysis of the circumstances giving rise to specific kinds of crime, it introduces discrete managerial and environmental change to reduce the opportunity for those crimes to occur. Thus it is focused on the settings for crime, rather than upon those committing criminal acts. It seeks to forestall the occurrence of crime,

rather than to detect and sanction offenders. It seeks not to eliminate criminal or delinquent tendencies through improvement of society or its, institutions, but merely to make criminal action less attractive to offenders. Central to this enterprise is not the criminal justice system, but a host of public and private organizations and agencies—schools, hospitals, transit systems, shops and malls, manufacturing businesses and phone companies, local parks and entertainment facilities, pubs and parking lots—whose products, services and operations spawn opportunities for a vast range of different crimes.

Dozens of documented examples now exist of successful situational prevention involving such measures as surveillance cameras for subway systems and parking facilities, defensible space architecture in public housing, target hardening of apartment blocks and individual residences, electronic access for cars and for telephone systems, street closures and traffic schemes for residential neighborhoods, alcohol controls at festivals and sporting fixtures, training in conflict management for publicans and bouncers, and improved stocktaking and record keeping procedures in warehouse and retail outlets (cf. Clarke, 1995).

Many of these successes were obtained by hard-pressed managers seeking practical ways to solve troublesome crime problems confronting their businesses or agencies. Only rarely were they assisted by criminologists, who, excepting a small handful of government researchers overseas, have generally shown little interest in situational prevention. In addition, situational prevention has rarely been accorded attention in policy debates about crime control, especially those in the United States.

This neglect stems from two mistakes of modern criminology. First, the problem of explaining crime has been confused with the problem of explaining the criminal (Gottfredson and Hirschi, 1990). Most criminological theories have been concerned with explaining why certain individuals or groups, exposed to particular psychological or social influences, or with particular inherited traits, are more likely to become involved in delinquency or crime. But this is not the same as explaining why crime occurs. The commission of a crime requires not merely the existence of a motivated offender, but, as every detective story reader knows, it also requires the opportunity for crime. In Cohen and Felson's (1979) terminology, it also requires the availability of a suitable target and the absence of a capable guardian. Thus, crime cannot be explained simply by explaining criminal dispositions. It also has to be shown how such dispositions interact with situational factors favoring crime to produce a criminal act (Ekblom, 1994).

The second related mistake of modern criminology has been to confuse the problem of controlling crime with that of dealing with the criminal (Wilkins, 1990). The surest route to reducing crime, it has been assumed, is to focus on the offender or potential offender. Most textbook discussions of crime control have therefore distinguished only between two broad kinds of measures, formal and informal social control. Formal control refers to society's formally constituted legal institutions of the Law and the criminal justice system designed to sanction offenders, to confine or rehabilitate them, and to deter crime among the population at large. Informal social control refers to society's attempts to induce conformity through the socialization of young people into the norms of society, and through people's supervision of each other's behavior, reinforced by rule making, admonition and censure. Whether formal or informal, these controls are exclusively focused upon offenders, actual or potential.

It has been argued that one important consequence of failing to separate the problems of dealing with offenders and controlling crime has been to divert the criminal justice system from its essential purpose of dispensing justice (von Hirsch, 1976). More germane to the present discussion, however, is that this failure has also resulted in the criminological and policy neglect of a third important group of crime control measures, additional to formal and informal social controls, but intertwined with and dependent on them. These are the extensive "routine precautions" taken by individuals and organizations (Felson and Clarke, 1995). Every day, we all do such things as lock our doors, secure our valuables, counsel our children, and guard our purses to reduce the risk of crime. To this end, we also buy houses in safe neighborhoods, we invest in burglar alarms and we avoid dangerous places and people. Similarly. schools, factories, offices. shops and many other organizations and agencies routinely take a host of precautions to safeguard themselves, their employees and their clients from crime. It is into this group of crime control measures that situational crime prevention fits. Indeed, it can be regarded as the scientific arm of routine precautions, designed to make them more efficient and beneficial to society as a whole.

Criminologists and policy analysts have assumed that the principal value of these precautions is not in reducing overall crime rates, but in protecting individual people and agencies from victimization. This is partly because situational measures focused on particular places or highly specific categories of crime cannot make much impression on the overall crime statistics. It has also been assumed, however, that faced with impediments, offenders will merely displace their attention elsewhere, with no net reduction in crime.

This assumption flows directly from the dispositional error of modern criminology and, as shown below, is not supported by empirical research which has generally found rather little displacement. Reducing opportunities for crime can indeed bring substantial net reductions in crime. As this evidence becomes more widely known, and situational prevention is taken more seriously by policy makers, the debate will move on to the ethical and ideological implications of situational measures. This is already apparent in countries such as Britain and the Netherlands where situational prevention is becoming an integral, though still small, component of government crime policy. As Garland (1996) has argued, these countries have seen a shift in the discourse of crime control, which is no longer seen to be the exclusive province of the government, but something that must be shared with all sectors of society. Consequently, a multitude of public and private actors are now finding that their routine precautions are becoming a matter of public duty. More significantly, governments now seem to be promoting a range of precautionary measures that many people find objectionable. When video surveillance of public places and street closures in residential areas become part of official policy, fears of Orwellian methods of social control are unleashed. These concerns are reinforced by developments in technology that make people believe government control is becoming too pervasive, intrusive and powerful.

These worries about the application of situational controls are widespread, and have become entangled with diverse ideological objections from across the political spectrum. The Right, especially in America (cf. Bright, 1992), sees situational prevention as an irrelevant response to crime because it neglects issues of moral culpability and punishment. Moreover, it "punishes" the law-abiding by infringing freedom and privacy. The Left characterizes it as politically and socially naive in its neglect of the role of social and economic inequities in causation and of political muscle in the definition of crime (Young, 1988). Liberals assert that by "tinkering" with symptoms it diverts attention from the need to tackle the "root causes" of crime such as unemployment, racial discrimination, sub-standard housing, inadequate schooling and inconsistent parenting (Bottoms, 1990). Before exploring these points in more depth, however, a more detailed account of situational crime prevention and its theoretical background is needed.

Definition of Situational Prevention

Situational prevention comprises opportunity-reducing measures that (1) are directed at highly specific forms of crime, (2) involve the management, design or manipulation of the immediate environment in as systematic and permanent way as possible, (3) make crime more difficult and risky, or less rewarding and excusable as judged by a wide range of offenders.

Several features of the definition relevant to the more extended discussion of situational crime prevention below should be noted. First, it makes clear that situational measures must be tailored to highly specific categories of crime, which means that distinctions must be made, not between broad categories such as burglary and robbery, but rather between the different kinds of offenses falling under each of these categories. Thus, Poyner and Webb (1990) have recently argued that preventing domestic burglaries targeted on electronic goods may require different measures from those needed to prevent domestic burglaries targeted on cash or jewelry. This is because of the many differences that existed between the two kinds of burglary in the British city they studied. When the targets were cash or jewelry, burglaries occurred mostly in older homes near to the city center and apparently were committed by offenders operating on foot. When the targets were electronic goods such as TVs and VCRs, the burglaries generally took place in newer, more distant suburbs and were committed by offenders with cars. The cars were needed to transport the stolen goods and had to be parked near to the house but not so close as to attract attention. The lay-out of housing in the newer suburbs allowed these conditions to be met and Poyner and Webb's preventive suggestions consisted principally of means to counter the lack of natural surveillance of parking places and roadways in new housing developments. These suggestions were quite different from those they made to prevent burglary in the inner city, which focused more on improving security and surveillance at the burglar's point of entry.

The need to tailor measures to particular offenses should not be taken to imply that offenders are specialists (cf. Cornish and Clarke, 1988)—only that the commission of specific kinds of crime depends crucially on a constellation of particular environmental opportunities and that these opportunities may need to be blocked in highly specific ways. Indeed, the second important feature of the definition of situational prevention is the implicit recognition that a wide range of offenders, attempting to satisfy a variety of motives and employing a variety of methods, may be involved in even highly specific offenses. It is further recognized that all people have some probability of committing crime depending on the circumstances in which they find themselves. Thus situational prevention does not draw hard distinctions between criminals and others.

The third point deriving from the definition is that changing the environment is designed to affect assessments made by potential offenders about the costs and benefits associated with committing particular crimes. These judgments are dependent on specific features of the objective situation and determine the likelihood of the offense occurring. This implies some rationality and a considerable degree of adaptability on the part of offenders.

The definition recognizes, fourth, that the judgments made by potential offenders include some evaluation of the moral costs of offending. We may all be prepared to steal small items from our employers, but few of us would be willing to mug old ladies in the street. Not all offenses are equally reprehensible, even in the eyes of the most hardened offenders. This means that making it harder to find excuses for criminal action may be sometimes be an effective opportunity-reduction technique. It also means that differences in the moral acceptability of various offenses will impose limits on the scope of displacement.

Finally, the definition of situational prevention is deliberately general in that it makes no mention of any particular category of crime. Rather, situational prevention is assumed to be applicable to every kind of crime, not just to "opportunistic" or acquisitive property offenses, but also to more calculated or deeply-motivated offenses. Whether offenses are carefully planned or fueled by hate and rage, they are all heavily affected by situational contingencies (Tedeschi and Felson, 1994). Thus, rates of homicide are importantly influenced by the availability of handguns. All offenders, however emotionally aroused or determined, take some account of the risks and difficulties of particular situations.

With respect to crimes thought to be the province of "hardened" offenders, evidence is now accumulating of successes achieved by situational measures, including the virtual elimination of aircraft hijackings by baggage screening (Wilkinson, 1986) and substantial reductions in robbery achieved by target hardening measures in post offices (Ekblom, 1988b), convenience stores and banks (Gabor, 1990; Grandjean, 1990; Clarke *et al.*, 1991).

Crimes of sex and violence have been regarded as less amenable to situational controls because they are less common and less likely to cluster in time and space (Heal and Laycock, 1986; Gabor, 1990). However, some examples will be provided below of the successful control of violence through deflecting offenders (for example, by preventing the congregation of large groups of drunken youths at pub-closing time) or through situational controls on alcohol and weapons. One particularly instructive example of controls on a "crime facilitator" is provided by the introduction of Caller ID in New Jersey, which, by threatening the anonymity of callers, seems to have produced a substantial reduction in obscene phone calling. Without this evidence many people might have argued that obscene phone calling, a sexual crime that seems to strike at random, is precisely the kind of offense that would be unamenable to situational controls. A similar argument might have been made about domestic violence, but encouraging evidence is beginning to emerge from an experimental program in England that providing personal alarms to repeat victims may inhibit the aggressor (Farrell and Pease, 1993).

The lesson is that the limits of situational prevention should be established by closely analyzing the circumstances of highly specific kinds of offenses, rather than by theoretical arguments about the presumed nature of motives for broad categories of crime such as sexual or violent offenses.

The Four Components of Situational Crime Prevention

As mentioned, much existing activity failing under the definition of situational crime prevention represents problem-solving undertaken by managers in a variety of public and private agencies. In some instances, mistakes might have been avoided and less time taken to develop solutions had those involved been familiar with the elements of situational prevention. The knowledge obtained through these independent efforts show how the criminological framework provided by situational prevention enables the lessons learned from dealing with specific crimes in specialized contexts to be more broadly generalized. This framework has four components:

1. A theoretical foundation drawing principally upon routine activity and rational choice approaches.

2. A standard methodology based on the action research paradigm.

3. A set of opportunity-reducing techniques, and

4. A body of evaluated practice including studies of displacement.

Theoretical Origins—The Role of Situational Factors in Crime

The development of situational prevention was stimulated by the results of work on correctional treatments undertaken in the 1960s and 1970s by the Home Office Research Unit, the British government's criminological research department (Clarke and Cornish, 1983). This work contributed to the demise of the rehabilitative ideal (Martinson, 1974; Brody, 1976) and forced researchers in the Unit, charged with making a practical contribution to criminal policy, to review the scope and effectiveness of other forms of crime control. The review concluded that there was little scope for reducing crime through the essentially marginal adjustments that were practically and ethically feasible in relation to policies of incapacitation, deterrent sentencing, preventive policing or "social" prevention (Tilley, 1993c). But it did identify opportunity-reduction as a worthwhile topic for further research, largely on the basis of some findings about misbehavior in institutions. It had been discovered in the course of the work on rehabilitation that the probability of a youth's absconding or re-offending while resident in a probation hostel or training school seemed to depend more upon the nature of the institutional regime to which he

was exposed than on his personality or background (Tizard *et al.,* 1975). Particularly important appeared to be the opportunities for misbehavior provided by the institutional regime—opportunities that could be "designed out."

If institutional misconduct could in theory be controlled by manipulating situational factors, it was reasoned that the same might be true of other, everyday forms of crime. Though not consistent with most current theory, support for the Home Office position was found in criminological research that had found immediate situational influences to be playing an important role in crime, including: Burt's (1925) studies of delinquency in London, showing that higher rates of property offending in the winter were promoted by longer hours of darkness: Hartshorne and May's (1928) experimental studies of deceit, showing that the likelihood of dishonest behavior by children was dependent on the level of supervision afforded; geographical studies showing that the distribution of particular crimes is related to the presence of particular targets and locations such as business premises, drinking clubs, and parking lots (Engstad, 1975); and demonstrations that fluctuations in auto theft reflect the number of opportunities as measured by the numbers of registered vehicles (e.g., Wilkins, 1964).

The Home Office position was also consistent with psychological research on personality traits and behavior that was finding a greater than expected role for situational influences (Mischel, 1968), and with an emerging body of work on the sociology of deviance, including studies by: Matza (1964) who argued against deep motivational commitment to deviance in favor of a "drift" into misconduct; Briar and Piliavin (1965) who stressed situational inducements and lack of commitment to conformity; and Yablonsky (1962) and Short and Strodtbeck (1965) who evidenced the pressures to deviance conferred by working class gang membership.

Taken together, this body of work suggested that criminal conduct was much more susceptible to variations in opportunity and to transitory pressures and inducements than conventional "dispositional" theories allowed. It was also becoming clear from interviews with residential burglars (Scarr, 1973; Reppetto, 1974; Brantingham and Brantingham, 1975; and Waller and Okihiro, 1979) that the avoidance of risk and effort plays a large part in target selection decisions. This dynamic view of crime provided a more satisfactory basis for situational prevention and led to the formulation of a simple "choice" model (Clarke, 1977; 1980). This required information not only about the offender's background and current circumstances, but also about the offender's (i) immediate motives and intentions, (ii) moods and feelings, (iii) moral judgments regarding the act in question, (iv) perception of criminal opportunities and [the] ability to take advantage of them or create them, and (v) assessment of the risks of being caught as well as of the likely consequences.

This model, dubbed "situational control theory" by Downes and Rock (1982), was subsequently developed into the rational choice perspective on crime (see below), but it served initially to deflect criminological criticism of the theoretical nature of situational prevention and, more importantly, to guide thinking about practical ways of reducing opportunities for crime.

Defensible Space, CPTED, and Problem-Oriented Policing

While the concept of situational prevention was British in origin, its development was soon influenced by two independent (Jeffery, 1977), but nonetheless related, strands of policy research in the United States. These involved the concepts of "defensible space" (Newman, 1972) and "crime prevention through environmental design" or CPTED (Jeffery, 1971), both of which had preceded situational prevention, but, because of the trans-Atlantic delay in the dissemination of ideas, had not been the stimulus to its development.

Oscar Newman's "defensible space" ideas represented a brilliant attempt to use architectural form to rescue public housing in the United States from the depredations of crime. Newman, an architect, believed that the design of public housing developments discouraged residents from taking responsibility for public areas and from exercising their normal "territorial" instincts to exclude predatory offenders. In particular, he criticized the large scale of the buildings which made it impossible for residents to recognize strangers, the multitude of unsupervised access points that made it easy for offenders to enter projects and to escape after committing crime, the location of projects in high crime areas, and their stark appearance which contributed to the stigma attaching to them. Newman supported these criticisms with statistical analyses of crime in public housing. He also provided a wealth of detailed design suggestions for creating "defensible space" through reducing anonymity, increasing surveillance and reducing escape routes for offenders.

"Defensible space" has sometimes been described as merely an extension of Jane Jacobs' (1961) ideas about the relationship between crime and the layout of streets and land use in American cities. As noted by Coleman (1985), however, this fails to do justice to Newman's unique contribution. He was focused upon buildings and architecture rather than urban planning, he moved beyond description to undertake quantitative analyses of the relation between specific design features and crime, and he was deeply involved in implementing change through the introduction of design modifications in housing developments. Despite the theoretical and methodological criticisms made of his work (see Mayhew, 1979 for a review), Newman's ideas have greatly influenced the design of public housing all over the world (Coleman, 1985). In particular, they have helped to rid many cities of high rise public housing blocks. With regard to the present discussion, they also stimulated efforts by the Home Office researchers engaged on situational prevention to undertake some early tests of "defensible space" notions in a British context (Wilson, 1978; Mayhew et al. 1979).[1]

In addition to Jane Jacobs, other influences on Newman included architectural ideas about the relation between environment and behavior and ethological writings on "territoriality" by authors such as Ardrey (1966). This mix of ideas was rather different from that giving rise to C. Ray Jeffery's (1971) concept of "crime prevention through environmental design." Jeffery claimed that the failures of the criminal justice system (in terms of limited reformative capacity, cruelty and inequity) stemmed from a flawed model of crime, in which ". . . the genetic basis of behavior is denied and. . . the environments in which crimes occur are ignored" (Jeffery, 1977: 10). Drawing upon a "biosocial theory of learning," he argued that punishment and treatment philosophies had to be abandoned in favor of a preventive approach which took due account of both genetic predisposition and the physical environment.

American criminology has been unreceptive to genetic explanations of behavior and Jeffery's general theory of criminal behavior has enjoyed less success than his concept of CPTED. Encompassing a broader set of techniques than "defensible space" and extending beyond the residential context, CPTED was adopted by the Westinghouse Corporation as the more suitable designation for its ambitious program of research to extend the defensible space concept to school and commercial sites. Unfortunately, this research produced disappointingly meager results — perhaps because "territorial" behavior is less natural outside residential settings (Jeffery, 1977: 45)—and government and research interest in CPTED has lagged in America in the 1980s and 1990s. Nevertheless, CPTED has enjoyed much success at a practical training level among police, due largely to the work of Tim Crowe and his associates (Crowe, 1991; Crowe and Zahm, 1994). Jeffery's ideas also provided encouragement to the Home Office team and have been developed in empirical projects undertaken by some of his former students, including Patricia and Paul Brantingham and Ronald Hunter whose work is represented among the case studies included in this book.

"Problem-oriented policing" (Goldstein, 1979) constituted a somewhat later influence on the development of situational prevention. Goldstein argued that the route to greater operational effectiveness for the police was not through improvements in organization and management, but through the detailed analysis of the everyday problems they handle and the devising of tailor-made

solutions. This process requires "identifying these problems in more precise terms, researching each problem, documenting the nature of the current police response, assessing its adequacy and the adequacy of existing authority, and resources, engaging in a broad exploration of alternatives to present responses, weighing the merits of these alternatives, and choosing from among them" (Goldstein, 1979: 236).

This formulation of problem-oriented policing—captured in the four-stage SARA model, Scanning, Analysis, Response and Assessment—reflects the same action research paradigm underpinning situational prevention (cf. Goldstein, 1990:103; Hope, 1994; Clarke, 1997). Nevertheless, some important differences exist between the concepts. In particular, problem-oriented policing is not exclusively focused on crime and is primarily a police management approach; situational prevention, on the other hand, is a crime control approach that can be utilized within any organizational or management structure and is open, not just to the police, but to whoever can muster the resources to tackle the problem in hand.

With respect to crime control, therefore, situational prevention represents a broader approach than problem-oriented policing. Because it encompasses the entire range of environments (and objects) involved in crime and because it encompasses legal and management as well as design solutions, situational prevention is also broader than CPTED (which tends to be focused on design of the built environment). For example, server intervention programs to control drunken driving and the provision of "call trace" facilities to private telephone subscribers as a deterrent to obscene phone calling would more readily fall under the definition of situational, than CPTED measures.

The Rational Choice Perspective

The earlier "choice" model formulated to guide situational prevention efforts has more recently been developed into a "rational choice" perspective on crime (Clarke and Cornish, 1985; Cornish and Clarke, 1986). This borrows concepts from economic theories of crime (e.g. Becker, 1968), but seeks to avoid some of the criticisms made of these theories, including that: (i) economic models mostly ignore rewards of crime that cannot easily be translated into cash equivalents; (ii) economic theories have not been sensitive to the great variety of behaviors falling under the general label of crime, with their variety of costs and benefits, and instead have tended to lump them together as a single variable in their equations; (iii) the formal mathematical modeling of criminal choices in economic theories often demands data that are unavailable or can only be pressed into service by making unrealistic assumptions about what they represent; and, finally, (iv) the image in economic theory of the self-maximizing decision maker, carefully calculating his or her advantage, does not fit the opportunistic and reckless nature of much crime (Clarke and Felson, 1993).

Under the new formulation, relationships between concepts were expressed, not in mathematical terms as was the case in Becker's normative model, but in the form of "decision" diagrams (Clarke and Cornish, 1985; Cornish and Clarke, 1986). Concepts were adapted from the other disciplines involved in the analysis of criminal decision making, as well as economics, to give greater weight to non-instrumental motives for crime and the "limited" or "bounded" nature of the rational processes involved. It was assumed, in other words, that crime is purposive behavior designed to meet the offender's commonplace needs for such things as money, status, sex and excitement, and that meeting these needs involves the making of (sometimes quite rudimentary) decisions and choices, constrained as these are by limits of time and ability and the availability of relevant information.

A second important new premise was that a decision-making approach to crime requires that a fundamental distinction be made between criminal involvement and criminal events (a distinction paralleling that between criminality and crime). Criminal involvement refers to the processes through which individuals choose (i) to become initially involved in particular forms of crime, (ii) to continue, and (iii) to desist. The deci-

sion process at each of these stages is influenced by a different set of factors and needs to be separately modeled. In the same way, the decision processes involved in the commission of a particular crime (i.e., the criminal event) are dependent upon their own special categories of information. Involvement decisions are characteristically multistage and extend over substantial periods of time. Event decisions, on the other hand, are frequently shorter processes, utilizing more circumscribed information largely relating to immediate circumstances and situations.

Finally, and this is of special importance for situational prevention, it was recognized that the decision processes and information utilized could vary greatly among offenses. To ignore these differences, and the situational contingencies associated with them, may be to reduce significantly the scope for intervention.

Cornish and Clarke's formulation of the rational choice perspective has been characterized by Opp (1997) as a "wide" model compared with the "narrow" economic formulation. This wide model was primarily developed to assist thinking about situational prevention, but it was not intended to be limited to this role. Indeed, Cornish (1993) has argued that many features of the rational choice perspective make it particularly suitable to serve as a criminological "metatheory" with a broad role in the explanation of a variety of criminological phenomena.

Environmental Criminology, Routine Activities, and Lifestyles

Rational choice premises have generally been supported by recent studies in which offenders have been interviewed about motives, methods and target choices (Cromwell, 1996). The offenders concerned have included burglars (e.g. Walsh, 1980; Maguire, 1982; Bennett and Wright, 1984; Nee and Taylor 1988; Cromwell *et al.*, 1991; Biron and Ladouceur. 1991: Wright and Decker, 1994; Wiersma, 1996), shoplifters (Walsh, 1978; Carroll and Weaver, 1986), car thieves (Light *et al.*, 1993; McCullough *et al.*, 1990; Spencer, 1992), muggers (Lejeune, 1977; Feeney, 1986) bank and commercial robbers (New

South Wales Bureau of Crime Statistics and Research, 1987: Normandeau and Gabor, 1987; Kube, 1988; Nugent *et al.*, 1989) and offenders using violence (Indermaur, 1996; Morrison and O'Donnell, 1996).

These studies of offender decision making constitute one of two major analytic paths followed in the past decade by "environmental criminology" (Brantingham and Brantingham, 1991). The other path has involved "objective analysis of the spatial and temporal variation in crime patterns in order to discover aggregate factors influencing the patterns" (Brantingham and Brantingham, 1991: 239). When such analyses involve aggregate crime rates or "macro" level data for countries or states, they rarely produce findings with preventive implications. "Micro" level analyses, on the other hand, of specific categories of crime occurring in specific kinds of buildings or sites are generally the most productive in preventive terms (Kennedy, 1990).

Analyses at an intermediary "meso" level can also lead to useful preventive suggestions as shown by Poyner and Webb's (1991) study mentioned above of domestic burglary in two British communities. This study is also illustrative of research on the criminal's "journey to work" undertaken, among others, by Brantingham and Brantingham (1975), Maguire (1982) and Rengert and Wasilchick (1995). Among the findings of these studies are that the risks of commercial robbery may be increased by being located close to a main road and those of domestic burglary by being located on the outskirts of an affluent area. In both cases, the explanation is that the offender's target search time is thereby reduced.

Research on the criminal's journey to work is conceptually related to another body of criminological work—routine activity theory —which has also contributed to the theoretical base of situational prevention. The routine activity approach stated three minimal elements for direct-contact predatory crime: a likely offender, a suitable target, and the absence of a capable guardian against crime (Cohen and Felson, 1979). It avoids speculation about the source of the offender's motivation, which distinguishes it immediately from most other criminological theories. Instead, it focuses upon the convergence in space and time of the three elements of crime, that is to say upon the conditions favoring the occurrence of a criminal event, rather than the development of a criminal disposition. This reflects its intellectual roots in the human ecology of Amos Hawley (1950), who recognized that the timing of different activities by hour of day and day of week are important for the understanding of human society. These points are also central to the routine activity approach, which is focused upon changes from moment to moment and hour to hour in where people are, what they are doing, and what happens to them as a result (Clarke and Felson, 1993; Felson, 1994a). In support of their approach, Cohen and Felson (1979) sought to demonstrate that increases in residential burglary in the United States between 1960 and 1970 could largely be explained by changes in "routine activities" such as the increasing proportion of empty homes in the day (due to more single person households and greater female participation in the labor force) and the increased portability of televisions and other electrical goods.

Cohen and Felson's analysis also illustrates the relationship between routine activity theory and the victimological work on "lifestyles" stimulated by the flood of National Crime Survey data first released in the 1970s (Hindelang *et al.*, 1978). One of the tenets of "lifestyle" theory is that the differential risks of victimization are partly a function of differential exposure to offenders (Fattah, 1993). This exposure varies not only with the sociodemographic characteristics of the victim (age, race, place of residence, etc.), but also with the victim's lifestyle. A person's work and leisure activities that increase exposure to potential offenders (such as alcohol consumption in public places or late-night use of public transport) increase the risks of victimization. The implication of this is that risks might be reduced by modifying patterns of activity. A further important finding of victimological research, the implications of which are being explored in a series of recent studies by Ken Pease and colleagues (for a review, see Farrell and Pease, 1993), is that some people and targets are repeatedly subject to victimization and might therefore be prime candidates for preventive attention. A similar point has been made by Sherman *et al.* (1989) in relation to the "hot spots" of crime, places that are the source of repeated calls for assistance to the police.

Lifestyle and routine activity theories have both made opportunity a respectable topic of research in criminology and have helped attract serious scholarly interest to situational prevention. Both theories are still evolving and Felson himself has made some attempts to expand the scope of routine activity theory. He has defined minimal elements for some categories of crime other than direct-contact predatory offenses (Felson, 1992) and, in order to accommodate social control theory (Hirschi, 1969), has proposed a fourth minimal element for predatory crimes, "the intimate handler," or someone who knows the likely offender well-enough to afford a substantial brake on the latter's activities (Felson, 1986). Clarke (1992) has argued that the contribution of routine activity theory to crime prevention could be enhanced by adding a fifth element which he refers to as "crime facilitators." These are such things as automobiles, credit cards and weapons that comprise the essential tools for particular forms of crime.

The Opportunity Structure for Crime

Environmental criminology, the rational choice perspective and routine activity and lifestyle theories have all helped to strengthen situational prevention in different ways, reflecting their different origins and the purposes for which they were developed. By interviews with offenders and analysis of crime patterns, environmental criminology has provided rich information about the motives and methods of offenders, which has been valuable in thinking about counter measures. The rational choice perspective has provided a framework under which to organize such information so that individual studies produce more general benefits. As will be seen below, it has also assisted analysis of displacement. Lifestyle theory has focused attention on what victims might do to reduce their risks of crime. And routine activity theory has served to extend preventive options by directing attention to features of the three essential elements of crime and their convergence. For example, the idea of convergence has led to the suggestion that "deflecting offenders" be recognized as a distinct technique of situational prevention (Clarke, 1992).

Cusson (1986) has argued that the differences among the various theoretical approaches may turn out to be mainly of historical interest and that a synthesis is inevitable and desirable. The model of the opportunity structure for crime presented in figure 15.1 represents one such attempt at integration.

Under this model, which includes the dispositional variables of traditional criminology as well as the situational ones of the newer theories, there are three components of the *criminal opportunity structure*. These are *targets* (cars, convenience stores, ATM machines, etc.), *victims* (e.g. women alone, drunks, strangers) and crime *facilitators*. These latter include tools, such as guns and cars, as well as disinhibitors such as alcohol or other drugs.[2]

The supply of targets and their nature is a function of (i) the *physical environment*, including the layout of cities, the kinds of housing, technology and communications, transportation and retailing systems, the numbers of vehicles and the supply of drugs and alcohol, and (ii) the *lifestyles and routine activities* of the population, including patterns of leisure, work, residence and shopping; these patterns either hinder or facilitate guardianship. The physical environment also determines the supply of facilitators, while lifestyles and routine activities play a large part in supplying the victims of personal and sexual attacks. Physical environment and lifestyles and routine activities are themselves determined by the broader *socio-economic structure* of society, including demography, geography, urbanization and industrialization, health and educational policy, and legal and political institutions. The numbers of *potential offenders* and their motives is also partly determined by the socio-economic structure of society through many of the mechanisms (alienation, subcultural influence, neglect and lack of love, etc.) identified by traditional criminology, and partly by life-style and routine activities which impact upon the nature of social control afforded by "intimate handlers" and in other ways.

The opportunity structure is not simply a physical entity, defined at any one point in time by the nature of the physical environment and the routine activities of the population. Rather, a complex interplay between potential offenders and the supply of victims, targets and facilitators determines the scale and nature of opportunities for crime. Potential offenders learn about criminal opportunities from their peers, the media and their own observation, but they are differentially sensitized to this information as well as being differentially motivated to seek out and create opportunities. Thus, offender perceptions and judgments about risks, effort and rewards play an important part in defining the opportunity structure. These judgments also play a determining role at the subsequent stage of crime commission, where figure 15.1 stops short.

Figure 15.1
The Opportunity Structure for Crime

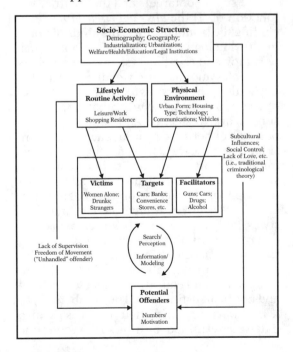

Before moving from the theoretical background of situational crime prevention to its other components, some questions about the scope and reach of situational prevention arising from the model of the opportunity structure should be addressed. The first is that, if everything seems to flow from the socio-economic structure, should not preventive effort be focused at that level? Could not large scale reductions in a wide range of crimes be achieved by tackling the disposition to offend through improved welfare and educational programs? Would this not be more efficient than undertaking the vast number of small-scale efforts to address highly specific crime problems implied by the situational focus?

One answer to these questions is that "social" crime prevention is already focused at the socio-economic level and that the opportunity structure requires attention in its own right. However, Morris and Hawkins (1970) and Wilson (1975) have noted that we do not know how to bring about some of the needed social changes, such as making parents love their children more. As for better welfare and education, these may be seen as desirable but often as demanding resources that society cannot afford. Finally, when Sweden and some other European countries enhanced welfare and achieved more equitable income distribution, this was followed not by reductions in crime but by increases (Smith, 1995).

A second question concerns deterrence and is as follows: Rather than attempting to manipulate the opportunity structure (with the attendant costs and inconvenience of this strategy), might it not be more efficient simply to raise the stakes of offending through heavier punishments? In fact, interviews with offenders have shown that they pay much closer attention to the immediate chances of getting caught than to the nature of the punishment they might receive later. Rather than increasing punishment, it is therefore more efficient to make the offender more fearful of being caught, and one component of situational prevention does indeed consist of increasing the risks of being caught through a process that Cusson (1993) refers to as "situational deterrence."

A final set of questions concerns the interplay between the objective reality of the opportunity structure and the way this is perceived by potential offenders. How do offenders learn about criminal opportunities and what factors come into play when they make decisions about which ones to pursue? What proportion of crimes are the result of opportunities seized, and what proportion of ones that are sought or created (Maguire, 1980; Bennett and Wright, 1984). At issue here is the question of whether opportunities for crime really are in infinite supply as some have argued. If so, this has serious implications for a strategy advocating their reduction. What matter the few reductions that can be achieved in criminal opportunities if these are infinite?

Consideration of the realities of crime helps provide an answer. While it may be true in theory that every dwelling and automobile provides not just one opportunity for crime, but, if considered over time, a set of almost endless opportunities, this ignores the fact that households and automobiles are afforded substantial guardianship for much of the time (Clarke, 1984). Even when unguarded, they may in actuality provide few rewards for crime. The average household contains only a few portable goods that can be converted into cash and there are limits to the number of stolen VCRs and television sets that the offender can store. It is also unclear how many such "hot" items can be off-loaded onto the market without provoking a determined response from law enforcement. Clarification of these issues needs to be sought in more research of the kind recently published by Cromwell et al. (1991), in which they undertook detailed interviews with residential burglars about their working methods.

The Action Research Methodology

The standard methodology for a situational project, situational prevention's second component, is a version of the action research model in which researchers and practitioners work together to analyze and define the problem, to identify and try out possible solutions, to evaluate the results and, if necessary, to repeat the cycle until success is achieved (Lewin, 1947). The influence of the action research paradigm can be seen in the following specification of the five stages of a situational prevention project (Gladstone, 1980):

1. collection of data about the nature and dimensions of the specific crime problem;

2. analysis of the situational conditions that permit or facilitate the commission of the crimes in question;

3. systematic study of possible means of blocking opportunities for these particular crimes, including analysis of costs;

4. implementation of the most promising, feasible and economic measures;

5. monitoring of results and dissemination of experience.

As mentioned, this is essentially the same problem-solving methodology used in problem-oriented policing as well as in many other forms of social intervention, and because of its extensive pedigree has required little modification for use in situational crime prevention. However, it represents an ideal not always followed in practice.

Sixteen Opportunity-Reducing Techniques

Unlike the action research methodology which has seen little modification, the classification of opportunity-reducing techniques, the third component of situational prevention, is constantly undergoing change. This is made necessary by developments (i) in theory which suggest new ways of reducing opportunities, (ii) in practice as new forms of crime are addressed by situational prevention, and (iii) in technology which opens up new vistas for prevention, just as it does for crime. The fact that the classification of techniques is constantly being refined is evidence of the vitality of the situational approach and, indeed, these re-classifications help further to stimulate its development by calling attention to new forms of opportunity-reduction.

In the first edition of [Clark's] book [1992] a classification of twelve opportunity-reducing techniques was introduced, itself a modification of an earlier classification proposed by Hough *et al.* (1980). In introducing the new classification, it was noted that the techniques served three purposes, implicit in the rational choice assumptions of situational prevention, of increasing the risks, increasing the difficulties, and reducing the rewards of crime.

This classification has recently been modified by Clarke and Homel (1997) to encompass a fourth purpose of situational prevention implicit in rational choice theory, which is to increase shame and guilt or, more particularly, to "remove excuses" for crime.[3] This reflects the fact that situational measures, having first been used to prevent a variety of "street" and predatory crimes, have more recently also been applied against income tax evasion, traffic offenses (including drunk driving), sexual harassment and theft of employers' property, which are as much the province of "ordinary citizens" as of "hardened offenders" (see Gabor's 1994 book, *Everybody Does It!* for a review of these crimes, and the earlier seminal paper by Ross, 1960, on traffic offenses as "folk crimes"). Opportunities for these offenses arise in the course of everyday life for most people and do not have to be sought in the same way as opportunities for autotheft or burglary. The very frequency of these opportunities, together with the generally higher social status of offenders, may contribute to the relative lack of moral opprobrium attached to taking advantage of them. This lack of condemnation and the relative ease of commission suggest that, rather than by increasing the risks of detection, these offenses might more effectively be prevented by increasing the incentives or pressures to comply with the law (Sparrow, 1994).

The addition of this fourth rational choice category represents more explicit recognition of the fact that offenders make judgments about the morality of their own behavior and that they frequently rationalize their conduct to "neutralize" what would otherwise be incapacitating feelings of guilt or shame thorough such excuses as, "He deserved it," "I was just borrowing it" and "I only slapped her." These rationalizations may

be especially important for ordinary people responding to everyday temptations to break the law. . . . The role of rationalizations was clearly identified in the original formulation of the rational choice perspective on which it was based (Clarke and Cornish, 1985; Cornish and Clarke, 1986).

Rationalizations are also given a central role by two other criminological theories, Sykes and Matza's (1957) social deviance theory of "techniques of neutralization" and Bandura's (1976) social learning theory of violence, which makes use of the concept of "self-exoneration" (Wortley, 1986). The parallels between these concepts are remarkable (though Bandura appears to have been unaware of Sykes and Matza's earlier work) and this degree of congruence gives further reason to think that removing excuses or rationalizations may be an important preventive strategy.

Clarke and Homel's (1997) modification of the classification. . . left eight of the original categories untouched, modified the remaining four and added four new ones for a total of sixteen techniques (see table 15.1).

In proposing the new classification, Clarke and Homel recognized a specific danger of including the manipulation of shame and guilt as a purpose of situational prevention. This is the danger of entangling situational prevention in attempts to bring about long-term changes in dispositions to offend—a fundamentally different approach to crime prevention (Newman, 1997). They justified their course by pointing out that a choice has to be made between maintaining the clarity of the situational approach but limiting its application, or extending its reach and complicating its definition. So long as the measures to induce guilt or shame are focused on highly specific categories of offending and are delivered at the point when criminal decisions are being made, they believe that the danger can be avoided of confusing the nature of situational prevention. For example, the message "Shoplifting is stealing" is much more likely to affect the situational calculus, and would thus qualify as a situational measure, when displayed in high risk stores than when displayed on school notice boards where it is intended to reduce the disposition to theft.

Before describing the sixteen techniques, and presenting examples of each, it should be noted that there is some unavoidable overlap among categories. For example, measures that increase the effort demanded for crime and delay the offender will also increase the risks of apprehension. This means that there is sometimes difficulty in deciding where a particular measure best fits into the classification in table 15.1, and indeed some measures can serve more than one purpose.

1. Target Hardening. An obvious, often highly effective way of reducing criminal opportunities is to obstruct the vandal or the thief by physical barriers through the use of locks, safes, screens or reinforced materials. Changes in design, including a slug rejecter device substantially reduced the use of slugs in New York parking meters (Decker, 1972)[4] and, more recently, in the ticket machines of the London Underground (Clarke et al., 1994). Transparent screens to shield the bus driver significantly reduced assaults on one transit system (Poyner *et al.*, 1988); anti-bandit screens on post office counters in London in the 1980s was conservatively estimated by Ekblom (1988b) to have cut robberies by 40 percent; and the installation of fixed and "pop-up" screens is believed to have been an important element in reducing over-the-counter robberies in Australian banks (Clarke *et al.*, 1991). A strengthened coin box has been identified in several studies as a significant factor in reducing incidents of theft and damage to public telephones in Britain and Australia (Wilson, 1990; Challinger, 1991; Bridgeman, 1997). . . .The introduction of steering locks on both new and old cars in Germany in 1963 produced a substantial decline in the rate of car theft for the country that has persisted to this day and that these locks have conferred similar benefits in Britain and America (Webb, 1994).

2. Access Control. Access control refers to measures intended to exclude potential offenders from places such as offices, factories and apartment blocks. The portcullises, moats and drawbridges of medieval castles suggest its preventive pedigree may be as lengthy as that of target hardening. It is also a central component of defensible space, arguably the start of scientific interest in situational prevention. A sophisticated form of access control lies in the use of electronic personal identification numbers (PINs) that are needed to gain access to computer systems and bank accounts. Poyner and Webb (1987b) found that a combination of access controls introduced on a South London public housing estate, including entry phones, fencing around apartment blocks and electronic access to the parking garage, achieved a significant reduction in vandalism and theft. They also found that the introduction of a reception desk on the ground floor of a tower block led to a marked reduction in vandalism, graffiti and other incivilities. The installation of entryphones, and the demolition of walkways linking buildings, significantly reduced robberies and purse-snatchings at Lisson Green, another London public housing estate.

3. Deflecting Offenders. At soccer matches in Britain, rival groups of fans have been segregated in the stadium to reduce fighting and their arrival and departure has been scheduled to avoid the periods of waiting around that promote trouble (Clarke, 1983). Scheduling the last bus to leave immediately after pub closing time is intended to interfere with another of Britain's less admirable traditions, the closing time brawl. Hope (1985) has suggested that crowds of drunken young people on the streets at closing time could also be reduced by avoiding the concentration of licensed premises in particular parts of the city. Bell and Burke (1989) show that the leasing of a downtown parking lot in Arlington, Texas, relieved severe congestion on weekend nights in nearby streets, and associated crime problems, by providing a venue for teenage cruising. These are all examples of "deflecting offenders" away from crime targets, a situational technique suggested by routine activity theory. Further examples are provided by case studies in this volume. Poyner and Webb (1987a) show that thefts from shopping bags at markets in Birmingham, England, were substantially reduced by reducing congestion around the stalls, which increased the difficulty of pickpocketing and other "stealth" thefts. Matthews

Table 15.1
Sixteen Opportunity-Reducing Techniques

Increasing Perceived Effort	Increasing Perceived Risks	Reducing Anticipated Rewards	Removing Excuses
1. Target hardening Slug rejecter device Steering locks Bandit screens	*5. Entry/exit screening* Automatic ticket gates Baggage screening Merchandise tags	*9. Target removal* Removable car radio Women's refuges Phonecard	*13. Rule setting* Customs declaration Harassment codes Hotel registration
2. Access control Parking lot banners Fenced yards Entry phones	*6. Formal surveillance* Red light cameras Burglar alarms Security guards	*10. Identifying property* Property marking Vehicle licensing Cattle branding	*14. Stimulating conscience* Roadside speedometers 'Shoplifting is stealing' 'Idiots drink and drive'
3. Deflecting offenders Bus stop placement Tavern location Street closures	*7. Surveillance by employees* Pay phone location Park attendants CCTV systems	*11. Reducing temptation* Gender-neutral listings Off-street parking Rapid repair	*15. Controlling disinhibitors* Drinking-age laws Ignition interlock V-chip
4. Controlling facilitators Credit card photo Gun controls Caller-ID	*8. Natural surveillance* Defensible space Street Lighting Cab driver I.D.	*12. Denying benefits* Ink merchandise tags PIN for car radios Graffiti cleaning	*16. Facilitation compliance* Easy library checkout Public lavatories Trash bins

Source: Adapted from Clarke and Homel, 1997.

(1990) shows that a road closure scheme to deflect cruising "Johns" contributed to the rehabilitation of a red light district in a North London suburb.

4. Controlling Facilitators. Saloons in the Wild West routinely required customers to surrender their weapons on entry because of the risk of drunken gun fights. In more recent times, the manufacture of "less lethal weapons" in the form of guns that shoot wax bullets, electricity or tranquilizers has been advocated (Hemenway and Weil, 1996). The Scottish Council on Crime (1975) suggested that in some pubs beer should be served in plastic mugs to prevent their use as weapons, and recent studies in Britain of the injury potential of different kinds of broken glass have led to the recommendation that toughened glass be used for beer glasses (Shepherd and Brickley, 1992). Controls on a range of other crime facilitators have been proposed including checks and credit cards (which facilitate fraud) and telephones (which may facilitate drug dealing, frauds and sexual harassment). To reduce drug dealing, pay phones have been removed from places where drug dealers congregate or have been altered to make them more difficult to use for dealing (Natarajan *et al.*, 1996). A new computerized phone system in Rikers Island jails substantially reduced illicit phone calls by inmates and also had the unexpected benefit of reducing fights over access to the phones (La Vigne, 1994). Two cases illustrate the value of other controls on telephones. Clarke (1990) showed that the introduction in New Jersey of Caller ID, a service which allows the person answering the phone to read the number calling, resulted in a reduction of about 25 percent in obscene and annoying telephone calls. Bichler and Clarke (1996) showed that re-programming pay phones at the Port Authority Bus Terminal in Manhattan prevented illicit access to toll lines and wiped out a multi-million dollar scam perpetrated by hustlers drawn to the building by the opportunities for fraud. Finally, Knutsson and Kuhlhorn (1981) have shown that the introduction of identification procedures in Sweden produced a dramatic decline in the number of reported check frauds.

5. Entry/exit Screening. Entry screening differs from access control in that the purpose is less to exclude potential offenders than to increase the likelihood of detecting those not in conformity with entry requirements. These requirements may relate to prohibited goods and objects or, alternatively, to possession of tickets and documents. Exit screens, on the other hand, serve primarily to deter theft by detecting objects that should not be removed from the protected area, such as items not paid for at a shop. Developments in electronics have resulted in the increasing use of these situational techniques in retailing, as evidenced by the spread of merchandise tagging, bar-coding and "electronic point of sales" systems (Hope, 1991). DiLonardo (1996) showed that electronic merchandise tags on clothing can achieve significant reductions in shoplifting of the order of 35–75 percent in American stores. Similar, though not as strong, effects were reported in Britain (Barrifield, 1994). Scherdin (1986) reports that the installation of book detection screens, as found in thousands of libraries, reduced thefts of both books and audiovisual materials at one University of Wisconsin library by more than 80 percent. The installation of automatic ticket gates on the 63 central zone stations of the London Underground resulted in a two-thirds reduction of fare evasion throughout the system (Clarke, 1993). In a "low tech" example of entry screening, the redesign of tickets to facilitate their inspection on Vancouver ferries produced a two-thirds reduction in fare evasion (DesChamps et al., 1991). Finally, the most famous example of this technique concerns the introduction of baggage and passenger screening at most major airports in the world during the early 1970s. This contributed to a precipitate reduction in the number of airline hijackings from about 70 per year to about 15 (Wilkinson, 1977, 1986; Landes, 1978).

6. Formal Surveillance. Formal surveillance is provided by police, security guards and store detectives, whose main function is to furnish a deterrent threat to potential offenders. One example. . .is the use of a security bike patrol to curb auto thefts from a commuter parking lot in Vancouver. The surveillance afforded by security personnel may be enhanced by electronic hardware, for example by burglar alarms and closed circuit television (CCTV). In their study of an afflu-

ent suburban community close to Philadelphia, Hakim et al. (1995) concluded that widespread ownership of burglar alarms reduced police costs by lowering burglary rates for the community at large. One element of "Biting Back," the preventive program focused on repeat victims of burglary in a[n] English town, included the temporary installation of silent alarms in victims' homes. In Australia, Homel (1993) reported that the introduction in 1982 of random breath testing (RBT) in New South Wales cut alcohol-related fatal crashes by more than a third relative to the previous three years, declines that persisted as a result of a continued high level of RBT enforcement. Also in Australia, Bourne and Cooke (1993) show that the widespread deployment of photo radar in the State of Victoria was the major factor in substantially reduced levels of speeding in 1991–92, contributing to an overall decline of 45% in traffic fatalities. An experiment with "red light" cameras in Scotland was also found to be successful in preventing motorists "running the red" (Scottish Office Central Research Unit, 1995)[5]. Several studies in Britain, two reproduced in this volume, have found CCTV cameras to be effective in reducing crime. When CCTV cameras were installed for the use of security personnel at a university's parking lots, Poyner (1991) found a substantial reduction in thefts. Appreciable reductions in a variety of crimes have been reported by Brown (1996) following installation of CCTV for police use in the centers of three British cities. Not all the successful examples of formal surveillance involve the use of technology. For example, rates of vandalism, assault and fare dodging on subways and trams in three Dutch cities were substantially reduced when 1,200 "VICs" were employed to serve as safety, information and control inspectors. Masuda (1992) showed that systematic, daily counting by security personnel of items of high risk merchandise, such as VCRs and camcorders, resulted in declines of between 80–100% in thefts by employees at a large electronics merchandiser in New Jersey. Lastly, ways of enhancing police surveillance by enlisting the help of the public are continually being expanded, including informant hotlines, "crime stopper" programs and "curfew decals" on automobiles, which indicate to patrolling police that the vehicle is not normally in use late at night (Clarke and Harris, 1992a).

7. Surveillance by Employees. In addition to their primary function, some employees, particularly those dealing with the public, also perform a surveillance role by virtue of their position. These include a variety of "place managers" (Eck, 1995; Felson, 1995) such as shop assistants, hotel doormen, park keepers, parking lot attendants and train conductors. All these employees assume some responsibility for monitoring conduct in their work-places. Canadian research has shown that apartment blocks with doormen are less vulnerable to burglary (Waller and Okihiro, 1979). In Britain, less vandalism has been found on buses with conductors (Mayhew et al., 1976) and on public housing estates with resident caretakers (Department of Environment, 1977). Public telephones in Britain which get some surveillance by employees, such as those in pubs or railway stations, also suffer fewer attacks (Markus, 1984). A two-thirds reduction in offenses at a parking lot in England followed the employment of attendants to cover high risks periods of the day (Laycock and Austin, 1992). Rewarding cashiers for detection of forged or stolen credit cards helped to reduce annual losses from credit card frauds by nearly $1 million dollars at an electronics retailer in New Jersey (Masuda, 1993). Once again, CCTV surveillance has been found effective when these cameras are provided for employee use. Cameras installed for use of station staff produced substantial reductions in muggings and thefts at four high risk stations on the London Underground (Mayhew et al., 1979). Vandalism of seats on a fleet of 80 double-deck buses in England was substantially reduced through the provision of CCTV for drivers, though only a few buses were equipped with the cameras (Poyner, 1988). Finally, Hunter and Jeffery (1992) report that ten out of fourteen studies they reviewed found that having two clerks on duty, especially at night, was an effective robbery prevention measure (see also Bellamy, 1996).

8. Natural Surveillance. Householders may trim bushes at the front of their homes and banks may light the interior of their premises at night in attempting to capitalize upon the "natural" surveillance provided by people going about their everyday business. Enhancing natural surveillance is a prime objective of improved street lighting (Tien et al., 1979; Ramsay, 1991a), of defensible space (Mayhew, 1979; Coleman, 1985), and of "neighborhood watch" (Bennett, 1990; Rosenbaum, 1988). Though results have not been uniformly positive, some successes in the use of all three measures have been reported. An "apartment watch" program combined with target hardening achieved an 82% reduction in reported burglaries in four apartment blocks in Ottawa (Meredith and Paquette, 1992). Cocoon neighborhood watch, whereby immediately surrounding homes were alerted after a burglary, was an element of the successful "Biting Back" scheme to reduce repeat burglaries. In his most recent publication, Oscar Newman (1996) reports some successes in reducing crime in public housing developments in the United States through application of defensible space principles. One component of a program that significantly reduced burglary on a commercial strip in Portland, Oregon, was improved lighting of the exterior of the stores (Griswold, 1984). Enhanced lighting in a public housing estate in Dudley, England, produced crime reductions with little evidence of displacement. In one "low-tech" example, components of successful robbery prevention in convenience stores in Florida included an unobstructed view of the store's interior from outside and location of stores near evening commercial activity (Hunter and Jeffery, 1992). Finally, "How's my driving?" decals with 1–800 telephone numbers displayed on the backs of trucks, and cab driver I.D.'s displayed for passengers, facilitate natural surveillance of the behavior of both groups of drivers.

9. Target Removal. A church in Northern Spain has recently installed a machine at its entrance that allows people to use their bank or credit cards to make donations. (In reporting this development, a local Spanish newspaper could not resist the headline "Through Visa Toward God," *New York Times*, February 1, 1997, p.172). The person making the donation has a receipt for tax purposes and the church may receive larger gifts. Since money is not being deposited, the church has also reduced its theft risk through "target removal." An earlier application of this same situational technique, quoted by Pease (1997), comes from the days of Californian Gold Rush. Plagued by robberies of stagecoaches, one mine started casting its silver into 400-pound cubes, about one foot on each side. These were simply too heavy for a robber, or even a gang of them, to carry off on horseback (Lingenfelter 1986). Other examples of target removal come from attempts to deal with attacks on public telephones in Great Britain and Australia (Bridgeman, 1997). Because the kiosk itself (specially the glass) is more frequently vandalized than the phone, kiosks in high risk locations have been replaced by booths. In addition, the smaller, highly vulnerable, glass panes in earlier kiosks have been replaced by larger panes in more recent designs. A third pay phone example is provided by the introduction of the phonecard, which by dispensing with the need for pay phones to store large sums of cash, has removed an important target for theft. A variety of cash reduction measures, including the use of safes with time locks, substantially reduced robberies of betting shops in Australia (Clarke and McGrath, 1990). Pease (1991) has shown that a package of measures to prevent repeat victimization of houses on a public housing estate in Britain, including the removal of gas and electric coin meters which were frequent targets for theft (Hill, 1986; Cooper, 1989), reduced burglaries on the estate from 526 in the year before intervention to 132 three years later. Cash reduction has consistently been found to reduce the risks of convenience store robbery. Perhaps the best known example of cash reduction, however, concerns the introduction of exact fare systems and safes on buses, which dramatically reduced bus robberies in New York (Chaiken *et al.*, 1974) and in 18 other cities in the late 1960s (Stanford Research Institute, 1970). Finally, a successful "low tech" application of target removal that consisted of persuading in-patients to surrender their valuables for safekeeping, or

not to bring them to the hospital, has been described by Moore (1987).

10. Identifying Property. Writing one's name in a book is a simple form of property marking . . . .The most developed programs of identifying property relate to vehicles. Registration of motor vehicles was required in some U.S. states from almost the beginning of the century and, subsequently, all vehicles sold in the United States were required to carry a unique Vehicle Identification Number (VIN). More recently, the Motor Vehicle Theft Law Enforcement Act [of] 1984 has mandated the marking of all major body parts of "high risk" automobiles with the VINs. One of the last U.S. states to require vehicle registration was Illinois in 1934, whereupon vehicle thefts declined from 28,000 in the previous year to about 13,000 (Hall, 1952). Although "operation identification" programs have had a checkered history in the United States (Zaharchuk and Lynch, 1977; Heller *et al.*, 1975), Laycock (1991) shows that property marking undertaken in three small communities in Wales, combined with extensive media publicity, nearly halved the number of reported domestic burglaries.

11. Reducing Temptation. In certain city streets it is unwise to wear gold chains or leave cars parked which are attractive to joyriders. (Throughout the 1980s, the Chevrolet Camaro constituted an American example of the latter, Clarke and Harris, 1992b). Some temptations are less obvious. For example, phone directories which are not gender-neutral might promote obscene phone-calls to women. It has also been found in extensive experimental research that the mere presence of a weapon, such as a gun, can induce aggressive responses in some people. Known as the "weapons effect" (Berkowitz and LePage, 1967), this gives further support to gun control. The weapons effect barely enters the subjective world of potential offenders and James Wise (1982) has argued that this is also true of many inducements to vandalism, for example, when the surface characteristics of a wall almost invite graffiti. Many of his suggestions for a "gentle deterrent" to vandalism consist of reducing such temptations. For example, he has suggested that the glass covering fire alarm handles should be mirrored because bad luck would follow its breaking. Another example of reducing temptation is "rapid repair" on the grounds that leaving damaged items unrepaired invites further attacks. Samdahl and Christensen (1985) provided support for this policy by demonstrating that picnic tables that had been scratched and carved were more than twice as likely to be damaged further than other tables. Zimbardo (1973) showed that a car left parked in poor condition in an inner city area rapidly attracted further depredation. Smith (1996) found that school boys in England who admitted recent similar vandalism acts, reported they would be more likely to damage fences or write on them when these already showed signs of vandalism and graffiti. Substantially reduced rates of crime and vandalism on the metropolitan railways of Victoria, Australia, were reported by Carr and Spring (1993) following the introduction of "Travel Safe," a program consisting of rapid repair of vandalism and graffiti as well as of more generally enhanced security. This advocacy of rapid repair and good maintenance has been taken a step further by Wilson and Kelling (1982) who have argued in their famous "broken windows" article that the failure to deal promptly with minor signs of decay in a community, such as panhandling or soliciting by prostitutes, can result in a quickly deteriorating situation as hardened offenders move into the area to exploit the break-down in control. Finally, Kuhlhorn shows how removing the temptation to understate income, by permitting income statements to be cross-checked by computer, reduced welfare frauds in Sweden.

12. Denying Benefits. Related to reducing temptation, but conceptually distinct, is denying the benefits of crime to offenders. The recent development of security-coded car radios that require a thief to know the radio's PIN before it can be used in another vehicle constitutes an excellent example of this principle. Cars fitted with these radios have been found to have lower theft rates in studies in Australia (NRMA Insurance Ltd., 1990) and in Germany and the United States (Braga and Clarke, 1994). These successes suggest that this principle might usefully be extended to VCRs and TVs so as to reduce the rewards of burglary. A further example of the principle in action is provided by "ink tags," which are designed to deny shoplifters the benefits of stealing. If tampered with, these tags release ink and indelibly stain garments to which they are attached, and these tags may be even more effective than the familiar electronic merchandise tags (DiLonardo and Clarke, 1996). Sloan-Howitt and Kelling (1990) document the remarkable success achieved within five years by the New York Transit Authority in ridding its subway cars of graffiti, an important component of which was a policy of immediate cleansing. This denied offenders the gratification of seeing their work on public display.

13. Rule Setting. All organizations find it necessary to have rules about conduct in their fields of governance. For example, most businesses regulate employees' telephone use and all retail establishments require their employees to follow strict cash handling and stock control procedures. Organizations such as hospitals, schools, parks, transportation systems, hotels and restaurants must, in addition, regulate the conduct of the clientele they serve. Any ambiguity in these regulations will be exploited where it is to the advantage of the individual. (Most attempts to avoid income tax relate to those sections of the IRS tax return that are more difficult to investigate Klepper and Nagin, 1987). One important strand of situational prevention, therefore, is rule setting—the introduction of new rules or procedures (and the clarification of those in place), which are intended to remove any ambiguity concerning the acceptability of conduct. For example, in attempting to reduce "no-shows," many restaurants will only accept reservations if callers leave a telephone number where they can be contacted if they do not appear. Some popular restaurants are now also requiring that reservations be accompanied by a credit card number against which a charge can be made for no-shows. A Manhattan restaurant reports that the scheme reduced no-shows at Thanksgiving from a total of 65 in the year before the scheme was introduced to zero in the two subsequent years (*New York Times*, January 31, 1996, p. C3). The same edition of the *New York Times* (p. 133) reports that taxicab fares from Kennedy airport to Manhattan have been fixed at a standard $30 to prevent visitors being cheated. Fishermen in California have also recently been required to wear their fishing licenses, rather than merely to carry them, in a successful effort to get more anglers to comply with license purchase requirements (*New York Times*, November 10, 1993, p.5). Not all such rules require the backing of the law. In an attempt to produce consensual crowd management at the Australian Motorcycle Grand Prix in 1991, riders were permitted to operate camp sites for their fellow motorcyclists and were encouraged to develop rules and procedures for use of the facilities. This helped to eliminate the brawls between the police and motorcyclists which had marred the event in previous years (Veno and Veno, 1993). Challenger (1996) demonstrates a marked reduction in "refund frauds" when new rules were introduced by stores in Australia requiring "proof of purchase" receipts.

14. Stimulating Conscience. This situational technique can be distinguished from society's more general informal social control by its focus on specific forms of crime occurring in discrete, highly limited settings (Clarke and Homel, 1997). Rather than attempting to bring about lasting changes in generalized attitudes to law breaking, these measures serve simply to stimulate feelings of conscience at the point of contemplating the commission of a specific kind of offense. For example, signs at store entrances announce that "shoplifting is stealing" and in the Port Authority Bus Terminal in Manhattan they proclaim that "Smoking here is illegal, selfish and rude." Mobile roadside speed monitors have been used to give immediate feedback (without issuing fines) to individual cars traveling above the speed limit (Casey and Lund, 1993). An example of a more intensive and coordinated attempt to increase such informal sanctions is provided by recent advertising campaigns mounted in Australia to reinforce the powerful deterrent impact of random breath testing (Cavallo and Drummond, 1994). These made use of the slogan, "Good mates don't let mates drink and drive." Finally, in Britain, government television campaigns that accompany crackdowns on

those who evade purchasing licenses required to own a television (the license fees help to finance the British Broadcasting Corporation) show those detected being treated by the police and courts as "common criminals." The British government has been repeating its advertising campaigns for more than two decades and claims (though without producing evidence) that applications for television licenses sharply increase whenever the campaigns are mounted.

15. Controlling Disinhibitors. Crime is not only facilitated by tools such as weapons, but also by psychological disinhibitors, which include: (i) alcohol and drugs, which undermine the usual social or moral inhibitions, or impair perception and cognition so that offenders are less aware of breaking the law (White and Humeniuk, 1994); (ii) propaganda, which can be directed at the dehumanization of target groups (such as Jews—see Bauer, 1990) and can provide the moral certainties and justifications that ordinary people need to commit atrocities and war crimes (Ellul, 1965); and (iii) television violence, which like propaganda, might "reduce or break down those inhibitions against being violent that parents and other socializing agencies have been building up in boys" (Belson, 1978: 17). The "V-chip," which under the Telecommunications Act of 1996 will become a feature of every new television set sold in America (Makris, 1996), allows parents to block reception of violent television programs. This is a situational response to the problem and constitutes an example of "controlling disinhibitors," though most examples of this technique relate to controls on drinking. Access to cars by intoxicated drivers can be restricted by breathalyzers built into the ignition, a measure that is sometimes mandated for recidivist drunk drivers (Jones and Wood, 1989; Morse and Elliott, 1990). A faculty-student committee at Rutgers University decided that beer should be served from kegs rather than cases at dormitory parties on grounds that (1) cases are easier to conceal and (2) in the words of a student: "If you have one keg and a line of 20 people behind it, people will get less alcohol than if you had a refrigerator and people were throwing out beer" (*New York Times*, September 13, 1991). The value of controls on drinking have been demonstrated in a variety of studies. Bjor et al., (1992) argue that "rationing" the amount of alcohol that individuals could bring into a Swedish resort town on Midsummer Eve helped to reduce drunkenness and disorderly conduct. Olsson and Wikstrom (1982, 1984) concluded that permanent closing of liquor stores on Saturdays in Sweden had reduced crimes of public drunkenness, assault and vandalism, and domestic disturbances in the summer months, and perhaps also for the remainder of the year. The introduction of a widely supported local ordinance banning the consumption of alcohol in public in Central Coventry in England was followed by large reductions in complaints of insulting behavior and in numbers of people who regarded public drinking as a problem in the city (Ramsay, 1991b). The promotion of responsible drinking practices and other attempts to control intoxication fed to a marked reduction in alcohol-related crime in the nightlife district in Surfer's Paradise, a large resort in Queensland, Australia (Homei, et al., 1997).

16. Facilitating Compliance. When Lombroso suggested in the 19th century that people should be locked up for publicly urinating in the streets, his pupil Ferri suggested an alternative more in keeping with the spirit of this book—the provision of public urinals (Hackler, 1978: 12). Ferri's suggestion constitutes an example of facilitating compliance, the sixteenth opportunity-reducing technique. This has wide application and includes subsidized taxi rides home for those who have been drinking, litter bins and "graffiti boards" (the latter of which are supplied for people's public messages), and improved checkout procedures in libraries, which remove delay and thus excuses for failing to comply with rules for book borrowing (Boss, 1980; Greenwood and McKean, 1985). Finally, Shearing and Stenning (1984) provide a fascinating glimpse into the ways in which sophisticated crowd control and management—involving the use of pavement markings, signs, physical barriers (which make it difficult to take a wrong turn) and instructions from cheerful Disney employees—

greatly reduce the potential for crime and incivility in Disney World.

Effectiveness of Situational Prevention

The examples of successful interventions mentioned in the course of describing the sixteen opportunity-reducing techniques, belong to its fourth component, the body of evaluated practice. This component also includes the evidence on displacement, but before moving to this topic it should be noted, in case a different message has been communicated through the cataloguing of successes, that situational prevention is not one hundred percent effective. Though reductions in crime may be considerable (often more than 50 percent), situational measures usually ameliorate, not eliminate a problem. In addition, situational measures do not always work as intended for a variety of reasons, including the following:

1. Measures have sometimes failed due to technical or administrative ineptitude, as when anti-climb paint to deter school break-ins was too thinly applied (Hope and Murphy, 1983), or when a scheme to defeat vandalism by replacing broken windows with toughened glass proved too complicated for school maintenance staff to administer (Gladstone, 1980).

2. Some measures have been too easily defeated by offenders, as in the case of the early steering locks in the U.S. and Britain which proved vulnerable to slide hammers (Clarke and Harris, 1992a), and that of the "smart" credit cards in France which could be disabled by stamping on the chip (Levi, 1992).

3. Too much vigilance has sometimes been assumed on the part of guards or ordinary citizens: Security guards rarely monitor CCTV systems as closely as designers expect; people pay far less attention to the street outside their homes than is sometimes assumed by neighborhood watch schemes and defensible space designs (Mayhew, 1979); and people rarely respond to car alarms so that the main result of their increasing use

has been to reduce further the quality of life in cities (Clarke and Harris, 1992a).

4. Measures have occasionally provoked offenders to unacceptable escalation as in the case of the bullet-proofing of token booths on the New York subway which resulted in some attacks on booths with gasoline-fueled fires (Dwyer, 1991).

5. Some measures have facilitated rather than frustrated crime: Ekblom (1991) cites the example of pickpockets on the London Underground who stationed themselves near signs warning of theft to see which pockets were checked by passengers on reading the signs; and one result of introducing traffic bollards in Vancouver to frustrate cruising "johns" was to give prostitutes somewhere to sit when propositioning clients who had slowed down (Lowman, 1992).

6. In other cases, measures have been defeated by the carelessness or idleness of potential victims. Residents routinely frustrate entry control systems on apartment buildings by propping open doors to save themselves from answering the doorbell. The preventive value of the early security-coded radios was reduced because car owners failed to enter their private codes, thus allowing the radios to revert to a standard code known to thieves (Braga and Clarke, 1994).

7. The preventive value of these radios was further reduced because thieves did not always know which were security-coded and continued to steal ones they could not use; this flaw was remedied by a continuously blinking light fitted to indicate that the radio was security-coded (Braga and Clarke, 1994).

8. Some inappropriate measures have been introduced because no proper analysis of the problem was undertaken. For example, Harris and Clarke (1991) argued that the parts marking provisions of the federal Motor Vehicle Theft Law Enforcement Act of 1984 were bound to fail because parts marking was restricted only to "high risk" automo-

biles; leaving aside the resultant scope for displacement, most of the defined "high risk" models are taken not for dismantling and sale of their constituent parts, but for joyriding which will not be deterred by parts marking.

9. Other measures have proved unsuitable because insufficient thought has been given to users' needs. For example, one security innovation left senior citizens "trapped inside a fortress of heavy doors and electronic card-key devices which they found difficult to understand and to operate, while neighbors were no longer able to keep a friendly eye on them" (Sampson *et al.*, 1988: 484).

10. Finally, some measures have had a detrimental effect on the environment. Weidner (1996) argues that floor-to-ceiling turnstile railings installed at one New York City subway station did reduce fare evasion, but only at the cost of creating what was in many people's view "a draconian, prison-like environment." This could have been avoided had other, possibly equally effective measures, been taken instead.

These examples (as well as others provided by Grabosky, 1996) make clear that situational measures do not always work in intended ways. In addition, measures that work in one setting may not do so in another. An example is provided by helmet-wearing laws that dramatically (but fortuitously) reduced motorcycle theft in Germany (see below), but which had little effect in the United States. This was because the laws were not universally applied as in Germany, but were introduced in a piecemeal and inconsistent fashion (Mayhew et al., 1989).

None of the failures of situational prevention seriously call into question the basic validity of the concept, but they suggest that matters may be more complex than those implementing measures sometimes appreciate. Measures must be carefully tailored to the settings in which they are applied, with due regard to the motives and methods of the offenders involved. Where the stakes are high, offenders must be expected to test the limits of the new defenses and to be successful sometimes in identifying vulnerabilities. This process may be assisted by the arrival on the scene of more resourceful or determined criminals than was previously the case. And this again may sometimes result in the greater use of violence. For the less serious forms of crime, measures that depend upon natural surveillance or the vigilance of employees may be expected to lose their value as people become more complacent.

That preventive measures may have a limited life is not a counsel of despair; rather, it is a fact that must influence the choice among preventive options of varying difficulty and cost. The challenge for research is to help practitioners avoid the pitfalls by providing a sounder base of knowledge upon which to act. All we know at present is that some measures work well in certain conditions. What we need to know is which measures work best, in which combination (Tilley, 1993c), deployed against what kinds of crime and under what conditions (Poyner, 1993). We also need to have much better information about the financial costs of particular crime prevention measures. As discussed below, this will require a greatly increased investment in evaluative research. It also means that the commitment to situational prevention has to be long term, which for many organizations and agencies will mean developing a permanent in-house capability.

Displacement of Crime

Under the dispositional assumptions of traditional criminological theory, situational variables merely determine the time and place of offending. Manipulating situations would thus simply cause offenders to shift their attention to some other target, time or place, change their tactics or even switch to some other categories of crime (Reppetto, 1976). Displacement has therefore been the Achilles' heel of situational prevention, but this has changed with the theoretical developments described above. Under the rational choice assumptions that now guide thinking about situational prevention, displacement is no longer seen as inevitable, but as contingent upon the offender's judgments about al-

ternative crimes. If these alternatives are not viable, the offender may well settle for smaller criminal rewards or for a lower rate of crime. Few offenders are so driven by need or desire that they have to maintain a certain level of offending- whatever the cost. For many, the elimination of easy opportunities for crime may actually encourage them to explore non-criminal alternatives. On the other hand, since crime is the product of purposive and sometimes inventive minds, displacement to other categories of offense would not be unexpected, so long as these new crimes served the same purposes as the ones that were thwarted.

Numerous examples of displacement have been reported, particularly in the early literature (Gabor, 1990). Street crimes increased in surrounding districts following a successful crackdown on these crimes in one New York City precinct (Press, 1971). The reduction in robberies following the introduction of exact fare systems on New York City buses was a accompanied by an increase of robbery in the subway (Chaiken et al., 1974). In Columbus, a police helicopter patrol (Lateef, 1974) and, in Newark, a street lighting program (Tyrpak, 1975) appeared to shift crime to precincts not covered by the new measures. The reduced risk of theft for new vehicles fitted with steering column locks in Britain was found to be at the expense of an increased risk for older vehicles without the locks (Mayhew et al., 1976). Gabor (1981) found that a property marking program in Ottawa may have displaced burglaries from the homes of participants to those of non-participants. Finally, Allatt (1984) found that the decrease in burglary on a British public housing estate which had undergone "target hardening" was accompanied by an increase of property crimes in adjacent areas.

Apart from these and other instances in which displacement was found, researchers may sometimes have failed to detect displacement that had in fact occurred. This is especially likely where the displacement involved kinds of crime other than the ones targeted. Thus, the reduction of aircraft hijackings in the 1970s achieved by baggage screening might possibly have resulted in an undetected increase in other terrorist activity, such as car bombings, assassinations and hostage taking. The methodological difficulty encountered in detecting such displacement has been explained as follows:

If, in truth, displacement is complete, some displaced crime will probably fall outside the areas and types of crime being studied or be so dispersed as to be masked by background variation. In such an event, the optimist would speculate about why the unmeasured areas or types of crime probably escaped displaced crime, while the pessimist would speculate about why they probably did not. No research study, however massive, is likely to resolve the issue. The wider the scope of the study in terms of types of crimes and places, the thinner the patina of displaced crime could be spread across them; thus disappearing into the realm of measurement error. (Barr and Pease, 1990: 293)

On the other hand, the uncritical acceptance of displacement might have meant that increases in crime, that would have occurred anyway, have sometimes been wrongly attributed to displacement. For example, London Underground officials believed that the appearance of a new kind of slug soon after ticket machines had been modified to prevent the use of an earlier, more primitive slug, was the result of displacement. However, Clarke, et al., (1994) showed that the new slugs were found in different stations from the earlier ones, which suggested that different groups of offenders were involved. They concluded that, even if action had not been taken against the original slugs, the new ones might still have appeared.

With the development of rational choice analyses, evidence has begun to accumulate of the successful application of situational measures with few displacement costs. Thus, after reviewing 55 studies of displacement, Hesseling (1994) concluded that displacement was not found in 22 studies, and was never 100 percent in the remaining studies (see also Gabor, 1990; and Eck, 1993; Ferreira, 1995).

Much of this evidence on displacement comes from studies reproduced in this book. For instance, Knutsson and Kuhlhom (1981) found no evidence of an increase in a range of "conceivable" alternative crimes as a result of the introduction of new identification procedures that greatly reduced check frauds in Sweden. Following the re-arrangement of market stalls and improved lighting which reduced thefts at covered markets in Birmingham, England, no evidence was found of displacement of thefts to other nearby markets. When Caller ID became available in some parts of New Jersey, there was little evidence of an increase of obscene calls in other areas, perhaps because obscene phone callers are generally not persistent random dialers, hoping to hit upon susceptible women. Rather, many appear to victimize only particular women of their acquaintance and, with the introduction of Caller ID in their local telephone areas, these individuals are unlikely to have begun calling more distant parts of New Jersey where they knew no one. Finally, Matthews (1990) found little evidence that prostitutes simply moved to other locations following successful action to close down the red light district in Finsbury Park, which he explained by a relative lack of commitment to prostitution among many of the women involved. As the environment in Finsbury Park became less hospitable ". . . it would seem that over a period of about one year, most of the girls gave up prostitution or moved back home or elsewhere. For many, their normal period of involvement in prostitution may have been three or four years and, therefore, the effect of intensive policing was to shorten that period for a year or two in most cases."[6]

In other cases cited above, the nature of the targeted offenses would have meant there was little point in looking for displacement. For example, it is unlikely that those deterred by random breath tests from drunken driving in New South Wales (Homel, 1993) or those deterred by speed cameras from speeding in Victoria (Bourne and Cooke, 1993) would have displaced these behaviors to some other time or place. People do not usually set out to commit these offenses, but will do so when circumstances dictate (Homel, 1993). One important circumstance is the perceived chance of arrest and, were the ubiquitous speed cameras or random breath testing patrols to be withdrawn, people would no doubt once again revert to their old ways.

Understanding Displacement

Deeper understanding of the motives and modus operandi of target groups of offenders, as obtained in Matthews' study, provides a way of dealing with the limitations of the statistical search for displacement discussed by Barr and Pease (1990). It may not always be possible to interview offenders, but in some cases insights into motivation and methods can be provided by closer analysis of patterns of offending. For example, Clarke and Harris (1992b) have shown important differences among automobiles in their risks for different forms of theft, which reflect the motives of offenders. Thus, new cars most at risk of "stripping" in the United States during the mid-1980s were predominantly European models with good audio equipment; those most at risk of "joyriding" were American-made "muscle" cars; and those at risk of theft for re-sale were mostly higher-priced luxury automobiles. These "choice structuring properties" (Cornish and Clarke, 1987) of the target vehicles are not difficult to understand in terms of the motives of offenders and would also help to direct the search for displacement if the security were improved for any subset of vehicles. Thus, if some "muscle" cars were made more difficult to take for joyriding it would make sense to confine the search for displacement only to others of the same group.[7]

Similar logic was followed by Mayhew et al. (1989) in their study of displacement following the reduction of motorcycle thefts in West Germany between 1980 and 1986, brought about by the progressive enforcement of helmet legislation. During this period, motorcycle thefts declined by more than 100,000 because the helmet requirement substantially increased the risks of opportunistic thefts for those offenders who were unable at the same time to steal a helmet.[8] Mayhew and her colleagues reasoned that since many opportunistic thefts would have been for purposes of joyriding or temporary use (for example, to get home late at night), the most likely result of the reduced

opportunities for stealing motorcycles would be an increase in thefts of cars and bicycles. In fact, as shown by table 15.2, there was little evidence of displacement to either category of target. Car thefts did rise over the same period, but only by a few thousand, while bicycle thefts declined (after an initial rise) to below their previous level. Bicycles may not usually provide a realistic or attractive alternative means of transportation, whereas cars may not provide the same joyriding thrills. They may also require more knowledge to operate and may be more difficult to steal.

Table 15.2
Thefts of Motorcyles, Cars, and Bicycles: Federal Republic of Germany, 1980–86

Year	Motorcycles	Cars	Bicycles
1980	153,153	64,131	358,865
1981	143,317	71,916	410,223
1982	134,735	78,543	453,850
1983	118,550	82,211	415,398
1984	90,008	72,170	376,946
1985	73,442	69,659	337,337
1986	54,208	70,245	301,890

Source: Mayhew *et al.* (1989).

A final illustration of the value of considering "choice structuring properties" is provided by the British gas suicide story (Clarke and Mayhew, 1988). The elimination of gas suicides in Britain in the 1960s and 1970s resulting from the introduction of natural gas (which contains no toxins) was not followed by substantial displacement to other forms of suicide. Consequently, the overall suicide rate for the country declined by about 40 percent. The lack of displacement was explained by Clarke and Mayhew in terms of the particular advantages of domestic gas as a form of suicide. It was readily available in every home, it was simple to use, and it was highly lethal. It was also painless, left no marks or blood, and required little courage. No other alternative possessed all these advantages and would therefore have provided an acceptable alternative for many people.

It has been argued that it will only be a matter of time before the suicidally-inclined in Britain displace to other methods and the suicide rate reverts to its former level. Indeed, there has been some increase in the suicide rate for males who have been making more use of other methods including car exhaust gases (Clarke and Lester, 1987). However, there is substantial evidence that for many people the urge to kill themselves is in response to situational stress (such as a bereavement) and may dissipate as depression is alleviated. The gradual increase in the male suicide rate may therefore reflect, not "delayed displacement" by people prevented from killing themselves by the detoxification of gas, but an independent increase in the motivation to commit suicide.

This argument about the consequences of gas detoxification should not be taken to mean that longer-term adaptations never occur in response to situational measures. Indeed, it is widely believed that car thieves have gradually found ways to defeat steering column locks and support for this can be found in the somewhat higher than expected rates of car theft in some countries, especially Britain, where the locks have been available for many years (Clarke and Harris, 1992a). On the other hand, the reduction in the rate of car thefts in West Germany, brought about by the introduction of steering column locks in the 1960s, has persisted to this day. One possible reason for this (apart from the possibly higher quality of the German equipment) is that theft was greatly reduced almost overnight because the locks were made compulsory for all cars on the road. Consequently, neophytes were deprived of the example and tutelage of experienced car thieves. This affords a marked contrast to the situation in Britain where the locks were introduced only for new cars at manufacture. Consequently, car thieves could continue to operate so long as they concentrated their efforts on older vehicles. This meant they could gradually learn ways of defeating the steering locks and could continue to pass on the tricks of the trade to novices.

Diffusion of Benefits

Even when displacement occurs, it may sometimes be "benign" (Barr and Pease, 1990), as in the case of preventive measures which bring relief to repeatedly victimized groups although at the cost of an increased risks for others. This observation guided the design of an experiment to reduce burglary in Kirkholt, a public housing estate in the North of England (Pease, 1991). Target hardening priority was given to houses that had recently experienced a burglary, with the result that, despite their higher risks, few of these houses experienced a repeat burglary in the follow-up period. Pease also noted that these preventive benefits permeated, through what he called a process of "drip-feed," to other households that were not target-hardened so that the burglary rate for the whole of the Kirkholt estate declined dramatically.

The "drip-feed" effect is, of course, the reverse of displacement in that preventive action led, not to an increase, but to a reduction in crimes not directly addressed by the measures. As Clarke and Weisburd (1994) observe, similar effects have been noted under a variety of other names. For example, Miethe (1991) has referred to the "free rider" effect when residents benefit from the crime prevention measures taken by their neighbors and Sherman (1990) to the "bonus" effect sometimes observed in police crackdowns when there is a carryover of the preventive effect beyond the period when the crackdown is in force. Scherdin (1986) used the term "halo effect" when reporting that book detection systems prevented thefts, not just of the electronically protected materials, but also of other materials as well. In some cases the phenomenon has been reported without giving it a name. Poyner and Webb found that measures to reduce thefts from shopping bags in particular city center markets seemed also to reduce thefts in other markets as well. In his evaluation of a CCTV system installed to reduce auto theft at a university, Poyner found an equal reduction of crime in the parking lot not covered as the ones that were covered by the cameras. In his study of CCTV on buses, he found that damage and other misbehavior was reduced, not only on five buses fitted with cameras, but throughout the whole fleet of 80 buses.

Despite the variety of terminology, in all these cases the same phenomenon has been observed. That is to say, reductions in crime have occurred which are difficult to attribute to the direct action of situational measures. Clarke and Weisburd (1994) have argued that the generality of the phenomenon demands a standard term and they have proposed "diffusion of benefits," since the geographical and temporal connotations of this term parallel those of "displacement of crime." They have defined diffusion as:

> the spread of the beneficial influence of an intervention beyond the places which are directly targeted, the individuals who are the subject of control, the crimes which are the focus of intervention or the time periods in which an intervention is brought. (Clarke and Weisburd, 1994:169)

They have also distinguished between two forms of diffusion which they call deterrence and discouragement. Deterrence was invoked by Scherdin (1986), for example, in explaining why the book detection system she studied also prevented thefts of items that were not electronically tagged, and by Poyner in identifying reasons for the general decline in damage to the fleet when only some of the buses were fitted with CCTV cameras: "The children have learned . . .that the cameras will enable misbehaving individuals to be picked out and that action will be taken . . .They appear to believe that most buses have cameras, or at least they are uncertain about which buses have cameras." (Poyner, 1988:50)

For diffusion by "discouragement," the key is not the judgment of risk, but the assessment of effort and reward. For example, one component of the successful action against burglary in Kirkholt was the removal of prepayment meters from many houses on the estate (Pease, 1991). This seems to have been enough to discourage potential burglars who could no longer be sure of finding a meter containing cash. Similarly, the drop in thefts at all Birmingham city center markets following the situational measures taken at only some of them may have been due to the fact that: "The general attractiveness of this area for thieves has [been] reduced." Ekblom (1988b) accounted for the fact that anti-bandit screens in London post offices had produced a reduction, not just in over-the-counter robberies, but also in other robberies

of staff and customers by speculating that would-be robbers may have received "the very general message that something had been done to improve security at the sub-post offices" (Ekblom 1988b: 39). Finally, Clarke, et al. (1991) have suggested that an intensive target hardening program in Australian banks brought about a general reduction in robberies of all commercial targets (including convenience stores, gas stations and betting shops) because robbers began to believe that this form of crime was no longer worth pursuing.

It would be difficult to overestimate the importance of diffusion of benefits if the phenomenon is as common as these various examples suggest. By showing that the preventive benefits of situational measures extend beyond their immediate focus, the debate about their value is transformed. It is also clear that much more needs to be discovered about ways of enhancing diffusion. Sherman (1990) has suggested that the "free bonus" of crackdowns might be increased by randomly rotating crackdowns and back-offs across times and places so as to lead offenders to overestimate the actual levels of risk in force on any particular occasion. He also advocated the deliberate use of publicity about imminent crackdowns to promote this uncertainty in offenders' minds. Clarke and Weisburd (1994) argue that these strategies might be employed to diffuse the benefits of other forms of "situational deterrence" (Cusson, 1993) than crackdowns, and they also identify other possible means of enhancing diffusion, such as concentrating preventive action on highly visible or attractive targets, so as to lead offenders to think that preventive measures may have been more generally applied.

Since these various strategies depend upon influencing judgments made by offenders, we need to learn more about ways that offenders obtain and process information about preventive initiatives and what role is played in this process by their own direct observation, their relationships with other offenders and information obtained through the media. Whatever the practical pay-off from such studies, it is likely that diffusion of benefits will soon supplant displacement as the principal focus for theoretical debate about the value of situational measures.

A Prescription for Evaluation

Because diffusion has been overlooked, cases may already exist in which the effects of situational measures have been underestimated. Most existing evaluations have made use of "quasi-experiments," or "natural experiments," in which researchers have taken advantage of new preventive interventions to examine effects on crime through use of time series data, or a comparison with "control" data from an untreated site. Increased crime in the controls is usually attributed to displacement resulting from the situational measures, rather than to some extraneous increase in crime. On the other hand, decreased crime in the controls has not generally been attributed to diffusion, but to some overall, extraneous *decline* in crime.

Even without the difficulties of measuring displacement and diffusion, the interpretation of situational evaluations is problematic. Though declines in crime may be large, one cannot be confident about the durability of success because follow-ups are often brief, sometimes less than one year. In some of the studies, several preventive measures were deployed at the same time and their relative contributions to the outcome are unknown. For example, Felson *et al.* (1996) list eleven different measures that were introduced at the Port Authority Bus Terminal to deal with misuse of the restrooms. Finally, competing explanations for reported reductions in crime (other than as the result of the situational measures) have been insufficiently investigated in many of these quasi-experimental studies.

The weaknesses of quasi-experiments led to calls for greater use of true experimental designs, involving random assignment of preventive measures between treatment and control groups (Sherman, 1996; Weisburd, 1997). However, while suited to the laboratory, these designs often involve serious ethical problems and are difficult and costly to implement in the real world (Clarke and Cornish, 1972; Farrington, 1983). These difficulties include: (i) attempts by practitioners,

who may have their own views of the intervention, to subvert randomization; (ii) the reactive effects of the experiment, with the particular danger of "Hawthorne effects" resulting from the difficulty of concealing the fact that some areas or groups are receiving new treatments; (iii) the commitment of those administering the experimental treatment which may play an important role in the results; (iv) differential rates of attrition that may result in the non-comparability of randomly selected experimental and control groups; (v) changes over time in the intervention, and (vi) ethical problems involved in providing different levels of service to experimental and control groups or areas.

More serious than any of these difficulties is that crime prevention interventions are not like drugs, i.e., treatments with precisely measurable and controllable chemical constituents. Rather, they consist of a complex interaction of several related social and physical elements. This makes it impossible to be certain about the precise cause of any effect demonstrated by the experiment. One example is provided by a rare experiment concerned with shoplifting (Farrington *et al.*, 1993), in which three measures (electronic tagging, redesign of merchandise layout, and security guards) were systematically compared for effectiveness. Each measure was introduced in two stores selling electronic merchandise, while three other stores served as controls. It was concluded that electronic tags and store redesign were effective in reducing shoplifting (at least during the brief follow-up of three to six weeks), but that store redesign was undermined by further changes made by clerks to increase sales. The security guards, on the other hand, were not effective though the researchers acknowledged that this may have been due to store layouts which made it difficult to watch customers, or to the inexperience, advanced age, unimpressive physiques and lack of training of the particular individuals concerned.

It is most unlikely that these possibilities could be systematically explored within the confines of a rigorous experimental methodology. Few if any retail stores would tolerate the interference in their operations demanded by the experiments (or, more likely, series of experiments). Unless employed to do so, few criminologists would want to devote so much effort to sorting out the minutiae of security guard effectiveness in preventing shoplifting in just one kind of store. Many other, more rewarding problems beckon them. Add to this the difficulties of studying displacement and diffusion, which experimental designs do not necessarily solve and may even exacerbate because of the greater interference in the real world that may be required, and it becomes clear that these designs will have to be reserved for cases where it is imperative to achieve as much certainty as possible.

A more appropriate evaluative strategy for situational prevention will need to recognize that the value of particular situational measures is highly contingent on the nature of the problem and the circumstances in which it arises. Something that works in one situation will not necessarily work in another. What is needed is some quick, and occasionally rough, indication of whether a newly introduced measure is working. Since situational measures often achieve large reductions in crime, a simple time series or a comparison with a control group will frequently suffice. Where measures appear not to have worked, some possible explanations for this are also needed. Armed with this information, the action-researcher knows whether something else should be tried and, perhaps, what this should be.

Given the vast number of natural experiments being conducted in all manner of settings, the optimal strategy therefore seems to be: (1) to undertake as many evaluations as possible, (2) to compensate for weaker designs with detailed observation of the process of implementation (the value of which is illustrated by Farrington et al. observations about the caliber of their security guards), (3) to include as much information as possible about the costs and practicability of the techniques studied, (4) to conduct periodic meta-analyses of results (for examples see Poyner, 1993; Hesseling, 1994, and Eck, in preparation), and (5) to piece together the findings with reference to a systematic classification of situational techniques. This accumulating body of empirical results contributes to the development of robust principles of opportunity-reduction, which will help in developing tailor-made solutions for new problems arising in fresh circumstances. This strategy seems consistent with other recent writings about the need for theory-based evaluations of community initiatives (Connell et al., 1995; Weiss, 1995).

The ultimate objective of the empirical evaluations is therefore not to document the precise value of particular interventions (say, security guards) observed under particular circumstances, but to build our detailed understanding of the principles of effective opportunity-reduction. Since situational crime prevention practitioners are constantly called upon to provide tailor-made solutions for new problems arising in fresh circumstances, they will be helped more by a robust and detailed theory of opportunity reduction than by attempts to catalogue the effectiveness of a host of variations on specific crime prevention measures.

Implementation Difficulties

Crime prevention is no longer the inoffensive and neutral activity it once was in the days when it consisted purely of publicity exhorting people to lock it or lose it, and advice from the police on locks and bars. Now it involves the police and central/local government seeking to influence the civil behavior of particular individuals, private companies and local authority departments responsible for the creation of criminal opportunities or motivation, instead of tackling the "common enemy crime," it cuts across conflicting public and private interests and policies, and has to compete for resources with other goals and needs, not always as a front runner. Reconciliation of all this conflict and competition means that crime prevention has to be slipped in by changing attitudes and expectations, by good salesmanship, clever design, close attention to cost effectiveness, sometimes piggybacking on other facilities and changes in an organization, and using data recording systems developed and maintained primarily for other purposes. (Ekblom, 1987a: 11–12)

This extended quote may be a useful corrective to the case studies reprinted in this volume which are largely silent about the difficulties encountered in implementing situational prevention. Rarely do the difficulties concern the identification of suitable measures since many alternative ways exist of blocking opportunities for specific classes of crime (cf. Hope, 1985; Smith, 1987). Rather, the difficulties of implementation usually concern acceptance of the responsibility for preventive action and issues of cost and coordination.

Because most situational prevention to-date has been undertaken in the public sector, discussion of implementation difficulties has focused largely on ways of achieving the necessary coordination among local government agencies (e.g., Gladstone, 1980; Hope, 1985; Ekblom, 1987a). Coordination is especially difficult when attempting to combine situational with "social" or "community" crime prevention measures (e.g. Blaug *et al.*, 1988; Sampson *et al.*, 1988; Liddle and Gelsthorpe, 1994; Gilling, 1996; Hughes, 1996; Sutton, 1996; Walters, 1996). However, with increasing recognition that much preventive action can be undertaken only by the private sector, for example, by credit card companies, bus operators, offices and shopping malls (cf. Felson and Clarke, 1997a), more attention is being focused on issues of responsibility and costs. Those in the private sector tend to see crime prevention as a police matter and are rarely willing to "acknowledge that their property or operations are generating, a substantial strain on police resources, accept that they have a duty, up to their level of competence, for the control of specific crimes, and take appropriate action" (Engstad and Evans, 1980:151). Acknowledging this responsibility would not only complicate the management task, but could involve the expenditure of significant resources. Analyses of these costs are therefore likely to play an increasingly important role in crime prevention (Burrows, 1991).

These points are illustrated by the familiar example of shoplifting, which is facilitated by some retailing practices including displays to encourage impulse buying. The risks of the ensuing "shrinkage" are accepted by most stores, which rely upon deterrence to contain the problem through the occasional arrest and prosecution of shoplifters. This results in significant costs being passed on to the criminal justice system, which are not borne by retailers except in an indirect way through taxation.

These practices will not be changed simply by government exhortation, which runs the risk of being dismissed as "blaming the victim" (Karmen, 1984). Nor could stores often be charged for police service when they have failed to adopt preventive measures (Pease, 1979). However, declining retail profits due to increased competition might force stores to take a more proactive role in prevention. This might also be facilitated by improved technology, which now permits instant credit checks (Levi *et al.*, 1991) and tighter stock control (Hope, 1991). The technology will always need to pass the retailer's cost-benefit scrutiny, but this will not take account of the criminal justice costs of failing to take preventive action. There will, therefore, be an increasing role for research such as that undertaken by Field (1993) on the costs of auto theft in the United States, which included analysis of criminal justice costs and of the potential savings that might result from government-mandated vehicle security standards.

Philosophical and Ethical Issues

When first introduced, the concept of situational prevention provoked fears about two unwelcome developments in society. In its more unattractive, "target hardening" forms (barbed-wire, heavy padlocks, guard dogs and private security forces) it suggested the imminence of a "fortress society" in which people, terrified by crime and distrustful of their fellows, barricade themselves in their homes and places of work, emerging only to conduct essential business (Davis, 1990). In its use of electronic hardware (CCTV, intruder alarms, x-ray scanning of baggage), it raised the specter of totalitarian, "Big Brother" forms of state control.

Experience of situational measures has dispelled some fears of the fortress society (though not all, cf. Bottoms, 1990). Many of the measures (such as parts marking of automobiles and the interior lighting of banks at night) are so unobtrusive as to be barely no-ticeable, while others (including street light-ing, defensible space architecture, and uni-formed security guards in shopping and lei-sure complexes) actually reduce the fear of crime. Yet other measures which enhance se-curity, such as bar coding of merchandise and central locking of automobiles, also have the advantage of increasing the convenience of everyday life.

This very unobtrusiveness and conven-ience feeds the second fear—that it may not be the fortress society that is imminent, but Huxley's "Brave New World." If America is the harbinger of change for the rest of the world, how much more true might not this be of Disney World? The unobtrusive yet powerful social control exemplified there, under which people willingly accept being corralled and shepherded from place to place, may soon be shaping much of our lei-sure behavior, if not our lives! Add to this the astonishing growth in the technological de-vices now available to the "new surveillance" (Marx, 1986), and the potential for state con-trol, not of the iron fist but of the velvet glove, seems frightening.

While credible under fascism or a dictator-ship, this scenario of a sheep-like populace gives altogether too little credence to the power of democracy. Visitors to Disney World might temporarily surrender some auton-omy, but only because they recognize that a degree of regimentation may be necessary if they are to enjoy the spectacles in safety and at reasonable cost. People may increasingly be willing to make this trade in their daily lives, but it will soon become apparent if they are not: Disney World will go broke. More-over, while they may welcome powerful new forms of surveillance in guaranteeing na-tional security or combating organized crime, they will fight its deployment in the everyday situations giving rise to most crime as soon as they perceive a threat to their civil liberties.

Nor is the vision, or perhaps nightmare, of a blanket application by the State of situ-ational controls on behavior consistent with the essence of situational prevention: Situ-ational measures cannot be applied whole-sale; they need to be tailored to the particular

circumstances giving rise to specific prob-lems of crime and disorder. Moreover, unlike most other measures of crime control, situ-ational measures are not the sole prerogative of the State. but need to be applied by par-ticular private or business organizations. Far from being enthusiastically embraced, they may be strongly resisted. Indeed, the prob-lem is less one of the sweeping application of situational measures, than of the failure to apply them when they should have been.

While ethical and legal questions sur-rounding particular situational measures, such as gun controls, have been extensively analyzed, there has, in fact, been compara-tively little general discussion of the ethics of situational prevention. This is because both critics and advocates have been preoccupied with its effectiveness. As evidence accumu-lates of its preventive value in a wide variety of crime contexts, the focus of debate is likely to move increasingly to ethical and philo-sophical questions (Homel, 1996).

Fears will no doubt continue to be ex-pressed about the fortress society and about Orwellian forms of surveillance, especially with the growing use of CCTV cameras in public places (Honess and Charman, 1992; Tilley, 1993c; Home, 1996; Davies, 1996a,b). Because situational prevention sees everyone as susceptible to crime opportunities, it will continue to be criticized for its essentially cynical and pessimistic character, even though it seems more morally defensible than the traditional view of crime as the prov-ince of a small group of criminal individuals. This can provide a device for scapegoating particular individuals and groups and for jus-tifying highly punitive or intrusive interven-tions (Seve, 1997). However, the debate about ethics in the next decade is likely also to en-compass a broader set of issues relating to "victim blaming" and to distributive justice.

Victim blaming was mentioned above in the context of persuading businesses to mod-ify criminogenic products and practices. An-other vocal group on this subject are victim advocates who resist any imputation of vic-tim responsibility because this might jeop-ardize the achievement of better rights and treatment for victims. However, most victims would no doubt prefer to have been protected from crime in the first place than to receive compensation or better treatment later. Most would also welcome sound advice on precautionary measures. Victim advocacy should therefore find a natural, symbiotic relationship with crime prevention, which neither compromises victim rights nor absolves offenders of responsibility. The position has been expressed as follows:

> The whole point of routine precautions against crime is that people can take responsibility without accepting criminal blame or even civil liability. Routine precautions by potential victims do not serve to exempt offenders from criminal responsibility. The citizen who reminds herself to lock her car door and does so still has a right to expect others not to steal that car, whether it is locked or not. . . . If crime opportunities are extremely enticing and open, society will tend to produce new offenders and offenses. By inviting crime, society will make it more difficult for the law enforcement system to prosecute and punish those who accept the invitation. With situational prevention, invitations to crime are fewer and hence it is more difficult for those who do offend to escape responsibility. (Felson and Clarke, 1997b)

One of the topics arising under distributive justice is the risk of displacement following preventive action—particularly displacement from the rich, who can afford situational prevention, to the poor who cannot. This concern, often raised in the context of "gated communities" (wealthy residential enclaves), is related to a second concern that situational measures can be used by the powerful to exclude undesirables—such as the poor, minorities and young people—from public places such as shopping malls, parks, town centers and particular neighborhoods (O'Maffey, 1994; White and Sutton, 1995).

On displacement from rich to poor, the issues are by no means straightforward. A wealthy neighborhood near to less affluent communities may provide a magnet for crime and, if it provides tempting targets and easy rewards for crime, may draw people into burglary who might otherwise not have become involved. On the other hand, reducing the opportunities for burglary may be un-

likely to drive offenders back to the less wealthy areas where the pickings may be more meager. There is even the possibility that the preventive measures taken in one community might benefit a neighboring one through a process of diffusion. Measures taken by the wealthy may thus sometimes benefit the less affluent. A concrete example is provided by LOJACK, a vehicle tracking system that consists of a small transmitter hidden in a car that can be activated to facilitate recovery when the car is stolen. LOJACK is too expensive for everyone to buy, but a recent study suggests that it brings general benefits in terms of reduced car theft (Ayres and Levitt, 1996). One reason is that car thieves do not know whether any given vehicle is equipped with LOJACK because police have made this a condition of collaborating in the retrieval of cars fitted with the transmitters.

In addition, many so-called exclusionary measures are not the prerogative of the rich. It may be the case that in New York, doormen are found only in apartment buildings for the wealthy, but in Europe concierges are found in many middle- and low-income apartment blocks. Many public housing estates have manned entrances and some poor communities make use of street barriers to exclude drug dealers and others who might prey upon residents (Atlas and LeBlanc, 1994). Indeed, Oscar Newman's (1972) original "defensible space" work, the start of scientific interest in opportunity-reduction, was undertaken in public housing and makes use of design to help residents police the public areas of the estate. More recently, he has described how the use of gates to create "mini-neighborhoods" in a down-town low-income rental community in Dayton, Ohio, substantially reduced traffic and crime problems (Newman, 1996).

In some cases, cultural attitudes will prevent the adoption of particular situational measures, even though they might have been accepted elsewhere. Thus, photo radar is widely used in Australia, but was recently made illegal in New Jersey (Clarke, 1995), while a scheme to reduce fraudulent checks requiring a thumbprint has been adopted in New Jersey (*New York Times*, March 23, 1997,

Sctn. 13, p. 1) when a similar scheme was rejected in Western Australia (Pidco, 1996). Even for the same population, what is found objectionable or intrusive can change over time. Witness changed attitudes to smoking or wearing seat belts.

Where situational measures are vetoed on ethical grounds or simply found objectionable. alternative situational measures can often be found that do not provoke these same reactions. Nevertheless, an improved understanding of ethical costs for the broad swathe of situational techniques would be of considerable value in planning interventions. Indeed, the greater attention being paid to these issues may result in general ethical guidelines, to be used together with improved information about the cost-effectiveness of particular measures, in tailoring responses to crime problems.

Political and Professional Constituencies for Situational Prevention

At the beginning of this introduction, it was argued that situational prevention is a radical new form of crime control focused not on criminals but on criminogenic situations, with all that implies for criminological explanation. Situational prevention can also be regarded, however, as a logical outcome of the precautions that people have always taken to protect themselves from crime and, seen in this light, it is little more than the systematization of a wide range of everyday, common sense practices. That two such divergent views can be taken of situational prevention helps to explain why it is widely practiced in all but name, while at the same time it is resisted by many criminologists and politicians.

Its lack of political support may be surprising: The Left might have welcomed its focus upon local problems and local decision-making. Liberals might have been attracted to its essentially non-punitive philosophy; and Conservatives might have been attuned to its message concerning the need for agencies and communities to take the initiative in dealing with their crime problems. Perhaps

the very breadth of this appeal means that situational prevention lacks a natural constituency among politicians, but they also have other reasons to resist it. It is too easily represented as being soft on crime and as blaming victims. It seems to demand new resources, in addition to those already allocated to the criminal justice system. It is easily characterized as demonstrating a failure of political will in dealing with the severe social and economic problems that confront society. Its essentially piecemeal approach affords little prospect of achieving immediate reductions in overall crime rates and its rational, analytic nature does not lend itself to eloquence in campaign speeches or political manifestos.

Politicians may indeed have a limited role in promoting situational prevention because particular measures often have to be initiated at a local level, sometimes by private sector organizations. The grass roots formulation of crime control must encourage cost-benefit appraisals of prevention and might result in more effective action, but it means that national politicians cannot claim the successes. When they do promote "situational" programs, such as neighborhood watch, there is the risk of this leading to the kind of unfocused efforts, out of keeping with the tenets of situational crime prevention, that result in disappointment and disillusionment. When central government intervention is indicated, as in the case of persuading vehicle manufacturers to improve security, this may not require laws enacted by politicians, but patient, "behind the scenes" negotiations conducted by civil servants to persuade reluctant parties to take preventive action.

Despite its lack of a political constituency, situational prevention has become a component, though a small one, of crime policy in some European countries (Willemse, 1994, Garland, 1996). This may be because civil servants can sometimes be more pragmatic than their political masters. Both in Holland and Great Britain, situational prevention is promoted by government crime prevention units and by a semi-autonomous governmental agency in Sweden. Its record of success and the resolution of ethical and theoretical dilemmas will mean that its policy role will grow, even in the United States where interest has been lagging. As mentioned above, this may be due partly to the disappointing results of attempts to implement CPTED in the 1970s. However, Bright (1992) has noted the absence of any crime prevention policy in America, which he attributes to a dislike of government intervention as well as to a strong ethos of personal responsibility that results in punishment being seen as the most appropriate response to law-breaking. Nevertheless, the recent federal government support for community and problem-oriented policing may signal a change, likely to benefit situational prevention.

Since the responsibility for much preventive action falls on the private sector, government officials promoting situational prevention will need to become familiar with a world that is now foreign to many of them. Their usual modes of governing, based upon fiscal control and parliamentary or Congressional authority, will have to be supplemented by other change strategies, including negotiation and persuasion (Burrows, 1997; Travis, 1997; van Dijk, 1997). Some difficult issues, discussed above in the context of shoplifting, will also have to be addressed concerning the role of government in helping to prevent crimes that impact profitability and which businesses might be expected to deal with themselves. Without a lead from government, however, many crime problems bringing harm to businesses and their clientele, or caused by business practices might never be addressed. Without government research funding, it is also unclear how the requisite body of knowledge about preventing crime in commercial establishments would be accumulated (Felson and Clarke, 1997a).

While its role in policy now seems assured, situational prevention still lacks a strong professional constituency. Since it can be used by such a wide range of public and private organizations, it will never be of more than marginal interest to any particular group of managers. The security industry also may resist an approach which could reduce the demand for guards and security hardware, the industry's main staples. Finally, police interest in situational prevention is likely to be subsumed under problem-oriented policing.

At the same time, situational prevention expertise is increasingly being sought in a wide range of settings, public and private. Towns and cities in Britain and Holland are beginning to appoint crime prevention or "community safety" officers, and some criminologists are already employed in a preventive capacity in business and industry (Burrows, 1997; Challinger, 1997). In America, Felson (1994b) has proposed that university departments of criminology and criminal justice should operate a crime prevention extension service based on the successful agricultural model.

These developments offer considerable training and employment opportunities for criminologists, but not without some changes of attitude. More young criminologists will need to define their theoretical goals more in terms of control than enlightenment, and will need to define control more in terms of reducing opportunities than propensities. They will have to become familiar with a host of social institutions—schools, factories, hospitals, rail and bus systems, shopping malls and retail stores—beyond the courts and the prisons. They must no longer disdain the business world, but must recognize its central role in the production and control of crime (Felson and Clarke, 1997a). Their role models will increasingly need to become traffic engineers and public health specialists—professionals employed to improve everyday life—rather than academics and social commentators. In short, a more down-to-earth, pragmatic approach will be required.

Sutton (1996) and O'Malley (1997) have argued that such pragmatism conflicts with the philosophy and values of criminology students, many of whom aspire to be social reformers seeking a reduction in inequality and deprivation. While these are admirable ambitions, equally rewarding and challenging careers await those who can shift their professional goals from long-term social reform to making an immediate reduction in crime—which, after all, harms the very people they seek to help.

Notes

1. Coleman (1985:16) is quite mistaken in describing the Home Office studies as being undertaken "to refute Newman's thesis." On the contrary, the limited support for his ideas provided by this research was a considerable disappointment to the researchers involved who included the present author.

2. The classification of 16 situational techniques makes a distinction between controls on facilitators and on disinhibitors (table 15.1).

3. Partly due to concerns raised by Wortley (1996) and Newman (1997), some further changes have been made here in Clarke and Homel's classification. Specifically, "removing excuses" has been substituted for "inducing shame and guilt," and "stimulating conscience" for "strengthening moral condemnation."

4. This work on slug use was undertaken in the Criminal Law Education and Research Center of New York University, under the direction of my colleague, G.O.W. Mueller, now at Rutgers. Sitting in his office is one of the old parking meters without slug-rejecter or coin window. Would that more criminologists had such tangible evidence of the practical value of their work!

5. The Insurance Institute for Highway Safety (1995) has been pursuing an alternative solution to this problem with some success by lengthening the yellow signal and/or the period during which the light is red in all directions.

6. As mentioned in the editor's note to *Case Study #3*, Lowman (1992) found extensive displacement of prostitution into nearby streets when a similar street-closure scheme was introduced in Vancouver. This seems to have been due to the Vancouver prostitutes' need for money to support drug habits. The implication is that similar preventive actions may have different displacement effects depending on the precise nature of the settings and offenders involved (cf. McNamara, 1994). A further example is provided by Curtis and Sviridoff (1994) who argued that street-level drug enforcement undertaken by police in three different areas of New York City had varying displacement effects because of differences in the social organization of the drug selling enterprises.

7. In line with this reasoning, Eck (1993) has postulated that displacement follows a "familiarity decay" function, in that it is most likely to involve similar times, places, targets and behaviors to the offenses blocked. Bouloukos and Farrell (1997) have taken this line of reasoning one step further and have used the concept of familiarity decay together with that of "crime scripts" (Cornish, 1994) in arguing that displacement is less likely to occur when repeat victimizations have been prevented.

8. Similar reductions in motorcycle theft have been reported in Britain (Mayhew *et al.*, (1976). Holland (Van Straelen, 1978) and Madras, India (Natarajan and Clarke, 1994) following the enactment of helmet laws.

References

Allat, P. 1984. Residential security: Containment and displacement of burglary. *Howard Journal of Criminal Justice* 23:99–116.

Ardrey, R. 1966. *The Territorial Imperative*. New York: Dell Publishing Co.

Atlas, R. and LeBlanc, W. G. 1994. The impact on crime of street closures and barricades. *Security Journal* 5:140–145.

Ayres, I. and Levitt, S. D. 1996. Measuring positive externalities from unobservable victim precaution: An empirical analysis of Lojack. Unpublished manuscript, Yale Law School.

Bamfield, J. 1994. Electronic article surveillance: Management learning in curbing theft. In M. Gill (ed.), *Crime at Work*. Leicester, UK: Perpetuity Press.

Bandura, A. 1976. Social learning analysis of aggression. In E. Ribes-Inesta and A. Bandura (eds.) *Analysis of Delinquency and Aggression*. Hillsdale, NJ: Lawrence Erlbaum Associates, Publishers.

Barr, R. and Pease, K. 1990. Crime placement, displacement and deflection. In M. Tonry and N. Morris (eds.) *Crime and Justice: A Review of Research* vol. 12. Chicago: University of Chicago Press.

Bauer, Y. 1990. The evolution of Nazi Jewish policy, 1933–38. In F. Chalk and K. Johassohn (eds.), *The History and Sociology of Genocide: Analysis and Case Studies*. New Haven: Yale University Press.

Becker, G.S. 1968. Crime and punishment: An economic approach. *Journal of Political Economy* 76:169–216.

Bell, J. and Burke, J. 1989. Cruising Cooper Street. *Police Chief*, January: 26–29.

Belamy, L. 1996. Situational crime prevention and convenience store robbery. *Security Journal* 7:41–52.

Bennett, T. 1990. *Evaluating Neighborhood Watch.* Aldershot, Hants: Gower.

Bennett, T. and Wright, R. 1984. *Burglars on Burglary.* Farnborough, Hants: Gower.

Bichler, G. and Clarke, R.V. 1996. Eliminating pay phone toll fraud at the Port Authority Bus Terminal in Manhattan. In R.V. Clarke (ed.), *Preventing Mass Transit Crime. Crime Prevention Studies,* vol. 6. Monsey, NY: Criminal Justice Press.

Biron, L.L. and Ladouceur, C. 1991. The boy next door: Local teenage burglars in Montreal. *Security Journal* 2:200–204.

Blagg, H., Pearson, G., Sampson, A., Smith, D. and Stubbs, P. 1988. Inter-agency co-ordination: Rhetoric and reality. In T. Hope and M. Shaw (eds.), *Communities and Crime Reduction.* London: H.M. Stationary Office.

Boss, R.W. 1980. The library security myth. *Library Journal* 105:683.

Bottoms, A.E. 1990. Crime prevention facing the 1990s. *Policing and Society* 1:3–22.

Bourne, M.G. and Cooke, R.C. 1993. Victoria's speed camera program. In R.V. Clarke (ed.), *Crime Prevention Studies,* vol. 1. Monsey, NY: Criminal Justice Press.

Braga, A. and Clarke, R.V. 1994. Improved radios and more stripped cars in Germany: A routine activities analysis. *Security Journal* 5: 154–159.

Brantingham, P.J. and Brantingham, P.L. 1975. The spatial patterning of burglary. *Howard Journal of Criminal Justice* 14:11–23.

Brantingham, P.J. and Brantingham, P.L. 1991. *Environmental Criminology.* (2nd ed.) Prospect Heights, IL: Waveland Press.

Briar, S. and Piliavin, I.M. 1965. Deliquency, situational inducements and commitment to conformity, *Social Problems* 13:35–45.

Bridgeman, C. 1997. Preventing pay phone damage. In M. Felson and R.V. Clarke (eds.), *Business and Crime Prevention.* Monsey, NY: Criminal Justice Press.

Bright, J. 1992. *Crime Prevention in America: A British Perspective.* Chicago, IL: Office of International Criminal Justice, The University of Illinois at Chicago.

Brody, S.R. 1976. *The Effectiveness of Sentencing.* Home Office Research Study No. 35. London: H.M. Stationary Office.

Brown, B. 1996. *CCTV in Town Centers: Three Case Studies.* Police Research Group Crime Detection and Prevention Series Paper 68. London: Home Office.

Burrows, J. 1991. *Making Crime Prevention Pay: Initiatives From Business.* Crime Prevention Unit Paper 27. London: Home Office.

Burrows, J. 1997. Criminology and business crime: Building the bridge. In M. Felson and R.V. Clarke (eds.), *Business and Crime Prevention.* Monsey, NY: Criminal Justice Press.

Burt, C. 1925. *The Young Delinquent.* London: University of London Press (reprinted 1969).

Carr, K. and Spring, G. 1993. Public transport safety: A community right and communal responsibility. In R.V. Clarke (ed.), *Crime Prevention Studies,* vol. 1. Monsey, NY: Criminal Justice Press.

Carroll, J. and Weaver, F. 1986. Shoplifter's perceptions of crime opportunities: A process-tracing study. In D.B. Cornish and R.V. Clarke (eds.), *The Reasoning Criminal.* New York: Springer-Verlag.

Casey, S. and Lund, A. 1993. The effects of mobile roadside spedometers on traffic speeds. *Accident Analysis and Prevention* 24:507–520.

Cavallo, A. and Drummond, A. 1994. Evaluation of the Victorian random breath testing initiative. In D. South and A. Cavallo (eds.), *Australian Drink-Drive Conference 1993, Conference Proceedings.* Melbourne, AUS: VicRoads.

Chaiken, J., Lawless, M. and Stevenson, K. 1974. *The Impact of Police Activity on Crime: Robberies on the New York City Subway System.* Report No. R–1424–N.Y.C. Santa Monica, CA: Rand Corporation.

Challinger, D. 1991. Less telephone vandalism: How did it happen? *Security Journal* 2:111–119.

Challinger, D. 1997. Will crime prevention ever be a business priority? In M. Felson and R.V. Clarke (eds.), *Business and Crime Prevention.* Monsey, NY: Criminal Justice Press.

Clarke, R.V. 1977. Psychology and crime. *Bulletin of the British Psychological Society* 30:280–3.

Clarke, R.V. 1980. Situational crime prevention: Theory and practice. *British Journal of Criminology* 20:136–147.

Clarke, R.V. 1983. Situational crime prevention: Its theoretical basis and practical scope. In M. Tonry and N. Morris (eds.), *Crime and Justice: An Annual Review of Research,* vol. 4. Chicago: University of Chicago Press.

Clarke, R.V. 1984. Opportunity-based crime rates. *British Journal of Criminology* 24:74-83.

Clarke, R.V. 1990. Deterring obscene phone callers: Preliminary results of the New Jersey experience. *Security Journal* 1:143–148.

Clarke, R.V. 1992. *Situational Crime Prevention: Successful Case Studies.* Albany, NY: Harrow and Heston.

Clarke, R.V. 1993. Fare evasion and automatic ticket collection on the London Underground.

In R.V. Clarke (eds.), *Crime Prevention Studies*, vol. 2. Monsey, NY: Criminal Justice Press.

Clarke, R.V. 1995. Situational crime prevention. In M. Tonry and D. Farrington (eds.), *Building a Safer Society: Strategic Approaches to Crime Prevention. Crime and Justice: A Review of Research*, vol. 19. Chicago: University of Chicago Press.

Clarke, R.V. 1997. Problem-oriented policing and the potential contribution of criminology. Report to the National Institute of Justice. Grant # 95IJCX0021.

Clarke, R.V., Cody, R. and Natarajan, M. 1994. Subway slugs: Tracking displacement on the London Underground. *British Journal of Criminology* 34:122–138.

Clarke, R.V., and Cornish, D.B. 1972. *The Controlled Trial in Institutional Research: Paradigm or Pitfall.* Home Office Research Study No. 12. London: H.M. Stationary Office.

Clarke, R.V., and Cornish, D.B. 1983. *Crime Control in Britain: A Review of Policy Research.* Albany, NY: State University of New York Press.

Clarke, R.V., and Cornish, D.B. 1985. Modeling offenders' decisions: A framework for policy and research. In M. Tonry and N. Morris (eds.), *Crime and Justice: An Annual Review of Research*, vol. 6. Chicago: University of Chicago Press.

Clarke, R.V. and Felson, M. (eds.), 1993. *Routine Activity and Rational Choice. Advances in Criminological Theory*, vol. 5. New Brunswick, NJ: Transaction Publisher.

Clarke, R.V., Field, S. and McGrath, G. 1991. Target hardening of banks in Australia and displacement of robberies. *Security Journal* 2:84–90.

Clarke, R.V. and Harris, P.M. 1992a. Autotheft and its prevention. In M. Tonry (ed.), *Crime and Justice: A Review of Research*, vol. 16. Chicago: University of Chicago Press.

Clarke, R.V., and Harris, P.M. 1992b. A rational choice perspective on the targets of auto theft. *Criminal Behavior and Mental Health* 2:25–42.

Clarke, R.V. and Homel, R. 1997. A revised classification of situational crime prevention techniques. In Lab, S.P. (ed.), *Crime Prevention at a Crossroads.* Cincinnati, Ohio: Anderson.

Clarke, R.V. and Lester, D. 1987. Toxicity of car exhausts and opportunity for suicide: Comparison between Britain and the United States. *Journal of Epidemiology and Community Health.* 41:114–120.

Clarke, R.V. and Mayhew, P.M. 1980. *Designing out Crime.* London: H.M. Stationary Office.

Clarke, R.V. and Mayhew, P.M. 1988. The British gas suicide story and its criminological implications. In M. Tonry and N. Morris (eds.), *Crime and Justice*, vol. 10. Chicago: University of Chicago Press.

Clarke, R.V. and McGrath, G. 1990. Cash reduction and robbery prevention in Australian betting shops. *Security Journal* 1:160–163.

Clarke, R.V. and Weisburd, D. 1994. Diffusion of crime control benefits: Observations on the reverse of displacement. In R.V. Clarke (ed.), *Crime Prevention Studies*, vol. 2. Monsey, NY: Criminal Justice Press.

Cohen, L.E. and Felson, M. 1979. Social change and crime rate trends: A routine activity approach. *American Sociological Review.* 44:588–608.

Coleman, A. 1985. *Utopia on Trial: Vision and Reality in Planned Housing.* London: Hilary Shipman.

Connell, J.P., Kubisch, A.C., Schorr, L.B. and Weiss, C.H. (eds.), 1995. *New Approach to Evaluating Community Initiatives.* Washington, DC: The Aspen Institute.

Cooper, B. 1989. Preventing break-ins to pre-payment fuel meters. *Research Bulletin* No. 26. Home Office Research and Planning Unit. London: Home Office.

Cornish, B. 1993. Theories of action in criminology: Learning theory and rational choice approaches. In R.V. Clarke and M. Felson (eds.), *Routine Activity and Rational Choice.* Advances in Criminological Theory, vol. 5. New Brunswick, NJ: Transaction Publishers.

Cornish, D.B. and Clarke, R.V. 1986. *The Reasoning Criminal. Rational Choice Perspectives on Offending.* New York: Springer-Verlag.

Cornish, D.B. and Clarke, R.V. 1987. Understanding crime displacement: An application of rational choice theory. *Criminology* 25:933–947.

Cornish, D.B. and Clarke, R.V. 1988. Crime specialization, crime displacement and rational choice theory. In H. Wegener, F. Losel and J. Haisch (eds.), *Criminal Behavior and the Justice System.* Berlin: Springer-Verlag.

Cromwell, P.F. (ed.), 1996. *In Their Own Words: Criminals on Crime.* Los Angeles, CA: Roxbury Publishing.

Cromwell, P.F., Olson, J.N. and Avary, D.W. 1991. *Breaking and Entering: An Ethnographic Analysis of Burglary.* Newbury Park, CA: Sage.

Crowe, T.D. 1991. *Crime Prevention Through Environmental Design: Applications of Architectural Design and Space Management Concepts.* Boston: Butterworth-Heinemann.

Crowe, T.D. and Zahm, D. 1994. Crime Prevention through Environmental Design. *Land Development* 7:22–27.

Cusson, M. 1986. L'analyze strategique et quelques developpments recente en Criminologie. *Criminologie* XIX: 51–72.

Cusson, M. 1993. Situational deterrence: Fear during the criminal event. In R.V. Clarke (ed.), *Crime Prevention Studies*, vol. 1. Monsey, NY: Cummings and Hathaway.

Davies, S. 1996a. *Big Brother: Britain's Web of Surveillance and the New Technological Order*. London: Pan Books.

Davis, M. 1990. *City of Quartz, Excavating the Future in Los Angeles*. London: Verso.

Decker, J.F. 1972. Curbside deterrence: An analysis of the effect of a slug rejectory device, coin view window and warning labels on slug usage in New York City parking meters. *Criminology* August 127–142.

Department of Environment. 1977. *Housing Management and Design*. (Lambeth Inner Area Study). IAS/IA/18. London: Department of Environment.

DesChamps, S., Brantingham, P.L. and Brantingham, P.J. 1991. The British Columbia transit fare evasion audit: A description of a situational prevention process. *Security Journal* 2:211–218.

DiLonardo, R.L. 1996. Defining and measuring the economic benefit of electric article surveillance. *Security Journal* 7:3–9.

DiLonardo, R.L. and Clarke, R.V. 1996. Reducing the rewards of shoplifting: An evaluation of ink tags. *Security Journal* 7:11–14.

Downes, D. and Rock, P. 1982. *Understanding Deviance*. Oxford: Clarendon Press.

Dwyer, J. 1991. *Subway Lives*. New York: Crown.

Eck, J.E. 1993. The threat of crime displacement. *Criminal Justice Abstracts* 25:527–546.

Eck, J.E. 1995. A general model of the geography of illicit retail marketplaces. In D. Weisburd and J. Eck (eds.), *Crime and Place. Crime Prevention Studies*, vol. 4. Monsey, NY: Criminal Justice Press.

Ekblom, P. 1987a. Crime prevention in England: Themes and issues. Unpublished paper presented at Australian Institute of Criminology, November 24, 1987. London: Home Office Crime Prevention Unit.

Ekblom, P. 1988b. Preventing post office robberies in London: Effects and side effects. *Journal of Security Administration* 11:36–43.

Ekblom, P. 1991. Talking to offenders: Practical lessons for local crime prevention. In O. Nel-lo (ed.), *Urban Crime: Statistical Approaches and Analyses*. Barcelona, Spain: Institute d'estudis Metropolitans de Barcelona.

Ellul, J. 1965. *Propaganda: The Formation of Men's Attitudes*. New York: Vintage Books.

Engstad, P. 1975. Environmental opportunities and ecology of crime. In R.A. Silverman and J.J. Teevan, Jr. (eds.), *Crime in Canadian Society*. Toronto: Butterworth.

Engstad, P. and Evans, J.L. 1980. Responsibility, competence and police effectiveness in crime control. In R.V. Clarke and J.M. Hough (eds.), *The Effectiveness of Policing*. Farnborough, Hants: Gower.

Farrell, G. and Pease, K. 1993. *Once Bitten, Twice Bitten: Repeat Victimization and its Implications for Crime Prevention*. Crime Prevention Unit Paper 46. London: Home Office.

Farrington, D.P. 1983. Randomized experiments on crime and justice. In M, Tonry and N. Morris (eds.), *Crime and Justice: An Annual Review of Research*, vol. 4. Chicago: University of Chicago Press.

Farrington, D.P., Bowen, S., Buckle, A., Burns-Howell, T., Borrows, J. and Speed, M. 1993. An experiment on the prevention of shoplifting. In R.V. Clarke (ed.), *Crime Prevention Studies*, vol. 1. Monsey, NY: Criminal Justice Press.

Fattah, E.A. 1993. The rational choice/opportunity perspectives as a vehicle for integrating criminological and victimological theories. In R.V. Clarke and M. Felson (eds.), *Routine Activity and Rational Choice, Advances in Criminological Theory*, vol. 5. New Brunswick, NJ: Transaction Publishers,

Feeney, F. 1986. Robbers as decision-makers. In D.B. Cornish and R.V. Clarke (eds.), *The Reasoning Criminal: Rational Choice Perspectives on Offending*. New York: Springer-Verlag.

Felson, M. 1986. Linking criminal choices, routine activities, informal control, and criminal outcomes. In D.B. Cornish and R.V. Clarke (eds.), *The Reasoning Criminal*. New York: Springer-Verlag.

Felson, M. 1992. Routine activities and crime prevention: Armchair concepts and practical action. *Studies on Crime and Crime Prevention* 1:31–34.

Felson, M. 1994b. A crime prevention extension service. In D. Wiesburd and J. Eck (eds.), *Crime Prevention Studies*, vol. 3. Monsey, NY: Criminal Justice Press.

Felson, M. 1994a. *Crime and Everyday Life: Insight and Implications for Society*. Thousand Oaks, CA: Pine Forge Press.

Felson, M. 1995. Those who discourage crime. In D. Wiesburd and J. Eck (eds.), *Crime and Place. Crime Prevention Studies*, vol. 4. Monsey, NY: Criminal Justice Press.

Felson, M., Belanger, M.E., Bichler, G., Bruzinski, C., Campbell, G.S., Fried, C.L., Grofik, K.C., Mazur, I.S., O'Regan, A., Sweeney, P.J., Ullman, A.L., and Williams, L.M. 1996. Redesigning hell: Preventing crime and disorder at the Port Authority Bus Terminal. In R.V. Clarke (ed.), *Preventing Mass Transit Crime. Crime Prevention Studies,* vol. 6. Monsey, NY: Criminal Justice Press.

Felson, M. and Clarke, R.V. 1995. Routine precautions, criminology, and crime prevention. In H.D. Barlow (ed.), *Crime and Public Policy.* Boulder, CO: Westview Press.

Felson, M. and Clarke, R.V. (eds.). 1997a. *Business and Crime Prevention.* Monsey, NY: Criminal Justice Press.

Felson, M. and Clarke, R.V. 1997b. The ethics of situational crime prevention. In G. Newman, R.V. Clarke and S.G. Shoham (eds.), *Rational Choice and Situational Crime Prevention: Theoretical Foundations.* Aldershot, UK: Dartmouth Publishing Company.

Ferreira, B. 1995. Situational crime prevention and displacement: The implications for business, industrial and private security management, *Security Journal* 6: 155–162.

Field, S. 1993. Crime prevention and the costs of auto theft: An economic analysis. In R.V. Clarke (ed.), *Crime Prevention Studies.* vol. 1. Monsey, NY: Criminal Justice Press.

Gabor, T. 1981. The crime displacement hypothesis: An empirical examination. *Crime and Deliquency* 26:390–404.

Gabor, T. 1990. Crime displacement and situational prevention: Toward the development of some principles. *Canadian Journal of Criminology* 32:41–74.

Gabor, T. 1994. *Everybody Does It! Crime by the Public.* New York: Macmillan.

Garland, D. 1996. The limits of the sovereign state: Strategies of crime control in contemporary society. *British Journal of Criminology* 36: 445–471.

Gilling, D. 1996. Problems with the problem-oriented approach. In R. Homel (ed.), *Crime Prevention Studies,* vol. 5. Monsey, NY: Criminal Justice Press.

Gladstone, F.J. 1980. *Coordinating Crime Prevention Efforts.* Home Office Research Study No. 47. London: H.M. Stationary Office.

Goldstein, H. 1979. Improving policing: A problem-oriented approach. *Crime and Deliquency* 25: 236–258.

Goldstein, H. 1990. *Problem-Oriented Policing.* New York: McGraw Hill.

Gottfredson, M.R. and Hirschi, T. 1990. *A General Theory of Crime.* Stanford, CA: Stanford University Press.

Grabosky, P. 1996. Unintended consequences of crime prevention. In R. Homel (ed.), *Crime Prevention Studies,* vol. 5. Monsey, NY: Criminal Justice Press.

Grandjean, C. 1990. Bank robberies and physical security in Switzerland: A case study of the escalation and displacement phenomena. *Security Journal* 1:155–159.

Greenwood, L. and McKean, H. 1985. Effective measurement and reduction of book loss in an academic library. *Journal of Academic Librarianship* 11:275–283.

Griswold, D.B. 1984. Crime prevention and commercial burglary: A time series analysis. *Journal of Criminal Justice* 12:493–501.

Hackler, J.C. 1978. *The Prevention of Youth Crime: The Great Stumble Forward.* Toronto: Methuen.

Hakim, S., Gaffney, M.A., Rengert, G., and Shachmurove, J. 1995. Costs and benefits of alarms to the community: Burglary patterns and security measures in Tredyffrin Township, PA. *Security Journal* 6:197– 204.

Hall, J. 1952. *Theft, Law and Society.* New York: Bobbs-Merrill.

Harris, P.M. and Clarke, R,V. 1991. Car chopping, parts marking and the Motor Vehicle Theft Law Enforcement Act of 1984. *Sociology and Social Research* 75:228–238.

Hartshorne, M. and May, M.A., 1928. *Studies in the Nature of Character (Vol. I): Studies in Deceit.* New York: Macmillan.

Hawley, A. 1950. *Human Ecology: A Theory of Community Structure.* New York: Ronald.

Heal, K. and Laycock, G. 1986. *Situational Crime Prevention: From Theory into Practice.* London: H.M. Stationary Office.

Heller, N.B., Stenzel, W.W., Gill, A.D., Kolde, R.A. and Schimmerman, S.R. 1975. *Operation Identification Projects: Assessment of Effectiveness.* National Evaluation Program, Phase 1, Summary Report. Washington, DC: National Institute for Law Enforcement and Criminal Justice.

Hemenway, D. and Weil, D. 1990. Phasers on stun: The case for less lethal weapons. *Journal of Policy Analysis and Management* 9:94–98.

Hesseling, R.B.P. 1995. Theft from cars: Reduced or displaced? *European Journal of Criminal Policy and Research,* 3:79–92.

Hill, N. 1986. *Prepayment Coin Meters: A Target for Burglary.* Crime Prevention Unit Paper 6. London: Home Office.

Hirschi, T. 1969. *Causes of Delinquency.* Berkeley and Los Angeles: University of California Press.

Homel, R. 1993. Drivers who drink and rational choice: Random breath testing and the process of deterrence. In R.V. Clarke and M. Felson (eds.), *Routine Activity and Rational Choice. Advances in Criminological Theory*, vol. 5. New Brunswick, NJ: Transaction Publishers.

Homel, R. (ed.), 1996. Editor's introduction. *Crime Prevention Studies*, vol. 5. Monsey, NY: Criminal Justice Press.

Honess, T. and Charman, E. 1992. Public drinking and violence: Not just an alcohol problem. *The Journal of Drug Issues* 22:679–697.

Hope, T. 1985. *Implementing Crime Prevention Measures*. Home Office Research Study, No. 86. London: H.M. Stationary Office.

Hope, T. 1991. Crime information in retailing: Prevention through analysis. *Security Journal* 2:240–245.

Hope, T. 1994. Problem-oriented policing and drug market locations: Three case studies. In R.V. Clarke (ed.), *Crime Prevention Studies*, vol. 2. Monsey, NY: Criminal Justice Press.

Hope, T. and Murphy, D.J. 1983. Problems of implementing crime prevention: The experience of a demonstration project. *Howard Journal* 83:38–50.

Horne, C.J. 1996. The case for CCTV: Should be introduced. *International Journal of Risk, Security and Crime Prevention* 13:3–18.

Hough, J.M., Clarke, R.V., and Mayhew, P. 1980. Introduction. In R.V. Clarke and P. Mayhew (eds.), *Designing out Crime*. London: H.M. Stationary Office.

Hughes, G. 1996. Strategies of multi-agency crime prevention and community safety in contemporary Britain. *Studies on Crime and Crime Prevention* 5:221–244.

Hunter, R.D. and Jeffrey, C.R. 1992. Preventing convenience store robbery through environmental design. In R.V. Clarke (ed.), *Situational Crime Prevention: Successful Case Studies*. Albany, NY: Harrow and Heston.

Indermaur, D. 1996. Reducing the opportunity for violence in robbery and property crime: The perspectives of offenders and victims. In R. Homel (ed.), *Crime Prevention Studies*, vol. 5. Monsey, NY: Criminal Justice Press.

Jeffery, C.R. 1971. *Crime Prevention Through Environmental Design*. Beverly Hills, CA: Sage.

Jeffery, C.R. 1977. *Crime Prevention Through Environmental Design*, 2nd edition. Beverly Hills, CA: Sage.

Jones, B. and Wood, N. 1989. Traffic Safety Impact of the 1988 Ignition Interlock Pilot Program. Oregon: Motor Vehicles Division.

Karmen, A. 1984. *Crime Victims: An Introduction to Victimology*. Monterey, CA: Brooks/Cole Publishing Co.

Kennedy, D.B. 1990. Facility site selection and analysis through environmental criminology. *Journal of Criminal Justice* 18: 239–252.

Klepper, S. and Nagin, D. 1987. The anatomy of tax evasion. Annual meeting of the American Society of Criminology, Montreal, November.

Knutsson, J. and Kuhlhorn, E. 1981. *Macro-measures Against Crime: The Example of Check Forgeries*. Information Bulletin No. 1 Stockholm: National Swedish Council for Crime Prevention.

Kube, E. 1988. Preventing bank robbery: Lessons from interviewing robbers. *Journal of Security Administration* 11:78–83.

La Vigne, N.G. 1994. Rational choice and inmate disputes over phone use on Rikers Island. In R.V. Clarke (ed.), *Crime Prevention Studies*, vol. 3. Monser, NY: Criminal Justice Press. '

Landes, W.M. 1978. An economic study of U.S. aircraft hijacking, 1961–1976. *Journal of Law and Economics* 21: 1–31.

Lateef, B.A. 1974. Helicopter patrol in law enforcement—An evaluation. *Journal of Police Science and Administration* 2:62–552.

Laycock, G.K. 1991. Operation identification, or the power of publicity? *Security Journal* 2:67–72.

Laycock, G. and Austin, C. 1992. Crime prevention in parking facilities. *Security Journal* 3:154–160.

Levi, M., Bissell, P. and Richardson, T. 1991. *The Prevention of Cheque and Credit Card Fraud*. Crime Prevention Unit Paper 26. London: Home Office.

Lewin, K. 1947. Group decisions and social change. In T.M. Newcomb and E.L. Hartley (eds.), *Readings in Social Psychology*. New York: Atherton Press.

Liddle, A.M. and Gelsthorpe, L. 1994. *Crime Prevention and Inter-Agency Co-Ordination. Crime Prevention Unit Series Paper 53*. London: Home Office.

Light, R., Nee, C. and Ingham, H. 1993. *Car Theft: The Offender's Perspective*. Home Office Research Study, No. 130. London: H.M. Stationary Office.

Lingenfleter, R.E. 1986. *Death Valley and the Amargosa: A Land of Illusion*. Berkeley: University of California Press.

Lowman, J. 1992. Street prostitution control: Some notes on the genesis of a social problem. *Canadian Journal of Criminology* 28: 1–16.

Maguire, M. 1980. Burglary as opportunity. *Research Bulletin* No. 10. Home Office Research Unit. London: Home Office.

Maguire, M. 1982. *Burglary in a Dwelling*. London: Heinemann.

Makris, G. 1996. The myth of a technological solution to television violence: Identifying problems with the V-chip. *Journal of Communication Inquiry* 20: 72–91.

Markus, C.L. 1984. British Telecom experience in payphone management. In C. Levy-Leboyer (ed.), *Vandalism Behavior and Motivations*. Amsterdam: Elsevier North-Holland.

Martinson, R. 1974. What works? Questions and answers about prison reform. *The Public Interest* 35(Spring): 22–54.

Marx, G.T. 1986. The iron fist and the velvet glove: Totalitarian potentials within democratic structures. In J. Short, Jr. (ed.), *The Social Fabric: Dimensions and Issues*. Beverly Hills, CA: Sage.

Masuda, B. 1993. Credit card fraud prevention: A successful retail strategy. In R.V. Clarke (ed.), *Crime Prevention Studies* vol. 1. Monsey, NY: Criminal Justice Press.

Matthews, R. 1990. Developing more effective strategies for curbing prostitution. *Security Journal* 1:182–187.

Matza, D. 1964. *Deliquency and Drift*. New York: Wiley.

Mayhew, P. 1979. Defensible space: The current status of a crime prevention theory. *The Howard Journal of Penology and Crime Prevention* 18:150–159.

Mayhew, P., Clarke, R.V., Burrows, J.N., Hough, J.M., and Winchester, S.W.C. 1979. *Crime in Public View*. Home Office Research Study No. 49. London: H.M. Stationary Office.

Mayhew, P., Clarke, R.V. Sturman, A. and Hough, J.M. 1976. *Crime as Opportunity*. London: H.M. Stationary Office.

Mayhew, P., Elliot, D., and Dowds, L. 1989. *The 1988 British Crime Survey*. Home Office Research Study No. 111. London: H.M. Stationary Office.

McCullough, D., Schmidt, T. and Lockhart, B. 1990. *Car Theft in Northern Ireland*. Cirac Paper No. 2. Belfast, UK: The EXTERN Organization.

Meredith, C. and Paquette, C. 1992. Crime prevention in high-rise rental apartments: Findings of a demonstration project. *Security Journal* 3:161–169.

Miethe, T.D. 1991. Citizen-based crime control activity and victimization risks: An examination of displacement and free-rider effects. *Criminology* 29:419–440.

Mischel, W. 1968. *Personality and Assessment*. New York: Wiley.

Moore, J. 1987. Safeguarding patient valuables: A case study. *Journal of Security Administration* 10:52–57.

Morris, N. and Hawkins, G. 1970. *The Honest Politician's Guide to Crime Control*. Chicago: University of Chicago Press.

Morrison, S. and O'Donnell, I. 1996. An analysis of the decision making processes of armed robbers. In R. Homel (ed.), *Crime Prevention Studies*, vol. 5. Monsey, NY: Criminal Justice Press.

Morse, B.J. and Elliot D.S. 1990. Hamilton County Drinking and Driving Study: 30 Month Report. Institute of Behavioral Science. Boulder, Co: University of Colorado.

Natarajan, M., Clarke, R.V. and Belanger, M. 1996. Drug dealing and pay phones: The scope for intervention. *Security Journal* 7:245–251.

Nee, C. and Taylor, M. 1988. Residential burglary in the Republic of Ireland: A situational perspective. *Howard Journal of Criminal Justice* 27:80–89.

New South Wales Bureau of Crime Statistics and Research. 1987. *Robbery*. Sydney: Attorney General's Department.

Newman, G. 1997. Introduction: Towards a theory of situational crime prevention. In G. Newman, R.V. Clarke and S.G. Shohan (eds.), *Rational Choice and Situational Crime Prevention: Theoretical Foundations*. Aldershot, UK: Dartmouth Publishing Company.

Newman, O. 1972. *Defensible Space: Crime Prevention Through Urban Design*. New York: Macmillan. (Published by Architectural Press, London, in 1973).

Newman, O. 1996. *Creating Defensible Space*. Washington, DC: Office of Policy Development and Research, U.S. Department of Housing and Urban Development.

Normandeau, A. and Gabor, T. 1987. *Armed Robbery: Cops, Robbers and Victims*. Springfield, IL: Charles C. Thomas.

NRMA Insurance Ltd. 1990. *Car Theft in New South Wales*. Sydney: National Roads and Motorists' Association.

Nugent, S., Burnes, D., Wilson, P. and Chappell, D. 1989. *Risks and Rewards in Robbery: Prevention and the Offenders' Perspective*. Melbourne: Australian Bankers' Association.

O'Malley, P. 1994. Neo-liberal crime control: Political agendas and the future of crime prevention in Australia. In D. Chappell and P. Wilson (eds.), *The Australian Criminal Justice System: The Mid-1990s*. Sydney, AUS: Butterworth.

Olsson, O. and Wikstrom, P.O. 1982. Effects of the experimental Saturday closing of liquor retail stores in Sweden. *Contemporary Drug Problems*, Fall: 324–53.

Olsson, O. and Wikstrom, P.–O. 1984. Effects of Saturday closing of liqour retail stores in Sweden. *Alcohol Policy: Journal of Nordic Alcohol Research* 1:95 (English Summary).

Opp, K.–D. 1997. Limited rationality and crime. In G. Newman, R.V. Clarke and S.G. Shohan (eds.), *Rational Choice and Situational Crime Prevention: Theoretical Foundations.* Aldershot, UK: Dartmouth Publishing Company.

Pease, K. 1979. Some futures in crime prevention. *Research Bulletin* No. 7. Home Office Research Unit. London: Home Office.

Pease, K. 1991. The Kirkholt project: Preventing burglary on a British public housing estate. *Security Journal* 2:73–77.

Pease, K. 1997. Predicting the future: The roles of routine activity and rational choice theory. In G. Newman, R.V. Clarke and S.G. Shohan (eds.), *Rational Choice and Situational Crime Prevention: Theoretical Foundations.* Aldershot, UK: Dartmouth Publishing Company.

Pidco, G. 1996. Check print: A discussion of a crime prevention initiative that failed. *Security Journal* 7:37–40.

Poyner, B. 1988. Video cameras and bus vandalism. *Journal of Security Administration* 11: 44–51.

Poyner, B. 1991. Situational crime prevention in two parking facilities. *Security Journal* 2:96–101.

Poyner, B. 1993. What works in crime prevention: An overview of evaluations. In R.V. Clarke (ed.), *Crime Prevention Studies,* vol. 1. Monsey, NY: Criminal Justice Press.

Poyner, B., Warne, C., Webb, B., Woodall, R. and Meakin, R. 1988. *Preventing Violence in Staff.* London: H.M. Stationary Office.

Poyner, B. and Webb, B. 1987a. *Successful Crime Prevention: Case Studies.* London: The Tavistock Institute of Human Relations.

Poyner, B. and Webb, B. 1987b. Pepys Estate: Intensive policing. In B. Poyner and B. Webb. *Successful Crime Prevention: Case Studies.* London, UK: Tavistock Institute (unpublished).

Poyner, B. and Webb, B. 1991. *Crime Free Housing.* Oxford, UK: Butterworth Architect.

Press, S.J. 1971. *Some Effects of an Increase in Police Manpower in the 20th Precinct of New York City.* New York: Rand Institute.

Ramsay, M. 1991a. *The Influence of Street Lighting on Crime and Fear of Crime.* Crime Prevention Unit Paper 29. London: Home Office.

Ramsay, M. 1991b. A British experiment in curbing incivilities and fear of crime. *Security Journal* 2:120–125.

Rengert, G.F. and Wasilchick, J. 1985. *Suburban Burglary.* Springfield, IL: Chas. C. Thomas.

Reppetto, T.A. 1974. *Residential Crime.* Cambridge, MA: Ballinger.

Reppetto, T.A. 1976. Crime prevention and the displacement phenomenon. *Crime and Deliquency,* 22:166–177.

Rosenbaum, D. 1988. A critical eye on a neighborhood watch: Does it reduce crime and fear? In T. Hope and M. Shaw (eds.), *Communities and Crime Reduction.* London: H.M. Stationary Office.

Ross, H.L. 1960. Traffic law violation: A folk crime. *Social Problems* 8:231–241.

Sandahl, D. and Christensen, H.H. 1985. Environmental cues and vandalism: An exploratory study of picnic table carving. *Environmental and Behavior* 17:445–458.

Sampson, A., Blagg, H., Stubbs, P., and Pearson, G. 1988. Crime localities and the multi-agency approach. *British Journal of Criminology* 28:478–493.

Scarr, H.A. 1973. *Patterns of Burglary.* 2nd Ed. Washington, DC: U.S. Department of Justice, National Institute of Law Enforcement and Criminal Justice.

Scherdin, M.J. 1986. The halo effect: Psychology deterrence of electronic security systems. *Information Technology and Libraries* September: 232–235.

Scottish Council on Crime. 1975. *Crime and the Prevention of Crime.* Scottish Home and Health Department. Edinburgh: H.M Stationary Office.

Seve, R. 1997. Philisophical justifications of situational crime prevention. In G. Newman, R.V. Clarke and S.G. Shohan (eds.), *Rational Choice and Situational Crime Prevention: Theoretical Foundations.* Aldershot, UK: Dartmouth Publishing Company.

Shearing, C.D. and Stenning, P.C. (eds.). 1987. *Private Policing.* Beverly Hills, CA: Sage.

Shepherd, J. and Brickley, M. 1992. Alcohol-related hand injuries: An unnecessary social and economic cost. *Journal of the Royal College of Surgeons* 75:69.

Sherman, L.W. 1990. Police crackdowns: Initial and residual deterrence. In M. Tonry and N. Morris (eds.), *Crime and Justice: A Review of Research,* vol. 12. Chicago: Chicago University Press.

Sherman, L.W. 1996. Policing Domestic Violence: The Problem-Solving Paradigm. Paper prepared for the conference on Problem-Solving as Crime Prevention, Swedish National Police College, Stockholm, September 1996.

Sherman, L., Gartin, P. and Buerger, M. 1989. Hot spots of predatory crime: Routine activities and the criminology of place. *Criminology* 27:27–55.

Short, J.F., Jr. and Strodtbeck, F.L. 1965. *Group Processes and Gang Deliquency*. Chicago: University of Chicago Press.

Sloan-Howitt, M. and Kelling, G. 1990. Subway graffiti in New York City: "Gettin' up" vs. 'meanin' it and cleanin' it." *Security Journal* 1:131–136.

Smith, D.J. 1995. Youth crime and conduct disorders: Trends, patterns, and casual explanations. In M. Rutter and D.J. Smith (eds.), *Psychosocial Disorders in Youth Populations. Time Trends and Their Causes*. Chichester, UK: John Wiley and Sons.

Smith, L.J.F. 1987. *Crime in Hospitals: Diagnosis and Prevention*. Crime Prevention Unit Paper 7. London: Home Office.

Smith, M.J. 1996. *Assessing Vandalism Cues in an Experimental Setting: A Factorial Design Involving State of Repairs, Presence of Graffiti, Target Vulnerability, and Target Suitability*. Ph.D. Dissertation, School of Criminal Justice, Rutgers, The State University of New Jersey.

Sparrow, M. 1994. *Imposing Duties. Government's Changing Approach to Compliance*. Westport, CT: Praeger.

Spencer, E. 1992. *Car Crime and Young People on a Sunderland Housing Estate*. Crime Prevention Unit Paper 40. London: Home Office.

Stanford Research Institute. 1970. *Reduction of Robbery and Assault of Bus Drivers*. Volume III: Technological and operational methods. Stanford, CA: Author.

Sutton, A. 1996. Taking out the interesting bits? Problem-solving and crime prevention. In R. Homel (ed.), *Crime Prevention Studies*, vol. 5. Monsey, NY: Criminal Justice Press.

Sykes, G.M. and Matza, D. 1957. Techniques of neutralization: A theory of deliquency. *American Sociological Review* 22:664–670.

Tedeshci, J.T. and Felson, R.B. 1994. *Violence, Aggression and Coercive Actions*. Washington, DC: American Psychological Association.

Tien, J.M., O'Donnell, V.F., Barnett, A. and Mirchandani, P.B. 1979. *Phase I Report: Street Lighting Projects*. Washington, DC: U.S. Government Printing Office.

Tilley, N. 1993c. *Understanding Car Parks, Crime and CCTV: Evaluating Lessons from Safer Cities*. Crime Prevention Unit Paper 42. London: Home Office.

Tizard, J., Sinclair, I. and Clarke, R.V. 1975. *Varieties of Residential Experience*. London: Routledge and Kegan Paul.

Travis, J. 1997. Foreward. In M. Felson and R.V. Clarke (eds.), *Business and Crime Prevention*. Monsey, NY: Criminal Justice Press.

Tyrpak, S. 1975. *Newark High-Impact Anti-Crime Program: Street Lighting Project Interim Evaluation Report*. Newark, NJ: Office of Criminal Justice Planning.

Van Dijk, J.J.M. 1997. Towards effective public-private partnerships in crime control: Experiences in the Netherlands. In M. Felson and R.V. Clarke (eds.), *Business and Crime Prevention*. Monsey, NY: Criminal Justice Press.

Veno, A. and Veno, E. 1993. Situational prevention of public disorder at the Australian Motorcycle Grand Prix. In R.V. Clarke (ed.), *Crime Prevention Studies*, vol. 1. Monsey, NY: Criminal Justice Press.

Von Hirsch, A. 1976. *Doing Justice*. New York: Hill and Wang.

Waller, I and Okihiro, N. 1979. *Burglary: The Victim and the Public*. Toronto: University of Toronto Press.

Walsh, D. 1978. *Shoplifting: Controlling a Major Crime*. London: Macmillan.

Walsh, D. 1980. *Break-Ins: Burglary from Private Houses*. London: Macmillan.

Walters, R. 1996. The dream of multi-agency crime prevention: Pitfalls in policy and practice. In R. Homel (ed.), *Crime Prevention Studies*, vol. 5. Monsey, NY: Criminal Justice Press.

Webb, B. 1994. Steering column locks and motor vehicle theft: Evaluations from three countries. In R.V. Clarke (ed.), *Crime Prevention Studies*, vol. 2. Monsey, NY: Criminal Justice Press.

Weidner, R.R. 1996. Target hardening at a New York City subway station. Decreased fare evasion—at what price? In R.V. Clarke (ed.), *Preventing Mass Transit Crime. Crime Prevention Studies*, vol. 6. Monsey, NY: Criminal Justice Press.

Weisburd, D. 1997. *Reorienting Crime Prevention Research and Policy: From the Causes of Criminality to the Context of Crime*. National Institute of Justice Research Report. Washington, DC: U.S. Department of Justice.

Weiss, C. 1995. Nothing as practical as good theory: Exploring theory-based evaluation for comprehensive community initiatives for children and families. In J.P. Connell, A.C. Kubisch, L.B. Schorr and C.H. Weiss (eds.), *New Approaches to Evaluating Community Initiatives*. Washington, DC: The Aspen Institute.

White, J. and Humeniuk, R. 1994. *Alcohol Misuse and Violence: Exploring the Relationship*. Canberra: Australian Government Publishing Service.

White, R. and Sutton, A. 1995. Crime prevention, urban space and social exclusion. *Australian and New Zealand Journal of Sociology* 3:82-99.

Wiersma, E. 1996. Commercial burglars in the Netherlands: Reasoning decision makers? *International Journal of Risk, Security and Crime Prevention* 1:217–228.

Wilkins, L.T. 1964. *Social Deviance.* London: Tavistock.

Wilkins, L.T. 1990. Retrospect and prospect: Fashions in criminal justice theory and practice. In D. Gottfredson and R.V. Clarke (eds.), *Policy and Theory in Criminal Justice.* Aldershot, UK: Avebury.

Wilkinson, P. 1977. *Terrorism and the Liberal State.* London: Macmillan.

Wilkinson, P. 1986. *Terrorism and the Liberal State,* 2nd ed. New York: New York University Press.

Willemse, H.M. 1994. Developments in Dutch crime prevention. In R.V. Clarke (ed.), *Crime Prevention Studies,* vol. 2 Monsey, NY: Criminal Justice Press.

Wilson, J.Q. 1975. *Thinking About Crime.* New York: Basic.

Wilson, J.Q. and Kelling G. 1982. Broken windows. *The Atlantic Monthly.* Orlando, FL: Orlando Police Department.

Wilson, P. 1990. Reduction of telephone vandalism: An Australian case study. *Security Journal* 1:149–154.

Wise, J. 1982. A gentle deterrent to vandalism. *Psychology Today* 16 (September):31–38.

Wortley, R. 1996. Guilt, shame and situational crime prevention. In R. Homel (ed.), *Crime Prevention Studies,* vol. 5. Monsey, NY: Criminal Justice Press.

Wright, R.T. and Decker, S.H. 1994. *Burglars on the Job.* Boston: Northeastern University Press.

Yablonsky, L. 1962. *The Violent Gang.* New York: Macmillan.

Young, J. 1988. Radical criminology in Britain: The emergence of a competing paradigm. *British Journal of Criminology* 28:289–313

Zaharchuk, P.G. and Lynch, J. 1977. *Operational Identification: A Police Prescriptive Package.* Ottawa: Ministry of Solicitor General.

Zimbardo, P.G. 1973. A field experiment in auto-shaping. In C. Ward (ed.), *Vandalism.* London: Architectural Press.

Reprinted from: Ronald V. Clarke "Introduction." *Situational Crime Prevention: Successful Case Studies,* 2nd ed. pp. 3–33. Copyright © 1997 by Criminal Justice Press. Reprinted by permission. ✦

Part IV

Implementing Change in Police Organizations

Organizational change is rarely self-executing, it typically occurs only with considerable time and effort and often meets resistance and difficulty. Such change is further frustrated and complicated by powerful forces *outside* the organization that strongly influence how employees behave and work. As police executives aim to transform their departments and to institutionalize new forms of policing as daily practice, their success will depend on thoughtful planning processes and implementation.

The ultimate test of successful change in an organization is how well the organization motivates new behavioral patterns in its employees. That is, change involves winning the support in those rank-and-file individuals doing the work. And, for this challenge innovative management methods are required. No longer can police leaders rely solely on staunch organizational control as their principal method of management. Instead, they need to employ a business approach to planning and implementation that emphasizes the future, while rethinking management, visible leadership, and staff involvement at all levels of the organization.

Unfortunately, there is no one best way or universal method to ensure a successful implementation. This lack is very clear from the varied experiences of police departments that are included in the readings in Part IV.

Although some departments are comfortable and adept at accepting new ideas and changing employee behavior, others have a limited capacity and tolerance for change.

The selections in this part provide a rich discourse about the complexities and challenges involved in moving an organization forward. Although a cookie-cutter approach is not recommended or suggested, several common themes and central elements for successful change emerge.

In the first reading, J. Zhao, Q. Thurman, and N. Lovrich examine the organizational characteristics of police departments. Drawing upon a nationwide survey of 281 municipal departments, the authors discuss the extent of organizational change and implementation of community policing throughout the United States. Specific attention is given to those attributes that promote or impede organizational change.

R. Glensor and K. Peak observe in the second reading that implementing change in organizations is no simple endeavor. They present four keys to success—leadership and management, organizational culture, field operations, and external relationships—for departments considering the transition to community-oriented policing and problem solving.

Changes in these areas are vitally important if, as A. Lurgio and W. Skogan discuss in the third selection, the department is going to be poised for "winning the hearts and minds" of the street officers. How do police departments undertake such an endeavor? Drawing on research on six cities, D. Weisel and J. Eck discuss the variations in the application of community policing. Their primary focus is on the methods that police departments undertook to persuade their officers to adopt and implement community policing.

A common assumption of community policing is that citizens and police must act collaboratively to solve problems. Inherent to this assumption is the notion that citizen perceptions of the police may affect this collaborative effort. For example, does an unwillingness to work with the police exist among those citizens holding negative attitudes toward the police? This question is examined by M. Reisig and A. Giacomazzi in the fifth reading. Through an assessment of neighborhood and individual-level data, these authors examine the relationship between citizen

perceptions of police and community-policing practices.

In the final reading, D.L. Carter and A.D. Sapp address the core issues surrounding effective evaluations of community policing. More specifically, they reveal the most common obstacles faced during evaluation and methods to overcome these problems. Instead of offering "one best method" of evaluation, the authors discuss the necessary procedures (e.g., defining community policing, operationalizing programs) for effective evaluations.

Collectively, the readings in Part IV strongly suggest that organizational change is not simple. Change cannot occur overnight; it requires a committed leadership as well as the involvement of motivated and dedicated people, both inside and outside the organization. When community policing is successfully implemented, however, it offers great potential for improving the police department and its services to the community. ◆

16

Community-Oriented Policing Across the U.S.

Facilitators and Impediments to Implementation

Jihong Zhao
Quint C. Thurman
Nicholas P. Lovrich

Change within any organization is difficult and probably more so in police departments. As police across the United States adopt new philosophies and begin to implement them, it is important to assess these departments as they evolve. Drawing upon a nationwide study of police departments, J. Zhao, Q. Thurman, and N. Lovrich analyze those factors that affect the implementation of community policing. As you read this selection, pay close attention to what impedes change as well as what facilitates change. In addition, ask yourself whether or not police departments can overcome the impediments for effective implementation. Why do they have such a difficult time with change? What type of organizational structure would be most likely to facilitate effective change? Is it possible for police departments to acquire these types of structures?

Citizen demand for responsive public services has grown considerably since the end of World War II. Similarly, Walker (1977) notes that the public's appetite for police services has increased as well over this time period, although not always at pace with the abilities of departments to respond.

While police executives will decry the dilemma of having to do more without signifi-

cant increases in resources, a long practiced reliance upon further police professionalization to deliver efficient services—often at the expense of effective outcome—has set the stage for re-examining how police agencies do their jobs and how they might wish to change in the 1990s. Similarly, many police scholars (e.g., Goldstein, 1987, 1990; Osborne and Gaebler, 1992; Kelling and Moore, 1988), have identified organizational change as a more pressing issue now than ever before in the history of modern American policing.

Skolnick and Bayley (1986) and Trojanowicz and Bucqueroux (1990) have noted that policing is in the midst of a time of transition from a bureaucratic model of operation to a Community-Oriented Policing (COP) model. Broadly defined, COP represents an ideal organizational form which emphasizes a set of new values and beliefs related to the coproduction of public order (Angell, 1971; Wasserman and Moore, 1988), modified organizational structures featuring employee empowerment and risk-taking, and essential operational activities relating to bridge-building between the police and the communities they serve (Brown and Wycoff, 1987; Lurigio and Skogan, 1994; Wycoff and Skogan, 1994).

However, despite considerable development of COP in the past twenty years, information regarding COP deployment and its consequences has been slow to emerge (Reiss, 1992). Most published research concerning COP falls into one of two broad categories. The first primarily centers on the discussion of COP values and change in general (e.g., Kelling and Moore, 1988; Mastrofski, 1988; Mastrofski and Uchida, 1993). The second approach largely focuses on the impact of COP programs in a few celebrated case studies. Sadly, a key issue—COP implementation in the process of change in American policing—has essentially been neglected. Such an oversight has resulted in the tendency to focus on "successful" programs (defined as those which demonstrate efficient service delivery) rather than to acquire important knowledge about the process of COP implementation.

Pressman and Wildvsky (1973) have highlighted the importance of implementation and have noted that programs often fail due to poor implementation. In a similar vein, Walker (1993) stresses the wealth of knowledge related to American policing that might be gained from past experiences involving the implementation of police innovations such as team policing. Other examples might include recent case studies reported by the Vera Institute of Justice involving Innovative Neighborhood Oriented Policing programs (INOP) in eight cities (Sadd and Grinc, 1994; Grinc, 1994).

To date there has been little attention paid to COP implementation beyond case studies of a few selected cities. One exception in this regard is a recent study by Greene (1993). Greene's study concerning the extent of COP implementation in the State of Florida addressed the process of organizational change from a bureaucratic model to a COP model in a single American state.

The present study builds upon the important scholarship of Greene and others to extend to a national scale the investigation of the extent of organizational change and COP implementation in American policing. In so doing we both explore the extent of COP training underway in the U.S. and identify the conditions which promote or impede COP implementation. While many policing scholars have highlighted the importance of these two areas of research in studying the transition from the bureaucratic model to the COP model (e.g., Trojanowicz and Bucqueroux, 1990; Goldstein, 1990; Greene, 1993), there has been little systematic research on this subject and none that we know of which has relied upon data from a national survey of police agencies.

Literature Review

Trojanowicz and Bucqueroux (1990:3) argue that a set of values relating to the proper role of the police in contemporary society is of primary importance for organizational change to COP (cf. Goldstein, 1977). Accordingly, Kelling and Moore (1988) have identified the central feature of COP as the shared empowerment of both the police agency and the community in controlling crime and reducing disorder. They believe that coproduc-

ing order in this way will result in strengthening public support for police work.

Sparrow (1988) and Moore (1992) both summarize the change in value orientation advocated in the COP reform model. Key to their arguments is the assumption that American police agencies inherently cannot be "neutral" entities with respect to their surrounding community. On the contrary, accountability to the local community is regarded as an essential feature of COP. Furthermore, there is a close linkage between value orientation and effective operational activities (vs. "public relations" programs) which particularly reflect these new values. Consequently, COP might be conceptualized as an expansion of the police role in American society beyond a more limited and narrowly-focused "crime fighting" function.

Operationally, Lurigio and Skogan (1994:315) point out that the COP philosophy "translates into a variety of specific operations and practices" (cf. Wasserman and Moore, 1988; Weisel and Eck, 1994; see Sparrow et al., 1990, for a discussion). As such, the examination of organizational change in policing should be firmly rooted in the structure of COP programs.

A review of the literature pertaining to COP programs suggests that the dimension of *externally focused change* (Huber et al, 1993) has been more frequently discussed and investigated than *internally focused change*. A reorientation of police operations in the form of crime prevention activities is illustrative of the former and reflects a police department's conscious effort to redefine its mission within the broad community while the latter is exemplified by an internal reorganization of the agency itself.

Many "re-oriented" police operations have been highlighted in professional journals. For example, the implementation of a foot patrol program is viewed as an important reorientation of police operations because of the patrol officers' direct involvement with the community through such programs (Skolnick and Bayley, 1986). Similarly, the use of special task units to address unique local problems is viewed as another strategy for the police to respond to the needs of a community (Goldstein, 1990). Furthermore, in their summary of COP programs in Houston, Brown and Wycoff (1987) emphasized the use of storefront stations, community crime prevention newsletters, and victim contact programs as effective examples of the reorientation of police activities toward COP goals. Other studies also have identified programs such as crime prevention education and permanent assignment of officers to a neighborhood as often useful methods of organizational change (e.g., Wycoff, 1988; Moore, 1992; Thurman, Bogen and Giacomazzi, 1993).

In a broad sense, the theme of community crime prevention represents the common denominator of externally focused change. Such an emphasis upon prevention over more efficient crime fighting implies the recognition of the supreme importance of the health of the community and the acknowledgment of the limited capability of police to control crime without the help of residents at large (Kelling and Stewart, 1989; Moore, 1992).

Some facilitators of and impediments to contemporary organizational change in American policing have been identified in the research literature. For example, two variables which might contribute to successful change are education and training (see Goldstein, 1977, 1990; Bittner, 1972). It is widely believed that a better educated and more highly-trained police officer can meet the essential requirements of contemporary organizational change.

Similarly, policing scholars and practitioners also have identified a number of variables that are regarded for their negative impact on organizational change. For example, Sherman (1975) pointed out that failure to win the support of middle management was the primary contributor to the end of the team policing movement in the early 1970s (cf. Walker, 1993). Similarly, the lack of understanding of COP by line officers is another important obstacle which is highlighted in the research literature (Goldstein, 1990; Kelling and Moore, 1988; Sadd and Grinc, 1994).

Methods and Measures

The data used in this analysis are derived from a national survey of police chiefs conducted by the Division of Governmental Studies and Services (DGSS) at Washington State University. DGSS has conducted mail-out and mail-back surveys in three-year intervals since 1978. The cities in the sample are selected from among those municipalities initially included in a representative national survey of chiefs of police in cities of over 25,000 population conducted by the International City Management Association in 1969. The sample size includes 281 municipal police departments in 47 states. In addition, this sample takes into consideration the representativeness of regions and sizes of cities. Included in the data base for this study is the sixth survey of municipal police departments conducted in 1993.

After three waves of mailings sent in 1993, 228 (81%) out of 281 police departments completed and returned a survey questionnaire. The survey instrument contained a wide variety of questions pertaining to COP programs implemented in each police department. Either a police chief or an appointed representative was asked to identify from a prepared list the presence or absence of COP programs elements compiled from a review of the relevant literature. Furthermore, information regarding interest in COP training and education and perceived major obstacles also was collected in the survey.

Externally focused change was measured by the presence of twelve commonly found COP programs identified from the research literature. These COP programs comprise both reorientation of police operations and efforts in crime prevention. The extent of COP training or education is assessed by a battery of fourteen items which cover COP philosophy and operational practices. Each item was rated based on a four-point scale varying from "not interested" to "very interested." Commonly hypothesized obstacles to COP implementation are represented by thirteen items which include both external and internal barriers to COP implementation. Each item was judged based on a similar four-point scale ranging from "no obstacle" to "a serious obstacle."

Findings

The frequency distribution presented in table 16.1 suggests that a majority of police departments across the nation report the implementation of some types of COP programs in the past three years. For example, foot patrol (88.4%), special task units (91.6%), education of the public (98.1%), and block watch programs (97.7%) are the most commonly adopted COP programs.

The average number of programs implemented in the survey is 9 out of a possible 12, with a standard deviation of 2.1. Furthermore, 66.7 percent of the police departments reported they have implemented new program in the past three years; 31 percent remained at the same level as 1990, and only 2.3 percent indicated that they have reduced the number of COP programs which were in operation in 1990.

In terms of interest in COP training and education, principal component factor analysis was used to identify any underlying themes which were of concern to police administrators using the usual method for determining the number of factors present among a number of like constructs (that is, the retention of factors with Eigen values

Table 16.1
Frequency Distribution of Externally Focused Change: COP Programs

	Yes	No
1. Community newsletter	49.8%	52.2%
2. Foot, horse patrol	88.4%	11.6%
3. Storefront station	41.4%	58.6%
4. Special task unit	91.6%	8.4%
5. Victim contact program	62.8%	37.2%
6. Education of public	98.1%	1.9%
7. Fixed assignment	87.0%	13.0%
8. Citizen survey	62.3%	37.7%
9. Block watch	97.7%	2.3%
10. Business watch	65.1%	34.9%
11. Block meeting	86.5%	13.5%
12. Volunteer program	68.4%	31.6%

n=215

Table 16.2
Factor Analysis: Interest in COP Training and Education*

Factor**	Loading[1]			Mean Rating***
	I	II	III	(SD)
1. Overall Performance Skills (INT1)				
a. Quality circles: an overview	.82	.09	.14	
b. Applying quality circles	.79	.16	.08	
c. Positive risk taking	.64	.33	.26	
d. Liability awareness	.52	.34	.16	
e. Excellence in community service	.50	.35	.24	3.29
				(.66)
2. Middle Manager Skills COP Principles (INT2)				
a. Middle management authority delegation	.24	.75	.08	
b. Survival strategies for managers	.40	.68	.07	
c. Comprehensive overview of COP principles	-.10	.66	.53	
d. Principles of neighborhood organizations	.22	.63	.11	3.42
				(.60)
3. Police Community Relations (INT3)				
a. Minority relations	.23	.12	.82	
b. Cultural awareness	.10	.05	.82	
c. Police ethics and values	.32	.27	.54	3.75
				(.43)

* Alpha level of all three factors>.70
** % of variance (Eigen Value) of three factors are: 40.5 (5.7), 9.8 (1.4), and 7.4 (1.0) respectively
*** Mean Rating: 1 = not interested, 2 = slightly, 3 = moderate, 4 = Very Interested

greater than one). Furthermore, a variable was selected if its factor loading correlated greater than .5 with a particular factor. Finally, the commonly used approach of varimax orthogonal rotation was adopted for presentation of these data since this approach is more appropriate than other techniques for undertaking exploratory analysis (Kim and Mueller, 1978:48–50).

Three distinctive factors were identified in the analysis. Mean ratings for these three factors are reported in table 16.2.

Findings from table 16.2 suggest that police departments across the nation tend to display similar kinds of interest in COP training and education. The underlying theme for the first factor noted reflects a broad interest in improving overall performance skills among police personnel. The second factor represents concern for the training and education of middle-level managers seeking to make the transition from a bureaucratic

agency toward COP. The final factor involves the improvement in police-community relations in the process of implementing COP programs, especially in culturally diverse communities. The overall ratings of themes composing each factor show that an interest in improving police and community relations is the top priority for the police chiefs surveyed in 1993.

Table 16.3 identifies the obstacles that can hinder the development and implementation of COP in police organizations. Once again, principal component factor analysis with the same approach as before was used. This generated three primary types of obstacles to COP implementation as noted by police administrators nationally.

The pattern of factor loadings for thirteen items indicated three underlying factors which appear to represent internal organizational obstacles, external community barriers, and inhibition as a result of the transition

Table 16.3
Factor Analysis: Impediments to COP Implementation*

Factor**	Loading[1] I	II	III	Mean Rating*** (SD)
1. Organizational Impediments (IMP1)				
a. Resistance from middle-management	.75	-.03	.05	
b. Line officers resistance	.75	.16	.08	
c. Departmental confusion of what COP is	.68	.15	.31	
d. Problem in line-level accountability	.66	.25	.22	
e. Officers' concern: COP is "soft" on crime	.63	.46	-.18	
f. Lack of COP training	.55	.24	.41	
g. Union resistance	.52	.51	-.18	2.41 (.76)
2. Community impediments (IMP2)				
a. Community resistance	.07	.71	.16	
b. Community concern: COP is "soft" on crime	.11	.69	-0.0	
c. Civil service rules	.13	.64	.10	
d. Pressure on chief to demonstrate COP reduces crime in short term	.23	.59	.34	
e. Lack of support from local government	.22	.56	.36	1.96 (.87)
3. Transition impediment (IMP3)				
a. Problems in balancing increased foot patrol activities while maintaining emergency response time	.11	.15	.84	2.98 (1.10)

* Alpha level of first two factors > .70.
** % of variance (Eigen Value) of three factors are: 36.9 (4.8), 10.7 (1.4), and 8.0 (1.0), respectively
***Mean Ratings: 1=no obstacle, 2=slightly, 3=moderate, 4=serious obstacles.

from a traditional paramilitary policing approach to the COP philosophy. The mean ratings associated with each factor suggest that police agencies are more concerned with internal organizational barriers than obstacles in their community. In particular, the factor labeled the "transition obstacle" is composed of one variable relating to the balancing of COP activities versus traditional crime fighting ones. This factor had the highest mean rating of the three factors identified.

The findings presented in table 16.4 present bivariate correlations obtained among training and education concerns, perceived obstacles to COP implementation, and the presence of externally focused COP programs in each police agency surveyed. The direction of these correlations suggests that the higher a police agency's interest in training and education, the greater the number of COP programs they implement. Conversely, the perception of serious obstacles is negatively associated with the level of COP program implementation as might be expected. These findings indicate that many police departments continue to be confronted with significant impediments to COP implementation, and as a result, these obstacles evoke considerable caution on the part of many po-

lice executives facing opportunities for organizational change.

As an exploratory study focusing on the extent of COP implementation at the national level, these findings suggest several important observations pertaining to both theoretical and practical issues. Theoretically, a key question emanating from these data is whether or not COP implementation represents (or at least is consistent with) the theme of organizational change. With respect to this issue, we think that it is important to discuss an essential concept concerning organizational change—the expansion of an organizational domain.

Meyer (1975:599) defines an organizational domain as "the technology employed, population served and services rendered by an organization." Scholars of American policing have long discussed whether or not COP represents the expansion of the police role in the society in terms of technology employed (Manning, 1992; Eck and Spelman, 1987; Eck, 1993; Goldstein, 1990), population served (Kelling and Moore, 1988; Mastrofski, 1988; Klockars, 1988), and services rendered (Skolnick and Bayley, 1986; Moore, 1992).

Based upon the number of COP programs implemented and the frequency distribution

Table 16.4

Correlation Coefficients of Externally Focused Change, Interest in Training and Education, and Impediments (N=171)

	EXTER (No. of CCP Prog.)	INT1	INT2	INT3	IMP1	IMP2
Perf. Skill (INT1)	.13[a]					
Mid-Mgmt. Skill (INT2)	.22[b]	.60[d]				
Pol.-Comm. Rel. (INT3)	.34[c]	.50[d]	.49[d]			
Org. Imped. (IMP1)	-.15[a]	-.16[b]	-.15[a]	-.14[a]		
Comm. Imped. (IMP2)	-.22[b]	.01	-.05	-.06	.56[d]	
Trans. Imped. (IMP3)	-.14[a]	-.09	-.07	-.08	.59[d]	.33[d]

[a]p<.05, [b]p<.01, [c]p<.001, [d]p<.0001

of COP development nationally, these data suggest that police departments across the U.S. have been expanding the organizational domain (or functions) in these three areas during the past three years (cf. Greene, 1993; Langworthy, 1992). In turn, such expansion in the organizational domain is consistent with organizational change in COP values that we might expect to see if police organizations indeed are moving toward the COP philosophy.

These data also indicate some disturbing trends in American policing with regard to impediments to organizational change. We speculate that many organizations are at a loss to move much further forward at this point in time beyond some incremental amount. Simply put, American police agencies do not appear to know what it is that they should be doing next.[2]

Operationally, growth is apparent in the implementation of foot patrols, special task units, and public education regarding the contemporary police mission. Similarly, we find that interest in COP training and education is positively associated with the expansion and implementation of COP programs, and that most important within the training area is line officer education with respect to police-community relations and particularly pertaining to law enforcement in racially diverse communities. All these developments reflect new requirements under the COP model for police personnel in terms of overall service skills and value orientation in a time of transition.

Sadd and Grinc's study (1994) of police agencies in eight cities identified several common problems that organizations face when implementing COP programs. These include: (1) confusion among line officers concerning what COP means, (2) lack of support from middle management, and (3) lack of support of the residents from a community (cf. Grinc, 1994).

In general, our national study of COP implementation identified similar obstacles to those previously mentioned. For example, the factor we identified as one consisting of organizational impediments was considered the most serious barrier to implementation. Key to the underlying theme of this factor

identified is the perceived resistance from police employees. Furthermore, the survey results suggest the widespread appreciation of the importance of middle management in COP implementation.[3]

Factor analysis also suggested that the issue of transition from a more traditional model of policing to the COP model uniformly has attracted the attention of administrators across the nation. Such concerns are not limited to the ideological sphere (e.g., soft on crime, etc.) but also include practical concerns such as the deployment of personnel (e.g., emergency response vs. foot patrol). This implies an important issue that often is overlooked by police administrations. Goldstein (1987) has pointed out that the traditional approach of policing focuses on incidents but neglects broader issues underlying such incidents. As such, organizational effectiveness instead of efficiency should be considered the top priority.

Based upon our findings, it seems that most police departments have difficulty emphasizing organizational effectiveness on par with efficiency (cf. Weisel and Eck, 1994). One of the reasons as pointed out by Sparrow et al. (1990) is that they lack the resources to achieve both simultaneously due to constraints imposed upon them by the increased demand for citizen services.[4]

In sum, it appears from our data that after nearly two decades of efforts, police agencies across the nation still are having difficulty transforming themselves from bureaucratic agencies into community-oriented ones at both theoretical and practical levels. Pfeffer (1982: 228) finds that the process of organizational change, by its very nature, is inescapably "traumatic and unsettling." This description may well depict the current state of organizational change in American policing. The traditional approach to policing still has a popular audience which has become attached to an "old, comfortable way of doing things."

Conclusion

As a first attempt to investigate COP implementation by focusing on externally focused change across the U.S., our findings highlight some policy-relevant issues which are important for both police administrators and future research. We found that organizational change in contemporary American policing has gained momentum in the past three years. It is clear, however, that this transition toward the COP model is not a matter of simple changes. This transition is affected by several dynamics present within a police organization and its surrounding environment. First, police officers' training and education is seen as an important area for successful implementation of COP innovations. Without the cooperation and support of all levels of police personnel, lasting and effective organizational change in policing is problematic. Under the present circumstances, it seems that training in ethics, police-community relations, and the principles of COP are recognized as important by police administrators nationally.

Furthermore, how to overcome impediments in the process of organizational change toward the COP model is another important area of study. We found that top priority must be afforded to the organizational problems which emerge during the change process. Particularly, the balance between the traditional approach versus a community-based orientation of policing is seen as critical: how might police organizations maintain adequate response time to calls for service while pursuing COP goals?

Findings from this study at the national level suggest several issues which might serve as foci for future studies concerning COP implementation. One issue concerns strategies of balancing the outcomes attributable to the traditional approach versus the expected benefits of the COP approach. Special attention should be given to identifying those police agencies which have been successful in striking such an effective balance. Similarly, employees' value orientation and change during a time of transition needs to be further investigated both within and across police organizations.

Successful organizational change toward the COP model should correspond with a change in values among police personnel as well. Furthermore, the relationship between facilitators and impediments involving COP implementation should be explored further in both aggregate studies as well as quali-

tively on a case-by-case basis. And lastly, longitudinal data should be collected to find out whether or not the same facilitators and impediments persist over time.

Notes

1. Two factors failed to reach the level of .5 on any of the three factors. Crime fighters v. peace keeper: Value conflicts was loaded .27, .46, and .43 while principles of neighborhood block organizations was .27, .46, and .43 on each factor respectively. The variable, Comprehensive overview: principles of COP, is placed in Factor 11 because of higher loading on the factor.

2. Twenty-six percent of the sample is derived from the Western part of the U.S., 30 percent originates from the North Central, another 30 percent from the South, and the remaining 14 percent represents the Northeast. Similarly, about 50 percent of the police agencies are located in cities with fewer than 100,000 populations (the sample also takes types of cities into consideration—e.g., rural, independent, and urban—as indicated in the *Municipal Year Book*, 1977). However, despite consistent findings regarding the variation between rural and urban law enforcement (e.g., Decker, 1979; Weisheit et al., 1994), smaller departments and larger ones, and variations by region (Warner et al., 1989; Meagher, 1985; Powell, 1990), it is interesting to note that the common obstacles identified by police agencies across the country are strikingly identical—all other differences among police departments across the nation disappear when the foci are obstacles to COP implementation.

3. Sherman (1975) has argued that the primary cause for the failure of numerous team-policing efforts in the early 1970s was the inability of middle management to handle the role conflict elements of change (cf. Walker, 1993). Based upon results from this survey, contemporary police administrators seem to have taken Sherman's proclamation to heart and realized the critical role of middle management in the transition to COP in American policing.

4. Kessler (1993) has refined this issue further based upon analysis of the patrol distribution in one district of the Houston Police Department. He noted a common problem is the lack of human resources to balance emergency calls with proactive COP activities. Par-

ticularly, the issue becomes one of management concerning how to prioritize calls for service and minimize patrol intervals between calls. Kessler found that a reduction from 15 to 14 officers on regular patrol duty has virtually little impact on the overall efficiency of police response time. Furthermore, by introducing other strategies such as teleserve and a combination of motorized patrol and foot patrol (e.g., response to different calls) considerable personnel resources can be reallocated to COP activities.

References

Angell, J. (1971). "Toward an Alternative to the Classic Police Organizational Arrangement: A Democratic Model." *Criminology,* 8:185–206.

Bittner, E. (1972). *The Functions of the Police in Modern Society: A Review of Background Factors, Current Practices, and Possible Role Models.* Rockville, MD: National Institute of Mental Health.

Brown, L. and M. Wycoff (1987). "Policing Houston: Reducing Fear and Improving Service." *Crime and Delinquency,* 33:201–18.

Decker, S. (1979). "The Rural County Sheriff: An Issue in Social Control." *Criminal Justice Review,* 4:97–111.

Eck, J. (1993). "Alternative Features for Policing." In D. Weisburd and C. Uchida (eds.), *Police Innovation and Control of the Police: Problems of Law, Order, and Community.* New York: Springer-Verlag.

Goldstein, H. (1977). *Policing a Free Society.* Cambridge, MA: Ballinger Publishing Company.

——(1987). "Toward Community-Oriented Policing: Potential, Basic Requirements and Threshold Questions." *Crime and Delinquency,* 33:6–30. (1990). *Problem-Oriented Policing.* New York: McGraw-Hill Publishing Company.

Greene, H. (1993). "Community-Oriented Policing in Florida." *American Journal of Police,* 12:141–55.

Grinc, R. (1994). "Angels in Marble: Problems in Stimulating Community Involvement in Community Policing." *Crime and Delinquency,* 40:437–68.

Huber, G.; K. Sutcliffe; C. Miller; and W. Glick (1993). "Understanding and Predicting Organizational Change." In G. Huber and W. Glick (eds.), *Organizational Charge and Redesign: Ideas and Insights for Improving Performance.* New York: Oxford Press.

Kelling, G. and M. Moore (1988). "From Political to Reform to Community: The Evolving Strategy of Police." In J. Greene and S. Mastrofski (eds.), *Community Policing: Rhetoric or Reality?* New York: Praeger.

Kelling, G. and J. Stewart (1989). "Neighborhoods and Police: The Maintenance of Civil Authority." *Perspectives on Policing,* No. 1. Washington, DC: National Institute of Justice and Harvard University.

Kessler, D. (1993). "Integrating Calls for Service with Community- and Problem-Oriented Policing: A Case Study." *Crime and Delinquency,* 39:485–508.

Kim, J. and C. Mueller (1978). *Introduction to Factor Analysis: What It Is and How to Do It.* Beverly Hills: Sage Publications.

Klockars, C. (1988). "The Rhetoric of Community Policing." In J. Greene and S. Mastrofski (eds.), *Community Policing: Rhetoric or Reality?* New York: Praeger.

Langworthy, R. (1992). "Organizational Structure." In G. Cordner and D. Hale (eds.), *What Works in Policing?* Operations and Administration Examined. Cincinnati, OH: Anderson.

Lurigio, A. and W. Skogan (1994). "Winning the Hearts and Minds of Police Officers: An Assessment of Staff Perceptions of Community Policing in Chicago." *Crime and Delinquency,* 40:315–30.

Manning, P. (1992). "Information Technologies and the Police." In M. Tonry and N. Morris (eds.), *Criminal Justice: A Review of Research.* Chicago: University of Chicago Press.

Mastrofski, S. (1988). "Community Policing as Reform: A Cautionary Tale." In J. Greene and S. Mastrofski (eds.), *Community Policing: Rhetoric or Reality?* New York: Praeger

Mastrofski, S. and C. Uchida (1993). "Transforming the Police." *Journal of Research in Crime and Delinquency,* 33:330–58.

Meagher, S. (1985). "Police Patrol Styles: How Pervasive is Community Variation?" *Journal of Police Science and Administration,* 13:36–45.

Meyer, M. (1975). "Organizational Domains." *American Sociological Review,* 40:599–615.

Moore, M. (1992). "Problem Solving and Community Policing." In M. Tonry and N. Morris (eds.), *Criminal Justice: A Review of Research* Chicago: University of Chicago Press.

Osborne, D. and T. Gaebler (1992). *Reinventing Government: How the Entrepreneurial Spirit is Transforming the Public Sector from Schoolhouse, City Hall to the Pentagon.* New York: Addison-Wesley Publishing Company.

Pfeffer, J. (1982). *Organizations and Organization Theory.* Boston: Pitman.

Powell, D. (1990). "A Study of Police Discretion in Six Southern Cities." *Journal of Police Science and Administration,* 17:1–7.

Pressman, J. and A. Wildvsky (1973). *Implementation*. Berkeley: University of California Press.

Reiss, A. (1992). "Police Organization in the Twentieth Century." In M. Tonry and N. Morris (eds.), *Criminal Justice: A Review of Research*. Chicago: University of Chicago Press.

Sadd, S. and R. Grinc (1994). "Innovative Neighborhood Oriented Policing: An Evaluation of Community Policing Programs in Eight Cities." In D. Rosenbaum (ed.), *The Challenge of Community Policing*. Thousand Oaks, CA: Sage Publications.

Sherman. L. (1975). "Middle Management and Police Democratization: A Reply to John E. Angell." *Criminology*, 12:363–377.

Skolnick, J. and D. Bayley (1986). *The New Blue Line: Police Innovations in Six American Cities*. New York: The Free Press.

Sparrow, M. (1988). "Implementing Community Policing." *Perspectives on Policing*, No. 9. Washington, DC: National Institute of Justice and Harvard University.

Sparrow, M.; M. Moore; and D. Kennedy (1990). *Beyond 911: A New Era for Policing*. New York: Basic Books.

Thurman, Q.; P. Bogen; and A. Giacomazzi (1993). "Program Monitoring and Community Policing: A Process Evaluation of Community Policing in Spokane, Washington." *American Journal of Police*, 12:89–114.

Trojanowicz, R. and B. Bucqueroux (1990). *Community Policing: A Contemporary Perspective*. Cincinnati, OH: Anderson Publishing Co.

Walker, S. (1977). *A Critical History of Police Reform* MA: D.C. Heath.

——(1993). "Does Anyone Remember Team Policing? Lessons of the Team Policing. Experience for Community Policing." *American Journal of Police*, 12:33–55.

Warner, R.; B. Steel; and N. Lovrich (1989). "Conditions Associated with the Advent of Representative Bureaucracy: The Case of Women in Policing." *Social Science Quarterly*, 70:562–578.

Wasserman, R. and M. Moore (1988). "Values in Policing." *Perspectives on Policing* No. 8. Washington, DC: National Institute of Justice and Harvard University.

Weisel, D. and J. Eck (1994). "Toward a Practical Approach to Organizational Change: Community Policing Initiatives in Six Cities." In D. Rosenbaum (ed.), *The Challenge of Community Policing: Testing the Promises*. Thousand Oaks, CA: Sage Publications.

Weisheit, R.; L. Wells; and D. Falcone (1994). "Community Policing in Small Town and Rural America." *Crime and Delinquency*, 40:549–567.

Wycoff, M. (1988). "The Benefits of Community Policing: Evidence and Conjecture." In J. Greene and S. Mastrofski (eds.), *Community Policing: Rhetoric or Reality?* New York: Praeger.

Wycoff, M. and W. Skogan (1994). "The Effects of a Community Policing Management Style on Officers' Attitudes." *Crime and Delinquency*, 40:37–43.

17

Implementing Change

Community-Oriented Policing and Problem Solving

Ronald W. Glensor
Kenneth J. Peak

Moving a police department from one that is incident-driven to one that proactively addresses problems is no easy task. R. Glensor and K. Peak examine four key areas in which departments must be recast: (1) leadership and management (including such tasks as developing new statements of mission, goals, and values, as well as ensuring that middle management and first-line supervisors are trained in and supportive of the transition); (2) organizational culture (developing new means for recruiting, hiring, training, evaluating, rewarding, and disciplining officers); (3) field operations (changing beat and shift assignments, finding time for officers to engage in problem-oriented policing); and (4) external relationships (developing working relationships with other city agencies, businesses, service providers, and the community). While reading, consider how departments might approach each of these four broad areas and where barriers or challenges to implementation may develop within each.

Concern over crime has become a national preoccupation, fueled by nightly media reports and political posturing. This trend belies the slight, but consistent, decline in crime rates recorded over the past four years.[1]

While the public's view of crime and actual crime statistics may seem contradictory, police administrators should consider the disparity more closely before assuming that the public's visible concern is largely unfounded. They need to consider the other factors that contribute to this consuming fear of crime.

A recent nationwide survey revealed that 44 percent of the respondents reported areas within a mile of their homes where they fear walking alone at night. Six of every 10 limit where they will go by themselves.[2]

Although violent crime and media accounts of violence spark much of this concern, public perceptions also play an important role. Neighborhood disorder affects the public's perception of safety as surely as crime does.

People express greater fear of strangers loitering near their homes than they do of random physical violence. Undoubtedly, they fear people they view as sinister: panhandlers, drunks, addicts, rowdy teens, mentally imbalanced drifters, and the homeless. But they also fear physical disorder: litter, abandoned buildings, graffiti, broken streetlights and windows, wrecked vehicles, and other indicators of neighborhood decline.[3]

The twin threats of violence and neighborhood disorder raise the public's fear of crime beyond the level that crime rates alone may seem to support. Over the past several years, these factors have led to a tremendous increase in calls for police service. Likewise, the rise in citizens' calls to the police has had a marked impact on the nature of policing itself.

The Nature of Policing

Several studies over the past three decades have succinctly described the reality of policing under the professional paradigm. Officers devote less than 50 percent of their on-duty time to responding to calls for service. They spend the remainder on administrative tasks. Of the calls responded to by officers, *over 80 percent are for noncriminal incidents.*[4] Clearly, officers deal with disorder and the fear of crime more than they deal with actual crime. As a result, they find themselves continually applying short-term solutions to the same long-term problems.

Ultimately, the strengths and weaknesses of the professional model rest with its method for measuring success. Under this model, agencies do not gauge success by determining whether a problem has been resolved fully. Rather, they measure success by tracking such quantitative indicators as response time, arrests, and crime clearance rates. This approach, while not without merit, assigns a great deal of weight to the accumulation of data. At the same time, it devotes too little effort to resolving problems long-term.

Granted, many incidents that the police confront require a one-time, short-term infusion of authority. But, as surveys and studies confirm, many calls for service require a far more comprehensive response.

Community-Oriented Policing and Problem Solving

To provide a structure to address the long-term factors that produce crime and disorder, hundreds of American law enforcement agencies have adopted two separate but interrelated strategies—community-oriented policing and problem oriented policing. To encompass the mutual ideals of these approaches, this article employs the term community-oriented policing and problem solving (COPPS).

COPPS is a proactive philosophy that promotes solving problems that are either criminal, affect the quality of life, or increase citizen fear of crime. It involves identifying, analyzing, and addressing community problems at their source.

Unfortunately, many individuals—both inside and outside of policing—believe that the goals of the COPPS model can be achieved by merely putting officers on foot or bicycle patrol, or by opening neighborhood mini-stations. Such approaches misrepresent the true potential of COPPS and establish unrealistically simplistic expectations.

Four Keys to Success

Moving an agency from the reactive, incident-driven mode to COPPS is no simple endeavor. Four principle components—leadership and management issues, organizational culture, field operations, and external relationships—must be rebuilt from the ground

up to provide a strong basis for the COPPS model.

Leadership and Management Issues

Successfully implementing COPPS requires a change in the management approach of an agency. Whenever law enforcement agencies adopt new programs or strategies, employees commonly want to know *why* the change is taking place. Administrators should understand that this is a valid concern.

To address employees' concerns, it is important to develop a mission statement that embodies new operating principles and long-term objectives. To be useful, the mission statement must articulate the basic values and goals inherent in COPPS. Attention must also be given to policies and procedures, management styles, planning and program evaluation, and resources and finances.

Police Leadership

In *Problem Oriented Policing*, Herman Goldstein argues that good leaders "must have a set of values a commitment, goals, and governing principles."[5] Chief executives who attempt to guide their agencies out of the purely reactive mode must create a climate conducive to change. To do this they themselves must become viable change agents.

When implementing COPPS, chiefs should avoid the "bombshell" technique—simply announcing that COPPS is now the order of the day without a carefully designed plan of implementation. The chief's job begins by involving the entire agency in developing a clear vision and mission statement that is consistent with the principles of COPPS. These guiding tenets should recognize that the police do more than merely enforce the laws. These principles should serve as the basis for establishing new values and goals.

Chief executives must remember that fully implementing the COPPS model takes years, not weeks or months. It requires careful and continuous planning to ensure that the organization's policies and procedures do not conflict with the basic principles of COPPS. Because the COPPS model places strong emphasis on street officers as primary problem solvers, chiefs also should carefully evaluate resource allocation to determine if any redistribution is necessary.

The larger the organization, the more time necessary to implement COPPS, especially if it is being implemented department-wide. This period of changeover may involve considerable turbulence. Chief executives should be prepared to face a reluctance to change from those comfortable with the status quo.

Mid-level Management

Mid-level police managers—lieutenants and captains—play a crucial role in the implementation of the COPPS model. Accordingly, they should be trained in the philosophy and methodology of the concept. Studies of the team policing initiatives of the 1970s found that many managers viewed that concept as a threat to their power. They subsequently "subverted and, in some cases, actively sabotaged the plans."[6]

Mid–level managers need not be a hindrance to innovation. Indeed, many researchers who study law enforcement agencies identify middle managers as the locus of innovation.[7] If COPPS is to be implemented successfully, mid–level managers must provide administrative support and remove any barriers that first–line supervisors confront.

First-line Supervisors

As first-line supervisors, sergeants wield a tremendous amount of influence on the attitudes and behaviors of officers. COPPS requires that sergeants allow their officers additional autonomy and authority to solve problems. This component of the COPPS model can seem threatening to first-line supervisors who, in turn, can create an enormous block to implementation. Supervisory training should define their new role as "facilitator" rather than "controller." Sergeants often must run interference for their patrol officers and give them the time required to perform problem solving. First-line supervisors can also assist by developing new COPPS activity forms and officer evaluation criteria that complement the new philosophy.

Organizational Culture

Reactive crime-fighting strategies and organizational values represent strong barriers to COPPS. Therefore, before meaningful transition can occur, the very core of an organization's culture must change. In this context, "culture" refers to a set of expectations and norms that guide employees behavior.

Organizations base their culture largely on history, officer experiences, organizational structure, leadership style, and past methods of handling change. To ensure that COPPS becomes a part of the organizational culture, and not simply a fleeting or peripheral "program," an agency must link COPPS to how it recruits, selects, trains, evaluates, promotes, rewards, and disciplines employees.

Agencies must review their recruiting literature and testing/selection processes to ensure that the skills, knowledge, and abilities used to select recruits are consistent with the desired traits of a COPPS officer. The training that recruits receive once they are hired becomes critical. Therefore, COPPS training must be integrated into the academy's curriculum fairly early in the implementation process.

In addition, both sworn and non-sworn employees should be taught in the COPPS philosophy to ensure common understanding. Personnel should receive practical training related to the problem-solving model and other crime prevention and analysis strategies. Personnel also need to be trained on effective ways to involve other government agencies, private businesses, public and private service organizations, and the community in general. Agencies should include this instruction in field training curricula and updated annual training.

COPPS also changes the way an organizations evaluate their officers. Evaluation criteria need not focus solely on efficiency, as indicated by citation and arrest figures. Under COPPS, agencies should recognize officers who maximize resources and exhibit initiative in solving seemingly intractable community problems. Administrators must remember that such activities often defy traditional numbers-oriented evaluation.

In fact, COPPS requires an evaluation system that measures whether attempted solutions successfully addressed community problems. Agencies must establish forms of assessment, such as community surveys and data analysis methodologies, that adequately gauge the effectiveness of individual problem-solving initiatives.[8]

In an organization devoted to the principles of COPPS, promotional exams should not focus solely on tactical orientation, nor should awards be restricted to recognizing only heroic deeds. Employees' knowledge about COPPS and their problem-solving performance must be reflected in an agency's promotional and reward systems.

Likewise, a department's disciplinary system is an important guide for employees' behavior. Agencies must uncover and swiftly deal with behavior that threatens their COPPS efforts.

Cultural resistance to implementing COPPS invariably encompasses officers' beliefs that responding to service calls leaves them insufficient time to engage in problem solving. COPPS training should explain that if officers do not engage in problems solving they will continue rushing from call to call like pinballs, achieving short-term results at best. Still, agencies can and should do a number of things to garner more time for officers to engage in problem solving.

Field Operations

Under COPPS, field officers become the focus of problem solving efforts; they identify problems, apply in-depth analysis of the underlying causes, employ creative and collaborative responses, and evaluate the results of their efforts. This philosophy often requires more time and effort from officers than incident-driven methodologies allowed.

An agency's administration might obtain more time for officers by analyzing calls for service and officers' workload and by evaluating what activities officers perform and how they spend their non-committed time. Agencies need to work toward taking more offense reports over the telephone or through mail-in reporting and consider the enactment of false alarm ordinances or other measures to reduce the number of unnecessary calls for police service. Agencies must also seek ways to reduce the amount of time officers spent performing non-police functions.[9]

Through better call management, supervisors can help by allowing officers to delay their responses to non–emergency calls. Supervisors in some agencies use cellular phones to contact complainants directly and handle their problems, thus eliminating the need for an officer's response.

Problem solving also requires acquiring reliable data and information about substantive problems. Centralized and accessible crime analysis information should provide officers with reliable and data on all calls for service, not merely Part I crimes. Identifying sites that yield repeat calls for service represents a vital component to establishing long-term response strategies.

Agencies often question whether to implement COPPS department-wide or through specialized units. Although specialized units may produce limited results more quickly, their long-range impact may prove detrimental to the organization if other personnel view COPPS as a temporary or specialized program. Consequently, there is a growing consensus that all personnel in an agency should be trained in and practice COPPS.

In addition, agencies must consider operational variables that impact the implementation of COPPS. Agencies that assign fixed shifts and beat assignments generally enjoy a higher success rate. Long-term and/or permanent beat and shift assignments—the ultimate form of decentralization—allow officers to learn more about people, places, issues, and problems within neighborhoods. Agencies may also need to examine and modify rank structure to accommodate COPPS and to ensure that communication is not filtered, doctored, or suppressed.[10]

External Relationships

While much can be debated about COPPS implementation, one thing is clear: COPPS requires changes in agencies' external relationships. The goal should be to establish new partnerships for sharing the information and resources necessary to solve neighborhood problems. As an integral component of this effort, law enforcement should foster a cooperative working relationship with city agencies, businesses, service providers, and the community.

Because a deteriorating neighborhood might require cooperation among health, police, fire, zoning, and social services agencies, key officials in each organization must be included early in the implementation process. The homeless, the mentally ill, and the victims of domestic violence often account for a high volume of police service calls. By working together, the police and other agencies can put victims in the hands of skilled practitioners and on the road to reclaiming their lives.

Other Considerations

Elected Officials

Soliciting and maintaining political support represents an essential element to implementing COPPS. Elected officials must provide sustenance and direction to any COPPS effort by allocating resources and developing strategic community-wide policies.

Unfortunately, political officials can be a very difficult group for police administrators to influence. Their knowledge of policing traditionally is grounded in Uniform Crime Reports' statistics, response times, and case clearance rates. They rarely think of the role of police beyond its law enforcement function.

The multi-agency cooperation inherent in COPPS represents a new concept for many public officials. Elected officials must understand that they cannot promise the community reduced response times and an officer's response to every type of call, or that drug-related crime, homelessness, and other social problems will be resolved within a finite time period. Both voters and elected officials should understand that to achieve long-term results, COPPS requires careful, thoughtful approaches with realistic time frames.

Detectives

To many officers, investigation represents the single most important function of a police organization. An inevitable by product of this vies is that uniformed officers are accorded less status than detectives. Thus, many patrol officers aspire to enter the investigative ranks. However, a shift to COPPS requires a new and enhanced role for line officers.

For this reason, detectives—who may feel that COPPS work is for uniformed officers alone—must be incorporated into the COPPS strategy. They should not view COPPS as an exclusive responsibility of the patrol force.

Detectives can feed intelligence information to the patrol division, while patrol officers can pass on relevant tips to detectives. In short, under COPPS, detectives are not the only crime-solvers in the organization, and patrol officers no longer limit their duties to report taking.

Unions

Is COPPS contrary to union interests? Does it conflict with contractual issues, such as shift staffing, work hours, and promotions? These questions pose serious barriers to many administrators, requiring careful thought and cooperation between labor and management before COPPS can be implemented.

If agencies exclude the unions from the COPPS planning process, officers may well perceive its implementation as a public relations gimmick to serve management's interests. Therefore, managers should explain their rationale and concerns to union leaders so that both groups can collaborate in planning the agency's future.

The implementation of the COPPS model is as important to labor as it is to management. Both sides desire a quality work environment for employees. COPPS fosters that and much more. It affords officers opportunities to use their talents creatively and to take control of their work environment through problem solving. COPPS also recognizes their cognitive abilities and rewards them for making lasting improvements in the community.

Case Study: COP+ in Reno

In the mid-1980s the Reno, Nevada, Police Department faced the challenges now confronting many law enforcement agencies. A lagging economy had forced administrators to make significant reductions in staffing and resources, while calls for service continued to rise dramatically.

As the department struggled to cope with these challenges, community support eroded. A survey taken in 1987 revealed that citizens viewed the police department as being uncaring and heavy-handed. Two municipal bond issues that would have replaced officers lost to attrition failed because of a lack of voter support.

Department administrators saw the need for broadbased change. In May, 1987, the Reno Police Department adopted a department-wide community policing strategy. Administrators realized that as part of COP+, the department must engage the community and city agencies in a shared approach to problem solving if it hoped to address the problems of increased crime and disorder.

First, the department decentralized patrol into three geographical sections, each commanded by an officer who assumed 24-hour responsibility for a specific area. The sergeants and officers assigned to the areas received more permanent beat assignments so that they could become familiar with residents and businesses and their respective problems.

Each area commander formed a neighborhood advisory groups (NAG). Made up of area residents, the NAGs reflect the unique socioeconomic makeup and ethnic balance of each area and relate the specific crime concerns of the residents. Newsletters distributed prior to each quarterly meeting inform residents of a variety of department issues and programs, as well as crimes in their area. Today, NAG meetings provide citizens the opportunity to meet with officers, exchange information, and develop problem solving strategies.

The department also established a quality assurance unit (considered the "plus" in COP+). Among other duties, this unit conducts biannual community surveys to identify citizens' concerns and evaluate the effectiveness of the department in resolving them. The survey results, which administrators use to make necessary operational or administrative policy adjustments, are presented to every department member, to the city council, and at community and NAG meetings.

To improve strained relations with the media, the department created a media advisory group. As part of this effort, the department appointed a public information officer to provide newscasters with a principal contact person in the agency. In addition, the depart-

ment's executive staff meets with members of the media twice a year to discuss policy issues and relations. The department also relaxed its press policy to encourage cooperation between officers and the media.

As community support grew for the department's efforts to solve problems through cooperation, residents began to take a more active part in problem solving. The department established neighborhood police stations in each of the three patrol areas. For the most part, these stations were funded through private community donations. Civilian report takers staff the stations to provide residents with a means to file police reports in their own neighborhoods. The stations also provide citizens a place to meet with officers to discuss neighborhood problems and to obtain information about a variety of community-based programs offered by the department.

City agencies and social service organizations also became vital to the police department's problem-solving efforts. Officers now routinely work with representatives from a variety of city agencies and offices, including planning, fire, streets, signs, and the city attorney to improve neighborhood conditions and eradicate specific problems.

The cooperative problem-solving approach led to the creation of several coalitions to address substantive community concerns. The gang alternative partnership (GAP) program brings together representatives from law enforcement, juvenile courts, probation, education, and citizens groups to establish gang enforcement policy and diversion programs.

A similar consortium of concerned stakeholders works together to help the homeless through the homeless evaluation liaison program (HELP). Comprised of police officers, university students, and volunteer residents, HELP identifies homeless persons and places them with a social service agency that can best assist them. HELP's efforts have significantly reduced homeless-related offenses and the male population of the county jail.

The efforts of the Reno Police Department to establish external problem-solving partnerships emerged as a critical component of its community policing strategy. While such an approach represents a significant departure for most law enforcement agencies, department leaders have found that the wide range of crime-related problems facing Reno can best be met through a broadbased community response.

Conclusion

Like any broadbased change to accepted practices, community oriented policing and problem solving should be implemented carefully. Chief executives who commit to the COPPS approach face two critical considerations—overcoming organizational resistance to innovation and gauging and managing the pace of change once it is undertaken. Police executives should understand that COPPS is evolutionary; it occurs as a result of refining past practices, implementing new strategies, and at times accepting small wins in lieu of major victories.

Agencies that provide a strong foundation for the COPPS model and nurture its growth will bring order to the chaos and fear often associated with organizational change. More important, these agencies will forge new relationships with city agencies and community members to resolve problems, not just respond to incidents.

Notes

1. "Preliminary Annual Uniform Crime Report," Federal Bureau of Investigation, Washington, D.C., released May 5, 1996.

2. George Gallup, Jr., *The Gallup Poll Monthly* (Princeton, N.J.: The Gallup Poll, March 1993).

3. James Q. Wilson and George L. Kelling, "Broken Windows: Police and Neighborhood Safety," *The Atlantic*, March 1982, p. 9.

4. See E. I. Cumming, I. Cumming, and L. Edell, "Policeman as Philosopher, Guide and Friend," *Social Problems*, 12, 1965, 276–286; T. Bercal, "Calls for Police Assistance," *American Behavioral Scientist* 13, 1970, 682; Albert Reiss, *The Police and the Public* (New Haven, Conn.: Yale University Press, 1971); R. Lilly, "What Are the Police Now Doing?" *Journal of Police Science and Administration*, 6, 1978, 51–60.

5. Herman Goldstein, *Problem-Oriented Policing* (New York: McGraw-Hill, 1990), p. 153.

6. Lawrence W. Sherman, *Team Policing: Seven Case Studies* (Washington, D.C.: Police Foundation, 1973), 10.

7. Rosabeth Moss Kanter, "The Middle Manager as Innovator," *Harvard Business Review*, July–August 1982, 95–105.

8. For a discussion of the evaluation process in several sites, see Dennis P. Rosenbaum (ed.), *The Challenge of Community Policing: Testing the Promise* (Thousand Oaks, Calif.: Sage, 1994).

9. See John J. Moslow, "False Alarms: Cause for Alarm," *FBI Law Enforcement Bulletin*, November 1994, 1.

10. Malcolm K. Sparrow, "Implementing Community Policing," *National Institute of Justice*, Research in Brief, 9, September 1988, 5.

Reprinted from: Ronald W. Glensor and Ken Peak, "Implementing Change: Community Oriented Policing and Problem Solving." In *Law Enforcement Bulletin*, 65 (7), pp. 14–21. 1996. ✦

18

Winning the Hearts and Minds of Police Officers

An Assessment of Staff Perceptions of Community Policing in Chicago

Arthur J. Lurigio
Wesley G. Skogan

The transition to community policing has certainly not been altogether smooth in all departments; as the following reading suggests, it has often entailed a battle for the hearts and minds of police officers, who often resist change. In order to shape and administer department implementation in a way that is more acceptable, A. Lurigio and W. Skogan suggest that planners of community-policing strategies would be wise to examine the feeling and attitudes of its staff in order to identify potential pockets of resistance. The authors provide a means for assessing, prior to putting the strategy into operation, how disposed the officers are toward the elements of community policing. The results are important for the city, and—perhaps just as significantly—the assessment is replicable for other similarly situated departments. As you read, contemplate what outcomes might result from such an assessment in your own city or country.

The success of community policing depends on the police officers who are responsible for implementing the programs. In essence, their attitudes, perceptions, and behaviors must be substantially changed before community policing can be put into practice. Chicago's community policing program, known as CAPS, became operational in March 1993 in five prototype districts. Before the program started, officers were surveyed about their job satisfaction, their supervisors, and their opinions regarding community policing. Results showed that officers were very ambivalent about CAPS. They were supportive of some CAPS-related activities (e.g., solving noncrime problems), but not others (e.g., foot patrol), and were dubious about the program's effects on crime and neighborhood relations.

The concept of community policing translates into a variety of specific operations and practices. Many of the directives of community policing are beyond the traditional capacities and roles of officers, who were initially selected and trained to perform only the basic activities associated with law enforcement, such as patrol, investigation, order maintenance, arrest, and report writing (Stone and DeLuca 1985; Walker 1992). Hence the transition to community policing is frequently a battle for the hearts and minds of police officers. Community policing requires them to do many of their old jobs in innovative ways: It forces officers to attempt unfamiliar and challenging tasks, to identify and solve a broad range of problems, and to reach out to elements of the community who were previously outside their purview.

The battle must always be waged, however, because police officers can be quite resistant to change. From their perspective, the battle is usually justified. Officers typically hear about new programs when they are announced from the highest levels of administration, and they feel that most initiatives are adopted without their input or prior acceptance. They are quick to observe whether civilians played a major role in instigating or planning department programs, which touches a deep and sensitive nerve in the police culture. They are resentful when the community is consulted about internal police business, and they are cynical about the role of politics in the appointment of their leaders and the definition of their missions. Officers who have survived previous policing reforms often derisively recall the acronyms that designated those projects and can recount the inevitable acrimony that eventually led to their failure. Police are particularly dubious about notions such as empowerment and participatory management; in reality, their agencies are managed mostly by the threat and fear of punishment from supervisors.

Effects of Community Policing on Officers

Although the battle for the hearts and minds of the police force can be spirited, community policing is supposed to be worth the effort because it produces a "new breed" of police officers who have greater knowledge about and expertise in problem solving and community engagement activities, and who experience greater job satisfaction, self-worth, and productivity. The few investigations examining community policing's effects on police personnel have reported favorable results (Lurigio and Rosenbaum 1994). For example, in an evaluation of a neighborhood policing project in Madison, Wisconsin, Wycoff and Skogan (1993) reported that involvement in the city's experimental police district changed the views of participating officers. Specifically, experimental district officers, compared to those assigned elsewhere, saw themselves working as a team, maintained that their efforts were supported by their supervisors and the department as a whole, and believed that the department was truly engaged in a process of reform. They were also more satisfied with their jobs, more strongly committed to the organization, more customer oriented, more invested in the principles of problem solving and community policing, and more pleased with their relationship to the community. Moreover, department records indicated that disciplinary actions, absenteeism, tardiness, and sick days were reduced in the experimental area.

These changes are consistent with those reported in Wycoff's (1988) interviews with officers doing community policing in several different cities. Generally, these officers thought that their work was more important, interesting, and rewarding, and less frustrating. They felt that they had more independence in and control over their jobs, two factors that are important determinants of job satisfaction. Finally, they tended to adopt a more benign and trusting posture toward the public.

Along the same lines, McElroy, Cosgrove, and Sadd (1993) found that officers assigned to New York's Community Police Officer Program (CPOP) had changed their attitudes toward community residents. CPOP officers reported that in walking their beats they were more exposed to "the good people" of the community, they got to know neighborhood residents as individuals, and their interaction with citizens was not limited to just crisis situations.

In Saad and Grinc's (1993) study of community policing in Hayward, California, officers reported that the community had gained a better understanding of the role of the police and had acquired more realistic expectations about what police could actually accomplish. In addition, officers became more knowledgeable about the community and more empathic toward neighborhood residents' problems. From their perceptive, residents found the police to be more receptive to change and more willing to help them with local problems.

Chicago Alternative Policing Strategy

Recognizing that many traditional policing practices are no longer effective, the city of Chicago commissioned the consulting firm of Booz, Allen, and Hamilton to conduct a study of the Chicago Police Department (CPD). Booz, Allen, and Hamilton recommended a series of operational changes designed to place more police officers on Chicago's streets to combat crime, drugs, and gang activity, and to pave the way for the implementation of a community policing program. Overall, they proposed a neighborhood-based strategy for CPD, which essentially represented a transition from incident-driven to community-oriented policing. As Chicago Police Superintendent Matt Rodriguez noted,

> These specific management changes will help make community policing work . . . . The police districts that we know today will be reconfigured to create efficient coordination of beat officers patrolling the streets and alleys of every neighborhood on foot and in patrol cars. They will be backed up by sector cars responding to

911 calls, specialized units, and tactical teams.

In January, 1993, Mayor Richard Daley announced the Chicago Alternative Policing Strategy (CAPS), which was initially implemented in five prototype districts that were chosen to reflect the diversity of Chicago's neighborhoods. At the planning stage, Chicago's community policing program had six basic features:

1. Neighborhood orientation. CAPS gives special attention to the residents and problems of specific neighborhoods, which demands that officers know their beats (i.e., crime trends, hot spots, and community organizations and resources) and develop partnerships with the community to solve problems.

2. Increased geographic responsibility. CAPS involves organizing police services so that officers are responsible for crime control in specific areas. A new district organizational structure using rapid-response cars to handle emergency calls allows newly created beat teams to engage in community policing activities. The beat teams share responsibility for specific areas under the leadership of a supervisory beat sergeant.

3. Structured response to calls for police service. A system of differential responses to citizen calls frees beat team officers from the continuous demands of 911 calls. Emergency calls are handled primarily by rapid-response sector cars, whereas nonemergency and routine calls are handled by beat officers or by telephone callback contacts. Sector officers also attend to community matters, and sector and beat teams rotate so that all officers participate in community policing.

4. Proactive problem-oriented approach. CAPS focuses on the causes of neighborhood problems rather than on discrete incidents of crime or disturbances. Attention is given to the long-term prevention of these problems and to the signs of community disorder and decay that are associated with crime (e.g., drug houses, loitering youths, and graffiti).

5. Community and city resources for crime prevention and control. CAPS assumes that police alone cannot solve the crime problem and that they depend on the community and other city agencies to achieve success. Hence part of the beat officer's new role is to broker community resources and to draw on other city agencies to identify and respond to local problems. The mayor's office ensures that municipal agencies are responsive to requests for assistance from beat officers.

6. Emphasis on crime problem analysis. CAPS requires more efficient data collection and analysis to identify crime patterns and to target areas that demand police attention. Emphasis is placed on crime analysis at the district level, and beat information is recorded and shared among officers and across watches.

Chicago's community policing program is expected to yield favorable results in several key areas. Specifically, CAPS is designed to (a) improve responses to calls for police service; (b) increase street presence of police (i.e., the number of officers visible on the beat); (c) optimize the use of crime information for problem identification and interventions; (d) facilitate law enforcement (i.e., increase the number of arrests and quality of clearances); (e) focus police efforts on resolving the underlying conditions that lead to neighborhood crime and disorder; (f) expand police capabilities by improving access to other resources in Chicago (e.g., community groups and other city agencies); and (g) reduce crime over a 3-year period.

The implementation of community policing in Chicago demanded dramatic modifications in CPD's entire approach to law enforcement, including its philosophy, structure, operations, and deployment strategies. The gradual evolution toward full-scale community policing essentially continues to redefine both the "means and ends" of policing (Moore 1992). Although all levels of the department have been affected by these changes, the onus of implementation devolved on the operational staff, whose roles were fundamentally reshaped in terms of problem solving and community relations. Community policing necessitated not only sweeping revisions in department policies and procedures, but also basic attitudinal and perceptual shifts by officers. Hence the program's success depends in part on the department's ability to prepare officers to make an effective adjustment to the unique rigors and demands of community policing.

This article examines police officers' views at the beginning of the CAPS program. Prototype officers completed questionnaires before they began their initial orientation training and before virtually anyone in the CPD knew much about the program. The survey probed their assessments of their jobs, their supervisors, and their relationships with the communities they served. The results provide insight into the potential impediments to the implementation of CAPS and a baseline for evaluating subsequent changes in officers' attitudes, perceptions, and behaviors.

Method

The survey included questions that formed 22 scales measuring the various components of factors such as job satisfaction, officers' relationships with peers and supervisors, and their attitudes toward police work and community policing.

Procedure

Arrangements were made with police academy staff to administer the instrument at the beginning of each orientation training session. Orientation sessions were scheduled on consecutive days from March 22 through April 1, 1993 (excluding Sunday). Sessions were held in three rooms at the police academy during the second and third watches, except for the final 2 days when sessions were held only during the second watch. Five make-up orientation sessions were later conducted for prototype personnel who could not attend the initial orientation training. The last day of training was April 20, 1993. A total of 24 orientation sessions were completed.

Surveys were distributed after attendance cards were completed by police trainees and after the trainers and training agenda were introduced by the training commander or his representative. In addition, the CAPS evaluation and its immediate staff were introduced prior to questionnaire implementation. To standardize the administration of the survey, evaluation staff were given a script, which they were told to follow (but not read verbatim) before distributing the questionnaire. The script contained the following key points:

- The purpose of the CAPS personnel survey is to give Chicago police officers a chance to have input into the CAPS evaluation. We really value your opinion and want to know how you feel about CAPS.

- Unless we hear from police officers and learn what they truly believe, we will not be able to determine whether CAPS is effective.

- The Chicago Police Department will never have access to your individual responses. Researchers will only report summary or aggregate statistics.

- Questionnaires are completely confidential. The only reason we are asking for your name is so that we can track you within the police department for a follow-up survey. Names will be kept secure by the research staff and will never be shared with the police department.

- Read the instructions preceding each group of items before filling them out. There are no right or wrong answers to the questions. In general, we want to know about your opinions or attitudes. Answer each item only once, and circle the one response that best fits your attitude or opinion.

Surveys were handed individually to respondents who were asked to fill out the first page of the instrument, which contained general instructions for completing the questionnaire, the respondent's identification number, the study identification number, and space for the officer's name, district, and star number. On top of each survey was a letter from CPD's superintendent, which stated his support for the evaluation and reassured the officers of the confidentiality of their survey responses. The trainees were also told to return the cover sheets immediately to the survey administrator, who placed them in an envelope that was promptly sealed to protect the identifying information. Respondents returned their completed surveys to an evaluation staff person. Completion times ranged from 10 to 40 minutes—the average completion time was 20 minutes.

Scale Analyses

Interim correlations were examined for each of the questionnaire's scales, with an initial alpha less than .60. Items with the lowest interim correlations were dropped, and the scales were recomputed until the .60 criterion was reached. Scales with final alphas less than .60 were not included in subsequent analyses. A total of 17 of the original 22 scales met the .60 standard; their alphas ranged from .60 to .95. Table 18.1 presents the alpha, mean, standard deviation, response option range, and N for each of these scales. Regres-

sion analyses were performed on some of the scale scores to test for differences based on officer age, rank, gender, and race.

Measures

Job Dimensions. Officers responded to a series of items relating to six scales of job dimensions: (a) Job Autonomy measures the degree to which employees believe that their jobs afford them discretion and independence; (b) Task Identity measures the extent to which work tasks have definite beginnings and ends and leave employees with a sense of having completed a whole job; (c) Skill Variety measures the amount of variation in the skills and responsibilities that employees experience in their daily assignments; (d) Peer/Supervisor Feedback measures the degree to which employees feel that their supervisors and coworkers provide them with information about their job performance; (e) Job Feedback measures the extent to which employees perceive that their jobs provide them with information about their performance, which is separate from peer or supervisor feedback; and (f) Working

Table 18.1
Chicago Police Scale Scores

Legend for chart:
A - Scale Name B - Alpha C - Mean D - Standard Deviation E - Minimum F - Maximum G - N

A	B	C	D	E	F	G
Job Autonomy	.72	3.52	.90	1	5	1,400
Task Identity	.61	3.12	.95	1	5	1,399
Skill Variety	.60	3.64	.87	1	5	1,403
Peer-Supervisor Feedback	.86	3.12	1.03	1	5	1,402
Job Feedback	.75	3.56	.82	1	5	1,403
Working With Others	.71	3.93	.80	1	5	1,404
Growth Need	.95	4.21	.82	1	5	1,401
Job Involvement	.70	3.45	.70	1	5	1,396
Mobility	.69	3.52	.99	1	5	1,408
Policy and Practice	.81	2.80	.85	1	5	1,385
Participatory Management	.64	2.72	.88	1	5	1,404
Orientation Toward Community Policing	.77	3.49	.61	1	5	1,407
Optimistic-CAPS Traditional	.87	2.09	.67	1	3	1,395
Optimistic-CAPS Nontraditional	.85	2.35	.61	1	3	1,395
Pessimistic	.71	2.69	.51	1	3	1,381
CAPS Capability	.84	2.83	.61	1	4	1,398
CAPS Resources	.83	2.92	.60	1	4	1,406

Note: CAPS = Chicago Alternative Policing Strategy

With Others measures the degree to which employees feel that their jobs require them to work cooperatively with other people. Participants scored each of the job dimension questions on a scale of 1 (strongly disagree) to 5 (strongly agree), which rated how closely each item correctly described their current job assignments.

Job Satisfaction and Participatory Management. Four scales examined officers' job satisfaction: (a) Individual Growth Need measures employees' needs for opportunities to be creative, independent, and imaginative in their work; (b) Job Involvement measures the extent to which employees feel that their job is enjoyable; (c) Extraorganizational Mobility measures employees' perceptions of how difficult it would be for them to leave their jobs; and (d) Organizational Policy and Practice measures employees' overall satisfaction with the organization and its management staff.

Respondents scored each of the questions on individual growth need on a scale of 1 (very undesirable) to 5 (very desirable), which rated how much they would like certain characteristics to be present in their current jobs. They scored each of the questions pertaining to job involvement, mobility, and policy and practice on a scale of 1 (strongly disagree) to 5 (strongly agree), which rated their agreement with items that described their attitudes and feelings toward work and management.

A separate scale measured participatory management, that is, employees' perceptions about the degree of influence they have over management decisions and job changes. Respondents also scored these questions on a scale of 1 (strongly disagree) to 5 (strongly agree).

CAPS-related Measures. Six scales were constructed to explore how police officers felt about community policing and the CAPS program: (a) Orientation Toward Community Policing measures officers' attitudes regarding contact with the community to jointly solve neighborhood problems; (b) Optimistic about CAPS–Traditional Measures officers' perceptions concerning the likelihood that CAPS will lead to favorable changes with respect to traditional police services; (c) Opti-

Table 18.2
Background Characteristics of Wave 1 Prototype Respondents

Characteristic	Percentage
District assignment	
Austin	18
Beverly	18
Englewood	23
Marquette Park	19
Rogers Park	21
Rank	
Patrol officer	86
Sergeant	11
Lieutenant	3
Captain or above	>1
Shift	
First shift	12
Second shift	22
Third shift	31
Rotating shift	35
Formal education	
High school graduate or GED	13
Some technical school, but did not graduate	2
Technical school graduate	2
Some college, but did not graduate	44
Junior college graduate	9
College graduate	16
Some graduate courses	8
Graduate degree	6
Gender	
Male	79
Female	21
Marital status	
Married	57
Married, but living alone	4
Unmarried	33
Unmarried, but living together	6
Current assignment	
Bureau of Operational Services	83
Bureau of Investigations	1
Bureau of Administrative Services	3
Bureau of Technical Services	4
Bureau of Staff Services	9
Race	
African American	26
Hispanic	9
White	63
Other	2

Note: N = 1,405. Category percentages may not total 100 due to rounding. GED = general equivalency diploma.

mistic About CAPS-Nontraditional measures officers' perceptions concerning the likelihood that CAPS will lead to favorable changes with respect to nontraditional services; (d) Pessimistic About CAPS measures officers' perceptions concerning the likelihood that CAPS will lead to unfavorable changes in police authority and autonomy; (e) CAPS Capability measures officers' perceptions concerning their ability to perform CAPS-related activities; and (f) CAPS Resources measures officers' attitudes regarding the allocation of police resources toward CAPS-related activities and services.

Survey Participants. A total of 1,405 completed surveys were collected during 22 of the 24 orientation training sessions. As shown in table 18.2, nearly 80% of the officers were male; 63% were White, 26% were African American, and slightly under 10% were Hispanic. The majority of respondents (57%) were married, and their ages ranged from 21 to 63 years with an average of 38 years. Most of the respondents (69%) had a 4-year college degree, had attended some college, or had graduated from junior college; 14% had a graduate degree or had taken some graduate courses.

The vast majority of police officers were assigned to the Bureau of Operational Services (83%). On average, officers had been in their current assignments for 8 years, with CPD for 12 years, and had joined the department when they were 27 years old. Officers' ages when they joined the department ranged from 19 to 55 years old. More than 85% of the respondents were patrol officers. Slightly more than one third were on a rotating shift, whereas slightly less than one third were on the third shift. Respondents were fairly evenly distributed among the five prototype districts, with about 20% participating from each.

Results

How Do Police Feel About Their Jobs?

Job Dimensions. The 5-point scale means ranged from 3.93 to 3.12. Officers rated their jobs highest with respect to working with others and lowest with respect to peer/supervisor feedback and task identity. For example, high percentages of officers either agreed or strongly agreed that their jobs required them to work closely (79%) and cooperatively (69%) with others. Considerably lower percentages of respondents either agreed or strongly agreed that their supervisors let them know how well they are performing (34%) and that their jobs provided them with a chance to complete all the tasks they had started (31%).

Officers rated the remaining job dimensions—job autonomy, skill variety, and job feedback—toward the upper limit of the middle (i.e., neutral) range of score values, from 3.52 to 3.64. More than one half of the participants either agreed or strongly agreed that their jobs gave them a lot of opportunities for independence and freedom in how they did their work (52%) and that their jobs provided them with information about their performance (56%). More than one third either agreed or strongly agreed that their jobs required them to use a number of complex and high-level skills (35%).

Job Satisfaction and Participatory Management. Most of the officers wanted their jobs to include the following experiences, which were rated either desirable or very desirable by the percentages of officers shown after each job characteristic: stimulating and challenging work (86%), a chance to exercise independent thought and action (87%), opportunities to learn new things (89%), opportunities to be creative and imaginative (86%), opportunities for personal growth and development (86%), and a sense of worthwhile accomplishment (89%).

The averages for extraorganizational mobility and job involvement were much higher than those for organizational policy and practices and participatory management. Nearly 60% of the respondents either agreed or strongly agreed with the statement that "staying with the police department is as much a necessity as a desire" and nearly 50% either agreed or strongly agreed with the statement that "it would be very hard for me to leave the department now even if I wanted to." In terms of job involvement, high percentages of officers either agreed or strongly agreed that they liked very much both the kind of work that they did (80%) and their fellow employees (74%), and that they enjoyed nearly all the things that they did on their jobs (66%). However, much lower percentages of officers either agreed or strongly agreed that they were personally involved with their jobs (41 %) or that the major or satisfaction in their lives came from their jobs (18%).

Although half or more of the officers either agreed or strongly agreed that the city's police department is a good organization to work for (58%) and that the department is one of the best in the country (50%), only 23 % either agreed or strongly agreed that management treats employees very well (less than 1% strongly agreed with this item) and that the department is open to suggestions for change, and only 6% had confidence that command staff pick the most qualified candidates for jobs. (The organizational policy and practice scale consisted of these items.) In relation to participatory management, the following percentages of officers either agreed or strongly agreed with these statements: "I have much say and influence over what goes on in regard to my job" (35%), "It is easy for me to communicate my ideas to management" (28%), and "My supervisor frequently seeks my opinion when a problem comes up involving my job environment" (24%).

How Do the Police Feel About CAPS?

Orientation Toward Community Policing. Participants rated each of the statements concerning police work and law enforcement in Chicago on a scale from 1 (strongly disagree) to 5 (strongly agree). Overall, officers' responses were neutral on this scale (M = 3.4). A large majority of them either agreed or strongly agreed that "the prevention of crime is the joint responsibility of the community and the police" (87%), "police officers should work with citizens to try and solve problems on their beat" (73%), and "assisting citizens can be as important as enforcing the law" (70%). However, much lower percentages either agreed or strongly agreed that "an officer on foot patrol can learn more about neighborhood problems than can an officer in a patrol car" (36%) and "police officers should try to solve noncrime problems in their beat" (28%).

Differences on this scale were analyzed by race (African American, Hispanic, White),

rank (patrol officers vs. sergeants and above), gender (men vs. women), and age (20s, 30s, 40s, and 50s+). African Americans scored higher than Hispanics and Whites (p≤.05), and Hispanics scored higher than Whites (p.≤05); higher-ranking officers scored higher than patrol officers (p≤.05); officers age 50 and over scored higher than officers in their 40s, 30s, and 20s (p≤.05); and officers in their 40s scored higher than officers in their 20s and 30s (p≤.05).

Optimistic About CAPS-traditional. Respondents scored these questions on a scale from 1 (less likely) to 3 (more likely) to rate the likelihood that a variety of positive changes in traditional police services would occur after CAPS was implemented. Overall, their average response was no change (M = 2.0). Approximately one fourth of the officers believed that more arrests, better responses to calls for police service, and a reduction in crime rates were more likely to occur after CAPS, whereas one third believed that expanded police capability, more effective use of resources, and a more balanced deployment of officers would be more likely to occur after CAPS.

Female respondents were more optimistic about traditional services occurring after CAPS (p≤.05); African Americans were more optimistic than Hispanics and Whites (p≤.05), and Hispanics were more optimistic than Whites (p≤.05); and older officers (age 50 and over) were more optimistic than officers in their 30s and 20s (p≤.05), and officers in their 40s were more optimistic than officers in their 20s (p≤.05).

Optimistic About CAPS-nontraditional. Respondents scored these questions on the same 3-point scale they used with optimism about CAPS-traditional. Overall, officers were only slightly more optimistic about nontraditional changes taking place after CAPS is implemented (M = 2.3). More than 60% believed that better police-community relations were more likely after CAPS; 48% and 47%, respectively, believed that a greater resolution of neighborhood problems and a more effective use of crime information were more likely after CAPS; and a little over 40% believed that a greater willingness of citizens to cooperate with the police was more likely after CAPS; but only 29% believed that better police relations with minorities were more likely after CAPS.

African American officers were more optimistic than White and Hispanic officers (p≤.05); sergeants and above were more optimistic than patrol officers (p≤.05); older officers (age 50 and over) were more optimistic than officers in their 40s, 30s, and 20s (p≤.05), and officers in their 40s were more optimistic than officers in their 20s and 30s (p≤.05).

Pessimistic About CAPS. Respondents scored these questions on the same 3-point scale that they used with the optimism about CAPS scales. On this scale, however, officers rated the likelihood that negative changes would occur after CAPS. The average scale score was 2.6, which indicated that they were quite pessimistic about such changes. Over 70% believed that community groups would place more unreasonable demands on police (73%) and that there would be greater citizen demands placed on police resources (72%) after CAPS. High percentages of participants also believed that greater burdens on police to solve all community problems (65%) and blurred boundaries between police and citizen authority (51%) were more likely to occur after CAPS. On this scale, a difference was found on only one of the subgroup variables: Whites and Hispanics were more pessimistic than African Americans (p≤.05).

CAPS Capability. Participants scored each of these questions on a scale of 1 (very unqualified) to 4 (very qualified) to rate their own ability to perform CAPS-related activities. Overall, officers felt fairly qualified to engage in such tasks (M = 2.7). At least 7 out of 10 respondents felt either qualified or very qualified to identify community problems (84%) and to develop (71%) and evaluate (77%) solutions to those problems. However, only 42% felt either qualified or very qualified to use the CAPS model to analyze problems.

African Americans felt more capable than Hispanics and Whites (p≤.05); higher ranking officers felt more capable than did patrol officers (p≤.05); and officers in the 50-and-

over age category felt more capable than did officers in their 20s and 30s (p≤.05).

CAPS Resources. Respondents scored these questions on a scale from 1 (none) to 4 (a large amount) to rate their opinions regarding the amount of resources that the department should commit to CAPS-related police activities. On average, officers felt that a moderate amount of resources should be devoted to such activities (M = 2.9). The following percentages of participants indicated that a large amount of resources should be committed to these CAPS-related activities: coordinating with other agencies to improve the quality of life in the city (43%), explaining crime prevention techniques to citizens (42%), getting to know juveniles (32%), working with citizen groups to resolve local problems (32%), understanding problems of minority groups (30%), researching and solving problems (30%), marketing police services to the public (22%), handling special events (8%), and patrolling on foot in neighborhoods (7%).

Female respondents were more likely than male respondents to want large amounts of resources devoted to CAPS (p≤.05); African Americans were more likely than Hispanics and Whites (p≤.05); and Hispanics were more likely than Whites to want large amounts of resources devoted to CAPS (p≤.05).

Summary and Conclusions

The current survey examined the views of police officers before CAPS was implemented in the prototype districts. Findings indicated that most respondents were looking for a job that allowed them to exercise independent thought and action, to be creative and imaginative, and to learn about new things. However, less than one half of those surveyed felt deep personal involvement in their present positions. Approximately one half of the officers reported that their jobs actually gave them opportunities for independence and control over how they did their work. Less than one third thought that the structure of their jobs enabled them to really see work through to its completion. Only about one quarter agreed that they had any influence over their jobs, that their supervisors sought their opinions, that management treated its employees well, and that they could easily communicate ideas to management. Only about one third felt that their supervisors let them know how well they were performing, and even less felt that the department was open to change.

Results also indicated that officers were very ambivalent about community policing in Chicago. At the outset, officers expressed only moderate enthusiasm for involving themselves in solving noncrime problems. They were not very keen on adopting new tactics such as foot patrol or on marketing their new services to the public. They were willing to devote department resources to community policing, but only in moderate amounts. They did not think that the program would have any marked impact on the crime rate or their ability to make arrests, or that it would improve their relationship with racial minorities. They were clearly concerned about the impact of community policing on the department's autonomy and on the nature and volume of work that would result from CAPS.

Finally, analyses of gender, race, age, and rank differences showed consistent trends in respondents' attitudes toward CAPS. In general, minority officers (especially African Americans), older officers, and higher-ranking officers expressed more favorable attitudes toward community policing in Chicago. They were more inclined to endorse CAPS-related police activities; they were more optimistic that CAPS would lead to positive changes in both traditional and nontraditional police services; they also were less pessimistic about CAPS leading to negative changes in policing; and, along with most female officers, they wanted larger amounts of resources devoted to CAPS.

In conclusion, the current findings indicate that police officers in Chicago are neither unanimously in favor of community policing nor are they equally disposed toward all the elements of such programs. Hence the data suggest the importance of a department examining the attitudes and feelings of staff before implementing community policing. At the outset, such an investigation can identify potential pockets of resistance among officers and can assist the administration to shape program operations to be more palatable to line staff and their supervisors. Furthermore, it would be useful to assess officers' relationships with peers and management as well as other factors concerning job satisfaction prior to program implementation. To be successful, community policing initiatives must be compatible with the existing culture and organizational climate in a department and with the basic concerns and needs of police personnel.

References

Lurigio, Arthur J. and Dennis P. Rosenbaum. 1994. "The Impact of Community Policing on Police Personnel." Pp. 147–63 in *The Challenge of Community Policing: Testing the Promises*, edited by D. P. Rosenbaum. Thousand Oaks, CA: Sage.

McElroy, Jerome, Colleen Cosgrove, and Susan Sadd. 1993. *Community Policing:* CPOP in New York. Newbury Park, CA: Sage.

Moore, Mark. 1992. "Problem-Solving and Community Policing." Pp. 99–158 in *Modern Policing*, edited by M. Tonry and N. Morris. Chicago: University of Chicago Press.

Sadd, Susan and Randolph Grinc. 1993. Issues in Community Policing: An Evaluation of Eight Innovative Neighborhood-Oriented Policing Projects (Final Technical Report). New York: Vera Institute.

Stone, Alfred R. and Stuart M. DeLuca. 1985. *Police Administration*. New York: Wiley.

Walker, Samuel. 1992. *The Police in America*. New York: McGraw-Hill.

Wycoff, Mary Ann. 1988. "The Benefits of Community Policing: Evidence and Conjecture." Pp. 103–20 in *Community Policing: Rhetoric or Reality*, edited by J. R. Greene and S. D. Mastrofski. New York: Praeger.

Wycoff, Mary Ann and Wesley G. Skogan. 1993. Quality Policing in Madison: An Evaluation of Its Implementation and Impact (Final Technical Report). Washington, DC: The Police Foundation.

This project was supported by Grant #90-DB-CX-00 17 awarded by the Bureau of Justice Assistance, Office of Justice Programs, U.S. Department of Justice. The Assistant Attorney General, Office of Justice Programs, coordinates the activities of the following program offices and bureaus: Bureau of Justice Assistance, Bureau of Justice Statistics, National Institute of Justice, Office of Juvenile Justice and Delinquency Prevention, and the Office for Victims of Crime. Points of view or opinions contained within this document are those of the authors and do not necessarily represent the official position or policies of the U.S. Department of Justice. Send correspondence to Dr. Arthur J. Lurigio, Associate Professor, Department of Criminal Justice, Room 715 Lewis Towers, Loyola University, 820 N. Michigan Avenue, Chicago, IL 60611.

19

Toward a Practical Approach to Organizational Change

Community Policing Initiatives in Six Cities

Deborah L. Weisel

John E. Eck

Organizational change is essential for community policing to be effective. In that vein, D. Weisel and J. Eck provide an extensive review of several very important, measurable attributes and activities that are associated with organizational shift to this strategy: the motivation for the change, the political structure and dynamics, police department culture and style, and the history of the city. In a comprehensive study of six municipal police departments, the authors look at how these elements are used to encourage police officers to carry out community-policing efforts. The implications of their findings are significant, particularly as they concern the kinds of efforts that are needed to induce a uniformed officer to buy into the community-policing philosophy. As you read, consider the level of difficulty that is involved with organizational change and whether each of the major elements for change that are discussed would be easily met in your community.

There is currently widespread interest in community policing. Whether one reads the extensive literature on the subject or reviews correct practices, however, there is no single articulated form of community policing. In-stead police agencies are engaged in a diverse set of practices united by the general idea that the police and the public need to become better partners in order to control crime, disorder, and a host of other problems. Although numerous police agencies are practicing some form of community policing, little is known about the variations of community policing being practiced or the reasons for these variations, the relative impact of these variations upon the objectives being sought, or the ways in which the behaviors of police personnel are altered in order to carry out the community policing efforts. One cluster of questions that has dominated practitioner discussions on community policing is how does one change an organization in order to get personnel to carry out the prescribed activities? Practitioners have been searching for guidance on the mechanisms useful for putting a particular form of community policing into place.

This chapter discusses one aspect from the findings of a comprehensive study of community policing that began with an extensive review to identify common measurable attributes and activities thought to be associated with community policing. These attributes were used to frame a study of community policing in six municipal agencies. Detailed information was collected on the actual practice of particular styles of community policing in Las Vegas, Nevada; Edmonton, Alberta, Philadelphia; Santa Barbara, California; Savannah, Georgia; and Newport News, Virginia. Although the variations cannot be fully addressed within the confines of this chapter—more fitting instead for the lengthier and descriptive case studies being developed as a primary product of this research—community policing initiatives varied among these sites. Some of the factors observed to be relevant in shaping the form of a city's community policing initiative included the precipitating motivation for community policing, such as tenuous race relations and potential for racial conflict; the political structure and dynamics of the city including the relationship between elections and crime rates; police organizational culture and style including leadership, openness, and degree of hierarchical structure; and the history of the city, including its approach to service delivery, among other factors.

This chapter looks primarily at the activities that police agencies used to enjoin, cajole, or direct uniformed police officers to carry out community policing efforts. These activities ranged from strategic planning that involved line officers, training efforts, and changes in promotional practices and performance evaluation. The chapter evaluates the impact of these various activities upon the outlook of line officers toward the future of community policing in their agency.

Research Methods

The agencies selected for study were all self-defined as engaged in some form or variation of community policing. As detailed later, these forms of community policing varied enormously and it should be emphasized here that there is no single model of community policing being identified, advocated, or studied. Consequently, a cross-site comparison of these highly variable programs represented a major research challenge. The primary method of research used was a case study method, employing experienced mid-ranking police practitioners teamed with researchers to collect background, programmatic, and other information. A comprehensive protocol was developed to ensure standardization of data collection across sites. The case study collection of extant documentation and interviews with key individuals was supplemented by a survey of line officers. The survey was intended to validate much of the qualitative data collected through other methods and to inform the cross-site analysis. The instrument was administered to all line personnel in Newport News, Santa Barbara, and Savannah (with response rates ranging form 68% to 86%) while a random sample of officers in Philadelphia, Edmonton, and Las Vegas were surveyed. Response rated for the identified samples ranged from 65% to 74%. Overall, a 75% response rate was achieved with a total of 866 surveys completed. Although attempts were made to quantify much of the data for the cross-site analysis, it should be noted that the richest findings from this study include both obser-

vations and impressions of the on-site researchers. Standardized case study protocols and other means do not obviate these impressions, which, although a product of a single point in time [of] data collection effort, represent years of accumulated experience in the field of community policing. Thus, throughout this chapter, much emphasis is placed upon both the line officer survey and the opinions of researchers regarding the relative merit of important issues in each site.

Specifically, the study documented a number of community policing issues including how each of the agencies defined community policing, identifying any changes in activities and responsibilities for patrol officers; determined the stimulus for the implementation of the effort; and developed a full description of the organizational mechanisms used to support or encourage community policing within and external to the organization. Data were collected through several methods including review of supporting documentation and direct interviews of patrol officers and supervisors engaged in community policing, police managers, and police executives as well as a limited number of city officials and community members.

One important element of the cross-site evaluation looked at the extent to which police agencies were able to implement their efforts successfully as reflected by the attitudes of each agency's patrol officers toward community policing. The research adopted a basic assumption that community policing involves an activity or embodies a philosophy of policing that, regardless of the form of the community policing effort, is reflected at the level of the line officer. In other words, most police agencies dedicated to community policing are primarily interested in modifying the way in which their primary point of contact with the public—patrol officers—conducts their business with citizens. This change is consistent with what Skolnick and Bayley (1988) identify as a "change in the practices but not the objectives of policing" (p. 90). The resultant behavioral change could range from addressing problems that officers or citizens identify, the way or form in which officers interact with citizens (such as through foot patrols or citizen reporting stations), or other patrol officer activities. It should be acknowledged that most community policing initiatives clearly are not defined by how officers view the approach. But many community policing efforts are defined de facto by the change in the conduct of most officers as reflected by their behaviors and activities. In this sense, officer behavior might be identified as the intermediate product while the ultimate product might be citizen attitudes to police, crime reduction, fear reduction, or other varied objectives, depending upon the organizational goals. Thus research about community policing efforts might suggest the following inquiries:

- What proportion of an officer's time is uncommitted? How are officers spending their uncommitted time that is not involved in answering calls for service? Where are officers spending this time?

- How do officers follow up on calls for service? Are calls handled as isolate incidents?

- How interactive are officers with members of the community? In what ways does the interaction occur—through meetings, door-to-door contacts, while on foot patrol, or in other ways?

- How interactive are officers with other agencies? How does this interaction occur?

- How are officers identifying and resolving crime, disorder, or fear issues with which they must deal?

In the context of this line of inquiry, a great many of the community policing implementation efforts of police agencies were specifically directed toward improving the skills and abilities of officers to carry out the specific community policing efforts desired. For example, many departments used formal mechanisms such as training, participative management, and modifications of performance evaluation and promotional structure in order to change or modify officer behavior. To what extent do these various implementation activities or tools have an impact on the acceptance by officers of the community policing initiative? This is a major research question that this chapter addresses.

Based on the assumption of officer behavior as the intermediate product of community policing (and because of research resource constraints), this research is absent any structured insight into the perceptions of citizens. If community policing behavior is indeed reflected primarily by officer actions, the absence of citizens input is not critical. It is only when behavioral actions are not sought as part of the process that the absence of citizen input becomes critical. It should be noted that one police agency in this study achieves its community policing goals primarily through the interaction of patrol captains with community residents. This department nonetheless has a valid claim that it is engaged in community policing. Citizens may feel safer, have greater access to police resources, and have other positive feelings that one might anticipate with a line officer-based community policing initiative. Nonetheless, because of the absence of line officer involvement, little can be said about the impact of such a program based on the research methods used in this study. This is a limitation of the study.

Overview of Study Sites

The six cities and their police departments in the study varied dramatically in their approach to community policing, a variance most apparent in the nomenclature used in each agency. The Santa Barbara Police Department primarily uses a special unit although virtually all of the agency' sworn and nonsworn personnel are engaged in the department's COPS (community-oriented problem solving) effort. The Metropolitan Las Vegas Police Department also uses a special unit known as Line Solution Policing, but the form looks significantly different from Santa Barbara's. The units take sole responsibility for problem-solving activities.

The police departments of Savannah (with its COP/POP initiative) and Newport News (with its Neighborhood Oriented Policing effort) developed generalist approaches to community policing based on a decentralization of dedicated police beats throughout each city. The community policing approach of the Edmonton, Alberta, Police Service is also decentralized, involving the development of service centers throughout the city. A different approach is embodied by Philadelphia, which conducts its community policing effort primarily at the captain level.

The cities varied in terms of geographic location, including one international city, Edmonton, Alberta, Canada, and five diverse U.S. cities. The cities included a variety of sizes, although three were clearly smaller cities with less than 200,000 population, and the remaining three ranged from more than half a million residents to three times that number.

The number of personnel varied widely, ranging from Philadelphia's 7,354 personnel to Santa Barbara's 228. The ration of sworn personnel to population also indicated the variation among the agencies. As indicated in table 19.1, the number of sworn personnel per 1,000 population ranged from Philadelphia's 4.4 to the 1.6 mark of Santa Barbara, Newport News, and Las Vegas. (The ratio was an important issue for community policing, for most agencies raised the issue of having an insufficient number of personnel to carry out the desired community policing tasks. These issues were as evident in departments with higher officer-to-citizen ratios as in departments with much lower ratios.)

Personnel varied in other ways. The ethnic composition of all sworn personnel in agencies ranged from Savannah's 38% representing persons of color to the 13% persons of color composition of the Las Vegas agency. (Persons of color in the departments were underrepresentative of the population in every city studied, although no data was

available for Edmonton.) Regarding educational level of officers, in Santa Barbara, 95% of all patrol officers reported having more than a high school diploma (43% had a college degree or more education) while in Philadelphia, 45% of patrol officers having only a high school diploma. The educational level of the other four agencies fell within these endpoints.

Santa Barbara

Santa Barbara is a relatively sleepy but picturesque city of less than 100,000 formal residents, overlooking the Pacific Ocean. Some 100 miles north of Los Angeles and 250 miles south of San Francisco, the community is sheltered from the urban woes that have challenged its larger neighbors. The city has a reputation for being an enclave to the rich and famous, although its largely working-class population struggles with a high cost of living (particularly for real estate) and problems related to incorporating and serving a large and unofficial immigrant population. Officially, the city's population consists of undocumented Mexicans, which contributes to latent ethnic tensions and significant language barriers with which the police department's mostly Caucasian force must often struggle.

The city's police department is led by the ebullient Richard Breza, a product of the city's own police force. Since taking the helm as chief in 1987, Breza, guided by a philosophical commitment to the idea of problem solving and community interaction, has molded the organization of 138 sworn personnel into an agency that is more integrated

Table 19.1
Demographic Characteristics of Study Cities

	Savannah	Philadelphia	Las Vegas	Edmonton	Newport News	Santa Barbara
City population	38,000	1,500,000	742,000	620,000	170,000	86,000
Total sworn personnel	326	6,532	1,162	1,095	263	138
Percentage of sworn personnel representing persons of color	38	26	13	N/A	17	15
Sworn personnel per 1,000 population	2.4	4.4	1.6	1.8	1.6	1.6

Source: Crime in the United States, 1990, Washington, D.C.: U.S. Department of Justice, Federal Bureau of Investigation.

in community activities, from working with small business groups to the local housing agency and a host of other city agencies.

The department's approach to community of policing includes the use of a team of six officers, known as beat coordinators, who focus their attention on specific problems within the six geographic beats that constitute the city. The beat coordinators are supplemented by other patrol officers and special units (such as the bicycle patrol) that alternately provide resources to the beat coordinators or conduct their own problem-solving efforts, using the beat coordinator for guidance and coordination. The beat coordinators are organizationally located within the department's Patrol Division in order to coordinate information and cooperation better among the beat coordinators and other patrol officers. Despite their existence as a special unit, the beat coordinators routinely handle calls for service for a portion of their shift.

Las Vegas

In stark contrast to Santa Barbara, Las Vegas is a town that never sleeps. The gambling industry, the city's economic foundation operates around the clock. But few of the city's crime problems are related to gambling, at least partially because the casinos maintain strict security systems and take steps to ensure the perceived and actual safety of their patrons.

The strong racial tension in Las Vegas between the city's black and white populations is palpable. During the aftermath of the Rodney King incident in Los Angeles, the city of Las Vegas was poised for massive protests and civil disorder among the minority residents. Indeed a period of civil disorder with rioting, fires, and attendant violence occurred in the spring of 1992. The tensions exist within a large and growing metropolitan area. With nearly three quarters of a million in population, the city is located in one of the fastest growing metropolitan areas in the United States, expanding by approximately 5,000 persons per month.

Policing in the metropolitan Las Vegas area occurs under a political umbrella. The agency is headed by an elected sheriff, who is reportedly retiring prior to the next election, and three political command-level appointees, who serve at the pleasure of the sheriff. The consolidated city-county jurisdiction provides a huge geographic service area; one can drive 2 hours down major highways and still be within the confines of the agency's service area.

The Las Vegas Police Department has also used a relatively decentralized special unit approach in its community policing effort. The department's Line Solution Policing (LSP) effort provides teams of officers to police area commands throughout the city who have the latitude to engage in proactive activities to address specific community problems—especially those related to gangs, drugs, and burglaries. The units were suspended in mid-1993 in an effort to expand the approach to all patrol officers within the agency. This change occurred following the conclusion of on-site data collection.

Savannah

The historic Spanish-moss swathed city of Savannah is nestled on the banks of the Savannah River near its mouth at the Atlantic Ocean. The narrow streets and numerous public squares as laid out by the city's founder, James Oglethorpe, in 1733 constitute the core of one of the nation's largest historic districts. Although tourism is not the city's major industry, it is a growing and important part of the local economy.

The city has been troubled by severe crime problems in recent years, including a high rate of violent crime and concomitant fear among the city's residents and businesses, particularly for the possibility of its adverse impact upon tourism. The city is predominately black (51%) with little other ethnic diversity, but most political power positions appear to be held by whites. The police department has made great efforts to include black representation; 36% of the department's personnel are black and blacks appear well represented throughout the command structure.

Ethnic tensions did not directly motivate Savannah's community policing initiative. It was driven instead by political sensitivity to the growing violent crime problem, which crested in 1991. The problem threatened the reelection and subsequently resulted in the loss of the mayor's seat by a 20-year incumbent. The political instability during the election period provided a forum for the city's manager and sitting mayor, in league with the chief of police, to craft and fund a full-fledged community policing effort. The department previously had implemented elements of such a community policing effort; the election-motivated initiative provided teeth and funding to buoy the previously ad hoc effort.

The Savannah Police Department's approach to community policing is based upon the decentralization of patrol activities to each of four precincts in a geographic area commanded by a captain. Each captain is responsible for using resources and encouraging officers to engage in problem-solving efforts. There appear to be some differences in the level in which problem-solving or community involvement activities occur within the city, based upon competing demands (such as heavy call loads) in each precinct and the personal approach of the patrol captain in carrying out the mandate in his area command. Savannah's most visible implementation activity in fulfilling the community policing initiative is a commitment to formal training of all personnel, civilian and sworn. Fully 95% of officer survey respondents indicated they had received formal training, and a third of those had received more than 17 hours of training in Community Oriented Policing/Problem Oriented Policing (COP/POP). This was significantly more training than occurred in any other agency.

Newport News

The approach to community policing in Newport News is similar to that of Savannah, for the department is utilizing generalist officers assigned to relatively fixed beats. The department has divided the city into geographic areas based upon workload factors; officers are assigned to permanent beats. Unlike Savannah, the patrol areas are much smaller and are designed to increase an officer's knowledge and familiarity with an area. Although the department has struggled with issues related to beat integrity—particularly in terms of limiting cross-dispatching of offi-

cers to other beats—additional resources were being sought in 1993 in order to alleviate the resource problem. In addition to the beat reconfiguration, patrol lieutenants (rather than captains) were given 24-hour responsibility for patrol areas. The city consists of two geographically distinct patrol divisions dividing the 22-mile-long city; a main headquarters and a patrol station serve as the focus of patrol functions for the department. In addition, efforts were being made to develop several community storefronts to serve citizens directly.

Newport News is a blue-collar city dominated by the shipbuilding industry and strongly influenced by the military installations in the adjacent city of Norfolk. Located on a peninsula jutting out into the southern end of the Chesapeake Bay of Virginia, Newport News is part of a huge metropolitan area of more than 1.4 million people.

Newport News was an interesting city for inclusion in this study because it represented something of an anomaly among community policing agencies. The department first experimented with and adopted the concept of problem-oriented policing in the mid-1980s under the leadership of its previous chief of police. The agency achieved something of a national reputation for its approach and became a model for departments implementing problem solving. Despite its perceived success, however, the approach examined in this study was the department's newer Neighborhood Oriented Policing effort, circa mid-1992. Although the department had not abandoned its problem-oriented policing approach, the agency's current chief, Jay Care, had envisioned the department's problem solving effort as being carried out at a highly decentralized level in order to provide greater and more systematic interaction between police officers and area residents. Care, chief since 1986, believes the decentralized approach will also enable officers to become more familiar with particular problems that cause citizens concern in their neighborhoods. The reconstituted Neighborhood Oriented Policing (NOP) effort in Newport News represented the "youngest" of the community policing initiatives studied.

Edmonton

More than 600,000 citizens live in Edmonton, the capital city of the province of Alberta in western Canada. Located roughly due north of Missoula, Montana, Edmonton is a city whose economy is built upon the oil and petrochemical industries and is sometimes referred to as the Houston of Canada. Following a boom period in the late 1970s and early 1980s, Edmonton suffered an economic slump with the decline of the oil business. The resultant financial pressure within the city resulted in major belt tightening in the city's police agency and contributed to pay cuts and a freeze on hiring.

By the early 1990s, restricted police growth had become incompatible with the city's burgeoning calls for service. The agency developed a unique form of community policing in order to get a handle on the excessive number of calls for police service that had burdened the agency and improve operating efficiency. The initiative was also developed as a means to being police officers closer to the community and to address specific community problems. The department created customer service centers scattered throughout the jurisdiction, which were designed to encourage citizen reporting as well as increase interaction with the police.

This service-oriented approach to citizens occurred at the behest of the Edmonton Police Commission, a policy-making group appointed by the mayor to provide direction to the police. The board used its major policy-making role—hiring the police department's chief—as a means to direct the department's future specifically toward community policing.

Philadelphia

Philadelphia is a traditional East Coast city and, like many of its sister cities, it was suffering from economic woes during the 1980s. Economic difficulties caused the police force to shrink dramatically during the period although the city still maintains a 4.4 officer per 1,000 population ratio, a staffing reinforced by the strong police union, the deep political roots of the police agency, and a steeply vertical organizational structure. The department is run by a commissioner of police who is appointed and serves at the pleasure of the city's mayor. There is no city manager form of government here; the elected mayor operates all of city government and key appointees serve at his will.

Philadelphia's community policing effort can be traced to a destructive bombing related to the urban cult group MOVE in 1985 that destroyed two city blocks and caused major conflict between the citizens and police. Commissioner Kevin Tucker, formerly of the Secret Service, was appointed as a reform commissioner. Serving from 1986 to 1988, Tucker was the first and only outside police commissioner ever to serve in that position.

The form of community policing in Philadelphia occurs primarily under the direction of police captains who command the dozens of patrol districts within the jurisdiction. In addition to patrol officers and detectives, each captain supervises what is known as Five Squad, consisting of specialized officers who deal with community problems. Within a district, the Five Squad includes Community Relations, Victims Assistance, Crime Prevention, Sanitation, and abandoned auto officers—each with specialized responsibilities and assigned to deal with common community problems. Regular patrol officers and detectives have not yet been integrated into community policing. However, the community policing effort is also structured to utilize Police District Advisory Panels, citizens groups that meet regularly and provide input to the district captains. The panels were created under Tucker and strengthened under Commissioner Willie Williams, who succeeded Tucker and served as commissioner until taking the helm of the Los Angeles Police Department.

Convergence and Variation

Six diverse cities and six unique approaches to loosely clustered objectives related to enhancing crime prevention, increasing police accountability, and coproduction of public safety produced community policing initiatives with wide variation but with some noteworthy issues of convergence. Based primarily upon the perceptions of researchers, the following issues emerged.

Catalyst. All six departments developed and implemented their community policing efforts for different but specific reasons. Some of the stimuli for community policing initiatives were apparent and reinforced through subsequent data collection; others were fleeting and desultory, reflecting only perceptions of researchers on site. Nonetheless, the perceived stimulus or precipitating event for implementation ranged from new leadership and adapting an agency for organizational efficiency to advancement of a philosophical commitment to the approach as an effective system for delivery of services to an effort to resolve potential or existing racial conflict within the community. The latter theme simmered in each agency to varying degrees. Each city, from Edmonton with its Aboriginal (equivalent to the United States' Native American) population to Santa Barbara with its influx of Latino immigrants to more traditional problems such as the relative isolation of blacks in Newport News, Savannah, Las Vegas, and Philadelphia, wrestled with the issues of developing police departments whose ethnic composition would be reflective of the community being policed; ensuring that patrol officers exhibited cultural sensitivity to ethnic groups; securing full access to police services for all populations; and addressing the potential for violence or disorder between ethnic communities and the police.

Regardless of the catalyst, the presence of a catalyst and the variation among cities suggests that different approaches to community policing efforts might be developed in order to address the varying objectives implicated by the variation in the catalyst. For example, a community policing effort designed to ease racial tension might look quite different from a community policing effort designed to reduce violent crime.

History. The departments in this study faced a set of organizational options defined by political and other systemic structures within their cities. Chief executives serving at the will of the mayor or publicly elected faced an entirely different set of constraints than those serving appointments under a council-manager form of government. At-large elections of city council members posed different political concerns than occurred in cities with single member districts whose representatives were in a position to lobby and demand additional resources for certain districts. Indeed, several cities anticipated transitions from at-large elections to single member elections in the future, all suggesting that such a move might have significant implications for their deployment of resources.

In several of the cities, an element of decision making about community policing was imposed on the department from outside. In Edmonton, the city's police commission formally tasked the department with implementing community policing; in Savannah an election-oriented mayor and his city manager pushed for and funded the city's COP/POP effort; and in Newport News, a decision to accept a federal grant kicked off efforts to implement the original POP efforts. These measures appear to have created a certain amount of demand or legitimacy for a concept that was already being advocated by leaders within the agencies.

It is important to note that the agencies were at different points in their evolution of community policing. This temporal dimension was not just chronological; some agencies with fewer years of experience appeared to be "further along" in their evolution than did others. But these agencies were "headed" different places to achieve different goals under varied circumstances. Most acknowledged that fully implementing a community policing initiative (whether the initiative as constituted as a program, philosophy, or a hybrid variation) takes a long period of time. However, almost all of the agencies had previous experience with concepts related in form to community policing; citizen liaison groups; park, walk and talk activities; Neighborhood Watch meetings; foot patrols; storefronts; bike patrol units; and other activities. For many of the agencies, adopting community policing meant integrating these and additional activities beyond special units, or establishing procedures to ensure that the activities would not terminate based upon political whim or funding constraints. Because of this evolving nature of community policing, one difficult dimension of the research was identifying the starting point of an agency's community policing effort. Indeed, based on the survey, officers within an agency were seldom in agreement on when their department"s community policing effort actually began.

Leadership. Data collection efforts revealed a wide variation in the amount and type of leadership and the intensity with which such leadership was used to promulgate community policing efforts. For example, the chief of police in Santa Barbara routinely and consistently reiterated the messages of community policing, and officers, even those at patrol level who may be distant from directives of the chief executive, left no doubt that the vision touted by the chief was well understood. In other agencies, the chief executives routinely incorporated the language of community policing into public statements, which were not of the depth to consistently reach to the troops. Several of these agencies had de facto community policing leaders at mid or upper ranks who assumed responsibility for pushing the concept of community policing within the agency. One agency even informally designated its mid-ranking leader as the "Community Policing Czar."

Implementation Activities

Given the wide variety of community policing efforts implemented, the variation in city size and location, and other important factors, it is not surprising that the police departments used a wide variety of strategies in order to implement community policing.

None of the agencies were directly involved in formal decentralization by flattening their organizations, although there were some efforts to increase accountability and responsibility at ranks deeper within [the] agencies. In all of the agencies, there was a heavy emphasis placed upon establishing geographic responsibility and accountability to police officers, establishing relatively permanent shifts and beats for personnel assignments, and limiting cross-dispatching of officers away from assigned areas—all within the general rubric of increasing an officers's familiarity with residents and knowledge of conditions and problems within specific areas.

Overall, there appeared to be only slight modifications in recruitment and selection practices as methods to increase hires of officers oriented toward community policing. Often these practices were informal and difficult to document. For example, in both Santa Barbara and Savannah, the chief of police routinely interviews all new police recruits. The interview provides an opportunity for department leaders to assist in selecting the "type" of officers who will fit in the direction the organization is headed. Many of the agencies had an increase in hires of college-educated officers and officers who were locally based or had some familiarity and connection with the local area.

Departments used various forms of internal communication to get the word out about the agency's community policing efforts. In Savannah, the agency's problem-solving committee included representatives from all the patrol areas in order to facilitate the dissemination of information. In Santa Barbara, white boards featuring efforts of the beat coordinators were prominently displayed in the patrol roll call room and beat coordinators routinely attended roll call to update other patrol officers about problem-solving efforts.

Across all six agencies, the most pervasive attention was given to four organizational approaches to getting community policing initiatives into action by altering or reinforcing officer behavior. These organizational approaches included:

- Using participative management styles, including seeking input from line officers into development of the community policing effort

- Changing promotional practices to reinforce officer involvement with community policing efforts

- Changing performance evaluation systems to support community policing

- Providing formal training to personnel

To one extent or another, every agency studied used these approaches to advance its community policing initiative (see table 19.2). For example, based on the officer survey, Newport News and Santa Barbara

Table 19.2

Use of Implementation Tools, Percent of Officers Responding Affirmatively

	Savannah	Philadelphia	Las Vegas	Edmonton	Newport News	Santa Barbara
Involved officers in planning	25	13	30	34	41	57
Formal training	95	35	47	79	36	66
Affect promotion potential	95	45	73	87	68	84
Community involvement in beat as a factor in performance evaluation	45	16	37	53	49	50
Number/quality of arrests as factor in performance evaluation	57	73	76	68	74	92

Note: Figures do not sum to 100 because respondents were allowed to select multiple answers.

ranked the highest for their involvement of patrol officers in planning of the community policing effort. Fully 41% and 57%, respectively, of patrol officer respondents felt officers had been included in the planning process. By contrast, only 13% of Philadelphia officers believed patrol officers had been involved in the planning process.

As mentioned previously, the Savannah Police Department extensively used formal training of its personnel in order to further community policing efforts. Some 95% of patrol officers indicated they had been trained. In contrast, 35% and 36% of respondents in Philadelphia and Newport News, respectively, felt they had received formal training in the community policing effort.

Philadelphia was also the low agency out in terms of the degree to which patrol officers felt that involvement in community policing affected promotional opportunities. This is likely a result of the positioning of the community policing effort at the captain level rather than at the patrol officer level. By contrast, however, nearly 95% of Savannah's patrol officer personnel thought COP/POP involvement affected promotional opportunities, while fully 87% and 84%, respectively, for Edmonton and Santa Barbara agreed that community policing involvement affected opportunities for promotion.

Changes in the performance evaluation systems of the departments studied did not indicate that this mechanism was widely used to reward officer involvement with the community. Indeed, arrests, technical skills (such as report preparation), and personal

appearance were the most highly rated factors used in performance evaluations in every department. Problem solving, ability to relate to citizens in the officer's beat, citizens complaints, and community involvement rated lowest as factors actually used for evaluation purposes. In table 19.2, the figures reflecting an officer's evaluation based upon his or her involvement with the community in the beat are included only to show the range of differences between agencies. For example, it is clear that community involvement of patrol officers is much less important in Philadelphia than in the other cities.

The continued emphasis on traditional performance measures (such as arrests) is noteworthy. Officers did not perceive, despite community policing efforts, that arrest had become a less important part of their work. Instead, in some agencies, other factors such as community involvement by officers may have become relatively more important. This distinction is critical, for many practitioners articulate a view that community policing suggests a lessened focus on arrests. Clearly, in the agencies in this study a reduced emphasis on arrests has not occurred or, at least, community involvement has not supplanted arrests as an evaluation criterion based upon officer perceptions.

The agencies in this study demonstrated a wide range in the use of the various implementation activities in order to encourage officer participation in community policing efforts. Because of that variation, an important question is, to what extent did the degree of departmental involvement in these various

Table 19.3
Police Perception of Future of Community Policing in Their Departments (in percent of respondents)

	Savannah	Philadelphia	Las Vegas	Edmonton	Newport News	Santa Barbara
Community policing is here to stay	68	79	80	78	73	64
Community policing fad/on way out	32	21	20	22	27	36

Columns are adjusted to 100 percent by eliminating nonresponses.

organizational activities affect the attitudes of officers? For example, did the strong commitment of the Savannah Police Department to train its personnel formally and extensively create more support for community policing? Did the involvement of officers in the planning process in Santa Barbara win officer support? Did the promotional opportunities in Edmonton, Santa Barbara, and Savannah win officer support for community policing? Or did the relatively weak involvement by Philadelphia in officer participation in planning, formal training, and use of promotional practices and evaluations negatively affect the extent of officer support in that city?

Despite the wide variation in implementation activities, the officer survey revealed remarkable consistency in the attitudes of officers toward community policing. At least two thirds of personnel (68%–80%) in each agency believed community policing, as currently practiced or in a varied form, was there to stay in their agency. (For convenience, this category of response is subsequently referred to as "positive view of community policing.") Only about 25% (20–32) felt community policing was either a fad connected with current political leadership or on its way out. (For convenience, this category is subsequently referred to as "negative view of community policing.") The positive views of the future of community policing were as strong in Philadelphia as in any other city despite the fact the Philadelphia rated lowest on all the measured implementation activities. The specific differences between departments in terms of officer perception of the future of community policing are detailed in table 19.3.

The consistency of positive views of community policing among officers—in light of

the variations in not only implementation activities but also in length of time involved with community policing, department-wide versus special unit approach, and other distinguishing programmatic characteristics— is surprising. One would anticipate that a much wider variation in officer attitudes would emerge among departments.

Why has this consistency emerged and what factors might account for the absence of variation between agencies in terms of officers' views about community policing?

One might anticipate that resistance from those with a negative outlook about the future of community policing would reflect certain demographic characteristics. The literature and popular practitioner opinion suggest that age of officers, length of service, and educational level may play a major role in their support of opposition to community policing efforts (see, e.g. Carter, Sapp, & Stephens, 1989; Skolnick & Bayley, 1988). Instead, this research shows that consistency of positive views of community policing remain regardless of years of service (partially a surrogate variable for age), education, race, sex, or experience in a fixed beat area. Positive views of community policing—disaggregated by demographic factors but consolidated across departments—fall, with only one exception, within the same percentage parameters (64%–80%) as did general support for community policing within the individual police agencies studied.

The one exception to the consistency of positive views occurs in the end points of length of service (table 19.4): Those officers with less than one year of service in policing exceeded the highest percentage of positive views in individual departments, while those

Table 19.4
View of Community Policing by Years of Service (in percent responding) *

	Less Than 1 Year	1–3 Years	4–5 Years	6–10 Years	11–15 Years	16–20 Years	20+ Years
Here to stay	86	78	71	64	69	77	63
On way out	14	22	29	36	31	23	37

officers with more than 20 years of experience in policing fell below the lowest level of positive views. This variation is consistent with the scant literature on the topic, indicating that support for community policing is higher among newer or younger officers and declines for personnel in subsequent years of service. This research shows, however, a marked about face among positive views over increasing years of service. Following a decline of positive views following the first year of service, a positive outlook for the future of community policing increases after the mid-career point of 6–10 years of service. Again, this upward trend remains consistent except for the 20+ years service group.

Other demographic variables in the study show far less variation than years of service in their impact on views of community policing. Educational level (table 19.5) showed no impact on support for community policing. Those personnel with only a high school degree were as likely to support community policing as were those with additional years of education, perhaps debunking the popular myth that officers with college educations might be more likely to embrace community policing.

Neither race nor sex was more likely to be identified with support of community policing (see table 19.6 and 19.7). White, black, and other persons of color were equally as likely to feel positive about the future of community policing in their agencies. Female and male officers shared similar attitudes; although the attitudes of females were slightly less positive, the percentage still falls within the range of positive views established earlier.

Table 19.6
View of Community Policing by Race (in percent responding) *

	White	Black	All Other Races
Here to stay	73	80	72
On way out	27	20	28

*Responses of all departments are consolidated.

Table 19.7
View of Community Policing by Sex (in percent responding) *

	Male	Female
Here to stay	75	66
On way out	25	34

*Responses of all departments are consolidated.

Table 19.5
View of Community Policing by Educational Level (in percent responding) *

	High School Only	Some College	College Degree or More
Here to stay	79	71	74
On way out	21	29	26

*Responses of all departments are consolidated

Table 19.8
View of Community Policing by Fixed Beat Assignment, in Last 4 Months (in percent responding) *

	No fixed beat	Fixed beat
Here to stay	75	72
On way out	25	28

*Responses of all departments are consolidated

The assignment of an officer to a fixed beat assignment within his or her police jurisdiction (within the last 4 months) also indicated little variation in terms of affected views of community policing. Although some practitioners speculate that a fixed beat assignment contributes to an officer's understanding of problems in the area and increases the officer's contact with citizens, this factor did not appear to affect officers' views about the future of community policing efforts.

Implications

The consistently positive views of the future of community policing within and across police agencies might lead a researcher intentioned with providing useful information to police practitioners in myriad directions. The research might reflect a general basic level of support for an apple-pie-and-baseball issue such as community policing. Perhaps a norm exists in policing, and the communication of information within the broader criminal justice field provides similar information to police officers despite the decentralized approach to policing that exists in this country. Perhaps, in fact, the concept of resistance to change is overrated and is less pervasive than widely assumed.

The research, however does beg the issue of what kind of effort it takes to get a uniformed police officer to buy into a new concept such as community policing and embrace or carry out such a change. Must a police department develop a remunerative system that financially rewards the officer for his or her support? Is educating the officer about the benefits of the effort sufficient to overcome potential resistance? Will involvement in the process of change ensure support? These are the questions that police agencies throughout the country are exploring as many agencies move toward implementation of the concept of community policing.

Despite the widespread variation in the form of community policing being implemented, questions related to implementation largely dominate many organizational efforts, particularly as related to their ability to address officer resistance to change. The concept of resistance to change frequently rears its head in community policing literature, although there is little description of such resistance in the literature on police organizational change (a noteworthy exception is Guyot, 1979). In community policing, individual-level factors such as age of personnel, tenure on job, and educational level and organizational characteristics such as police hierarchy, proliferation of rules, and centralization are often cited as factors contributing to resistance (Williams & Sloan, 1990).

In fact, this study showed that neither tenure, education, sex, race, nor assignment to a fixed beat affected the proportion of officers who felt positively about the future of community policing in their agency. An important dimension of implementation may be the existence of different types of police personnel within organizations. Goldstein (1990), for example, suggest that within police agencies, new concepts will have a range of employees including supporters, pacifists, and resisters or saboteurs.

> Many officers, whether experienced and set in their ways or new and recruited with certain expectations about policing, find it difficult to alter how they think about their jobs. If one sets out to effect changes that depend for their success on a change in attitude of all members of a police agency, the task is enormous; many people must be reached, and the effort is bound to be diluted by those who are either passive or—as is likely to be true especially of middle management—actively resist and perhaps even attempt to sabotage the efforts. Undertaken in this manner, planned change requires a long time frame, consistent and persistent efforts, facilitated by a gradual turnover in personnel. (p.173)

Goldstein's typology is consistent with those heard from the field and described in less academic prose. One police supervisor with more than two decades of experience in policing described police personnel as falling clearly into three flavor categories: vanilla, chocolate, and strawberry. (It should be noted that these "flavors" have nothing to do with skin color but are intended to represent different personality types of police officers that may be found within an organization.)

Vanilla officers are those personnel who are compliant, willing to follow direction, and, with sufficient training, will carry out to the best of their abilities the tasks that are sought by police administrators. Chocolate officers are a bit more complex: These officers need to be sold upon the merits of any organizational change. They are outspoken and may be critical until convinced of the value and logic of the change. Once convinced, however, these officers are stalwart supporters of the concept. The final flavor in the ice cream trio are the strawberry officers who are present in every organization. The strawberries are stubborn and resistant; no amount of training, inducements, direction, or other strategies will dislodge their position of resistance.

To the extent that these specific types of police officer personalities exist, these personalities contribute to the "culture" of the police agency. Sparrow, Moore, and Kennedy (1990) identify police culture as the single biggest obstacle facing those who desire to implement a new strategy of policing. But, importantly, the disaggregation of personality types as delineated suggests that there is not a single type of officer characterized by Skolnick's (1966) classic view of the "working personality" of the police officer as characterized by his or her distinctive way of looking at situations and events.

These types may affect the attitude of police officers so that, indeed, resistance may be limited to a small number of police personnel. If so, resistance may be overrated and the vast majority of officers will be willing to go along with new approaches to police work.

To the extent that different personality types such as those described occur naturally within organizations, there are implications for implementing any type of organizational change. The data in this research suggest that regardless of type and longevity of community policing effort, and the variety and intensity of implementation activity, a solid core of personnel (about 75%) believe community policing is here to stay and their behaviors are likely to reflect that perception. Indeed, one might expect to see a concurrent increase in the behaviors sought within community policing. Such an observation could be significantly informed via a pretest-posttest study of officer behavior. Without such research, we can only speculate about changes in the conduct and deportment of line personnel.

What does the research suggest about the solid core of individuals—the strawberries or saboteurs who may be obstructionists for community policing initiatives? In a practical sense, perhaps the best approach for advocates of community policing is to simply ignore or wait out the detractors and move ahead with community policing efforts. Because the relative importance of different implementation efforts in overcoming resistance to change appears minimal, an organization's time may be better spent by forging ahead. As the German physicist Max Planck observed: "A new scientific truth does not triumph by convincing its opponents and making them see the light, but rather because its opponents eventually die, and a new generation grows up that is familiar with it." The observation is consistent with the approach advocated by some management analysts as a bias for action, suggesting that the most important activity in implementing change may be simply to move forward and avoid laboriously concentrating on process variables. Indeed, the single most important activity for changing the police agency and institutionalizing community policing may be simply to move ahead and get new people on board the community policing agency.

References

Carter, D., Sapp, A. D., & Stephens, D. W. (1989). *The state of police education: Policy direction for the 21st century*. Washington, DC: Police Executive Research Forum.

Federal Bureau of Investigation. (1990). *Crime in the United States*. Washington, DC: Department of Justice.

Goldstein, H. (1990). *Problem-oriented policing*. New York: McGraw-Hill.

Guyot, D. (1979). Bending granite: Attempts to change the rank structure of American police departments. *Journal of Police Science and Administration*, 7(3), 253–384.

Skolnick, J. H. (1996). *Justice without trial*. New York: John Wiley.

Skolnick, J. H., & Bayley, D. (1988). *Community policing: Issues and practices around the world*. Washington, DC: National Institute of Justice.

Sparrow, M., Moore, M. H., & Kennedy, D. M. (1990). *Beyond 911: A new era for policing*. New York: Basic Books.

Williams, J., & Sloan, R. C. (1990). *Turning concept into practice: The Aurora Colarado story*.

East Lansing: University of Michigan, National Center for Community Policing.

Reprinted from: Deborah Lamm Weisel and John E. Eck, "Toward a Practical Approach to Organizational Change: Community Policing Initiatives in Six Cities." In *The Challenge of Community Policing: Testing and Promises*, pp. 53–72. Copyright © 1994 by Sage Publications, Inc. Reprinted by Permission. ✦

20

Citizen Perceptions of Community Policing

Are Attitudes Toward Police Important?

Michael D. Reisig
Andrew L. Giacomazzi

A fundamental belief that underlies community policing is that the police cannot unilaterally combat crime and disorder; citizens must successfully mobilize residents of neighborhoods in order to coproduce order. What if, however, the citizens are not favorably disposed toward their local police? Will this lack of positive attitudes severely undermine or totally destroy officers' efforts in community policing? Can citizen attitudes vary from one neighborhood to the next? These are important questions for any police department that is contemplating a shift to community policing. M.D. Reisig and A.L. Giacomazzi examine whether or not less-than-favorable public attitudes will preclude the effective implementation of change. The study results may surprise some readers.

Introduction

Locally-based responses to fear, disorder, and crime (e.g., crime prevention efforts and multi-level collaborative police-community partnerships) involving both citizens and the police have increased substantially over the last decade under the rubric of community policing. These responses largely have been the result of two overlapping trends: first, the realization that local police cannot successfully combat crime and related forms of disorder in the absence of citizen assistance (Cirel et al., 1977); and second, the increased availability of federal funds to assist community crime prevention and neighborhood revitalization efforts.

The community policing movement represents a philosophical shift in the operational mission of policing. Rather than simply enforcing laws, community policing emphasizes the importance of mobilizing neighborhood residents and establishing police-community partnerships to address crime and its related correlates. Accordingly, citizens are encouraged to unite and assist police (both individually and collectively) in addressing a wide range of community problems rather than relying solely on police services.

For some time now it has been assumed that police efforts to mobilize neighborhood residents and develop meaningful ties in the name of "co-production of order" were dependent on positive attitudes toward the police (Hahn, 1971; Frank et al., 1996; Stipak, 1979, p. 49). The present study assessed the relationship between citizen attitudes toward police performance (officer demeanor and citizen-police relations) and perceptions of an important facet of community policing (collaborative police-community partnerships) in a small, northwestern town.

Review of the Literature

The dominance of the community policing movement is reflected not only by the growing body of literature on the topic, but also by the resounding endorsement of community policing by the national police research organizations, and by the proliferation of community policing in practice (Eck and Rosenbaum, 1994, p. 3). Several factors have combined to serve as the impetus for this reorientation of the police role. For example, the results of traditional police practices (e.g., the isolation from the public, the ineffectiveness of police as crime fighters, and research that has called into question Wilson's police management principles) led many police executives and academics to call for a new approach to policing (Skolnick and Bayley, 1986).

In practice, community policing takes many forms, including increased accessibility of police officers to the public through foot and bicycle patrols; the decentralization of police operations through the use of neighborhood substations; the implementation of crime prevention programs; and the long-term assignment of officers to specific beats in an attempt to establish collaborative police-community partnerships to address neighborhood crime-related problems (see Mastrofski, 1993).

The long list of programs and initiatives that fall under the general heading of community policing has generated strong criticism. Some have argued that the lack of a unitary concept of community policing limits the external validity of evaluation research and promotes the use of "community policing" as a slogan for enhancing a police department's public image (Green and Taylor, 1988; Klockars, 1988; Mastrofski, 1988; Weatheritt, 1988). Despite this criticism, community policing has emerged as the dominant paradigm in policing today. And at its core, community policing requires, among other things, an organizational commitment to problem solving and customer satisfaction (Rosenbaum and Lurigio, 1994).

Police-Community Partnerships

One of the goals of community policing is to enhance the citizen's role in addressing neighborhood crime-related problems. Such active involvement may take place on two levels: first, citizens may act individually to assist police by reporting suspicious behavior; and second, neighborhood residents may act collectively by participating in various programs sponsored by local policing agencies (e.g. Block Watches) (Rosenbaum, 1988, p. 325).

The extent to which citizens are willing partners in the co-production of order appears, however, to be the product of a number of factors. As Grinc (1994) found in an analysis of eight community policing sites, neighborhood residents tend to express little desire to become partners in community policing.

Grinc (1994) cited a number of explanations for this lack of involvement, including fear of retaliation and poor pre-existing relations between the police and neighborhood residents (see also Sadd and Grinc, 1994), apathy, the ambiguous role of citizens in community policing, the highly disorganized nature of some community policing areas, and intra-group conflict between community leaders and other residents. In addition, Walker (1992) notes that large, heterogeneous, transient populations that make up many inner-city neighborhoods have few ties to their neighborhoods, and thus are difficult to mobilize.

Research has also revealed that other demographic, crime-related, and community context variables are important indicators of citizen participation in community policing programs. For example, minority individuals have been found to be more likely to participate in neighborhood-based anti-crime efforts (Lavrakas and Herz, 1982). Additionally, indicators of higher social class (e.g., income and education) have been found to increase the likelihood of citizen participation in neighborhood activities (Haeberle, 1987).

There is a lack of consensus concerning the effects of crime-related variables. For example, while it is possible that increased levels of fear may increase the likelihood of citizens assisting police, Wilson and Kelling (1982, p. 32) note that high levels of fear may result in citizens retreating to the safety of their homes. In general, community context variables also are thought to have an impact on citizens' willingness to assist police. Simply put, if residents feel as though neighborhood problems (e.g. social and physical disorder) are in need of attention, then they will be more likely to get involved. However, if citizens feel as though such problems are under control, then they are more likely to rely on the police to maintain the order that already has been established (Lavrakas and Herz, 1982).

Public attitudes toward the police traditionally have been thought to have a direct impact on whether citizens will co-operate with the police and engage in collaborative partnerships to address crime-related issues (Bell, 1979; Brandl and Horvath, 1991; Hahn,

1971; Reisig and Correia, 1997; Scaglion and Condon, 1980; Stipak, 1979; Thurman and Reisig, 1996; Wycoff, 1988). However, contrary to conventional wisdom, in a recent analysis, Frank et al. (1996) found little support for the hypothesis that attitudes toward the police are an important predictor of whether or not citizens will engage in co-productive behaviors with the police.

Attitudes Toward the Police

Conflicting evidence exists regarding the relative impact of demographic characteristics such as education, income, and gender on attitudes toward the police (Correia et al., 1996, pp. 18–19; Decker, 1981). However, age and race have repeatedly been found to affect citizens' attitudes. Most studies report a positive relationship between attitudes toward the police and the respondent's age (Hadar and Snortum, 1975; Walker et al., 1972). Attitudinal differences concerning police have been thought to be reflective of different value structures between age groups. While mature residents value safety and security, younger residents have been found to value freedom. Because younger citizens perceive the police as attempting to restrict their independence, they tend to hold more negative attitudes toward the police when compared to their more mature neighbors.

Overall, research indicates that whites tend to hold more favorable attitudes toward the police when compared to nonwhites (Carter, 1985; Furstenberg and Wellford, 1973; Peek et al, 1978). More recent evidence has suggested, however, that the race effect is closely related to community context and crime-related variables. For example, Cao et al. (1996, pp. 12–13) initially found racial differences in the level of confidence in the police; however, they also found that this relationship was suppressed once perceptions of physical and social disorder were included in their model. Additionally, Murty et al. (1990, p. 225) found an association between crime rates and public attitudes toward the police. In particular, the authors reported that residents from low-crime neighborhoods were found to express more positive images of the police.

Researchers also have noted the importance of neighborhood characteristics in re-lation to attitudes toward the police. For example, Jacob (1971, p. 78) argued that evaluations of the police were rooted to some degree in is "neighborhood cultures," operationalized by way of racial and class differences between neighborhoods. Dunham and Alpert's (1988) analysis of five distinct neighborhoods in Dade County, Florida underscored the importance of Jacob's earlier findings. Dunham and Alpert found considerable variation in public attitudes of the police between different ethnic neighborhoods. Differences in the qualitative nature (e.g., culture, crime and disorder) of neighborhoods and its apparent relationship to attitudes toward the police have led researchers to conclude that neighborhood context is an important factor (Webb and Marshall, 1995, p. 58–59).

Research Objective

The objective of the study presented here was to assess the hypothesis that positive attitudes toward police performance are a necessary precursor to meaningful police-community partnerships. This longstanding assumption was assessed in a two-step process. First, neighborhood-level data were used in a series of post hoc comparisons to evaluate whether neighborhoods where attitudes toward police performance were relatively negative were less supportive of policing strategies that were reliant on public co-operation. Second, the effects of attitudes toward police performance on perceptions of collaborative policing strategies were assessed at the individual-level, controlling for important demographic characteristics, crime-related, and community context variables. It was reasoned that the two-step procedure was necessary since community policing entails co-operative relations between citizens and the police at both the individual level, and as a collective group (i.e., neighborhood groups).

Methods

Sample

Reported here are the results from a random probability sample of adult residents from a small town (population approximately 25,000) located in a northwestern state. A modified version of Dillman's (1978) Total Design Method was employed as the data collection procedure. This approach entailed a careful pretesting of the survey instrument, and repeated mailings to nonrespondents. Surveys were distributed over a three-month period during the spring of 1995. Of the 514 individuals included in the initial sample, 365 people returned usable surveys resulting in a response rate of 71 percent.

Research Setting

The sample was drawn from a town that is home to one of the nation's many land grant universities (student enrollment approximately 17,000). Like most college towns, a wide array of student housing (both university and privately owned) is available. While such accommodations exist throughout the area in question, a sizable majority of apartment complexes and rental homes are confined to two particular neighborhoods.

For a number of reasons (e.g., construction zoning laws, geography, etc.), the town is largely segregated by age and social class. In so doing, many of the demographic characteristics are unevenly distributed. The researchers were able to identify four different neighborhoods. College Park and McGee Bluffs generally consist of residents who were relatively young, less educated, lower income and renters, who recently had moved to the town to attend school. In contrast, residents of Sunnyside Acres and Military Heights were generally older, better educated, higher income, long-term area residents who own their homes.

The four neighborhoods were also found to vary along crime-related and community context characteristics. For example, residents of Military Heights and Sunnyside Acres reported lower levels of fear of crime, victimization, disorder, and higher levels of neighborhood integration when compared to residents of College Park and McGee Bluffs (see tables 20.1 and 20.2). The differences between these neighborhoods justified the researchers' aggregating these data accordingly for a series of post hoc comparisons of

attitudes toward police performance and perceptions of community policing.

Measures

Dependent Measures. Two additive scales were used to assess "police performance:" officer demeanor and citizen-police relations. Two additional variables were used to measure citizen perceptions of "community policing:" problem-solving orientation and crime control responsibility.

Principal components analysis using varimax rotation revealed that each of [the] survey items was associated with each of the hypothesized factors (see table 20.1). Specifically, each factor had an Eigenvalue greater than 1.0, which satisfied the traditional rule used to determine the appropriate number of constructs (Kim and Mueller, 1978, pp. 43–44). The strength of the factor loadings were quite high (i.e., from 0.62 to 0.87), suggesting a high level of internal consistency. Additionally, the magnitudes of the internal consistency, as indicated by Cronbach's alpha (i.e., from 0.54 to 0.88), suggest a moderate to high level of reliability (Carmines and Zeller, 1979, pp. 43–48).

Independent Variables. Several demographic, crime-related, and community context variables were used in this analysis. Age was the respondent's age measured in years. Race was coded "0 = non-whites," and "1 = whites". Income was an ordinal scale ranging from "1 = less than US $7,000" to "9 = more than US $74,999" yearly household income. Gender was coded "0 = males," and "1 = females." Finally, education was an ordinal scale ranging from "1 = not a high school graduate" to "7 = graduate degree."

Three crime-related variables also were included in this study. First, "fear of crime" was measured using a two-item scale ($r = 0.51$) that asked respondents to rate their perception of safety when walking alone in their neighborhood (a) during the day, and (b) at night. Each item featured a five-point ordinal scale with "1 = very safe" and "5 = very unsafe." Second, "perception of crime" was measured using a single survey item that asked participants about crime in their neighborhood over the previous two years. This item employed a seven-point ordinal

Table 20.1
Description of Dependent Measures

Constructs and items	Factor loading
Officer demeanor	
Officers are usually fair	0.83
Officers are usually courteous	0.87
Officers are usually honest	0.84
Officers treat all citizens equally	0.75
Officers show concern	0.73
Eigen value = 3.97	
Cronbach's Alpha = 0.88	
Item-to-item correlation coefficient range = 0.52-0.70	
Scale range = 5-25	
Scale mean = 17.21	
Scale standard deviation = 3.91	
Citizen-police relations	
There are dependable ties between police and public	0.67
Officers interact with citizens	0.76
Friendship between citizens and officers is easy to develop	0.62
Eigen value = 1.07	
Cronbach's Alpha = 0.54	
Item-to-item coefficient range = 0.25-0.34	
Scale range = 3-15	
Scale mean = 8.54	
Scale standard deviation = 2.02	
Problem-solving orientation	
Police should spend more time informing people about available services	0.76
Police should spend more time talking to people about problems	0.81
Police should spend more time solving problems related to public safety	0.70
Eigen value = 1.85	
Cronbach's Alpha = 0.66	
Item-to-item correlation coefficient range = 0.35-0.47	
Scale range = 3-15	
Scale mean = 10.06	
Scale standard deviation = 1.93	
Crime control responsibility	
Only the police can control crime	–
Range = 1-5	
Mean = 1.97	
Standard deviation = 0.94	

scale with "1 = crime problem getting better" and "7 = crime problem getting worse." Finally, "victimization" was a dichotomous variable indicating whether the respondent had been a victim of a crime (e.g., assault, burglary, and robbery) over the six months prior to the study (1 = victim, and 0 = not a victim).

In addition, two community context variables were used in the analysis. Disorder was measured using an eight-item scale (alpha = 0.85) that included indicators of physical disorder (e.g., garbage and litter in the streets) and social disorder (e.g., illegal drug use and teen vagrancy) (see Skogan, 1990)[2]. Integration was measured using a two-item scale (r = 0.49) that included the following items:

(1) Do you feel your neighborhood is:

- just a place to live; or

- more of a real home?; and

(2) Would you describe your neighborhood as:
- a place where people go their own way; or
- a place where people mostly help one another?

Statistical Procedure

The correlation coefficients among the four dependent measures indicated that they were independent from one another (see Appendix, table 20.2). In the absence of a meaningful relationship between these measures, one-way analysis of variance (ANOVA) was employed to assess differences in attitudes at the neighborhood level. The *F*-ratio was used to measure systematic differences between group means. The Bonferroni multiple comparison test was used to assess post hoc differences between specific neighborhoods (see Kirk, 1995, pp. 137–43). Finally, multiple regression analysis was employed to assess the effects of demographic, crime-related, and community context variables on each of the dependent measures at the individual-level.

Results

The ANOVA for "officer demeanour" revealed significant differences between neighborhoods; F (3, 318) = 8.52, *p* < 0.001. More

specifically, table 20.2 shows that differences existed between residents of College Park and Sunnyside Acres, as well as between those living in College Park and Military Heights. As noted previously, these two neighborhoods were densely populated with university students. Comparing the mean scores across neighborhoods, the two neighborhoods housing the greatest number of students evaluate officer demeanour lower than the other two neighborhoods. Nevertheless, all four residential groupings reported attitudes in a positive direction.

The ANOVA for "citizen-police relations" also revealed significant differences between neighborhoods; F (3, 322) = 3.56, $p<0.05$. The Bonferroni multiple comparison test showed a significant difference between inhabitants of College Park and Sunnyside Acres. In general, the mean scores indicated that the entire sample rated the relationship between the citizens and the police relatively low. It should be noted that, as a group, the only neighborhood to rate the state of citizen-police relations positively was Sunnyside Acres. Once again, however, evaluations were more negative in the neighborhoods where students reside when compared to neighborhoods housing long-term residents.

The analysis failed to find significant differences between neighborhood residents concerning perceptions of community polic-

---

Table 20.2

Means, Standard Deviations, One-way Analysis Of Variance, and Bonferroni Multiple Comparisons by Dependent Measure

	College Park	Sunnyside Acres	Military Heights	McGee Bluffs	F-ratio
Officer demeanour	15.91	18.27[a]	18.44[b]	17.12	8.52***
	(4.3)	(3.8)	(3.3)	(3.5)	
Citizen-police relations	8.16	9.05[a]	8.82	8.36	3.56***
	(1.9)	(2.4)	(1.9)	(1.8)	
Crime control responsibility	1.93	1.86	2.00	2.16	1.32
	(0.9)	(0.9)	(1.1)	(1.0)	
Problem-solving strategy	10.09	9.93	9.76	10.56	2.45
	(2.0)	(1.8)	(1.7)	(1.8)	

Notes:
[a]Bonferroni multiple comparison test significant (at 0.05 level) between Sunnyside Acres and College Park
[b]Bonferroni multiple comparison test significant (at 0.05 level) between Military Heights and College Park
*p < 0.05; **p < 0.01; ***p < 0.001
Higher means indicate higher levels of positive response. Standard deviations for each group mean are presented in parentheses.

ing. More specifically, results from the ANOVA for "crime control responsibility" showed that, as a whole, neighborhood residents disagreed with the notion that only the police could control crime in their town. Additionally, the ANOVA for "problem-solving orientation" revealed no significant differences between neighborhood residents. In other words, all mean scores for neighborhoods revealed that a measurable level of support existed for community policing in general, and the development of police-community collaborative partnerships specifically, despite the differences between these residential settings. At the neighborhood-level, the findings reported here do not support the hypothesis that positive attitudes toward the police are a necessary precursor of collaborative police-community partnerships. . . .

Discussion

To summarize the findings, significant differences were noted between residents of different neighborhoods concerning attitudes toward officer demeanour and the state of citizen-police relations. In general, residential areas where long-term, older, higher income, white, highly educated home owners who reside in well integrated and orderly neighborhoods rated police performance higher than their short-term, younger, less educated, lower income neighbors from other less integrated and more disorderly neighborhoods. Again, what was interesting about these findings was that these distinct settings did not result in differences concerning perceptions of crime control responsibility, nor were differences detected concerning the support for a problem-solving orientation. In fact, the results indicated that there was support for such an approach in each of the four neighborhoods under observation, despite existing and sometimes negative attitudes toward the police. When analyzed at the individual level, these existing attitudes had no measurable effect on either of the two variables used to assess perceptions of a community policing strategy, that, by definition, relies heavily on police-community collabo-

rative partnerships to address crime-related problems.

Previous studies have demonstrated that public attitudes toward the police and preferences for policing strategy can vary significantly by residential setting Dunham and Alpert, 1988; Jacob, 1971). These studies were conducted in major metropolitan areas (i.e., Milwaukee and Miami). The site of the analysis presented here, in comparison, was relatively small and homogeneous. As a result, the indicators of "neighborhood culture" were limited to age and social class (e.g., family income, occupation, and housing). However, as Dunham and Alpert (1988, p. 521) point out, "it appears that neighborhood differences that are significant to policing go beyond traditional ethnic distinctions." What is important to recognize is that attitudes toward police not only vary in large cities, but also in small town America as well; however less-than-favorable attitudes may not necessarily preclude the effective implementation of community policing. The findings reported above indicate that attitudes toward the police do not result in citizen attitudes reflecting an unwillingness to be partners in the co-production of order.

In fact, instead of viewing pre-existing negative attitudes toward the police as barriers to the successful implementation of community policing initiatives, individual and neighborhood-level attitudinal data should be used and understood by police executives and line-level officers, and, if necessary, proactive measures should be taken in an attempt to reduce the social distance between citizens and the police—neighborhood by neighborhood, citizen by citizen. Indeed, these findings suggest the proclivity toward meaningful partnerships from the point of view of most residents despite pre-existing, less-than-favorable opinions regarding the police in some neighborhoods. Also others through evaluation research of citizen-police, collaborative partnerships (e.g. Peak *et al*, 1992) have found that in time, pre-existing negative attitudes toward the police can be improved with well conceived community policing initiatives.

The research findings reported here are limited to some degree given the method of data collection. Through survey research the researchers elicited attitudes and opinions for each of the dependent variables. The findings suggest that attitudes toward the police are not significant when it comes to forging productive partnerships between citizens and the police. But the continuing debate over the correspondence between attitudes and behaviors highlights the limitations of this research, and suggests the need for observational methods in this area in the future. While Adzes and Fishbein (1977, p. 912) conclude that "the relation between attitude and behavior only appears to be inconsistent," (rather than no correspondence as critics might suggest) the authors remain skeptical—given the existing literature—that positive attitudes concerning the role of citizens and police as coproducers of order using a problem-solving approach easily manifest themselves in meaningful police-citizen partnerships, especially when attitudes toward the police in general are somewhat negative (see Frank *et al*, 1996).

According to Yin (1986), the key to successful community-based efforts to reduce crime and fear of crime, and to improve neighborhood conditions is the active involvement of the police in educating citizens about crime prevention and working collaboratively with citizens in solving neighborhood problems. The extent to which citizens will become active, collaborative partners in the community policing process, however, is more problematic (Grinc, 1994). The first step toward participation is the belief that the police are not solely responsible for crime control, but rather should be active problem-solving partners working collaboratively with the police. The residents within distinct neighborhood contexts in a small northwestern city observed in this study overwhelmingly reported attitudes that were consistent with this sentiment, even though their neighborhood context resulted in varying attitudes toward the police in general.

Notes

1. Crime control responsibility was measured using one survey item; hence this measure was not included in the principal components analysis.

2. Because each of the neighborhoods in question could be characterized as low disorder areas, the natural log was calculated for the disorder variables so as to better approximate a normal distribution.

References

Ajzen, I. and Fishbein, M. (1977), "Attitude-behavior relations: a theoretical analysis and review of empirical research," *Psychological Bulletin*, Vol. 84, pp. 888–918.

Bell, D. (1979), "Police and public opinion," *Journal of Police Science and Administration*, Vol. 7, pp. 196–205.

Brandl, S. and Horvath, F. (1991), "Crime victim evaluation of police investigative performance," *Journal of Criminal Justice*, Vol. 19, pp. 293–305.

Cao, L., Frank, J. and Cullen, F (1996), "Race, community context and confidence in the police," *American Journal of Police*, Vol. 15, pp. 3–22.

Carmines, E. and Zeller, R. (1979), *Reliability and Validity Assessment*, Sage, Newbury Park, CA.

Carter, D. (1985), "Hispanic perception of police performance: an empirical assessment," *Journal of Criminal Justice*, Vol. 13, pp. 487–500.

Cirel, P, Evans, P, McGillis, D. and Whitcomb, a (1977), *An Exemplary Project: Community Crime Prevention Program, Seattle, Washington*, Law Enforcement Assistance Administration, Washington, DC.

Correia, M., Reisig, M. and Lovrich, N. (1996), "Public perceptions of state police: an analysis of individual-level and contextual variables," *Journal of Criminal Justice*, Vol. 24, pp. 17–28.

Decker, S. (1981), "Citizen attitudes toward the police," *Journal of Police Science and Administration*, Vol. 9, pp. 81–7.

Dillman, D. (1978), *Mail and Telephone Surveys: The Total Design Method*, Wiley-Interscience, New York, NY.

Dunham, R. and Alpert, G. (1988), "Neighborhood differences in attitudes toward policing: evidence for a mixed-strategy model of policing in a multi-ethnic setting," *The Journal of Criminal Law and Criminology*, Vol. 79, pp. 504–23.

Eck, J. and Rosenbaum, D. (1994), "The new police order: effectiveness, equity, and efficiency in community policing," in Rosenbaum D.(Ed.), *The Challenge of Community Policing. Testing the Promises*, Sage, Thousand Oaks, CA, pp. 3–23.

Frank, J., Brandl, S., Worden, R. and Bynum, T. (1996), "Citizen involvement in the coproduction of police outputs," *Journal of Crime and Justice*, Vol. 19, pp. 1–30.

Furstenberg, F. and Wellford, C. (1973), "Calling the police: the evaluation of police service," *Law & Society Review*, Vol. 7, pp. 393–406.

Greene, J. and Taylor, P, (1988), "Community-based policing and foot patrol: issues of theory and evaluation," in Greene, J. and Mastrofski, S. (Eds), *Community Policing:Rhetoric or Reality*, Praeger, New York, NY, pp. 195–223.

Grinc, R. (1994), "Angels in the marble: problems in stimulating community involvement in community policing," *Crime & Delinquency*, Vol. 40, pp. 437–68.

Hadar, I. and Snortum, J. (1975), "The eye of the beholder: differential perceptions of police and the public," *Criminal Justice and Behavior*, Vol. 2, pp. 37–54.

Haeberle, S. (1987), "Neighborhood identity and citizen participation," *Administration and Society*, Vol. 19, pp. 178–96.

Hahn, H. (1971), "Ghetto assessments of police protection and authority," *Law and Society Review*, Vol. 6, pp. 183–94.

Jacob, H. (1971), "Black and white perceptions of justice in the city," *Law and Society Review*, Vol. 6, pp. 69–89.

Kim, J. and Mueller, C. (1978), *Factor Analysis: Statistical Methods and Practical Issues*, Sage, Newbury Park, CA.

Kirk, R. (1995), *Experimental Design: Procedures for the Behavioral Sciences*, Wadsworth, Belmont, CA.

Klockars, C. (1988), "The rhetoric of community policing," in Greene, J. and Mastrofski, S. (Eds),*Community Policing: Rhetoric or Reality?* Praeger, New York, pp. 239–58.

Lavrakas, P. and Herz, E. (1982), "Citizen participation in neighborhood crime prevention," *Criminology*, Vol. 20, pp. 479–98.

Mastrofski, S. (1988), "Community policing as a reform: a cautionary tale," in Greene, J. and Mastrofski, S.(Eds), *Community Policing Rhetoric or Reality?* Praeger, New York, NY, pp. 47–67.

Mastrofski, S. (1993), "Varieties of community policing," *American Journal of Police*, Vol. 12, pp. 65–77.

Murty, K., Roebuck, J. and Smith, J. (1990), "The image of the police in black Atlanta communities," *Journal of Police Science and Administration*, Vol. 17, pp. 250–7.

Peak, K., Bradshaw, R. and Glensor, R. (1992), "Improving citizen perceptions of the police: back to the basics' with a community policing strategy," *Journal of Criminal Justice*, Vol. 20, pp. 25–40.

Peek, C., Alston, J. and Lowe, G. (1978), "Comparative evaluation of the local police," *Public Opinion Quarterly*, Vol. 42, pp. 370–9.

Reisig, M. and Correia, M. (1997), "Public evaluations of police performance: an analysis across three levels of policing," *Policing: An International Journal of Police Strategy and Management*, Vol. 20, pp. 311–25.

Rosenbaum, D. (1988), "Community crime prevention: a review and synthesis of the literature," *Justice Quarterly*, Vol. 5, pp. 323–95.

Rosenbaum, D. and Lurigio, A. (1994), "An inside look at community policing reform: definitions, organizational changes, and evaluation findings," *Crime & Delinquency*, Vol. 40, pp. 299–314.

Sadd, S. and Grinc, R. (1994), "Innovative neighborhood oriented policing: an evaluation of community policing programs in eight cities," in Rosenbaum, D. (Ed.), *The Challenge of Community Policing*, Sage Publications, Thousand Oaks, CA, pp. 27–52.

Scaglion, R. and Condon, R. (1980), "Determinants of attitudes toward city police," *Criminology*, Vol. 17, pp. 485–94.

Skogan, W. (1990), *Disorder and Decline: Crime and the Spiral of Decay in American neighborhoods*, University of California Press, Berkeley, CA.

Skolnick, J. and Bayley, D. (1986), *The New Blue Line: Police Innovation in Six American Cities*, Free Press, New York, NY.

Stipak, B. (1979), "Citizen satisfaction with urban services: potential misuse as a performance indicator," *Public Administration Review*, Vol. 39, pp. 46–52.

Thurman, Q. and Reisig, M. (1996), "Community-oriented research in an era of community-oriented research," *American Behavioral Scientist*, Vol. 39, pp. 570–86.

Walker, D., Richardson, R., Williams, O., McGaughry, S. and Denyer, T. (1972), "Contact and support: an empirical assessment of public attitudes toward the police and the courts," *North Carolina Law Review*, Vol. 51, pp. 473–79.

Walker, S. (1992), *The Police in America*, McGraw-Hill, New York, NY.

Weatheritt M. (1988), "Community policing rhetoric or reality?" In Greene, J. and Mastrofski, S. (Eds), *Community Policing: Rhetoric or Reality*, Praeger, New York, NY, pp. 153–75.

Webb, V. and Marshall, C. (1995), "The relative importance of race and ethnicity on citizen attitudes toward the police," *American Journal of Police*, Vol. 14, pp. 45–66.

Wilson, J. and Kelling, G. (1982), "Broken Windows," *Atlantic Monthly*, Vol. 127, pp. 29–38.

Wycoff, NL (1988), "The benefits of community policing; evidence and conjecture," in Green, J. and Mastrofski, S. (Eds), *Community Policing: Rhetoric or Reality*, Praeger, New York, NY, pp. 103–20.

Yin, R. (1986), "Community crime prevention: a synthesis of eleven evaluations," in Rosenbaum, D. (Ed.), *Community Crime Prevention: Does it Work?* Sage, Beverly Hills, CA, pp. 294–308.

Appendix 20.1
Neighborhood Characteristics

	College Park (n = 110)	Sunnyside Acres (n = 83)	Military Heights (n = 80)	McGee Bluffs (n = 71)	Chi-Square value
Age (years)					125.18***
< 26	61.5	9.8	19.2	47.9	
26–35	16.5	14.6	16.7	39.4	
36–50	7.3	14.6	21.8	11.3	
51+	14.7	61.0	42.3	1.4	
Race					14.93***
White	83.0	91.4	88.2	67.9	
Nonwhite	17.0	8.6	11.8	32.1	
Gender					7.06
Male	55.0	63.4	72.2	54.9	
Female	45.0	36.6	27.8	45.1	
Education					52.16***
High school graduate	65.1	24.1	20.8	23.9	
College graduate	29.0	24.1	42.9	46.5	
Graduate degree	15.0	51.9	36.4	29.6	
Family income					79.35***
<US $10,000	22.7	1.3	10.3	45.9	
US $10,000–19,999	20.4	17.3	14.1	26.2	
US $20,000–29,999	9.1	12.0	14.1	18.0	
US $30,000–49,999	17.0	26.7	26.9	3.3	
US $50,000+	30.7	42.7	34.6	6.6	
Housing					124.62***
Homeowner	21.0	80.2	61.3	2.9	
Renter	79.0	19.8	38.9	97.1	
Occupation					94.03***
Blue-collar	1.7	6.6	5.3	0.0	
White-collar	16.4	47.3	39.5	7.0	
Unemployed	1.7	2.2	4.0	4.2	
College student	71.6	15.4	35.5	88.7	
Retired	8.6	28.6	15.8	0.0	
Years in Community					137.45***
1–5	80.0	17.5	36.3	95.8	
6–10	5.5	8.8	8.8	2.8	
11+	14.5	73.8	55.0	1.4	
Victim					8.19*
Yes	20.2	8.9	7.7	11.4	
No	79.8	91.1	92.3	88.6	

Note: $^*p < 0.05$; $^{**}p < 0.01$; $^{***}p < 0.001$; $N = 365$

Appendix 20.2
Means, Standard Deviations, One-way Analysis of Variance by Crime-related and Community Context Variables

	College Park	Sunnyside Acres	Military Heights	McGee Bluffs	F-ratio
Fear of crime	4.06	2.94	3.13	3.93	14.80***
	(1.5)	(1.0)	(1.2)	(1.6)	
Perception of crime	4.36	4.41	4.32	4.23	0.43
	(0.8)	(0.9)	(0.9)	(1.0)	
Neighbourhood disorder	13.17	9.62	10.61	12.33	11.80***
	(3.9)	(3.0)	(2.5)	(3.6)	
Integration	2.87	3.52	3.17	2.65	17.63***
	(0.8)	(0.7)	(0.9)	(0.8)	

Notes:
$*p < 0.05; **p < 0.01; ***p < 0.001$
Higher means indicate higher levels of integration, neighbourhood disorder, fear of crime, and concern with community crime problems. Standard deviations for each group mean are presented in parantheses.

Appendix 20.3
Bivariate Relationships Between Demographic Crime-related, Community Context and Dependent Measures

Variables	1	2	3	4	5	6	7	8	9	10	11	12	13	14
1. Age	1.00													
2. Race	-0.10	1.00												
3. Gender	-0.17	-0.06	1.00											
4. Income	0.44	-0.15	-0.8	1.00										
5. Education	0.20	0.13	-0.21	0.14	1.00									
6. Fear of crime	-0.21	0.03	0.33	-0.19	-0.20	1.00								
7. Perception of crime	0.06	-0.04	0.12	0.11	-0.05	1.00								
8. Victim	-0.14	0.01	-0.03	0.04	-0.05	0.11	0.06	1.00						
9. Disorder	-0.30	0.10	0.06	-0.21	-0.08	0.33	0.07	0.11	1.00					
10. Integration	0.47	-0.08	-0.03	0.36	0.02	-0.35	-0.00	-0.06	-0.22	1.00				
11. Officer demeanour	0.38	0.02	0.02	0.12	0.11	-0.17	-0.11	-0.12	-0.17	0.23	1.00			
12. Citizen-police relations	0.25	0.02	0.03	0.13	0.07	-0.15	-0.13	-0.12	-0.01	0.25	0.46	1.00		
13. Problem-solving orientation	-0.12	0.17	0.09	-0.06	0.02	0.13	0.06	0.17	0.10	-0.08	-0.11	-0.19	1.00	
14. Crime control responsibility	0.02	0.20	-0.09	0.01	-0.02	0.00	-0.02	0.02	-0.06	0.01	0.05	-0.01	0.01	1.00
Mean	38.76	0.16	0.39	5.39	5.05	3.55	4.33	0.12	11.47	3.05	17.21	8.54	10.06	1.97
Standard deviation	18.87	0.37	0.49	2.75	1.79	1.45	0.88	0.33	3.56	0.86	3.91	2.02	1.93	0.94

21

Community Policing Evaluation

David L. Carter
Allen D. Sapp

Did it work? That is the question that we all ask whenever a fundamentally new and different initiative has been attempted. In order to determine whether or not a community-policing initiative has succeeded, it is necessary to conduct, as an integral part of the problem-solving process, a formal assessment. Traditional measures of police effectiveness—numbers of arrests and calls for service, citations issued, and so on—are neither appropriate nor acceptable for today's policing strategy. The formal evaluation of community-policing efforts, however, is a step in the process that has often been neglected and is a frequently cited shortcoming of community policing. Granted, a proper evaluation is not simple; one must take into account a number of variables that are to be evaluated, how the evaluation will be structured, and methodologies for acquiring the necessary information. This reading by D.L. Carter and A.D. Sapp is significant in that it "sets the table" for evaluating community policing. Perhaps without blatantly saying so, the authors demonstrate the importance of planning an effective evaluation prior to the implementation of community-policing strategy. As you read, consider how you might structure an evaluation of community-policing efforts in your area.

Introduction

Evaluating community policing policies and practices poses some difficult problems. Community policing has been implemented in a wide variety of ways depending on the police department's vision, different communities' demands and characteristics, resource availability, and an array of other factors that contribute to the uniqueness of any given community-based initiative. Moreover, community policing is not a program or a uniform set of tasks. Rather, it is a *philosophy* of management and service delivery that makes the operationalization of an evaluation even more difficult. While certain practices may be transferred between departments, even those practices must be amended to meet the characteristics of specific jurisdictions.

A further problem is that community policing requires administrators, managers, supervisors, and officers to think about their responsibilities differently. Reactive and "incident-driven" policies are cleared away for implementation of proactive, innovative, "problem-driven" officer behaviors. As a result, evaluations cannot simply "count beans"—that is, merely tabulating the number of calls answered, response time, tickets written, reports written, and so forth will not accurately measure goal realization under the community policing philosophy.

Finally, there is a problem of unanimity. Community policing has different names around the country, as well as different ways of being implemented. Beyond the question of the types of activities (or tasks) community police officers perform, there is significant variation in allocation and deployment schemes—some departments use community policing department-wide, while others experiment with the philosophy based on shift or location.

The reader must keep these issues in mind in developing a community policing model, as well as in evaluating it. To manage these issues, this model begins with the premise of definitions. Critical terms for both the development and implementation of community policing will be presented, as well as definitions for different steps in the evaluation. It is inherent in any research endeavor that operational definitions be used. These are consistent, measurable descriptions of phenomena that enhance the overall quality of program development and evaluation. It is in this spirit that the definitions are presented.

In the authors' opinions, simply providing a single model description of how to evaluate community policing will leave many questions remaining. Thus, this chapter addresses core issues related to both the development and evaluation of the community policing philosophy. Beyond descriptions of processes, the authors have appended some sample instruments to assist in an assessment.

Before effective evaluation can occur, one must first have a foundation against which measured criteria can be compared. This relates to the conceptual development of a community policing philosophy, as well as the specific operational activities that will be used.

Community Policing Defined

There are a number of definitions for community policing. For this model, community policing is defined as a philosophy, not a tactic. It is a proactive, decentralized approach to policing, designed to reduce crime, disorder and fear of crime, while also responding to the community's explicit needs and demands. Community policing views police responsibilities in the aggregate, examining problems, determining underlying causes of the problems, and developing solutions to those problems (amended from Trojanowicz and Carter 1988, and Spelman and Eck 1987).

Among the fundamentally synonymous terms for community policing are problem-oriented policing (POP), community problem-oriented policing (CPOP), neighborhood-oriented policing (NOP), community-oriented policing and problem solving (COPPS), police area representatives (PAR), citizen-oriented patrol experiment (COPE), experimental policing (EP), neighborhood foot patrol, and community foot patrol. While there are some variations in these concepts' proffered definitions, for the purpose of this model, all these concepts are defined the same as community policing is above.

Operational Context for Evaluation

Of necessity, the evaluation of any policy or activity actually begins with the development of the policy. In this regard, it is essential that administrators and managers conceptualize how the community policing philosophy integrates with the police department's organizational existence. That is, the core values and implementation strategies of community policing policies must be clearly linked to the organization's purpose. The purpose can be viewed as having two elements: the department's *mission*, and the department's *goals*.

> *Mission*—The mission is the role the organization or unit fulfills—it specifies in general language *what* is intended to be accomplished.

It establishes the organization's *direction and responsibility*, which all other administrative activities are designed to fulfill. Thus, the administrative philosophy of policing and all organizational policies and functions should be guided toward fulfilling the mission.

It should be noted that mission goes beyond a statutory obligation. That is, statutes that empower police departments state that the police are responsible for law enforcement and crime repression—they generally do not stipulate any responsibilities for public order. However, city commissions, mayors or the public in general may require the police to fulfill additional responsibilities of providing public service, maintaining order and generally enhancing the quality of life in the community.

> *Goal*—The goal is the end to which all organizational activity is directed.

A goal is broad-based, yet *functionally* oriented. It must be *specific* enough for all department members to clearly understand it, it must be measurable, it must be reasonably *attainable* in the time period allotted it, and it must be *mission-related*—that is, accomplishing goals supports the department's mission. Since a department's mission will typically be comprehensive and incorporate diverse functions, multiple goals will typically be set. Goals will also likely vary between areas within a jurisdiction, and perhaps even between shifts.

In that the community environment will change over time, as will crime patterns and community problems, goal statements should be reviewed yearly and changed or revised to reflect current issues and trends.

Planning—Planning anticipates situations, estimating organizational demands and resources needed to handle those situations, and initiating strategies to respond to them.

Particularly in community policing activities, planning is an ongoing responsibility of all organizational members. Middle managers and administrators are primarily responsible for *strategic* or long-range planning. This includes budget planning, facilities and equipment planning, and staff development. Planning projections should include multiple stages for up to 10 years. In these cases, information gained from program evaluations should be incorporated in the plans so appropriate changes can be made.

Community police officers and first-line supervisors are generally responsible for tactical planning. Tactical planning addresses problems, crime and quality-of-life issues affecting the community. The time frame for tactical plans is usually one year or less-accomplishing tactical planning objectives contributes to the department's overall goals. Once again, program evaluation assesses the tactics' efficiency and effectiveness.

Viewed in a different way, strategic plans could be viewed as *macro* plans that address the department's mission and goals. Tactical plans could be viewed as *micro* plans that are operationalized by units at the line level.

Evaluation and planning are interactive in that new plans (and, consequently, goals) depend on information gained from the department's evaluations. From a substantive perspective, planning issues can be classified based on

- organization and development issues,
- administrative issues, and
- operational issues.

Within this tripartite model, those responsible for planning should use the following questions as a checklist for program development

1. *Organization and Development Issues*

- How extensive will resource allocation to various programs be in comparison with that for the department as a whole?
- Do the jurisdiction's crime patterns and service demands warrant specializations? If so, what types?
- Regarding specializations, are the anticipated size, structure, goals, and responsibilities consistent with the crime and service demands?
- How do community policing activities relate to other department activities?
- Will changes be needed in the authority and responsibility for community policing activities?
- How comprehensive will community policing activities be?
- What growth patterns, if any, are expected in community policing activities, and what expertise will be needed to respond to growth?
- What are the anticipated equipment needs, depending on changes in size, crimes, service demands, and community policing goals?

2. *Administrative Issues*

- What criteria and procedures will be used to target community policing activities and problems?
- What type of progress reports are expected, and when?
- What will be the relationship and extent of resource allocation and demonstrable results of community policing efforts?
- On what criteria will community policing goals be changed or revised?

3. *Operational Issues*

- How extensively will community policing activities permeate all departmental activities? Divisions? Shifts? Selected officers? Department-wide?
- What will the performance measures be, and why?
- Obviously difficult to assess—performance measures depend on department's and jurisdiction's goals, needs and unique characteristics.

- Performance measures determine
- whether goals are being met,
- whether tasks and activities officers perform are *functionally* related to goals, and
- whether tasks are cost-effective.
- Performance measures, to have a true evaluative impact, must *not* be designed to weigh individual accountability, but *should* be designed to ensure that policy activities are responding to needs.
- How can ongoing, forward-looking goal preparation best be accomplished?
- Based on changing police service needs, are any unique staffing patterns emerging?
- Are new training programs needed or anticipated based on new and emerging officer responsibilities associated with community policing?
- Do changing responsibilities indicate the need for formal links with specialized agencies or groups?
- How can community policing activities integrate with non-patrol activities?

Operationalizing Programs Within the Community Policing Framework

While community policing is a management and operations philosophy, a number of elements in most community policing initiatives are fairly consistent. Just as there should be evaluation of the total community policing initiative, there should be "micro-evaluations" for critical elements of the initiative. The following sections provide a summary discussion of those elements that can help guide a community policing evaluation.

Neighborhood Watch. Neighborhood Watch was not originally intended to establish a strong police-community alliance—it was viewed as a means to help prevent burglaries and increase the probability of apprehending criminals. The concept evolved to include safe havens for children and to address other crime-related problems (such as vandalism) present in the neighborhood.

An obvious inherent element in Neighborhood Watch is to involve the community in crime deterrence and apprehension strategies. Organizing structured groups in neighborhoods not only increases the acquaintances among residents, but also provides a forum for the police to address the community on crime prevention techniques or other issues that may arise. Thus, it increases the quality of the relationship between the police and the community. Any assessment of Neighborhood Watch activities should be certain to include additional benefit.

Crime Stoppers. Like Neighborhood Watch, Crime Stoppers was designed as a crime suppression and apprehension program, with no explicit intent to ally the police and the community. Crime Stoppers is a joint venture among citizens, the media and the police to identify and locate serious offenders (typically when there is a limited amount of evidence for investigators). Selected crimes are highlighted through descriptions and reenactments on television (or radio). Citizens may make anonymous calls to report information they have on the "focus crimes" or any other crime. They may receive a cash reward for information leading to an arrest and/or conviction.

It is difficult to say whether Crime Stoppers works, because it is initially very probabilistic: Someone must have information about a crime, *and* that crime must be chosen to be described on a Crime Stoppers program, *and* that person must see the program and recognize the crime *and*, finally, that person must call the hotline. Despite these delimiting probabilities, Crime Stoppers has been surprisingly successful nationwide. This suggests that citizens are aware of crimes and are sufficiently concerned about them to both watch the program and provide information to the police.

One may infer that Crime Stoppers has served as an electronic means to develop stronger community relationships. While it lacks the traditional elements of face-to-face contact and individual "bonding" between officers and citizens, it nonetheless provides an avenue of understanding and involvement that can support other community alliance efforts.

Volunteers. For various reasons related to constrained resources, community relations and community activism, police departments began using volunteers to help with a wide range of organizational functions. At one end of the spectrum, volunteers were used as "reserve" or "auxiliary" officers to assist in law enforcement activities. Even these programs vary widely—some reserve officers are used simply for traffic control, while in Kansas City, MO., and San Bernardino County, Calif., for example, reserve officers have full police powers and responsibilities. At the other end of the spectrum, volunteers do odd jobs at the department on an irregular or unscheduled basis.

Volunteers can be a valuable resource for a police department both because of the money saved in salaries and because of the expertise they can provide. For example, the American Association of Retired Persons (AARP) has a structured process for soliciting, screening and training volunteers to work with police departments. Retired accountants, psychologists, teachers, lawyers, and other professionals can provide a department with expertise that may not otherwise be available.

An obvious additional advantage of using volunteers is community alliance. Volunteers can provide a "citizen's perspective" of issues as well as serve as a sounding board for policies and practices. Ideally, they also serve as a community resource for police department matters.

Volunteer programs contribute to a police department's profile. Unfortunately, most organizations do not take complete advantage of the opportunities afforded through volunteers. Instead, there is a tendency to treat them as interlopers. This attitude will likely have a negative effect on the police-community relationship. Assessments should focus on how volunteers are used, as well as on their direct and indirect impact on the total police function.

Crime Prevention. The sociologically based concept of crime prevention was generally a long-term approach aimed at young offenders. The hypothesis was that potential criminal behavior would initially manifest itself in youth. Juvenile delinquency was a precursor—an early warning system, perhaps—for adult criminality. Thus, to prevent future

crime, one needed to identify young offenders and change their behavior. There are both theoretical and pragmatic limitations to this hypothesis. However, the basic premise appears to ring true. Unfortunately, because of legal, financial and practical restrictions, this hypothesis cannot be tested. Certainly, however, research in this vein contributed to greater thought about ways to *prevent* crime, not just apprehend offenders.

The 1970s saw a tremendous growth in the "physical crime prevention" movement. A very pragmatically oriented approach—sometimes known simply as "locks and bolts"—physical crime prevention initially relied on the premise that the more difficult it is for a thief to get access to and steal property, the less likely it is that he or she will commit the crime. The concept grew to include programs such as Operation Identification, wherein the premise was that a thief is less likely to steal property if he or she knows that the property is clearly marked and recorded, thereby making it more difficult to "fence." Variations of this theme grew in popularity among police departments.

From a theoretical perspective, this movement relied on a likely fallacious assumption: that the crime would be *prevented*. In fact, the likelihood is that the crime would still be committed, just not at the initially intended location: the phenomenon of *displacement*. Despite this theoretical concern, police departments embraced the concept, because as long as the community had been comprehensively canvassed with crime prevention surveys and "protections," displacement to another jurisdiction was fine. Indeed, most police administrators accept crime displacement as a legitimate goal.

Just as police departments embraced the concept, so did the public. The program seemed logical, and it provided physical evidence of behavior designed to reduce the probability of crime and, consequently, fear of crime. As with Neighborhood Watch, crime prevention programs helped police open doors to "law-abiding" citizens and perform a service they wanted. While physical crime prevention has many positive aspects, it lacks depth to deal with problems to any substantive degree. Instead, it provides a cushion on which concerns about victimization and fear of crime may rest.

From an evaluation perspective, a department obviously cannot measure prevented crime. Other variables can be measured, such as reductions in reported crime (which has a number of problems in itself), crime rate changes in adjacent areas or jurisdictions (which may indicate displacement), changes in levels of fear of crime, and changes in 911 calls or calls for service in the targeted areas.

Police-Community Relations. With its roots at the National Center for Police Community Relations at Michigan State University, in the 1950s, led by the late Louis Radelet, the police-community relations (PCR) movement tried to resolve the tension between law enforcement and citizens by opening lines of communication. While PCR was initially intended to develop a means to exchange information, it evolved to emphasize teaching officers about communications with the public, teaching the public about the challenges of police work, and developing empathy between law enforcement and the community.

The PCR movement was the first initiative to truly try to reach the community. The initial aim was to identify community leaders as a focal point for establishing a liaison with citizens. Positive relations between community leaders and the police, it was theorized, would "trickle down" (to borrow a Reaganomics term) to community members. At the outset, PCR was largely one-sided—its focus was predominantly on changing the community's view of the police and on making citizens more supportive and understanding of police actions (President's Commission 1967). By the 1970s, virtually every police department of any size had a police-community relations unit (or officer), and PCR courses had become a staple in law enforcement/criminal justice college curricula (Radelet and Carter 1994).

As the movement matured, the focus became somewhat more reciprocal. It was felt that police officers needed to learn more about social-psychological dynamics affecting their relationship with the community. Moreover, all officers needed to practice PCR, not just those assigned to a PCR unit. As a result, police training was emphasized as a means to get all officers to be more communicative—sometimes civil—with the public. Particularly in the late 1970s, police departments also regularly incorporated crime prevention programs and Neighborhood Watch with the PCR unit. It was felt that this additional step would help the police and community communicate, as well as make an effort to reduce crime (Radelet and Carter 1994).

PCR was the first comprehensive effort to try to resolve the issues inherent in community alliance. The movement recognized that disequilibrium existed between the police and the community, and it developed programmatic strategies to address this dissonance. The goal of PCR was to establish an effective dialogue between citizens and law enforcement and, consequently, develop better support for the police, as well as enhance police accountability to the public.

Without question, PCR efforts were focused mainly on minority communities, . . . where the greatest disequilibrium existed between the police and citizens. The need for better relations with minorities became evident in the 1960s. With the force of the civil rights movement punctuated by civil disturbances and protest marches, it became evident that police practices had to change. The National Advisory Commission on Civil Disorders, the National Commission on the Causes and Prevention of Violence, and the President's Commission on Law Enforcement and Administration of Justice all cited problems in police-community relations—particularly excessive force, deprivation of constitutional rights, rudeness, insensitivity to minorities, and discriminatory practices. As a remedy to these and other strains in the police-community relationship, each commission recommended that police departments develop aggressive PCR programs.

The PCR concept is by no means dead, but it is being rethought. Police executives were concerned that PCR did not delve deep enough. Despite the intent, PCR appeared to have become a veneer for police inadequacies—a predominantly *reactive* method to deal with problems. PCR's proactive elements were limited and generally shallow.

Based on the evolving body of research on police practices and the increasingly apparent limitations of PCR programs, practitioners and theoreticians alike felt that the endemic issues of policing in general—not simply those related to community alliance—were not being effectively addressed. This is the framework from which the embryo of community policing was conceived.

A positive police-community relationship is obviously desired in community policing, although the focus and approach are different from the traditional PCR model's. That relationship must be redefined to include many of the issues discussed above, as well as such factors as respect and support for the police, numbers of complaints against officers, satisfaction with police service, and other quality indicators. Collectively, evaluating these variables can provide important insights on the success of community policing vis-a-vis the police-community relationship.

The Political Dimension

Police involvement with the community in a new, proactive relationship is inherently a political dynamic. The political elements of program development and evaluation should not be ignored.

Crime—and the need to prevent it—has consistently received such substantial attention from politicians simply because it is of major concern to citizens. Several explicit reasons come to mind when considering why crime is a political factor.

First, crime is an emotional issue that affects feelings of safety and security for oneself and one's family. The political process feeds on emotion, as evidenced by political advertisements both for and against the "Brady Bill" handgun purchase waiting period. A tug on the heartstrings has far more political clout than the weight of empirical evidence.

Second, crime will touch most people, either directly or indirectly, at some point in their lifetime. Nearly every American will be a victim or know a victim; consequently, crime is something the public can relate to with near unanimity. This comprehensive experience gives the politician a good frame of reference for communicating with his or her constituency.

Third, crime is one issue on which nearly all people can agree to some extent, regardless of political position, race, ethnicity, age, gender, or lifestyle—people do not want crime. Democrat or Republican, black or white, young or old, man or woman, gay or straight: all agree that crime and violence must be controlled. Consequently, it is politically safe to oppose crime and offer *reasonable* initiatives to control it.

Fourth, citizens are willing to make some sacrifices for protection against criminals. Fear of crime is pervasive, fueled by media reports, political perspectives, and gossip and assumptions. To abate this fear, many people are even willing to pay more taxes. For example, the citizens of Flint, Mich., voted by a two-thirds majority to increase their taxes to support community policing (Kelling and Moore 1988). In Texas, citizens voted to spend over $2 billion to build prisons, even though the state's financial status was lean. The point is that increased expenditures for crime control are relatively easier to justify than other government initiatives, because crime control efforts are not generally seen as a "pork barrel." Spending money on issues of popular concern can be an important way to gain "political chips," as will be discussed later.

Finally, crime is visible and piques a morbid curiosity among people. News reports about murder and mayhem, television programs depicting "real crime," and nonfiction books on "true crime" are all evidence of this. As another illustration, people still go to rural Waco, Texas, where the Branch Davidian compound stood, just to see the sight of that calamity (and buy T-shirts). Crime draws public fascination, particularly when the crime is senseless or an atrocity. Thus, crime makes great fodder for politicians to decry, examine, comment about, and act on.

While there is a common ground surrounding the concern for crime and the need to control it, there are also notable disagreements on the proper responses to it. For example, opinions vary widely on such questions as the following:

- Should police authority be increased to deal with crime?

- Should some legal rights be temporarily "suspended" in order to deal more effectively with criminals, notably drug dealers?

- What is the best way to prevent crime—educational programs, physical crime security, more police officers, stiffer prison sentences, youth diversion programs, the death penalty? All of the above? Some of the above? None of the above?

- Will crime be more effectively prevented (and will justice be more effectively served) if convicted criminals are punished or rehabilitated?

- Is punishment vs. rehabilitation a legal issue, professional issue or political issue?

- Should drugs be legalized to cut down on drug-related crime?

- Is crime a racial problem? A youth problem? An urban problem? A poverty problem? A media problem? A parental problem? A "fill in the blank" problem?

These questions present a number of controversial issues. Importantly, these questions—and the way they are answered—reflect political perspectives and beliefs far more than substantive knowledge and research. Several examples come to mind. Because violent crime has become a pervasive issue for the public, Congress and state legislatures have attempted to respond with a number of "get tough" measures to deal with the problem.

The label of "get tough" is important from a political perspective. Citizens are both tired and fearful of crime, consequently holding elected officials accountable for doing "something" (particularly as reflected in the November 1993 elections). With such explicit political sentiment, politicians recognize that some action must be taken, and that they cannot be viewed as being "soft" on crime or criminals. Consequently, opening youth boot camps, providing federal support for hiring up to 100,000 more community police officers, increasing the range of offenses for the death penalty, making life sentences mandatory for career criminals, increasing mandatory penalties for offenses involving firearms, and building more prisons have been among the common responses. Indeed, the creation of the Community-Oriented Policing Services (COPS) agency in the U.S. Office of Justice Programs in 1994 illustrates the political influence of crime in general and of community policing in particular. The political dynamic comes into play not because of actual knowledge about these measures' effectiveness, but because they lessen the political heat from the public.

Developing a new crime control strategy can be yet another political move. This is where community policing comes into play, and where the concept is jeopardized.

Increasingly, politicians are embracing community policing as the means to more effectively deal with crime and to provide better service to the public, with special concern for increasing the quality of life. In reality, there are probably few politicians who truly understand the philosophy. Despite this, they are providing their heartfelt support (in a political sense) for the concept because it addresses crime, strengthens the bond between the police and the community, and shows that community concerns are being addressed.

This is not meant to sound cynical or accusatory; rather, it is pragmatic. Most politicians realize they have an ethical responsibility to address public concerns. The fact that one's future is tied to this responsiveness is not inconsequential. It is, of course, the nature of the beast. Unfortunately, any new initiative—such as community policing—is also politically fragile, because if no "successes" can be shown, support will dwindle. Defining and measuring "success" is an inherent part of program evaluation, yet the political dynamics cannot be completely ignored.

Performance Evaluations

. . .[A] common issue that emerges in assessing community policing is performance appraisal. Because of this issue's prominence, the authors will address it in this discussion.

Wycoff and Oettmeir (1994), in addressing the need for personnel evaluation, identified six primary reasons for it:

- *Administration.* To help managers make decisions about promotion, demotion, reward, discipline, training needs, salary, job assignment, retention, and termination.
- *Guidance and counseling.* To help supervisors give feedback to subordinates and help them in career planning and preparation, and to improve employee motivation.
- *Research.* To validate selection and screening tests and training evaluations, as well as to assess the effectiveness of interventions designed to improve individual performance.
- *Socialization.* To convey expectations to personnel about both the content and the style of their performance, and to reinforce other means of organizational communication about the department's mission and values.
- *Documentation.* To record the types of problems and situations officers are addressing in their neighborhoods, and how they deal with them. This provides for data-based analysis of the resources and other managerial support needed to address problems, and allows officers the opportunity to have their efforts recognized.
- *System improvement.* To identify organizational conditions that may impede improved performance, and to solicit ideas for changing the conditions.

To fulfill these criteria, a system must be developed to validly and reliably measure individual activities. Unfortunately, this has been difficult to achieve. Police agencies seek a system that has the ease and objectivity of "bean counting," but also the substantive flexibility and ability to be reasonably subjective, as is found in qualitative or narrative evaluations.

Any policy that seeks effective performance evaluations must address several points:

- Who is to be evaluated?
  + Probationary officers
  + Patrol officers
  + Supervisors
  + Managers
  + Administrators
  + Nonsworn personnel
  + Volunteers
- How frequently will personnel be evaluated?
- Who will do the evaluations?
- What kind of training will evaluators need?
- What form will evaluations take (e.g., qualitative, quantitative, narrative, self-evaluation)?

Based on input the authors have received from various police managers seeking to evaluate community police officers, the following factors have consistently emerged:

- Does the officer have a clear sense of objectives?
  + Understands the department's mission and goals
  + Understands his or her role in achieving the department's goals
  + Has objectives he or she wants to accomplish in the job assignment
  + Has a sense of direction in work, rather than just "occupying space"
- Does the officer understand operational policies and procedures?
- What has the officer done for professional self-improvement (e.g., taken college courses; taken advantage of training opportunities; become familiar with research, current thought, issues, and trends in policing; applied diverse knowledge and research to his or her working environment)?
- What kind of feedback is received about the officer (e.g., commendations from the public and department, complaints from the public and department, informal feedback from peers)?
- What duties must the officer perform (e.g., write reports, identify and report

problems, get involved with the community)?

- How does the officer perform his or her duties (e.g., competently, with understanding of the job, confidently, proactively, with professional pride)?

Expanding on the idea of performance assessment, the authors suggest that there be an opportunity for officers to evaluate "up the organization." That is, officers should be able to provide some input on survivors' and managers' effectiveness. Inherently qualitative in nature, factors in this upward assessment may address the following:

Leadership— Does the manager
- set a good example?
- motivate, using positive reinforcement?
- take risks and experiment when appropriate?

Communication—Does the manager
- provide information critical to successful performance?
- provide constructive criticism?
- choose the right time to deliver messages?
- sense others' mood and respond appropriately?
- exhibit compassion and sensitivity?

Teamwork—Does the manager
- treat employees equally?
- encourage group problem solving?
- share credit with all team members?
- hold effective team meetings?

Quality—Does the manager
- set a good example by constantly trying to improve?
- provide training opportunities?
- have a good sense of the customers and their needs?

Planning—Does the manager
- ask for help in planning?
- set realistic, attainable goals?
- follow through with the plan?
- celebrate accomplishments?

While supervisors and managers may resist this form of evaluation, the organization will benefit from the practice. Each organization will need to refine specific procedures for the process to maximize its benefit and ensure that it is used equitably.

Police agencies should develop a broad range of flexible criteria that can accurately assess community police officers' performance. The criteria should be flexible to adjust to the officers' various duties. The criteria should also be evaluated subjectively. The process of developing a performance evaluation policy should also include a component for personnel to evaluate supervisors and managers (see Carter 1995a).

The Evaluation Structure

Evaluation has been defined in many ways—regardless of the definitions, it can be classified in two categories, depending on the general purpose:

Outcome evaluation—The process of determining the value or amount of success in achieving a predetermined goal by

- defining the goal in some qualitatively or quantitatively measurable terms,
- identifying the proper criteria (or variables) to be used in measuring success in attaining the goal,
- determining and explaining the degree of success, and
- recommending further program actions to attain the goal.

Process evaluation—The assessment of procedures used to attain goals under the following criteria:

- Do the procedures substantively contribute to the goal?
- Do the procedures effectively utilize resources?
- Are the procedures coordinated with other elements in the implementation process?
- Are staff members properly trained to execute the procedures?

More simply, each of these evaluations is characterized by the following questions:

- *Outcome evaluation:* Are the goals being accomplished?
- *Process evaluation:* Are the methods for accomplishing goals working with maximum utility?

Essentially, evaluation is a scientific process that involves making comparisons between "conditions." These conditions may range from reported burglary rates to levels of fear of crime to levels of satisfaction with how courteous officers are when speaking to citizens. Regardless of the nature of the comparison, it must address some police department activities that support its goals as related to the mission.

When one says that evaluation is a "scientific" process, that means that it is logical, it is objective, and it has inherent procedures of quality control to try to ensure the accuracy of the information collected, analyzed and interpreted. These procedures are referred to as research methods or the evaluation's methodology. The type of methodology used will vary based on the nature of the program or activities being evaluated. Initially, this largely relates back to the idea of "comparisons"—the factors against which comparisons are made are typically built into the *development* of a program so that an effective *evaluation* can be made. The comparisons made in law enforcement evaluations include the following:

- *"Real" vs. "expected" outcomes*—Serves as a means to assess the accuracy of projections and forecasts. It can be used to assess the accuracy of hypotheses, conclusions and recommendations. Actual or "real" results of a program or activity as determined by the evaluation are compared with the expected results developed in the planning and development phases.
- *"Before" vs. "after" status*—Examines whether specific activities have had an impact or contributed to a change in the goals or the phenomena peripheral to the goals. Measurements are taken before a new program is implemented, and again after a defined period of operation. Changes in the measured variables are attributed to the program's effects. (For example, one would measure burglary rates and citizens' perceptions of safety before a Neighborhood Watch was started, and then after the program had been in effect for a year. Changes, if any, in the burglary rates and/or the feelings of safety would be attributed to the Neighborhood Watch.)

- *Comparison of reactions to operations and administrative expectations*—Determines whether perceptions and quality (value) of community policing activities are consistent with expectations of administrative and operational consumers of the activities. Simply put, great ideas do not always work as planned—this comparison attempts to measure whether they do.

- *Contributory value*—Attempts to assess the degree to which the program activities contributed to goal attainment. A program may have some effect, but it may not necessarily be goal-related. For example, a community outreach program initiated by the police department may make citizens more aware of the public schools' or city recreation department's needs. While this may be viewed as a positive effect, it is not related to the police department's goals.

- *Quality control assessment*—Is an overall, broad-based assessment of the utility, accuracy, general value, and orientation of the community policing philosophy and its related programs. It may be learned that initial ideas and policies related to the philosophy are unrealistic for the department and/or community. As a result, "fine tuning" may be required to ensure that program and activity quality are reasonably attainable.

- *Processes and outputs*—Is an internal assessment of the correlation of expended efforts and procedures compared with the type and quality of output produced by the community policing activities.

The 'Character' of Evaluation Methods

It was noted above that while sophisticated evaluation techniques should be used, they should be limited to conditions and times that require them. Supervisors or designated evaluators can use less rigorous methods for effective "evaluative sensing." When problems appear, then formalized evaluation may be warranted. For informal evaluation to work, it must be performed

- purposely,
- routinely,
- comprehensively, and
- critically.

Importantly, evaluation should be viewed as a positive, constructive activity to make the community policing policies more valuable to the organization—evaluation should not be viewed as "faultfinding".

At the heart of any evaluation is the identification and assessment (measurement) of relevant variables. In a formal evaluation, the variables must be critically selected from the particular activity being assessed. Informal evaluation can take a more generalized approach. To maintain an intuitive base of understanding about the philosophy, programs and activities to be evaluated, there are several types of variables and questions that may be asked during informal evaluations.

1. *Protocols of Officers' Tasks*
- Are the proper or best activities being selected for the designated community policing needs?
- Are personnel properly trained to interpret and utilize the data being collected via the protocol used?
- Is the protocol fully within the agency's capability, or are resources and expertise being stretched?

2. *Information Processing*
- Is information being adequately collected and assessed to evaluate the community policing goals?
- Is the quality of information being adequately controlled and assessed?

- Is too much raw, noncontributory (e.g., high-interest but low-utility, or simply "bean counting") information being introduced into the evaluative process?

3. *Analysis*
- Are the best and most appropriate analytic techniques being used for evaluative purposes?
- Are logical conclusions being drawn?
- How accurate are hypotheses and interpretations of collected data/information?
- Is the analysis providing useful information for decision making?

4. *Reporting*
- Are evaluation reports understandable?
- Are they comprehensive?
- Are they meeting their intended purpose?

5. *Dissemination*
- Are the right people receiving the needed information (e.g., are community police officers and decision makers receiving the information needed to fulfill their responsibilities)?
- Is the information being promptly disseminated?

6. *Personnel*
- Are all staff members—e.g., community police officers, supervisors, evaluators—properly trained for their tasks?
- Is the supervision of community police officers a style that is compatible with the proactive, innovative approach they must use?
- Is officer expertise sufficiently diverse to meet the stated goals?
- Do personnel have effective relations and communications with other organizations that contribute to community policing activities?

The answers to these questions can pose significant challenges for successful program evaluation. The evaluation process is not simple: It requires *planning, expertise* and *thought*. Of these three, perhaps the most difficult is careful, logical, critical thought about the transition from a community policing philosophy to action. . . .

Common Problems to Focus Evaluations

This section addresses some of the more common problems found in police operations as they relate to the evaluation process.

> The department becomes too enmeshed in daily activities and has difficulty changing procedures to respond to fast-breaking or special needs.

Most police departments are bureaucratic, paramilitary organizations. As such, they rely heavily on uniform procedures, allowing limited discretion. Moreover, rigid accountability to the letter of procedures tends to take precedence over the spirit of procedures (embodied in the policy). Consequently, daily activities become routinized. Community policing requires greater flexibility, discretion and innovation. This change is difficult for personnel to accept. Human behavior is inherently dogmatic; thus, change is difficult. Yet, change is essential for community policing to succeed. Ideally, planning and leadership will promote change, and evaluation will measure it.

> Little feedback, positive or negative, is given to the department's various units on the quality and value of community policing activities.

There is a tendency to keep evaluation results—particularly those that are intermediately collected in ongoing programs—among the administrative staff. Sometimes, supervisors in programs being evaluated do not receive the results. This information *must* be communicated to supervisors and line-level employees performing the community policing activities. This not only helps in "fine-tuning" activities to make them more workable, but it can also help in team building and enhancing the program participants' *esprit de corps*. Providing feedback is not only good for program development and implementation, but it is also good management.

Commonly used procedures for responding to calls for service and order-maintenance situations become institutionalized, allowing limited creativity.

More attention should be given to creative problem solving—it must, however, go beyond training and include good *leadership*. There should be an ongoing awareness of the need for proactive efforts and innovation in dealing with all responsibilities. When there is disagreement about the best alternative to use to deal with a problem or situation, personnel frequently *compromise* rather than present their various positions and supporting arguments to decision makers. Doing so would permit *informed leadership*, which, in turn, would contribute to more robust program development.

> There must be ongoing communications between all department units—line and staff—to make community policing work most efficiently and effectively.

Communications must be two way—both horizontal and vertical. Not only must leaders and line-level personnel communicate (and *listen*), but there must also be lateral communications between units. For example, a community police officer may be trying to deal with an increase in "destruction of property" complaints in his or her assigned area. The officer should be able to ask the department's crime analysts to conduct a special analysis of the complaints and receive a cooperative, rapid response. If crime analysis personnel do not understand their role in community policing *and* the need to respond rapidly to such requests, then the potential effect of the officer's activities will be minimized. *All* units must share information, thoughts and ideas as related to their responsibilities and department's goals. Evaluations should be designed to measure communications related to the program and activities in question.

> Program evaluators must avoid "circularity" in facts—that is, not lose perspective and believe that earlier suggestions or assumptions are now fact.

When there is significant investment in a philosophy and in activities that support that philosophy, there is an obvious desire to see one's beliefs confirmed. Program evaluation is a way to objectively measure those beliefs. Because of the desire for success and the reinforcement provided by continued discussion and consideration of the program activities, it is easy to confuse reinforced belief with scientific fact. Thus, care must be taken to avoid this "circularity."

In sum, evaluation of community policing activities should ensure that activities and processes are

- *effective*—they accomplish what is intended; they contribute to goals;
- *efficient*—they are effective without waste or undue resource expenditures;
- *accurate*—they are valid and reliable;
- *timely*—they produce information within time frames that are useful for decision making; and
- *relevant*—they are all directly related to the department's mission and goals.

Because community policing requires substantially different personnel utilization, program evaluation is also critical for effective personnel allocation and deployment.

Allocation—The long-term assignment of personnel by function, geography and shift/duty tour, along with the commitment of required supporting resources to deal with crime and police service demands in the most efficient and effective way.

Deployment—The short-term assignment of personnel to address specific crime problems or police service demands.

Many departments, when initially adopting the community policing philosophy, will *deploy* officers to perform activities that support the philosophy. There is greater flexibility in experimental deployment, which leads to further program and policy development. When policies and practices have been tested and "fine-tuned," resources are *allocated* to fully operationalize the philosophy. In many ways, *allocation* can be viewed as a *strategic* activity, and *deployment* as a more *tactical* activity. In both cases, evaluation plays an important role in continued policy application.

Methodologies Used in Program Evaluation

In all cases, the first methodological issue is to decide *what information is wanted or needed in the evaluation*. The desired information must be clearly articulated so that the best method may be used to collect it.

Administrators and policymakers may sometimes simply say "I want to know about. . . " with no further delineation. In such cases, it is common that an idea is being explored, but that not enough is known to formulate specific questions. Evaluators and administrators must solidify the issues and formulate them into "researchable" questions.

Once it is determined *what information is wanted*, the methodology is selected based on a wide range of factors. In selecting the methodology, the evaluator must examine

- the variables that will yield the information desired, either
- individually,
- collectively (in the aggregate), or
- interactively;
- the ability to access and measure the variables;
- the reliability of the variables;
- the validity of the information obtained.

Identifying and understanding variables are critical in the evaluation process.

Variable—Any characteristic on which individuals, groups, items, or incidents differ.

Examples of variables that may be measured in the evaluation of a community policing program include:

- types of community problems;
- alternative solutions to the problems;
- solutions that have been implemented;
- quality of the relationship between the police and other departments and agencies;
- fear of crime;
- "signs of crime" in the community (the "Broken Windows" analogy);

- citizen satisfaction with police;
- employee job satisfaction;
- degree of citizen involvement in program implementation and problem-solving activities;
- complaints about police behavior (not the numbers of complaints, but the types of complaints);
- responsiveness to citizen demands;
- effectiveness of the management system;
- efficiency of the management system;
- crime patterns;
- patterns in the flow and distribution of unlawful commodities; and
- changes in demographics.

The reader will note that most of these variables are *qualitative*—that is, they are factors that are *described* rather than *counted*, per se. This is because community policing focuses on prevention, problem solving and resolution of issues, rather than documentation of activity. Moreover, community policing is concerned about the *quality of life* both in the community and in the police department. These factors simply cannot be quantified. The problem with qualitative information is that it is much more difficult to collect, analyze and base decisions on. Yet, qualitative dynamics are at the heart of community policing initiatives. This is not to say that quantitative data is never collected in community policing programs. Rather, it is a caveat of which one should be aware.

As a related point, one may asked, "Why should new data be collected if existing data may answer the questions at issue?" It is true that new information does not necessarily have to be collected to evaluate a program. Existing data can be used, but considered in light of the following points:

- How *available* are the data, and can they be obtained for research?
- How *valid* are the data (e.g., do the data measure what is wanted)?
- Do the data *reflect the universe* or a selected, nonrepresentative subset?

- How reliable are the data (e.g., would the same results be found time after time)?

If these questions can be answered to the satisfaction of the policymakers and research team, then there are distinct advantages of using existing data:

- It is *inexpensive*.
- It is more *rapidly available*.

In most cases, new data will need to be collected. Beyond the methodological issues involved, policymakers and researchers must also be concerned with:

- maintaining data confidentiality,
- protecting human subjects,
- maintaining public service/safety obligations,
- getting the staff's cooperation, and
- avoiding the collection of too much data.

In addition, a *methodology* must be selected.

Methodology—A set of scientifically based procedures used to

- collect information from the variables,
- control the information collection for validity and reliability,
- analyze the information to describe the subject/target,
- analyze the information to make inferences about the subject/target,
- direct the interpretations of the analysis, and
- report the information.

There is an inherent difference between quantitative and qualitative methods. The essential difference is that quantitative methods collect and analyze information that can be "counted" or placed on a measurement scale that can be statistically analyzed.

Qualitative methods collect and analyze information given in narrative or rhetorical form and draw conclusions based on the cumulative interpreted meaning of that information. Thus, the nature of the methodology will depend on:

- the *variables' characteristics* and/or
- *how* the information will be collected.

Methodologies and analytic procedures that can be used include:

- survey research (both of citizens and of department members);
- case studies;
- qualitative descriptors based on interviews;
- expert analysis (such as the delphi technique);
- operations research (queuing theory, decision theory, modeling, simulation, gaming theory);
- experimental and quasi-experimental design;
- descriptive and inferential statistical analysis (including probability–based projections);
- econometric models;
- spatial analysis (location/geography and associated patterns of crimes, people, commodities);
- temporal analysis ("time," e.g., monthly, weekly, daily, and hourly measures of incidents and changes in the targeted entity).

While many research methodologies are available, these are among the most useful for program evaluation. Obviously, many of these methods require specialized training to perform them properly. Others require less technical knowledge; personnel who have taken college courses on research methods may be able to conduct the research. However, it should be cautioned that most research is far more complex than many believe. For example, survey research program evaluations requires expertise in item construction and analysis; case studies require, careful analytic skills; interviewing requires controls in both questioning and inter–rater reliability. As a result, administrators must be aware of these concerns when making decisions based on research results. No methodology is "pure" or "conclusive"—[each] requires the evaluator's interpretation. Thus,

the best-prepared evaluators will produce the best output.

Reporting the Results of a Program Evaluation

Once data have been collected in an evaluation, they must be put in a form that can be used for both administrative and operational purposes. The results from the evaluation can be used to make *administrative decisions* concerning program financing, personnel allocation and deployment, program continuance, and related issues. The information can also be used for *operational decisions* that reflect the specific activities, policies and approaches to be used in applying the community policing philosophy. Various evaluation report models can be used to meet different needs. Generally speaking, any evaluation report should have three component parts:

- *Descriptive*—The report describes the issues and processes that are subject to the analysis. The information and data are presented objectively.
- *Interpretative*—The evaluator interprets the data with respect to the issues or activities involved.
- *Available alternatives*—In light of the interpretations, the resources available, the community policing activities used, and the agency's capabilities/expertise, the evaluator recommends alternative actions and strategies for the future.

The general types of evaluation reports that may be written include the following:

- *Cost-effectiveness reports*—These show ratios of costs to results.
- *Comprehensive evaluations*—These show the correlation between program activities (i.e., independent variables) and the results of the activities (i.e., dependent variables).
- *Status and information reports for extradepartmental dissemination*—These are primarily prepared to inform non-law enforcement government administrators and legislators about community policing activities in general.

Caveats Regarding Program Evaluation

Despite sophisticated methodologies and analytic methods, program evaluations have limitations about which administrators should be aware. The results of evaluative efforts are only as good as:

- the quality of raw data/information collected,
- the appropriateness of the methodology(ies) selected,
- the quality of all portions of the data collection process, and
- the quality of the analysis and data interpretation.

Program evaluation is not conclusive—it relies on samples of information and data that are generalized. As a result, it is always possible that the evaluation's findings are incorrect. While good research methods can significantly reduce this possibility, it nonetheless remains. Moreover, evaluations are also subjective, based on the experience of the evaluator(s) and decision maker(s), particularly when qualitative variables are measured (as is frequently the case in evaluating community policing). This subjectivity is both positive and negative. While on the one hand it permits the use of *experience* in the evaluation, it also introduces *emotion*, which can cloud objectivity.

Overall, program evaluation is *descriptive,* not *prescriptive.* That is, it can tell "what is" and "what may be." It can also provide *alternatives* for action. However, it cannot tell *what actions* to take. Decision making remains a human responsibility.

Evaluation is *program*-oriented, not *individually* oriented. That is, it examines aggregate issues—the cumulative effects of a program, policy or activity, not individual steps in the process.

Finally, program evaluation is a function that supports organizational goals—the evaluation's output is *not a goal in and of itself.*

A Final Note

Effective program evaluation largely depends on how well an initiative is developed. Thus, it is critical at the outset to establish a framework that will be the basis for operations, in order to have clear criteria to assess. The message, of course, is to comprehensively plan an initiative so that a meaningful evaluation can be performed.

There is no recipe for evaluating community policing, because the philosophy is conceived and implemented in widely varying ways. However, understanding the critical elements can provide a road map to assist in an assessment.

Program Evaluation Steps in a Nutshell

I. Program Development

A. Clearly and concisely state the following:

1. *Who* is involved in the program:
- Officers
- Segments of the community
- "Target" criminal types
- Classes/groups of people who need a defined service
- Volunteers
- Representatives from other departments or agencies

2. *What* the program is intended to accomplish:
- Goal(s)
- Objectives

3. *When* the program is to be implemented:
- Time frames for planning and development
- Time line for employee, organizational, and resource preparation and allocation

Dates for program initiation Dates for initial program monitoring review
- Dates for data gathering
- Time line for analysis and preparation of evaluation reports

4. *Where* implementation and evaluation will be made:
- Unique community characteristics
- Unique geographic boundaries

5. *Why* the evaluation is proceeding (special evaluation requirements):

- Management decisions on effectiveness (with specific criteria delineated)
- Management decisions on efficiency
- Political issues/dynamics that influence the program
- Need for evaluation due to grants and/or experimental program funding

6. *How* the evaluation is proceeding:

- Research methods being used
- Adherence to timetable
- Personnel responsible for program design, implementation and evaluation

B. Convert all applicable factors in the program into measurable variables.

C. Complete the following steps:

1. Select data-gathering methods.
2. Finalize and gain approvals for evaluation time frame.
3. Provide necessary training to program participants.
4. Set up the management structure and policies for the program.

II. Program Implementation

A. Put program policies into effect.

B. Have supervisors audit activities to ensure that:

1. everyone is doing what they are supposed to, and
2. activities and duties are being performed correctly.

C. Begin data gathering (depending on research methods used).

D. Make program adjustments as necessary.

III. Evaluation

A. Complete data gathering.

B. Analyze data.

C. Write reports.

D. Disseminate results.

E. Have command staff review evaluation results in consultation with the research team:

1. Draw operational conclusions.

2. Discuss results, validity and reliability.

3. Discuss possible program amendments.

IV. Post-Evaluation Decisions

A. Is further data collection and analysis needed?

B. What strengths and weaknesses were found in the program?

C. How can the program be amended?

D. Should the program be dropped?

V. Evaluation Starts Over As Appropriate

References

Babbie, E. 1962. *Survey Research Methods.* 6th ed. Belmont, Calif: Wadsworth Publishing Co.

Baltimore County Police, Field Operations Bureau. 1988. *Community Foot Patrol Officer Guidelines and Procedures.* Towson, Md.: Baltimore County Police Department.

Bohigian, H.E. 1971. *The Foundations and Mathematical Models of Operations Research With Extensions to the Criminal Justice System.* Doctoral dissertation in the School of Education, New York University.

Bureau of Justice Statistics. 1988. *Report to the Nation on Crime and Justice.* Washington, D.C.: U.S. Department of Justice.

Cahn, M., and J.M. Tien. 1980. *An Evaluation Report of an Alternative Approach in Police Response: The Wilmington Management of Demand Program.* Cambridge, Mass.: Public Systems Evaluation Inc.

Carter, D.L. 1989. *Research in Support of the Community Policing Concept.* Training document, FBI Academy, Quantico, Va.

———. 1995a. *Keystone Human Resource Issues for Community Policing.* Paper presented at the NIJ/BJA Annual Conference on Criminal Justice Research and Evaluation, Washington, D.C.

———. 1995b. "The Politics of Community Policing." *Public Administration Review* 191:6–26.

Carter, D.L., and A.D. Sapp. 1993. "A Comparative Analysis of Clauses in Police Collective Bargaining Agreements as Indicators of Change in Labor Relations." *American Journal of Police* 122:17–46.

Carter, D.L., A.D. Sapp, and D.W. Stephens. 1991. *Survey of Contemporary Police Issues: Critical Findings.* Washington, D.C.: Police Executive Research Forum.

Couper, D.C. 1991. *Quality Policing: The Madison Experience.* Washington, D.C.: Police Executive Research Forum.

Dolbeare, K.M., ed. 1975. *Public Policy Evaluation.* Beverly Hills, Calif: Sage Publications.

Eck, J.E., and W. Spelman. 1987. *Problem-Solving: Problem-Oriented Policing in Newport News.* Washington, D.C.: Police Executive Research Forum.

Farmer, M. 1981. *Differential Police Response Strategies.* Washington, D.C.: Police Executive Research Forum.

Franklin, J.L., and J. Thrasher. 1976. *An Introduction to Program Evaluation.* New York: John Wiley and Sons.

Greene, J., and R. Worden. 1988. "Community–Based Policing and Foot Patrol: Issues of Theory and Evaluation." In J. Greene and S. Mastrofski, eds., *Community Policing: Rhetoric or Reality?* New York: Praeger Press.

Hartmann, F.X., L.P. Brown, and D.W. Stephens. 1989. *Community Policing: Would You Know It If You Saw It?* East Lansing, Mich.: National Center for Community Policing.

———. 1976. *Program Analysis for State and Local Governments.* Washington, D.C.: Urban Institute Press.

Hatry, H.P., et al. 1981. *Practical Program Evaluation for State and local Governments.* Washington, D.C.: Urban Institute Press.

Kansas City, MO., Police Department. 1977. *Response Time Analysis: Executive Summary.* Kansas City: Board of Police Commissioners.

Katzer, J., et al. 1978. *Evaluating Information: A Guide for Users of Social Science Research.* Menlo Park, Calif.: Addison-Wesley Publishing Co.

Kelling, G.L., and Moore, M.H. 1988. "The Evolving Strategy of Policing." *Perspectives on Policing,* (4).

Kelling, G. 1981. *The Newark Foot Patrol Experiment.* Washington, D.C.: Police Foundation.

Kelling, G., et al. 1974. *The Kansas City Preventive Patrol Experiment: Technical Report. Washington, D.C.: Police Foundation.*

Kerlinger, F. 1973. *Foundations of Behavioral Research.* 2d ed. New York: Holt, Rinehart and Winston.

Larson, R.C., and M. Cahn. 1985. *Synthesizing and Extending the Results of Police Patrol Studies.* Washington, D.C.: National Institute of Justice.

Levine, M., and J.T. McEwen. 1985. *Patrol Deployment.* Washington, D.C.: National Institute of Justice.

McEwen, J.T., et al. 1969. *Evaluation of the Differential Police Response Field Test.* Washington, D.C.: National Institute of Justice.

Morris, L.L., and C. Fitz-Gibbon. 1978. *How to Deal With Goals and Objectives.* Beverly Hills, Calif.: Sage Publications.

Nagel, S.S., and M. Neef. 1975. *Operations Research Methods.* Beverly Hills, Calif.: Sage Publications.

National Institute of Justice. 1991. *Evaluation Plan: 1991.* Washington, D.C.: U.S. Department of Justice.

President's Commission on Law Enforcement and Administration of Justice. 1967. *Task Force Report: The Police.* Washington, D.C.: U.S. Government Printing Office.

Radelet, L., and D.L. Carter. 1994. *The Police and the Community.* 5th ed. New York: Macmillan Publishing Co.

Skolnick, J,and D. Bailey. 1986. *The New Blue Line.* New York: The Free Press.

Spelman, W., and D. Brown. 1984. *Calling the Police: Citizen Reporting of Serious Crime.* Washington, D.C.: National Institute of Justice.

Spelman, W., and J. Eck. 1987. *Problem-Oriented Policing: The Newport News Experiment.* Washington, D.C.: Police Executive Research Forum.

Thierauf, R.J., and R.C. Klekamp. 1975. *Decision Making Through Operations Research.* 2d ed. New York: John Wiley and Sons.

Trojanowicz, R.C. 1990. "Community Policing Is Not Police-Community Relations." *FBI Law Enforcement Bulletin.* October: 6–11.

Trojanowicz, R., and B. Bucqueroux. 1990. *Community Policing.* Cincinnati: Anderson Publishing Co.

Trojanowicz, R., and D.L. Carter. 1988. *The Philosophy and Role of Community Policing.* East Lansing, Mich.: National Center for Community Policing.

Weidman, D.R., et al. 1975. *Intensive Evaluation for Criminal Justice of Planning Agencies.* Washington, D.C.: U.S. Department of Justice/Law Enforcement Assistance Administration.

Whitaker, G., et al. 1982. *Basic Issues in Police Performance.* Washington, D.C.: National Institute of Justice.

Whitmire, K., and L.P. Brown. Undated. *City of Houston Command Station/Neighborhood-Oriented Policing Overview.* Houston: Houston Police Department.

Wycoff, M.A., and T.N. Oettmeier. 1994. *Evaluating Police Officer Performance.* Washington, D.C.: National Institute of Justice.

Part V

Epilogue: Future Trends and Challenges

We live in a dynamic world where people, things, and ideas are constantly changing. Given this unpredictable world, can anyone believe that the future is likely to be tranquil or that we can enter the future with our eyes fixed firmly on the methods of the past? In truth, we are probably moving into some of the most tempestuous and challenging years in the history of this nation; the police must anticipate and plan for what is coming.

This is an exciting time in which to be engaged in the policing field; any officer who seeks to be challenged at the workplace, and who is fortunate enough to be a part of an innovative department, would be hard pressed to find a more exhilarating era in the history of formal policing. The emergence of a "new policing," vested in partnerships and problem solving, provides knowledge and tools to effect more long-term solutions to recurring community problems. At the same time, this perspective affords officers a much higher degree of closure and job satisfaction than was obtainable under the older "professional" model.

The first reading in Part V, by W. L. Tafoya, uniquely presents the thoughts of six major thinkers in community policing—three academics and three executives. These individuals discuss a wide range of related subjects, including the origins and the future of community policing. The second reading, by S.

Greenberg, describes several future police issues and challenges including community policing, the drug trade, citizen fear, and violence.

As the readings in Part V emphasize, police executives are being taught how to allocate resources. They need to prepare their departments to meet the challenges of ongoing change in the form of rapid technological advancements and increasingly complex social environments. Diversity—cultural, gender, and ethnic—will increasingly characterize the police of the future. Success will come to intelligent, analytical officers who are supported by information, technology, the community, training, and internal support systems that reward and motivate them in their problem-solving efforts. To name a few challenges, police accreditation, a more civilian approach, and budgetary constraints are issues that will be critical.

Given that the landscape of policing is strewn with the bones of "innovations" attempted and abandoned, one might wonder whether community-oriented policing and problem solving have staying power and can survive in the long term. The answer is in the hands of time. However, the readings presented thus far, and those that follow, have surely provided a rational basis for these new approaches. ✦

22

The Current State and Future of Community Policing

William L. Tafoya

It is important in any discipline to learn from some of its major figures—those who influence a body of knowledge and its growth, direction, and conventional wisdom. Community policing has developed several such luminaries; W. L. Tafoya affords an opportunity to hear from six such persons, three of them academics and three of them police executives. As you read, consider the common themes of their responses in terms of the following: What are major contributions to policing? Who are some of the major founders of community policing? What is its potential and what are some major challenges for the future?

Over the past two decades a great deal of research has been undertaken in an effort to determine the effectiveness about various conceptions that today have been subsumed under the rubric of Community Policing. To gain a viewpoint of the implications of this important concept, OICJ has conducted interviews with six individuals who have made important contributions to Community Policing. All are scholars in their own right. Three are university professors: Dennis Rosenbaum (University of Illinois at Chicago), Gary Cordner (Eastern Kentucky University), and David Carter (Michigan State University). Three carry a badge: Dennis Nowicki (Chief of Police, Charlotte, North Carolina), Charles Moose (Chief of Police, Portland, Oregon), and Joseph Harpold

(Supervisory Special Agent, FBI Academy, Quantico, Virginia).

Their responses to a series of questions follow.

1. What Factors Preceded and Prompted Your Interest in Community Policing (CP)?

David Carter

We have a great body of research about policing and preventive patrol, response time, differential police response, directed patrol, and so forth, going back to the early 1970s. The research was "tight" and innovative. Yet, it seems it was used very little. There was virtually no translation of this new body of knowledge to policy. Community policing seems to do this. It takes the product of research and experimentation and applies it to operations. Another reason for my interest in community policing was that it did not seem that what we were doing in patrol was working. The whole idea of quality management, increased efficiency and effectiveness and, particularly, re-engineering the organization seems to fit well with community policing. It is the application of contemporary management to the police environment.

Gary Cordner

On a personal level what is now being called CP is consistent with the way I always looked at the role of the police and how I tried to do policing when I was a practitioner. On a professional level, I was fortunate enough to serve as an evaluator of the COPE Program in Baltimore County in the early 1980s. This was one of the first "official" CP evaluation projects. As it evolved, POP was incorporated into COPE. In fact, Herman Goldstein became an advisor to that project. That I filled this role enabled me to benefit from exposure to Neil Behan and Herman Goldstein because of association with that project.

Joe Harpold

I began getting involved in the precursor to community policing in 1972 when I was a police officer in Kansas City. I had undertaken a research project that resulted in a large community effort to combat rape through crime prevention and victim assistance initiatives. What was then viewed within policing circles merely as community relations gave me an appreciation for the value of community involvement. When I joined the FBI, I found myself involved in crime resistance, crime analysis, and community relations programs in Cleveland, Ohio. In 1984, I joined the faculty at the FBI Academy. There I began teaching community crime prevention that is central to community policing. Community policing offers a style of policing that affords an opportunity to make suggestions, volunteer, and solve community problems. I believe people like the feeling of being involved. It also provides an opportunity for a more personalized relationship with police officers.

Charles Moose

Traditional policing was not being very successful and was doing a great deal to destroy the trust between the police and the community. We were becoming a separate group and failing at our task. Instead of solving problems, we were causing situations to explode and then simply leaving everything to get worse. The concept that the police and the community could work together not only made sense, it sounded rewarding.

Dennis Nowicki

Many years ago, primarily through my membership in PERF, I met Herman Goldstein. His ideas, especially his 1979 "Crime & Delinquency" article, caused me to start thinking about what we were doing. At the time, I was a lieutenant in the Chicago Police Department. I started thinking of myself as a manager and not just as a cop. Community Policing made a lot of sense. By the time I was deputy superintendent in Chicago, I tried to move the department in that direction. For example, we made revisions in the way we had been policing with differential response. Together with the deputy superintendent of technical services, we made other changes when I was deputy superintendent at the Police Academy. Later, as chief of police in Joliet, Illinois, I re-engineered that agency using POR. Today the Joliet Police Department continues to use that model.

Dennis Rosenbaum

I have been studying community crime prevention for many years. CP is a logical extension of that initiative. It provides a context between the police and community. As an evaluator for more than 20 years, I enjoy trying to document and evaluate reform efforts.

2. Are Community Policing, Community-Oriented Policing, Problem-Oriented Policing (POP), and Neighborhood-Oriented Policing Synonymous Terms or Is There a Substantive Difference?

David Carter

This is where I probably differ with many others, but I would say now that they are. Each of these ideas, when introduced, had a different methodology in mind to meet a common end: improved police service delivery and more productive use of the police patrol work force. As these concepts have evolved, I see them merging into a synonymous ideology which can be tailored to a given community. Call it quality policing, what David Couper called it in Madison, Wisconsin.

Gary Cordner

All the terms except POP are synonymous. POP is substantively distinct although compatible and overlaps significantly the other variants. The main thrust of CP seems to be in developing a relationship between the police and the community, whereas for POP the thrust is on how police officers think about and do their work.

Joe Harpold

In the courses I teach, I say that there is substantive difference. I do not believe there is much of a difference between community policing and community-oriented policing. But I believe there is a major difference between problem-oriented policing and neighborhood-oriented policing. I also expand on Herman Goldstein's definition. I emphasize that to grasp the difference it is essential that the problem and not just the symptoms be well understood. The focus is different in traditional policing than in problem-oriented policing. In the latter the emphasis is on the problem-solving process.

Charles Moose

One can argue that you can have POP without the community. For the Portland Police Bureau it has made sense to have problem-solving as a value of community policing. This allows us to focus on solving problems while always having the community as the foundation of everything we do. The other values that surround our decision-making are partnership, empowerment, accountability and service. The other three terms seem synonymous although I prefer the term community policing.

Dennis Nowicki

Those labels do not have meaning until you define them. In Charlotte, we use the term community problem oriented policing. We define it through our mission statement and in the way we go about our business. We will build problem-solving partnerships with our citizens to prevent the next crime and enhance the quality of life throughout our community.

Dennis Rosenbaum

A number of years ago, America was policed differently than it is today. Today there is a growing consensus about what the police should be doing. Because POP is the process of solving neighborhood problems, it has become a central activity in policing. We now understand that engaging the community in the CP process is essential. Therefore, emphasis is correctly placed on neighborhoods. When CP first came out in the late 1970s, I was disappointed in the lack of a clearly defined role for the community. At that time, the police did everything. Now that has changed. Community involvement is now central to successful CP initiatives.

3. What Could Be Done to Correct the Commonly Held Perception Among Practitioners That Community Policing Is 'Old Wine In a New Bottle'?

Gary Cordner

I don't think it is entirely a misconception. There is a lot in CP that is similar to what has been done before. But, there is more in CP than traditional policing. One thing that would help demonstrate that CP is more than old wine would be to continue to provide police officers with more and more examples of some of the innovative things that others are doing. It is also important to respect and value the experience and wisdom of police officers. It is important to acknowledge what police officers have learned over the years and work that into CP rather than replacing their experience with someone else's notion of CP.

Joe Harpold

We haven't communicated the new concept of CP in a language that has been well understood. Unless we tell people that CP is an enhancement to traditional policing, and not merely an addition, it is very difficult for citizens or police officers, for that matter, to accept CP as different because the incomplete explanation does not make CP seem to be REAL police work. In terms of "old wine in a new bottle," we want the relationship that the police once had with the community; that police officers know my name and I know theirs. What makes this wine new is that whereas before the patrolman was given a badge and a gun and put out there, now we're training police officers in new concepts, techniques of analysis, and problem-solving strategies.

Charles Moose

We need to remind ourselves that the police and our poorer minority communities have never worked well together and we have never been seen as a problem-solving partner in these communities. This history is the old wine. Just putting out a couple of bike patrols does not constitute community policing.

With community policing, the relationships determine if one is really doing community policing. This is the new wine.

Dennis Nowicki

There are certain elements that make up wine, old or new. Community policing is not really old wine because it is arranged differently than traditional policing. We are mixing it all differently than in the past. All the ingredients that were in the old wine are there, but in different quantities. Ask those who ask the question; ask what gets measured. In Charlotte we have de-emphasized rapid response. That is not the "bottom line" as it was in the old days. Now what is important is that we solve problems. We still respond as promptly as possible, but that is no longer a measurable.

Dennis Rosenbaum

This is a partially true statement. But CP brings back the best of the old way of policing while adding some important new dimensions. CP is bringing back the old contact with the community: this is an important element. If you start with the notion that information is the basis for solving crime, then the need for the police to work with the community becomes crucial. More importantly, in CP there is something new. CP gets officers out there to try it. It is easy to be critical of CP when one has not tried it. "Doing" CP will help both the police and citizens to cross the bridge. The "something new" that has been added to traditional policing is that CP enables community input to be taken seriously. CP is increasingly structured to provide opportunities for community input. CP is a little better planned and more organized than was the case when it was first introduced. Another important aspect of CP is that policing is going through a technological revolution. Thus, the door is now open for CP to move to the next level. We now have new tools, such as laptop computers that enhance CP initiatives. As we consider police organizational structure, CP is not old wine. We are breaking down the quasi-military structure of police organizations. We are seeing a more responsive delivery system. Internally and exter-

nally, there is some new wine to be consumed.

4. What Percentage of the 16,000 American Law Enforcement Agencies Are Today Making Use of Community Policing?

Gary Cordner

Nobody really knows. A wild guess is that 75% are doing something akin to CP. Some aspects or elements of CP are in use. The number of agencies that have whole-heartedly adopted all the elements of CP is much smaller. National surveys by NIJ's COPS Office, the Police Foundation, and the Police Executive Research Forum (PERF) are underway to discover to what degree CP is being practiced.

Joe Harpold

This is a very difficult question to answer. No one really has a true answer. We recently completed a research project in which 686 agencies were sent surveys. We had an 81% (546) return rate. From that survey, we can only comment on perceptions. Whether or not the respondents are really doing CP cannot be answered from a mail-in survey. Respondents use different definitions of what CP means to them when they answered our questions. Some people reported that they are doing CP; others say they think they're not doing CP; 42% (229 of 546) say that they are doing CP right. In a smaller study, 245 agencies were sent surveys. In that study, 66% (98 of 148) of respondents said they had CP right now. In that survey others said that while they are not doing CP now, they plan to do so in the future. Using their own definitions there were some commonalities, but it is quite logical to expect that there are also differences, which depend on the communities themselves.

Dennis Nowicki

It is probably very small. A police chief goes through a five-stage process in bringing about community policing: (1) Discovery and exploration, (2) preparation, (3) program, (4) actualization (everything done is consistent with the philosophy), and (5) renewal. I do not know of any department that has actualized. My department is as close as any.

Dennis Rosenbaum

Presently this is an impossible question to answer. National survey data indicates that police agencies are involved in CP at different levels. Complicating the research initiative is the fact that individuals are not necessarily good reporters of change. This is a methodological problem. No one person can give an accurate assessment of CP. CP means different things to different people. Thus, a definition problem persists. Given that dilemma, the percentage of agencies making use of CP is relatively small. That is, the number of agencies that are doing what should be done. A lot of agencies are doing a little in the way of CP and a few agencies are doing a lot of CP.

5. Recently Released FBI Statistics Reflect a Decline in Violent Crime Over the Past Five Years in the U.S. What Part Has Community Policing Played in This Decline, If Any?

David Carter

The crime drop is a product of many factors. Certainly police programming of different types has contributed to it, but so have things such as demographic trends, changes in social values, the economy, and perhaps incarceration policies. To say that community policing alone has caused the crime rate drop is naive. We need to look at the big picture. Society is complex and changes in social phenomena, such as the crime rate drop, require complex explanations.

Gary Cordner

Some part. It is widely understood that we have had several fortuitous developments in the time since CP has been used. Some factors include beneficial demographic shifts, e.g., a smaller proportion of young adults, a strong economy, etc. There are also other developments within policing beside CP. Teasing out independent effects is pretty difficult.

Joe Harpold

First, this decline may be a false "positive." That is, this trend may not hold, In *Varieties of Police Behavior* in 1968, James Q. Wilson reported that political culture, socio-economic characteristics of a community, and so forth, reflect the type of behavior of the police in their interactions with the public. In 1985, Wilson and Richard J. Hermstein, in *Crime and Human Nature*, talked about "constitutional" factors, such as sex, age, intelligence, and personality, which may differentiate the criminal from the non-criminal. What is the relationship between violent crime and those who commit that crime, those who are predominately kids age 15 to 24? In 1986, police futurist William L. Tafoya completed a landmark research project. He forecasts that violent crime will dramatically increase before the end of this decade. I agree that through the remainder of this century we're going to be looking at an increase instead of a decrease in violent crime. CP will not prevent all the violent crimes. In our survey we looked at the impact of CP on violent crime. Almost 100% said that CP did impact violent crime and does address fear of crime. It is really interesting, I think, that traditional policing does not change the fear factor. With CP, citizens as well as police officers themselves report feeling safer and police departments report that CP does reduce crime.

Charles Moose

Crime is down because of low unemployment, the population shift with regard to young people, and several other social factors. Community policing is a philosophy that has had its impact and in many cases advocated for many of the other influencing social factors. But presently there is no clear way to judge the impact of community policing. This is a tough question that needs to be answered.

Dennis Nowicki

Partly, but we cannot give CP all the credit. This is a complex issue. There is no one, simple solution. As we define it, CP is a powerful concept and it is having positive results. In those neighborhoods where we have strong partnerships that result in focusing energies on solving problems, we are showing greater reductions than in those neighborhoods where those partnerships have not yet been developed. Every district is having its own successes and failures. The key is strong neighborhood organizations.

Dennis Rosenbaum

CP has played a small yet significant role. If crime statistics are evaluated based on the premise that the forces which determine a decrease in crime include those beyond the control of the police, then this is a strong statement. It means that when the police work together with the community and use a wide range of tools to solve crime to mobilize the community, this can have a powerful effect if efforts are targeted and intensive. However, there are competing explanations for the decline in crime. One is the stabilization and aging of the drug market. Thus far, we are actually lost for a meaningful explanation of the decline in crime. But CP is a plausible explanation in some communities. In cities such as New York and Chicago, for example, there is some reason to believe that joint police and community efforts seem to be related. Therefore, CP seems to have contributed to the decline in crime in those communities. Of course, the same may be true elsewhere.

6. What Were the Contributions of Robert Trojanowicz?

David Carter

Bob first started discussing Community Policing—which he called Neighborhood Foot Patrol—in the mid-1970s, with little notice. He got his first grant to study the concept in Flint, Michigan, in 1978, from the Mott Foundation. That was ground-breaking in terms of the development of Community Policing. Bob had worked with many police departments experimenting with the concept well before it came into vogue. While many are familiar with his work in the area, particularly via his books and the Harvard University Executive Sessions, I think there is a general lack of knowledge abut how deep-

rooted and long-lasting his impact has been on Community Policing.

Gary Cordner

His influence was very important, especially in the early years of the 1980s. For many police departments, foot patrol was the precursor to the more full–fledged CP. One of Bob's most important contributions was that he enthusiastically supported the simple— not simplistic—notion that for CP to succeed, it is necessary for administrators to take a more humanitarian approach to policing in general.

Joe Harpold

Trojanowicz wrote landmark publications in CP, such as *Community Policing in Contemporary Perspectives* and *How to Get Started*. I would say that his contribution was very significant and brought about a change in the climate of law enforcement. He helped start the winds to blow in the right direction of this change. He talked about the "BIG 6" which was necessary in CP because it required the police, citizens, media, politicians, public and private organizations and business communities in partnership to enhance the quality of life in the community.

Charles Moose

He set the table with clear, understandable documentation of community policing. His definition, with Bucqueroux in 1990, is enlightening. Community policing is a contemporary perspective; is very workable and understandable by police officers and community members. We could go on and on with many other accomplishments, but let's keep it simple.

Dennis Nowicki

His ability to stimulate our thinking. In Charlotte we are developing an "organizational filter" that is consistent with our CP philosophy. Bob did not talk about such a concept, but the idea is based on his ideas.

Dennis Rosenbaum

He had a special ability to bring practitioners together. He opened a dialogue that by itself helped to advance policing in the U. S.

7. What Have Been the Contributions of Herman Goldstein?

David Carter

Herman has contributed so much to policing in many different venues; he has truly changed the landscape of policing in America. His classic 1977 book, *Policing in a Free Society*, although 20 years old, still has a great deal of relevant concepts. And, of course, his 1990 book, *Problem-Oriented Policing*, forged new ground into the analysis of police responsibilities and responses. In looking at Herman's contributions, I think we need to look at all of his work. Collectively, it has shaped his view on how to modernize all police practices and we need to rethink the role and responsibilities of the police in American society.

Gary Cordner

His prominence has been extremely significant. His "invention" of POP and continued elaboration of the concept has resolutely inspired a lot of police officers and academics to take seriously the philosophy. POP has changed the way police officers do their work.

Joe Harpold

Goldstein also wrote landmark publications on Problem-Oriented Policing. He has gained the respect of many, many police executives who are beginning to understand that CP offers the means to bring about needed change.

Charles Moose

His contributions are on-going. He continues to ask the tough questions, while demanding that we continue to think about community policing and problem-solving policing. Otherwise, we get busy with budgets and personnel issues. Without Goldstein, there is no evolution of the philosophy. Goldstein also has that rare ability to be meaningful to both the practitioner and the academician. He is very difficult to dismiss; he is well rooted and practical. Also, he continues to be available and visible.

Dennis Nowicki

His ideas are tremendous. They have had great influence. I need to point out that the concepts of these two pioneers are in no way contradictory: their ideas are in fact complementary.

Dennis Rosenbaum

Enormous. He was really the first—he is considered the pioneer of POP—who forced us to begin thinking about responding to problems rather than continuing in the mindless mode of incident-driven policing. He provided the theoretical framework for the switch which gradually has occurred.

8. Who Are Some of the Major Contributors?

David Carter

Darrel Stephens, Dennis Nowicki, Gil Kerlikowski, Neil Behan, and the late Keith Bergstrom.

Gary Cordner

Among the practitioners, Lee Brown, Neil Behan, David Couper, and Darrel Stephens come to mind. They each have had a major impact on the positive image of CP over the past two decades.

Joe Harpold

Among the most notable scholars are Dave Carter, Gary Cordner, Mark Moore, Francis Hartmann, Malcolm Sparrow, George Kelling, and others. Among the practitioners, Lee Brown, Reuben M. Greenberg, Darrel Stephens, Bill Bratton, and too many small town police chiefs and sheriffs than you have space for me to list.

Dennis Nowicki

George Kelling, John Eck, Bill Geller, Wes Skogan, and Dennis Rosenbaum.

Dennis Rosenbaum

Among the scholars are Wesley Skogan and George Kelling. They put disorder on the front burner across the country. They helped us to realize that a big part of what needs to be done is to reduce disorder, both physical and social. They helped us to understand that neighborhoods decline when local residents and the police fail to address or attend to what are seemingly the less serious problems, such as broken windows, graffiti, garbage, and loud music. The reality is that these problems are the most offensive to urban residents. They enhance fear significantly which sets in motion a cycle of neighborhood decline. That process has to be arrested.

9. What Are Some of the Most Significant Publications on Community Policing?

Gary Cordner

Bob's 1983 evaluation of the Neighborhood Foot Patrol Program in Flint, Michigan and his 1990 book with Bucqueroux, *Community Policing: A Contemporary Perspective*. Of course, Herman's 1979 "Crime & Delinquency" article, as well as his 1990 book, *Problem-Oriented Policing*. Another important publication is *Community Policing: Rhetoric or Reality*, edited by Jack Greene and Steve Mastrofski in 1988. This book stimulated a great deal of thinking about the pros and cons of CP: it highlighted the distinctions between the articulation and the basis in fact of CP.

Joe Harpold

The publications of Trojanowicz and Bucqueroux, Herman Goldstein, Carter and Radelet, as well as documents published by the National Institute of Justice, among others. There are actually so many worthwhile CP publications out there that it would be impossible to describe all of them.

Dennis Nowicki

Herman's 1979 "Crime & Delinquency" article as well as his 1990 book, *Problem-Oriented Policing*. Bob and Bonnie Bucqueroux's 1990 book, *Community Policing: A Contemporary Perspective, Disorder in Decline, Beyond 911* by Mark Moore, *Police As Problem Solvers*, and PERF's many publications on POP.

Dennis Rosenbaum

George Kelling and Catherine M. Coles' 1996 book, *Fixing Broken Windows*; Wesley Skogan and Susan M. Hartnett's 1997 book,

Community Policing Chicago Style, is also an important contribution to enhancing our understanding of the impact of CP.

10. What Have Been the Major Contributions of Community Policing to Policing in the Past 18 Years?

Gary Cordner

Because of CP, police officers and police departments are much more likely today to think of themselves and their role in terms of working with the community rather than in an "us vs. them" framework. With respect to POP, police departments today are being much more creative in the way they tackle specific crime problems and disorder. In many cases, they are are also being much more effective.

Joe Harpold

You can almost measure these contributions with a video camera. Neighborhoods have turned around. A lot of places start with clean up campaigns, which restore a community's pride and esteem. You can measure it in terms of people's behavior and how the neighborhoods look. The real contribution is that it facilitates police and community working together to solve these problems in a more meaningful long lasting way. CP prevents a lot of communities from getting as bad as they might. CP gets "good people" together with the police and in some places it keeps the bonds tighter between these people and the police. People need a personalized relationship with their police. CP facilitates a personal relationship between law-abiding citizens and keeps anonymity from creeping in.

Dennis Nowicki

Major re-engineering of police departments is going on across the country. This involves decentralization, flattening the pyramid, structural changes, operational strategies, and POP as the basic unit of work. All of this is value-driven because of the concept of CP is very visible. We are more open as organizations. We are more willing to let outsiders in. We are more involved in other departments within our jurisdiction in the delivery of government services. We are not as isolated as we used to be from other government services.

Dennis Rosenbaum

CP has permanently changed the paradigm in policing. The value of preventive patrol, for example, has been replaced by neighborhood-based problem solving. The focus on order-maintenance and community participation will require some organizational change and education.

11. What Are the Major Impediments to Community Policing in America?

David Carter

Organizational change. It takes time to change the organization toward a new philosophy and overcoming dogmatism is extraordinarily difficult. Measuring effectiveness is also difficult. We are trying to quantify quality; this is very subjective. Moreover, how do we measure crime and problems we prevented? Patience. Both the police and the public have to recognize that community policing strategies are inherently long-term. This is a factor that is not really consistent with American life today. Political will. Changing a philosophy of policing and maintaining the commitment to see it through requires exceptional political will. Not every police chief can survive this.

Gary Cordner

We read a great deal about police culture and resistance to change. Middle-management has been described as being a primary impediment to progress. I am not sure whether or not that type of resistance is predictable. Given the rather heavy-handed ways in which CP has sometimes been implemented, suspicion and distrust are natural preliminary outcomes in hierarchically structured organizations. The main obstacles are simply insufficient imagination and in some cases, a lack of nerve or managerial sophistication.

Joe Harpold

The problem with implementing CP in America is not CP The problem is we. It has to do with our perception of policing. But frontline police officers and their supervisors are the ones who are going to make it or break it. Everyone must have the same common belief in order for CP to work. When it gains acceptance from the police agency, then it is going to work. But if everyone is not for it or in it, then it will not work. Internal acceptance of the change has to happen. Then the chief executive can put all this together and accept recommendations on how to provide better service to law-abiding citizens.

Charles Moose

The media and the American love affair with instant solutions. The Portland Police Bureau has been evolving as a community policing organization for seven years. Yet, our local media and many of our community members still focus on a quick fix formula and expect us to operate independently. But refusing to see the need for a holistic approach, they still think that the police alone can solve our community problems. Our funding is still a moving target and thus the goal of institutionalization is difficult.

Dennis Nowicki

The short time line of politicians. Transforming an organization takes time. Lack of understanding of the change process in a police organization is problematic. Complexity is a major component within the organization as it is in the community. An educational process is essential. Some politicians do not have a capacity to understand or deal with this kind of complexity.

Dennis Rosenbaum

Organizational structure and the culture of policing are dominant obstacles. Major changes in quasi-military structures are needed to make this happen. Some police departments are further along than others. Too many have made only cosmetic changes. The key point is that the ability to sustain a new paradigm will be determined by organizational readiness. That is, to what extent is the organization ready—at all levels—to deliver a new style of policing? Major changes still have to be made in their standards. Organizations need to be flattened and decentralized. Police departments need to be geobased. They need to empower not just the officer, but also sergeants and lieutenants, to affect the quality of policing in the neighborhood. Police organizations need to make decisions without the fear of bureaucratic punishment. Another element is the police culture. The police have spent so many years battling the bad guys, they have developed an "us vs. them" mindset. Too many have become disillusioned. Such officers need to be "jump started" to get them to believe CP is the right thing to do. For good things to accrue to the police and to the public, deep skepticism has to be overcome. In some cases, it is just a matter of resistance to change. Now, seemingly all of a sudden, they are expected to put down their defenses. It is not that easy. We should not underestimate the time it will take to shift from the old to the new paradigm. We must not think in terms of months or years to bring about CP, but rather decades.

12. What Are Your Impressions of Community Policing in Other Countries?

David Carter

I have worked with the police in England, Thailand, South Korea, China, and several eastern European countries concerning implementation of community policing. In addition, I have corresponded with the police in Brazil, South Africa, Zambia, and Bosnia about the concept. Needless to say, there are many obstacles to address, ranging from budgets to political ideology. Also, we must recognize that the problems to be solved are quite different. Despite this, I have found the police in different countries are exploring the ideology of community policing and seeing how the concept integrates with their culture and legal systems. We should not be presumptuous and attempt to simply transplant American community policing to another country. Indeed, it should be tailored to the country and the community from the

"ground up," just as we try to apply the concept in the United States.

Gary Cordner

I have no first hand knowledge of such endeavors elsewhere. I am impressed, however, with what I have read and heard about the initiatives in Canada. Given their similarities to us, we could learn a great deal from their experience with CP.

Joe Harpold

CP in other countries? Absolutely! This is not confined to the U.S.A. Many countries in the world are working with the concepts: Australia, England, Japan, Singapore, Norway, Iceland, and others.

Dennis Nowicki

I have very little to assess efforts in other countries, although I will soon travel to Poland and will have an opportunity to think about how CP might work there.

Dennis Rosenbaum

I am not that familiar with CP efforts elsewhere. As I understand it, Canada is doing a lot of interesting things. We can learn from them and they from us. Canadians have taken the role of community further than have we. They focus on preventing crime as opposed to reacting to crime. We have a great deal to learn about how to mount serious programs that deal with "at risk youth," for example, as has been successfully achieved in Canada.

13. What Is Your Prediction for the Future of Community Policing?

David Carter

An ideological change in the method of police service delivery is difficult. While we have COPS hiring incentives and training available, and while the concept is in vogue, it will continue to evolve. However, when the hoopla is gone and the federal monies dry up, the true test of administrative and political resolve will emerge. It is then that we will begin to assess the resilience of the concept.

Gary Cordner

I am optimistic that CP will continue to be a good fit with what communities want as well as with the needs and desires of police officers. My only concerns are, if CP is seen simply as a response to the federal crime bill, what will happen when the federal money runs out? Second, if crime reverses its current downward trend and starts to go back up, will CP be blamed? If that happens, will police departments regress to the legalistic style of policing that preceded CP?

Joe Harpold

I am hoping that it is going to proliferate throughout America. The key to success has to be that executives believe in it. If executives do not, the troops do not believe in it either. The programming of CP has to be designed by the police and must be based on the perceived need from both sides of the fence. Citizens have to "own" the program if it is to be supported locally. The citizens invest their time and talent; they volunteer their services to make CP work.

Dennis Nowicki

Where the police and the community work together, both get hooked on it. Once a community gets a taste of CP, there is no turning back.

Dennis Rosenbaum

It still remains uncertain because we sometimes underestimate the extent of resistance to change in police organizations. In high crime communities, where there are poor relations between the police and African Americans and Latinos, there is a need to build trust. Things are changing on a large scale in thousands of police organizations, but it is slow. The key lies in police leadership. Police organizations need chiefs who will push their organizations forward. They need to do so consistently and firmly and with an understanding of the reservations expressed by those opposed to this new paradigm. A major mitigating factor, however, is that there is no job security for change agent police chiefs. Until multi-year contracts are awarded to chiefs of police, most will not push the new paradigm at a faster pace.

Reprinted from: William L. Tafoya, "The Current State and Future of Community Policing." In *Crime & Justice International*, 13 (6), pp. 7–14. Copyright © 1997 by Crime & Justice International. Reprinted by permission. ✦

23

Future Issues in Policing

Challenges for Leaders

Sheldon Greenberg

Strategic planning can mean many things to police administrators; at its core, it is intended as a long-term effort toward defining future issues—normally in a three- to five-year time span. This reading by S. Greenberg begins by identifying 36 issues considered by police executives to be important for the future. Certainly these broad questions loom large for today's police executives—how to implement community policing, reduce citizen fear, address the burgeoning drug market, reduce the "new" violence (that for many criminals today is a desired end, rather than a means), and allocate resources within the police department. As you read, consider how you might address each of these considerations, bringing to bear your own education (up to this point) in the discipline. What should the police be doing today in order to prepare for challenges of the future?

"The future never just happened. It was created."

—Will Durant

Defining future issues facing American police service is not easy. Just as the future is different for individuals, it varies significantly for law enforcement agencies. Factors such as locale, political environment, economics, and others determine how an agency and its employees will view and react to the future.

Definition of the term *future* also comes into play when discussing key issues. For some police leaders, the future is the next fiscal year. For others, it is a three- to five-year

span of time toward which they have set into motion a strategic planning process. Yet, for others, the future is next Friday and surviving without a crisis until their next day off. Any discussion of future issues in policing must consider the short term as well as the long term and must give attention to operational issues, administrative issues, the community, and the basic philosophy of policing.

The *Encyclopedia of the Future* (Macmillan, 1996), identified numerous important issues facing the police, political leaders and the community. This analysis drew upon a wide spectrum of information, ranging from reviewing current research, discussions with police executives, to studies conducted on policing agencies. Listed below are 36 of the issues identified as important (not ranked by priority):

- Reducing citizen fear
- Reducing violence and sustaining the reduction
- Maintaining and demonstrating integrity and ethics
- Community policing
- Accountability for 100,000 additional police officers
- Declining federal funding for local police
- Federal agencies dictating local police strategies
- Viability of crime control models (such as the NYPD model, COMPSTAT)
- Police infringement on individual rights as a byproduct of zero tolerance
- Independent civilian review boards
- The value of the police agencies to communities
- The role of the police in economic development
- Infusing new technology into police service—Over-reliance on technology to cure all ills
- Technology-related crime
- Changing nature of narcotics use and trafficking
- The loss of experience in police agencies

- Patrol officers as leaders in identifying and handling crime patterns
- Crimes against children (pornography, child abuse, drugs, alcohol)
- Changing community demographics
- Competition for highly qualified police recruits
- Changing nature of suburbia Mandating higher education for police (the national Police Corps experiment)
- Proliferation of small criminal factions (independent gangs, pseudo gangs)
- Urban terrorism in United States Modifying police academy curricula (adult education, maximizing time)
- Accreditation of police agencies
- Resource allocation—improving efficiency and productivity
- Political influence on local police
- Changing police work schedules
- Reliance on early warning systems to identify potentially troubled officers
- Reducing ranks—flattening the structure
- Changing role of first-line supervisor
- Developing police leaders
- Labor/management relations
- Marketing the police
- Need for research, experimentation, innovation at the local level

Police leaders need to consider these and other issues relevant to their agencies and communities. Occasionally, command meetings and discussion groups with supervisors, officers, and civilian employees should center on an issue of importance. Personnel matters, policy matters, internal affairs cases, and budget concerns should be put aside during the meetings to allow open dialogue on how the agency copes with the issue. Such sessions are invaluable in formulating new approaches and assessing existing activities. The following pages address some of the key issues that police leaders will face. Many of the discussions pose questions rather than suggest answers.

Accountability to the Public for 100,000 Police Officers

One of the most pressing near-term issues that will be shared by large and small police agencies is the anticipated demand by the public for accountability for the millions of dollars spent to place 100,000 more police officers on the streets of the nation's cities, counties, and towns. The current downturn in violent crime has afforded police agencies, particularly those in large urban centers, with a temporary reprieve. The newness of community policing and problem solving to the public provides an additional reprieve.

Several factors may change the public's attitude and place increased and significant pressure on police agencies and executives to "make good" on their commitment to the public for the additional officers. The most significant will be any sustained increase in violent and other serious crime. It will be a relatively short period of time before the media and politicians, especially those out to replace their chief of police or sheriff, begin to probe to determine if COPS (Office of Community Oriented Policing Services, U.S. Department of Justice) grant objectives have been met. Regardless of size, those agencies that failed to commit adequately to community policing, or used COPS officers to supplant hiring, may suffer politically, legally, and within the community.

Reducing Citizen Fear

Serious crime is down. Violent crime is down. Many of the nation's large and small jurisdictions have been publicizing the reduction of crime for five or more years. Yet, the reduction in crime has had minimal, if any, effect on reducing citizens' fear of crime. Reducing fear—not simply crime statistics—will be a major challenge facing police leaders in the future.

For generations, police officials have espoused that policing to the public's perception or fear of crime is as important as policing to the reality of crime. However, few police leaders and officers know anything about fear. What is it? How does it work? What is the cycle of fear? How can a police officer or deputy intervene to break the cycle? Why is fear contagious? What do the police do as a matter of routine to spark fear? Do problem solving, partnering, and the implementation of crime control strategies and tactics reduce fear?

An exploratory survey of 28 police academies revealed that not one offered recruits or in-service personnel a course of instruction on fear. Several police academy officials noted that *fear of crime* was addressed in courses on patrol techniques, victim assistance, and community policing. These academies presented information on the goal of the police to reduce fear of crime. None addressed the social and physical disorder [which are] the primary determinants of fear. Addressing fear of crime is not, necessarily, related to fear.

Recently, a police officer handling a theft from an auto call told the victim that he would have arrived sooner if the dispatcher had not made a mistake in broadcasting the address. He went on to talk about the police department being short of personnel and the lack of sufficient officers to handle the community's demands. In another recent situation, a deputy sheriff responding to a routine vandalism call told the victim that such calls were not a high priority and that the agency had to focus its resources on more serious crimes. What effect did this officer and deputy have on citizens' fear? What effect did they have in building public confidence in the police?

There is a need for every officer, regardless of rank or position, to be trained in the practical aspects of fear. They should be taught to assess causes and levels of individual, neighborhood, and community fear. They should be taught intervention techniques so that, during a simple conversation, they may alleviate rather than exacerbate the victim's or witness's apprehension.

Fear is a disease, and if untreated it fosters and slowly infects and takes over its host the community. It inhibits normal functioning and paralyzes the citizens. It has several causes, most related to a person's environment, experience, and values. Fear is a complex phenomenon that has many causes, including those involving the environment and personal experiences and values.

Police have long thought that fear and crime were directly related. That is, a reduction in criminal behavior, as evidenced by crime statistics, would be followed by a reduction of fear. Unfortunately, this is not the case. Simple reductions in criminal behavior may not lead to reductions in fear. To cure the disease, the police first need to understand the underlying causes.

Changing Drug Trade

United Nations and other intelligence reports have indicated that the South American drug cartel has moved heavily into growing poppy for the purpose of producing heroin. Further evidence suggests that the cartel has a price-fixing strategy to convert cocaine users to the longer-lived addiction to heroin.

Heroin is quickly reclaiming its place as a "common" commodity—a leading drug of choice. In addition to being reasonably priced, new forms of heroin allow users to ingest [it] through smoking and other means. These new methods of use create a new market among users who may have feared the pain, scarring and disease associated with the more traditional "shooting up" with needles. As a result of new ways to use heroin, a rapidly increasing number of young women are turning to the drug, increasing the likelihood of adversely affecting children. In the past, heroin was a drug used predominantly by men.

In explaining the reduction in drug related violence over the past several years, many police and government leaders make reference to successful enforcement, problem solving, and educational efforts that reduced the use of crack and other forms of cocaine. Few, however, pose questions about where the former cocaine users have gone.

Most police agencies remain reactive to the drug trade. Traditional approaches prevail. These include street corner sweeps, arresting users and low level dealers, relying on specialists (narcotics units) to assume primary responsibility for enforcement, and participating in regional task forces (generally when funded by the federal government).

Police leaders will have to "think out of the box" in the future in response to a changing drug market. A well-planned, strategic approach to the drug trade and problem solving related to drugs will be needed in every sized agency. More agencies must become involved in teaching employees about drug market analysis and forecasting. Police leaders will have to embrace and lobby for rehabilitation of offenders. While it brings few awards to politicians who support it, rehabilitation on a larger scale will be a primary tool in reducing crime caused by the drug market.

Two factors set apart the coming heroin epidemic from problems caused by heroin trafficking in years past. First, as stated, new forms of heroin use have emerged. Others will evolve that make it easier and cheaper to use. People—particularly young people—will be provided with an array of alternatives for consuming heroin. Second, while property crimes will increase, those committing the crimes will have grown up in an environment more prone to violence. It is feasible that a confrontation with police that may have caused a burglar or other perpetrator of property crime to run may now result in aggression or injury.

Should a police agency change its procedures and tactics? What are police agencies doing to prepare officers—particularly patrol officers—for the heroin "epidemic?" How will heroin users react when confronted by a police officer? What medical dilemmas does the heroin user pose? How will the drug affect women? These are but a few of the questions the changing drug trade poses for the foreseeable future.

Violence

In both the immediate and distant future, police will continue to deal with "the new violence" that has emerged over the past five to ten years. Far too many police executives have relished in and taken credit for the reduction in violent crime that has been realized in most jurisdictions. On the other hand, few are focusing on the nature of the violence that has been occurring.

In the past, violence was an end to a means. Revenge, robbery, and jealousy were among the many reasons that people resorted to violence. Today, an entire culture has emerged that sees the use of violence as an end unto itself. The people who make up this culture—gangs, pseudo gangs, well-armed young people, and others—are not going to change their way of thinking or relax their hostility and aggression simply because there is a fluctuation in drug usage or a switch from cocaine to heroin.

For many, violence has become a way of life, just as for others peace has become a way of life. For these people, the wanton use of violence—aggression for the sake of aggression—is not considered abhorrent behavior. Taken in combination, these factors present challenges for police leaders. Police will have to be trained and educated to understand violent behavior far beyond what they are given today.

Community Policing

"Community policing has changed the way police do business," stated a chief of police during a conference sponsored by a regional community policing institute. At the same conference, another chief said, "Community policing is a patient in critical condition whose survival looks bleak."

Determining whether community policing is a philosophy that forges the foundation of quality police service or simply a "flavor of the month" to be referenced in the history books is one of the most challenging and important significant issues facing executives in police service. Since passage of the Crime Bill, much of the growth and progress in law enforcement has been connected to community policing. The President's commitment to placing 100,000 more police officers on the nation's streets is tied directly to community policing. Extensive technical assistance, training, and research have been funded by federal agencies to support community policing. Thousands of police agencies have publicly embraced community policing.

Yet, many questions remain. For example, how many police agencies have made a commitment to community policing? How many agencies have demonstrated the link between community policing and the quality of the communities they serve? How many have embraced community policing to gain a share of available federal dollars? Will community policing endure without federal funding?

The Office of Community Oriented Policing Services of the U.S. Department of Justice has been a primary source of funds and support to police agencies. Federal legislation mandates that the Office of Community Oriented Policing Services be dismantled in the year 2000. Will the legacy of the COPS office be sustained? Will community policing prevail as a philosophy and road map for the future? Or will it fade and become yet another failed policing innovation?

Hard questions must be asked as police leaders look to the future. What expectations have police and political leaders set for community policing? Are they realistic? What are the motives? How is community policing being entrenched within the organization? Do supervisors and officers embrace community policing? Do they simply manipulate the system or go through the motions to meet community policing mandates?

Partnerships

As part of community policing and doing good business, police agencies have turned to creating partnerships with neighborhoods, community organizations, businesses, and others. Partnerships have been emphasized in literature, policy, education and training programs, and news and popular media. Much of society has come to realize that the police cannot function independently to address crime and disorder and are willing to create partnerships. In many jurisdictions, beat officers have been mandated to "partner" as part of their regular duties.

There is, however, more to creating and sustaining effective partnerships. As they currently exist in most jurisdictions, many partnerships are ineffective. In fact, they may be more detrimental than helpful in effecting long-term positive change. The challenge to leaders, now and in the future, is to develop meaningful and lasting partnerships rather than the superficial relationships that exist in most communities. Far too many agencies

have entered into partnerships because they seemed right. Others have entered into partnerships with neighborhood groups and community organizations because they provide short-term public relations benefits or meet the requirement of federal grants. Few have entered long-term partnerships oriented toward the alleviation of crime and fear of crime.

Community policing calls for police officers to be "empowered" and many police executives contend that empowerment has been bestowed. Yet, few officers and deputies feel comfortable exhibiting authority on behalf of their agency or making significant decisions when attending neighborhood or community meetings.

For many police officers, the concept of partnership means simply attending occasional neighborhood association meetings or occasionally visiting neighborhood leaders who live on their beat. Other officers feel frustrated because they know that partnerships are important but believe their role to be one of public relations hype rather than substance.

Neighborhood residents and business people who attend community meetings and get to know officers tend to have their expectations raised toward some additional or extraordinary performance by the police. They believe their needs are going to be met in a better way.

Partnerships for the sake of partnership do not endure. Partnerships only work when the mutual benefits to the parties involved are well defined, well understood, and attainable. In fact, superficial partnerships backfire. For example, at a community meeting, residents expressed their concern about several thefts from garages and sheds that occurred over a brief period of time. Little had been stolen. They asked if patrols could be increased in the area. The police officer in attendance responded by telling the audience about the police department being short-handed. The officer went on to tell the people that there was little chance of their crimes being solved and that the police department was targeting violence reduction as its priority. While the officer achieved his goal of attending and participating in the meeting, little good came from the encounter. The officer believed he was being candid. He gave little thought to the frustration he caused or fear he reinforced.

This scenario is repeated with far too much frequency. As police leaders look to change the nature of partnerships, emphasis must be placed on quality. Endurance, too, is important, but only if the goals of the partnership require a long-term commitment. Executives must grasp that not all partnerships should be everlasting. There are ways to achieve quality and endurance. Toward this end, several important questions must be asked before any partnership is forged:

- What is the purpose of the partnership and what are the projected outcomes?
- Who are the key players in the partnership?
- What is the experience of the key players in working with partners?
- What do the partners stand to gain or lose by participating?
- Are both partners worthy of participating in the partnership?
- Are the right players involved in the partnership (neighborhood leaders, residents, local business people, police officers, police supervisors)?
- Are officers comfortable with their position and authority to make the decisions necessary, support the outcomes of the partnership?
- Are the outcomes of the partnership well stated?
- How will the success of the partnership be measured?
- Are employees trained and well versed in the nature of partnerships?
- How much time will be allowed before the assessment occurs and a determination is made to continue or disband the partnership?

Resource Allocation

If the quality of policing is to progress, a greater number of police leaders will need to know more about resource allocation than currently exists. At a conference involving 125 police executives, questions were posed about knowledge and experience in allocating resources. The questions focused on workload analysis, scheduling, and beat alignment. Only 25 of the executives acknowledged that they had hands-on experience allocating resources through analysis. Only 15 of the 25 believed that the process adequately placed officers where they were needed most.

With the decline in federal funding for additional police officers, combined with local, state, and federal belt-tightening, greater emphasis will be placed on using available resources as efficiently as possible. Yet, few police executives and supervisors receive education and training in resource management and personnel allocation.

Some executives have grown in agencies in which resource allocation is handled by computer. Others have functioned in environments in which the number of officers provided to the agency is dictated by fiscal or political authorities. Many officials have committed simply to placing all available resources in patrol, often to the detriment of specialty units.

All police leaders, regardless of rank, should be versed in resource allocation skills. Analysis of workload and resources should be part of every supervisor's and executive's routine functioning. Justifying resources should be based on more than perception, statistics such as increased calls for service, and a simple belief that more is better. Once learned, resource allocation is neither overwhelmingly time consuming nor difficult. It becomes second nature. With the predicted reduction in federal funds for local police and a tightening of local budgets, a commitment to quality allocation of resources is essential.

Closing Comment

This is an exciting and challenging time in the history of police service. No matter what issues lie ahead, the public will continue to expect a high degree of service from its police. And this expectation will be met as it has always been met. Any time of day or night, citizens will receive quality response from professional police officers. Officers and deputies will continue to care, perform their tasks diligently, and meet whatever challenges are presented to them. Exceptions will continue be rare.

Today's leaders and those who follow will determine whether police agencies embrace their communities or return to being distant and aloof. They will look at the value of police service in new ways and demonstrate the positive effect a police or sheriff's department has on the overall quality and economic viability of neighborhoods. They will deal with unforeseen problems caused by new drugs, small but hostile groups of extremists, young people who were raised in an environment of violence, and more. They have the opportunity to deal with these issues supported by advanced technology, highly evolved information resources, better trained officers and deputies, and a heightened commitment to interjurisdictional cooperation.

"The best preparation for good work tomorrow is to do good work today."

—Elbert Hubbard